THE ROUGH GUIDE TO

Conspiracy Theories

ROUGH GUIDES

www.roughguides.com

Credits

The Rough Guide to Conspiracy Theories

Contributing editor: Neil Foxlee
Editors: Greg Ward, Andrew Lockett
Layout: Michelle Bhatia, Dan May and Link Hall
Picture research: Suzanne Bosman
Proofreading: Orla Duane
Production: Julia Bovis and Katherine Owers

Rough Guides Reference

Series editor: Mark Ellingham
Editors: Peter Buckley, Duncan Clark,
Daniel Crewe, Matthew Milton,
Joe Staines
Director: Andrew Lockett

Publishing Information

This first edition published September 2005 by
Rough Guides Ltd, 80 Strand, London WC2R 0RL
345 Hudson St, 4th Floor, New York 10014, USA
Email: mail@roughguides.com

Distributed by the Penguin Group:
Penguin Books Ltd, 80 Strand, London WC2R 0RL
Penguin Putnam, Inc., 375 Hudson Street, NY 10014, USA
Penguin Group (Australia), 250 Camberwell Road, Camberwell,
Victoria 3124, Australia
Penguin Books Canada Ltd, 10 Alcorn Avenue, Toronto, Ontario,
Canada M4V 1E4
Penguin Group (New Zealand), Cnr Rosedale and Airborne Roads,
Albany, Auckland, New Zealand

Printed in Italy by LegoPrint S.p.A

Typeset in Veljovic, Berthold Akzidenz Grotesk and Helvetica Neue
to an original design by Henry Iles

© James McConnachie and Robin Tudge
432 pages; includes index

A catalogue record for this book is available from the British
Library

ISBN 10: 1-84353-445-2

ISBN 13: 978-1-84353-445-7

7   9   8   6

THE ROUGH GUIDE TO

Conspiracy Theories

by
James McConnachie & Robin Tudge

Contents

General introduction   ix

Assassinations and downfalls

Introduction   3
Tutankhamun and the curse of the pharaoh   4
Jesus of Nazareth and the case of the missing penis   7
A great reckoning in a little room: Christopher Marlowe   8
The poisoning of Mozart   11
Frank Olson   15
Marilyn Monroe   17
The CIA and Castro   20
John F. Kennedy   23
Malcolm X   32
Dr Martin Luther King Jr   34
Robert Kennedy   37
Harold Wilson   41
Salvador Allende   43
Elvis Presley   46
Pope John Paul I   48
Suicided at Blackfriars Bridge: Roberto Calvi   50
A living sacrifice: Archbishop Romero   52
John Lennon   55
Paul McCartney is dead   58
Death of a princess: Diana   59
Kim Jong-il: a very quiet coup   64
Dr David Kelly   64

Mega-conspiracies and master plans

Introduction 71
Knights of the shadows: the Templars 73
Freemasonry: centuries of conspiracy? 76
The Illuminati 85
The Rosicrucians 87
The Blood Libel: the longest-running conspiracy theory of all 89
Conspiracy of fear: satanic ritual abuse 92
Holocaust denial 94
Anne Frank: teenager or face of an international conspiracy? 96
The Armenian genocide 98
The Protocols of the Elders of Zion 100
Daniel Pipes and the Hidden Hand 104
The British royal family 105
The Central Interference Agency 109
The military-industrial complex 112
Men in Black 114
The military-entertainment complex 115
Currency codes: from Masonic dollars to ten-agora coins 117
Italy: land of conspiracy 122
Wrestling with the Octopus: Danny Casolaro 128
The Gemstone File 131
California's queen of conspiracy: Mae Brussell 132
The EU 135
The Council on Foreign Relations 137
The Trilateral Commission 139
Organized crime 141
Secret services 144

Miracles, secrets and lies: conspiracies of religion

Introduction 149
The great conspiracy: patriarchy and the Great Goddess 150

The New World Religion conspiracy 153

Dead Sea cover-up 154

Miscellaneous for sale 154

The Jesuits 158

Jesus the myth 160

The suppressed Apostle: Mary Magdalene as feminine divine 164

The Cathars 166

Benedict XVI: The Panzer Pope 170

Opus Dei: the holy Mafia 171

The Land of the Free

Introduction 175

Watergate: a third-rate burglary 176

Jonestown 181

Ronald Reagan and the October Surprise 185

Iran-Contra: no theory 186

October surprises 191

MK-ULTRA 192

The White Alliance: the CIA, the Contras and cocaine 196

Did not snort: Clinton and the "Mena" Affair 198

Gangland peninsula 200

Clintongates: ruining people is considered a sport 202

The Clinton body count 204

Waco 207

OKC: the Oklahoma City bombing 212

The elections of George W. Bush 216

The great election robbery of 1876 217

Skull, Bones and Bush 221

Corporate clampdown

Introduction 225

The international banking conspiracy 226

Nazi gold 231

   The New World Order 234
   The World Economic Forum 237
Perpetual war on perpetual energy 240
The eternal light bulb and the Phoebus Cartel 243
Microsoft 245
Cyberdisease and Y2K 248
   Bar codes 250
ECHELON and the world wide web 251
Fluoride 253
A cure for cancer 257

Real weapons of mass destruction

Introduction 265
The Black Death 266
The Philadelphia Experiment 268
Port Chicago 271
Chemical cover-ups 274
AIDS 277
   SARS 282
Secret bases 283
HAARP 287
   Microwaves 289
   The origins of HAARP 291

Sea, air and space: calamities and cover-ups

Introduction 295
   The Titanic 297
   The Lusitania 299
Lockerbie 301
TWA 800 306
Roswell and Majestic-12 311
   Alien Abductions 313
The Apollo moon landing 316

Commie cosmonauts 321

Warplay

Introduction 325
The USS Maine and the Spanish-American War 327
Operation Northwoods 329
Pearl Harbor 330
The Invasion of Poland 335
Odessa and the Org 335
The Cold War conspiracy 338
The Gulf of Tonkin incident and the Vietnam War 343
The Israeli attack on USS *Liberty* 348
The Kremlin and the Chechen rebels 353
The Great Game: Afghanistan and Caspian gas 359
9/11 360
Iraq: the case for war 371
The first Gulf War 372
Iraq: the real reasons for war? 380
The Project for the New American Century 381
The capture of Saddam Hussein 388
Saddam and the CIA 391

Conspiracy Theory Archive

Books 393
Conspiracy Movies 397
Websites 402

Picture credits 407

Index 409

Introduction

"And I began to question everything around me: the houses, the shop signs, the clouds in the sky, and the engravings in the library, asking them to tell me not their superficial story but another, deeper story, which they surely were hiding."

Umberto Eco, *Foucault's Pendulum*

To *conspire* once meant to "breathe together". It is an image of the most intimate and secretive complicity, perfectly conjuring smoky political backrooms, sinister whisperings and passionate plots. Today, "conspiracy" means a very particular kind of plan. It must involve more than one person – no "lone gunman" can make up a conspiracy of one. It must have goals that are either criminal, hostile or nefariously political – no one can conspire to forgive Third World debt or feed the homeless. And it must be secret – conspirators do not announce their manifestos to the world.

But this is a guide not to *conspiracies*, but to conspiracy *theories*. It doesn't freshly unveil hidden agendas or dramatically unmask sinister conspirators – though there's endless material here that you won't easily find published elsewhere. It doesn't presume to tell you who really shot JFK, whether Princess Diana's car crash was definitely an accident or if Neil Armstrong actually walked on the moon. We don't announce the Truth According to Rough Guides. Instead, this guide presents the world according to *conspiracists*, unleashing accusations, allegations and extreme explanations that are by turns brilliant, absurd, insightful, witty, nonsensical and sometimes outright insane.

Some of the authors, journalists, bloggers and whistleblowers this book cites believe their own theories passionately, while others undoubtedly have hidden reasons for claiming what they do. Some are even accused (by other conspiracy theorists) of being the public face of a conspiracy to discredit conspiracy theories. Many just revel in the sheer creative and iconoclastic energy of the conspiracist world. Either way, they are all given plenty of rope here. Some inevitably hang themselves - with others we've been delighted to give a gentle tug. But readers should beware: even where we haven't explicitly challenged or ridiculed a particular theory (after all, we can't begin every sentence with "supposedly" or "allegedly") it doesn't mean we think it's true or that we are presenting it as the truth. Of course there are a few exceptions and for the avoidance of doubt let's name them explicitly: the politically-motivated plots to kill Fidel Castro, the "Iran–Contra" affair, the barely-legal rigging of the US presidential elections in 1876 and, most heinously, the Nazi conspiracy to murder millions of European Jews – despite the disturbingly motivated attempts of Holocaust Deniers to claim that this is the world's greatest conspiracy theory, rather than an actual conspiracy. We can also add to these some conspiracies to provoke conflict and blame it on an opposing party: Hitler in Poland, and the US in respect of the Gulf of Tonkin incident in Vietnam. With all the other theories in this book, again, beware! **Though we have tried to be open-minded and judicious while seeking out the best-substantiated accounts of events, that still doesn't mean you should treat any of the other theories (or any of the "facts" related by us in our discussion of them) with anything other than complete disbelief.**

But it's not always easy to stay dry and rational. Entering the world of conspiracy theories can be as disorientating as, say, underwater diving. Once you've left behind the reassuringly two-dimensional dry land of believing what the government or the media or indeed anyone else tells you, you're in a new and infinitely more complex world. It's hard to keep track of where you're heading, or even to know when you're facing up or down. Everybody seems to have an agenda, no one can be trusted – your field of vision is constricted by the mask of ideology, and looking down into the murkier depths, it's easy to give way to panic and paranoia. And this is not the only danger: it's just as easy to be lured by the seductive intricacy of the conspiracy reef; stay down too long, and you may succumb to a fatal narcosis. As Umberto Eco puts it in *Foucault's Pendulum*, one of the great conspiracist novels, conspiracy theorists "are people lost in a maze: some choose one path, some another; some shout for help, and there's no telling if the replies they hear are other voices or the echo of their own". Calling for help underwater is still lonelier.

In a postmodern world where one version of history is supposedly as valid as another, conspiracy theories are often treated as a kind of game, or as the flowering of a fascinating but ultimately irrelevant subculture. Does it matter who believes what about JFK any more? Is it even possible to know what really happened? This book may of course lead you to think that to dismiss conspiracy theories is the greatest danger of all. You only have to look at the anti-Semitic "Blood Libel" (which is perhaps the longest-lived conspiracy theory of all) or the fraudulent screed known as "Protocols of the Elders of Zion" (which is perhaps the most internationally widespread) to see how conspiracy theories can be supremely dangerous. It could be said that the Holocaust was allowed to happen only because ordinary German people had been persuaded that the Jews were a genuine threat.

Nazi Germany was, admittedly, one of history's most conspiracist regimes. But other totalitarian governments – Fascist Italy, Soviet Russia, Cuba and many contemporary Middle Eastern states, for example – have been equally conspiracist in their thinking. (In the case of Cuba, of course, this has been largely justified.) Perhaps Hitler saw the world as a conspiracy because he himself behaved like a conspirator. Perhaps whipping up fear of external (or better still, internal) threats is simply the best way to suppress dissent: just ask Senator Joseph McCarthy or President George W. Bush.

It is curious that the majority of conspiracy theories seem to emanate from the right – notably when right-wing beliefs are combined with fundamentalist religion. Extremist Muslims and ultra-evangelical Christians share much in this respect. It seems that people with absolutist, black-and-white worldviews tend to believe that the powerful operate in an equally absolutist way. People who desire patriarchal governments cannot conceive that their opponents might not act in a patriarchal way. If a political enemy is seen as basically evil – rather than, say, misguided or incompetent – then all their actions must surely be the result of sinister machinations. And all "accidents" are therefore the result of conspiracy, not cock-up.

Liberals or left-wingers prefer to imagine that they are above "naïve" conspiracist thinking, that they are relative sophisticates who understand the real workings of government – socialism grew out of Marx's profoundly intellectual analysis of history, after all. And yet the further left you go, the more conspiracist thinking creeps in. Anti-globalization campaigners typically caricature the workings of Western governments or multinational institutions as profoundly conspiratorial, and ultra-liberals and fascists alike share a belief in the corporate capture of politics.

Whether on the right or the left, it seems that the world's most conspiracist cultures tend to be those where the people feel most disenfranchised. Without any chance to witness the chaotic workings of the machinery of power, it's easy to believe that political affairs can be driven by sinister, implacable forces. Where there is no understanding of history, conspiracy theories are sucked in to fill the intellectual vacuum.

Ever since the Warren Commission into Kennedy's assassination, such inquiries themselves have often been seen as cover-ups or whitewashes – part of the original conspiracy. Yet all too frequently, the term "conspiracy theory" has provided those in power with a convenient way of brushing serious allegations aside, with the result that the official version of events prevails.

In these days of the Internet, however, the "official version" of events is subject to ever-increasing scrutiny. With access to a computer and a phone line making it possible for all and sundry to broadcast their opinions to the world (and without the ben-

efit of editorial fact-checking), conspiracy theories have become an accelerating global phenomenon. Today, they stoke fear and outrage in the Middle East. They inspire homespun "patriot" movements in the US (and actual terrorist attacks in Oklahoma). They make liberal Europeans cynical and apathetic. They influence the politics of the entire Italian nation. They spawn computer games ("Deus Ex"), card-trading games ("Illuminati"), hip-hop albums (Public Enemy's *Fear Of A Black Planet*), films (*Conspiracy Theory*, *JFK* and so on) and a whole sub-genre of fiction ranging from the intellectual games of Eco, Don DeLillo and Thomas Pynchon to the *Illuminatus!* trilogy and Dan Brown's *The Da Vinci Code* – a global publishing phenomenon in its own right.

Conspiracy theories have also given birth to a miniature academic industry. Where once serious historians avoided the word "conspiracy" like a disease, cultural critics and sociologists are now documenting conspiracism in popular culture, dissecting the politics of conspiracist thinking and analysing what is sometimes called the "paranoid style" – interestingly, a term borrowed from clinical psychology. A few historians are now willing to lash themselves, like Ulysses, to the mast and expose their ears to the siren voices of the conspiracy version of history. The idea that long ago it was great men's deeds that drove world affairs gave place to the notion that much bigger historical and social forces were at stake. Now, once again, it is being recognized that plans, projects, conspiracies and even conspiracy theories can change the world.

Assassinations

Tutankhamun and the curse of the
pharaoh
John F. Kennedy
Pope John Paul I
Death of a princess: Diana

Assassinations

Forty years after John F. Kennedy was shot dead in Dallas, in November 1963, his death has become more famous as a source of conspiracy theories than as an actual presidential assassination. Even the shock that so famously caused a generation to remember exactly where they were at the time has itself become part of the mythology: the actual feelings have long been forgotten, while JFK has become "JFK". After forty years of investigations and speculations, the incident has spun itself into a massive conspiracy tornado, sucking in an ever-increasing cast of suspects and spitting out an ever-mounting flow of print.

The JFK maelstrom easily encompasses the other notorious assassinations of America's "Civil Rights Era": black activist Malcolm X, shot dead in February 1965; civil rights leader Martin Luther King, shot dead in April 1968; and JFK's brother, presidential hopeful Robert F. Kennedy, shot dead in June of the same year. Even the 1962 "suicide" of Marilyn Monroe is dragged into the same vortex, largely thanks to her relationships with both

Kennedy brothers. The names of the same mobsters and Washington insiders crop up in theory after conspiracy theory, with mantra-like repetition substituting for lack of evidence. In every case, the witnesses are said to be mistaken or lying, and the forensic evidence supposed to have been destroyed, tampered with or misrepresented. Powerful interests were behind the killing. The truth was covered up. The gunman was not alone. One conspiracy theory shifts and slides smoothly into another.

The conspiracy theories of 1960s America all finger the "usual suspects": the Mafia and the CIA. Both organizations, of course, are conveniently secretive, and in the absence of reliable information, theory steps in. The CIA, in particular, is widely accused of orchestrating assassinations both before and after JFK. One early victim, it is claimed, was Frank Olson, one of the CIA's own agents, who was allegedly defenestrated in murkily hallucinogenic circumstances in 1953. On the international front, practically any dead leader in the Americas has been a supposed CIA target, from Chilean premier Salvador Allende, found mysteriously full of bullets after a coup in September 1973, to outspoken Archbishop Oscar Romero of El Salvador, gunned down at the altar in March 1980. Only Cuban leader Fidel Castro has proved elusive – despite a baroque array of proven CIA plots against him.

Even the death of Elvis Presley in 1977 has been linked – by some – to the notorious Agency. Elvis's death is perhaps the best example of a constant in conspiracy theorizing: the refusal by fans to accept that the beloved icon could die before their time. Saints are supposed to be immortal, after all. A man whose case was genuinely more suspicious than Elvis's – and who was genuinely closer to sainthood – was Pope John Paul I, who died in 1978 after just 33 days in office. (Some connected his death to the Vatican Bank scandal, which culminated in the apparent "suicide" of Italian banker Roberto Calvi in London in 1982.) Quasi-religious outraged disbelief was also in evidence in the wake of the deaths of ex-Beatles singer John Lennon, shot by a supposedly mind-controlled assassin in 1980, and Princess Diana, killed in a sordid Paris underpass crash in 1997. Further back in history, fans of "poisoned" composer Wolfgang Amadeus Mozart and "assassinated spy" (and sixteenth-century playwright) Christopher Marlowe have proved just as reluctant to believe their heroes' early deaths could be accidental.

Some say Princess Diana was bumped off by the British Secret Intelligence Service. "MI6", as the service is usually known, may be no rival to the CIA in conspiracy circles, but if two conspiracy theories are to be believed, its hands are far from clean. MI6's grubby-mac-wearing brother MI5 is rumoured to have actually brought down Prime Minister Harold Wilson in 1976 – admittedly a political assassination rather than an actual one – while some sources have linked the services to the alleged suicide of Iraqi WMD expert David Kelly in 2003.

In fact, you don't have to be a saint or a genius for people to suspect that your murder was not the work of a lone madman. You just have to be a high-profile leader who dies in a high-profile way. As for the death of the Egyptian pharoah Tutankhamun, in the 1320s BC, no one knows if it launched conspiracy theories at the time.

Most bizarre of all are two assassinations that may not even have happened. So thick is the bamboo curtain around North Korea, that for all anyone in the West knows, rumours of assassination plots against "Dear Leader" Kim Jong-il may even have succeeded. As for another Beatles member, Paul McCartney, most of the world would undoubtedly be very surprised to hear that "in fact", he died back in 1966. Why does he still appear to be alive? It is, of course, a conspiracy.

Tutankhamun and the curse of the pharaoh

Before Tutankhamun's dazzling tomb in Egypt's Valley of the Kings was opened by the archeologist Howard Carter in November 1922, the pharaoh familiarly known as "King Tut" had been largely lost to history. Even today, Egyptologists remain uncertain as to exactly who he was, though most accept that he was the twelfth ruler of the eighteenth dynasty.

That would make him either the son or the half-brother of Amenhotep IV, otherwise known as Akhenaten, the "heretic pharaoh". Tutankhamun was born in around 1341 BC, and died at the age of eighteen or so, having ruled for roughly nine years. The big question is: why did the cosseted ruler of a civilized kingdom steeped in medical knowledge die so young? The first person to suggest an answer – at least, the first for some three millennia – was Ronald Harrison, a researcher at the University of Liverpool, who in 1968 took a series of X-rays of Tutankhamun's skull. He found fragments of bone dislodged within the brain cavity, and a thickening at the base of the skull that hinted at a heavy blow to the back of the head. More surprising still was the complete removal of the mummy's ribcage. Had the ribs been badly damaged? Was it murder?

Heretic pharaohs

Abnormalities about Tut's burial seem to endorse the homicide theory. Despite the presence of such amazing golden artefacts as the inner coffin and mask, his tomb was smaller than usual, and partly unfinished. Some of the artefacts that stunned the world even seemed to have been "borrowed" from other tombs – here and there, names had been painted out and replaced with "Tutankhamun". Had the young king died suddenly, before his funeral could be properly prepared? Or was his reign something of an embarrassment, to be quickly forgotten?

If Tutankhamun was indeed Akhenaten's son, he may have been tainted by association. His father has been credited with founding the world's first monotheistic religion, by turning away from the old Egyptian gods in favour of worship of the Aten sun-disc. Indeed, Tutankhamun's name was originally Tutankhaten, "the living image of the Aten"; he changed it, or his advisors changed it for him,

in what was presumably a bid to dissociate himself from the discredited "Atenist" regime of his father. As Tutankhamun, "the living image of Amun", the boy king reinstated the traditional worship of the god Amun, abandoning the new city of Akhetaten to return to the former religious and political capital at Memphis. But was that enough to establish the authority of his brief rule? Tutankhamun's name, like his father's, is glaringly absent from the "king list" in the Temple of Seti at Abydos.

Suspects – and a murdered Hittite prince

It would appear that someone set out to write Tutankhamun out of history. A leading suspect is Horemheb, a powerful courtier under Akhenaten who continued to wield influence as a military leader during Tutankhamun's minority rule. After the apparently sudden death of the boy king, Horemheb took responsibility for the restoration of the ancient temples, having his own name carved and painted over Tutankhamun's – even where the relief image obviously depicts a young man.

Even more suspicious is Ay, who was probably Tutankhamun's grandfather and acted as a kind of vizier or Prime Minister. Was an increasingly grown-up Tutankhamun trying to assert his authority? Did Ay and Horemheb conspire to remove him from the throne? Ay came to power after the boy king's sudden death – a wall painting in Tutankhamun's tomb shows him performing the Opening of the Mouth ceremony, a ritual traditionally carried out by the heir to the throne. Horemheb in turn became king after Ay. It also seems that Ay married Tutankhamun's widow, Ankhesenamun. In the aftermath of her husband's death, Ankhesenamun wrote to the Hittite King Suppiluliumas I, complaining that "they" were trying to marry her off to one of her servants, and would he please send a son as a more worthy husband. As Prime Minister, was this "servant" none other than Ay? Some Egyptologists argue that the letter was actually from Akhenaten's widow (perhaps the legendary beauty Nefertiti, who may have been Tut's mother), rather than Tutankhamun's, but it's hard to be sure. One thing is certain: the fate of the Hittite bridegroom, Zannanza, who was murdered at the Egyptian border.

It's possible, for that matter, that Ankhesenamun was behind Tutankhamun's murder herself. Queens could inherit the throne, after all. Two mummified fetuses were found in Tutankhamun's tomb. Were these stillborn children? Had the boy king failed to provide Ankhesenamun with a child and heir?

Medical evidence

After 3300 years, there's more theory than substance to this conspiracy. Although wall paintings, letters and inscriptions have been used to build a serious case, the conspiracy's foundations still rest on sandy ground. Recent studies of the original X-rays – notably Richard Boyer's 2003 study *The Skull And Cervical Spine Radiographs Of Tutankhamen: A Critical Appraisal* – have found no evidence of a traumatic or homicidal death, or have claimed that any injury could just as well have happened after death as before it. It was reported, however, that Tutankhamun might have suffered from Klippel Feil Syndrome, which produces abnormal curvature in the spine and fuses the upper vertebrae. It would only take a small shove to knock over and seriously injure a sufferer… As Utah police crime analyst Mike King commented for Atlantic's Discovery Channel documentary, *Mummy Autopsy*, "it was like having a bowling ball on top of a pool cue". Another study showed that he suffered from "fatty hips", which might explain the customary, bizarre depiction of Akhenaten as a deformed and androgynous-looking figure.

Serious Egyptologists tend to sniff at the X-ray story, but in early 2005, Zahi Hawass, Secretary General of the Egyptian Supreme Council for Antiquities tried to produce more solid evidence. He subjected Tutankhamun's mummy to a CT scan, a sophisticated kind of X-ray capable of building up a three-dimensional map of the skull – the same technology that revealed that Oetzi, the 5200-year-old hunter-gatherer found preserved in an Alpine glacier, had been shot in the shoulder with an arrow and had a fresh gash on his hand. (This evidence produced the media-friendly theory that Oetzi had been shot in the back while escaping a violent pillaging raid.) Excitingly, a photofit of Tutankhamun's face was created from the scanned images, but things didn't look so good for the murder theory. After a few tense weeks in the Egyptology community, Zahi Hawass finally announced in March: "We don't know how the king died, but we are now sure it was not murder. The case is closed. We should not disturb the king any more." The bone fragments in Tutankhamun's skull were blamed on careless embalmers, or the rough handling of Howard Carter and his team.

The curse of the press

No skull-bludgeoning, no murder. No murder – no story. If there's a real conspiracy wrapped up in Tutankhamun's bandages, it has less to do with ancient Egypt and more to do with the modern media, which happily turned Tutankhamun into a whodunnit to boost sales. From 1922 onwards, the press conspired to concoct a better story than the mere uncovering of a tomb. The original problem was that the expedition leaders, Lord Carnarvon and Howard Carter, gave exclusive coverage to *The Times*, leaving rival newspapers with little to say. Luckily, a bright journalist – perhaps influenced by *Lost In A Pyramid: The Mummy's Curse*, Louisa May Alcott's little-known sequel to *Little Women* – came up with the Curse of the Pharaoh.

The story usually goes that Howard Carter found a clay tablet whose hieroglyphs were deciphered as reading: "Death will slay with his wings whoever disturbs the peace of the pharaoh." Fearing that panic would spread among the superstitious workers, Carter destroyed the tablet – as archeologists are wont to do. But somehow the press got hold of the story. As you'd expect – given that the curse was entirely made up – there are scores of variations on the wording. One "curse" was borrowed from a real Anubis shrine, inscribed: "It is I who hinder the sand from choking the secret chamber. I am for the protection of the deceased." To that, some creative hack added "and I will kill all those who cross this threshold into the sacred precincts of the Royal King who lives forever".

It was a brilliant story, and pretty much eclipsed the actual tomb in fame. And it could run and run – every time an expedition member died, newspapers would speculate about the cause. It even surfaced in 2005, when a desert wind supposedly began to blow as the mummy was being transferred from the tomb, and when the CT scanner stopped working for a couple of hours. Occultologists still swap lists of dead archaeologists, one popular Internet conspiracy theory claiming that 26 people from Carter's team died within a decade of the tomb being opened. (The true figure is six.)

Conveniently for the theorists, Lord Carnarvon died of pneumonia in April 1923. All the lights in Cairo were said to have gone out at his death, while at home in England his dog Susie allegedly put up her muzzle, howled and died. Unfortunately for the curse theory, Howard Carter survived until 1939, dying at the respectable age of 64, while Alan Gardiner, the supposed translator of the curse, made it until 84.

Horemheb and the foreigners

An investigation of Horemheb's tomb at Saqqara in 1975 uncovered a message from the general to his brother Egyptians. Protesting his loyalty to the dead pharaoh, he exhorted the people not to trust foreigners and "to remember what they did to Tutankhamun". Was this just misinformation? Or did it explain Tutankhamun's death? The young pharaoh

JESUS OF NAZARETH AND THE CASE OF THE MISSING PENIS

The most baroque Tutankhamun conspiracy theory focused on his penis. Small, but clearly visible in the photographs taken in 1926, it had vanished by the time Ronald Harrison removed the mummy from the tomb again in 1968 (as had the right ear, but that's somehow less significant). Carter and his crew, it turned out, had crudely hacked about the mummified body and entirely failed to replace its bandages. But had they really stolen the royal penis? Obviously, it would make a magnificent talk-ing point on some millionaire art-collector's mantelpiece.

Some theorists believed that the mysterious castration is more ominous. Tutankhamun, they say, was the first god-king, the model for a certain Jesus of Nazareth 1300 years later. Extreme theorists even claim the two to be one and the same person – the original stories about Tutankhamun were simply displaced 1300 years into the future and a few miles down the road to Palestine. Just as Tutankhamun/Tutankhaten was "the living image of the Aten", so Jesus was "Adon", the Lord, the Son of God. Jewish circumcision is a ritual memory of the seasonal castration and rebirth of the Egyptian god Osiris – and Tutankhamun's golden coffin depicts him as Osiris, holding the royal symbols of the crook and flail. Tutankhamun's penis, therefore, is a potent ritual object representing the very wellspring of life, and its absence is a sure sign that dark forces are at work in the world. Whoever holds the penis of Tutankhamun, it appears, holds great power… Conspiracy theorists wondered what Howard Carter's descendants knew. Unfortunately, the conspiracy line turned out to be a dead end, as the CT scan of 2005 revealed that Tut's penis was in fact present, though not in the usual place – it was revealed to be lying in the sand tray in which the mummy rested.

is known to have conducted unsuccessful wars; perhaps he was injured on the battlefield. A lesion on his jaw is known to have begun to heal before he died, so one theory proposes that he was struck in the face in battle and fell, hitting his head and crushing his ribs, perhaps under a chariot. He then succumbed to his injuries slowly enough for his jaw to heal, but quickly enough for his tomb not to be ready.

It's possible. Unless another, near-contemporary tomb is found by a modern-day Howard Carter, it seems unlikely that the secret of Tutankhamun's death will be definitively unmasked, whatever the CT scans show. There's too much media interest at stake.

SOURCES

Books

Bob Brier **The Murder Of Tutankhamen: A True Story** (1998). A paleopathologist traces the conspiracy behind the killing of a pharaoh. Paced like a breathy thriller.

Howard Carter and A.C. Mace **The Discovery Of The Tomb Of Tutankhamen** (1933). Carter's memoirs, with some extra material. Fascinating – but there's nothing about dismembering the mummy here…

Gregory M. Cooper and Michael R. King **Who Killed King Tut? Using Modern Forensics To Solve A 3300-Year-Old Mystery** (2004). Utah-based police criminal profilers investigate the case of Tutankhamun. Reads like the TV script it is.

Christiane Desroches-Noblecourt **Tutankhamen: Life And Death Of A Pharaoh** (1965). A classic biography.

Paul Doherty **The Mysterious Death Of Tutankhamun** (2002). A thriller-writer's threadbare speculation that Tutankhamun died of Marfan's syndrome.

Websites

⊛ www.ashmol.ox.ac.uk/gri/4tut.html "Tutankhamun: Anatomy Of An Excavation" – the complete records of Howard Carter's dig online, including Carter's diaries and Harry Burton's original photographs.

A great reckoning in a little room: Christopher Marlowe

The handsome and preposterously talented English poet-playwright Christopher Marlowe was only 29 years old when he died, but he had already been hailed as one of the greatest writers of the age. On May 30, 1593 he went to Deptford in southeast London to drink, dine and talk with three men, Ingram Frizer, Nicholas Skeres and Robert Poley, in a house owned by the widow Eleanor Bull. The four spent the day quietly, talking and walking in the garden, but after supper a dispute broke out about the "recknynge", or bill. "Malicious words" were spoken, tempers lost, and Marlowe, who had been lying down, apparently leapt up, snatched Frizer's dagger, and slashed twice at his head, possibly with the hilt. Frizer's wounds were not serious, but in the ensuing struggle, he stabbed Marlowe in the right eye, killing him outright.

Popular legend has it that the incident was nothing more than a bar-room brawl – a myth that conjures up a colourful vision of Elizabethan roistering, worthy of a macho literary golden age before poets turned into daffodil-contemplating navel-gazers. Even Shakespeare was scarcely respectful of his rival's demise, punningly referring to it as "a great reckoning in a little room" in his play, *As You Like It*. The official inquest – which opened immediately, on June 1 – agreed that it was all the result of a drunken fight, and found that Frizer had indeed killed Marlowe in self-defence. Less than a month later, Queen Elizabeth I granted Marlowe a posthumous pardon for charges of blasphemy that Marlowe was on bail for. Was this Elizabethan efficiency or suspicious haste to close the case and any lingering questions about it? Was there something unusual about Marlowe that meant his death was unlikely to have been "just a pub fight"? Was he really an atheist? And a secret agent?

Historical detectives

With a few variations, the writings of near-contemporaries largely bear out the official story. Thomas Beard, writing in 1597, alleged that the incident took place in a London street and was because of a grudge; Francis Meres wrote in 1598 that Marlowe "was stabd to death by a bawdy Serving man, a rivall of his in his lewde love"; William Vaughan noted in 1600 that "as he meant to stab with his ponyard one named Ingram, that had invited him thither to a feast, and was then playing at tables, he quickely perceyving it, so avoyded the thrust, that withall drawing out his dagger for his defence, hee stabd this Marlow into the eye, in such sort, that his braines comming out at the daggers point, hee shortlie after dyed."

Although the seventeenth-century biographer John Aubrey accused another poet-playwright, Ben Jonson, of murdering Marlowe, it was only after 1925, when J. Leslie Hotson published *The Death Of Christopher Marlowe*, that the vultures really began to circle round Marlowe's corpse. A review article by a certain Eugénie de Kalb suggested that Audrey Walsingham, the wife of Marlowe's patron, had instigated the killing as part of an elaborate plot involving the succession of the Scottish King James VI to the English throne. In 1926, Samuel Tannenbaum's *The Assassination Of Christopher Marlowe* set out to prove that Walter Raleigh had bumped Marlowe off to stop him betraying the secret of Raleigh's atheism – a capital offence in those days.

An exhaustively researched but no less fantastical counterthrust to Tannenbaum was delivered in Charles Nicholl's *The Reckoning* in 1992. This untangled the complex strands of Elizabethan espionage and court factions, only to weave together a tight web of a story in which Marlowe was killed to clear the way for a conspiracy to slander Raleigh. Nicholl originally thought the plot was the work of the powerful Earl of Essex, but later changed his mind.

Marlowe as atheist

But why should so many commentators have imagined that Marlowe's death was no accident? The answer lies in the timing. Just ten days before his death, Marlowe had been arrested and bailed by the Privy Council on charges of atheism, blasphemy and sedition. These were considered serious crimes, tantamount to treason, and a number of witnesses – or plotters and slanderers, according to the theorists – had testified against him. The most famous evidence was given by Richard Baines, who claimed that Marlowe believed "that Moyses was but a Jugler & that one Heriots, being Sir W. Raleigh's man, can do more then he ... That the first beginning of Religioun was only to keep men in awe ... That all protestants are Hypocriticall asses ... That if he were put to write a new Religion, he would undertake both a more Exellent and Admirable methode and that all the new testament is filthily written." And, for good measure, "That all they that loue not Tobacco & Boies were fooles." If Marlowe did even think any of this, let alone say it, or persuade others it was true – as was alleged – it was staggeringly bold of him. Such beliefs risked undermining the whole structure of society, right up to the Queen herself; in the right hands, however, evidence of such beliefs could bring down Marlowe and all his circle, the so-called School of Night and its patron, Walter Raleigh.

Marlowe as secret agent

The idea of Marlowe as some kind of early-modern Bond is widespread. He apparently went AWOL from his degree at Cambridge. While that was not uncommon in those days, on his return, finding his degree in peril, he persuaded the highest powers in the land – including the Archbishop of Canterbury – to write a letter certifying that he had in fact "done Her Majesty good service, & deserved to be rewarded for his faithful dealing". Some claim that he had gone undercover among Catholic students in exile in France, listening out for rumours of the Babington plot against the Queen's life – a role certainly played by Robert Poley, one of the Deptford Four. Curiously, Skeres and Ingram, the other two men present at Marlowe's death, had links with Sir Francis Walsingham, Elizabeth's spymaster. Conspiracists allege that Marlowe was meeting fellow agents, and was probably lured to his death.

Other evidence is more circumstantial. The leniency with which Marlowe was treated after many of his numerous misdemeanours does seem surprising. In 1589, he got into a brawl with one William Bradley, who ended up being stabbed by Marlowe's companion in circumstances suspiciously similar to those of Marlowe's own death. In 1592, he was caught counterfeiting Dutch shillings in Flushing, a capital offence, but was freed in a matter of months. And of course he was arrested for sedition shortly before his death, but quickly released; fellow dramatist and alleged atheist Thomas Kyd, by comparison, was tortured into a confession. And Marlowe's play *The Massacre At Paris* features a non-speaking role for an "English Agent". Was he drawing on personal experience?

Marlowe as ... Shakespeare

One group of conspiracists believes that Marlowe never died at Deptford. Why? Because Marlowe was Shakespeare! Propounded by the Marlowe Society, this thesis found its most articulate and committed exponents in Calvin Hoffman, who wrote *The Man Who Was Shakespeare* in 1955, and A.D. "Dolly" Wraight. Hoffman believed that Marlowe's lover Thomas Walsingham, cousin of the spymaster Francis Walsingham, faked the playwright's death to save him from execution. Dolly Wraight works backwards, beginning with the clues found in "Shakespeare's" Sonnets (which, if read in the right way, apparently fit every detail of Marlowe's life – notwithstanding the fact that such sonnet sequences were rarely autobiographical) and ending with a faked death at Deptford. Marlovians have variously explained away the problem of the corpse by introducing substitute bodies or wilfully mistaken identities into the equation. Inconsistencies in Elizabethan name spellings provide rich soil for conspiracy theorists, who conveniently bump off the "original" William Shakespeare, allowing Marlowe to slip straight into his shoes.

SOURCES

Books

Calvin Hoffman **The Man Who Was Shakespeare** (1955). The original Marlovian theory. Out of date and out of print, but too classic too miss.

Charles Nicholl **The Reckoning** (1992). The best book on Marlowe's life and death and a great introduction to the underbelly of Elizabethan England. Well researched and excitingly written.

M. J. Trow **Who Killed Kit Marlowe?** (2001). Harps on a similar string to Nicholl, but accuses spymaster Lord Burghley instead.

Websites

⊛ www.marlowe-society.org The dark heart of the Marlowe-was-Shakespeare propaganda machine.

The poisoning of Mozart

The story that his fellow-composer Antonio Salieri poisoned Mozart because of insane professional jealousy has been circulating for centuries. According to Niemetschek's biography of Mozart, written just seven years after the composer's death, Mozart even believed it himself. He apparently lapsed into a sick melancholy after returning to Vienna, fresh from the success of his Masonic-themed opera, *The Magic Flute*, and told his wife that the new Requiem Mass he was writing was for himself. "I am sure I have been poisoned", he told her, with tears in his eyes, "I cannot rid myself of this idea." In late November he was overcome by a fever that lasted for a fortnight, causing his hands and feet to swell up painfully. On the morning he died, December 5, 1791, his wife's sister Sophie recalled that he again joked that the Requiem was for himself, vomited in "a brown arc" and died two hours later. His last conscious act was apparently to "express with his mouth the drum passages in the Requiem".

Mozart's wife and aqua toffana

Mozart's wife, Constanze, later recalled that the composer "was impressed with the horrid idea that someone had poisoned him with aqua toffana". Invented in seventeenth-century Naples, this arsenic-based poison was originally sold as a miraculous cosmetic that supposedly issued from the tomb of St Nicolas of Bari, patron of healing, and was allegedly widely used by women to poison their unwanted husbands. Mary Novello, who interviewed Constanze in 1829, discovered that during his illness Mozart had claimed that one of his enemies had administered the terrifying poison, but recanted when he felt a little better, saying: "I was ill to have had such an absurd idea of having taken poison; give me back the Requiem and I will continue with it."

Rumours abounded in Vienna, however. In 1791, a Berlin newspaper reported that many found the swelling of Mozart's body after death suspicious, adding that "he was constantly the object of cabals, which at times may well have been provoked by his carefree manner". According to Constanze's second husband Nissen, who wrote a seminal biography of the composer, she didn't believe the poisoning theory, and blamed Mozart's death on illness and overwork. Other evidence suggests that she wasn't so sure, however. Constanze wrote a letter to a Munich official in which she commented that her son "would not, like his father, have to fear envious men with designs on his life".

Forensic evidence

Most of Mozart's many biographers believe that he was killed either by acute rheumatic fever, or by uraemia following kidney poisoning. Advocates of the kidney-disease theory claim that the swelling of the body and the poisonous taste Mozart described in his mouth fit the bill, as does his earlier medical history of streptococcal infections. More bizarre diagnoses have included hyper-thyroidism, based on a portrait described as revealing the telltale "staring, rather frightened look, the swelling of the upper eyelid and the moist glaze of the eyes" and trichinosis – a recent allegation based on a diary note written six weeks before Mozart's death, in which he refers to having eaten a meal of pork cutlets. Whatever actually killed him, it's clear that Mozart was less than robust. Based on the detailed letters of his father, Leopold, the composer has been post-diagnosed as suffering from tonsillitis (1765), typhoid (1765), smallpox (1767), severe frostbite (1770), hepatitis (1771), a dental abscess (1774) and bronchitis (1780). More spiritually minded biographers attribute the composer's early death to his almost maniacal work rate, as though a flame that burned so brightly could not have burned for very long.

Doctors, biographers and conspiracy theorists Dieter Kerner and Gunther Duda of Germany point to a contemporary report that the composer died of mercury poisoning. Whether this was deliberate or not is another matter. Other authorities claim that Mozart may have overdosed while attempting the mercury treatment for syphilis – or indeed kidney disease. One objection to the mercury theory is the absence of any sign of tremor in Mozart's handwritten compositions.

The Salieri theory

It was only some years after Mozart's death that anyone pointed the finger at his rival, Antonio Salieri. The lyricist Da Ponte, who had worked with both composers, passed on gossip that the Emperor Leopold had said: "Salieri is an insufferable egoist. He wants successes … only for his own operas and his own women … He is an enemy of all composers, all singers, all Italians." In an attempt to quell the growing rumours, Eduard Guldener von Lobes, a colleague of the two doctors who treated Mozart in his final illness, wrote that Mozart "fell sick in the late autumn of a rheumatic and inflammatory fever, which being fairly general among us at that time, attacked many people". He also said that "the statutory examination of the corpse did not reveal anything unusual" – though it seems strange that Vienna's death registers do not back up his claim that there was an epidemic, and Mozart's son Karl claimed that after death, the corpse's "internal disintegration … increased to the extent that an autopsy was rendered impossible".

In 1823, rumours began to spread that Salieri had gone mad, confessed to the poisoning and tried to cut his own throat. The "conversation books" of the deaf composer Beethoven, a former pupil of Salieri, reveal that both his nephew and his secretary asked about the story. Sadly, Beethoven's replies, which did not need to be written down for the benefit of his visitors, are not recorded. It's likely that Salieri's "confession" never occurred. In 1825 his two attendants, who were with him day and night in his final illness, vowed that they had heard no such thing. Ignaz Moscheles, a pupil of both Beethoven and Salieri, records Salieri's own comments from October 1823: "Although this is my last illness, I can assure you on my word of honour that there is no truth in that absurd rumour; you know that I was supposed to have poisoned Mozart. But no, it's malice, pure malice."

The main problem with the Salieri theory is lack of motive. Much has been made of Mozart's 1789 letter to a fellow Freemason, Michael Puchberg, in which he writes of "Salieri's plots". But was his plotting so very sinister? Mozart and his father, it seems, believed that Salieri had conspired at court to undermine Mozart's operas *The Abduction From The Seraglio* and *The Marriage Of Figaro*, while in a letter to his father, Mozart accused Salieri of preventing him from signing up the princess of Württemberg as

Wolfgang Amadeus Mozart

a piano pupil. Hardly the work of an evil assassin...

Alexander Pushkin's 1830 play, *Mozart And Salieri*, depicts a Salieri riven by jealousy of the younger composer. But Salieri had no reason for envy – at the time, he was the more popular of the two. He held the top post in Vienna, as Kapellmeister at the Italian Opera, and basked in the patronage of the Austrian emperor, Joseph II. And the two composers appear to have been on friendly terms: they loaned each other scores, referred to each other's work and collaborated on an operatic double-bill. Mozart even took Salieri to a performance of *The Magic Flute* – and Salieri loved it.

The Grey Stranger

The legend of the Grey Stranger was given a major fillip by the advertising campaign for Milos Forman's 1984 film *Amadeus*, written by the playwright Peter Shaffer. The trailer depicted a grey-clad, ghost-like figure pressing Mozart to finish the Requiem Mass, and thereby hounding him to his grave. The story dates back to 1798, and an anecdote told by Friedrich Rochlizt, a music journalist. In the summer of 1791, he wrote, "a carriage drew up, and a stranger was announced ... [a] somewhat ageing, serious, imposing man, of a very respectable appearance." He apparently commissioned a requiem from Mozart on behalf of an anonymous employer, and Mozart "began at once to work on the commission. His interest in it seemed to grow with every bar: he wrote night and day. His body could not stand the strain: on a few occasions he fell fainting over his work." Prague biographer Franz Niemetschek notes that the messenger was dressed in grey, and adds that he appeared again "like a ghost" just as Mozart was leaving for Prague to work on *La Clemenza Di Tito*.

The stranger, we now know, was sent by Count Franz Paola Joseph Anton von Walsegg-Stuppach, who wanted the requiem to be sung on the anniversary of his own death. The only sinister aspect of the commission – other than the fact that it was soon after beginning this funeral mass that Mozart lapsed into depression, and his final illness – was that Walsegg-Stuppach wanted to pass it off as his own work. Shaffer's spin on the story – that the messenger was sent by Salieri to provoke Mozart's depression and paranoia, and thereby his death – is pure fiction.

Isis and Osiris: the Masonic connection

Mozart was a Freemason. He even wrote hymns for his lodge, including one that became the Austrian national anthem after World War II. The problem was that he wasn't a very good Mason: some theorists, particularly in Germany, have believed that he was murdered by an outraged lodge for having betrayed Masonic secrets in his last opera, *The Magic Flute*. Certainly, the Masonic imagery of the opera could hardly be clearer, and some have argued that despite its apparently pro-Masonic plot, the subtext evinces a troubling sympathy for Tamino's attempt to rescue Pamina from captivity in the lodge-like home of her Mason-captor, Sarastro.

But did this operatic "betrayal" result in Mozart's death? The theory has murky origins in the Nazi era, when it was popularized by General Ludendorff and his wife, who were as paranoid about Freemasons as they were about Jews. According to them, the two groups collaborated in poisoning the composer, though quite why they were so closely in cahoots, when Jews were largely excluded from Masonic lodges in the eighteenth century, is never made clear. For good measure, Mathilde Ludendorff imagines an anti-German conspiracy, in which Mozart was killed to prevent him from establishing a German (rather than Italian) opera in Vienna. Again, why the Masons would object any more than, say, the Italians, is less than apparent. She adds that Mozart was denied a proper burial as a breaker of Masonic laws – in fact, his burial, while simple and ill attended, conformed to laws established by the Emperor to prevent over-elaborate and over-costly ceremonies.

A more appealing riff on the Masonic thesis comes from Dieter Kerner's 1967 book on Mozart's death, though it owes a lot to the Ludendorffs. Apparently, the frontispiece of the first libretto of *The Magic Flute* – an engraving created by a Freemason – contains eight allegories of the Roman god Mercury, and it was mercury that Kerner believes was used to poison Mozart. As does an Austrian postage stamp from 1956 – proof of a long-lived secret conspiracy to suppress the truth. And in alchemy, the number eight is linked with the colour grey, which is in turn linked with the planet Mercury. The Grey Stranger, therefore, was a Masonic envoy sent to warn Mozart of his death – hence his sudden and fearful embarkation on the writing of his own Requiem.

SOURCES

Books

Peter J. Davies Mozart in Person: His Character And His Health (1989). Written by a British doctor, this is the last word in theorizing about Mozart's death.

H.C. Robbins Landon 1791: Mozart's Last Year (1999). Not just the death scandal, but the story of the composer's last tumultuous year, from Salieri to sexual scandal via Freemasonry and the Requiem.

David Weiss The Assassination Of Mozart (1970). Bizarre thriller in which a contemporary American couple discover that Salieri forms only part of a wider conspiracy by the Austrian regime to murder Mozart.

Websites

ⓦ www.openmozart.net Privately-run Mozart discussion site, with a good discussion board as well as FAQs on burning issues such as "was he murdered?" and "did he really write *Twinkle, Twinkle, Little Star*?"

Frank Olson

On November 28, 1953, US Army scientist Dr Frank Olson hurtled through the window of his tenth-floor room in New York's Hotel Statler, and plummeted to his death. According to the inquest, it was suicide. Richard Lashbrook, a CIA colleague who was with Olson at the time, testified that he had been unable to stop Olson killing himself.

The official story stayed that way for 23 years. Then, in 1975, the Rockefeller Commission into illegal operations by the CIA uncovered "Operation Artichoke", an ultra-secret research programme investigating drugs and interrogation methods, in which both Olson and LSD were in some way involved. Olson hadn't fallen victim to his own foolhardy experimentation: the LSD had been slipped to him a few days prior to his death. The doctor had become prone to psychotic episodes, and was in New York to get treatment for shock effects induced by taking LSD.

President Ford invited the Olson family to the White House to apologize, while CIA director William Colby explained the circumstances surrounding his death over lunch, and later released numerous related CIA documents. Congress also rapidly put together a $750,000 cheque for the family.

But *The New York Times* called the Colby documents "elliptical, incoherent, and contradictory", and said they contained "deletions, conflicting statements [and] unintelligible passages". Combined with the previous secrecy over the role of drugs in Olson's death, such rapid contrition from the government had a strong stench of further conspiracy to it.

The son takes up the case

After his mother's death in 1993, Frank's son Eric, who remained unsatisfied with the official explanations, began to investigate his father's death. Experts told Eric that his father would have had to run at 20mph to hurdle a radiator and smash through the hotel's heavy plate-glass windows and blinds.

Eric arranged for his father's body to be exhumed. Scientists from George Washington University failed to find any of the cuts or damage recorded by the first autopsy over four decades earlier, nor any traces of LSD. Instead, they noted a previously unremarked wound on his skull, consistent with his having been repeatedly struck from behind before the fall.

This sparked interest from the New York district attorney and the assistant DA Steve Saracco was assigned to reinvestigate Olson's death as homicide. Key witnesses subpoenaed from US and UK intelligence, such as Lashbrook, Gottlieb and Colby, were among those to be interviewed. (Colby, however, disappeared from his Maryland holiday home on April 27, shortly after being subpoenaed. His body was found face down in a river by police eight days later; a verdict of death by accidental drowning was returned.) The investigation also revealed that the Frank Olson case was taught as a case of "perfect murder" at the assassination training unit of the Israeli secret service organization Mossad, for its success in making murder look like suicide.

Lashbrook, who was looking after Olson, was shown to have made a phone call to someone immediately after the fall, saying only "Olson's dead". Eric also uncovered a CIA manual on "dropping" people, which paralleled his father's death. But after five years, scores of interviews and sifting hundreds of CIA records, the case was left open. "We could never prove it was murder," says Saracco, even though he and Eric continue to believe that's exactly what it was.

From Korea with anthrax

According to the German TV documentary and book *Codename Artichoke – The Secret Human Experiments Of The CIA*, Olson had worked on "Operation Artichoke", which was related to MK-ULTRA (see p.192), investigating the effects of LSD and its use in torture and interrogation. During the Korean War, Olson was based at Fort Detrick, where the US developed biological weapons such as anthrax for use against the Koreans and Chinese. Here too, ex-Korean War GIs who had been captured and "brainwashed" were debriefed using LSD treatment, in a recklessly experimental culture which to say the least achieved mixed results.

Olson also visited the UK's own bio research centre, Porton Down (see p.276), and elsewhere witnessed brutal interrogations based on techniques picked up from former Nazis and Soviet citizens. On his return to the US in the summer of 1953, he told a colleague that he was disgusted by the work, and informed his boss, brainwashing expert Sidney Gottlieb, who was the head of the CIA's Technical Services Division, that he wanted to leave. According to American political magazine *Counterpunch*, Gottlieb was involved in drug experiments, backed by the Rockefeller Foundation, that were worthy of Dr Josef Mengele. Gottlieb allegedly spiked Olson's drink at a party in Maryland in mid-November, and arranged for Olson to take the ultimate high jump a few days later.

Revelations get buried

Eric Olson believes that his father had had enough of the increasingly psychotic capers that the Army was paying him to work on. As he told the *New York Times* in 2001, the US biological weapons programme and the use of such weapons in North Korea may have been the key to his father's decision to quit, and ultimately his murder. He also pointed to the simultaneous persecution of Manhattan Project scientist Robert Oppenheimer as evidence of the fate of those who turned against the military's weapons programmes.

Interestingly, both Dick Cheney and Donald Rumsfeld were young lions in President Ford's short-lived administration at the time "Operation Artichoke" came to light. Documents unearthed by California university professor Kathryn Olmstead link them to the decision not to sanction any new inquest into Olson's death at the time of the payout. A White House memo dated July 11, 1975, said that such an inquest might make it "necessary to disclose highly classified national security information", ie information relating to bio-warfare programmes.

In September 2001, the *New York Times* reported that the US was pursuing research in violation of a 1972 treaty that prohibited the development of weapons that spread disease. When the paper reported further evidence that the US military had covertly developed anthrax and other germ bombs, interest was clouded by other events on the day of publication – September 11, 2001.

SOURCES

Books

James E. Starrs and Katherine Ramsland
A Voice For The Dead: A Forensic
Investigator's Pursuit Of Truth In

The Grave (2005). Starrs digs for dirt by literally digging up famous corpses, commenting on the smell and even sticking the bones in aircraft overhead bins before

he decides whether they died as reported. He also confirms the Hollywood myth that pathologists spend their time eating doughnuts over cadavers.

Websites

❀ www.frankolsonproject.org/Contents.
html Set up by Eric Olson, this provides a

host of links to reports on Frank Olson's life
and the aftermath of his untimely death.

❀ **www.counterpunch.org/gottlieb.html** A

speedy, non-too reverential obituary of the
invidious Dr Gottlieb.

Marilyn Monroe

Hollywood film star and all-American sex symbol Marilyn Monroe was found dead of a massive drugs overdose on the night of August 4, 1962. Her bloodstream contained enough chloral hydrate and barbiturate Nembutal to kill fifteen people. Although to the world Monroe symbolized glamour and easygoing sexuality, some on Hollywood's inside circuit gossiped that she was an emotional wreck and an alcoholic. She already had a string of broken marriages and failed relationships behind her, while her career appeared recently to have stalled with her dismissal from the film *Something's Got To Give* (an ironic title in the circumstances). The Los Angeles County Coroner's court considered her sufficiently depressed to declare a verdict of suicide.

Things weren't so bad

However, some say that the suicide theory just doesn't add up. They argue that Marilyn was getting back together with her first husband, baseball star Joe DiMaggio; indeed her stepson, Joe Jr., phoned

her on August 4 and said she sounded fine. She was also re-contracted to Twentieth Century Fox, on better money, to return to *Something's Got To Give*.

What's more, the manner of her death was odd. Although there was a police station less than three miles away, the police weren't summoned to Monroe's side until 4.30am on August 5, six hours after her publicist had been called to the house. One policeman said that Monroe's body was so neatly laid on the bed, with pill bottles tidily arranged beside it, that it was "the most obviously staged death I have ever seen".

The bed linen had already been laundered by Monroe's housekeeper, and her notes and diaries were all gone. An autopsy showed that, despite all the empty pill bottles and the massive dose that killed her, her stomach was devoid of tablet residue. Nor was any explanation given about the bruising on her body. Other tissue sent for analysis mysteriously disappeared.

High life and low lives

Marilyn Monroe moved in the very highest of circles. She was as glamorous as the number-one political family she hung around with, the Kennedys, and their glitzy circle of super-cool stars such as Rat-Packers Frank Sinatra and Peter Lawford (who had married into the Kennedy family and provided Monroe with her initial entrée). According to conspiracy theorists, all this was becoming too dangerous for comfort by 1962, when Kennedy brothers Jack and Robert were enjoying public power as US President and Attorney General respectively, while both privately enjoying Monroe's sexual favours. The Kennedys therefore unceremoniously set about ditching Monroe before the affairs could be revealed. For her part, Monroe felt shabbily treated, and was reportedly about to "blow the lid off of Washington" before she died.

So was it the Kennedys?

According to the most persistent theory, the Kennedys had Marilyn bumped off on the evening of August 4. During her final 48 hours, she was bombarded with phone calls from Robert and another woman telling her to "leave him alone", while she's said to have had a row with Robert at her house on the day of her death. Monroe's first husband Joe DiMaggio went to his grave believing that the Kennedys were responsible. However, there are different versions of precisely how the deed was done.

The first ambulance driver to arrive at Monroe's house, James Hall, subsequently wrote *Peter Lawford: The Man Who Kept The Secrets*. He contended that Robert Kennedy persuaded Monroe's psychiatrist, Dr Ralph Greenson – who arrived with the ambulance – to inject her with a lethal dose of Nembutal. "Just as Marilyn started coming around, the doctor arrived ... I believe it was Dr. Greenson. He ... pushed her breast to one side and gave her an injection." That would account for the lack of tablet residue.

According to Robert Slatzer's book *The Marilyn Files*, on the other hand, Robert Kennedy ordered

Secret Service and CIA agents to kill Monroe, on the grounds that information she'd picked up from the Kennedys as pillow talk made her a threat to national security. Marilyn's phone records were then seized by the police. Frank Capell, in his 1964 book *The Strange Death of Marilyn Monroe*, blamed the Communists, though agreeing they were hired by order of Robert Kennedy.

Marilyn Monroe at JFK's birthday party

Another twist has it that the FBI did it on Robert's orders, ostensibly to bail out the executive, but in reality because FBI boss J. Edgar Hoover wanted to have something he could hold over the boys in the White House. The trouble with this theory is that Hoover already knew of the Kennedys' relationship with Monroe, so why would he need to embroil himself with complicity in her murder?

The mob did it to help the Kennedys

Joe DiMaggio's belief in the Kennedys' guilt derived from his claim to have read Monroe's diaries after her death – diaries that then supposedly disappeared. Monroe is said to have had detailed conversations with Robert Kennedy about the CIA's plans to poison Fidel Castro with the aid of the Chicago gangster Sam Giancana, as well as ongoing investigations into union leader Jimmy Hoffa's relationship with the Mafia. She then told Frank Sinatra, who unbeknown to her passed the details on to Giancana. In *DiMaggio: Setting The Record Straight*, Morris Engelberg and co-author Mary Schneider report that Monroe told Joe DiMaggio Jr. on the day of her death that she was seriously considering telling all, not just about her relationships with the Kennedy brothers but about the other plots afoot.

At that point, the Kennedys called in their long-standing Mob connections to get rid of Monroe before she exposed both the Kennedys and their Mafia associates. One intriguing aspect of this hypothesis is that administering chloral hydrate by enema was a known feature of Mafia-related killings. The lack of tablet residue and the bruising on Marilyn's body, indicative of a violent struggle, would thus be explained.

The mob did it to get the Kennedys

Or did the mob do the deed not at the behest of the Kennedys, but in order to get at them? Family patriarch Joe Kennedy had made his millions as a bootlegger during the Prohibition era, aided by Mafia boss Frank Costello, while JFK was only elected in 1960 thanks to Mob-assisted vote rigging. Once in office, however, the Kennedy boys bit the hand that had fed them, and Robert Kennedy's crackdown on organized crime came as a humiliating slap in the face. It's said that as a result, besieged Chicago mob boss Sam Giancana enlisted the aid of Teamsters' leader Jimmy Hoffa to get RFK out of office by bugging Monroe and exposing their affair. When that failed, the theory goes, they killed Marilyn, hoping to implicate the Kennedys in her death; in any case, killing a Kennedy moll was satisfying enough in itself. The witness is a good one – Chuck Giancana, Sam Giancana's younger brother, as interviewed in the 1992 book *Double Cross*.

No more questions

Scores of books have been written about the death of Marilyn Monroe, while hundreds of websites still speculate about the possibilities. However, no reinvestigation seems imminent, and the suicide verdict still stands. Perhaps those who refuse to believe it are simply too dazzled by Marilyn's beauty, fame and fortune. Nonetheless, lingering questions continue to surround her final hours, and there's something compellingly mysterious about the death of a woman with such murky connections to the leaders of both the free world and the criminal underworld.

SOURCES

Books

Frank Capell The Strange Death Of Marilyn Monroe (1964). An anti-Red rant nailed onto Marilyn Monroe's death.

Morris Engelberg DiMaggio: Setting The Record Straight (2003). Contains some bits of interest on Monroe but focuses mainly on the world's greatest baseball player.

James Hall Peter Lawford: The Man Who Kept The Secrets (1991). Not as enthralling as you might expect, considering Lawford's dual status as the president's brother-in-law and a Ratpacker.

Robert Slatzer The Marilyn Files (1991). The most comprehensive work on the subject.

The CIA and Castro

Were he the leader of any country but Cuba, Fidel Castro would look like the world's most paranoid premier: he believes that the US government and its CIA agents have been hellbent on the destruction of both him and his regime ever since he came to power in 1959. But Castro is right. And, for once, not only right, but proven right. A CIA report released in 1967 let slip some choice titbits; more was revealed in the Church Committee's 1975 Senate enquiry into "Alleged Assassination Plots Involving Foreign Leaders"; and in 1993, key CIA files were declassified as part of Congress's investigation into the JFK assassination, the Assassinations Record Review Board, or ARRB. A baroque array of plots and plans was revealed, aimed at destabilizing Cuba and taking out Castro. Most were subsumed under the codename Operation Mongoose, which was set up in late 1961 in the wake of the disastrous Bay of Pigs invasion. Conspiracy theorists were elated. If all their suspicions about the CIA and Cuba were justified, what else might not be true?

Psyops: Operation Mongoose

Operation Mongoose started out small, with plans to drop leaflets over Cuba offering a reward for Castro's murder. The CIA's ingenuity was soon put to work, however, with Operation Dirty Trick, a disinformation scheme to blame the failure of the Mercury rocket launch – if it did fail – on Cuban electronic interference. A psyop (psychological operation) dubbed "Good Times" envisaged disseminating postcards of a fat, smug Castro living the decadent high life, which, it was noted, "should put even a Commie Dictator in the proper perspective with the underprivileged masses". Operation Free Ride would have dropped one-way tickets to Mexico City all over Cuba, though it was noted sensibly that "the validity of the tickets would have to be restricted" – there's always a catch. In 1963, the CIA envisaged creating a fictitious Cuban opposition leader to whom "humorous antics" could be credited, as well as "exploits of bravery (à la Zorro)". Even brighter were alleged plots to undermine Castro's persona as a revolutionary hero: perhaps they could spray the area around a radio studio with an hallucinogen before one of his lengthy revolutionary speeches, or lace one of his cigars with a disorienting substance, or make his famously virile beard fall out by contaminating his shoes with thallium salts.

There's something childish and slightly suspect about all of this. Even the CIA recognized as much in 1967, calling it "fruitless and, in retrospect, often unrealistic plotting". They blamed excessive pressure from the Kennedy administration. And not unreasonably so: in January 1962 Robert Kennedy publicly stated that deposing Castro was "the top priority of the US government; all else is secondary; no time, money, effort, or manpower is to be spared". Apparently, the tradition of futile machinations continues to this day. In 2003, a Miami newspaper reported that US officials had been harassed by Cuban government agents who had urinated into their homes, made nuisance phone calls in the early hours and, worst of all, retuned their car radios to pro-Castro stations. But perhaps this was just black anti-Castro propaganda...

"Devices which strain the imagination": ZR/RIFLE

In 1975, when the Church Committee published its report into "Alleged Assassination Plots Involving Foreign Leaders", it found evidence of a darker side to the CIA's plans for Cuba. It cited eight separate plans to kill Castro drawn up between 1960 and 1965 – plots that "ran the gamut from high-powered rifles to poison pills, poison pens, deadly bacterial powders, and other devices which strain the imagination".

One early scheme, before the accession of JFK

involved using the Mafia, which had its own grievance against the revolutionary regime for shutting down its casinos and prostitution rackets in Havana (as portrayed in the film *The Godfather Part II*). Conveniently, the CIA could be covered by a chain of association that would seem increasingly improbable as it became longer and apparently more tenuous. The CIA's Colonel Sheffield Edwards got in touch with ex-FBI man Robert Maheu, who contacted underworld figure Johnny Roselli, who recruited Chicago syndicate mobster Sam Giancana – who had supposedly shared a girlfriend with JFK – and Cuban Mafioso boss Santos Traficante. They in turn were supposed to recruit a Cuban with access to Castro who would do the deed, but nothing came of the plans.

After the debacle of the abortive US-backed Bay of Pigs invasion in April 1961, the Kennedy brothers upped the pressure for results. The CIA set up a top-secret assassination programme, codenamed ZR/RIFLE, and again prompted Roselli and his associates into action, supplying them with poison pills, weapons and explosives. Again, nothing happened, although the Mafia was presumably grateful for the free equipment.

Another CIA faction turned to the CIA's Medical Services Division, headed by the controversial Dr Sidney Gottlieb – also accused of testing LSD on unsuspecting US citizens as part of the MK-ULTRA programme (see p.192). The plans read like the work of a Bond villain. Castro was known to enjoy a cigar, so a box was contaminated with botulinum and delivered to "an unidentified person" in February 1961 – whereupon they vanished from the record. Castro was also known for his love of diving, so an alluring exploding conch shell was devised, the idea being to drop it at one of the Cuban leader's favourite dive spots.

Another scheme envisaged lacing the breathing apparatus of Castro's diving suit with TB bacilli while, for good measure, dusting the whole suit with a virulent fungus that would, according to the

Church Committee's report "produce a chronic skin disease (Madura foot)". Before the plan could be put into action, however, Castro was given a good Yankee wetsuit – minus germs and fungi – by an American lawyer. Finally, a Cuban army major, Roland Cubela, knocked on the CIA's door offering to kill Castro. He was promptly codenamed AM/LASH, supplied with a poison pen and promised a rifle to follow. Fortunately for Castro, Cubela's meeting with CIA agent Desmond Fitzgerald took place on the same day that JFK was shot in Dallas, and the plans were shelved.

No cigars for Fidel

At the time of writing, Fidel Castro remains alive and well: still delivering lucid, marathon speeches, without any signs of flashbacks, and still walking without a Madura-foot limp. He has, however, given up cigars. The CIA hasn't come off quite so well, and neither has the reputation of the Kennedys. The Church Committee hauled CIA executives and directors, especially Richard Helms, over the coals. Their 1975 "Interim Report" found evidence of CIA involvement in the assassinations of the Congo's Patrice Lumumba, Vietnam's Ngo Dinh Diem, Rafael Trujillo, of the Dominican Republic, and the Chilean leader, René Schneider, but after a lot of buck-passing and mutual accusations, its conclusions were fairly mild. The CIA, the report concluded, had problems with accountability, and it was recommended that the US should stop trying to kill foreign leaders. President Ford's Executive Order 11905 duly declared that "no employee of the US government shall engage in, or conspire to engage in, political assassination". Ultimately, nobody's career suffered much. Least of all Castro's.

Fidel Castro: very much alive

SOURCES

Books

William F. Buckley Jr. Mongoose, R.I.P: A Blackford Oakes Mystery (1998). Cuba, 1963. Yankee James Bond gets caught up in Operation Mongoose. A good thriller.

Fabian Escalante The Cuba Project: CIA Covert Operations Against Cuba 1959–62 (1995). As the former head of Cuban counterintelligence and the director of Cuba's 1978 investigation into the Kennedy assassination, Escalante knows a thing or two.

Claudia Furiati and Maxine Shaw ZR Rifle: The Plot To Kill Kennedy And Castro (1994). More on Kennedy than Castro, but only because it claims that the same cabal of Cuban exiles, CIA and Mafia was behind both plots.

Websites

ⓦ **www.aarclibrary.org/publib/church/contents.htm** The full text of the Church Committee's "Interim Report: Alleged Assassination Plots Involving Foreign Leaders". Covers Patrice Lumumba, Rafael Trujillo, Ngo Dinh Diem and René Schneider, as well as Castro.

John F. Kennedy

One question defines a decisive moment for a generation: where were you when John F. Kennedy was shot? If you were in downtown Dallas, Texas, on Friday, November 22, 1963, the chances are that you either have been or will be named in some dark conspiracy to kill the President of the USA.

Had it not been for the murder of JFK, this book might never have been published. The sudden, violent death in a bright, open public space of the world's most powerful man, and the murky circumstances that surrounded not only the assassination but also the ensuing investigation, which seemed to grow murkier with every new line of enquiry, kick-started the whole modern conspiracy-theories industry. (Though of course that's not to say that the conspiracy theory industry wanted Kennedy dead in order to raise its public profile...)

Successive investigations into Kennedy's death in the US Congress, courts, newspapers, books, films and scientific academies have not settled, for the American public at least, the question of who killed him. In 2003, an ABC TV News poll showed that just 32 percent of Americans believed that Lee Harvey Oswald acted alone in killing Kennedy; the Discovery Channel reported just 21 percent believing it was only Oswald; and the History Channel a mere seventeen percent. So up to four out of every five Americans think there was a bigger conspiracy going on.

What's known

While almost everything about the Kennedy killing has been questioned at some point, a few hard facts remain undisputed. John Fitzgerald Kennedy and his wife Jackie arrived in Dallas on November 22, 1963, and joined Texas governor John Connally in an open-top limousine. They were driven downtown, past cheering crowds. Secret Service agents drove behind, and a third car carried Vice President Lyndon B. Johnson, also from Texas, and his wife Lady Bird.

At 12.30pm, the motorcade was rounding Dealey Plaza. Kennedy was in the back right-hand seat, flanked by Jackie, with Connally in front of him. In the course of a few seconds, as the President's car pulled away from the imposing Texas Book Depository, bullets drilled into both Connally and Kennedy. Connally was badly injured, while much of Kennedy's brain splattered from the back of his skull. The whole group raced to Parkland hospital. Kennedy was declared dead at 1pm, though doctors conceded that he'd died before he ever got there.

As the world was informed of the killing, the presidential plane waited for Mrs Kennedy to arrive with her husband's coffin. On board, at 2.39pm, LBJ was sworn in as the 36th president of the United States. Lady Bird and the widowed Mrs Kennedy looked on.

Meanwhile, a police search of the Depository revealed that one employee was missing, having left minutes after the shooting. Across town, at about 1.15pm, an assailant shot and killed policeman J. D. Tippit. An hour later, Lee Harvey Oswald was traced and captured in a movie theatre and charged with Tippit's murder. The next day, he was charged with Kennedy's killing. Oswald denied both.

On November 24, as police bustled Oswald through a throng of guards and journalists at the Dallas city jail, in order to transfer him to the county jail, Dallas strip-club owner Jack Ruby stepped forward and shot Oswald. Again, the shooting was caught live on TV, and like Kennedy, Oswald was pronounced dead at Parkland hospital. Jack Ruby was convicted of his murder in 1964, but the conviction was overturned in 1966. He died while awaiting a new trial.

JFK shortly before his assassination

The Warren Commission

Just a week after the killing, President Johnson set up a commission to investigate the assassination. Headed by Chief Justice Earl Warren, it also included future president Gerald R. Ford; Allen Dulles, former director of the CIA; and the father of the CIA, John J. McCloy, himself a former adviser to President Kennedy. It delivered its verdict – the so-called Warren Report – in September 1964. According to the report, Lee Harvey Oswald was the killer and had acted alone. He shot Kennedy from a sixth-floor window at the Book Depository, where a sniper's rifle was found among boxes that bore his handprints. Oswald fired three shots in the space of something between 4.5 to 7 seconds. The first passed through Kennedy and into Connally; the second, seconds later, hit Kennedy's head; and the third missed. Oswald escaped and killed Tippit, but died in turn at Ruby's hands.

The report painted a picture of Oswald as a misfit, and a major-league one at that. A high-school dropout with strong Marxist leanings, he had been discharged from the Marines and subsequently defected to the USSR, where he was initially refused Soviet citizenship. In 1962, he somehow managed to return to the US with his Soviet-born wife, Marina, where he set up as the sole activist for the New Orleans branch of the Fair Play For Cuba Committee. He stated his support for Fidel Castro in a TV interview, and in mid-1963 applied in Mexico City for a visa to visit Cuba. The Commission could not ascribe to Oswald "any one motive or group of motives", but noted that Oswald had "an overriding hostility to his environment", "perpetual discontentment" and a "hatred for American society"; he sought "a place in history", yet acted "without regard to the consequences" of his actions. Having considered Oswald's relations with the Russian community in Fort Worth, Texas, his life and work with the Soviets, and the idea that he may have been a government agent (the FBI interviewed him three times on his return from Moscow), and also investigated whether he already knew Ruby (the conclusion was that he didn't), "no credible evidence" of a conspiracy was found. Oswald had acted alone.

Doubts set in

Although the Warren Commission gave its verdict in 1964, it took thirty years, under a schedule instigated by LBJ, for its twenty-six volumes and sixteen thousand pages of evidence to dribble into the public domain. The painfully slow, piecemeal way in which the report was released was sufficient to arouse suspicion in itself, but the dribs and drabs that gradually emerged were found to contain more and more holes. Articles and books disparaging the report appeared with increasing frequency in the later 1960s, and titles such as *Rush To Judgement* by attorney Mark Lane, and *Inquest* by Edward J. Epstein, became bestsellers.

The most glaring problem was that the chief suspect, Oswald, had never reached trial. Instead, he was gunned down in public. While it seemed implausible that a lowlife like Jack Ruby could have been outraged enough to kill Oswald, it was astounding that this petty mobster, known to the police, could get within a *mile* of the chief suspect, let alone *two feet*. What were the Dallas police thinking... or plotting? Furthermore, the police at Dealey Plaza at the time of Kennedy's shooting were said to have been so "fazed" that they failed to record dozens of witness statements, and thereby left Warren to depend on FBI material.

On the other hand, no one actually *saw* Oswald shoot the President, and it's hardly surprising that his prints were found at the depository – he worked there. Then there was the supposed murder weapon, a $12 bolt-action World War II rifle with sights bought by mail order. Was it accurate enough at the range and capable of being repeatedly reloaded in the few seconds Oswald had to kill Kennedy? And was Oswald himself a good enough shot? Or was he, as he told Dallas police, "just a patsy"?

Photographs and X-rays from Kennedy's autopsy were deemed by persons unknown to be too "gruesome" even to be submitted to the men on the Commission. Instead, the investigators relied on artists' impressions, which further compromised their dubious conclusion that one single bullet had entered Kennedy's back, exited his neck and then pierced Connally's chest, hitting his wrist and entering his thigh. That "magic bullet" – exhibit 399, which was noted to be in mighty fine condition – became infamous, and helped to taint medical examinations that already appeared to be contradictory.

The Parkland doctors wrote of a big hole at the back of the head, which would suggest a shot from the front, and thus a second assassin, as did a bullet *entry* wound on the front of Kennedy's neck. However, the autopsy said that the head wound was nearer the front, and thus the result of a shot from behind and above – Oswald's location – while the neck wound was an exit wound. Were wounds actually made to fit what became the Oswald theory, which would mean the doctors were complicit in the conspiracy – or were there perhaps two bodies, as some speculated? For that matter, were there two killers? Witnesses spoke of a man with a rifle seen leaving a "grassy knoll" just in front of the President's limo, and described the mysterious arrest of "three hoboes" who were on the scene.

The Garrison investigation

The Warren Report made a passing reference to a phone call that a lawyer received from one "Clay Bertrand" in New Orleans, during the few hours between the two killings, urging him to represent Oswald. That prompted New Orleans District Attorney Jim Garrison, with the backing of a solitary US senator, Russell Long, who had doubts about the Warren Report, to launch his own investigation in 1967. Finding that Clay Bertrand didn't exist, Garrison insisted that the name was a pseudonym for homosexual businessman Clay Shaw. Shaw was arrested and charged with supposed involvement in an elaborate conspiracy with another homosexual, David Ferrie. Garrison claimed that both men were friends and conspirators with closet homosexual Oswald, as well as being CIA agents, and that Oswald's Fair Play For Cuba office was located in a building full of CIA-backed anti-Castro operatives. Over a five-week trial, Garrison portrayed a gay/CIA/FBI Johnson-backed conspiracy to kill Kennedy, with shots from the grassy knoll and the three hoboes as contracted killers.

The jury took 45 minutes to clear Shaw, agreeing with Garrison's chief investigator William Gurvich, as he told Robert Kennedy, that the case was "rubbish". Garrison accused Robert Kennedy of conspiring to obstruct his case, despite the fact that Robert would surely want to know who killed his brother more than anyone. Many observers saw the trial as proving that Garrison was a paranoid egotist of epic and megalomaniac proportions. Even so, it gave an "official" voice to theories blasting the government and intelligence agencies – and it also allowed the public, for the first time, to see the film of the shooting captured by Abraham Zapruder.

Zapruder

The Garrison/Shaw trial brought the Zapruder film to prominence as the most important single piece of evidence in the shooting of JFK. A short, jiggly home-movie sequence that captured the violence of Kennedy's death in horrible colour, it had been seen by the Warren Commission and used for timings and reactions, but its graphic horror had hardly been conveyed by the dry words of the Warren Report. The 1975 Rockefeller Commission's investigation into illegal activities and assassinations by the CIA, which cleared the organization of involvement in the killing, concluded from its review of Zapruder that the President had not been shot from the front. For most of the American public, on the other hand, who saw the movie for the first time on TV's *Goodnight America*, the footage of Kennedy's head and brain matter being projected backwards seemed to confirm the very opposite. If the bullet came from the front, Oswald could not have fired the fatal shot.

The Church Committee and the HSCA

The 1975 Senate "Church Committee" also looked into illegal activities by intelligence agencies, including the plot against Castro – something Allen Dulles, sacked by Kennedy over Cuba, had failed to mention to the Warren Commission. It was perturbed enough to order another investigation: the 1976 House of Representatives' Select Committee on Assassinations (HSCA), which reinvestigated the assassinations of JFK, his brother Robert and Martin Luther King. Its fourteen-volume report, released in 1978, concluded that Kennedy "was probably assassinated as the result of a conspiracy". Oswald fired the fatal shots, but someone else was probably involved. On a police motorcyclist's recording of events at Dealey Plaza, acoustics experts counted *four* gun shots: two from the Depository, and at least one from the grassy knoll. Warren Report photos of Oswald holding a rifle and left-wing magazines were also revealed as fakes.

Most of the suspicion centered on the Mafia. Among those assigned possible roles were people like Teamsters' boss Jimmy Hoffa, and big Dons like Santos Trafficante, Johnny Roselli, New Orleans godfather Carlos Marcello and Chicago's Sam Giancana. Both Trafficante and Roselli were called to appear before the Committee, but died violent deaths before they could do so. In the end, the HSCA absolved Castro, the CIA, the FBI, the Mafia and the USSR. By blaming no one, however, their report only raised more doubts.

One consequence was that in 1981, Oswald's body was dug up, to dispel rumours that he had never actually returned to the US and had been replaced by a Soviet agent. The exhumed body, however, was confirmed as Oswald's.

Further suspicions raised by the HSCA's report were allayed when its acoustics evidence was discounted by the National Academy of Sciences, while an Ohio musician got fifteen minutes of fame after he analyzed a freebie recording of the tape and showed that it had been made minutes *after* the shooting.

The Communists

Among the earliest theories about the assassination, advanced for example by Edward J. Epstein in *Legend* and *Plot and Counterplot*, were that Oswald was a KGB agent who shot Kennedy on Soviet orders. Another variation has it that Fidel Castro, livid over the Bay of Pigs incident and the Cuban missile crisis, but not feeling unduly threatened by Kennedy's efforts to kill him (see p.21), simply got his shot in first, hiring Oswald to do the deed. By that reckoning, Castro correctly anticipated that the CIA and FBI would sit on any evidence rather than risk another confrontation with Cuba, which was under the Soviet umbrella, and so Johnson directed the Warren Commission to pin the blame on Oswald alone.

According to Robin Ramsey in *Who Shot JFK?*, there were indeed moves to stifle investigations into the alleged Communist conspiracy, possibly in order to head off a violent reaction against the well-armed Soviets. For their part, the Soviets claimed that the theory was itself a right-wing conspiracy. The strongest argument against it runs that Kennedy was considering making moves to harmonize relationships with Cuba, and that it's hard to imagine Castro or Khrushchev risking such a huge provocation as shooting the US President.

The CIA and FBI

Further theories focus on the roles of the FBI and CIA. There's certainly a case for suggesting that while the FBI may not have been involved in the assassination itself, it had a strong interest in pressuring the Warren Commission to deliver a whitewash verdict. After all, the FBI had somehow allowed one of the country's most public Communist agitators – Lee Harvey Oswald, whom the G-men had been following since 1960 – to kill the President in broad daylight.

Much more damning speculation has it that Oswald's New Orleans' Fair Play For Cuba Committee may have been a CIA trap to snare commie sympathizers, and that the CIA killed Kennedy using Oswald as a decoy. The CIA is said to have hated Kennedy for blaming them first for losing Cuba, and then for failing to get it back.

Questions have also been raised about the Secret Service men who were supposedly protecting Kennedy. Why was he in an open-top car, with its bulletproof bubble unattached, grinding slowly past crowds of people? Why were there no marksmen overlooking the Plaza – apart of course from the one(s) who shot Kennedy? And why, in the seconds that followed the first shot, did the car neither accelerate nor take evasive action?

LBJ

Perhaps the most basic of all theories poses the simple question: who gained the most from the assassination? It was Vice President Lyndon Johnson who ascended to the presidency, and who, as a Texan, would have known the right people in Dallas to pull off the hit; and it was Johnson who stopped all the other investigations in favour of the unreliable Warren Commission. JFK had supposedly never liked or trusted Johnson, and may have been planning to drop him from the presidential ticket for the next election. Texas oil barons, smarting from the loss of their Cuban assets, supposedly saw Johnson as a president who wouldn't also forfeit the riches of Vietnamese oil. According to Mark North's *Act of Treason*, the plot was aided by Kennedy-hater J. Edgar Hoover and his FBI. North contends that Hoover was tipped off about possible plots on Kennedy's life, but in a murderous dereliction of duty, did nothing to prevent them, or even to warn the president.

The Vietnam connection

Shortly before his death, JFK is said to have indicated plans to withdraw US troops from Vietnam. Johnson, by contrast, scaled up American involvement in Vietnam just four days after stepping into the bloody presidential breach. According to Peter Dale Scott in *Crime And Cover-up: The CIA, The Mafia And The Dallas-Watergate Connection*, the military-industrial complex was alarmed by Kennedy's desire to cut defence expenditure, and an end to the US presence in Vietnam would have cost them dearly. The CIA too was making money from intelligence funding and drug trafficking in Southeast Asia, while for good measure the Mafia were profiting from the drug trade as well...

Richard Nixon

According to A. J. Weberman and Michael Canfield, in *Coup d'Etat In America*, convicted Watergate burglar E. Howard Hunt (see p.177) was one of the infamous "three hoboes" who were arrested on the grassy knoll at Dealey Plaza on the day JFK was shot. Hunt's presence in Dallas was apparently confirmed by a self-proclaimed co-conspirator's confession to the British *Sunday Times* in 1977. To some minds, that's enough to suggest a connection to "Tricky Dicky" himself, Richard Nixon, who was in Dallas between November 20 and 22, attending a Pepsi Cola convention (whereas Kennedy drank Coke). Supposedly, Nixon's motive was to gain revenge for his narrow defeat by Kennedy in the 1960 presidential election. What's more, the subsequent assassination of Robert Kennedy in 1968, just as he appeared to have secured the Democratic presidential nomination, meant that the Democrats had lost their two most charismatic leaders within five years – which paved the way for Nixon's own election as president.

The Mafia

As noted above, the 1976 House of Representatives' Select Committee on Assassinations, the HSCA, pointed a finger of suspicion at the Mafia, and the Mob's putative links with the CIA, the FBI, anti-Castro operatives, Cuba and the Kennedy family. One theory holds that Mafia bosses wanted a president who would help them get their lucrative Cuban casinos back, not one who made deals with Castro. In addition, many mobsters hated the Kennedy brothers for their war on organized crime, especially as the Mob had helped them attain power in the first place. The role of Jack Ruby, as a small-time gangster on the Mob payroll, was to plug Oswald before he could sing.

Mark North, in *Act of Treason*, adds that J. Edgar Hoover was tipped off about a plot by New Orleans mobster Carlos Marcello in 1962. He goes on to suggest that far from preventing it, the FBI boss was a racist who actively colluded in the plan – which also involved the Ku Klux Klan – to get rid of a president seen as sympathetic towards civil rights.

National security and pillow talk

One twist to the possible involvement of the CIA and/or FBI argues that John Kennedy was brought down by his own sexual promiscuity. His pillow talk may have so compromised national security that it became necessary to kill him. Supposedly, JFK's liaisons with Ellen Rometsch, who was suspected of being a Stasi agent, were on the point of being investigated by Congress before the shooting. Along the same lines, there's also another link with the Mafia, in that JFK also trysted with Judith Campbell, the girlfriend of Chicago boss Sam Giancana.

The Nazis

Conspiracy theorist Mae Brussell outlined an almost senselessly elaborate theory that put Nazis behind Kennedy's killing, with Nazi hitmen hired through the Org (see p.335). In 1971, a French paper headlined a news story – "Martin Bormann behind the Kennedy murders" – pointing at an international band of killers in Texas, while a 1977 *Guardian* report, "Bormann Linked With Kennedy Murder" (based on *Treason For My Daily Bread* by Mikhail Lebedev) placed Hitler's deputy, missing since 1945, behind the killing. By this account, anticipated cuts in missile programmes under Kennedy led to anger among the ex-Nazi scientists working on NASA's space programme, and they, with the FBI, military-industrial complex and the Las Vegas Mob had Kennedy shot. In *NASA, Nazis And JFK: The Torbitt Document And The Kennedy Assassination*, William Torbitt and Kenn Thomas claimed that the firms involved in the killing were also behind the failed attempt on Charles de Gaulle's life in 1962. When de Gaulle realized that the companies behind the assassination bid against him were the same ones who supplied NATO, he took France out of the pact.

JFK the movie

In 1992, Oliver Stone's movie *JFK*, which is said to be filled with subliminal imagery suggesting Masonic and homosexual links to the assassination, brought the Garrison trial back to public attention shortly before the thirtieth anniversary of Kennedy's death. The American Bar Association conducted a mock trial of Oswald, while Congress approved the JFK Assassination Records Collection Act to ensure the speedy declassification of all files. "Speedy" in this context, however, means that the records needn't be made public until 2017, and that date can be postponed if "the President certifies" that release could "harm the military, defense, intelligence operations", and/or "outweighs the public interest in disclosure".

The big picture? The Masons and other strange phenomena

For a truly global conspiracy, how about the idea that the assassination of JFK was a Masonic coup to get rid of the first Catholic president, who but for the Pope was the most powerful Catholic in the world? Lyndon Johnson, Earl Warren, and J. Edgar Hoover were all Masons. So too were Gerald Ford, who "edited" the Warren Report, and another leading member of the commission, former CIA director Allen Dulles.

Other notably left-field suggestions include the following: Kennedy, who was a much sicker man than the public knew, arranged his own shooting so that he could die a martyr before his various ailments claimed him; he faked his own death to escape the burden of the presidency; Jackie Kennedy was sufficiently tired of JFK's philandering to take out a contract on her own husband; and finally, the Roswell aliens (see p. 311) shot Kennedy to prevent his space programme from revealing all their interstellar secrets.

Next comes the odd "0" coincidence. Every president elected in a year ending zero has died in office: William Harrison, elected in 1840; Abraham Lincoln, 1860; James Garfield, 1880; William McKinley, 1900; Warren Harding, 1920; Franklin Roosevelt, 1940; John Kennedy, 1960. Ronald Reagan, 1980, bucked the trend, but only by a hair's breadth, when he survived an assassin's bullet in 1981. George W. Bush, 2000, has yet to dispel the curse.

Further bizarre coincidences link Kennedy to Abraham Lincoln. Kennedy's vice-president was Lyndon B. Johnson, while Abraham Lincoln's was Andrew Johnson. Both Johnsons were Southerners, while Lincoln and Kennedy were Northerners. Kennedy had a secretary called Lincoln; Lincoln had a secretary called Kennedy. Both Kennedy and Lincoln were noted for their commitment to civil rights.

Back to square one

And still the debate continues. Forty years after the killing, as if to complete the circle, the BBC broadcast a documentary that came down in favour of the original story: Oswald was a lone Marxist sniper. Notes from his years in the Marine Corps prove that Oswald was a crack shot even without telescopic sights. Kennedy was clearly visible, and the limo was moving so slowly that shooting him was easy. Oswald didn't need to take three shots in the few available seconds, just two – the so-called "magic bullet" could indeed have followed the trajectory described in the Warren Report if, as a computer simulation showed, and the limo's design makes plausible, Connally was placed slightly inboard and down from Kennedy. That said, anyone can programme a computer to do anything, and it remains just one theory among hundreds.

The theories continue

So far, around two thousand books have been devoted to the assassination of JFK, creating a self-sustaining sub-industry that also includes TV documentaries, websites, films, essays, magazine and newspaper articles, PhDs, memorabilia and sheer conjecture. Every year, researchers and conspiracy enthusiasts meet in Dallas for the "November in Dallas" convention, sounding out new theories and evidence. Dallas even has its own Conspiracy Museum. Over thirty gunmen have been named as acting either in cahoots with or separately from Oswald, and a hundred witnesses are said to have been killed as a result of the conspiracies that surround the deaths of Kennedy, Oswald and Ruby.

While the assassination was a spectacular and deeply affecting event in itself, a more subtle dislocation in the minds of the American public began to set in with the shootings of Malcolm X, Martin Luther King Jr. and Robert Kennedy later that decade. It became increasingly hard to believe in Oswald as a "lone nut". Just how many "lone nut" killers, and successful ones at that, could there be? As the later deeds of the CIA and FBI were revealed, atrocities in Vietnam were televised, and the Watergate scandal saw the President of the United States incontrovertibly linked to a grubby burglary and an even grubbier cover-up, the potential depth of the government's duplicity seemed limitless.

Multiple investigations, whether Congressional, judicial, intelligence agency or simply private, have pored over not only the assassination but also every previous investigation. Every item of evidence, and every conclusion drawn from it, has been examined and re-examined from every angle. Doubts have been cast on everything from the "magic bullet" to the autopsy X-rays; has even the Zapruder film been altered? (Doubts have also been cast on the death of JFK's son John Kennedy in a plane crash in 2000, but that's another story).

So, anyway, where were *you* when Kennedy was shot?

SOURCES

Books

Stewart Galanor Cover-Up (1998). A concise outline of the cover-up in government and the press over key elements of Kennedy's death.

Mikhail Lebedev Treason For My Daily Bread (1977). One of the more fringe theories, though a bit dry to read.

Jim Marrs Crossfire: The Plot That Killed Kennedy (1989). A fascinating tour of the big theories behind Kennedy's assassination, cited by Oliver Stone in *JFK*.

Sylvia Meagher Accessories After The Fact (1967/1992). One of the first big conspiracy works, imbued with the sense of wide-eyed disbelief that such a thing could be lied about.

Mark North Act of Treason (1991). J. Edgar Hoover's involvement, or lack of it, in events preceding Kennedy's death. Could he have warned the president?

Gerald Posner Case Closed (1994). A somewhat overly confident book that triumphantly proves Oswald did it alone.

Robin Ramsay Who Shot JFK? (2000). An excellently researched, tightly written tour through the thinking (or lack of it) behind Kennedy's assassination. Ramsay's *Conspiracy Theories* (2000) is of a similar calibre. (See p.395)

David Schiem Contract On America (1988). "It wuz da Mob."

Peter Dale Scott Crime And Cover-up: The CIA, The Mafia And The Dallas-Watergate Connection (1977). The same names seem to keep cropping up in all these political scandals, and Scott refuses to accept that this is a "coincidence".

Anthony Summers Conspiracy (1980). Another highly praised summary of the main theories around Kennedy's death.

A.J. Weberman and Michael Canfield Coup D'Etat In America (1975). The focus here is on the three hoboes and the grassy knoll.

Websites

ⓦ www.newsmakingnews.com/ mbnaziconnect.htm Devilishly convoluted theory that puts a cabal of Nazis behind the killing.

ⓦ www.archives.gov/research_room/ jfk/warren_commission/warren_ commission_report.html The report that started it all – all 888 pages of it.

Malcolm X

In the late 1950s and early 1960s, Malcolm X was the most visible spokesman of radical black America. Establishing a powerful public persona as the principal mouthpiece of the Nation Of Islam, he rejected the passive civil disobedience advocated by Dr Martin Luther King Jr., and argued that it was up to blacks to resist oppression "by any means necessary". In 1964, he split with the so-called "Black Muslims" and set up his own Organization Of Afro-American Unity. Reaching out to other domestic and international leaders, he appeared to espouse the idea that it might after all be possible for different races to live in equality in the US. On February 21, 1965, however, immediately after delivering a speech, Malcolm X was shot dead on stage at the Audubon Ballroom in New York City. Three men – Talmadge Hayer, Thomas "15X" Johnson and Norman "3X" Butler – were convicted of his murder in March 1966.

However, Hayer always maintained that the others were innocent, and there were doubts as to whether Johnson and Butler were even at the meeting. Whereas initial press reports said that two people had been rescued from the furious crowd, including Hayer, who had himself been shot, both press and police said later that Hayer was the only one arrested. Although there was usually a high police presence at Malcolm's speeches, almost none were there that fateful day. The police claimed that Malcolm had turned down their protection, but his widow, Betty Shabazz, insisted that was a lie. It took half an hour for help to arrive from a hospital directly across from the theatre. Finally, short-

Malcolm X

ly after Malcolm's death, an Organization activist announced that he had evidence of government involvement. The activist collapsed and died the following day from "epilepsy", although he'd never suffered from the condition before.

The FBI and the CIA

According to Roland Sheppard, who attended many of Malcolm X's lectures and had at different times a presence in both the Organization and the Nation, Malcolm X had by 1965 become the focus of a high-level conspiracy within the government. His conviction that American capitalism was irredeemably rooted in racism, and that the struggle for civil rights was just part of a larger economic and social struggle, combined with his opposition to the war in Vietnam to attract the attention of the FBI.

Then there was the international company that Malcolm was keeping. He met with Castro and Che Guevara in 1964, and planned to petition the International Court in the Hague with a list of abuses against blacks in both the US and South Africa. In addition, Ahmed Ben Bella of Algeria had invited Malcolm X, along with other independence leaders, to the Bandung conference in March 1965, at which Malcolm X intended to make a consorted effort to create a global black power base. This in turn was anathema to the CIA, which was desperate to hold on to its raft of friendly states in Africa, where Western and Soviet agencies were fighting a covert but deadly serious battle to maintain their spheres of influence.

In *The Judas Factor*, Karl Evanzz of *The Washington Post* contends that the CIA decided to "neutralize" Malcolm. Both Evanzz and Sheppard believe that the FBI and/or the CIA infiltrated agents into the Nation of Islam to disrupt its activities, and possibly precipitated the split between Malcolm and its leader, Elijah Muhammad. Evanzz argues that one key high-level informant, the "Judas", was largely

responsible, and that circumstantial evidence suggests that he was none other than Nation secretary John Ali. That said, even if there was a conspiracy to stir up trouble in the Nation, there's no sign of the proverbial "smoking gun" – a documented order to kill Malcolm X.

Drugs and the Klan

There were also rumours that Malcolm X was killed by Chinese drug traffickers who stood to lose out from his campaigns against inner-city drug abuse. Another rumour suggested that Malcolm X was killed by the Nation members because he was going to reveal that the Nation had received monies from the American Nazi Party and the Ku Klux Klan (on the basis that the Nation, the Nazis and the KKK all agreed with the idea of racial segregation).

Turf war

Hayer himself never denied pulling the trigger. He was a member of the Nation of Islam, and the most popular theory continues to ascribe Malcolm X's murder to a straightforward act of vengeance. Malcolm had founded the Organization while on suspension from the Nation, ostensibly for the controversy he had aroused by saying of the assassination of JFK that "chickens coming home to roost never did make me sad", but also because X had publicly alleged that the Nation's leader, Elijah Muhammad, had fathered numerous illegitimate children. Muhammad, livid at both that charge and X's defection, reportedly said in 1964: "It's time to close that nigger's eyes."

Equally outraged was a one-time supporter of Malcolm, Louis Farrakhan, who called Malcolm a traitor and wrote two months before the killing that "such a man is worthy of death." Michael Friedly outlined the likelihood that the shooting was an inside job in *Malcolm X: The Assassination*, pointing out there had been four attempts on Malcolm's life in the weeks preceding the shooting. Malcolm's widow Betty Shabazz publicly accused Farrakhan of involvement in his murder, and that suspicion remained strong enough for Malcolm's daughter Qubilah to attempt to hire a hitman – who turned to be an FBI informant – to kill Farrakhan in 1994.

Admission and contrition

In 2000 Farrakhan, who by then had been leading the Nation for some years, told CBS News and Malcolm X's daughter Atallah Shabazz: "I may have been complicit in words that I spoke leading up to February 21 [1965] ... I acknowledge that and regret that any word that I have said caused the loss of life of a human being." Atallah replied "My father was not killed from a grassy knoll", and said she still believed that the FBI were involved, even if it was young black men who shot him.

Nonetheless, while Farrakhan has made his peace with the Shabazz family, and has also acknowledged that "I know that members of the Nation were involved in the assassination of Malcolm X", some theorists continue to believe that he was himself directly involved. Which doesn't, of course, preclude the possibility that government agencies also played a part. The FBI is still refusing to release the 45,000 documents it holds on Malcolm X.

SOURCES

Books

Karl Evanzz The Judas Factor (1992). While holding the Nation responsible, Evanzz also charts the shadowy influence of the FBI and CIA, in a detailed write-up that covers Malcolm's life and works.

Michael Friedly Malcolm X: The Assassination (1992). A neat summary of the many theories around Malcolm's death, this concludes that the Nation of Islam was responsible (and as a result has been decried by some as an FBI cover-up).

Films

Malcolm X (Spike Lee, 1992). Denzil Washington captivates as the eloquent, angry Malcolm.

Dr Martin Luther King Jr.

While civil rights leader Dr Martin Luther King Jr. could draw crowds of millions, and bring them to tears with his impassioned vision of black and white living in harmonious equality, his vision also drew murderous hate. On April 4, 1968, while King was visiting Memphis to mediate in a strike by local authority workers, he was shot dead on the balcony of the Lorraine motel. A single shot went through his neck, severing his spinal cord and killing him almost instantly.

Martin Luther King, Washington

a warrant was put out for his arrest. By now, Ray was on a complicated and expensive fugitive flight through Canada, England and Portugal. He was finally detained, after two months on the run, at London's Heathrow airport, en route to start a new life as a mercenary in southern Africa.

This inept car thief appeared to have done his best to get caught. As well as leaving his prints everywhere, he had also dropped a bundle of personal effects on the sidewalk as he fled the apartment building. At his trial, Ray pleaded guilty, and thereby avoided a full trial, which he was told would end in his execution.

After a worldwide manhunt, the man blamed for the killing, petty criminal James Earl Ray, was charged and convicted of King's murder and sentenced to 99 years. Accusations and rumours of conspiracies have continued to rumble ever since.

The case against Ray

Moments after King was shot, someone was seen to leave an apartment building opposite the motel, and race away in a white Mustang. The shot was later traced to the bathroom of one apartment, a classic "sniper's nest" equipped with binoculars and a rifle with telescopic sights, and enjoying a perfect view of the motel balcony. All, police later claimed, were covered in the fingerprints of James Earl Ray, and

Questions arise

Three days after his conviction, Ray began to protest his innocence, saying that he'd been framed by a gun-smuggler called "Raul" or "Raoul". Questions were in any case being asked. Where had this habitual petty criminal obtained the ten thousand dollars needed to fund his globetrotting escapade, and how had he managed to pull off a major assassination, only to leave such incriminating evidence at the scene? How come his prints were neither all over the boarding-house room nor on a box of bullets? Why did Memphis police withdraw police protection for King the day before he died, despite fifty-odd death threats? Hours before the shooting, two firemen and a detective posted near the motel were sent off on spurious tasks. The infamous photo of King lying on the balcony, taken moments after the shooting, shows all his aides pointing up to the motel roof opposite, not across the way towards the apartment. In addition, the only witness who identified the mystery Mustang man as Ray, Charles Stephens, was an alcoholic who later retracted his story, while his similarly unreliable wife Grace said that Charles couldn't see the mystery man from where he was at the time, whereas she could – and it wasn't Ray. She was later put in a mental hospital. Furthermore, it was no secret that FBI boss J. Edgar Hoover had hated King for years, hounding him in the hope of destroying his reputation. FBI investigators took more than two weeks merely to announce that they had found Ray's things in the street, shortly after the car sped off.

The House points to conspiracy

The 1977–78 House Select Committee on Assassinations found that, while Ray did the deed, there was a "likelihood" he did not act alone. The House considered whether the CIA was involved in framing Ray, in view of the numerous fake IDs and documents found on him when he was arrested. One alias, which he'd used before the shooting, belonged to a Canadian named Galt. Galt strongly resembled Ray, and was a crack shot into the bargain. However, Ray's initial escape to Canada, where a "fat man" gave him the money to get to England, was the first time he had ever visited the country.

Jowers "confesses"

Another twist came in 1993, when Loyd Jowers, the owner of a grill bar opposite the motel, told ABC TV that he had been asked to help in the assassination, and had been told there would be a decoy, namely Ray. Jowers said that a cast of Memphis police and government agents met in his restaurant in the days prior to King's death; that a mobster dropped off money there; and that a man named Raul arrived the day before, and left a rifle which reappeared, smoking, after the shooting.

The story unravels

Ray's lawyer, William Pepper, accused the Green Berets of carrying out the killing. In his 1995 book *Orders To Kill: The Truth Behind The Murder Of Martin Luther King*, he says that members of the 20th Special Forces Group, including several with experience of CIA missions in Vietnam, were scattered in and around Memphis in the period leading up to the shooting.

An FBI agent came forward in 1998 and claimed that he had once had papers from Ray's car with FBI phone numbers and "Raul" written on them, which were subsequently stolen. In August that year, Attorney General Janet Reno ordered the Justice Department to reinvestigate King's death. Focussing mainly on the Jowers story, they completed their report in 1999. Their conclusion? Ray did it, and there was "no reliable evidence that Dr King was killed by conspirators who framed James Earl Ray". They continued "nor have any of the conspiracy theories advanced in the last thirty years … survived critical examination". It was Ray and Ray alone.

The Kings say it wasn't Ray

In December 1999, on the other hand, a Memphis jury in a wrongful death suit determined that there was a conspiracy to kill King by Loyd Jowers and "other unknown conspirators" – understood to mean government agents of some kind – and awarded the King family a symbolic $100. The trial was a civil suit because the intelligence agencies can only be tried in criminal courts with Federal government consent, which wasn't forthcoming. Coretta Scott King and King's son Dexter have also said that they believe their father was killed in a larger conspiracy, involving the CIA, FBI, Army and President Johnson. Dexter visited Ray in jail in 1997 to say that he and the Kings believe in his innocence. Ray himself has since died. Both the Lorraine motel and the "sniper's nest" in the apartment building are now open to visitors as memorials to Dr King and his death, and an exhibition approved by the King family lays out assorted conspiracy theories in copious detail.

SOURCES

Books

William Pepper Orders To Kill: The Truth Behind The Murder Of Martin Luther King (1995). The fact that the charges come from a source as close to the facts, and the family, as King's lawyer renders them all the more extraordinary.

Websites

ⓦ www.consortiumnews.com/2000/ 022100a.html Plenty of Martin Luther King conspiracies.

ⓦ www.usdoj.gov/crt/crim/mlk/part1. htm The official verdict of the Justice Department in 1998.

Robert Kennedy

For a brief, heady moment in 1968, it looked as though Robert F. Kennedy was going to fill the presidential shoes of his slain brother John. The great white hope of liberal America, Robert had recast himself as a handsome, idealistic young knight, crusading across an America that was bitterly divided over civil rights and the worsening situation in Vietnam. It's hardly surprising that when Robert was shot dead on June 4, 1968, a mere two months after the killing of Dr Martin Luther King Jr., three quarters of Americans are said to have believed he was the victim of a conspiracy.

That day, RFK won the crucial Democratic primary election in California, which made him the front-runner to become the Democrats' presidential nominee that fall. As the results came in, he celebrated at Los Angeles' Ambassador hotel. At 12.15am, engulfed by a throng of supporters, press, guards and others, he was being escorted out through the hotel pantry when someone managed to get a clear shot at him. A hail of bullets left RFK bleeding to death on the floor.

A small Palestinian man, Sirhan Bashira Sirhan, gun in hand and firing wildly, was wrestled down by the security men who had so palpably failed to protect Kennedy. Sirhan was subsequently put on trial, and convicted of murder in the first degree. A "lone nut", who had apparently snapped on seeing RFK's pro-Israeli statements in late May, he was sentenced to life imprisonment.

A case riddled with holes

For many observers, however, too much about the case simply didn't add up. For a start, although the would-be president was appearing in front of two thousand people, and despite the fate of his brother, his only protection came from a private security firm, Ace.

On top of that, there were too many bullets. Sirhan's pistol held eight rounds, but RFK took three wounds, one bullet went through his clothing, and five others were also fired... which makes nine bullets. According to the Los Angeles Police Department, some bullets must have hit more than one person. However, the *Los Angeles Free Press* newspaper then reported, with photographic proof,

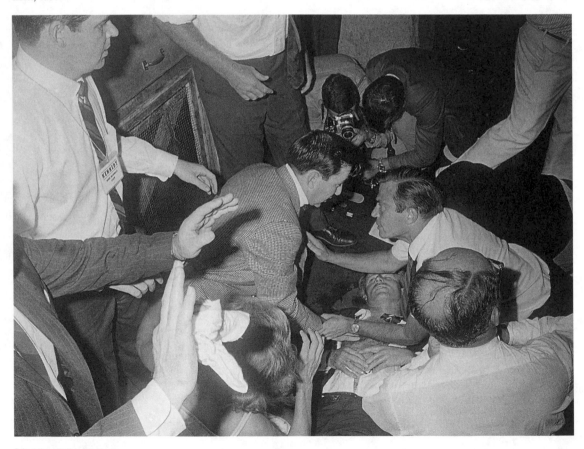

Robert Kennedy lies dying

that more bullets were lodged in a doorframe in the pantry. Indeed the total fired reached thirteen, and thus pointed to the presence of at least one more gunman. It was shown that the police had indeed documented the extra hits, but had failed to disclose that information at the trial, after which the doorframe and all forensic evidence had been destroyed. On that basis, Congressman Allard Lowenstein attempted unsuccessfully to start a reinvestigation in 1974, backed by Hollywood celebrities such as Robert Vaughn. Lowenstein was later shot dead in his law office by "a disgruntled client".

According to Court TV, Lowenstein's investigation was largely sabotaged by the intransigence of the LAPD. After much media pressure, the LAPD released its crudely censored records of the events in 1986. Further pressure led to the release of fifty thousand more documents in 1988, but these still excluded not only the doorframe evidence but also the trial testimonies of seven forensic experts.

Bullets from the wrong direction

Crucially, the coroner, Thomas Noguchi (who also attended the corpses of Marilyn Monroe and John Belushi), reported that the fatal wound was caused by a .22 bullet that went into the back of RFK's head. Powder burns indicated that the gun was fired from a distance of no more than three inches. However, every witness put Sirhan several feet *in front* of RFK, and no one said that Kennedy had turned away. Noguchi, who examined the bullet-ridden doorframe, later wrote: "The existence of a second gunman remains a possibility. Thus, I have never said that Sirhan Sirhan killed Robert Kennedy."

Sirhan remembers nothing

Sirhan himself said after the trial that he had no memory of the shooting. Although a psychiatrist working for the defence, Bernard Diamond, diagnosed Sirhan as a paranoid schizophrenic, the trial judge didn't allow Sirhan to use the defence of insanity. Diamond did not rule out hypnosis, which another doctor who examined Sirhan in jail said was utterly credible.

In *RFK Must Die*, former *Time* correspondent Robert Blair Kaiser, who also worked for Sirhan's defence team, wrote that Sirhan was programmed to kill Robert Kennedy and then forget his programming. Dr Eduard Simpson examined Sirhan in prison and believed he had been hypnotized. Notebooks presented by the prosecution at the trial, which supposedly belonged to Sirhan and in which he wrote "RFK must die" and "must be assassinated", were claimed to be forgeries. Ex-FBI agent William Turner lent his support to the theory that Sirhan was a so-called "Manchurian candidate" (see p. 192).

Half a dozen witnesses reported seeing a "girl in a polka-dot dress" fleeing the scene, screaming "We shot him!"; asked "who?", she replied "Senator Kennedy!". Sirhan's last memory prior to the shooting was of drinking coffee with a woman, who he said wore a polka-dot dress. The theory runs that the woman gave Sirhan his final preparations, using techniques mastered under the CIA hypnosis program, MK-ULTRA.

If the CIA was involved in hypnotizing Sirhan, a possible motive might be fear that if RFK reached the White House he would order a proper investigation into his brother's death, and thus discover the part played by the CIA. But that doesn't answer the riddle of the point-blank shots fired from behind him.

The security guard

Many observers saw Ace security guard Thane Cesar standing right behind Robert Kennedy, and even described him drawing a gun. As Cesar admitted, he was in a perfect position to shoot Kennedy at point-blank range. Despite being a crucial witness, however, he was not called to testify at Sirhan's trial.

Cesar told the LAPD that he'd possessed a .22 pistol that he had sold before the shooting; it was subsequently proved that he'd sold it afterwards. Interviewed in 1994 by Dan Moldea, the author of *The Killing Of Robert Kennedy*, he passed a polygraph test in which he denied shooting Kennedy. But had he been programmed as well?

The CIA, the Mafia and the arms industry

So who wanted Kennedy dead? It wasn't beyond the CIA to get the Mafia to do the job, but equally it wasn't beyond the Mafia to do it themselves. As Sam Giancana's brother and grandson wrote in *Double Cross*, the mob hated Robert Kennedy for his war on organized crime as both senator and attorney general. The Giancanas also charged that Marilyn Monroe's death was a bid by the Mafia to topple Robert Kennedy (see p.17). In 2004, Court TV reported that Giancana's supposed ally in bumping off Monroe, Teamsters' union leader Jimmy Hoffa, had told an informant in 1967 that he had a contract on RFK and he'd be dead if he ever won a primary.

Another much-touted suspect is the "military-industrial complex", which didn't want Kennedy to end the lucrative Vietnam war. It has to be said that the president who ended the war, Richard Nixon, wasn't killed... but then he did resign in disgrace. For that matter, neither did neo-Nazis want an advocate of civil rights in the White House, and they may have been aided by FBI boss J. Edgar Hoover. In 2005, one writer linked the CIA, FBI and Aristotle Onassis in the plot to hypnotize Sirhan, but again failed to address the bullet-from-behind conundrum.

Case unsolved

Whoever was behind the killing – and more to the point, whoever was behind Kennedy when the killing was done – Sirhan continues to protest his innocence from jail. The belief of his lawyer, Lawrence Teeter, that Sirhan was hypnotized might seem absurd, but it's no more absurd than the fact that Sirhan was convicted despite the problem of the extra bullets.

In the minds of many Americans, the case is still unsolved, and the actions of the LAPD in disposing of the forensic evidence hardly allay suspicion. Nonetheless, the official story, as reiterated by a 1997 Congressional hearing on the killing, remains the same. Sirhan did it, and he acted alone.

SOURCES

Books

Sam and Chuck Giancana Double Cross: The Explosive, Inside Story Of The Mobster Who Controlled America (1992). This book is a must-read, not only for the vignettes of Mafia-speak, but also because it plausibly identifies a handful of Mafiosi as the men behind many 1960s assassinations.

Robert Blair Kaiser RFK Must Die! (1970). A contemporary account.

William W. Turner and Jonn G. Christian The Assassination Of Robert F. Kennedy: The Conspiracy And Coverup (1993). This raises a lot of questions about the LAPD and CIA, but the biggest mystery is the lack of outcry from the US public.

Websites

ⓦ www.crimelibrary.com/terrorists_spies/assassins/kennedy/2.html A detailed, soberly written tour through the failures and questions surrounding RFK's death.

ⓦ www.ss.ca.gov/archives/level3_rfkguide.html The Californian government's opinion about the RFK killing.

Harold Wilson

What do you do when your own spies turn against you? British Prime Minister Harold Wilson was faced with that question in a conspiracy, which, if it didn't kill him, is said to have put an abrupt end to his career. Wilson could boast the enviable achievement of winning more general elections for the Labour party than any other leader, in 1964, 1966, and twice in 1974. No one in the party challenged his leadership. When he suddenly announced his departure, on March 15, 1976, the official explanation was that the sixty-year-old was too tired to go on; he'd simply had enough. However, within weeks, stories began to surface that a broad right-wing conspiracy had been plotting against Wilson and his aides throughout his years in office.

"Dark forces"

The source of these stories was Wilson himself. In May 1976, he gave a series of speeches alleging "subversion from the Right" of Britain's democratic parties. In lengthy recorded interviews, he told two journalists, Barry Penrose and Roger Courtiour, that "dark forces" with unlimited slush funds were undermining democracy, targeting the Labour party and especially himself. Wilson spoke of a coup that had been planned in 1968 by Lord Mountbatten and others, and described malicious rumours that had been circulated of a pro-Soviet cell in 10 Downing Street under his tenure. He also directed the Press Commission towards a series of break-ins at his family and aides' residences in the months preceding his resignation, and charged that extreme right-wing forces in the UK's domestic intelligence service MI5 were behind the attacks.

"Cock and bull"

Unfortunately, the style in which the allegations were written up was not entirely conducive to their being taken seriously. Wilson claimed that because Penrose and Courtiour were inexperienced, and unable to distinguish between fact and humour, the stories they published had been "cock and bull". He also denied reports elsewhere in the press that No. 10 had been bugged. The fact that Wilson appeared to be rubbishing his own bizarre delusions meant that few people took his accumulated charges at all seriously.

The confessions of a British spy

Ten years later, however, Peter Wright, the former deputy director of MI5, had much to say on the subject of Wilson as the target of "dirty tricks". In his 1985 autobiography *Spycatcher*, Wright stated that there was indeed a conspiracy to topple Wilson by "exposing" him as a Communist. Wilson's pedigree at Oxford University in the 1930s, when it was almost *de rigueur* to be a Marxist, aroused the conspirators' suspicions, but they were particularly interested in his trip to Moscow in 1947. As a junior minister at the Board of Trade, he was involved in selling aero-engines to the USSR; but rumour had it that he was compromised in a love tryst that kept him in hock thereafter to the KGB. Both MI5 and the US intelligence agencies were also alarmed by his views on the Korean War, which he felt could be settled without necessarily destroying the North Korean state.

According to Wright, most suspect of all was the death of Wilson's predecessor as leader of the Labour party, Hugh Gaitskell, in 1963. Gaitskell's doctor is said to have approached MI5 with concerns about his disease, *lupus disseminata*, which was quite alien to the UK. Gaitskell had recently visited Russia, and word soon filtered back through a defector, Anatoli Golitsin, that the KGB had plotted to bump off a major European leader and "get their man in place". In the UK in 1963, the existing Conservative government was clearly imploding in a welter of corruption, and power seemed to be Gaitskell's for the taking – until he died, and it passed instead to Wilson. As Wright put it, this fitted Golitsin's story rather too neatly for MI5 to dismiss.

Comrade Wilsonski

But was Wilson really Moscow's man in London? Golitsin's allegation was made when he was on a substantial retainer from MI5; he had, however, not bothered to mention it to US intelligence while he was in their hands during the preceding years. And Wilson had not exactly ingratiated himself with MI5, making it one of his first jobs in 1964 to order the spooks to stop wire-tapping MPs. According to London MP and mayor Ken Livingstone, MI5 feared that Wilson might dismember the service because of its failures in the earlier Burgess/Maclean/Blunt/Philby spy scandals. Livingstone told the House of Commons in 1996 that seven of Wilson's cabinet and three Labour MPs were deemed to be spies or security risks. Ben Pimlott, in his biography of Wilson, wrote that a pernicious strain of anti-Semitism ran through the security services, and named Peter Wright in particular. MI5 is said to have hated the Jewish business friends whom Wilson made while at the Board of Trade, many of whom were eastern European.

During the 1970s, further aggravated by increased union "extremism", MI5 is said to have fed the press,

notably *Private Eye* magazine, with a steady drip of smear and innuendo about Wilson's supposed Soviet links and his alleged "affair" with his aide Marcia Williams. According to the chief of MI6, Sir Maurice Oldfield, MI5's chief Sir Michael Hanley went "white as a sheet" when Oldfield told him about the campaign, "learning that half of his staff were up to their necks in a plot to get rid of their prime minister." Pimlott argues that Army intelligence hated Wilson too, citing the belief of one officer that Wilson and his crew were puppets of the pro-IRA Soviets. Supposedly, the Soviets were also behind civil unrest and strikes not only in Ulster, but throughout the UK. Wilson had to be brought down by any means. At one stage, Wright even tried to enlist CIA director James Jesus Angleton to expose the ultimate KGB front man.

It has also been alleged that MI5 was deeply involved with Britain's main opposition party, the Conservatives, in engineering Wilson's departure. By the time *Spycatcher* appeared, Margaret Thatcher's Conservative government was in power. It didn't so much counter Wright's allegations as exhaust itself spending two years trying to prevent its publication in the UK, and thereby helped turn a less-than-enthralling tome into a global bestseller. The third edition of the government's official *MI5: The Security Service* says that the plot to undermine Wilson "was exhaustively investigated", and "no such plot had ever existed". The booklet points out that even Wright told BBC1's *Panorama* programme that his account was "unreliable", but it has itself been called a whitewash.

Just because you're paranoid...

If a country's secret services have their own politicized agenda, then there's little anyone can do about it, especially if the country's leader is not only kept out of the loop but is in fact the target.

In the public mind, Harold Wilson shot down his own original claims. His former chancellor, Denis Healey, said that Wilson's capacity for self-delusion "made Walter Mitty look unimaginative", and that he was obsessed with illusory plots and conspiracies whenever things went wrong. However, the big guns of MI5 have told the world that they considered Wilson to be a Soviet man even if they couldn't prove it, and that they spread rumours and innuendo in the hope of getting rid of him.

Thus there was indeed a conspiracy against Wilson, though as Pimlott argues, whatever the intelligence services had on Wilson when he was in office wasn't enough to shut him up when he left it. If both the target and the conspirators are paranoid, it becomes impossible to know who to believe. To this day, however, there has never been a truly convincing explanation of quite why Harold Wilson resigned when he did.

SOURCES

Books

Ben Pimlott **Harold Wilson** (1992). A brick-thick, but incisively written tome on the life and

times of Labour's most elected prime minister.
Peter Wright **Spycatcher: The Candid Autobiography Of A Senior Intelligence**

Officer (1987). More hype than substance, and sadly not as revealing as the mass government efforts to censor it suggested.

Salvador Allende

It's not known who exactly pulled the trigger to kill President Salvador Allende on September 11, 1973, during a bloody military coup in Chile. It remains a mystery whether he was cut down by the troops of General Augusto Pinochet as they stormed the presidential palace, which had already been bombed by airforce jets, or whether Allende took his own life in defiance. What's no longer in dispute is that the US was behind the coup, in a plot that can no longer simply be dismissed as a "conspiracy theory".

The official US version, in the days that followed the coup, was that Allende's bad leadership had obliged the Chilean military to step in and rescue the country. As President Richard Nixon put it in his memoirs, Allende's inefficient socialist government, in power since late 1970, had caused crippling strikes that resulted in an inflation rate of 350 percent by 1973. The army could no longer stand by.

The CIA and Nixon

However, it was hard to believe that the US had played no part in Allende's downfall, given that it had tried so hard to stop him getting into office in the first place. Richard Nixon, who was in office at the time of both Allende's accession and his death, wrote that Kennedy and Johnson had spent almost four million dollars ensuring Allende's defeat in Chile's 1962 and 1964 elections, while in 1970, when Allende won, he received $350,000 from Cuba. Nixon followed his predecessors' lead, instructing the CIA to support Allende's opponents in the Chilean Congress. "As long as the Communists supply external funds to support political parties, factions or individuals in other countries, I believe that the United States can and should do the same and do it secretly so that it can be effective ... To me it would have been the height of immorality to allow the Soviets, the Cubans and other Communist nations to interfere with impunity in free elections while America stayed its hand."

The election of Allende established Cuba and Chile as a "red sandwich", which Nixon feared might export revolution elsewhere in the continent. Even so, the US appeared to accept the will of the Chilean people, until Allende's overthrow in 1973 ushered in the seventeen-year dictatorship of Augusto Pinochet, whose regime didn't so much interfere with free elections as outlaw opposition on the pain of murder.

The problem with Allende

Salvador Allende nationalized Chile's banks and copper industry, and received aid from both Cuba and the USSR. By contrast, the US government curtailed its trade with Chile, and cut off aid, while at the same time the CIA increased its support to the Chilean military in terms of arms and advice, and encouraged right-wing paramilitary groups. Once the pro-capitalist Pinochet was installed, US trade and aid with Chile resumed. Pinochet cut government spending and social subsidies, lowered tariffs, and opened Chilean markets to massive imports, causing wages to fall and industries to close. As the working poor faced starvation, the US government propped up the Pinochet junta with financial aid.

Keep your enemies closer: Augusto Pinochet and Salvador Allende

The smoking guns

While this was all common knowledge, it amounted to no more than circumstantial evidence that the CIA was behind the coup. Then the Clinton administration declassified the relevant CIA documents in 2000. US strategy at the outset was summarized in a memo dated September 27, 1970, which outlined a programme of economic, political and psychological warfare against and within Chile that might ultimately bring down Allende, with the final pointer: "Surface ineluctable conclusion that military coup is the only answer. This is to be carried forward until it takes place ... [but in production being] diffuse, denatured, and ineffective ... Eventually we may use propaganda to persuade the military that it is their constitutional duty to prevent Allende from holding power." CIA director Richard Helms said that he intended to "make the Chilean economy scream".

In September 1973, the plan came off. The reason Nixon declined to take credit for the coup is revealed in a transcript of what national security adviser Henry Kissinger told him on September 16, 1973. US newspapers were "bleeding because a pro-Communist government had been overthrown ... I mean instead of celebrating – in the Eisenhower period we would be heroes," Kissinger lamented.

The documents also revealed that in 1964, the CIA had not considered Allende to be all that dangerous, or regarded him as a genuine ally of the Soviets. "The US has no vital national interests within Chile", it reported, or at least none that could be threatened by distributing free milk or national-izing industries, or even by expanding trade with the Soviets.

Suspicions proven

The declassification of the CIA documents confirmed beyond doubt the extent of the US government's determination to bring down Allende. Under the ensuing Pinochet dictatorship, 130,000 Chilean citizens were placed under political arrest; 3100 "disappeared" and torture was widespread. True, inflation was brought under control and some economists cited Chile as a model for other Latin American countries; it also, however, came to rank seventh in the world for inequality of income distribution. Despite the support of powerful friends, among them Margaret Thatcher, Pinochet has since been the subject of court action in Spain and the UK, and has recently been stripped of his immunity from prosecution in Chile.

SOURCES

Books

Richard Nixon The Memoirs Of Richard Nixon (1978). A good read, and an insight into what the world's most powerful man will choose to delete, forget or subliminally reappraise.

Websites

Ⓦ www.worldpress.org/Americas/1591.cfm
A brief, political summary of events; there's more detail (although uncorroborated), at www.rrojasdatabank.org/coup1.htm

Elvis Presley

Elvis Presley, "The King" of Rock'n'Roll, was found dead in the bathroom at Gracelands, his home in Memphis, on August 16, 1977. Tributes poured in from around the world, from The Beatles to The Beach Boys, and President Jimmy Carter made a statement.

The medical examiner in Shelby County reported the cause of death as heart failure, brought on by chronic heart disease. However, Elvis was only 42, and rumours ran rife that he'd simply faked his own death to escape his unrelenting, obsessive fans.

Those rumours have snowballed into a veritable industry, as magazines like *National Enquirer* publish a steady stream of bread-and-butter stories that Elvis has been spotted everywhere from Antarctica to the Moon.

Chips and fixes

Compared to the young sex-god who had shown America's teens what hips were really for during the 1950s and 1960s, Elvis had by the 1970s be-

The President meets the King: Richard Nixon and Elvis

come a physical and mental wreck. He both dealt with and exacerbated his decline by ingesting copious quantities of food and prescription drugs. The same evergreen core of devotees who went to his shows, and thus provided him with the audiences he craved, also staked out his mansion, flooding his mailbox with letters, flowers, tributes and declarations of undying love. All of which served to fuel Elvis' paranoid fantasies that he too would fall victim to a lone nut.

When he stayed in hotels on tour, Elvis often used the pseudonym John Burrows. Just days after the King was announced dead, someone with that name, who very much resembled Presley, was supposedly seen buying a ticket for South America. Had Elvis chosen to escape from his own glamorous but destructive existence for a life of anonymity?

Elvis meets Nixon

Although some have suggested that Elvis was murdered by right-wing government elements, Elvis considered himself to be very much in line with that mindset. So much so that he took himself to Washington DC in 1970, to meet first Vice President Spiro Agnew and then, a few weeks later, Richard Nixon. He told the president how America's youth was being morally degraded by rock degenerates such as The Beatles, and offered his services. Nixon responded by appointing him as "Federal Agent at Large" against drugs.

Elvis messes with the CIA

Did Elvis's desire to help the government run deep enough to allow the CIA to use Graceland as the cover for a massive secret underground installation? The very idea was so ludicrous, of course, that no one would ever suspect the truth. Then Elvis,

forgetting quite who he was dealing with, is said to have threatened to expose the scheme unless the CIA moved out from beneath him – paying the price with his life. Equally ludicrously, some have blamed Elvis for assassinating JFK, having been enraged by the way that the handsome President was barging into his limelight. Elvis was then killed in revenge.

Elvis on drugs

Perhaps, on the other hand, Elvis died of an overdose of prescription drugs. It's been alleged that Elvis's father Vernon was so afraid that the news would tarnish his son's anti-drugs image forever that he bribed medical officials to say that he'd died of a heart attack. *The Washington Post* reported the coroner's verdict that "there was no sign of drug abuse": a striking observation to make if it had simply been a heart attack. Vernon's widow Dee has told of seeing autopsy papers that blamed drugs for Elvis's death. However, while the Shelby County Commission has filed for a second autopsy, the Elvis estate has resisted such a move. According to the website www.elvispresleynews.com, "the secrets surrounding Elvis' autopsy is [sic] still to be laid to rest".

There was only one Elvis – and he's gone

The reason there have been so many Elvis sightings is very simple: there's a lot of money, entertainment, and just plain comfort to be derived from reporting yet another sighting, even decades after his death. On top of that, of course, countless men the world over still pay homage to the King by dressing up and singing like him – it's hardly surprising some of them get "spotted".

Ultimately, heart failure makes the most sense, given Elvis's extraordinary appetite. This was a man who considered a dozen two-foot baguettes, stuffed with pounds of bacon, jam and peanut butter, literally worth flying to Las Vegas for. His frenetic stage performances also forced him into an horrendous see-sawing cycle of weight gain and loss. In the end, it was a question of time which organ would shut down first, as the world's most famous star gorged himself to death.

SOURCES

Books

Paul Simpson **The Rough Guide To Elvis** (2002). Contains a very detailed overview of the many theories and rumours that surround the death of the King.

Websites

ⓦ**www.deadoraliveinfo.com/dead.nsf/ pnames-nf/Presley+Elvis** For those who suspect that Elvis isn't even dead.

ⓦ**www.elvispresleynews.com** and **www. elvis.com** For die-hard fans.

ⓦ**www.nationalenquirer.com** For those who know that Elvis isn't dead.

Pope John Paul I

When Albino Luciani, a humble, almost timid man without a high-profile career in the Vatican hierarchy, was elected Pope on August 26, 1978, the cardinals in the papal conclave seemed as surprised as Luciani himself. But he was proudly acclaimed as "God's candidate", and soon acquired the nickname of the "Smiling Pope". Catholics all over the world responded warmly to his modesty – at his coronation, he refused the customary papal tiara and only reluctantly agreed to be carried aloft on the traditional gestatorial chair. Shortly after 5am on September 28, however, just 33 days after his election, Pope John Paul I was found dead in the papal lodgings. The Vatican initially claimed that his body was found by his papal secretaries, Magee and Lorenzi

– propped up in bed with a copy of Thomas à Kempis's *Imitation of Christ* – but afterwards revealed that he was discovered by a nun who had brought him his morning coffee. The papal doctor, Renato Buzzonetti, declared him dead of a heart attack. At 5.15pm, the Signoracci brothers, embalmers to the Vatican, were summoned. They began work within two hours. There was no autopsy.

For any Pope, let alone such a popular one, to die just a month after his election was unimaginable. Conspiracy theories abounded, the most persuasive and persistent of which were eventually researched, tidied up and presented in David Yallop's 1984 bestseller, *In God's Name*. The book accused an unholy trinity of Vatican conservatives, Mafia bankers and right-wing Italian Freemasons, claim-

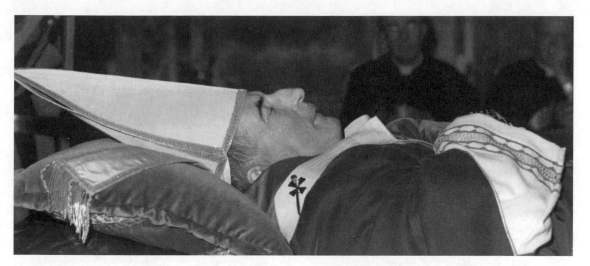

John Paul I lies in state

ing that Luciani had been poisoned with digitalis heart medicine.

Vatican conservatives

The Second Vatican Council of 1962–65 proclaimed a new, more open Catholic church, and finally permitted a vernacular rather than a Latin liturgy. But the church was riven by factions. Some thought "Vatican II" had been dangerously liberal, others that it hadn't gone far enough. Although birth control was outlawed, the election of a liberal pope might change that. John Paul I, according to Yallop, was that liberal pope, and was on the brink of authorizing contraception when he was killed.

But was Luciani really a liberal? Yes, he apparently rejected some traditions by toning down his coronation and by referring to himself as "I", not "we", but these might simply have been the actions of a modest man, rather than a reformer. Yallop alleges

that Luciani had advised Paul VI – in a document never found by any other researcher – not to outlaw contraception in his bull *Humanae Vitae*. Although publicly Luciani always supported the conservative line on birth control, Yallop's supporters claim that John Paul's speeches on the subject were subtly censored in the Vatican mouthpiece newspaper, *L'Osservatore Romano*, which did, it is true, change his "I"s to "we"s.

God's bankers

According to Yallop, Luciani's allegedly liberal views on contraception were only a side issue. He says the real danger was his desire to clean up the *Istituto per le Opere Religiose* (IOR), the Vatican Bank. The story is murky, complex and highly disputed. Sicilian tax expert and international financier Michele "the Shark" Sindona had apparently become a key middleman between the IOR, which

SUICIDED AT BLACKFRIARS BRIDGE: ROBERTO CALVI

In 1982, a stock-market slide caused the secretive financial walls around Roberto Calvi, a director of the Milan-based Banco Ambrosiano, to collapse, exposing the foundations of his self-built banking castle as nothing but $1.3 billion's worth of sheer air. He was sacked on June 17, and expected to face prosecution. Privately, he knew he faced a worse fate, as he and his co-conspirators in the Vatican Bank had been ripping off the Mafia on the side for years, and had earned the enmity of Michele "the Shark" Sindona – allegedly the financial middle-man between the Vatican Bank and the Mafia – for failing to bail out Sindona's beleaguered Franklin Bank back in 1974. Calvi's rumoured attempts to negotiate a financial rescue package from the right-wing Catholic organization Opus Dei (Calvi's son Carlo claims he even met John Paul II) came to nothing.

On June 18, Calvi was found hanging below London's Blackfriars Bridge on the end of a noose of orange rope, with $15,000 dollars stuffed into his pockets. Some observers saw Masonic significance in the choice of venue – a "black friar" is supposedly one of the symbols commonly used in Italian Freemasonry… A British coroner, who perhaps hadn't come across many Mafia or indeed Masonic killings, recorded a verdict of suicide. Coincidentally, Calvi's secretary committed suicide in Milan on the same day.

The initial British verdict was finally overturned by an Italian court in 2002. It certainly looked like a punishment killing. Calvi had been hung from an iron ring, his feet in the water and bricks in his pockets; he would have died slowly and agonizingly as the tide dropped away beneath him. In 1992, Mafia supergrass Francesco Mannino Mannoia declared that Calvi had been strangled by one Francesco Di Carlo, the Mafia's man in charge of London's heroin operation, on the orders of Cosa Nostra boss and Mafia "ambassador to Rome", Pippo "the Cashier" Calò. In April 2005, three alleged Mafia men (including Calò) and a woman were charged with Calvi's murder in a Roman court. Calvi's son Carlo is sure that he was killed to protect the powers behind the Vatican Bank – Archbishop Paul Marcinkus in particular – and the institutional conspiracy that lay behind the right-wing Masonic lodge, P2 (see p.125). A dead man can't squeal, and neither can he blackmail his former co-conspirators.

As for the black hole left in the Vatican's finances by Banco Ambrosiano's collapse, persistent (and just as persistently denied) rumours claim that the right-wing Catholic organization Opus Dei (see p.171) footed the bill, thus buying its way into the heart of Vatican counsels. In Italy, allegations that the membership of Opus Dei crosses over with that of P2 have dogged the group. Certainly, there's a significant correlation in terms of personality profile – high-achieving, authoritarian and conservative. The same is true for CIA agents, a disproportionate number of whom are said to be Opus Dei members. Conspiracy theorists claim that Ronald Reagan helped to plug the Vatican's finances (and not incidentally bought himself "the Catholic vote") with three hundred million dollars of CIA discretionary funds.

was seeking to limit its new tax liabilities, and the Mafia, which needed its money laundered – preferably through an opaque, hard-to-touch financial institution. Sindona's key instrument was Roberto Calvi (see above), who handled the IOR's riskier and shadier speculations through the Milan-based Catholic bank, Banco Ambrosiano, including the transfer of billions of dollars into ephemeral and sometimes non-existent offshore accounts, allegedly in partnership with the American Archbishop and IOR director, Paul Marcinkus.

Nicknamed "God's banker", Marcinkus has always denied any involvement; at the time of writing, he was working as a priest in Arizona, with no threat of prosecution – thanks partly to John Paul II granting him special immunity. Equally, the Vatican never accepted responsibility for Ambrosiano's collapse under Calvi, though it paid out some $250m to creditors – allegedly with the help of Opus Dei (see p.171). Sindona's fraudulent banking deals, by contrast, were exposed when his Franklin Bank collapsed in 1974 – the largest bank failure in US history. Sindona was later forced to fake his own kidnapping by "left-wing terrorists" in order to escape criminal charges, but eventually went on trial in Italy. There, he arranged the contract killing of a prosecution witness, a classic Mafia crime for which he was convicted by an Italian court in 1986; that same year, while in prison, he was murdered with a cup of poisoned coffee.

figures. Roberto Calvi and Michele Sindona were on the list too, but curiously, no Vatican prelates were named. This doesn't bother Vatican conspiracists, as self-confessed repentant P2 member and tabloid journalist Mino Pecorelli claimed in 1978 that both Marcinkus and Villot had in fact been members. As the sole witness to have come forward, Pecorelli is less than reliable, though perhaps his credibility rose after he was killed in March 1979 – the first of a number of implicated figures and investigators who were murdered that summer.

A thief in the night: Cornwell's counter-claims

In the wake of the scandal that surrounded *In God's Name*, Vatican officials asked English journalist John Cornwell to conduct a thorough, independent investigation, and write it up in popular form. Written like a thriller, *A Thief In The Night* appeared in 1989. Pope John Paul I, it said, had died of a pulmonary embolism. Cornwall's evidence was persuasive. Luciani was known to have had severely swollen feet. He complained of feeling unwell the day before he died. He suffered a bad bout of coughing in front of his papal secretaries. And he unwisely ran to answer the telephone that evening. Sure-fire grave-fodder, then. All this, Cornwell claims, points to the development of an embolism that was dislodged and finally reached the heart at around 9.30pm. Cornwell convincingly demolishes some key points in Yallop's argument – especially his claims that Cardinal Villot called the embalmers in before he let anyone else in the Vatican know about the Pope's death, and disposed of the Pope's allegedly vomit-stained glasses, slippers and heart medicine. His own theory has one weak point, however: it relies on the papal secretaries having manoeuvred the Pope's body into a more dignified position in bed and having lied about it forever after.

Roberto Calvi

Masons in the Vatican

Blowing the whistle on the Vatican Bank was the least of Luciani's threats. Millions of people in Italy – almost a third, some polls suggest – believe he was also poised to expose the existence of a powerful Masonic cabal within the Vatican. Among the Masons, it is claimed, were Cardinal Villot – as the Vatican Secretary of State, number two to the Pope – and Archbishop Marcinkus. They are supposed to have belonged to *Propaganda Due*, better known as P2 (see p.125), which was half quasi-Masonic network, half murderous terrorist cell dedicated to the establishment of a fascist state. A police raid in 1981 turned up a list of members that included countless powerful state officials, police chiefs, businessmen and media

Gibson, Lefebvre and the sedevacantists

The death of John Paul I continues to have political reverberations within the Catholic church. Arch-traditionalist "sedevacantists" (such as Mel Gibson), who believe that all Popes since Vatican II have been false Popes, are as ready to believe in conspiracies as left-wingers. As early as August 28, 1978, maverick sedevacantist French bishop Marcel Lefebvre claimed that the papal conclave had elected its candidate with suspicious haste, given that the necessary two-thirds majority had been achieved at only the third ballot. Some Lefebvrists even went on to claim that Pope Paul VI had been replaced by an impostor.

As for Luciani's successor, Pope John Paul II, he was at various times dubbed a Communist sympathizer on the one hand, and a tool of liberal capitalism – personally responsible for the collapse of the Eastern Bloc – on the other. It's a question of political sensibility. The Left is sure that the CIA was behind Luciani's death, while the Right is convinced the KGB were involved. Catholics smell Masonic plots, while secular Italians see the machinations of the Vatican. Like so much in Italy, Italian history seems to be a matter of taste.

SOURCES

Books

John Cornwell A Thief In The Night (1989). A thriller-writer's authorized counter-blast to Yallop.

David Yallop In God's Name (1984). The chief conduit by which the conspiracy theories raging in Italy and the Catholic world reached the Anglo-Protestant hemisphere. Not big in Catholic bookshops.

A living sacrifice: Archbishop Romero

Of all the 75,000 political murders that took place in El Salvador between 1980 and 1991, the most shocking and iconic was the killing of Archbishop Oscar Arnulfo Romero y Galdámez, shot dead at the altar as he celebrated a memorial mass in March 1980. Romero was a gadfly, relentlessly criticizing the right-wing junta that had ruled El Salvador since a military coup in 1979, speaking out in defence of the poor and exposing the activities of the notorious, military-backed death squads fighting the left-wing insurgents against the regime. He was aware of the danger, telling a newspaper: "You can tell the people that if they succeed in killing me, that I forgive and bless those who do it."

On the morning of March 24, 1980, a red Volkswagen pulled up immediately outside the open west doors of the chapel of the Hospital de la Divina Providencia in San Salvador, where Romero was celebrating a memorial mass. A bearded gunman leaned out with a rifle and calmly, expertly shot Romero dead as he stood at the altar. The following day, the Carter administration sought congressional approval for $5.7m worth of military equipment to be sent to El Salvador, while officials simultaneously accused Cuba of direct involvement in the insurgency. Amid bomb explosions and flying bullets, fifty thousand mourners turned out for the Archbishop's funeral. There's no doubt that there was a conspiracy to kill Romero, and small doubt that the right-wing military was behind it. More contentious is the idea that the CIA had a hand in the murder too.

The campaigner

Romero hadn't won his elevated post by being a radical. In March 1977, however, he experienced a Damascene conversion after one of his more outspoken priests, a Jesuit campaigning for the rights of the poor, was murdered in mysterious circumstances. As there was no official investigation, Romero began his own enquiries. By May 1979, he had gathered enough material to present the recently elected Pope John Paul II with a dossier detailing hundreds of murders and other human rights abuses. The Archbishop helped start up a San Salvador radio station that broadcast the names of the missing and the killed, and spoke out passionately from the pulpit, telling soldiers: "I beseech you, I beg you, I order you, in the name of God, to stop the repression!"

In February 1980, Romero even wrote directly to President Carter, pleading for him to stop supplying the governing regime with arms, money and "counter-insurgency" training, on the grounds that they "increase injustice here and sharpen the repression

that has been unleashed against the people's organizations fighting to defend their most fundamental human rights". In 1993, a UN Truth Commission reported that the US delivered almost six billion dollars in aid to El Salvador during the 1980s. It also claimed that 85 percent of all "disappearances" were carried out by neither left-wing rebels nor right-wing "Contras" (see p.186), but by the Salvadoran military itself. This was the force Romero was trying to oppose.

D'Aubuisson and the CIA

Although the US publicly vowed to pursue the Archbishop's killers, the local investigation was hampered from the beginning – the presiding judge escaped an assassination attempt and subsequently fled the country. The prime suspect was Roberto D'Aubuisson, a former army major who had previously run ANESAL, El Salvador's CIA-trained intelligence agency. The Salvadoran authorities raided his estate in May, but claimed they uncovered no evidence against him – although it later emerged that they had found the infamous "Saravia Diary", written by former army Captain Alvaro Rafael Saravia, which contained information about Romero and details of the supply of exactly the sort of rifle that was used to kill him.

While publicly denying all knowledge of army-sponsored murders, the CIA privately admitted that they had put up with "a few bad apples", because removing them might cause the Salvadoran government to fall apart. In any case, the CIA had knowledge of a trail that led back to D'Aubuisson. In 1983, journalist Tom Gibb found declassified CIA files that "named D'Aubuisson's top former internal security agent, Oscar Perez Linares, as a member of a four-man National Police squad which murdered Romero". Gibb also cited a private source from a D'Aubuisson death squad who had overheard Linares boasting about killing Romero.

Linares was finally arrested in Guatemala in 1986 by a US-backed special police unit investigating human rights abuses, including Romero's murder, and was murdered on his return to El Salvador. Sceptics wondered whether his death was accident, punishment or silencing.

Motives

It's universally accepted that the death squads and the military were, at the least, closely intertwined, and that the military was funded and supported by the CIA, which on its own admission turned a blind eye to abuses. El Salvador was suffering from a classic cold war by proxy. Because of political bias, deliberate misinformation, or perhaps just ignorance of local conditions, the US government was convinced that the insurgency had international Communist backing – or, according to some, found it useful to *appear* to be convinced of this. To quote from the State Department's notoriously skewed White Paper: "the insurgency in El Salvador has been progressively transformed into another case of indirect armed aggression against a small Third World country by Communist powers acting through Cuba" – a commie conspiracy, no less. The excesses of a right-wing regime fighting a secret civil war by means of semi-official death squads could therefore be tolerated, and even funded. Some cynics allege a less ostensibly noble motive, claiming links between CIA operatives and cocaine smugglers (see p.196).

SOURCES

Books

James R. Brockman Romero: A Life (1982). Hagiography, but stirring stuff nonetheless. Later filmed as *Romero* (1989) by John Duigan, with financial backing from US Catholic organizations and with Raul Julia in the lead role.

Websites

🌐 www.usip.org/library/tc/doc/reports/el_salvador/tc_es_03151993_toc.html
Hosted by the US Institute of Peace Library, this is the full report of the UN Security Council's Commission on the Truth for El Salvador, entitled "From Madness To Hope: The twelve-year War In El Salvador". A section is dedicated to Romero.

John Lennon

There has never been any mystery as to who fired four bullets into John Lennon's back, outside the Dakota apartment building in New York City, on December 8, 1980. Indeed, as the former Beatle and prominent anti-war activist lay dying in the arms of his wife Yoko Ono, the man with a revolver, Mark David Chapman, relaxed his military-style shooting stance, and, instead of fleeing, began to read *The Catcher In The Rye*. A witness asked him if he knew what he'd done. "I just shot John Lennon", Chapman replied, having flown in from Hawaii, with the revolver, to do just that. A few months later, Chapman, officially deemed to be a "deranged fan", with the catch-all loser motive of "wanting attention", pleaded guilty and was sentenced to twenty years to life. Lennon appeared to have been slain by a lone nut. But was he?

It was strange of Chapman suddenly to plead guilty, after lawyers had spent six months preparing his defence. He did so, he said, on orders from a "voice" he heard in his cell. A psychiatrist for the defence, Dr Bernard Diamond, who coincidentally had also testified on behalf of Robert Kennedy's assassin Sirhan Sirhan, called Chapman a "paranoid schizophrenic".

Nonetheless, Chapman was deemed rational enough to stand trial, and was sent not to a mental institution but to a normal jail. One detective commented that there was something vacant or "programmed" about Chapman on the day of the killing, adding that Chapman "did not want to talk to the press from the very start", which he said cast doubt on Chapman's supposed craving for attention. Chapman has since agreed to just one single press

interview, in which he said: "He [Lennon] walked past me and then I heard in my head, 'do it, do it, do it', over and over again ... I don't remember aiming" – and that he felt "no emotion, no anger".

It's also puzzling why Chapman made no attempt to escape. With a couple of bullets left, credit cards and two thousand dollars in cash, he could have got a long way. In any case, where did he get the money? And where did an untrained civilian learn to shoot like that?

Lennon, Nixon, Chapman and the CIA

One theory, proposed by author Fenton Bresler in *Who Killed John Lennon?* and supported by radio journalist Mae Brussell, suggests that Chapman's madness was the result of being a brainwashed CIA assassin, who was put up to kill Lennon by right-wing elements within the US government. They argue that Chapman, while working as a children's counsellor in refugee camps for World Vision from Laos to Beirut, fell into the clutches of just the sort of covert operatives you'd expect to find in such war zones – the CIA.

Chapman's sojourn in Beirut coincided with the presence of CIA assassination squads, while in 1976 he appeared in Hawaii, a centre for CIA and Special Forces operatives, where mental ill-health and hospitalization caused him to drift from job to job. Somewhere along the way, it's speculated that the CIA hypnotized and drugged Chapman under their MK-ULTRA programme, as revealed to the Senate in 1975, and brainwashed him into killing Lennon. Although Chapman was certifiable, no paperwork prevented him from buying a gun, and there was

John Lennon and Yoko Ono: dangerous extremists

no metal detector to stop him from taking it to the mainland. Somehow, this indolent lunatic had the funds in October 1980 to travel to Switzerland and Georgia, and from Hawaii to New York and back, on what was perhaps an abortive killer-run, in which he managed to resist the "master inside himself". In December, however, he succumbed, and killed Lennon.

So why would the government want a hippy singer like Lennon dead? Because John Lennon was much more than that. He was an outspoken activist, demonstrating against the Vietnam war, marching for the IRA and CND and supporting striking shipbuilders. During the 1970s, John and Yoko supported radicals like jailed White Panther John Sinclair, and the anti-establishment Yippies (the pro-pot "Youth International Party"), and planned a series of anti-war concerts across the US.

To President Nixon's right-wing administration, anti-war meant anti-them. And Lennon, allegedly able to "draw out one million anti-war protestors in any given city in 24 hours", seriously threatened their ability to mobilize for war. FBI boss J. Edgar Hoover wrote on Lennon's file "ALL EXTREMISTS SHOULD BE CONSIDERED DANGEROUS." G-men tapped Lennon's phone and stalked him everywhere. Right-wing senator Strom Thurmond urged that Lennon's 1968 marijuana conviction in the UK – a set-up bust in itself – should be used to stop Lennon's contested immigration to the US. Later, Senator Frank Church's committee hearings outlined the dangers of the anti-war "new Left", and cited Lennon as a prominent member.

Lennon remarked in 1972 that "if anything happens to Yoko and me, it was not an accident". As the continual threat of deportation, and harassment by the FBI, strained Lennon's career and marriage, the birth of son Sean in 1975 pushed the Lennons into seclusion.

But then John got his green card, and after 1976, his 300-page FBI file gathered dust. Either the fact that he was keeping quiet was keeping everyone off his case, or maybe it was simply because Nixon had left office in 1974, and the Republicans were dumped in 1976.

1980 saw the relaunch of Lennon's career with the *Double Fantasy* album, and the return of the Republicans, when Ronald Reagan won the White House on the back of CIA chief-to-be William Casey's election campaign. Their plan to square up to the USSR, flood the Pentagon's coffers, and kick off numerous covert operations in Central America wouldn't have been popular with the rabble-rousing likes of Lennon. At the time, Ms Brussell said "the old assassination teams are coming back into power". The very next day, the drugged-up Chapman cut Lennon down.

Spooky lyrics

According to a spokesman for Lennon's record label Parlophone, certain of Lennon's songs contain "spooky" clues that predicted his death. Some read significance into the US release of The Beatles' *Magical Mystery Tour*, which showed a picture of Lennon next to a sign that read "The best way to go is by MD & C" – Chapman's initials. The lyrics from The Beatles' "Helter Skelter" formed part of Charles Manson's twisted logic in the brutal killing of the

The Fab Four – or should that be three?

pregnant Sharon Tate. And Tate's husband, film director Roman Polanski, made the film *Rosemary's Baby* about the birth of the anti-Christ at the Dakota Building in New York! Even more eerily, CNN reported in 2000 that Lennon apparently foresaw his own death in the 1980 song, "Help Me To Help Myself": "The angel of destruction keeps on hounding me" and "Oh help me, Lord".

Still believing

Brussell and Bresler's story is a fantastic concatenation of events and themes. Bresler obtained his information on Nixon and the FBI's pursuit of Lennon through the Freedom of Information Act, but as no files on Chapman have surfaced, Bresler doesn't claim that his theories about Chapman amount to anything more than speculation. In any case, Chapman's mental state seems parlous enough for

PAUL MCCARTNEY IS DEAD

With John Lennon and George Harrison both dead, Ringo Starr and Paul McCartney are the only Beatles to survive. Or is Starr the only true survivor? According to a rumour that spread like wildfire during the late 1960s, McCartney was actually the first to die, killed in a fiery car crash in 1966. As that would have finished the Fab Four, a look-alike replacement named Billy Shears (see below) was found. With a little plastic surgery and the growth of some scar-covering facial hair – matched by George, Ringo and John for the sake of fashion consistency – The Beatles kept on rocking. The ongoing aversion of "McCartney" to spontaneous photography is said to be owing to his fear that the cover-up will be rumbled.

However, The Beatles couldn't keep the truth hidden, and their post-Paul songs and albums are riddled with hints at Paul's death. Thus the photo on the cover of the *Abbey Road* album depicts The Beatles crossing the road with Lennon dressed in white, like a minister; Starr in black, like a pallbearer; and Harrison wearing the garb of a gravedigger. The barefoot McCartney is walking out of step with the others because … he's dead. The number plate of a VW car reads 28IF LMW: Paul would have been 28, *if* he'd been alive to make *Abbey Road*, as *Linda McCartney Weeps*. The line "Come together / Over me" from "Come Together" refers not to a kinky sexual fantasy, but to the three remaining Beatles standing over Paul lying in state, while "Your Mother Should Know" somewhat tactlessly points to the most qualified person to distinguish Paul from the impostor.

The famous sleeve of *Sergeant Pepper* is even more explicit, showing a crowd of famous dead people, with The Beatles centre, all facing Paul, behind a BEATLES wreath. War figures of the band stand overlooking a grave. Splitting the words on the drum with a mirror reveals HE ^ DIE, pointing at Paul. There's also a left-handed bass guitar, as played by Paul, with three sticks to symbolize the remaining Beatles, and a doll in a red-lined dress, holding a toy car: that's a blood-soaked Jane Asher in the car Paul died in.

Inside, the sleeve shows Paul wearing an armpatch with the letters OPD: Officially Pronounced Dead. The lyrics tell it all: "Let me introduce to you the one and only Billy Shears / And Sergeant Pepper's Lonely Hearts Club Band." "She's Leaving Home" reveals the time and day of the accident to be "Wednesday morning at five o'clock". That's confirmed in "Good Morning, Good Morning" – "Nothing to do to save his life", "People running around / It's 5 o'clock" – which also describes how Paul's loss of concentration caused the crash, "Watching the skirts you start to flirt / Now you're in gear". The climactic "A Day In The Life" tells of a man who "blew his mind out in a car", while "A crowd of people stood and stared / They'd seen his face before". Of course they had: it was Paul McCartney.

The so-called Paul Is Dead theory has circulated since Michigan University student and musician Fred LaBour made it up in the *Daily* newspaper in 1969. LaBour's Byzantine version also mentioned "I Am The Walrus", claiming that "walrus" means death in Greek – which it doesn't – while a hand apparently visible behind Paul's head was a mystic sign of his death. LaBour told the *Nashville Tennessean* years later that people used to call him to ask if Paul was really dead. "How did I know? I was just a college kid!" he laughed.

---

him to have committed any kind of psychotic behaviour – such as killing Lennon on his own initiative. His madness is so readily apparent that the killing has never been reinvestigated at any official level – but then, if there was a conspiracy, that's exactly what the plotters would be banking on.

Whether or not they buy Bresler's version, Yoko and Sean have armed minders to this day. Sean Lennon told the *New Yorker* in April 1998: "He [Lennon] was dangerous to the government. If he had said, 'Bomb the White House tomorrow', there would have been ten thousand people who would have done it. These pacifist revolutionaries are historically killed by the government."

SOURCES

Books

Fenton Bresler Who Killed John Lennon?
(1989). This well-sourced book makes a swift and fascinating read.

Jack Jones Let Me Take You Down: Inside The Mind Of Mark David Chapman, The Man Who Killed John Lennon (1992). Considering that Chapman claimed he never did it for the publicity, this insight into the man seems to have had a lot of assistance from the said killer.

Death of a princess: Diana

On the morning of August 31, 1997, the normally phlegmatic British public woke to receive a profound shock. While driving through an underpass beside the River Seine, in Paris, Princess Diana and her new boyfriend, Dodi Al-Fayed (son of the controversial Harrods' owner, Mohamed), had been killed in a cataclysmic car crash along with the driver, Henri Paul. Only their bodyguard, former British soldier Trevor Rees-Jones, had survived.

In the aftermath, the nation surpassed itself in the public display of emotion. The more distress people felt – the more images of weeping families along the Mall screened on TV, the more bunches of flowers seen piled up outside Kensington Palace – the more important Diana came to be seen as an icon of late twentieth-century Britain. It appeared that the British were at last rejecting the chilly formality embodied by the royal family. Although Diana would never be queen, she was quickly dubbed the "queen of hearts" – by the new, young and then popular Prime Minister Tony Blair, no less. In the weeks following the accident, the scale and significance of the public reaction to Diana's death seemed to dwarf the banality of a car crash. Could something so profound really have been caused by something so simple?

Henri Paul and the Mercedes S-Class

While driving from the Ritz hotel to the Al-Fayed apartment, the couple had taken a circuitous route to avoid a relentless pack of paparazzi. In his powerful Mercedes S280, Henri Paul attempted to outrun a persistent group of motorcyclist photographers – early reports, later discredited, estimated his speed at well over 100mph – only to lose control. Entering an underpass tunnel beneath the Place de l'Alma, the Mercedes clipped a white Fiat Uno, then skidded alongside it for 19 metres with two wheels in the air. As he fought to regain control, Paul turned to the right to get ahead of the Fiat, but found the path blocked by a Citroën BX. When he over-corrected to the left, the car entered another skid, and headed straight for the infamous thirteenth pillar, which it struck head-on with devastating impact before rebounding into the tunnel wall. The airbags inflated, saving the bodyguard in the passenger seat, but Paul was killed outright by the steering column. Without seatbelts, the two celebrity passengers in the rear stood no chance: Dodi was killed and Diana terribly injured. When the paparazzi caught up they took a gruesome sequence of photographs and called an ambulance – in which order remains highly disputed. Off-duty doctor Frédéric Mailliez was the first qualified person to reach Diana; she was alive but barely conscious, trying to move an arm and a leg and muttering "My God, what's happened?" Mailliez and the arriving emergency medical team treated her at the site for an hour, before loading her into an ambulance on its way to the Pitié-Salpetrière hospital. The journey took 43 minutes – the ambulance had to stop twice en route to allow Diana's ruptured heart to be given emergency massage – and the princess died shortly before entering surgery.

At the close of the official French inquiry, the prosecutor, Mme Coujard, summed up: "The direct cause of the accident is the presence, at the wheel of the Mercedes S280, of a driver who had consumed a considerable amount of alcohol, combined with

... medication, driving at a speed ... faster than the maximum speed-limit in built-up areas." The decision was upheld by that conclusion.

Unanswered questions

At first, everyone blamed the paparazzi. Some were even charged under France's "good Samaritan" law for failing to give proper help. Many fled the scene; some had taken photographs. But this wasn't so much a conspiracy as just criminally irresponsible behaviour. They may have hounded Diana to her death, but the last thing they would have wanted was to slay the goose that laid the golden eggs.

Doubts began to be raised when the focus of the French inquiry moved to driver Henri Paul, who was declared to have had three times the legal limit of alcohol in his blood. Was that really it? Was it just an accident caused by a drunk and speeding driver?

Surely not. Suddenly everyone was asking questions. Why were the CCTV cameras on the underpass turned off "for repair"? Where was the driver of the white Fiat Uno? Where were the two motorcyclists allegedly seen by witnesses blocking the exit just before the tunnel (which, it seemed, would have been the quicker route for Henri Paul to have taken)? Where was the other motorcyclist allegedly seen harassing the Mercedes in the tunnel? What was the bang allegedly heard by some witnesses immediately before the sound of the crash? Why were abnormal carbon monoxide levels discovered in Henri Paul's blood test? Why did the Parisian authorities clean the tunnel so thoroughly after the accident? Why did the ambulance take so long to get to hospital? Why didn't it go to a closer hospital anyway? Why was Diana's body embalmed and sent back to England before a UK post-mortem could be carried out?

Other rumours were wilder: was it really true that the bodyguard had conveniently lost his tongue in the accident? (It wasn't, though his multiply broken jaw was wired shut.) Why had he been wearing a seatbelt, against the rules of his profession? (He hadn't, though he had tried to buckle it in the final seconds of the skid.) Why did all of Paris's police radios go dead moments before the crash? (They didn't.) Was Diana pregnant with Dodi's child? (No, said the French doctors.)

MI6 assassination?

The official answers certainly weren't good enough for Dodi's father, Mohamed Al-Fayed. A wealthy Egyptian-born UK businessman and long-term opponent of the British Establishment, he'd previously brought down a Tory MP who had admitted to receiving money from him in return for political influence, in the so-called "cash for questions" scandal. Almost single-handedly, Al-Fayed fomented the conspiracists' chief line of attack: it was the British secret services, in league with the royal family. This argument had already found widespread favour in Egypt and the Middle East. Pregnant or not, surely the British Establishment could never accept a Muslim as the husband of the mother of the heir to the throne – MI6 would have stepped in to prevent it. Maverick ex-MI6 agent Richard Tomlinson even told the judge in charge of the French inquest that Henri Paul had been passing on gossip to the secret services, and added that the death bore a striking similarity to a 1992 plan to assassinate Slobodan Milosevic. Furthermore, two MI6 officers were reported as having been staying in the British embassy in Paris at the time of the accident. Others claimed that the bodyguard, Trevor Rees-Jones, was involved, citing (falsely) a service history in the secretive and elite SAS regiment. There were also stories that the Mercedes had been tampered with – the French inquiry found that it hadn't, though the usual chauffeur, Olivier Lafaye, pointed out that the brakes were faulty and "it didn't hold the road well".

In September 1999, a documentary presented by an eminent lawyer, Anthony Scrivener QC, claimed that moments before the crash, witnesses saw a bright flash of light set off from a motorcycle that subsequently powered its way through the tunnel. Was this a blinding strobe gun rather than the flash of a camera? Did MI6 stooge Henri Paul deliberately take the Alma route to bring his car within range? Did he meet up with his French intelligence handler earlier that afternoon, as alleged by US reporter Gerald Posner, citing US intelligence sources? Were the five unexplained 40,000-franc deposits found in Paul's account payments from the DGSE, the French equivalent of the CIA?

The establishment has taken the conspiracists' allegations seriously. In 2004, Michael Burgess, the Coroner to the Queen's Household, commissioned an inquiry codenamed Operation Paget. Its head, retired London police chief Sir John Stevens, has analysed the 6000-page French report, interviewed M16 agents, scanned the Alma tunnel with lasers and even talked to the Queen. His report has been delayed by the London bombings of July 2005, but is still expected to be delivered in 2006, just before the official British inquest is resumed.

James Andanson and the white Uno

Despite a giant-scale search, the French police never managed to trace the white Uno that was the apparent catalyst of the accident. It became a totem for the failure of the investigation to provide a convincing explanation. Suspicions of a cover-up were fuelled in May 2000, when the body of paparazzo James Andanson was found in a burned-out car in the south of France. Suicide provoked by marital difficulties was the official cause of death, but something looked fishy. Andanson had been investigated as the owner of a white Uno at the time of

the Paris crash, and one report had even matched his car with the traces of paint on the Mercedes. Suspiciously, the Fiat had been prepared for respray soon after the crash. Yet Andanson – who some investigators alleged had links with the British secret services – had simply given an alibi and been released. And is it stretching coincidence that the offices of Andanson's photo agency were burgled by three masked and armed men after his death? Many claimed the *modus operandi* of the intruders duplicated security-service methods. Were they removing evidence that linked Andanson to the crash?

The Windsors

Nine days after the crash, Mohamed Al-Fayed announced that Dodi had bought a $200,000 ring in the Repossi jewellery store on the Place Vendôme. The couple were supposed to have picked it out while on a yachting trip the previous week, though their bodyguard, Trevor Rees-Jones, strenuously denies they would have had time. Was it an engagement ring? Diana never told anyone she was getting married – unless you believe rumours that she confessed as much in a phone call to a friend in Washington that was tapped by the CIA. One Al-Fayed retainer claims that Dodi told him to "have the champagne ready" as he was going to ask Diana on the night she died. Even if this is true, would it really have necessitated her death? Some conspiracists state that her marriage to a Muslim would have provoked a constitutional crisis, as her eldest child, William, was heir to the throne and the title of Supreme Governor of the Anglican church. And if she in turn converted her children to Islam... Others spin a simpler yarn, that Diana had finally had enough of the Windsors, and was going to reveal their murky or at least mucky secrets, triggering so much public outrage and disgust that the monarchy would fall.

A sensational twist in the tale came in October 2003, when Diana's disgruntled and much-vilified

Diana, Princess of Wales

butler, Paul Burrell, published a letter from Diana in the tabloid *Mirror* newspaper. "This particular phase in my life is the most dangerous," she wrote, "XXX [the name was blanked out in the published version] is planning 'an accident' in my car, brake failure and serious head injury in order to make the path clear for Charles to marry." Burrell refused to say whether he thought it was a coincidence or something more sinister. Others charge that the suspicious coincidence is that Burrell released the letter to coincide with publication of his book, *A Royal Duty*, rather than when the accident originally happened.

Landmine-producers' cabal? Frankish sacrifice? Bin Laden?

Some suspect that Diana, through her charitable work with the Halo Trust, an anti-landmine organization, had become a threat to organizations with an interest in continued landmine production. While enticingly plausible, such a view rather overstates her influence as a celebrity figurehead. The Canadian government, chief instigator of the 1997 Ottawa Convention, was probably more of a danger.

A truly bizarre theory claims that the death of Diana was in fact a ritual sacrifice. Isn't her name that of the goddess worshipped by the ancient Franks? Isn't the place de l'Alma built over an underground chamber dedicated to Diana-worship? Isn't the torch monument on the spot an ancient sacrificial symbol? Isn't Diana associated with Hecate, whose satanic sacrifices are traditionally held on August 31, at a major crossroads such as the place de l'Alma? Wasn't Diana's Spencer family related to the Stuart royal family, which was in turn related to the French Merovingian dynasty, itself descended directly from Jesus and Mary Magdalene? Didn't Diana bleed to death, as prescribed in ritual sacrifice? Didn't the car hit the thirteenth pillar? The fact that the answer to all these questions – except the fact that she bled to death and the car hit the thirteenth pillar – is a resounding "no" doesn't stop the Internet speculation.

In the wake of 9/11, a sublime theory pointed the finger at none other than Osama bin Laden. He was apparently very worried that Muslim women were identifying with Diana, and that her marriage – how did he know? – to well-known devout Muslim and international playboy Dodi Al-Fayed would apparently "give her more of an entrée" into Muslim society.

SOURCES

Books

Martyn Gregory Diana: The Last Days (2004). A sceptic's response to Al-Fayad. Get the 2004 updated edition.

Jon King and John Beveridge Princess Diana: The Hidden Evidence (2001). Four hundred-plus pages of pure Diana conspiracy.

Trevor Rees-Jones The Bodyguard's Story: Diana, The Crash And The Sole Survivor (2000). Would be interesting as a bodyguard's-eye view of Diana's strange world, even if it weren't for the eyewitness crash details. Lots on Rees-Jones himself.

Websites

Ⓦ **www.alfayed.com** The official site of showman, arch-conspiracist and grieving father Mohamed Al-Fayed. Packed with Diana-related material.

Ⓦ **www.davidicke.com** Search the site for a plethora of Diana-related opinion pieces pushing Icke's inventive "reptilian Windsors" line.

Ⓦ **www.dianaconspiracy.com** Good overview of the main "unanswered questions" and conspiracy theories relating to Diana's death. Ignores the wackier allegations.

Ⓦ **www.londonnet.co.uk/ln/talk/news/diana_conspiracy_news.html** A travel guide to London is an odd place to host a website devoted to Diana's death and the conspiracy theories around it, but there are lots of useful pages nonetheless, with regularly updated news.

Ⓦ **www.public-interest.co.uk/diana/dianawhydie.htm** Useful Diana conspiracy site featuring postings of lots of news articles related to her death.

Dr David Kelly

Dr David Kelly, British microbiologist and biological weapons expert, was found dead in woods near his Oxfordshire home on July 18, 2003. His death marked the pinnacle of a spectacular row over the British government's justification for a war on Saddam Hussein's Iraq. Officially, Kelly killed himself. However, many people think that the man who blew the whistle on the case for war just wasn't the kind to commit suicide.

In late 2002, Britain's Labour government was busy trying to convince parliament and the UK public that Iraq posed a clear and immediate threat to the world through its possession of "weapons of mass destruction" – weapons that it should have destroyed after the 1991 Gulf War, but had instead not only hidden but continued to manufacture. According to the government, sanctions, bombing and endless weapons inspections had had no effect. It published two dossiers outlining the Iraqi threat. The first, in September 2002, created headlines throughout the world by claiming that Iraq had weapons of mass destruction that were deployable within 45 minutes. The second, in February 2003, described Iraq's secret network of arms programmes.

The February dossier swiftly became known as the "dodgy dossier", when it was exposed as being largely based on an article by a postgraduate student that had been published on the Internet. Even so, the Iraq War began in March, with the UK's involvement backed by both Parliament and, to a lesser extent, the public. Then the September dossier began to look suspect too. On May 29, journalist Andrew Gilligan told BBC Radio's *Today* programme that a senior source at the Ministry of Defence had told him that the government had "sexed up" the September dossier with its 45-minute claim. Gilligan went further in a newspaper article on June 1, by saying government spin doctor Alastair Campbell was responsible for the sexing-up. The BBC's *Newsnight* also cited a senior MoD source as stating that the government had inserted the 45-minute claim.

Infuriated, the government insisted that the BBC should reveal the source of this outrageous allegation. Meantime, Dr David Kelly told his MoD superiors that he had spoken to Gilligan. The government announced on July 8 that the source had been found; then, in a highly controversial move, Kelly was "named" by the MoD to the press on July 9. (As an indication of the kind of petty game-playing that was going on, Kelly's name was confirmed when a journalist read through a list of suspects, and Kelly's was the one to which an MoD official didn't respond by saying "no".) On July 15 and 16, Kelly was grilled by a House of Commons Foreign Affairs Select Committee and the Intelligence and Security Committee. He said he didn't think he was the source of the "sexing-up" allegation. On July 17, Kelly left his Oxfordshire house for an evening walk. After he failed to return, searchers found his body in woods two miles away the next day. The BBC confirmed on July 20 that Kelly had been their source.

An autopsy led by Dr Nicholas Hunt reported that Kelly was discovered with his left wrist slashed, and had also taken a large quantity of Coproxamol painkillers. The verdict: suicide. Senior judge Lord Hutton subsequently conducted an inquiry into the circumstances that led to Kelly's death and the role of the BBC and the government in the lead-up to the tragedy. In his January 2004 report, Hutton castigated the BBC and largely exonerated the government of plotting to expose Kelly. He drew attention to Hunt's conclusion that "I am satisfied that Dr Kelly took his own life" and that no other person was involved. Instead, the exposure of "such a

David Kelly: the police investigate

private man" and the possible jeopardizing of his career, caused Kelly to withdraw into himself, with fatal consequences.

Who said it was suicide?

However, the verdict cited by Hutton was not that of an official inquest. Neither was Hutton's inquiry given the remit to investigate Kelly's death as such, only the actions of the government and the BBC that preceded it. The inquiry was not given tribunal powers to subpoena new witnesses, or to call for new evidence. Of three hundred witness statements concerning Kelly's death, only seventy were submitted to the Hutton Inquiry.

The crucial point was that the *inquest* into Kelly's death, as opposed to the autopsy, had not delivered a final verdict; the Lord Chancellor had ordered the inquest adjourned for the duration of the Hutton Inquiry. And the inquest never did deliver a verdict. Oxford coroner Nicholas Gardiner said on March 16, 2004, that the inquest into Kelly's death would not be resumed. The verdict, as Hutton said, was suicide. Those who questioned that view were, said Gardiner, "conspiracy theorists".

"Conspiracy theorists"

Some of those supposed "theorists", including doctors and barristers, formed the Kelly Inquiry Group and demonstrated outside the coroner's court. Among them was lawyer Michael Shrimpton, who, the BBC reported, asked why the forensic report could not confirm whether Kelly had taken 29 Coproxamol tablets. Somehow, Kelly had managed to perform the dextrous feat of slashing his ulnar artery but not the radial one, and still bleed to death.

Three doctors, anaesthiologist Searle Sennett, trauma specialist David Halpin, and radiologist Stephen Frost wrote to the *Guardian* newspaper on January 27 to express their doubts, and were followed on February 12 by a letter from vascular surgeon Martin Birnstingi, pathologist Dr Peter Fletcher, and public health consultant Dr Andrew Rouse. All agreed the stated primary cause of Kelly's death, bleeding to death from a severed ulnar artery, was "highly improbable". The idea was "against classical medical teaching". The toxicologist who measured Kelly's Coproxamol level said it was just a third of what was usually regarded as a fatal dose. A concurrent debate in the *British Medical Journal* mentioned that Kelly had "ischaemic heart disease" and the possibility that he had died of heart failure, but the pathologist Dr Nicholas Hunt had ruled that out.

Shifting evidence

The Indymedia website reported that the two volunteer searchers who first found Kelly, Louise Holmes and Paul Chapman, discovered his body propped against a tree. On their way to tell Abingdon police, they met three "plain-clothes detectives", who continued on to the body. Witnesses later placed the body flat on its back, away from a tree, and the post-mortem reported that Kelly must have died on his back. Paramedic Vanessa Hunt reported finding very little blood at the scene, either in quantity or sprayed around, whereas a fatal hemorrhage usually amounts to five pints. Scratches and bruises suggested that Kelly had been "stumbling around" in the undergrowth, but police found no trampled vegetation. Why had a police support operation, codenamed Mason, begun nine hours *before* Kelly was reported missing?

According to the *Daily Mirror*, there was no suicide note. Channel 4 reported that the day before he died, Kelly emailed a friend: "Hopefully it will soon pass" he wrote "and I can get to Baghdad and get on with the real work." The Ananova website stated that he had mentioned "many dark actors playing games" in an email to a journalist written hours before his suicide. Then there were Kelly's own alleged dark comments, supposedly made in February 2003, that "if Iraq is attacked, then I might be found dead in the woods".

If it was murder, who did it?

Allegations that Kelly was murdered centre on the belief that Kelly was seen as a loose cannon, who needed silencing. He was certainly an expert in biological warfare and weapons, having worked at the Institute of Virology at Oxford and the Ministry of Defence's Porton Down research centre (see p.276), before becoming an advisor to the MoD and Foreign Office. As a UN weapons inspector, he visited Iraq nearly forty times to investigate its WMD programmes. If he was prepared to tell the press that the government case for war was full of holes, what else might he spill?

UK national security lawyer Michael Shrimpton told US listeners to the Alex Jones radio show in February 2004 that although 29 Coproxamol tablets were apparently missing from the blister packs found beside his body, Kelly's stomach contained less than a fifth of one. He argued that Kelly was injected with traceless succinyl choline, and that his wrist was cut to cover the injection site. The assassination, he suggests, was probably carried out by French intelligence services. Alex Jones's prisonplanet.com states that Shrimpton believes the UK media covered up the assassination, one reason being they didn't want to depose the pro-Europe Prime Minister Tony Blair, as this could thwart plans for the UK to adopt the euro.

A theory by conspiracy theorists

Michael Shrimpton is the only person to have pointed at anyone for Kelly's murder, and the fact that he has only been able to make his accusation on the Internet, as he himself acknowledges, is significant. Use of the word "murder" seems to be restricted to the major "alternative" news sources, such www.propagandamatrix.com, Alex Jones's prisonplanet.com and www.rense.com. Although many newspapers have raised serious doubts over Kelly's death, none has taken these doubts to any conclusion, except to report that, as Hutton talked through his findings, he was interrupted by criminology psychologist Patricia Rodrigues-Walsh, who shouted that Kelly had been murdered.

As time has gone by, the story has been buried by larger events. The Hutton Inquiry's biggest impact was on the BBC: Gilligan, the director-general and chairman all resigned, and the government seized the opportunity to rein in the BBC's proclivity for questioning the state. Even so, no weapons of mass destruction have ever been found in Iraq.

Could a modern government really kill someone like Kelly so audaciously, in the midst of a media maelstrom? Perhaps only a government also audacious enough to base its public case for going to war on shamelessly inadequate intelligence. It does seem strange that the press, which usually lays siege to anyone in the public eye, was not surrounding Kelly's home in sufficient strength to deter him from going out that night.

As coroner Nicholas Gardiner remarked: "This hearing will do little to put an end to the controversy relating to the death of Dr Kelly." Kelly was a scientist who lost his life after exposing government spin in justification of a controversial war, and having his painstaking, dangerous work for the UK, UN and intelligence services meddled with and squandered by governments with their own agendas. However, his Baha'i faith prohibited him from having any political affiliation. Baha'i also forbids suicide.

SOURCES

Websites

ⓦ en.wikipedia.org/wiki/David_Kelly A succinct summary of Kelly's life, work and tragic death.

ⓦ www.guardian.co.uk/letters/story/0,3604,1131833,00.html Doctors cast doubt over "suicide" verdict.

ⓦ www.rense.com/general49/kelll.htm US radio-show presenter Alex Jones talks to Michael Shrimpton, who asserts that Kelly was assassinated.

ⓦ www.the-hutton-inquiry.org.uk The official version as to who was to blame for outing Kelly.

Mega-conspiracies and masterplans

Knights of the shadows: the Templars
Blood Libel: the longest-running
conspiracy theory of all
The British royal family
The EU

Mega-conspiracies and master plans

Mega-conspiracies aren't so much about specific events, or even strings of conspiratorially connected events, as the groups supposedly behind them – and indeed, behind everything else going on in the world. The paranoia of mega-conspiracy theorists is reflected in the megalomania they attribute to those who hold power, especially when that power appears to be concealed from public view. The theories often concern centuries-old secret societies, so it's no surprise that the theories themselves are often centuries old too.

One group that has recently attracted the attention of a new generation of conspiracy theorists is the Knights of the Templar. Originally a corps of French mercenary knights during Europe's Christian crusades, the Templars subsequently dispersed across the continent, where their wealth made them the object of much ill feeling. They'd otherwise probably be forgotten, if not for their reappearance in the background of Dan Brown's thriller *The Da Vinci Code,* which links them to an elaborate cover-up in which the "real" Jesus Christ escaped crucifixion to live with Mary Magdalene and have a child. A longer-running theory is that many of the Templar orders simply reinvented themselves as the society of Freemasons.

Freemasons, also simply called Masons, are seen as mega-conspirators in their own right. For most of us, Masonry conjures up images of men wearing aprons, with rolled-up trouser legs and weird handshakes, meeting in their "lodge" bedecked with strange symbols of eyes and pyramids, and quietly running the police, the local council or golf club. Some conspiracy theorists, however, believe that Freemasons run the planet, dominating governments, supra-national corporations and banks. Haven't a dozen US Presidents been Masons? And why are the movement's arcane motifs emblazoned all over the country's currency, making a dollar bill a veritable manifesto of Masonic influence?

Equally obsessed with odd rites, rituals and signs are the world's various Mafias. The Chinese Triads are named after their triangular sign, while Japan's Yakuza can be recognized from their lack of fingers and the Russian Mafia by their little black caps, adopted in homage to their Italian-American and Sicilian counterparts. When you read about the activities of the CIA, KGB or Mossad, though, you can't help wondering who the real bad guys are. Assuming they exist in the first place, it's a question that can also be asked of the "Men in Black": are they government agents fighting stellar aliens, or working with them?

Talking of aliens, David Icke claims that the British royal family themselves are from outer space. Others say the Windsors are the chief cabal of a British Commonwealth that's still seething over the loss of its American colonies and is plotting to bring the latter to heel. But that overlooks other theories that bodies like Britain's Royal Institute of International Affairs and the US's Council on Foreign Relations are sister institutes in an Anglo-American conspiracy to rule the world – unless other pan-Continental groups like the Trilateral Commission or European Union beat them to it. Whether they're all in it together or are all out for themselves depends on the theorist.

While the EU is presented by many British tabloid newspapers as a "conspiracy" of Brussels bureaucrats, some Americans see it as a vast economic plot to bring down the US. In their view, the concept of global warming is an EU invention designed to hamper American economic growth. If so, the EU would also be taking on the US military-industrial complex, whose growing influence was the subject of a warning by ex-general and US president Dwight Eisenhower – but not until he was leaving office, perhaps to escape reprisals himself. The premature deaths of Mae Brussell, whose conspiracy archive included the notorious Gemstone File, and journalist Danny Casolaro, whose Octopus theory embraced everyone from Tehran to Washington, are seen by some as evidence that they were getting too close to the truth.

Some secret groups only exist as fantasies. One 17th-century conspiracy theory that spread like wildfire across Europe concerned the Rosicrucians, a quasi-Masonic religious sect supposedly bent on spreading religious reformation across the world. The only problem was that there was no evidence of their existence – which didn't stop new groups calling themselves Rosicrucians from being set up. By then, however, there was another movement with branches scattered across Europe: a proliferation of pompous academic circles calling themselves *Illuminati* or "enlightened ones". The name was also adopted by a somewhat malevolent anti-Jesuit group whose rituals and secrecy led the Illuminati to be lumped together with the Masons, a confusion that continues today.

A lethal and even older conspiracy theory is that of the "blood libel", a term used to describe the medieval belief that Jews regularly abducted, crucified and ate Christians (mainly children). Disturbingly, it's a theory that is still held in certain Middle Eastern circles, while in 2005 it was revived by some MPs in the Russian parliament. In the West, meanwhile, similar practices have been ascribed to Satanists. In the 1980s, one astounding trial in the US ground on for six years, without anyone being convicted (not even those who had fabricated the evidence).

Sadly, the blood libel is just the tip of the iceberg as far as anti-Semitic conspiracy theories are concerned. In 1890, a piece of black Russian propaganda called *The Protocols Of The Learned Elders Of Zion* outlined a Jewish plot to take over the world. People like Henry Ford and Hitler fell for it, and the forgery helped to fuel the hatred that led to the murder of six million Jews. This hasn't stopped anti-Semitic Holocaust deniers like David Irving from claiming that the Holocaust never happened: works such as Anne Frank's *Diary* are themselves dismissed as part of a Zionist conspiracy. It's despicable claims like this that drive academics such as Daniel Pipes to distraction.

Murder and denial, it seems, go hand in hand. The Turkish government, for example, still officially denies the genocide of some 1.5 million Armenians under the Ottoman Empire during World War I. For a country where conspiracies and conspiracy theories are part of the culture, however, you have to look to Italy, where corruption seems endemic and the long-standing political battle between Left and Right has given rise to a succession of scandals and rumours concerning assassinations, banking, Mafia connections and terrorist attacks. For some, the government of Silvio Berlusconi has made politics itself into a giant conspiracy – but in the land of Machiavelli and the Borgias, perhaps it always has been.

Knights of the shadows: the Templars

Two kinds of histories describe the Knights Templar. The first is historians' history, based on documents and contemporary descriptions. The second blends in a potent mixture of conspiracy theory, fiction, and occult and esoteric "knowledge". For different reasons, the crucial date in both histories is 1312, when Pope Clement V officially dissolved the order in the Papal Bull *Vox In Excelso*. According to historians, that was that for the Knights. According to conspiracists, the Templars and their secrets survived in hiding – and continue to wield great power today.

Eastern origins

As the official version has it, the Poor Fellow Soldiers of Christ and the Temple of Solomon were established in 1118, when eight (or some say nine) French noblemen made a vow to Baldwin II, the Crusader King of Jerusalem, to defend pilgrims to the Holy Land. They took their name from the Temple quarter of Jerusalem where they had their base – just as their rivals, the Knights Hospitaller, were named after the Hospital of St John, whose inmates they cared for. Donations of property in Europe quickly made the Templars extremely rich, while donations of younger sons in search of a role in life made them more numerous. At the height of their power there were around four hundred Knights in Jerusalem, plus many more lightly mounted "Serjeants" and other hangers-on.

To assist the Templars' defence of the pilgrim passes into the Holy Land, the crusading nations entrusted the great frontier castles to their care. This wasn't philanthropy: by the latter half of the thirteenth century, the Mamelukes were threatening the Holy Land, and the Templars were gradually forced out of stronghold after stronghold. Finally abandoning their walled city of Tortosa in August 1291, they fled to the offshore island of Arwad, where they held on for another eleven years. After 1302, however, the Templars became refugees in Europe – albeit rich ones, thanks to developing a successful second career as bankers and moneylenders. This made them no more popular than it had the Jews.

Accusations

Rumours began to spread that the Templars had been strangely corrupted by the Mohammedan ways of the East and had discovered "secrets" while excavating on the site of the Temple of Solomon. They were accused of heresy, sodomy, worshipping cats or a mysterious head called "Baphomet", and performing strange initiation rites – denying Christ and the crucifixion, spitting on the cross, and kissing on the buttocks, mouth and penis. A mysterious "secret test" that guaranteed loyalty and silence provoked further suspicion. On October 13, 1307, Philippe IV "Le Bel" of France pounced, sending

A medieval fresco of a Knight Templar

agents to arrest all the Templars in his kingdom on the same day. They were charged with heresy, but it was their money Philip was after. Confessions were tortured out of the arrested Knights, and the rest of Europe followed the French lead. Within five years the Pope had outlawed the order, and on March 11, 1314, the Grand Master, Jacques de Molay, was burned at the stake in Paris. He allegedly cursed Philippe IV and Pope Clement V as he died; both followed him to the grave within the year.

Secret survival – the Da Vinci codswallop

The Templars' property was either seized or turned over to the rival Knights Hospitaller. As for the Templars themselves, those who weren't burned were forced to join other orders, or quietly disappear. They vanished from history. Unless, that is, you believe the "alternative histories" propagated by various pseudo-historians and a handful of modern neo-Templar orders. One of the most prominent, the Sovereign Military Order of the Temple of Jerusalem, for example, lays claim to a "Charter of Transmission" and a list of Grand Masters that traces their current chief back to de Molay. These claims are almost as dubious as those of Freemasonry, which at a certain point in the eighteenth century decided that its supposed roots among medieval masons weren't glamorous enough. Instead, it was alleged that the Templars had fled to Scotland, either joining Robert Bruce's army or establishing their own orders, which in due course became Masonic.

Even more absurd is the claim, reiterated in Dan Brown's thriller, *The Da Vinci Code*, that the Templars were a mere front organization for a "Priory of Sion" which survived the Knights' downfall unscathed. According to Brown and his sources – notably a French neofascist hoaxer called Pierre Plantard, and

the books *Holy Blood, Holy Grail* by Baigent, Leigh and Lincoln, and *The Templar Revelation* by Picknett and Prince – the Priory of Sion was the guardian of the Templars' true secret: that Jesus had a child with Mary Magdalene. This "holy blood" or *sang réal* is supposedly the true origin of the myth of the Holy Grail, on the grounds that the medieval French for "Holy Grail" was the similar-sounding *san graal*. (For a fuller discussion of this topic, see p.166.)

The Templars today

Templar occultists like to link the Knights to every other hermetic mystery or conspiracy theory around. The head of Baphomet is often said to have been what later turned up in church history as the Turin Shroud – which is a historical possibility. Other Templar occultists claim that the Shroud represents not Jesus, but Jacques de Molay. Others still hold that Baphomet is a mishearing for "Mahomet", or Mohammed – or even the alchemical symbol known as the Caput Mortum or "Dead Head".

Once you get this deep into unsourced speculation, you can pretty much say what you like. Which is probably why today the Templars are variously claimed to be responsible for building Europe's Gothic cathedrals and discovering America in the thirteenth century, orchestrating the French Revolution in the eighteenth, and pulling the strings of the New World Order (see p.234) in the twenty-first. However, the order has not existed in any meaningful sense since Pope Clement V dissolved it – without papal sanction, a Templar "order" isn't anything more than a club with a fancy name, a few fragments of empty iconography and a wishful claim to historical antecedents. If the Templars are to be found anywhere today, it's only in their surviving round churches, modelled on Jerusalem's Holy Sepulchre, and the ruined, empty castles of Palestine: Chastel Blanc, Chastel Pèlerin, Crac des Chevaliers, Safèd...

SOURCES

Books

Malcolm Barber **The Trial Of The Templars** (1993). A serious study of the Templars' downfall.

Peter Partner **The Knights Templar And Their Myth** (1990). Detailed and serious account not just of Templar history, but of the order's fantastical after-history too – hence the "myth" part of the title. Not for beginners.

Lynn Picknett and Clive Prince **The Templar Revelation: Secret Guardians Of The True Identity of Christ** (1998). Even before **The Da Vinci Code** bumped this back onto the bestseller list, it was required reading for devotees of the "alternative" version of Templar history. Mad – it calls itself "a quest through time and space" – but highly enjoyable.

Piers Paul Read **The Templars: The Dramatic History Of The Knights**

Templar, The Most Powerful Military Order Of the Crusades (2001). Highly readable popular history, but more a general survey of the crusading era than a detailed account of the Templars.

Websites

ⓦ **www.ordotempli.org** Home page of one of the many groups that likes to pretend it's the real heir of the Templars. Packed with popular pseudo-history.

Freemasonry: centuries of conspiracy?

Freemasonry attracts so many conspiracy theories for exactly the same reason that it attracts so many Freemasons – it has "secrets". The sheer popularity of Freemasonry just adds another dimension: the greater the number of conspirators, the greater the scale of the conspiracy. In fact there are roughly five million Freemasons worldwide, all signed up to a creed that sounds harmless enough. As the Scottish Rite puts it: "Human progress is our cause, liberty of thought our supreme wish, freedom of conscience our mission, and the guarantee of equal rights to all people everywhere our ultimate goal."

For conspiracy theorists, however, there must be a more sinister agenda hidden away in all those "secrets". And the more influential the conspirators are,

the more dangerous their conspiracy must be. Lists of powerful Freemasons – past and present – are posted up all over the Internet. Most of the lists are exaggerated and highly speculative, but there *are* some remarkable facts. Well over a dozen US presidents, for instance, were definitely Freemasons, from George Washington to Gerald Ford by way of William Taft, Franklin D. Roosevelt, Harold Truman and Lyndon B. Johnson. Can any other secret society claim so much?

Stonemasons and Freemasons

Freemasonry famously claims that it's not a secret society, just a society with secrets. And the biggest secret of all is where it came from. The respected historian Frances Yates even wrote that "the origin of Freemasonry is one of the most debated, and debatable, subjects in the whole realm of historical enquiry." Plenty of writers claim to have found the answer to the mystery, however, so the legendary history of Freemasonry has easily expanded to fill the real-world vacuum.

For Freemasons, there's an obvious allure in having exotic ancestry; for opponents, long, furtive histories simply back up their darkest allegations. Some have said that Freemasonry is a descendant of the Mystery Schools of the ancient world, or Rome's Collegia, or the Knights Templar; others that it is the visible face of more secretive societies still, such as the "Priory of Sion", the Illuminati or the Rosicrucians. According to the Orientalist Sir Richard Burton, Freemasonry was nothing less than a western offshoot of Islamic Sufism.

The most common explanation, however, is that Freemasons were once medieval masons, the word "free" referring to their skill in the working of freestone, or fine-grained stone such as sandstone or limestone. These techniques were passed on from master to apprentice, and jealously guarded in order to differentiate skilled masons – the architects of their day – from ordinary labourers. Guilds, the medieval equivalent of unions, grew up, and gradually – so the story goes – these "lodges" of "Operative masons" began to accept non-mason members, who became known as "Speculative" or "Accepted" Masons, or just "Freemasons".

Unfortunately, there's no hard evidence of any connection between the (stone)masons of the fifteenth century – the time from when the latest records of stonemasons' guilds date – and the (Free)masons of the mid-seventeenth century (from when the earliest records of Freemasonry date). In lieu of proof, many writers cite medieval documents such as the early-fourteenth-century Holkham Bible, with its image of a Masonic-style "architect god", or the Regius Poem from the 1390s, with its Masonic-sounding phrases. It's just as likely, however, that Freemasonry adopted medieval symbolism as it is that it inherited an almost invisible medieval tradition. As for the "tradition" of secret signs, it seems unlikely that medieval stonemasons would have needed them to identify themselves to each other, as most lived on site.

Freemasonry breaks cover

The fact that there's no proof that Freemasonry existed at all before the mid-seventeenth century counts for some as further proof of its malignancy. Surely on ly an awesomely powerful organization could have covered its traces so well... The earliest firm evidence of Freemasonry records the admission of a Scotsman, Robert Moray, into an Edinburgh-based, military-oriented Masonic lodge in 1641, and the acceptance of an Englishman, Elias Ashmole, into another lodge in 1646. Curiously, both were key founders of the Royal Society, which established the formal study of science in England. Both were also known for their interest in Rosicrucianism, an occult pseudo-scientific fad of the era (see p.87), which is sometimes accused of having been "behind the Masons". (In this, Rosicrucianism has much in common with other groups such as the Illuminati and the Templars.)

In the later seventeenth century, Freemasonry spread rapidly among young gentlemen in England and Scotland alike. It may have owed its success partly to its alluring secrecy, partly to the enticing admixture of Enlightenment philosophy with the occult. For reasons never discovered, four London lodges "went public" in 1717, declaring themselves to be a united or Premier Grand Lodge of England, with jurisdiction over all the other lodges. Once the cat was out of the bag (and once it looked as if it wasn't about to be strangled), other lodges declared themselves too, initially in England, but soon all over Europe. Many politicians declared at the time (and some still say now) that this was proof of a deep-rooted and wide-ranging secret network finally revealing itself. Others believed Freemasonry was just another genteel European fad, like Humanism or coffeehouses.

Higher degrees

In 1725, the original two "degrees" or levels of Freemasonry were augmented by a third. Only when members had learned the mysteries of the first two degrees could they progress to the great secrets possessed by a (third-degree) Master Mason. In 1737, French Masons went one – or rather thirty – better, adding higher degrees up to the thirty-third level and calling their new system the *Rite Ecossaise*, or "Scottish Rite", after the man they believed had invented it, a Scotsman called Andrew Ramsay.

More conservative Masons, confusingly called the "Moderns", and disturbed by the thought that the "Antients" might consider themselves above their Masonic cousins, described the new levels as "side degrees". For the Antients, however, there was nothing in the past that couldn't be plundered to make Freemasonry ever more complex and exciting. The stonemason-origin story wasn't enough. Freemasonry's key foundation myth was now that it descended from the masons who built Solomon's Temple. This, then, was one of the secrets that aspiring Masons would discover once they had successfully schmoozed their way into a lodge: theirs was the most ancient club in the world.

Masonic secrets: Hiram Abiff and the Juwes

Another "secret" was the elaborate third-degree initiation ritual, which in some Masonic rites re-enacts the main event in this legendary Temple history. You won't find the story in the Bible, but according to one account, the three "Juwes" (whose names have nothing to do with Judaism, but derive from the cod-Latinate, quasi-magical-sounding Jubela, Jubelo and Jubelum) sought out Hiram Abiff, the master architect of the Temple, to discover his secrets. Hiram, of course refused to divulge what he

knew, and was murdered. Solomon sent the Juwes back to open Hiram's coffin, on the safe grounds that the first thing they found there would surely be the Secret of the Temple. The Juwes found Hiram's hand – which is one origin of the famous Masonic secret handshake.

It's an odd story (particularly as the Bible names a different Hiram – Hiram of Tyre – as the builder of the Temple) and makes little sense without a detailed explanation of the symbolism hidden in the narrative – which is exactly what initiates are given. Even odder, perhaps, is the image of adult men acting out a murder as part of their initiation (and you thought rolling up a trouser leg was weird). Of course not every Masonic lodge follows the same ritual, but the sheer creepiness of these kinds of narrative helps explain much of the resentment and suspicion that attaches itself to the Masons. It also explains a lot about the macabre rituals of later societies such as Yale's Skull and Bones (see p.221). Presumably the frat boys' dads hadn't kept their Masonic secrets too well.

Templar theories

Staking a claim to a Biblical heritage was not enough for the early Freemasons. Calling himself the "Chevalier", Andrew Ramsay delivered an "Oration" to Paris's Grand Lodge in March 1737 that set out another theory. The Masons, it seems, were the latter-day resurgence of the medieval warrior-monks, the Knights Templar – who took their name from their medieval base in Jerusalem, on the site of Solomon's Temple. Despite a complete lack of evidence of the existence of either Templars or Masons in the four centuries between 1312 (the date of the Templar suppression) and 1717 (when Masonry emerged in public), the idea caught on. Ramsay linked Masonry's early popularity in Scotland with that country's acceptance of Templar refugees in the fourteenth century – an idea later elaborated upon by conspiracy-historians Michael Baigent and Richard Leigh in *The Temple And The Lodge*.

Another modern author, John J. Robinson, outlines a different theory to explain the four-hundred-year gap in his book *Born In Blood*. He requires historians "to have one mental band tuned to the wavelength of the Masonic connection"; it's very much a conspiratorial bandwidth. Robinson sees the Masonic heritage cropping up repeatedly in various conspiratorial activities from the anticlerical Lollard movement of the fourteenth century and the Peasants' Revolt of 1381 to the publication of Sir Francis Bacon's *New Atlantis* in 1627, which described "an unknown island guided by a learned society, told from the viewpoint of a shipwrecked gentleman". The New Atlantis, according to Robinson, was a Masonic Utopia. The shipwrecked gentleman represents a Templar fleeing persecution, washed up on the coast of Scotland, and "guiding" the society he found there towards higher learning...

A twist in the argument for a Templar origin of Freemasonry was introduced in Germany. The Scottish Rite had been introduced there by Karl Gotthelf, aka Baron von Hund, in 1755. His "Strict Observance" movement was soon joined by one Johann August Starck, who claimed to have knowledge of alchemy (much like the Rosicrucians) and to have evidence of Freemasonry's direct descent from the Templars' clergymen, who were, he said, the Order's secret masters. (A similar idea was later revived by a French Fascist called Pierre Plantard, the hoaxer behind the Priory of Sion, which later achieved worldwide fame via Dan Brown's *The Da Vinci Code*.)

For Christopher Knight and Robert Lomas, the Hiram legend is proof of the Masonic–Templar link. Their bestseller, *The Hiram Key* (another of Dan Brown's favourite sources) identifies a Pharaonic mummy with the corpse of Hiram, thanks to three "ritually placed" wounds. The Egyptians' Hebrew slaves, it seems, proudly maintained their former masters' ancient wisdom, and they employed the secret symbolism of Egyptian architecture when they built the Temple for Solomon. As a Jew and a rabbi, Jesus was also privy to these secrets, and his followers practiced the Resurrection ritual of Hiram. When the Knights Templar uncovered the ruins of the Temple during the Crusades, they surely discovered Hiram's secret too, which they then passed on to their Freemason descendants. It's a great story, but so flimsy that it hasn't "shaken the Christian world to its very roots", despite what the book's blurb promised. The authors' professional backgrounds – one was a consumer psychologist with a degree in advertising and graphic design, the other a lecturer in marketing trained as an electrical engineer – and their status as practising Masons didn't help their cause.

Revolutionary agenda: Freemasonry in France

The apotheosis of the myth of Templar origin came during the French Revolution, when the storming of the Bastille was blamed on a Templar element in the Masonic movement. Almost five hundred years after the suppression of their order by the French king Philippe IV and the immolation of their Grand Master, Jacques de Molay, in Paris, the Knights were still thirsty for revenge.

The Templars as a kind of Masonic Marine Corps is an alluring idea, and these kinds of accusations weren't limited to a loony fringe. An influential book published in 1798 by a conservative French clergyman, the Abbé Barruel, *Mémoires pour servir à l'histoire du Jacobinisme*, blamed Freemasons not just for the Bastille episode, but for the entire French Revolution. With the addition of a Jewish conspiracy, his book later became the basis for the infamous "Protocols of the Elders of Zion" (see p.100), in which an "Elder" states: "The Masonic Lodge throughout the world unconsciously acts as a mask for our purpose."

Many subsequent writers agreed with Barruel that Freemasons had inflamed the deliberations of the Third Estate, the parliament of landowners that set the French Revolution in motion, and believed that they had formed the backbone of the revolutionary-minded Club Breton, which became the notorious Jacobin Club. These allegations were made both by anti-Masons, eager to expose what they saw as a dangerous force in French society, and by Masons themselves, keen to lay claim to exactly this kind of power. Historians still argue the point today.

In fact, the French Revolution went too far for most bourgeois-liberal Freemasons, who tended to support the idea of a constitutional monarchy. By 1792 most French lodges had lost their members to emigration. And yet, right across Europe, Barruel's notion of a mega-conspiracy turned out to be self-fulfilling. As the idea that Freemasonry had sponsored an anticlerical, egalitarian and progressive revolution spread, *real* revolutionaries were attracted to Freemasonry. Italy's Giuseppe Mazzini and Giuseppe Garibaldi were just two examples. Plenty more were to be found on the other side of the Atlantic.

Another revolution: early Freemasonry in America

Freemasonry had spread to North America by the 1730s, and swiftly became popular among the political classes. Benjamin Franklin jumped on the bandwagon as early as 1731, while George Washington was initiated a little later, in 1752. It seems, however, that Washington took little interest in Masonic affairs thereafter, despite his leading role in the most notorious Masonic incident of all, the laying of the foundation stone of the Capitol on September 18, 1793. For that occasion he wore a Masonic apron, and used a Mason's silver gavel and trowel.

The symbolism could not have been more explicit.

And that symbolism runs deep, pervading the very geography of Washington DC, according to many accounts. The first overall architect of the city, Pierre-Charles L'Enfant, was an associate of the French revolutionary and committed Freemason, the Marquis de Lafayette. Although there's no evidence that L'Enfant himself was a Freemason, his design for Washington was certainly informed by the kind of esoteric ideas propagated by the Masonic movement. Endless US-based websites now display maps and satellite photos of Washington DC, enhanced or marked up to reveal geometric patterns – notably a pentagram with its point at the (phallic) Washington Monument – in the street layout. Their interpretations draw on anything from pseudo-Egyptian occultism to all-out Satanism to explain the "Masonic" origins of the design. (Erecting a five-sided structure explicitly called "the Pentagon" during World War II, of course, was sheer Masonic chutzpah.)

Similarly, books and websites alike crawl with allegations, usually exaggerated, such as the "fact" that the US Constitution was based on Freemasonry's 1723 "Ancient Charges", otherwise known as "Anderson's Constitutions", or that the design of the dollar bill is proof of a Masonic conspiracy at the heart of the US's foundation (see p.119). Participants in the Boston Tea Party are said (without any evidence) to have been Freemasons, and indeed practically anyone with any role in the War of Independence has been similarly "outed" at some point. Although lodge membership was widespread, however, it wasn't ubiquitous. Of the 55 signatories of the Declaration of Independence in 1776, it's often said that only six were not Freemasons; in fact, a mere eight (or possibly nine) were. Similarly, of the 39 men who approved the Constitution in 1787, just thirteen are known to have been Freemasons.

The publication in 1797 of *Proofs Of A Conspiracy Against All The Religions And Governments Of Europe Carried On In The Secret Meetings Of Free Masons, Illuminati And Reading Societies*, written in Edinburgh by a Secretary of the Royal Society, Professor John

Robison, helped to whip up rumours of a conspiracy in Europe and America alike. Curiously, many influential Freemasons in America joined up precisely because they'd heard the rumours – becoming a Mason was seen as a way of involving oneself with the cause of independence. Membership of a lodge is often hyped up by the conspiracy-minded as proof of commitment to some Masonic agenda, but in fact most American Freemasons joined primarily for social reasons. It was the ultimate fashionable gentleman's club – albeit one with a worthy political edge. Of course, membership wouldn't hurt their careers, but a little ambition doesn't turn a Founding Father into an Agent of Satan.

Masons vs Christians

It's easy to understand why conservative, eighteenth-century French monarchists would mistrust Freemasons, given that they were supposed to have been responsible for the French Revolution. What's less clear is why modern Americans would be so suspicious. If Freemasonry was a conspiracy to kick out the British and establish a democracy, it's hard to see where the problem is.

The answer lies in Freemasonry's rationalist roots in the Enlightenment and, perhaps, its status as a potential rival to the church. Right from the start, the Vatican was hostile. Freemasonry's alleged complicity in the French Revolution, which dethroned a divinely appointed king and promoted a brotherly egalitarianism, was a bad start, and the bourgeois liberalism of the typical Freemason didn't mix too well with conservative Catholicism. Worse still, the Masonic conception of God as the "Architect of the Universe" smacked of rationalistic deism – anathema to a Catholicism founded on the church's apostolic authority. Some lodges were even openly atheist.

One of the earliest and most famous anti-Masonic documents was a flysheet distributed in London in 1698 that warned "all Godly people" against Freemasonry. "For this devillish sect are Meeters in secret which swere against all without their Following", it read. "They are the Anti-Christ which was to come leading them from Fear of God. For how should they meet in secret places and with secret Signs taking care that none observe them to do the Work of God; are not these the Ways of Evil-dom?"

The definitive religious tract against Freemasonry was published by the conservative Pope Leo XIII in 1884. His encyclical, *Humanum Genus*, openly accused Freemasonry of being in league with the devil. It is heavily conspiracist in tone. Freemasonry's "ultimate purpose", it declares, is "the utter overthrow of that whole religious and political order of the world which the Christian teaching has produced, and the substitution of a new state of things in accordance with their ideas, of which the foundations and laws shall be drawn from mere naturalism." "By means of fraud or of audacity", Freemasonry had apparently gained "such entrance into every rank of the State as to seem to be almost its ruling power."

The relationship hasn't mellowed much since then. Paul VI, Pope from 1963 to 1978, declared that Freemasonry was "the smoke of Satan ... penetrating and fogging the temple of God". But then, he did have P2 to contend with (see p.125). Today, Catholics are forbidden to become Freemasons in many countries (though the reverse is not true), and rival Catholic fraternities such as the Knights of Columbus vie with Masonic lodges for membership around the world.

Anti-Masonic feeling in America

In America, the most vehement anti-Masonic conspiracism dates back to the well-publicized disappearance in 1826 of a renegade Mason, William Morgan, who had claimed he was about to write an exposé of Masonic secrets. It is probable that he was murdered by local Freemasons, and certainly this is what most Americans believed at the time, leading to widespread anti-Masonic feeling, and even riots.

Although Protestant churches have tended to be more tolerant than the Catholic Church, in America the alignment of Freemasonry with Satanism has been enthusiastically espoused by the more rabid wing of the evangelical movement. To the evangelical ultra-right, the esoteric symbolism employed by Freemasonry is like a red rag to a bull. According to one conspiracist website, theforbiddenknowledge. com, the "meaning" of Washington DC's street plan "is all too clear". By using such symbols as the Goathead of Mendes and the Devil's Pentagram, it seems that "occultists planned for the White House to be controlled by Lucifer in accordance with his occultic power and doctrine."

Part of the blame for this Satanic reputation can be laid at the door of Albert Pike, the great embellisher of American Freemasonry in the nineteenth century. Conspiracists love to cite his 1871 magnum opus, *Morals And Dogma Of The Ancient And Accepted Scottish Rite Of Freemasonry*, as evidence of Freemasonry's alleged atheism, or worse. "The God of the Christian world", Pike wrote, "is only Bel, Moloch, Zeus, or at best Osiris, Mithras or Adonai, under another name." At one point, Pike hails "Lucifer, the Light Bearer! ... Lucifer, the Son of the Morning! Is it he who bears the Light?"

Utah's Church of Latter Day Saints, or Mormon Church, has proved a longstanding opponent of Freemasonry, despite the remarkable parallels between certain rituals performed in Mormon Temples and Freemasonic lodges. Some Mormons claim this is because they share a common heritage in the secrets of the Temple of Solomon, but it's more likely because the Mormon founder Joseph Smith and other church leaders were Freemasons themselves. Either way, the allegation that the mob that killed Joseph Smith and his brother Hyrum (note the name) in Carthage, Illinois, in 1844, was in fact a Masonic mob has been repeated for generations.

UK and European conspiracy theories

In the UK, many conspiracy theories have focused on the royal family. Prince Charles, it seems, is the first male heir to the throne not to be a Mason for two hundred years. The Masonic angle is regularly blended in with wild allegations of the Windsors' involvement in global power-politics (see p.105). Or with notorious murder cases ... Stephen Knight's *Jack The Ripper: The Final Solution* (1976) produced an elaborate theory that linked Queen Victoria's grandson, the Duke of Clarence, to the famous murders of East End prostitutes by Jack "the Ripper". The gruesome killings were supposedly ordered by the Prime Minister, Lord Salisbury (a Freemason), to cover up the Duke's marriage to a Catholic commoner – the prostitutes were apparently witnesses. It seems the actual killer, royal doctor Sir William Gull, left ample evidence of his guilt in the form of carefully constructed Masonic symbolism.

Most British conspiracy theories tread a more measured line. In the early 1980s, Knight went on to write the virtual textbooks of UK anti-Masonic theories, *The Brotherhood* and *Inside The Brotherhood*, setting out the standard allegation that Freemasons have a policy of mutual preferment. They help each other into jobs and contracts, it's said, and out of jail. Freemasonry, it seems, is popular in the police force and the judiciary.

In 1990, the Labour government tried to push through a bill demanding that all British Freemasons publicly declare their membership. MPs' legislative zeal had been stoked by the publication in 1989 of Martin Short's *Inside The Brotherhood: Further Secrets Of The Freemasons*, which mixed testimony from disgruntled Masonic widows and divorcees with political allegations, such as the claim that the Conservative party was "riddled" with Freemasons. Short even implied that Freemasons had murdered his predecessor Stephen Knight (in fact, Knight died of a brain tumour in 1985). England's United Grand Lodge responded to the parliamentary challenge by declaring that no democracy would ever countenance forcing individuals to declare their religious beliefs, say, or their membership of a golf club. Short retorted that Freemasonry wasn't like other clubs in that it had five disturbing features: a code of mutual aid; ritual threats directed at potential whistleblowers; rituals involving "menacing objects or disorienting devices"; secret passwords and signs; and lastly, "widespread public concern". Short also pointed out that only seven members had been expelled from the Grand Lodge for criminal convictions in the thirty years to September 1988. It didn't help. Labour's bill failed.

Over on the Continent, European Freemasonry has a more profoundly conspiracist edge – partly thanks to its profoundly more political history. In French lodges, political discussion had always been allowed, whereas in Britain, it had been resolutely banned. In France, each year brings a new crop of books containing fresh allegations about the baleful influence – historical or contemporary – of *la franc-maçonnerie*. In Italy, Freemasonry has been tainted by its apparent connection with the *Propaganda Due* affair (see p.125), though in fairness it seems vastly more likely that P2's masters were making use of Masonic networks than the other way round, and P2 was later expelled by the Italian Grand Lodge. Many Italians claim that Freemasonry has "infiltrated" the Vatican, to the extent that some blamed the "murder" of Pope John Paul I on Masons in the Holy See.

Racism, sexism – and persecution

The most disturbing allegations against Freemasonry aren't actually conspiracy theories. They relate to sexism and racism. On the first count, it's true that women are excluded from most lodges in the UK and US. According to authors R. A. Gilbert and John Hamill (both enthusiastic Freemasons), wom-en are banned because that's what the "Ancient Landmarks", or Masonic rules, prescribe. Most Masons, they say, would "echo the sentiments" of a certain John Coustos, who told the Portuguese Inquisition in 1743 that women were excluded in order "to take away all occasion of calumny and approach" – ie to pre-empt any accusations of orgiastic practices and general immorality – and because "women had, in general, been always considered as not very well qualified to keep a secret; the founders of the Society of Free-Masons, by their exclusion of the other sex, thereby gave a signal proof of their prudence and wisdom".

On the racism front, lodges today do not exclude people on the grounds of race. Not explicitly, at least. In the American South, many lodges do not recognize members of the (black) Prince Hall Lodge as fellow Masons. As author John J. Robinson remarks, "it is difficult to wrap one's mind around the concept of a limited universal brotherhood". Historically, there are many connections in the white South between Freemasonry and the Ku Klux Klan, with their parallel systems of symbols, signs and chivalric orders, and their odour of anti-Catholicism.

For their part, many Freemasons equate conspiracy theories about Freemasonry with similar anti-Semitic or racist arguments. Germany's defeat in World War I was widely blamed on a "Judaeo-Masonic" conspiracy. Publications such as future Nazi General Erich von Ludendorff's *The Extermination Of Masonry By The Exposure Of Its Secrets* (1928) only fanned the flames, as did the Nazis' dissemination of the "Protocols Of The Elders Of Zion" – which was almost as virulent in its hatred of Freemasonry as of Judaism. Mussolini's Italy banned Freemasonry in 1925, while Nazi Germany sent thousands of Masons to concentration camps – where they wore blue forget-me-nots as a secret sign of recognition.

The implicit warning, of course, is that something similar could happen again, if conspiracy theorists continue attacking Freemasonry. It does, however, seem difficult to compare anti-Masonic rhetoric with the naked hatred directed against Judaism worldwide. For all the conspiracy theories, the usual stereotype of Freemasonry is of a rather dusty gentleman's club where men can enjoy genteel, boozy dinners, indulge in philanthropy, and take part in rather wacky male-bonding rituals. These days, Freemasons seem more like Shriners or Rotarians than Jacobin revolutionaries.

One episode of *The Simpsons* featured a famous parody that says a lot about modern public attitudes to Freemasonry. Every Wednesday, the "Ancient Society of Stonecutters" – which numbers virtually every man in Springfield – meets in a large, forbidding pyramid. Safe in their lodge, they pay homage to a Sacred Parchment before getting drunk, playing wild games of table tennis and singing their sinister song: "Who keeps the metric system down? We do! We do! Who leaves Atlantis off the maps? We do! We do! Who keeps the Martians under wraps? We do! We do!"

SOURCES

Books

Michael Baigent and Richard Leigh The Temple And The Lodge (1991) Recounts the pseudo-history of the Masonic influence on Scotland, the main evidence being supposed Templar graves. Throws in some material on the Masons in the American Revolution, and the architecture of Rosslyn Chapel. Not much on Masonic conspiracies, though – the authors say the contemporary controversies are "a storm in a teacup".

David V. Barrett Secret Societies: From The Ancient And Arcane To The Modern And Clandestine (1999). Excellent primer, with encyclopedia-style articles ranging from neo-Platonism and Hermes Trismegistus (from whom we get the word "hermetic", meaning sealed or secret knowledge), through brief histories of the Rosicrucians and Illuminati, right through to Nazis and modern Triads.

R. A. Gilbert and John Hamill World Freemasonry: An Illustrated History (1992). From the official, Masonic Aquarian Press. Holds that Freemasonry descends "directly or indirectly" from medieval stonemasonry. As much a history of Masonic persecution as of Masonry itself.

Christopher Knight and Robert Lomas The Hiram Key: Pharaohs, Freemasonry, And The Discovery Of The Secret

Scrolls Of Jesus (2001). Described in detail on p.78.

Stephen Knight The Brotherhood (2001). Described in detail on p.82.

David Ovason The Secret Architecture Of Our Nation's Capital: The Masons And The Building Of Washington, D.C (2002). Plenty of good research on architecture and Masonic history, but overlaid by a wacky astrological angle that strays deep into speculation.

Jasper Ridley The Freemasons (2000). Authoritative, balanced and well-written history; dry at times, but good on anti-Masonic conspiracy theories.

John J. Robinson Born In Blood: The Lost Secrets Of Freemasonry (1990). The first half of the book is a history of the Knights Templar; the second "unlocks" the symbolic secrets of Masonry to discover their true meanings – and they have nothing to do with guilds of medieval stonemasons. Fascinating but fanciful.

Martin Short Inside The Brotherhood: Further Secrets Of The Freemasons (1990). Picks over the pernicious influence of Freemasonry in UK society, especially in the police and judiciary, notably in the Woolard and Stalker "Affairs". Gives airtime to the Evangelical argument suggesting Freemasonry is Satanic. Gilbert and Hamill (see above) call it a "venomous attack", full of "long exposed fables and lies".

Frances Yates The Rosicrucian Enlightenment (2001). A serious work by one of a generation's greatest and most fascinating historians. Traces the history of esoteric philosophy behind the Rosicrucians, and gently – but cogently – puts forward some ideas about the origins of Freemasonry.

Websites

ⓦ anti-masonry.info/alt.illuminati_FAQ.html The Grand Lodge of British Columbia and Yukon has pooled lots of links to articles and sites dismissing anti-Masonic theories.

ⓦ www.catholicculture.org/docs/doc_view. cfm?recnum=1244 Pope Leo XIII's anti-Freemasonry broadside, *Humanum Genus*, in English.

ⓦ www.freemasonry.bcy.ca/fiction/cinema. html An excellent list of Freemasonry in films, with short reviews and brief details of Masonic Moments.

ⓦ www.freemasonry.org/psoc/ masonicmyths.htm A page from an official Freemasonry site which aims to counter myths about Masonic influence on American Independence.

ⓦ www.freemasonrywatch.org Begins by approvingly quoting JFK: "the very word 'secrecy' is repugnant in a free and open society; and we are, as a people, inherently and historically opposed to secret societies, to secret oaths and to secret proceedings." Ends in the wilder fringes of conspiracy.

⊛ **www.grandlodge-england.org** Homepage of the original United Grand Lodge of England.

⊛ **www.masonicinfo.com** Sets out the main arguments and conspiracy theories ranged against Freemasonry, and then attempts to counter them. Unusually balanced, for the most part.

⊛ **www.rosicrucian.org** The homepage of AMORC, one of many fraternal organizations claiming to be the true heirs of the Rosicrucians.

⊛ **www.theforbiddenknowledge.com/ chapter3/** The Luciferic symbolism of Washington DC, luridly explained.

Films

From Hell (Allen and Albert Hughes, 2001). Horrific thriller based on the theory that Freemasons were behind the Jack-the-Ripper killings in nineteenth-century East London. Excellent casting, with Ian Holm, Heather Graham, and Johnny Depp as an opium-fuelled Scotland Yard detective. Based on a graphic novel by Alan Moore and Eddie Campbell.

The Illuminati

Groups calling themselves *illuminati*, after the Latin word for "enlightened", have come and gone for centuries. The earliest had loosely Gnostic beliefs (see p.164): the *alumbrados* of sixteenth-century Spain, for example, believed that the soul could communicate directly with the divine. They quickly fell foul of the Inquisition. In France, various sects have called themselves *illuminés*; the Martinists for example, a Christian mystic sect that originated in the eighteenth century, still survive today.

However, the first group to actually call itself "the Illuminati" was closer to Freemasonry than Gnosticism. In 1776, a Bavarian university professor, Adam Weishaupt, founded an "Order of Perfectibilists", or Illuminati. They were basically an anti-Jesuit club, with anti-monarchist and egalitarian beliefs mixed up with a Masonic-style culture of esoteric symbolism – in fact, Weishaupt and his

colleague Baron von Knigge recruited mostly from Masonic lodges within Baron von Hund's popular Strict Observance rite. At first, with just five members, it seemed there weren't too many Perfectible men in Bavaria, but within ten years the group had grown to a few hundred strong, mostly in German-speaking Europe.

By the mid-1780s, the activities of the Illuminati and other "secret societies" – for which there was a pan-European fad – had attracted the suspicion of Bavaria's ruler, the Elector Prince Karl-Theodor. Warned by informers that these kinds of groups were stirring up political trouble, if not outright Jacobinism, Karl-Theodor banned all secret associations in Bavaria in June 1784. In March 1785 he followed up by condemning Freemasonry and the Illuminati by name. Weishaupt fled Bavaria, and the Illuminati were disbanded.

Afterlife: growth of a conspiracy theory

Despite the order's official closure, the reputation of the Illuminati lived on, and even grew, in the burgeoning conspiracy-theory culture of late eighteenth- and early nineteenth-century Europe. The group's alleged reach was most famously exaggerated by the controversial healer, occultist and Freemason, "Count" Cagliostro (who inspired the character of the Masonic enchanter Sarastro in Mozart's *The Magic Flute*). After being arrested in Rome in 1789, Cagliostro quickly confessed the "secrets" of the Templars, Masons and other groups to the Inquisition. As extravagant under duress as he was in high-society parties, Cagliostro declared that the Illuminati were plotting to overthrow first the Bourbon monarchy and then the Papacy.

In Europe, conservatives' fear of secret societies was inflamed by the Abbé Barruel's *Mémoires* (see p.79) of 1797, which blamed the Illuminati (along with Freemasonry in general) for the French Revolution. The following year conspiracy theories in Britain and North America were stoked by John Robison's *Proofs Of A Conspiracy* (see p.81), which was as unsparing of the Illuminati as it was of Masons. Slowly the Illuminati were mythologized as a kind of arch-Masonic group, an elite conspiracy behind a conspiracy. In 1803, a former colleague of Baron von Hund's, Johann August Starck, published his *Triumph der Philosophie im Achtzenten Jahrhundert*, an early mega-conspiracy theory tracing the growth of evil from Greek philosophy through medieval heresy and culminating in that by-now-typical whipping boy of the era – the Illuminati. (Though Starck fingered the more mystically oriented Knigge as the villain of the piece, rather than Weishaupt.)

Despite a complete lack of any proof of the Illuminati's existence, the group continued to be blamed for all manner of conspiracies well into the nineteenth century. Federalists accused Thomas Jefferson of being controlled by European Illuminati (though he wasn't even a Freemason), largely on the grounds that he had expressed sympathy for Weishaupt for living "under the tyranny of despots and priests". In fact, Jefferson had written in a letter to a friend that if Weishaupt had lived in America he would have had no need for secrecy.

The Illuminati today

In 1924, the publication of Nesta H. Webster's *Secret Societies And Subversive Movements* catapulted the myth of the Illuminati out of the eighteenth century and right into the twenty-first. Although Webster had merely repeated the stale gossip of post-French Revolutionary Europe, *Secret Societies* became a staple reference work of the twentieth century; over eighty years after its publication, the Illuminati are once again widely tipped as the ultimate conspiracy organization.

Perhaps because of the complete lack of any evidence for who the Illuminati actually are, they have simply become whatever conspiracists want them to be; the traces of their existence are the very conspiracies theorists believe they have unmasked. Most common is the thesis that Freemasons are the unwitting dupes of the Illuminati. It's as if conspiracy theorists fire off their anti-Masonic accusations with such force that they overshoot what's actually there. It's not a problem: beyond the Masons lie the Illuminati. Alternatively, the hierarchical system of Freemasonry is offered as proof of the existence of the Illuminati: only when Masons penetrate beyond the thirty-third degree, it's alleged, do they learn that the Illuminati are the master architects presiding over the grand plan. Only the most devoted Freemasons get that far, and thus the secret is safely preserved.

Oddly, ever since conspiracism took off on the Internet, scores of sub-Rotarian private clubs have suddenly cropped up, all claiming to descend in an unbroken (but hitherto unaccountably secret) line

THE ROSICRUCIANS

In 1614 a pamphlet was published anonymously in Germany with the ambitious title *The Universal And General Reformation Of The Whole Wide World*. It announced the existence of a secret Brotherhood of the Rosy Cross – *rosae crucis* in Latin, hence the English "Rosicrucian" – which would set about just that bold project. (The name was a nod and a wink to those with a working knowledge of alchemical symbolism: the rose signifying female sexuality – or, alternatively, the mystical alchemical *ros* or dew of regeneration – the cross symbolizing the male organ.) Within two years, further anonymous "manifestos" followed: the *Fama Fraternitatis Rosae Crucis*, the *Confessio Fraternitatis*, and *The Chemical Wedding Of Christian Rosenkreutz*. They revealed a mysterious organization that had supposedly been founded in 1407 by a German monk, "Christian Rosenkreutz", who had learned the secrets of Arab science and medicine during his travels around the Mediterranean. On his return to Germany, he had founded a secret society of eight members to preserve this knowledge, and built a temple named after the Holy Spirit to which all eight would return, in secret, once a year. This "Sanctus Spiritus" was also Rosenkreutz's grave. When it was unsealed, after 120 years,

a hidden seven-sided chamber was supposedly revealed, containing books, alchemical instruments and Rosenkreutz's fresh and undecomposed body.

The effect of the "manifestos" on European intellectual circles was something like the impact of Chubby Checker's "The Twist" on early 1960s America: soon everyone was dancing to the new tune. "Occult" sciences such as alchemy were deeply fashionable in the higher echelons of society, especially when polished up with an antique patina, and pamphlets were published answering the Rosicrucian call, challenges were issued and addressed, accusations levelled and denied, and open letters written calling on the secret society to reveal itself – and its secrets, whatever they were. Some scholars actually went off in search of the "Sanctus Spiritus".

Although the clamour spread across Europe – reaching Britain in 1625 or so, if the published record is anything to go by – the Rosicrucians themselves responded with a deafening silence. Perhaps this was because they were a *secret* society, after all. Or perhaps because they were nothing more than a witty invention – a *ludibrium* or plaything. That, at least, was the word used for the "manifestos" by the man most widely suspected of

having written them, the theologian Johann Valentin Andreae, who was born in 1586. As the admirable British historian, Frances Yates, puts it in *Rosicrucian Enlightenment*, "The right way of looking at the question may thus be to give up the hunt for 'real' Rosicrucians and to ask instead whether the Rosicrucian movement *suggested* the formation of secret societies." (As she also noted: "when, as is often the case, the misty discussion of 'Rosicrucians' and their history becomes involved with the Masonic myth, the enquirer feels as though they are sinking helplessly into a bottomless bog.")

Even if the legend behind the secret brotherhood was a fiction, Rosicrucianism as a scientific and philosophical ideal – promoting learning and spiritual improvement, and challenging ignorance and the abuse of religious authority – was certainly real. Proto-Enlightenment Europe *was* becoming acquainted with Arab scholarship and alchemical science, and even if thinkers and specialists in Hermetic mysteries like Giordano Bruno, John Dee, Philip Sidney, Francis Bacon and Robert Fludd weren't members of a "Rosicrucian brotherhood", it was only for want of the name.

It wasn't long before Rosicrucian societies were being set up for real, the first appearing in

Holland in the 1620s. It was scarcely any longer before they were denounced, with pamphlets appearing in Paris in 1623 accusing the "Invisibles" of entering into a pact with the devil. The eighteenth-century re-inventors of Freemasonry (see p.76) added a sprinkling of Rosicrucian terminology and symbolism to give their efforts a high-minded flavour, while in the late nineteenth and early twentieth centuries a number of "Rosicrucian" brotherhoods were set up. Some still exist, many claiming to be authentic inheritors of Rosenkreutz's "original" tradition. Of course, they can't all be right. You could say none of them is, but this doesn't mean they're any less "real" than the Dutch brotherhood of the 1620s. Today, you can try to join any of the Ancient Mystical Order Rosae Crucis (AMORC), the Confraternity of the Rose Cross, the Fraternitas Rosae Crucis, the Societas Rosicruciana and the Rosicrucian Fellowship, to name just a few. Ideals vary from sincere Christian philanthropy to mystifying astrological hocuspocus. Some conspiracy theorists see these organizations as mere shams. The descendants of Rosenkreutz's eight Brothers are surely too busy setting about The Universal and General Reformation of the Whole Wide World to mess around with frat clubs…

from Weishaupt's original organization. None is any more credible than similar "Templar" groups.

In certain authors' hands, the power of the

Illuminati has grown with impressive virulence. On website after Christian Identity website, the Illuminati are blamed for world Communism or, more recently, one-world-government projects. The Illuminati are Satanists, international capitalists, Zionists. They run the CIA, the Vatican, the Freemasons, the Wide Awake Club. They murdered Lincoln, shot JFK, and put the phoney "face" on the surface of Mars. For self-styled intelligence insider Milton William Cooper, author of the right-wingers' apocalyptic mega-conspiracy bible, *Behold A Pale Horse* (1991), the Illuminati are the cutting edge of a grand plan to impose an anti-libertarian one-world government. For British arch-conspiracist David Icke, they are just another name for the power-wielding elite behind the New World Order conspiracy, the Bushes, Saddams and Windsors of the world, and are thus a tool and synonym for the sinister, shape-shifting Reptilians (see p.107). Curiously, both writers invert the Illuminati's historical reputation as revolutionary and anti-establishment.

The Illuminati are almost as popular in full-blooded fiction as they are in the half-reality of mega-conspiracy literature. Robert Shea and Robert Anton Wilson's cult *Illuminatus!* trilogy depicts them as a repressive, quasi-Fascistic force, locked in constant struggle with the chaotic, liberated "Erisians" for domination of the world. Umberto Eco weaves them into his scintillatingly cerebral *Foucault's Pendulum*, while Dan Brown's infinitely more lowbrow (and more engagingly plotted) *Angels And Demons* imagines them as a cabal of ultra-scientists (founded by Galileo, no less) pitted against Vatican philistines in a hyper-modern outburst of the ancient conflict between faith and reason. *Angels And Demons* also gave the world that visually pleasing, reversible-cal-ligraphy rendering of the word "Illuminati", which has so boosted the organization's ubiquity on the Web. Every secret society needs a logo, after all, and there's no story without a picture.

The most satisfyingly extravagant anti-Illuminati conspiracy theory, however, belongs to "former MI6 agent" John Coleman. And Coleman says it is no fiction. His Illuminati, aka the "Committee of 300", has a very broad agenda indeed. On a number of websites, Coleman helpfully breaks down their "Targets" into 21 bullet points. It begins with the destruction of "national identity and national pride", as well as "the Christian religion", and ends with the establishment of a "New World Order" (see p.234) backed by the IMF, UN and World Court. To achieve this goal, mind control will be used to help achieve drastic population reductions, with the help of "religious cults such as the Moslem Brotherhood, Moslem Fundamentalism and the Sikhs". Meanwhile, "the youth of the land will be encouraged by means of rock music and drugs to rebel against the status quo, thus undermining and eventually destroying the family unit". Devised by the Tavistock Institute, this programme is known as the "Aquarian Conspiracy". This totalitarian agenda culminates in the Illuminati "taking control of education in America with the intent and purpose of utterly and completely destroying it. By 1993, the full force effect of this policy is becoming apparent, and will be even more destructive as primary and secondary schools begin to teach 'Outcome Based Education'". A formidable threat indeed.

SOURCES

Books

John Coleman **Conspirator's Hierarchy: The Committee Of 300** (1992). "Can you imagine an all-powerful group, that knows no national boundaries, above the laws of all countries, one that controls every aspect of politics, religion, commerce and industry, banking, insurance, mining, the drug trade, the petroleum industry, a group answerable to no one but its members?" Coleman can.

Milton William Cooper **Behold A Pale Horse** (1991). Possibly the maddest mega-conspiracy book ever written. Unsummarizable, but as one online reviewer put it, "this Book has made me paranoid and explained all the visions and dreams I have had as far as the battle over Good vs. Evil". Oddly, the title was stolen from a 1964 film starring Gregory Peck and Omar Sharif. In May 2001, Cooper was shot dead by police. He was wanted for assault and had fired first. At least, that's what the police say.

Robert Shea and Robert Anton Wilson Illuminatus! Part1: The Eye In The Pyramid (1987). *The Hitchhiker's Guide to the Galaxy* meets the world of conspiracy counter-culture. A favourite among computer hackers, apparently.

Fritz Springmeier Bloodlines Of The Illuminati (2002). In mocking imitation of the Twelve Tribes of Israel, Satan set up his own dozen. And a thirteenth, whose modern-day descendants are still obscenely powerful. The book is filled with all the usual suspects:

Kennedy, Rothschild, Onassis, Rockefeller, McDonald, Disney etc. Written by a Christian "Patriot" jailed for a bank robbery.

Websites

Ⓦ **illuminati-order.com** One of a number of groups claiming to be the original Illuminati. "Some have tried to discredit our authenticity because we are not as secret as we are supposedly required to be. So, let us be clear here and now that we are only as secret as necessary to exist relatively unimpeded." That's solved that one, then.

Ⓦ **100777.com/myron** Audio downloads

of the "Myron Fagan tapes", which have long circulated in right-wing groups. Fagan delivers a deeply conspiratorial lecture on the Rothschild-backed Illuminati plot to establish a One World Government through the medium of the nefarious Council on Foreign Relations. Describes income tax as a "cancer".

Ⓦ **www.illuminati-news.com** Click on the Illuminati link and you'll be taken to a page on "Shadow Government". Also features a revolving version of Dan Brown's calligraphic rendition of the word Illuminati – just hover your mouse over it and it spins!

Blood Libel: the longest-running conspiracy theory of all

Forget about conspiracy theories that a blood-sucking government wants to drain your life away in the form of taxes, the "Blood Libel" or "Blood Accusation" is the real thing: the paranoid belief that Satanists, Protestants, Catholics, witches or – most frequently – Jews are actually out for your blood. Or rather your children's blood, supposedly collected in ritual sacrifices and drunk as wine or blended with other ingredients to make festival cakes.

Lost boys: William of Norwich, Little Hugh, Simon of Trent

Around 40 BCE, according to the historian Josephus, the grammarian Apion accused Alexandria's Jewish community of sacrificing a Greek boy every year and eating his entrails. Apion worked the resulting uproar to his own political advantage. Before the Roman Empire adopted Christianity, similar accusations were regularly made by Roman authorities against Christians – who weren't helped by the fact that their principal ritual involved consuming the "body" and "blood" of their founder.

However, the Blood Libel was first infused into the mainstream of European history in Norwich, England, at the Easter festival of 1144, when a tanner's apprentice called William disappeared. His body was never found, but local Jews were accused of torturing, hanging – crucifying by some accounts – and perhaps eating him. Although the Sheriff dismissed the claims, mob violence drove the Jews out of town. In 1255 the story bobbed up a few miles away, when "Little Hugh" of Lincoln was found dead in a cesspool belonging to a Jew named Jopin. Had he fallen? Or was he, as the crowd insisted, the victim of a ritual crucifixion? After confessing under torture, 81 Jews were arrested; eighteen were hanged.

The Blood Libel flowed all too easily into the well of Christians' darkest fears about Jews: were they not responsible for the crucifixion of Jesus? (Never mind that it was the Romans; that Jesus was a Jew himself; and that without the cross Christianity would be just another Jewish cult...) The story spread across Europe like an epidemic. In 1267, fishermen found a seven-year-old girl's body washed up near Baden. Miracles such as blood flowing fresh from the wounds "proved" the Jews were responsible. Similar cases soon surfaced all over Germany and beyond. In 1475, the Blood Libel was officially endorsed, after a boy from Trent called Simon disappeared during Holy Week. Again, the Jews were accused of kidnapping the child, crucifying him to express their implacable enmity towards all Christians, then butchering him and collecting his blood. Again, confessions were extracted under torture. Such was the outcry that a papal enquiry was eventually set up. It concluded that Simon had been killed following "rabbinical law" to celebrate Passover with blood-leavened breads – ignoring the fact that he disappeared on the day *after* the feast. Simon was soon canonized as a martyr by Pope Sixtus V (and only de-canonized in 1965).

In late fifteenth-century Hungary, Jewish men were driven to confess, after torture, that the Blood Libel was true. And why? Because, they revealed, male Jews menstruate like women and therefore need to replenish their blood supply. (Oddly, Christian women seem to get by without regular infusions.) Seventeenth-century pogroms in Poland were inspired by the Blood Libel to such an extent that one Rabbi Siegel ruled that the wine used at ceremonial Passover meals – traditionally red – should be changed to white, so as not to provoke neighbours who had heard about the Blood Libel.

The Blood Libel in the Middle East

The "Damascus Affair" of 1840 saw the arrival of the Blood Libel in the Middle East, after a Capuchin monk named Father Thomas disappeared in the city. The French consul, Ratti Menton, made the old accusation, backed up by the British and American consuls. Jews were rounded up and imprisoned, but eventually released (apart from four who had died) after the pasha of Egypt made an official declaration that the ritual murder claim was a nonsense.

One hundred and fifty years later, in March 1991, the accusation broke out again, when a Syrian UN Human Rights Commission delegate recommended that members should read *The Matzah Of Zion*, a book published in 1983 by the Syrian statesman and onetime defence minister, Field Marshal Mustafa Tlass. The cover showed a man whose throat had been cut (with a menorah, the traditional Jewish candelabrum, in the 1986 second edition), and whose blood is being collected in a basin. The book describes the Damascus Affair and presents the Blood Libel as accurate – Father Thomas's blood having apparently been used in the preparation of Jewish *matzah* bread. As the introduction puts it (according to a translation published on the website of the pro-Israeli Middle East Media Research Institute), "Damascus was shocked by this loathsome crime ... now every mother warns: 'Be careful not to stray far from home unless the Jew comes, puts you in his sack, takes you, slaughters you and drains your blood in order to prepare the '*matzah* of Zion'."

In March 2002, a storm brewed up after Umayma al-Jalahma, a teacher at King Faisal University in Al-Dammam, Saudi Arabia, published an article in the Saudi Arabian daily *Al-Riyadh*. Describing "The Jewish Holiday Of Purim", it claimed that "Jewish people must obtain human blood so that their clerics can prepare the holiday pastries ... [The victim's] blood is taken and dried into granules. The cleric blends these granules into the pastry dough; they can also be saved for the next holiday." On return from a visit to the Lebanon, the editor commented that the article had "slipped through the cracks".

The Blood Libel even crops up on television: in 2003 the TV series *Al-Shatat* on the Lebanese Al-Manar satellite channel notoriously included an episode in which a "rabbi" character cuts the throat of a Christian child and collects his blood in a basin. In the next scene the rabbi offers a Jewish man a *matzah* that is "tastier and holier because it was kneaded with pure blood".

Fighting back

That the Middle East Media Research Institute translated and Web-published parts of Mustafa Tlass's book is typical of the efforts of a number of websites keen to expose the truth about Arab anti-Semitism (as they'd put it), or to slander their enemies (as their opponents would counter). MEMRI rightly points out that few Arab media sources are translated into English – unfortunately, this makes it hard for non-Arabic-speakers to check the original sources. Sites ranging from the moderate, Arab-Israeli mideastweb.org to the influential Anti-Defamation League and the frankly conspiratorial trackingthethreat.com all spotlight anti-Semitic slanders emanating from the Middle East.

Some conspiracists have seized on an unfortunate parallel with conspiracy theory websites, in that the same allegations crop up again and again. Reports of what this or that Palestinian Authority figure may or may not have said, for instance, get cut-and-pasted so many times that it's sometimes alleged that these are not genuine reports of modern manifestations of the Blood Libel but amount to a conspiracy in themselves – a Zionist conspiracy to convince the world that Arabs are dangerous conspiracists and potential *génocidaires*. But then this kind of thinking is disturbingly close to the anti-Semitic fable of the all-powerful "Jewish lobby" (see p.229). There's undoubtedly a powerful moral imperative to expose these myths. The precedents of eastern European pogroms and of course the Holocaust (see p.94) are always close to mind, as the Blood Libel has always been an undercurrent of the most dangerous anti-Semitic rhetoric. The Nazi mouthpiece, *Der Stürmer*, for instance, was full of references to it.

While the Blood Libel itself is fairly unusual outside conspiratorial circles – whether ultra-right or anti-Zionist – its subtler manifestations, however, are disturbingly common. Arab newspaper cartoons, for instance, may show caricatures of Israeli politicians stalking through the ruins of Palestine, their hands dripping with blood, while liberal attacks on Israel's interventions in the West Bank often focus on the deaths of Palestinian children or teenagers. You could see these as fair – if robust – attacks on Israel's policies. You could also see them as sinister takes on the old Blood Libel – Israel is, after all, a Jewish state. A libel case in 1985 became a landmark in US law, when then-General Ariel Sharon sued *Time* magazine after a cover story in February 1983 accused him of conspiracy in the massacres at Sabra and Shatila camps, conducted by Christian Phalange militia during the Lebanese Civil War. The case was widely reported as a "blood libel". (For the record, the court found the *Time* article to be false, and the product of "negligent and reckless" reporting. It wasn't, however, malicious – and therefore wasn't libel.)

CONSPIRACY OF FEAR: SATANIC RITUAL ABUSE

A modern twist on the Blood Libel seems to have emanated from an unholy conjunction of the psychiatrist's couch and the fundamentalist's newsletter. In the 1980s, using "recovered memory" techniques, psychotherapists "helped" hundreds of adults to "remember" that they had been sexually abused as children. In many cases, the abuse was blamed on the ritual practices of "Satanists" – whatever they were supposed to be. Some linked belief in devil-worship to paranoid fundamentalist Christians with imaginations stimulated by the old Blood Libel stories. (Others blamed hysterical feminists convinced that just as all men were rapists, so all fathers were abusers.)

Whatever the cause, the most serious consequence of the sudden growth in belief in Satanic Ritual Abuse (SRA) was a spate of so-called Multi-Victim, Multi-Offender (MVMO) cases, most famously the McMartin Pre-School scandal in Manhattan Beach, California. This kicked off in August 1983 when an alcoholic paranoid schizophrenic mother accused a part-time school worker of molesting her son. The DA dropped the case for lack of evidence, but a local chief of police wrote to some two hundred parents asking them to question their children. The media quickly took up the hue and cry, as did the (Catholic) American Martyrs Church. Panic spread, and hundreds of children were interviewed using techniques now known to be highly suggestive, including leading and repeated questions. By the spring of 1984, it was declared that 360 children had been abused. Their interviews revealed a story of teachers belonging to a "Satanic Church" who ritually murdered other babies and drank their blood. The children were molested on highways, buried in coffins, flushed down toilets and abused in underground networks of secret tunnels.

After six years and fifteen million dollars' worth of trial costs, however, the McMartin jury failed to make a single conviction. Perhaps because of the publicity the affair generated, however, MVMO cases spread all over the US and beyond. Childcare professionals gave seminars on SRA and evangelical churches galvanized their members to warn others of the dangers. In the UK, these combined efforts led to almost a thousand cases of organized abuse and 86 cases of ritual abuse being brought between 1988 and 1991, including the Cleveland, Rochdale and Orkney scandals. In the last-named affair, children were forcibly removed from their homes in dawn raids. In an official UK government report, completed in 1994, Professor Jean La Fontaine concluded that Christians in opposition to new religious movements had been "a powerful influence encouraging the identification of Satanic abuse".

From the early 1990s, the interviewing techniques that led to MVMO cases began to be discredited. False Memory became the new buzzword in psychological circles. Yet some still saw conspiracies of Satanic abusers at large. Elizabeth Loftus, author of the 1996 book *The Myth Of Repressed Memory*, was told that her work was "on the same level as those who deny the existence of the extermination camps during World War II". And as late as 2003, a group of New Agers on the predominantly Free Church (Christian fundamentalist) island of Lewis, off the west coast of Scotland, were accused of SRA – including blood-drinking, orgies with children and animal sacrifice. By July 2004, however, all the charges had been dropped.

One of the accused, a self-styled white witch or pagan, described the experience as "like a seventeenth-century witch-hunt", inevitably inviting comparisons with the late Arthur Miller's play *The Crucible*, itself a dramatic response to the madness of MacCarthyism (see p.338). The message is clear: whether the finger is pointed at witches or Jews, Communists or suspected child-abusers, some conspiracy theories can all too easily tip over into collective hysteria.

The Blood Libel today

Over two thousand years after Apion's Alexandrian accusations, the old wound is still bleeding. On January 25, 2005, twenty members of the Russian parliament from the Motherland and Communist parties signed a declaration demanding that Jewish organizations be banned throughout Russian on the grounds of their hostility to the Russian people and their practice of ritual child murder. Somehow, it's not surprising that they also bemoaned the fact that "the whole democratic world is today under the financial and political control of international Jewry" – a reference to the hoary "Elders of Zion" myth (see p.100).

And the accusation has spread beyond Judaism. In 1996, Evangelical Christians persuaded Senator Jesse Helms of the House Foreign Relations Committee to investigate stories that Chinese people eat aborted fetuses for their medicinal benefits, for example. And pro-life groups frequently equate abortion with the Holocaust, characterizing feminists and other campaigners for women's rights as bloodthirsty servants of evil – terms disturbingly reminiscent of the Blood Libel.

SOURCES

Books

Alan Dundes The Blood Libel Legend: A Casebook In Anti-Semitic Folklore (1991). This collection of academic essays is one of the few serious studies of the phenomenon.

Ronald Florence Blood Libel: The Damascus Affair Of 1840 (2004). Pacy and fascinating account of the Damascus Blood Libel. For a really detailed and scholarly version, go for Jonathan Frankel's 1997 doorstopper, **The Damascus Affair**.

Debbie Nathan and Michael Snedeker Satan's Silence: Ritual Abuse And The Making Of A Modern American Witch Hunt (2001). Wise and considered telling of the story of Satanic Ritual Abuse scares, advocating more rights for children. One Amazon reader claims the book helped them resume contact with a family they'd believed ritually abused them.

Marvin Perry and Frederick Schweitzer Anti-Semitism: Myth And Hate From Antiquity To The Present (2002).

Fascinating and scholarly survey of the history and origins of anti-Semitism, ranging from the myths of the Blood Libel (in chapter 2) and the Protocols of the Elders of Zion, to modern-day Holocaust denial and the attitudes of the Nation of Islam.

Websites

ⓦ **www.adl.org/css/mix_blood_libel.asp** The 1986 cover of Mustafa Tlass's **Matzah Of Zion** book – just one of the blood libelling, anti-Semitic cartoons archived at the Anti-Defamation League's site.

ⓦ **www.amprom.org/trent** The website of America's Promise Ministries, from Sandpoint, Idaho "in the beautiful Northwestern United States". Their beliefs, however, are far from beautiful: "Hundreds of thousands of children disappear every year in the world, perhaps some of them victims of Zionist ritual murder which remain undiscovered."

ⓦ **www.holywar.org/txt/RitualMurder/ jrm_toc.html** The full text of **Jewish**

Ritual Murder, an extraordinary, hate-filled book-length justification of the Blood Libel, published in London in 1938. The author, former jailbird Arnold Leese, believed he was "killing a rat with a stick". From a bizarre and offensive European anti-Semitic site.

ⓦ **www.memri.org** "Bridging The Language Gap Between The Middle East And The West" – albeit with an agenda to show the West how anti-Semitic the Arab Middle East is. Click on "videos" to see the blood-libelling episode of **Al-Shatat**, among other clips.

ⓦ **www.thewatcherfiles.com/jewish_ sacrifice.htm** Headlines such as "Jewish Murder Plan Against White Christians Exposed" give some idea of the flavour of this long screed, written by one Willie Martin with endless pseudo-historic citations of the Blood Libel. Comes from one of Sherry "Soldier in the Army of God" Shriner's hysterical conspiracy websites.

Holocaust denial

Denying that the Holocaust ever happened is a conspiracy theory because it requires you to believe not only that all the survivors of the death camps were lying, but that they were complicit in an intricate conspiracy to agree on a story – a conspiracy that somehow embraced the scores of Nazis who admitted involvement in the death camps in the post-war Nuremberg trials. Typically, the idea that such a conspiracy exists neatly confirms Holocaust deniers' darkest and oldest fears about Jewish people – the very fears that Hitler fuelled as he marched to power in Germany.

The Holocaust: some facts

The Nazi's genocidal attempt between 1941 and 1945 to eliminate European Jewry – along with the Roma (gypsies), gay men, Jehovah's Witnesses, Communist leaders, dissenters, and the physically and mentally disabled – is usually called the Holocaust. In practice, the sheer numbers of Jews killed – six million is the conventionally accepted figure – means that the term is often used for the Jewish Holocaust, or what the Nazis called the *Endlösung der Judenfrage*, the "final solution of the Jewish question". The phrase is known from the infamous Wannsee conference of January 20, 1942, where German leaders promised Reinhard Heydrich, deputy to SS chief Heinrich Himmler, that they would help set up – and supply – seven new *Vernichtungslager*, or extermination camps: Auschwitz-Birkenau, Belzec, Chelmno, Majdanek, Maly Trostenets, Sobibór and Treblinka II.

The origins of the Final Solution date back to the mid-1930s, with the increasing persecution of Jews and their incarceration in ghettos. Mass killings began even before Wannsee, as the ruthless *Einsatzgruppen* execution squads followed the German army's advance into Soviet territory from June 1941. Secret meetings between Himmler, Heydrich and Adolf Eichmann, the SS officer in charge of the Gestapo's Jewish Office, are known to have taken place in mid-October 1941. Around that time, Himmler banned all Jewish emigration, the first gas chambers were built at Belzec and Chelmno, and the first experiments with Zyklon B gas were conducted at Auschwitz-Birkenau.

Jews and Hebrew speakers today often talk about the Shoah, or "calamity". Around sixty percent of all Europe's Jews were killed, or a third of the entire Jewish population of the world. In all, somewhere between twelve and 26 million people died as a result of Nazi persecution, including many millions of non-Jewish Slavs and Poles.

Conspiracy theorists in denial

A small, very vocal minority dispute these basic facts. For them, the "history" of the Holocaust is a gigantic conspiracy to present the Jews as victims and to blacken the reputation of the Nazis. Ever since French Nazi-sympathizer Paul Rassinier began claiming in the late 1940s that the figures for the dead were grossly exaggerated, these "revisionists", as they call themselves, have presented their arguments as a contribution to the real historical debate about the exact number of Jewish deaths. Opponents, however, call them Holocaust deniers, claiming that their arguments spring not from fresh examination of the evidence, like genuine revisionist historians, but from blind and poisonous prejudice.

When "revisionist" publications are laden with anti-Semitic language, it's easy to draw that conclusion. Increasingly, however, Holocaust deniers present themselves more subtly, as champions of freedom of speech, as underdogs challenging the established, entrenched hierarchy, as seekers after truth against a conspiracy of dogma or silence. Their enemies are legion: the Allied military men who "staged" war-film footage of "death camps"; the post-war governments intent on demonizing Germany in order to boost their own power-share in Europe; the Zionist factions bent on justifying and sustaining the creation of a Jewish homeland in the Middle East; the European Jews eager to reap spectacular profits in reparations; and the campuses filled with academics anxious to protect their own profitable Holocaust-industry careers.

Most of all, Holocaust deniers just blame the sheer malevolence of Jewish people. As Harold Covington, leader of America's National Socialist White People's Party, wrote to supporters in July 1996: "Take away the Holocaust and what do you have left? Without their precious Holocaust, what are the Jews? Just a grubby little bunch of international bandits and assassins and squatters who have perpetrated the most massive, cynical fraud in human history."

Zionist conspiracy?

Some on the left point to the massive disparity between the amount of time and money spent on remembrance of Jewish deaths – through museums, newspaper articles, television programmes and so on – as opposed to the relatively unpublicized murders of Roma (gypsy) people, gays and people with disabilities. This is seen as evidence of a Jewish or Zionist conspiracy to infiltrate the media and promote their own cause at the expense of others. Such thinking is particularly common in the Middle East, fuelled perhaps by resentment or hatred of Israel. As Palestinian Authority newspaper *Al-Hayat Al-Jadeeda* put it on July 2, 1998: "The persecution of the Jews is a deceitful myth which the Jews have labelled the

Holocaust and exploited to get sympathy."

Or as French philosopher Roger Garaudy has argued, Israel uses "the myth of the six million to build its state and justify attacks on Palestinians". A former Communist who converted to Islam late in life, Garaudy was lionized by the Egyptian press when he toured the country in November 1996. In January 1998, however, he was tried for breaking the French law against Holocaust denial, and specifically for "complicity in the questioning of crimes against humanity", in his book *The Founding Myths Of Israeli Politics*. Despite the help of volunteer lawyers from Egypt and the Lebanon, and Garaudy's own claim that "My adversaries confuse Judaism, which is a religion that I respect, and Zionism, which is a policy that I fight", he was fined 240,000 francs – roughly US $40,000 at the time.

Hot air and gas chambers

In the aftermath of World War II, Allied troops recovered letters, lists, reports, orders, photographs, films and blueprints detailing exactly how the Holocaust was arranged. All forgeries, say the deniers. The Allies also discovered trucks, chambers and mass graves packed with emaciated, sometimes tortured bodies – the result of typhus or cholera epidemics, according to the deniers.

Following the line of French literary professor and leading Holocaust denier, Robert Faurisson, it's claimed that the Nazis were technically incapable of mass murder on such a huge scale. Cleverly, this approach chimes with the sense of appalled disbelief that anyone studying the Holocaust encounters. In a book with a foreword by Noam Chomsky (defending the right to free speech), Faurisson claimed Zyklon-B was used only for delousing detainees.

"Evidence" was provided, much later, by the infamous, self-published *Leuchter Report*, a 1988 tract by layman Fred A. Leuchter, who tested the Auschwitz gas chambers for cyanide and found no significant

ANNE FRANK: TEENAGER OR FACE OF AN INTERNATIONAL CONSPIRACY?

Anne Frank: The Diary Of A Young Girl was written by a Jewish girl who remained hidden in a secret annex of an Amsterdam house between 1942 and 1944. She died of typhus in Bergen-Belsen in March 1945, a month before the camp was liberated. After the war, her manuscript was published by her father, Otto Frank – the sole family member to survive the death camps.

Although some 31 million copies have now been sold, some Holocaust deniers allege that Otto Frank was selling a scam, a forgery designed to provide a convenient focus for public sympathies and to help publicize the "myth" of the Holocaust. These allegations have been tested in the courts a number of times, first in Lübeck in 1959 – where the German court ruled, after tests, that the *Diary* was genuine and the claim was withdrawn. A flush of cases came to a head in the late 1970s: a certain Werner Kuhnt wrote in a far-right monthly that the diary was a fraud; a pamphlet by one Erwin Schönborn said it was "the product of Jewish anti-German atrocity-propaganda to support the lie of six million gassed Jews and to finance the State of Israel"; and one Ernst Römer was prosecuted for giving out the pamphlet *Best-Seller – ein Schwindel* outside a theatre showing a dramatic version of the diary. The courts allowed the first two cases to pass, on the basis of free speech, but the third went ahead. As part of the investigation, the Bundeskriminalamt (BKA), or German Criminal Court Laboratory, examined the manuscripts and commented in their four-page report that all the materials were of genuine wartime origin, except for some "later corrections made on loose-leaf pages written in black, green and blue ballpoint pen".

There were no ballpoints in Amsterdam in 1945, a fact that didn't escape an article in *Der Spiegel*, the leading German weekly. Troubled by a growing public furore, the Dutch government commissioned a detailed report from the Gerechtelijk Laboratorium (State Forensic Science Laboratory) in 1980. It ran to 250 pages and concluded that the diaries were certainly written by one person using paper and ink that dated exclusively from the early 1940s. The ballpoint pen additions were indeed later changes – added to help keep the pages in the right order.

In 1989, the *Revised Critical Edition* of the *Diary* was published, revealing the original unedited version along with Anne Frank's own edit, which she'd completed in 1944 as part of her efforts to write an autobiographical novel she called *Het Achterhuis* ("The Secret Annex"). The new edition also revealed that Anne's father had made some cuts, but mostly just short passages where Anne criticized her mother or made sexually suggestive or crude remarks. Of course, this hasn't stopped Holocaust deniers using them as "evidence" that the diary is a forgery.

residues. (With no forensic training – unless you count his job as a builder of execution apparatus in the US – and after an interval of almost fifty years, it would be surprising if he had.) Similarly, a photograph circulates on the Internet showing a "flimsy" door on a gas chamber: in fact, this photo shows a chamber that *was* used for delousing. Most damningly, a former associate of Faurisson's, Jean-Claude Pressac, turned against his own theories after undertaking one of the most detailed studies ever published, the massive *Auschwitz: Technique And Operation Of The Gas Chambers* (1989). The "shower rooms", Pressac pointed out, had gas-tight doors and lacked water connections.

Hitler's Orders

One favourite tactic of Holocaust deniers is to allege that there is no proof that Hitler ordered the genocide. (Evidently, Zionist conspirators managed to forge a mountain of evidence besmirching other Nazi leaders but somehow forgot to implicate the Führer.) Like the exact figures of the dead, this claim is cleverly passed off as a contribution to a genuine historical debate: which Nazis decided what, and when? While there's no signed and dated order saying "kill all the Jews", there's no doubt that Hitler was involved in planning the genocide. As early as January 30, 1939, he was telling the Reichstag: "If international Jewish financiers inside and outside Europe again succeed in plunging the nations into a world war, the result will not be the Bolshevization of the earth and with it the victory of Jewry, but the annihilation of the Jewish race in Europe." Empty rhetoric, deniers say. Empty? Really? Coming from the man who *started* a world war by invading half of Europe later that year?

Once the war was fully underway, Hitler's intentions became increasingly clear. The head of the Gestapo's Jewish Office, Adolf Eichmann, wrote in his memoirs that in July 1941 SS intelligence chief Reinhard Heydrich had told him that Hitler ordered the "physical destruction" of the Jews. Himmler recorded a meeting with Hitler on December 10, 1942, in which they discussed the "6–700,000" Jews in France; next to the item on the agenda is a tick, and Himmler's note *"abschaffen"* ("get rid of"). At the first Klessheim conference of April 17 and 18, 1943, Ribbentrop stated in Hitler's presence that the Polish Jews "must either be exterminated or brought to concentration camps". Hitler commented: "They should be treated like the tubercular bacillus ... even innocent creatures of nature like hares and deer must be killed so that they cannot damage others."

The counter-evidence is flimsy, to say the least. Leading Holocaust denier David Irving (see below) has claimed that a note of a telephone call between Himmler and Hitler on November 30, 1941, for instance, states there will be "no liquidation" of the Jews. In fact, the note says "Jewish transport from Berlin. No liquidation." – clearly referring to a specific case, and – taken out of context – ambiguous to say the least (an order? a statement of fact? a reprimand?). As for Eichmann's "physical destruction" note, Irving comments that "you've only got to change one or two words and you get a completely different meaning". Which words? "Physical destruction", perhaps?

Whether or not Hitler was the driving force behind the genocide, and when exactly it became Nazi policy, it was certainly ordered. In October 1943, SS chief Heinrich Himmler gave a speech to senior Nazis, saying "I regard myself as having no right to exterminate the men – in other words, to kill them or have them killed – and to let the avengers in the form of the children grow up for our sons and grandsons to deal with. The difficult decision had to be taken to make these people disappear from the earth." But then, according to David Irving, "Hitler couldn't be bothered with much that Himmler was up to. I think there was a certain lack of affinity between the two."

David Irving: anti-Semite

The frontman for Holocaust denial is the best-selling British writer David Irving. In his own words: "People say to me, 'Mr Irving, do you believe in the Holocaust?' I say that I mistrust words with a capital letter. They look like a trademark, don't they?" In 1993, his work was targeted in historian Deborah Lipstadt's seminal book, *Denying The Holocaust*. In response, Irving sued her and her publisher, Penguin, for accusing him of "distorting evidence and manipulating documents to serve his own purposes", and calling him "right-wing" and "an ardent admirer of the Nazi leader".

Cambridge historian Richard Evans was hired to defend Lipstadt's case, and after two years of detailed research into Irving's work he reported that Irving had indeed used documents he knew to be forgeries or inadequate material – such as the Leuchter Report – as sources. Judge Charles Gray firmly decided in favour of Lipstadt and Penguin (and Evans), declaring that comments made by Irving such as "Jews are amongst the scum of humanity" and "Jews scurry and hide furtively, unable to stand the light of day" make it "undeniable" that Irving is anti-Semitic. He concluded that "Irving has for his own ideological reasons persistently and deliberately misrepresented and manipulated historical evidence; that for the same reasons he has portrayed Hitler in an unwarrantedly favourable light, principally in relation to his attitude towards and responsibility for the treatment of the Jews; that he is an active Holocaust denier; that he is anti-Semitic and racist and that he associates with right-wing extremists who promote neo-Nazism."

More deniers in the dock: Zündel and the IHR

Over in North America, legal squabbles have focused on Ernst Zündel. Until 1985, when he was sent to prison by an Ontario court for "disseminating and publishing material denying the Holocaust", Zündel ran a small Canadian publishing house producing pamphlets such as *Did Six Million Really Die?* His conviction was overturned by Canada's Supreme Court in 1992 on the grounds that the "false news" law was unconstitutional – thus allowing Zündel to parade himself as the champion of free speech against a repressive, conspiratorial government. In January 2002, Canada's Human Rights Tribunal decided that his website contravened the Human Rights Act, and ordered him to shut it down. Sympathetic websites now push his beliefs and his status as a victim of oppression, declaring that they are "fighting the New World Order" (see p.234). One such site, the Zundelsite (see p.100), features a stirring cartoon of the eagle of Truth swooping down on the dragon of the "Holocaust Lie".

Online, the loudest mouthpiece of Holocaust denial is the Institute for Historical Review (see p.100), founded in 1978 by Willis Carto – "America's leading anti-Semite", as detractors have dubbed him – and

British National Party founder, Dave McCalden, aka Lewis Brandon. David Irving has been a key contributor. In 1979, the IHR offered a US $50,000 reward to anyone who could prove that Jews were gassed at Auschwitz. A year later, one Mel Mermelstein, Auschwitz survivor number A-4684, submitted affidavits detailing the deaths of his mother, father, brother and two sisters. When the IHR refused to pay, Mermelstein sued them. Both sides agreed to settle for a summary judgement, in which the court forced the IHR to apologize formally and pay Mermelstein the $50,000, plus a further $40,000 for causing emotional distress.

The Upshot

Historians will continue to debate the precise scale of the killings, the exact workings of the death camps, and the division of responsibility among the Nazi leadership, the German population in general and European churches and governments. But Holocaust denial itself is entirely discredited. In Israel, Switzerland and seven European Union countries, including France and Germany, claiming that the Holocaust never happened is actually illegal.

Holocaust denial uses techniques familiar to anyone interested in conspiracy theories, in which evidence is used piecemeal to buttress a case whose merits were decided far in advance. The effect is similar too: whether or not there's any substance to the theories, the fact that they're "out there" in the media leaves non-experts wondering if there's some truth to them. It allows cynical politicians like the French nationalist leader Jean-Marie Le Pen to claim that the Holocaust is "a detail in the history of the Second World War" (though he was fined 1.2 million francs for doing so), and creates statistics such as the one which surfaced in Italy's *Corriere della Sera* in January 2005 – that twelve percent of Italians believe the Holocaust never happened. This leaves commentators with an ethical problem: does refuting Holocaust deniers only give them airtime they don't deserve? In this guide, for instance, should we even have mentioned the "Anne Frank fraud" theory, even if only to say it's not true? Once established, it's hard to make these kinds of myths go away.

Many historians believe that they should, like the Buddha, maintain a noble silence, just as many evolutionary biologists refuse to share platforms with Creationists on the grounds that it would give their opponents a legitimacy they don't deserve. Deborah Lipstadt, however, believes the "lunatic fringe" must be vigorously challenged: "We must function as canaries in the mine once did, to guard against the spread of noxious fumes. We must vigilantly stand watch against an increasingly nimble enemy. But unlike the canary, we must not sit silently by waiting to expire so that others will be warned of the danger."

SOURCES

Books

Christopher R. Browning The Origins Of The Final Solution (2004). Still in any doubt that the Nazis planned it? Here are 615 pages that trace the decision in painstaking detail from the initial idea to its implementation.

Arthur R. Butz The Hoax Of The Twentieth Century: The Case Against The Presumed Extermination Of European Jewry (1992). Quasi-textbook for Holocaust revisionists, which caused a huge uproar in 1977. Its author, a professor – of electrical engineering – at Northwestern University, is now associated with the IHR (see opposite).

Richard J. Evans Lying About Hitler: History, Holocaust, And The David Irving Trial (2002). Not always spot-on-accurate on the complexities of German history, but an excellent English writer on Holocaust denial, and a key witness in the David Irving trial.

Norman G. Finkelstein The Holocaust Industry: Reflections On The Exploitation Of Jewish Suffering (2003). Widely vilified as a Holocaust denier, (Jewish) academic Finkelstein is no such thing. He is, however, a vocal campaigner against what he calls the exploitation of the Holocaust for

financial gain, through compensation cases, fraudulent claims and so on.

Daniel Jonah Goldhagen Hitler's Willing Executioners: Ordinary Germans And The Holocaust (1997). Deeply controversial naming of names, a nightmarish account of the Holocaust from the side of the perpetrators.

Raul Hilberg The Destruction Of The European Jews (1985). The first and most influential historical account of the Holocaust, with detailed sources.

David Irving Hitler's War (1990 o/p). Hard to find these days, except in second-hand bookshops, though even the judge in the Lipstadt trial agreed that he was a fine military historian. Details the war from Hitler's point of view – from which he apparently couldn't see the plan for genocide.

Deborah Lipstadt Denying The Holocaust: The Growing Assault On Truth And Memory (1994). Written by a professor at Emory University, **Denying The Holocaust** sparked the David Irving trial. Offers a passionate overview of the recent debates, and anatomizes who supports Holocaust denial, and why.

Peter Novick The Holocaust And Collective Memory (2001). A fascinating angle on the context and the afterlife of the

Holocaust, protesting against the way in which the scale of the Jewish genocide has masked the killings of other groups, such as gays and the mentally ill.

Michael Shermer, Alex Grobman and Arthur Hertzberg Denying History: Who Says The Holocaust Never Happened And Why Do They Say It? (2002). Historians' examination not only of the evidence for the Holocaust, but also how "counter-evidence" has been manipulated by Holocaust deniers.

Websites

🌐 **alt.revisionism** The main Usenet newsgroup devoted to debate – often impassioned – on Holocaust denial.

🌐 **motlc.wiesenthal.com/resources/ education/revision/** Point-by-point refutation of revisionists' "factual" arguments.

🌐 **remember.org/image/** A large collection of photos and other images of the Holocaust.

🌐 **www.annefrank.org** Homepage of the Anne Frank house, in Amsterdam.

🌐 **www.holocaustdenialontrial.org** The full transcripts of the Irving–Lipstadt trial. If you're in any doubt about David Irving's motives, click the tab "the Judgment" and read part IX, "Justification: The Allegation That Irving Is An Anti-Semite And A Racist".

⊛ **www.holocaust-history.org** Compelling and authoritative site presenting essays on the Holocaust and Holocaust denial, along with scanned versions (and translations) of key Nazi documents and death-camp photographs.

⊛ **www.ihr.org** Website of the deeply controversial Institute for Historical Review devoted to "challenging" the accepted view of the Holocaust.

⊛ **www.nizkor.org** Anti-Holocaust-denial website maintained by American anti-revisionist Ken McVay, a non-Jewish ex-gas-station manager with a cause.

⊛ **www.yadvashem.org.il** Jerusalem's Holocaust Martyrs' and Heroes' Remembrance Authority. A serious archive.

⊛ **www.zundelsite.org/101.html** "Revisionist Articles Offered As A Detoxification Program To Cure The Politically Correct Of The Hollywood Version Of The Holocaust". You can find the "66 Q&A" elsewhere on the site – described as an "early" IHR document, though it's apparently an abridged form of the 1983 *120 Questions And Answers About The Holocaust*. (One wonders what the 54 questions and answers *not* good enough for the final cut were like.)

Films

Anne Frank Remembered (Jon Blair, 1995). From the director behind the original documentary that inspired Schindler's List. Narrated by Kenneth Branagh and Glenn Close, with powerful interviews – one with Anne's father – and even some film footage of Anne herself.

The Holocaust On Trial (Channel 4, 2000). Gripping courtroom drama-documentary re-enacting British historian David Irving's libel trial against American academic Deborah Lipstadt. Includes interviews with Holocaust experts.

Never Forget (Joseph Sargent, 1991). Straight-to-video dramatization of the Mel Mermelstein / IHR case, starring Leonard Nimoy.

Shoah (Claude Lanzmann, 1985). "The most comprehensive account of the Holocaust available on film." Haunting, painstaking, shattering nine-hour documentary using interviews with survivors, perpetrators, bystanders and historians, and film of extermination sites today rather than archive footage. For a list of other films about the Holocaust, with detailed reviews, go to www.jhvc.org/video_library/index.html and click on "Holocaust".

The Protocols of the Elders of Zion

The *Protocols Of The Learned Elders Of Zion*, to give the text its full title, first appeared in Russia in the late 1890s. It purported to be a series of lectures by the leaders of a Jewish world-domination conspiracy, in which they revealed a Machiavellian plot to prepare the grounds for a world socialistic revolution, a revolution they would ultimately control for their own purposes. The text incorporated age-old anti-Semitic ideas like the Blood Libel (see p.89). The *Protocols* have since been published and republished, and are accepted as genuine in large areas of the world. Even where the work isn't known, the idea that a Zionist, Jewish or Semitic bankers' scheme exists to control the world is now a common-place.

The Protocols of the Elders of Zion: required reading for Nazis

Genesis of the Protocols

Frustrated at the global success of a shabby forgery, scholars have traced the genesis of the *Protocols* with exacting care. In fact, the so-called "lectures" were probably cobbled together by the Okhrana, the Tsarist secret police, in Paris in the wake of the Dreyfus case in France. Printed privately in Russia in 1897, the first public edition was produced by a minor Tsarist official called Sergei Nilus in 1905. (It's thought that he privately knew them to be a forgery while believing that the basic idea behind them was sound.) It's almost certain that the *Protocols* were created with the specific political aim of discrediting Marxism and its offshoots, and consolidating the po-

sition of Tsar Nicholas II by whipping up hysteria about an implacable and alien external threat. (Anyone with half an eye on contemporary politics will recognize a familiar manoeuvre.) In Russia, the end result was the pogroms. If there was an international conspiracy, therefore, it was a Tsarist not a Zionist one.

The *Protocols*' Russian authors used a bizarre miscellany of sources, mostly French. Some of the basic ideas and phrasing were drawn from a four-volume work written in 1797-98 by a clergyman called Augustin de Barruel, *Mémoires pour servir à l'histoire du Jacobinisme*. This argued that the French Revolution had been secretly sponsored by Freemasons, and was highly influential in publicizing the idea that dangerous secret societies were pulling the strings behind world affairs. The idea that the Freemasons in their turn were the puppets of a sect of power-hungry Jews was a later twist, drawn from the so-called "Simonini Letter" sent to Barruel in response to his book's success.

The Okhrana's key source, however, was a satire written in France in 1865 by a lawyer called Maurice Joly, the *Dialogue aux Enfers entre Montesquieu et Machiavel* ("Dialogue in Hell between Montesquieu and Machiavelli"). A good fifteen to twenty percent of the *Protocols* is closely paralleled by Joly's text, its wry representations of the political machinations of the Emperor Napoleon baldly translated into the actions of the "Elders of Zion". Other sources of the *Protocols* are still more bizarre: many sections can be traced to an 1868 novel written in Prussia by a certain Hermann Goedsche under the pen-name of "Sir John Retcliffe". One chapter described how the elders of the twelve tribes of Israel would meet every hundred years to plot world domination; this section was widely reprinted in Russia as a factual tract. Another key influence was French historian Gougenot des Mousseaux's 1869 *Le Juif: le judaïsme et la judaïsation des peuples chrétiens* ("The Jew: Judaism And The Judaeofication Of Christian Peoples"). This, by contrast, was at least a work of history – albeit a deeply flawed one – rather than outright fiction.

Hitler and Henry: the Protocols between the wars

Most likely, the *Protocols* would never have amounted to more than an obscure relic of Russian anti-Semitism had it not been for two men: Adolf Hitler and Henry Ford. Ford was apparently persuaded of the document's authenticity by a Russian émigré, and had parts of it republished in the *Dearborn Independent* through much of the 1920s. "They fit in with what is going on", he commented. "They are sixteen years old, and they have fitted the world situation up to this time. They fit it now." It's a pity he never read Lucien Wolf's 1920 debunking, *The Jewish Bogey And The Forged Protocols Of The Learned Elders Of Zion*, which first set out the evidence of Russian forgery.

The Nazis simply wove the *Protocols* into their hate literature, presenting them as authentic. No fewer than 120,000 copies of a German edition were sold in a single year. In 1935, the text was utterly discredited in the Swiss trial of two Nazis accused of peddling it. The presiding judge declared the Protocols "nothing but ridiculous nonsense". Ironically, he added: "I hope that one day there will come a time when no one will any longer comprehend how in the year 1935 almost a dozen fully sensible and reasonable men could for fourteen days torment their brains before a court of Berne over the authenticity or lack of authenticity of these so-called Protocols."

The judgement did nothing to slow their success. Hitler himself cited the *Protocols* as evidence that "the whole existence of this people is based on a continuous lie". In *Mein Kampf*, he makes the conspiracists' classic connection to Zionism, portraying the goal of a Jewish state in Palestine not as a place to live, but as "a central organization for their international world cheating, withdrawn from others' reach – a refuge for convicted dregs and a college for aspiring swindlers". It's not in fact certain whether Hitler actually believed the *Protocols* to be authentic. One leading anti-Jewish propagandist, Count Ernst zu Reventlow, privately admitted they were "a clumsy hoax" – while continuing to make use of them in public.

Nazi publications drew directly on the Tsarist example of the propaganda of fear, using the text to attack not just Jews but a supposed cabal of Jews, international financiers and Communists. It's hard to imagine representatives of the three groups sitting round a boardroom table, cigars in hand. Soviet-era propaganda, by contrast, tended to portray Jews as lackeys of the capitalist counter-revolution.

The Protocols in the Far East

Nazi anti-Semitism is a given. More surprising is the use of similar propaganda in imperial Japan. During the war, the same Tsarist material was publicized there for the same purposes – with utterly bizarre success, given the almost complete absence of Jews from Japanese territory. Equally strange is the success of the *Protocols* in contemporary Southeast Asia. In Malaysia, for example, the document was first published – as fact – in 1983. Within a few years, conspiratorial and anti-Zionist rhetoric crept into public discourse, notably in the mouth of the brash, confrontational Prime Minister Mahathir Mohamad, who led the country for 22 years.

In October 2003, just days before he resigned, Mohamad addressed the tenth summit of the Organization of the Islamic Conference (IOC). As part of a typically undiplomatic speech aimed at giving Muslim leadership a kick in the pants, he declared "We are up against a people who think ...They invented and successfully promoted Socialism, Communism, human rights and democracy so that persecuting them would appear to be wrong ...With these they have now gained control of the most powerful countries and they, this tiny community, have become a world power." The words could have been drawn straight from the *Protocols* – and indeed probably were. Non-Jews haven't escaped his wrath and suspicion either: in the same years he labelled "Anglo-Saxon Europeans" as proponents of "war, sodomy and genocide".

The Protocols in the Middle East

The *Protocols of the Learned Elders of Zion* have found an unintended, but enthusiastic audience in the modern Middle East. Legend has it that the text had arrived in the region before World War I was over – the Jerusalem leader Musa Kazim al-Husayni supposedly asked Chaim Weizmann whether he and the other Zionist leaders were the same thing as the "Elders". The story is almost certainly apocryphal, as Arabic translations only emerged in the 1920s. Persian editions appeared after World War II. Modern editions in Arabic and other languages are now regularly republished – and even distributed free by the Saudi government in one notorious 1980s incident. Certainly, the general idea of a world conspiracy to promote Zionism is extremely widespread.

It's curious that what was once a specifically European idea, an answer to suspicions about the forces behind European revolutions, was able to morph into a general cultural prejudice, and then be retranslated into another, entirely different political situation – the issue of Israel's position in the Middle East. European liberals rightly protest against the conflation of anti-Israeli policies and cultural anti-Semitism, but it's far harder to unpick the two strands of thought on the ground in Palestine or Tehran.

The controversial US academic Daniel Pipes (see box overleaf) claims that the *Protocols* are "the most important single vehicle for transmitting Christian anti-Semitism to the Muslim world" – and for passing on conspiracist thinking to boot. Pipes has collected numerous examples of *Protocols*-influenced Middle Eastern conspiracism on his website and in his book, *The Hidden Hand*. He describes how a 1985 Tehran edition of the *Protocols* included a commendatory introduction, as well as a map called the "Dream of Zionism" showing the supposed boundaries of "Greater Israel". He reports on how Shimon Peres's book promoting regional cooperation, *The New Middle East*, was given a new introduction in an Egyptian edition, declaring "when the *Protocols of the Elders of Zion* were discovered about 200 years ago ... the international Zionist establishment tried its best to deny the plot ... And now, it is precisely Shimon Peres who brings the cutting proof of their validity." He points out how Hamas's Charter portrays Freemasonry as a Jewish tool, citing the *Protocols*. He quotes an academic at Cairo's prestigious Al-Azhar University, Salih Hasan al-Maslut, as writing in 1995 that Freemasonry is "a Jewish international organization seeking to destroy non-Jewish nations and governments ... as defined by the Zionists' *Protocols*". Pipes reports the professor as going on to say that the Masons weren't an effective enough tool, so the Jews went on to establish the Rotary Clubs...

DANIEL PIPES AND THE HIDDEN HAND

Anyone investigating Middle Eastern conspiracies will soon stumble across the name of Daniel Pipes. Some view him as a ruthless opponent of anti-Semitism who uses his website (www.danielpipes.org), lectures and ever-growing bibliography to expose the worst excesses of Middle Eastern rhetoric. Pipes is an undoubted authority on Middle Eastern politics, and on conspiracism in general – his 1996 book *The Hidden Hand: Middle East Fears Of Conspiracy* is near the top of the reading list. He says that his "mantra" is "militant Islam is the problem, moderate Islam is the solution", and he is absolutely right to point out that "the twentieth century's terrible history should expunge the impression that conspiracy theories are trivial".

And yet his strong links with conservative groups that promote an aggressively pro-Israeli US foreign policy have troubled some commentators, as have his self-pro-moting "name and shame" campus campaigns against academics guilty of what he sees as anti-Semitism. The Orientalist scholar Edward Said described Pipes in 1996 as a pundit who sought to "make sure the (Islamic) threat is kept before our eyes, the better to excoriate Islam for terror, despotism and violence". Other critics have seized on statements such as the one Pipes made in *USA Today* after the Oklahoma City bombing: "People need to understand this is just the begin-ning. The fundamentalists are on the upsurge and they make it very clear they are targeting us. They are absolutely obsessed with us." There's undoubtedly something ironic about Pipes, the analyst of the "paranoid style" in politics, accusing "fundamentalists" of being obsessed with "us". The harsher irony, of course, is that the Oklahoma bombers turned out to be right-wing American funda-mentalists, not Islamic ones.

SOURCES

Books

Norman Cohn **Warrant For Genocide: The Myth Of The Jewish World Conspiracy And The Protocols Of The Elders Of Zion** (1996). The definitive story, proving the *Protocols* a forgery once and for all.

Marvin Perry and Frederick Schweitzer **Anti-Semitism: Myth And Hate From Antiquity To The Present** (2002). See review on p.93.

Daniel Pipes **The Hidden Hand: Middle East Fears Of Conspiracy** (1998). See box above.

Websites

ⓦ **users.cyberone.com.au/myers/toolkit.html** Pro-Protocols attempt to discredit the "forgery" line. This highly conspiracist and racially charged site loses sight of the bigger picture as it triumphantly discovers minor errors in the main argument, but provides surprisingly handy source material on the way.

ⓦ **www.danielpipes.org** See the box "Daniel Pipes and the Hidden Hand" above.

ⓦ **www.holywar.org** Lurid European site dedicated to "combatting Jewish terrorism", with lots on the *Protocols*. Claims, highly unconvincingly, to be "100 percent anti-hate".

ⓦ **www.memri.org** The Middle East Media Research Institute: a source of Arab-language articles otherwise unavailable in English, though readers may note that the bulk of its translations somehow show only a disturbing side of Arab culture.

The British royal family

When the British Empire was at its height, to accuse the royal family of being behind a mega-conspiracy to rule the world would not have been entirely unreasonable. Over a hundred years later, however, most people would say that the map of world power has changed more than a little. To be sure, the Windsors have been fingered as the conspirators behind scandals as disparate as the Jack the Ripper murders of the 1880s, and the death of Princess Diana (see p.59), but two arch-conspiracy theorists paint an altogether more sinister picture. American political activist and conspiracy king Lyndon LaRouche accuses the royal family of being the puppet-masters

behind a host of international agencies and corporations, while prolific conspiracy author, ex-footballer and self-proclaimed Messiah, David Icke, believes that the real issue is that Windsors are reptilian shape-shifters.

Prince Philip, the WWF and the ODA

In LaRouche's own words, "the Queen runs from the top down, through a Privy Council. Number One on the Privy Council, after the Queen, is the Church of England, the head of the Church of England, and then a whole lot of other people, about 500.

The British royal family: gang of lizards?

These 500 people run the British Empire, including the apparatus of its old Colonial Office. The Colonial Office was never disbanded. They call it the Overseas Development Office now."

As an offshoot of the Foreign Office, with a relatively tiny budget spent largely on aid and development projects, the ODA (now the Department For International Development) is an odd choice of villain. But then it turns out that the DFID is a pawn in a much larger global game. According to LaRouche and his co-theorists, the Windsors wield power through an assortment of agencies. As President Emeritus of the World Wildlife Fund, Prince Philip – apparently "the Doge of London" – "leads the world in orchestration of ethnic conflict and terrorism". To date, successes of the WWF have included the Rwandan genocide, which was not, as you may blindly believe, the work of marauding, machine-wielding bands of Hutu extremists, but in fact executed by trained soldiers from Ugandan President Yoweri Museveni's army. (Don't be fooled by Uganda's apparent support for the opposing Tutsi rebels.) These soldiers were all trained in camps set up under the guise of WWF gorilla-protection programmes. Given that the Overseas Development Agency "controls" Museveni, the troops were in fact little more than proxies for the British.

By this account, Rwanda is far from being the only WWF operation. Anything from African coups and rebellions to ecological protests (such as those against French nuclear testing in the South Pacific) are actually the work of the SAS, the British Army's elite special operations commandos. The SAS is behind what Lyndon LaRouche calls the Afghansi terrorist network (better known today as that all-powerful and ultra-evil demon, "Al Qaeda", which, according to most Western pundits and politicians, magically controls and coordinates world terrorism). According to LaRoucheites, the regiment "operates outside the British government command structure, and is directly beholden to the Sovereign". If that got out, it would be a big shock to the Ministry of Defence.

Prince Philip and the Club of the Isles

You may wonder why Prince Philip, in cahoots with the WWF, ODA and SAS, would have wanted the Rwandan genocide to happen. According to LaRoucheites, it stems from his historical role as the unofficial leader of the "Club of the Isles", an informal and highly secretive association of corporate and European aristocratic interests. According to one website, the Club of the Isles lords it over "an estimated $10 trillion in assets". Associated businesses include Shell, ICI, Lloyds of London, Unilever, Lonrho, Rio Tinto Zinc and DeBeers; as a result, the Club controls most of the world's raw materials. This oligarchy is so nefarious, according to one writer on LaRouche's website, that it even manipulates the world's food supplies, a policy that results in the deaths of tens of millions every year from "the most elementary lack of their daily bread".

The Club of the Isles, it seems, inherits its power from "Mesopotamian-Roman-Venetian" trade networks. More specifically, it represents "a new, more virulent, Anglo-Dutch-Swiss strain of the oligarchic system of imperial Babylon, Persia, Rome, and Byzantium". (US corporations may sometimes seem aggressive, but they are philanthropic in comparison.) But this doesn't explain the Rwandan genocide. It was, it seems, just one element in a super-plan drawn up by the Royal Institute for International Affairs, aka Chatham House (see p.138), as part of a "blueprint for the consolidation of one-world empire". To rule this empire according to the feudal model – and nothing else would be acceptable to Prince Philip and his blue-blooded friends in the City of London – would apparently require that the world's population be reduced fivefold to one billion people…

…Starting with Lyndon LaRouche. According to a 1999 article in the LaRouche magazine *Executive Intelligence Review*, the publication of a distinctly negative article in the budget UK women's magazine *Take A Break* was apparently the first step in an MI6 campaign to assassinate him. One wonders why Prince Philip didn't use the SAS.

The Windsors, the Commonwealth and the UN

As a challenge to American corporate hegemony, the Club of the Isles conspiracy theory could be compared to the highly conspiracist conception of the EU that emanates from ultra-right America (see box on p.135). It's also distinctly reminiscent of conspiracists' accusations about the UN. And indeed the Commonwealth. After all, as one conspiracy site's blogger puts it "there really is no real reason for the UK to have the Commonwealth except to control the UN through the Commonwealth. Its goals are exactly those of the UN."

Joan Veon, author of *Prince Charles: The Sustainable Prince*, has noted that "every time a country was granted independence from Britain, they were given a vote at the UN". Strange, that. Equally, according to Veon, the Senate's ratification of the UN Charter meant that it simply reverted to British overlordship. Like LaRouche's co-conspiracists, Veon sees Prince Philip as the *eminence grise* behind the throne – and behind the UN too, "a key, behind-the-scenes mover and shaker" who follows the goals of arch-colonial capitalist and diamond baron Cecil Rhodes. (Not incidentally, he is also "responsible for the radical environmental agenda that perverts Genesis 1, 2, and 3 and puts the earth above man and not man above the earth as God intended.")

Drugs, The Beatles and Diana

The decimation of the world population envisaged by the Club of the Isles will obviously have seriously negative social consequences. But according to LaRoucheites, the conspirators have an ingenious plan to deal with this. By fostering a "drug-rock-sex counterculture", potential protestors will be effectively silenced. According to LaRouche devotee and self-confessed former British spy, David Coleman, The Beatles were just one thrust of this campaign, designed by the Club of Rome and Tavistock Institute for Human Relations to create a drugged-out and conspiracy-minded population with no inclination towards effective activism.

Meanwhile, Queen Elizabeth has been busy writing science fiction (under various pseudonyms), aimed at distracting and disorienting the young and impressionable. If that isn't enough, environmental youth groups (fostered, of course, by Prince Philip's WWF) will act as a kind of Hitler Youth. The WWF's vicious "Pandas", in their distinctive Black-and-White-Shirts, will face a debilitated enemy, racked by drug use. The Windsors, it appears, control the global drug trade – a continuation, it seems, of Britain's role in China's Opium Wars. Triads and Colombian drug cartels are mere lackeys in their thrall.

David Icke and the Reptilians

There's no way that a mere summary of his arguments can do justice to the fantastical conspiracy cocktail that has become the world view (and chief source of income) for former footballer David Icke since he first reported seeing visions in 1990. Icke incorporates all and any other conspiracy theories in his mega-system, but the conspiracists' usual explanations, he claims, never go far enough. Icke puts it in quasi-Buddhist terms, saying that we are too habituated to "false reality". Icke, of course, can always see a deeper conspiracy lurking behind the one that other theorists claim to have exposed. The result, of course, is that his "ultimate" conspiracy is far more dramatic than anything anyone else could possibly believe in.

Humanity, Icke says, is being controlled, manipulated and in some cases actually drained of blood by alien reptiles. These "reptilians" are something like dinosaurs and something like dragons, only vastly more intelligent. Thanks to their origins as a consciousness from the Fourth Dimension, they are also able to change shape at will. While Icke's evidence ranges across human and mythological history, from ancient snake worship to modern "eyewitnesses", his proof rests finally on the visions experienced by him and his supporters.

Using their ability to shapeshift (as well as the relatively conventional practice of inter-marriage), the reptilians have worked their bloodline (or, more specifically, their "reptilian-mammalian DNA combination") into everything from the all-powerful Illuminati to powerful families such as the Bushes, the Rockefellers, the Rothschilds – and the Windsors. (Some suspect that beneath Icke's idea of a racial – albeit lizard-race – conspiracy involving powerful banking and political families lies a deeply anti-Semitic subtext. Others think his idea is so mad that he must be the front man for a conspiracy to give conspiracy theories a bad name.)

According to Icke, the Windsors "are not the top of the pyramid by any means", but "they are very much involved in the global agenda and in the sacrificial ritual that always goes with it". These sacrificial rituals apparently included the death of Princess Diana at the thirteenth pillar of the Alma tunnel (see p.63). One writer on the Icke-ite website reptilianagenda.com claims that Balmoral, the British royal family's Scottish summer residence, is a "very, very nasty place. That's somewhere they want to dig underground. They will find reptile fossils, it goes back that far." Scotland's other conspiracy landmark, the "Templar" Rosslyn Chapel, pales into insignificance.

As Icke admits, the Windsors Are Lizards theory is "quite something to absorb from our conditioned version of reality". But how can you gainsay an eyewitness who claims to have seen an extra membrane momentarily flicking across Queen Elizabeth's eyes? Or one who observed the Queen Mother actually transforming into a lizard? The secret of the Windsors' abilities, according to reptilianagenda.com, is not gin and tonic, horseracing and unimaginable wealth, but "microcurrents". Apparently, "it's much easier for them to do Frankenstein shit than it is for us. The different bodies are just different electrical vibrations and they have got that secret, they've got the secret of the microcurrents, it's so micro, so specific, these radio waves that actually create the bodies." Fortunately, these microcurrents aren't entirely negative. As the website's contributor goes on to add: "These are the energies I work with when I'm healing."

SOURCES

Books

David Icke **The Biggest Secret: The Book That Will Change The World** (1999). It may not have changed the world, but it has done wonders for Icke's bank balance. Alternately mad, funny and shoddily written. A few of the main arguments are summarized above.

Joan Veon **Prince Charles: The Sustainable Prince** (1997). This former businesswoman and now devoted conspiracy theorist campaigns against the UN by means of the bi-monthly newsletter **UN Watch!** Her book traces the conspiratorial links between the one-world global agenda of the UN and the environmental activism of Prince Charles.

Websites

ⓦ www.davidicke.com. Hilarious Icke takes on the news of the moment, and lots of advertising for his many books.

ⓦ www.larouchepub.com Lyndon LaRouche's website, featuring the online publication *Executive Intelligence Review*. As with the absence of WMD in Iraq, this gives a whole new meaning to "intelligence".

ⓦ www.reptilianagenda.com. Staggeringly detailed elaboration of Icke's "reptilian agenda" theory from fans around the world with an equally tenuous hold on what most of us think of as reality.

The Central Interference Agency

The Central Intelligence Agency, or CIA, has been accused of just about every conspiracy going, from trafficking drugs, covering up the existence of UFOs and leaking Watergate to assassinating JFK, RFK, Martin Luther King and Malcolm X – to name just the most famous alleged hits. It's surely the world's largest intelligence agency, though its budget, structure and even the number of staff it employs are known only to the president, to whom it reports, the National Security Council, and the congressional and senate committees that oversee its activities. At least its objectives are known – to track and disrupt terrorism, drugs trafficking and organized crime, all of which are aspects of its brief to evaluate and challenge foreign threats to national security – it is forbidden to carry out investigations on the "homeland".

The first fifty years

For the first fifty years, however, the CIA seemed to see only one threat to national security: Communism. Its roots might have something to do with this monomaniacal focus. The CIA grew out of Roosevelt's wartime Office of Strategic Services (OSS), and was formally established in 1947 (much to the annoyance of the FBI). Its first real chance to prove itself came in 1950, with the Korean War. Thereafter, it swiftly expanded its fight against Communism into what was then called the "Third World". In 1953 the CIA pulled off one of its first coups with the installation of the Shah of Iran, while a year later it was actively promoting a Fascist coup in Guatemala – with the help of a kill-list and training for assassins – which ushered in a procession of murderous dictators and 36 years of civil war. At the same time, its Science and Technology Directorate, headed by Sidney Gottlieb, was experimenting with mind-control drugs – including LSD – under the MK-ULTRA program (see p.192–195).

By the 1960s, the CIA was ready to provoke its own wars. Unfortunately for "the Company", as it became known, its promotion of the invasion of Cuba in 1961, at the Bay of Pigs, was an embarrassing failure. The Cuban campaign was sidelined into absurd plots aimed at Fidel Castro, as part of Operation Mongoose (see p.20). Assassination plots aimed at foreign leaders with CIA backing continued apace: Patrice Lumumba of the Congo was executed against a tree on January 17, 1961, while Rafael L. Trujillo of the Dominican Republic was shot by two carloads of gunmen on May 30, 1961. The Vietnam war offered further opportunities: through the 1960s and into the early 1970s the CIA was in the thick of the "Secret War" in Laos, supplying the so-called Secret Army with a private fleet of aircraft flying under the patriotic banner of "Air America". Meanwhile, the agency was supporting a coup in the Middle East led by a certain Saddam Hussein, and funding a bloody guerrilla war in Angola.

In the 1970s and 1980s, the CIA turned its chief attentions to Latin America, helping to overthrow Chile's Salvador Allende in favour of a military dictatorship (see p.43), and funding and arming Nicaragua's drug-running, torturing Contra guerrillas. It suffered two major setbacks, however. First was the 1975 Church Committee (see p.27), which uncovered scores of assassination plots, including some of the "successes" of the 1960s. The Church Committee's report resulted in the signing of Executive Order 11905 by President Ford, which ruled that "no employee of the US government shall engage in, or conspire to engage in, political assassination". Next came the 1983 Boland Amendment, which indirectly caused the most scandalous project to date – the Iran–Contra affair (see p.186). By throwing Lieutenant Colonel Oliver North to the wolves, the agency itself dodged the fallout, though it's widely assumed that then-Director Bill Casey had backed the scheme himself. Watergate reporter Bob Woodward even claimed that Casey had confessed as much on his deathbed, in 1987, with the words "I believed" (though no one believed Woodward). Associated rumours that the CIA was involved in the Contras' drug-trafficking have proved hard to suppress (see p.196).

9/11 and the CIA

The CIA's failure to predict the collapse of the Soviet Union or the 9/11 attacks (see p.360) proved extremely damaging – not that anyone was sacked – as did the agency's role in the Iraqi Weapons of Mass Destruction debacle (see p.371). In July 2004, the US Senate Intelligence Committee reported that the CIA had described the WMD danger in "an unreasonable way, largely unsupported by the available intelligence". But wasn't intelligence the CIA's job, not decision-making? In the ensuing political fallout, it wasn't just left-wingers and conspiracy theorists who were wondering what the CIA had been up to, but congressional leaders and senators as well. The CIA's support for Afghanistan's Mujahadeen fighters – whose resistance to the Soviet invasion had previously been trumpeted as one of the agency's greatest successes – suddenly seemed deeply ill-considered: the CIA had trained the very same Islamic militants who planned the World Trade Center attacks.

On September 15, 2001, then-CIA Director George Tenet presented a memorandum to George W. Bush asking for permission to engage in "lethal covert action". Bob Woodward even claimed that Tenet presented a "Worldwide Attack Matrix" which would, if activated, set in motion the assassination of some eighty targets around the world. A number of suspicious deaths certainly followed, most obviously the killing of "Al Qaeda" operatives in Yemen on November 5, 2002, whose car was destroyed by a "Predator drone", a missile from a high-altitude, remote-controlled CIA aircraft. These kinds of operations went directly against President Ford's Executive Order (and President Reagan's clarification of it, Executive Order 12333, that "no person employed by *or acting on behalf of* the United States Government shall engage in, or conspire to engage in, assassination"), but were justified on the grounds that both excluded wartime activities. And, as President George W. Bush repeatedly reminded his electorate, he was fighting a "war on terror".

The CIA today

The CIA's current budget is a secret, but it can be assumed that it's not all that different from the budget of 1997, which was made public after a lawsuit sponsored by the Federation of American Scientists. The figure was $26.7 billion – a figure neatly matched by Chile's foreign debt, US arms exports, and the global expenditure on pesticides in the same year. (At the time of writing, the same figure applies to the GDPs of Argentina and the city of Beijing, the total US debt on personal credit cards and, curiously enough, the budget set for the new Department of Homeland Security.) Critics claim that this secret budget goes against the constitutional requirement for federal spending to be published openly.

It's thought that the CIA currently has some sixteen thousand employees, most of whom work at its base at Langley, Virginia. At the time of writing, the Director, or DCI, was Porter Goss, nominated by President George W. Bush in 2004. He oversees four Directorates: Intelligence, Science and Technology, Administration and Operations. While intelligence is the most important function, it's Operations – whose chief is always anonymous – that has most attracted the world's attention. Most notorious is Covert Operations, officially defined as those "conducted or sponsored by this Government against hostile foreign states or groups or in support of friendly foreign states or groups but which are so planned and executed that any United States government responsibility for them is not evident to unauthorized persons and that if uncovered the United States government can plausibly disclaim any responsibility for them". (These guys obviously hate commas as much as they hate commies – or perhaps they can't tell the difference.)

George W. Bush's "War on Terror" will guarantee jobs for field agents and technical surveillance teams alike for years to come (raising the question whether his father, ex-CIA director George H.W. Bush, has ever lobbied for funding for the organization). Even if the CIA could wash its hands clean of its history, its fatal combination of secrecy, power and ideology – what its mission statement calls "quiet patriotism" – will ensure that it remains the subject of endless conspiracy theories. If history is anything to go by, a lot of them will be right.

SOURCES

Books

William Blum Killing Hope: US Military And CIA Interventions Since World War II. The first part of the title leaves you in no doubt which side of the fence Blum is on.

Ronald Kessler Inside The CIA. Amazingly dull, given the subject matter. Full of facts – the journalist had unprecedented cooperation – but short on the agency's darker past. Dated, but still authoritative on the agency's internal workings.

H. Westerfield (ed) Inside The CIA's Private World : Declassified Articles From The Agency's Internal Journal, 1955-1992. The real thing: formerly classified CIA reports, in your own hands, and all the more fascinating for it.

Websites

Ⓦ www.cia.gov You can click on "Who we are and what we do" and "What's new at the Central Intelligence Agency", but don't expect to get many answers. There is, however, a "CIA homepage for kids".

Ⓦ www.gwu.edu/~nsarchiv/index.html Homepage of the National Security Archive of the George Washington University: lots of declassified CIA material.

The military-industrial complex

In January 1961, the departing President Dwight D. Eisenhower gave his farewell speech to the nation. Astonishingly, with the Cold War at its height, Eisenhower – a former Allied Supreme Commander, a man with years of experience of exercising power at the very highest level and a Republican to boot – took this opportunity to warn that the US arms industry had grown to an unprecedented size: "This conjunction of an immense military establishment and a large arms industry is new in the American experience. The total influence – economic, political, even spiritual – is felt in every city, every State house, every office of the Federal government ... We must guard against the acquisition of unwarranted influence, whether sought or unsought, by the military-industrial complex. The potential for the disastrous rise of misplaced power exists and will persist."

As Eisenhower's speech shows, the "military-industrial complex", a concept that permeates conspiracy-theory talk, was born at the highest levels of civilian and military governance. The following year, President Kennedy and his Secretary of State Robert McNamara would blame the complex for promoting myths about a "missile gap" and a "bomber gap" between the US and USSR, pushing military spending to unprecedented levels. (While there were indeed gaps, they were in the US's favour – see p.340.) Some conspiracy theorists link Kennedy's subsequent assassination (see p.23) to his call for cuts in military expenditure and for the token US presence in Vietnam to be withdrawn, citing as evidence his successor Lyndon Johnson's immediate increase of US involvement there, especially after the fabricated Gulf of Tonkin incident (see p. 343).

More recently, director Eugene Jarecki has placed the military-industrial complex at the heart of his Sundance award-winning documentary *Why We Fight*, which suggests that it is behind many of the US's forays abroad in the past fifty years. It's thought that the complex may actually foment wars – and fabricate threats to justify wars – in order to secure profitable contracts and more taxpayer funding. "Threats" from Iraq, Iran and North Korea (see p.371) have been exaggerated – demonstrably so in the case of Iraq's WMD – or provoked, like intimidating the North Koreans so that they resume atom-bomb production, thus helping to justify, for example, the otherwise redundant (and unworkable) National Missile Defense system, part of the Strategic Defense Initiative (SDI).

In 2005, fifteen years after the end of the Cold War, the taxpayer-funded US discretionary military budget reached $420 billion – 51 percent of the total budget; seven times bigger than that for the next biggest sector, education; only fractionally less than the rest of the world's military spending put together; four times the joint total of America's fabled foes Russia, China, Syria, Iran, Libya, Cuba and North Korea; and 42 times the annual spending of all the agencies of the United Nations. This budgetary expansion, a 45 percent increase on 2000, has mostly come in the wake of the 9/11 attacks, but the policy think-tank Project for a New American Century (see p.381) – whose founders included Dick Cheney, Donald Rumsfeld, Paul Wolfowitz and George W. Bush's brother Jeb – had advocated big increases in military spending since the late 1990s.

Indeed, in 2000 the alarming PNAC policy document *Rebuilding America's Defenses* (www.newamericancentury.org/RebuildingAmericasDefenses.pdf) said that a "catalyzing event – like a new Pearl Harbor" might be needed to galvanize increased spending on hi-tech weaponry, ensuring that the US can fight wars better than anyone and everyone. Despite the fact that the attacks involved just nineteen men aboard four airliners, 9/11 provided just such a catalyst. Spending on new jet fighters, tanks, satellites and NMD, meanwhile, benefits defence giants such as Lockheed Martin, Northrop Grumman, Boeing & Rockwell, Raytheon and Litton – all big contributors to the Democratic and Republican parties, but favouring the latter by 2 to 1.

Such political lobbying is evidence of what – as *Why We Fight* reminds us – the first draft of Eisenhower's speech referred to as a "military-in-dustrial-*congressional* complex". Jarecki's film suggests that "defence" industries and their suppliers are deliberately spread throughout the US to spread their wealth-creating and political lobbying power (Lockheed Martin claims it has facilities in all fifty US states). Local economies, the funding of political parties and local politicians' careers are all dependent on their success.

It used to be said that what's good for General Motors is good for America (economically speaking, that is). As Michael Moore's 1989 debut film *Roger And Me* dramatically demonstrated, however, GM and other civilian manufacturers have shut down plants, leaving derelict, "rustbelt" towns. In *Fahrenheit 9/11*, Moore argues that for many of the young urban poor left behind, their best chance of paid employment, let alone a college education or healthcare, is to join the Army. The alternative is welfare-to-work programmes, run by companies like US defence giant Lockheed Martin. In this scenario, Americans simply become the tax-paying subsidizers and slave-wage workers of a system that's immune from the checks and balances of the peace-seeking electorate – because it owns them and their representatives.

According to the *Christian Science Monitor* of February 13, 2002, the "Iron Triangle" of the Pentagon, defence firms and Congress extends directly into the White House through the Carlyle Group, an investment firm with billions of dollars in military and aerospace. The Group is chaired by Ronald Reagan's former Defense Secretary Frank Carlucci, a confidant of Donald Rumsfeld, and employs former President George H.W. Bush (and at one time, his son George W. in an airline food subsidiary), his advisor and former Secretary of State James Baker, and former British prime minister and Bush senior's partner in the Gulf War, John Major.

Other Web sources reveal that between 1994 and 2001, Vice President Dick Cheney's wife Lynne earned six figure fees as a board director of Lockheed Martin – the world's largest weapons manufacturer, which "in the past two years alone", Bill Hackwell of the International Action Center wrote in 2003, "has received prime Pentagon contracts totalling $30 billion". Perhaps the man who best embodies the new military-industrial complex, however, is the less well-known Bruce P. Jackson, Lockheed's Vice President for Strategy and Planning from 1999 to 2002 (and Finance Chairman for the 2000 Bush election campaign).

During this time Jackson – a board director of the Project for the New American Century – not only founded the US Committee for NATO and the Project

US Vice President Dick Cheney

MEN IN BLACK

If you've recently been abducted by aliens and maybe had a mind-control chip implanted to boot, you should expect a visit from the Men In Black some time soon. The "MIB" are the *X Files* version of the CIA, the stormtroopers of a ubiquitous, sinister agency dedicated to covering up the existence of aliens. Some think the Men In Black actually *are* government agents, perhaps thanks to their rather formal dress code of black, badly made suits, stiff white shirts and plain black ties – the uniform, coincidentally, of any self-respecting secret agent from the 1950s.

Some witnesses have reported seeing MIB travelling in 1950s Cadillacs (which, apparently, "smell new" rather than "vintage"), while others have spotted MIB using blacked-out limos or even the more up-to-date black helicopters – also the transport of choice for hi-tech agents of conspiracy ranging from the CIA to the UN, according to popular ultra-right-wing legend. Alleged MIB victims have reported more obviously extra-terrestrial features such as "shiny skin", "pointy chins", "hands without fingernails" and metallic, inhuman voices.

As it turns out, Men In Black do come from the 1950s, or at least from a 1956 book melodramatically entitled *They Knew Too Much About Flying Saucers*. The author, a West Virginian theatrical film booker (and notorious hoaxer) called Gray Barker, claimed that he had been visited by a trio of terrifying dark-dressed men who had warned him off relaying details of his UFO experiences. The story drew heavily from early 1950s UFOlogy, which typically incorporated sinister government agents on a mission to suppress The Truth. (In fact, CIA files later released showed that in the 1950s the Agency had indeed mounted disinformation campaigns related to UFO sightings, partly to conceal the existence of early spy planes such as the U2.)

West Virginia was again the setting for the big entrance of MIB into popular culture, via the "Mothman" hysteria of 1966–67 Point Pleasant, as documented by John Keel's book, *The Mothman Prophecies*. As well as the "Mothman" himself, townsfolk were soon reporting visits from endless dark-suited men – some at least of whom were undoubtedly Barker himself, or his friends, playing pranks.

If Men In Black are what their eye-witnesses clearly think they are – aliens conspiring to cover up evidence of UFOs – then it seems odd that they'd adopt such a time- and culture-specific costume. As a fiction, however, it's a good hook, pulling on all sorts of subconscious strings related to powerful but faceless authority figures. Bluntly, the MIB are right out of a comic book, and in fact they were later turned into cartoon characters by Lowell Cunningham – whose books were in turn adapted as the comic film *Men In Black*, starring Tommy Lee Jones and Will Smith.

The movie version had the distinctly neo-Fascist twist that the Men In Black are actually *good* cops protecting the world from an invasion of aliens – like a paranormal Department of Immigration, perhaps. By contrast, the "sentient agents" of *The Matrix* are faithfully drawn from MIB mythology, right down to their sinister service of an inhuman master – the "Machines". If the Matrix itself stands for faceless bureaucracy, the Men In Black are its federal agents. They are the men from nowhere, the waking nightmare of the disenfranchised and the fearful, whose lonely lives only mean something when these insidious government agents invade them.

Tommy Lee Jones and Will Smith sport the mythological uniform of Men in Black in the 1997 film

THE MILITARY-ENTERTAINMENT COMPLEX

Some would say that the reach of the complex is such that there is no escape from it, even in mindless escapism, thanks to the military-entertainment complex. World Socialist Website reported that the Pentagon, CIA and US Air Force all have "film approval" offices or liaison officers to assist films that show them in a favourable light (hence credits thanking the Department of the Navy/Army/Air Force). The lavishly assisted *Top Gun* helped increase naval aviation recruit-

ment five-fold, aided by recruitment booths in cinemas, while Paramount offered the Pentagon advertising space for recruitment on the videos of *Flight Of The Intruder* and *The Hunt For Red October*.

Computer games have also been given a military tie-in, with some deliberately designed as recruiting tools. The Common Dreams website notes that "Full Spectrum Dominance", a Microsoft Xbox game about

attacking the fictional central Asian "haven for terrorists" of "Tazikhstan", had been developed in conjunction with the US Army and took its name from the Pentagon's 2000 "Joint 20/20" plan for fighting future wars. The Department of Defense, US Army and Marines have worked with the University of Southern California, the Institute for Creative Technologies and companies like Paramount Pictures to produce simulators such as "Advanced Leadership",

tank simulator "Spearhead" and "Tom Clancy's Rainbow Six: Rogue Spear". And the online game "America's Army", which has attracted some two million registered users since its launch in 2002, was a US Army co-production with Epic Games and *Star Wars* creator George Lucas's company Lucasfilm Ltd. But then it was *Star Wars* that supplied the nickname – and who knows, perhaps the idea – for Ronald Reagan's Strategic Defense Initiative.

for Transitional Democracies, but also (wait for it)... chaired the Republican Party's subcommittee on foreign policy. All of these bodies, Stephen Gowans noted in a November 2002 article in the e-zine *What's Left*, advocated more defence spending – from which Jackson's employer Lockheed, more than any other company, stood to gain. To cap it all, between 2002 and 2003 Jackson was the Chairman of the Committee for the Liberation of (you guessed it) Iraq.

From another viewpoint, it's been argued that the military-industrial complex goes hand in hand with a foreign policy dedicated to preserving US supremacy and the American way of life in an increasingly competitive world. In his 1998 book *Hidden Agendas*, award-winning Australian journalist John Pilger quotes a secret (but now declassified) memo written in 1948 by George Kennan, head of the US State Department Policy Planning Staff. Noting that the US had half the world's wealth but only six percent of its population, Kennan said that the real task ahead was to devise "a pattern of relationships which will permit us to maintain this position of disparity without positive detriment to our national security". Referring to the Far East – though clearly the same principle could be said to apply elsewhere – Kennan argued that this

would mean dumping "unreal objectives" like "human rights, the raising of living standards, and democratization" and instead dealing in "straight power concepts".

Writing in 1999, US author William Blum noted that since World War II, the US had carried out "extremely serious interventions" – from supplying arms for military coups to actual invasions – in more than 70 countries. These included Cambodia, China, East Timor, Korea, the Philippines, Vietnam, Chile, Cuba, the Dominican Republic, El Salvador, Grenada, Guatemala, Nicaragua, Panama, Afghanistan, Iran and Iraq – to name but "Third World" countries. Today, a US military presence "defends American interests" in over 140 states worldwide.

On the business side, US arms make up around fifty percent of global arms sales, and war zones provide a perfect showcase for the latest weapons. US firms, along with several from Western Europe, armed both sides of the Iran-Iraq war in the 1980s. The US media have been accused of unquestioningly promoting the brilliance of US-made smart bombs and Patriot missiles during the first Gulf War in 1991 – which, predictably, gave a massive boost to Israeli and Saudi Arabian demand for US arms. The publication *Foreign Policy In Focus* reported that

Boeing, Lockheed Martin and Textron all lobbied for the expansion of NATO in the late 1990s as a "golden opportunity" for increased arms sales, although the move also antagonized Russia and undermined arms control talks (which the George W. Bush administration put the boot in on anyway).

As recently as March 2005, Condoleezza Rice was in India discussing closer ties with the US on practically the same day that 22 F-16 fighter jets were sold to India's neighbour Pakistan – a move hardly calculated to ease the longstanding tension between the two countries. For the military-industrial complex, it would seem, business is business, regardless of the human consequences – and not just abroad. According to a 2005 UNICEF report, the US has the highest proportion of children growing up in poor households of any OECD country – 21.9 percent, nine times the rate in Denmark. As Eisenhower pointed out in 1953, at the *beginning* of his presidency: "Every gun that is made, every warship launched, every rocket fired signifies, in the final sense, a theft from those who hunger and are not fed, those who are cold and are not clothed."

SOURCES

Books

Helen Caldicott The New Nuclear Danger: George W. Bush's Military-Industrial Complex (2002). Giving the military-industrial theory a modern context, Caldicott argues that the complex has used its connections to Congress and successive White House administrations to hurdle the post Cold War downturn in fortunes and turned 9/11 into a once-in-a-lifetime business opportunity. Resultedly, the complex is spending more and tightening its grip on America's government and society more than at any time since WWII.

Aaron L Friedberg In the Shadow of the Garrison State (2000). Friedberg doesn't actively support a complex as a good thing per se, but contends its size and growth during the Cold War has not led to a garrison state (phew!).

Indeed, the process of investment in arms, technology, and supportive political institutions and individuals has created a stable, economically unbeatable political-economic set-up. But whether that means it is a model for economic growth the world should follow, he doesn't say.

Films

Eugene Jarecki Why We Fight (2005). Taking Eisenhower's "military-industrial complex" speech as its starting-point, Jarecki's film adopts an altogether more sober approach to its subject than Michael Moore's *Fahrenheit 9/11* and is all the better for it. Essential viewing.

Websites

ⓦ **www.eisenhower.archives.gov/farewell. htm** The text of Eisenhower's seminal speech.

ⓦ **schema-root.org/commerce/corporations /military/** Covers 38 military industry topics, each with a current news feed.

ⓦ **www.sourcewatch.org/index. php?title=Military-industrial_complex** SourceWatch describes itself as a collaboratively written "encyclopedia of people, issues, and groups shaping the public agenda". The article includes dozens of links to follow up.

ⓦ **www.thirdworldtraveler.com/Blum/ US_Interventions_WBlumZ.html** "A Brief History of US Interventions: 1945 To The Present" (*Z Magazine*, June 1999), by William Blum, author of *Killing Hope: US Military And CIA Interventions Since World War II*.

Currency codes: from Masonic dollars to ten-agora coins

Coins and banknotes are so familiar that people scarcely notice what's on them. Most people, that is. The conspiracy-minded, by contrast, are able to tease out a wealth of arcane imagery and symbolism that reveals some disturbing truths: that Masons run the US government, that 9/11 is written all over a twenty-dollar bill issued in 1998, that Israel plans to colonize three-quarters of the Middle East, and that John McEnroe is the front-man for some pretty dark forces...

The almighty dollar: Masonic myths

Ever since 1935, the reverse side of the one-dollar bill has carried a pair of strange images framed by circles on either side of the word "ONE". To quote the State Department's official heraldic description, the one on the left shows: "A pyramid unfinished. In the zenith, an eye in a triangle, surrounded with a glory proper." The Roman numerals for the date of independence, 1776, are carved into the base of the pyramid, which has thirteen steps. Above the eye is the Latin motto *Annuit Cœptis*, while below the base of the pyramid a banner reads *Novus Ordo Seclorum*. The image on the right shows a Bald Eagle holding a banner reading *E Pluribus Unum*, and clutching an olive branch and arrows in its talons.

Together, these odd drawings make up the Great Seal, the official symbol of the United States of America. Conspiracy theorists, however, especially those on the religious right, see them as powerful proof that Masonry captured the heart of the republic right from the start. Never mind the slogan "IN GOD WE TRUST" written in capitals across the centre of the note, the Masons were – still are – conspiring to build an atheistic, self-interested state on the ruins of what was once the new promised land. *Novus ordo seclorum*, it's said, stands for "New World Order", the much-feared Grand Plan to establish an authoritarian, probably left-wing and certainly ungodly world regime (see p.234). Latin scholars can bleat in vain that the phrase really means "a new order of the centuries", *seclorum* being a short form of *saeculorum* (some have argued that the abbreviation has numerological significance), and is adapted from Virgil's fourth Eclogue, where the line "*Magnus ab integro seclorum nascitur ordo*" trumpets the hope that "a mighty order of ages is born anew" for the Roman empire. Which is, not coincidentally, just what the founding fathers hoped for the American republic back in MDCCLXXVI – that it would begin a new era in which monarchies would become a thing of the past. (Now that's a real conspiracy.)

Above the pyramid, the phrase *Annuit Cœptis* translates as "He favours our undertaking" – "He" being God, who apparently looked on people born in a certain part of North America with the same indulgence he once granted the Israelites. This divine favour, the official version has it, also explains the eye in the top of the pyramid, described as the "Eye of Providence". Mason-watchers, however, see a very different interpretation. The blazing eye, they claim, is in fact a secret symbol for the Great Architect of the Universe, the "light-filled" Deistic

George Washington in his Masonic Apron

bols. Turn over the dollar bill, however, and there are more clues. The US Treasury Seal shows scales, a chevron representing a carpenter's square, and a key. Do these represent a balanced budget, judicious accounting and monetary security, as conventional accounts would have it? Or do they represent Masons, Masons and Masons?

George Washington was not the only high-placed Mason in the early years of the Republic. Benjamin Franklin is known to have rolled up a trouser leg as well, and it turns out that he was actually on the committee that designed the Great Seal. But then so too were Thomas Jefferson and John Adams – and there are no records of either being a Freemason, despite what conspiracy theorists believe. With the help of an artist named Pierre Eugene du Simitière, Franklin, Jefferson and Adams created some of the main elements of the Seal, including the Eye of Providence and the date of independence, along with the thirteen-striped shield and the motto *E Pluribus Unum*. By 1782 the design of the Seal had gone to a Third Committee, which devolved the hard work to William Barton, a Philadelphia lawyer and heraldic enthusiast who added the eagle – not yet bald – and the pyramid.

Barton was almost certainly not a Mason, though a contemporary with the name William Barton apparently was – a fact that has led to rich confusion. Mason or not, numerologists and symbol buffs have had plenty of fun with his designs. One of the wings of the eagle has 32 feathers – that's the number of degrees in Scottish Rite Freemasonry! Its tail has nine feathers – that's the number of degrees in the York Rite! Best of all, as freemasonrywatch.org has it, "the total number of feathers in the two wings is 65, which, by gematria – the assigning of numerical values to the letters of the Hebrew alphabet – is also the value of the Hebrew phrase YAM YAWCHOD (together in unity). This phrase appears in Psalm 133 as follows: 'Behold, how good and how pleasant it is for brethren to dwell together in unity,' and is used in the ritual of the first degree of Freemasonry."

divinity or "Supreme Being" in which Deistic Freemasons are traditionally supposed to believe. The light emanating from it is nothing less than the light of Masonic knowledge – the original light of "the Enlightenment".

For once, symbol-readers aren't entirely barking up the wrong pyramid. The eye turned up on the Masonic apron worn by George Washington when he laid the foundation stone of the Capitol in 1793. But when it comes to proof, symbols are as elusive as eels – it's counter-claimed that in the late eighteenth century the "eye" symbol was used outside Masonic circles as much as within them, so the designers of the Seal and the Freemasons were just drawing on a common stock of quasi-spiritual sym-

But then you can prove almost anything with numbers.

As for the pyramid, those versed in Masonic lore believe it represents the unfinished Jerusalem Temple, begun by the legendary ancestors of the Masons. Or as Henry Agard Wallace, vice president to Franklin D. Roosevelt during World War II and 32nd-degree Mason, wrote in his 1934 work, *Statesmanship And Religion*: "It will take a more definite recognition of the Grand Architect of the Universe before the apex stone is finally fitted into place and this nation in the full strength of its power is in position to assume leadership among the nations in inaugurating 'the New Order of the Ages'." It was Wallace who took the decision to put the Seal on the dollar bill – by his own account at the prompting of Roosevelt himself, a fellow Mason.

A truly sinister reading of the pyramid image sees a hidden code within it implicating Jews in the conspiracy (whatever that conspiracy is). The image can be made to reveal a Star of David, as follows: one equilateral triangle is drawn using the lines of the pyramid, with its base on the letters N and M of "N*ovus ordo secloru*M"; the second, inverted triangle has its base on A*nnuit Coepti*S, and its point on *ord*O. And the anagram thus created reads "A MASON"... And the official view? It comes from Charles Thomson's report to Congress on the work of the three committees, from June 20, 1782. His "Remarks and Explanation", as quoted by the State Department, declares: "Reverse. The pyramid signifies Strength and Duration: The Eye over it & the Motto allude to the many signal interpositions of providence in favour of the American cause. The date underneath is that of the Declaration of Independence and the words under it signify the beginning of the New American Era, which commences from that date" (although the right-wing think tank Project for the New American Century might argue such an era really starts with them).

Masonic symbolism on the US dollar

The twenty-dollar prophecy

This one's a little complicated, and you'll need to have an old twenty-dollar bill in front of you (or go to snopes.com, see p.405, to see how it's done). If you fold the note in half to show the top half of the White House, then fold both the left and right halves of what you're left with up underneath themselves so they point upwards at ninety degrees, you're left with a composite image apparently showing the Pentagon ablaze – just like the famous image from 9/11. Spookily, if you turn the folded note over, a tower with black smoke pouring out of it is revealed. (In both cases the smoke is dark green shrubbery from the original image.)

If you were in any doubt that something very iffy is going on, try this: a concertina-style fold allows you to spell out "Osama" from "20 *united States of*

AM*eric*A". And here's the clincher: the note was a redesign introduced in September 1998, but it was replaced *again* as soon as October 9, 2003. But what's the conspiracy here? Did the Treasury know at least three years in advance what was going to happen on September 11, 2001? If so, it's a shame officials didn't tell the President – or did they (see p.366)?

The ten-agora coin: map of Greater Israel

During the early 1990s, Yasser Arafat is said to have carried around Israel's ten-agora coin in his jacket pocket. Not in case of parking emergencies but to offer "proof", as he would put it, of an Israeli conspiracy to colonize the entire Middle East. On May 25, 1990, he even spoke to the UN Security Council on the issue, showing the coin to representatives specially assembled in Geneva. The coin is engraved with the image of an ancient coin dating back to the Roman siege of Jerusalem, in the reign of the last Hasmonaean king, Mattathias Antigonus II. It is stamped with the image of a seven-branched candlestick, the Jewish menorah, and its shape is distinctive, with a broken left-hand edge curving out to a point on the lower left side.

Suspicious-minded Palestinians saw a familiar outline in that edge – it was the profile of the eastern Mediterranean shore! If the rest of the coin was superimposed on a map of the Middle East, then the right-hand side of the coin would cover half of the Middle East, stretching from the Red Sea three quarters of the way across Iraq and Saudi Arabia – almost to the Gulf. This coin, then, was nothing less than a coded reference to "Greater Israel". As Arafat put it, it was "a glaring demonstration of Zionist aspirations".

This "Greater Israel" notion didn't spring from nowhere. Early Zionists had indeed planned a much larger Jewish state. Theodor Herzl, for instance, believed the Jews should settle in Palestine and Syria, and even considered settlements in Mesopotamia – modern-day Iraq. This was on the basis of two Biblical passages: in Genesis 15:18 Abraham is told "Unto thy seed have I given this land, from the river of Egypt unto the great river, the river Euphrates", while at Deuteronomy 11:24 Moses declares "Every place whereon the soles of your feet shall tread shall be yours: from the wilderness and Lebanon, from the river, the river Euphrates, even unto the uttermost sea shall your coast be". From the Euphrates to the sea? Or to the "river of Egypt" – the Nile? Jewish scholars may explain that these vague territorial claims are superseded by later, more precise Biblical delimitations of the land of Israel (and that in any case the river called "Euphrates" may in fact be a small river in Syria, while the so-called "river of Egypt" is probably another minor watercourse in the north of Sinai) but Palestinians aren't much comforted. Israel's sudden seizure of the West Bank, Gaza and, for a time, Sinai, in the wake of the Six-Day War, and the actions of Jewish settlers, seem to tell a different story – of expansion not defence.

And then there's the issue of the Israeli flag, which shows the state of Israel, represented by a blue Star of David, standing between two blue stripes. Officially, these stripes are taken from the traditional pattern of Jewish prayer shawls. According to conspiracy lore, however, they show how Israel has designs on all the land "from the river to the river" – from the Euphrates to the Nile. Exactly as depicted on the ten-agora coin.

The ten-quid secret

When Charles Darwin elbowed Charles Dickens off the rear of Britain's ten-pound note, it was officially on the grounds that the great scientist's beard was bushier and therefore harder for forgers to copy than the less hirsute – though still impressively endowed – novelist's. If it had been the ten-

dollar bill that had swapped Dickens for Darwin, it's not hard to imagine the conspiracy theories that would have quickly flooded the Internet. Was the reserve bank run by a cabal of Masonic atheists parading their evolutionist hero in the faces (or at least the wallets) of the righteous? This being tolerant, atheist-minded Britain, however, there was no such outcry – but a secret code was soon found nonetheless. With a bit of care, the lower half of the Queen's face, from the front of the note, can be folded so that it aligns with the upper part of Darwin's. The result is striking. It's John McEnroe. Complete with earring. The attendant conspiracy theory hardly needs to be explained – first Wimbledon, tomorrow the world? As McEnroe himself would say: you can *not* be serious!

SOURCES

Books

David Ovason **The Secret Symbols Of The Dollar Bill** (2004). A trove of arcane information, from numerology to etymology, by way of early American history.

Richard S. Patterson and Richardson Dougall **A History Of The Great Seal** (1976). Released by the Department of State, this weighty official history tells you everything you might want to know (and probably a good deal more) about the origins of the seal.

Daniel Pipes **The Hidden Hand: Middle East Fears Of Conspiracy** (1998). The last word on the subject, though admittedly from a distinctly pro-Israeli perspective.

Includes a map of "Greater Israel" as depicted on the ten-agora coin.

Websites

ⓦ www.danielpipes.org/article/247 Article-type treatment of the ten-agora affair by Daniel Pipes, *the* authority on Middle Eastern conspiracy theories.

ⓦ www.freemasonrywatch.org/ onedollarbill.html Virtuoso freestyling on the Masonic symbolism of the dollar bill.

ⓦ www.legendinc.com/Pages/ MiscellaneousPages/USDollar.html A good online image of the dollar, with a short key to what's on it.

ⓦ www.mideastweb.org/log/ archives/00000132.htm Contains an image of the ten-agora coin.

ⓦ www.moneyfactory.com/ Official website of the Treasury's Bureau of Engraving and Printing, with lots on the development of dollar banknotes.

ⓦ www.snopes.com/rumors/20bill.htm Perfect illustration of how to fold a $20 bill to reveal the 9/11 atrocities.

ⓦ www.srmason-sj.org/council/journal/ uzzel.html Full Masonic biography of Henry A. Wallace, Vice President and Freemason.

ⓦ www.state.gov/www/publications/ great_seal.pdf Brief official history of the Great Seal.

Italy: Land of conspiracy

Everything is political in Italy, and everything is a conspiracy – history included. The country is divided between left and right in a way that makes the American divide between pro- and anti-Bush camps look shallow and inconsequential, and for decades, right and left alike have issued frantic warnings of the dangers of Communist or Fascist coups or covert action. A politician convicted of corruption or outright criminality can easily survive until the next trial by appealing, and claiming that "Communist justice" has conspired to slander him. Or, like President Silvio Berlusconi, by rewriting Italian law to create immunity from prosecution and to halve the statute of limitations.

As an integral part of Italian politics and culture, conspiracies are a topic of discussion as hot as football. There's even a word in Italian for conspiracy theorizing: *dietrologia* – "the study of what lies behind". Adriano Sofri, the convicted murderer of the anarchist Pino Pinelli, gives author Tobias Jones one of the sharpest soundbites on conspiracy theories anywhere. "*Dietrologia* is an air that you breathe in Italy", he says. "It's the result of paranoia and jealousy, and it simply exalts an intricate intelligence. It's like Othello with Desdemona's handkerchief: one innocent object can spark off endless suspicions. It's a game which people play, almost to show off."

Communists vs Fascists

Italy's Communists and Fascists were fighting it out long before the end of World War II, as left-wing partisans harried the retreating Nazis and the remnants of Mussolini's collapsing armies. As elsewhere in Europe, the Allies quickened the pace of their invasion, alarmed by the possibility of a Communist takeover. In Italy, the proto-CIA did its bit for peace and security by setting up a "stay-behind" network of trained anti-Communists under Operation Gladio (its name taken from a Roman stabbing sword), with caches of weapons ready for use in the event of a left-wing government coming to power. Until 1990, when scandal-dogged Prime Minister Giulio Andreotti admitted to the Italian parliament that the programme had indeed existed, "Gladio" had been regularly dismissed as the most absurd of conspiracy theories. Unlike in France, where the *épuration* helped to purge the country of its political tensions, Italy remained split into two semi-warring camps, with Fascist-era officials still largely in power.

By the late 1960s, the pressure had only intensified. Italy's neighbours in the Mediterranean – Spain, Portugal and Greece – were all run by fascist, military dictatorships, and the Italian left was in a constant state of paranoid alarm about an imminent right-wing coup. Conspiracy theories were rampant – and largely justified. The right and the conservative establishment seem to have collaborated on what has become known as a "strategy of tension", to work on public fears of left-wing or anarchist terrorism. With Greek – and possibly US – support, the far right attempted to create the conditions for a coup, preparing the ground by claiming that Italy just wasn't ready for democracy – a claim reminiscent of apartheid-era statements about Africans.

Piazza Fontana and the Anni di Piombo

The *autunno caldo* or "hot autumn" of 1969 saw some 145 explosions. It was just a prelude. On December 12, 1969, a huge bomb exploded in Milan's Piazza Fontana, killing sixteen and injuring 88. The ensuing decade of terrorism and political semi-chaos was dubbed the *anni di piombo*, or "leaden years", and Piazza Fontana became the centre of a conspiracy vortex, sucking in endless court cases and political careers, and leaving an ever-mounting death toll of murdered witnesses and judicial officials. Whether Piazza Fontana was the work of anarchists or Fascists became the ultimate test of Italian political loyalties, but the more the bombing was investigated, the harder it seemed to become to establish the truth. As Tobias Jones puts it: "There are so many words. Words everywhere, and not a shred of common sense. Documents multiply amongst themselves, which sire new pieces of paper, loosed from all logic. The longer I spent following the trial, the more it seemed like something out of Kafka."

The most notorious eddy of the Piazza Fontana tornado was the furore surrounding the death of a young anarchist and pacifist, Giuseppe "Pino" Pinelli, an event made famous by Dario Fo's brilliant farce *Accidental Death Of An Anarchist*. Pinelli was arrested shortly after the bombing, and held for 72 hours in custody in Milan, before he apparently threw himself from a window and died in the courtyard below. The *questore* in charge of the investigation called his leap "a sort of self-accusation". All suicides are open to conspiricization, of course, and yet this one looked particularly iffy. No one heard Pinelli scream, there was evidence of a blow to the back of his neck, and he had no injuries to his arms – although even suicides usually instinctively protect their heads. And why was a window wide open in winter?

The police commissioner in charge of Pinelli's case, Luigi Calabresi, was murdered in "revenge" in May 1972, and bombing campaigns followed throughout the 1970s. An army colonel announced that his troops were "the only bulwark against disorder and anarchy" – in reality, the far right, including more than a few military elements, was behind the destabilizing events. The *anni di piombo* culminated in the bombing of Bologna railway station in August 1980, in which 85 bystanders were murdered. Like the less murderous bombs that had preceded it, the Bologna bomb was at first pinned on radical left-wing terrorists, but many Italians were never convinced, and theories that the bombings had in fact been the results of a right-wing conspiracy – to discredit the left and set a right-wing coup in motion – were widespread.

The Slaughters Commission and the Ordine Nuovo

In the late 1980s, the parliamentary *Commisione Stragi* or "Slaughters Commission" investigated Piazza Fontana. A far-reaching right-wing conspiracy with the alleged collusion of the Ministry of the Interior and the Italian (and possibly US) secret services was reluctantly dragged out of the underworld and into Italy's sunshine. Without actual convictions, however, the shadows of the past seemed just to dissipate, the evidence buried rather than revealed by the million-odd court documents.

Finally, in 2001, Delfo Zorzi, Carlo Maria Maggi and Giancarlo Rognoni were convicted of the Piazza Fontana bombing. Zorzi and Maggi had been members of *Ordine Nuovo*, an ultra-Fascist group then led by a robust operator called Pino Rauti, and were rumoured to be secret agents with connections to the CIA – in 2000, Italian newspapers reported that Rauti had received cheques from the US embassy in the early 1970s, though this issue remains typically unresolved. As for Rauti, he went on to lead another entirely legal neo-Fascist party, the Tricolour Flame.

Murder of a president: Aldo Moro

Iconic Piazza Fontana may be, but it was overshadowed by the most shocking event of the *anni di piombo*, an incident that has been compared in its impact on the national psyche – and on conspiracy theorizing – to the assassination of JFK. On March 16, 1978, Italy's centrist, Catholic President, Aldo Moro, was kidnapped at gunpoint by members of one of the "Red Brigades", devoted to the violent overthrow of the state. He had been on his way to a meeting sanctioning a new government that, for the first time, would include Communist representation in a broad coalition. Moro was held for two months, during which time he sent letters begging Prime Minister Giulio Andreotti to negotiate. Andreotti refused. Moro's bullet-ridden body eventually turned up on the Via Caetani in central Rome.

One effect was more like September 11 than JFK: a war on terrorism was unleashed (this time, with the full backing of the Communists). Equally, a flood of speculation was unleashed. The Italian public had been horrified by its government's uncharacteristic refusal to negotiate with the kidnappers, and its rather less surprising failure to locate and free their hostage. Right-wing elements in government, including Andreotti himself, were accused of wanting Moro dead rather than alive, in a deliberate attempt to keep the Communists out of government. Investigators revealed that the Red Brigades had been heavily infiltrated by the secret services, while the security forces themselves were in the grip of sinister forces (later identified as the P2 group – see opposite). Some newspapers claimed that the CIA effectively ran certain Brigade cells. (For many, their suspicions were confirmed when Brigade members Mario Moretti and Giovanni Senzani – both probably secret service plants – were

allowed to travel to the US, at a time when all Italian Communists were routinely denied visas.) A parliamentary commission even suggested that the Interior Ministry might have actually located the apartment where Moro was held, and diverted police searches to protect it.

The Vatican Bank scandal: Licio Gelli revealed

Exactly which elements in government might have wanted Moro dead only emerged in the wake of the death of an Italian banker, Roberto Calvi, who was found hanging below London's Blackfriars Bridge on June 18, 1982. As chairman of the traditionally Catholic Italian bank, Banco Ambrosiano, Calvi had presided over an elaborate drug-money laundering scam on the behalf of Sicilian Mafia figures, using the Vatican Bank as a conduit (a story covered in full as part of the background to the death of Pope John Paul I on p.50). Foolishly, he'd also been swindling the Mafia on the side, and had threatened to reveal the involvement of powerful political figures; his death, then, was not exactly surprising.

One of the first magistrates sent to investigate Banco Ambrosiano – he had previously tried to investigate Pino Rauti for the Piazza Fontana murders – ended up dead, killed by "terrorists". Another magistrate sniffing around the finances of Calvi's co-conspirator, Sicilian tax expert and banker Michele Sindona, was also murdered. But slowly, the links between the various cases were pieced together, despite the outright obstruction of powerful figures in government. (Calvi, it seemed, had been paying off all of Italy's political parties for years, including making two payments totalling seven million dollars to Bettino Craxi, who became Italy's first socialist Prime Minister in 1983.) As magistrates approached the centre of the web, a certain Licio Gelli emerged as the key political fixer behind the whole Calvi–Sindona–Vatican affair, bribing and blackmailing politicians and Mafia grandees alike to protect the operation.

The Italian press promptly nicknamed Gelli *Il Burattinaio* – "The Puppet-Master". A committed Fascist and SS officer in the war, he had escaped to Argentina, where he formed a close political association with the dictator Juan Perón and dealt in arms. Conspiracists have fingered him for involvement in anything from the flight of Nazi's criminals, including Klaus Barbie, to South America and the death of Pope John Paul I (see p.48), to the assassination of Swedish Prime Minister Olaf Palme and Reagan's October Surprise (see p.185). Certainly, Gelli's range of contacts was impressive, extending to Pope Paul VI and George H. W. Bush, never mind Juan Perón. Italian Prime Minister Giulio Andreotti even claimed that at Perón's inauguration in 1973, he saw the new Argentinian president kneel and kiss Gelli's ring.

P2 unmasked

Gelli, it seems, was the dark side of Italy's right wing, the point at which it shaded off into the Mafia – he was widely quoted as saying "the doors to all bank vaults open to the right". When his homes and business addresses were raided in March 1981, an extraordinary document was found in a safe. It listed 953 powerful names in politics, business and the military and judiciary – including 38 MPs, fourteen judges, two cabinet members, all the heads of the Italian armed services and a certain businessman called Silvio Berlusconi (see overleaf). All were supposedly members of a secret, quasi-Masonic lodge called *Propaganda Due*, or P2. Freemasonry buffs have tried to concoct lurid histories for P2, involving connections with a nineteenth-century "Egyptian rite" and tales of oaths made in Tuscan villas with Nazi decor to hooded officials, but the organization is thought by most to have been founded in the 1970s, allegedly with CIA support, and to

be less a Masonic lodge than a political network. P2's aims lay somewhere between the promotion of Gelli's own Mafia-style mini-empire, by means of bribery, blackmail, murder and ferocious networking, and the overthrow of the Italian state and its replacement with a Fascist regime.

Shortly after the discovery of the list, a manifesto was discovered underneath a false bottom in Gelli's daughter's briefcase, setting out "A Plan For The Rebirth Of Democracy". It involved suspending unions, controlling the media and generally putting Italy back on its Fascist feet. (Post-Berlusconi, the scheme doesn't look all that unlikely.) Never mind Piazza Fontana – for conspiracists, this was the Holy Grail, proof that a powerful, well-connected and well-hidden hand had long been directing the course of Italian affairs for its own advantage, under the cover of democracy. If P2 existed, what else might not be true? P2 was quickly linked to Sindona's faked kidnapping, the failure of Andreotti's government to negotiate for Aldo Moro, the infamous Bologna railway bombing of August 1980, and indeed with most of the unsolved and unresolved outrages of the *anni di piombo* that had previously and so unconvincingly been laid at the door of ineffectual anarchists.

P2 obscured; Licio Gelli on the run

This being Italy, the euphoria of a conspiracy unmasked didn't last long. Slowly, the list has been chipped away, many of the names denying ever having "joined", others turning out to have had only distant connections. Or so they have claimed. Like the so-called "Mafia", P2 has proved to be less an organization than a coincidence of interests; less a Masonic club – with rules, code words, curious costumes etc – and more a networking opportunity. Some commentators have even said that P2 was nothing more than a chimera, a sop thrown to the left to distract its attention from the real locations of power. And yet ... Gelli and his associates did repeatedly engage in the planning and execution of very real terrorist murders.

Gelli himself went on the run. He was arrested in Switzerland in 1987, probably while scrabbling together some of the missing millions for his drug-running Mafia cronies, but escaped from prison – with astonishing ease – and made for South America. Eventually extradited to Italy, he fled house arrest, only to be arrested again in Cannes in 1998, and sent back home to face a twelve-year prison sentence.

The Mafia on trial

Less the family-run crime gang of popular legend, and more an unholy alliance of "black shirts" and "white collars", the Italian Mafia has cast an obscuring smog of disinformation across the face of Italian history. So many Mafia-inspired lies have now been told in Italian courts, so many perjured confessions made by so-called *pentiti* (supergrasses), so many investigations obfuscated, and so many judges and witnesses murdered that it is almost impossible to verify anything. The so-called "maxi-trials" of the late 1980s only led deeper into confusion, as government figures were half unmasked by *pentiti*, and new lines of judicial assault opened. Seven-times Prime Minister Giulio Andreotti was accused of exchanging an infamous kiss of association with "boss of bosses" Salvatore "Toto" Riina – who was allegedly behind the deaths of elite anti-Mafia judges Giovanni Falcone and Paolo Borsellino, murdered by huge bombs in May 1992. The judges' landmark assassinations finally revealed the extent of government collusion with the Mafia: only someone with high-level inside information could have got through the judges' security. As with the scandals of the 1970s, the most outrageous allegations of so-called conspiracy theorists were revealed to be true.

Clean Hands and Silvio Berlusconi

The Mafia trials soon morphed into the *Mani Pulite* or "Clean Hands" investigation led by Milanese judge Antonio di Pietro. The ensuing *tangentopoli* or "bribesville" scandal revealed the breathtaking extent of corruption in the established political parties, the Christian Democrats and Socialists. Again, conspiracy theorists were vindicated. Into the power vacuum swooped the charismatic multi-billionaire media magnate, Silvio Berlusconi, who set up his own political party, Forza Italia, or "Come on Italy". Berlusconi was not the refreshingly unpolitical outsider he claimed to be. Aside from his inclusion on the notorious P2 list (see p.125), he was a former crony of Bettino Craxi, one of the politicians most deeply tainted by *tangentopoli*, and later played a leading role in discrediting Antonio di Pietro. Berlusconi has also been accused of long-term involvement with the Mafia, to the extent that the Milan headquarters of his Finninvest holding company were raided by anti-Mafia investigators in 1998. In August that year, he was sentenced to almost three years in jail for corruption, although he was later acquitted.

In May 2001, Berlusconi bounced back as the leader of a new coalition with a huge majority. The 1970s and 1980s may have been the most extravagant era of Italian conspiracy theorizing, but under Berlusconi's premiership, contemporary Italy comes a respectable second. At times, the Italian Prime Minister's career seems designed to provoke the conspiracy machine. There are the conflicts of interest between his roles as the ultimate boss of the state media network, RAI, and as the owner of the main rival private channel, Mediaset. There are the links between his financial holding company, Finninvest, and a plethora of individuals with Mafia ties (although it's true that any big fish in Italy swims in a murky pond).

And then there are the actions of Berlusconi's Forza Italia government, which not only voted to halve the statute of limitations on false accounting to seven and a half years – thus wiping Berlusconi's

Silvio Berlusconi: clean hands

own pre-office record legally clean – but also declared their Prime Minister to be officially immune from prosecution ... while he was actually in the middle of being tried for bribing a judge during a takeover deal. The immunity law didn't last long, being overturned by a constitutional court in January 2004. But then, as his Forza Italia colleague Carlo Taormina commented, "only a Communist could conceive such a ruling". Blaming the so-called "red togas" – judges named after the colour of their politics, not of their judicial robes – is a typical move. Any setback in Italy, it seems, must be the result of a conspiracy.

SOURCES

Books

Giuseppe Genna In The Name Of Ishmael (2004). Complex literary thriller featuring two Italian detectives' investigations steadily converging on a mysterious arch-villain, Ishmael, who seems to be at the centre of forty years of European conspiracies and ritual murders.

Paul Ginsborg A History Of Contemporary Italy: Society And Politics, 1943–1988 (2003) and **Italy And Its Discontents** (2003). Ginsborg is the pre-eminent historian of postwar Italy, and the best

guide to the background of its conspiracy theories. His most recent publication is a compelling, insightful and hostile study of the Berlusconi era, *Silvio Berlusconi: Television, Power And Patrimony*.

Tobias Jones The Dark Heart Of Italy (2005). Not just a portrait of postwar Italy, or a book about conspiracy theories, or just another "my year in the sun" publication – although it is all three. Instead, like a piece of travel literature, it describes the author's own fascinating journey into the world of conspiracy theorizing.

Leonardo Sciascia The Moro Affair And The Mystery Of Majorana (2004). An enthralling indictment of the Italian state and of the Christian Democrats in particular by a Sicilian novelist and member of the parliamentary commission investigating the Moro murder.

Websites

ⓦ **www.americanatheist.org/pope99/calvi. html** Full exposition of the Calvi–Gelli–Marcinkus–Sindona–John Paul I affair, with black-and-white photos of the protagonists.

Wrestling with the Octopus: Danny Casolaro

On August 10, 1991, a would-be investigative writer called Danny Casolaro was found dead in a motel bathtub in Martinsburg, West Virginia, with a dozen slashes to his wrists and a note that read "please forgive me for the worst possible thing I could have done". Local police officers concluded that his death was suicide, and the county coroner released the body to an embalmer the same evening. Technically, this was illegal, as the dead man's next of kin had yet to be notified – and had it not been too late, his family might well have called for an autopsy. Danny's brother Anthony claimed that Danny had told him he was on the trail of a dangerous story, and was about to interview a source who would finally give him conclusive proof of the existence of a mega-conspiracy he called "the Octopus". Danny, Anthony said, was euphoric. He had warned his brother that if he died suddenly it would not be suicide.

The head of the Octopus

Danny Casolaro nicknamed his dangerous story "the Octopus" for a simple reason: it had so many tentacles. Reeling it in was proving a hard job. Casolaro's starting-point was the conspiracy theories most beloved by US counter-culture, from BCCI to the Bay of Pigs, and from the CIA in Angola to Iran–Contra and the October Surprise.

His own theory featured dozens of the usual conspiracy suspects, from E. Howard Hunt to Colonel Oliver North, and from CIA directors George H. W. Bush and William Colby to Attorney General Edwin Meese. All, Casolaro claimed, were part of an elite network of ex-intelligence agents that was controlling world events in order to extend the wealth and power of its members.

Danny Casolaro

It sounds like real James Bond stuff, and Casolaro's overwrought "Octopus" manuscript, which survived his death, doesn't make his theory look any more convincing than a thriller. It regurgitates familiar gems of "alternative history" in the best stream-of-consciousness tradition of conspiracy theorizing, leaping from one topic to another using coincidences of names and places as the sole stepping-stone on the way. Casolaro's problem seemed to be less a matter of finding the head of the Octopus than getting himself tied in knots by its many tentacles.

His problems were compounded by his contacts with an "informant" called Michael Riconosciuto, a self-publicizing character who touted himself as an operative moving on the murkier fringes of the intelligence world. He claimed to have developed gene warfare technology for the CIA and infrared sensors capable of "saturation surveillance". He also bragged that he had laundered money for the Mena drug-running operation (see p.198) and told one writer that he had witnessed the famous Roswell autopsy (see p.311). In short, he was as steeped in conspiracy culture as Casolaro himself. In his journals, Casolaro nicknamed Riconosciuto "Danger Man".

The PROMIS case

Riconosciuto also claimed to be a brilliant software engineer who had made secret modifications to a piece of Department of Justice database-integration software called PROMIS. (The setting for his efforts was supposedly the Cabazon Indians' tribal lands in Indio, California – an area touted by conspiracists as being "near" the notorious secret airbase, Area 51.) He told Casolaro that he had been given a pirated copy of the software by Earl Brian, an associate of Ronald Reagan's Attorney General Ed Meese, who had in turn received a knock-off copy as payment for brokering the October Surprise between Reagan and the Ayatollah Khomeini (see p.185).

Whatever the truth of Riconosciuto's claims, PROMIS did at least actually exist. It had been developed by a software firm called Inslaw, in association with the Department of Justice, to manage crime statistics. Its unique feature was that it was able to co-ordinate separate databases (on criminals, legal cases etc) without requiring the manual re-entry of data, thus allowing officials to track disparate pieces of data held on separate systems. A contentious dispute over rights to the software developed between Inslaw and the Department of Justice, which suspended payments and effectively drove its own contractor out of business.

Inslaw's boss, Bill Hamilton, relentlessly pursued the DoJ through the courts. He won a multi-million-dollar lawsuit –though the verdict was later overturned by the DC Circuit Court of Appeals. The bullying criminality of the Department of Justice's behaviour – as described by the House Judiciary Committee's Investigative Report, of August 1992 – explains the notoriety of the PROMIS case in Washington circles. The case's journey into the realms of conspiracy theory, however, needs more explanation. On one level, the PROMIS case was perfect fodder for the libertarian wing of the conspiracy fraternity, reinforcing the belief that the hungry federal machine is bent on ripping off the small guy. Similarly, as a piece of software able to search databases by individuals' names, PROMIS was seen as a threat to liberty.

Tools of international surveillance

In the hands of conspiracy theorists, PROMIS has morphed into an enviably powerful piece of software, able to "track Soviet submarines in previously untraceable marine trenches near Iceland", according to one website, and "predict patterns and establish trends on the world's stock and financial markets", according to another. The ensuing profits are so vast that knowledge of the application is apparently restricted to the President, Vice President and Secretaries of State and Defense. (And, presumably, one lone conspiracy theorist.) An "enhanced" version of PROMIS called "Brainstorm" is able to "track individuals by predicting their thoughts and future actions". These are the kinds of claims more usually made of ECHELON (see p.251); PROMIS must really have filled up those early-1990s floppy discs.

Predicting the future aside, PROMIS was as useful for intelligence as it was for police work, and part of Inslaw's case rested on the allegation that it had been sold on to intelligence agencies around the world. It wasn't so much the ethical principle; Inslaw wanted payment for the rights. The 1992 House Judiciary Committee declared that the software had indeed been distributed "to further the intelligence and foreign policy objectives of the United States". Israeli secret intelligence agency Mossad had it (supposedly through the good offices of media mogul Robert Maxwell), as did the Pakistanis and Interpol – not forgetting the Canadian Mounties. In such hands it could be used to keep track of dissidents and terrorists. More sinister still was Riconosciuto's claim that he had re-engineered the software with a "backdoor" to allow the CIA to access the files and monitor the file-searching activities of all its international users. Hence the DoJ's extreme reluctance for an ordinary company like Inslaw to claim the rights.

Consequences

The Judiciary Committee's Investigative Report recommended an immediate investigation of the Justice Department's treatment of Inslaw. "As long as the possibility exists that Danny Casolaro died as a result of his investigation into the INSLAW matter", the report's authors declared, "it is imperative that further investigation be conducted." Attorney General William Barr appointed a retired federal judge, Nicholas Bua, as Department of Justice Special Counsel – not the independent counsel requested by the report's authors. Bua reported on PROMIS in June 1993, clearing Justice officials of any wrongdoing and finding Casolaro's death to have been suicide.

Danny Casolaro was evidently in over his head, caught up in a highly political court case and in the warped world of a notorious fraudster. (Riconsciuto may have been trying to muddy the waters relating to impending narcotics charges, for which he was later sentenced to thirty years in a federal prison; he presumably wanted to make it look as if he was the victim of a conspiracy to silence him – and many conspiracists, of course, believe exactly that.) Whether Casolaro's interest in or indeed understanding of PROMIS was sufficient cause for him to be murdered is debatable. For conspiracists, it just has to have been an assassination. Casolaro's death has become a kind of proof that theorizing isn't futile, and that lone researchers can come close enough to the Octopus to make it lash out – thereby forcing it to prove its own existence.

SOURCES

Books

Kenn Thomas and Jim Keith **The Octopus: The Secret Government And The Death Of Danny Casolaro** (2003). The full story, with all the conspiracy ramifications filled out – including the 1999 death of co-author Jim Keith "in mysterious circumstances".

Websites

⊛ www.usdoj.gov/opa/pr/Pre_96/ September94/555.txt.html DoJ press release detailing (and publicizing) Special Counsel Nicholas Bua's favourable conclusions.

⊛ www.webcom.com/~pinknoiz/covert/ inslaw.html A collection of documents relating to Inslaw, including parts of the Investigative Report submitted to the House Judiciary Committee (which recommends further investigation of Casolaro's "suicide") and Inslaw's rebuttal of Bua's report.

The Gemstone File

The so-called Gemstone File is the original mega-conspiracy theory, a radical reinterpretation of postwar history along deeply conspiratorial lines. It sucks in everything from the deaths of JFK and Mary Jo Kopechne to the empires of Howard Hughes and Aristotle Onassis – the arch-villain of the piece. But what's really fascinating about the theory is the subversive way it was originally disseminated. You might have been sitting in a California campus coffee bar, when an excited-looking fellow student surreptitiously and yet somehow melodramatically passed you a sheaf of scrappy photocopied papers entitled "The Skeleton Key To The Gemstone File". After reading right through the night, slack-jawed in astonishment at the power of the forces manipulating the world outside, you passed the document on to another campus contact in your turn.

Sadly, the actual content of the Gemstone File is relatively unthrilling. At least, it may have seemed radical and exciting when it first emerged, in the mid 1970s, but these days it looks more like an oddball synthesis of rather-too-well-worn conspiracy theories. Perhaps Gemstone's arch-villain groove has been carved too deep, thanks to a host of fictional clones, from Ian Fleming's Ernst Stavro Blofeld to *The X Files'* Cigarette Smoking Man. (Curiously, Blofeld actually dates back to 1956, the year Fleming published *Diamonds Are Forever*, and conspiracists have seized on this fact as evidence that Fleming, with his background in British Intelligence, was aware of Onassis's true status. Sceptics point out that it's just as possible that the Gemstone File was influenced by the film version of *Diamonds Are Forever*, which came out in 1971.)

Bruce Roberts, costume jeweller

The Gemstone File began life as a series of letters written in the early 1970s by a San Francisco Bay Area resident called Bruce Roberts. He sent them to a local conspiracy researcher and minor media pundit, Mae Brussell, who stored them in her archive. The "Skeleton Key" later claimed that these letters amounted to a cache of some thousand pages. Roberts – whom some have said was a costume jeweller by training, though he seems to have worked as a roofer during the 1970s – claimed to have invented a method of synthesizing rubies. Unfortunately, his techniques were stolen in 1960 by the Howard Hughes Corporation – which needed them for "laser weaponry research". When Roberts began to investigate the theft, he uncovered a web of corruption and conspiracy on an epic scale – which he in turn revealed to Mae Brussell in his letters.

Brussell, however, thought Roberts was little more than a crank, and failed to pass his revelations on to a less-than awestruck world. In 1974, however, a minor freelance journalist called Stephanie Caruana, who moved on the fringes of Brussell's circle, wrote a couple of articles with Brussell for *Playgirl* and other publications that partially drew on Roberts' theories. According to Caruana's own account, Brussell had at first discouraged her from looking through the "Roberts" file – which was stored in a manila envelope marked "Gemstone" – and indeed when she first took a look her reaction was "Hey, this guy is a paranoid schizophrenic!"

For some unaccountable reason, Caruana's first reaction didn't stick. She decided "to read the material with an open mind" and found that "it all held together – from first to last page". She went to see Roberts himself, and was persuaded that he was a credible character, a player in a high-octane world of espionage and covert commerce. Roberts told her that he sold his artificial gemstones (wrapped in pieces of conspiracy-theory-inscribed paper he called "whys") to powerful figures around the world in exchange for inside information.

Caruana's skeleton key

By now seriously impressed, Caruana worked up what she claimed was a summary of Roberts' theories. She called it "The Skeleton Key To The Gemstone File", a title redolent of locked cabinets, stolen treasure, wisdom and insight – and of course skeletons in the cupboard. Based around a historical timeline, with asides related to Roberts' own life, the "Key" was concise, urgent and assertive in tone, and its total lack of any kind of sourcing or evidence only made it appear more mysterious and gnomic. (Another journalist, Jim Moore, disputes Caruana's authorship, claiming that he himself wrote "The Skeleton Key". This was shortly after he "designed and built spy satellites, most notably Project OBSAT". According to Moore's resumé, OBSAT was able to detect Soviet nuclear tests using "Extremely Low Frequency energy". Sadly for Moore, he "lacked the security clearance at seventeen to even know whether or not the thing was actually in orbit".)

The original 24 photocopied pages hit the campuses in 1975, just a year before Roberts' death from a malignant brain tumour. The "Key" quickly became a conspiracy phenomenon, thanks to a pre-Internet version of viral distribution. Its concluding words appealed to the bottom-line nationalism of its enthusiastic American readership: "At present the only way to spread this information here in America is hand to hand. Your help is needed. Please make 1, 5, 10, 100 copies or whatever you can, and give them to friends or politicians, groups, media. This game is nearly up. Either the Mafia goes or AMERICA goes." Surprisingly perhaps, "The

CALIFORNIA'S QUEEN OF CONSPIRACY: MAE BRUSSELL

Until JFK was assassinated in November 1963, southern California resident Mae Brussell was more concerned with bringing up her five children than with politics. Convinced that Lee Harvey Oswald had not acted alone, however, she bought all 26 volumes of the Warren Commission report and began reading. It was the start of a vast archive of conspiracy-related material, and of Brussell's transformation into California's best-known conspiracy theorist. Brussell's viewpoint was unusual in that she saw the "hidden hand" as belonging to not a cabal of bankers and Jews, as was more commonly believed in her day, but to the remnants of European fascism. The urgency this conviction provoked in her was engaging and persuasive, and she held a guest spot on the Carmel, California local radio station KLRB for almost seventeen years. Her rough-voiced, rambling broadcasts earned her followers – nicknamed "sprouts" – and detractors in equal measure.

Since her death from cancer in 1988, aged 66 (a death somewhat predictably ascribed by some of her fans to foul means), the Brussell legend has only grown. As has her archive, which was passed around the California area before finally ending up in the possession of conspiracy writer Virginia McCullough. Formally named the "Mae Brussell Archive", according to conspiracy researchers who claim to have browsed its rich contents it contains "38 four-drawer file cabinets, over 10,000 books and countless boxes of newspapers, magazines and unfiled articles".

Mae Brussell's international fame is principally linked to her role in the dissemination of the so-called Gemstone File – some say she wrote it herself. Referencing Mae Brussell has become a way for conspiracists to corroborate their versions of history – conveniently skating over the important distinction between a primary source with inside contacts, and a secondary commentator on and collator of conspiracy theories. Brussell's sources, let it not be forgotten, were mostly other conspiracy theorists.

Skeleton Key" soon travelled abroad, making a big hit in the Middle East. It was quoted in a number of magazines, and an anonymous New Zealand conspiracist eventually expanded it into an even vaster (and more up-to-date) mega-conspiracy sometimes called the Opal File, or "Kiwi Gemstone", which dragged in BCCI (see p.230) and Danny Casolaro's Octopus (see p.128).

Now that anyone can download "The Skeleton Key" from the Internet, the romance has gone. There's no longer the sense that a secret has somehow made its way unerringly into your hands, no implication that it's your responsibility to guard it and pass it on. No sensation of risk. The nearest you might get to the original frisson is to try to lay hands on the elusive CD-Rom that Caruana has tried to hawk on the Internet. It is said to contain Roberts' original Gemstone File.

Casting gemstones before swine

The world, according to "The Skeleton Key To The Gemstone File", was run by the Mafia. Not the Sicilian families of the Cosa Nostra, or Vegas crime syndicates, or Russian gangster-capitalists, but a new kind of Mafia under the leadership of Greek shipping magnate Aristotle Onassis. Onassis, it seems, controlled the Democrat and Republican parties, as well as the CIA and other US government departments. His only rival was multi-millionaire Howard Hughes. The solution was simple: in 1957 Hughes was kidnapped and replaced with a double. Soon after, Onassis set the Vietnam war in motion to protect his business empire. When JFK came to power, the young president tried to rebel, but was promptly murdered – Jackie Kennedy subsequently became Jackie O in a kind of bizarre revenge re-marriage. Other Kennedys proved equally troublesome, leading to the deaths of Mary Jo Kopechne – supposedly murdered on Chappaquiddick island at the hands of Onassis loyalist Teddy Kennedy –

and RFK, who was assassinated by a "Manchurian candidate".

Meanwhile, Bruce Roberts' "gemstones" (both literally, in the sense of his artificial rubies, and metaphorically, in the sense of his revelations) were apparently making waves internationally. The Chinese made use of his files to force their way into the United Nations; FBI chief Hoover was poisoned after Onassis discovered he had been in contact with Roberts. In 1972, Nixon's Watergate "plumbers" team overheard Roberts holding court on his theories in a San Francisco bar – hence the supposed name of their Campaign to Re-Elect the President, aka CREEP, aka "gemstone". Nixon was furious – his rant against Roberts was so vehement that all eighteen minutes of it had to be deleted from the White House tapes.

There's plenty more, including asides that inspired generations of conspiracy theorizing – notably the allegation familiar from Dan Brown's *The Da Vinci Code* that the Council of Nicea was responsible for the destruction of "old copies of the Bible". Some sections are subtly anti-Semitic, notably the derogatory claim that Pope Paul VI's mother was Jewish, while other points are plain absurd, in particular the assertion that Howard Hughes's handwriting was faked by a computer (in 1957!) and that Hoover and others were killed using a rat-poison derivative called "Sodium Morphate" – a poison about as plausible as the test tube of "Sodium Asturbate" (geddit?) that Cary Grant picks up in the 1952 film *Monkey Business*. But like Bible-bashers defending the non sequiturs of the Old Testament, conspiracists have an easy answer to these kinds of problems: they are the fault of the transcriber, not the author. When the original Gemstone File comes to light, all manner of things shall be well.

Loose Cannon

During 1994 and 1995, Mae Brussell's archive was apparently in the hands of a Californian mail-order bookseller, Tom Davis. According to vehement conspiracy-debunker Martin Cannon, in this period he was finally able to locate the original Gemstone File (well, Brussell's photocopies of Roberts' letters, at least – the originals had either been returned or "gone missing"). It amounted to 351 pages ... of psychotic ranting. There were no sources, no evidence of any research, no new "Key" that would unlock the secrets of the File. The "File" was less of a complete theory than the supposed précis that was the "Key".

In a Web-published article on Virginia McCullough's Brussell-archive site, newsmakingnews.com, Cannon quotes from Roberts' letters at length. It makes sad and fascinating reading at the same time, a kind of ultimate extrapolation of the paranoid edge of conspiracy writing. An extrapolation that leads straight over the edge, in fact. Robert's prose has recognizably conspiracist features – breathless iteration of proper names, barely suppressed violence and wheeling, leapfrogging sentence structure – but it lacks order or argument. Of course, conspiracy researchers with a vested interest in Gemstone and/or a history of Gemstone-related research have been quick to expose Cannon as a plant, a government agent (or

MMORDIS agent, perhaps?) with a brief to discredit the Gemstone File.

Among Cannon's quotations is a supposedly key passage on the "Enemy Within", ie Onassis's Mafia, an organization Roberts nicknames MMORDIS. (Curiously, Caruana failed to repeat the acronym in her "Skeleton Key".) "There's a deadly disease running around: It's called MMORDIS – Mouldering Mass Of Rotten Dribbling Infectious Shit. Have a happy day. Hierarchy of shit – sustained by a society of shit. Sucking on Onassis' heroin-chancered thing, sitting on Montini's 'Holy Crusade' – brave, free, Americans eating Grecian and Roman shit for dessert. Melting Pot? Yes indeed. Rejects from every corner of the world – too rotten to correct the shit in their own native area – run to America – the US of Mafia – and from that gutless breed comes the creeping crawling cancer that today composes a necrophiliac nation dead-fucking on Mary Jo's grave – now escalated to the horror of a 1972 'free' election between Onassis-Montini-Kennedy-Chappaquiddick-'Hughes'-Teddy McGovern – and Onassis-Montini-Chappaquiddick-'Hughes'-Dickie – in a joint Hand-Maiden-Vatican, Mafia-Mafia election process. All of them running now – from these papers. Double cross, triple cross – anything to continue the run toward other crosses that wait – empty. Gangbang on Christ vs Universal Fuck of God." Yeah, right...

SOURCES

Books

Gerald A. Carroll Project Seek: Onassis, Kennedy, And The Gemstone Thesis (1994). As one Amazon reviewer puts it: "This book digs up so much dirt your mind will never be clean again."

David Hatcher Childress and Kenn Thomas Inside The Gemstone File (1999). From the publisher of the top conspiracy magazine **Steamshovel Press**, a collection of essays on the Gemstone File and the theory it presents, with an unmissable piece on the

Blofeld connection.

Jim Keith The Gemstone File (1992). Includes the original "Skeleton Key" along with a history of its distribution, and various articles, the last of which has the title "Is Gemstone A Hoax?" Do you really need to ask?

Websites

ⓦ **www.newsmakingnews.com/ mcgemstoneexposedatlast.htm** Martin Cannon's demythologizing broadside

– largely directed at Stephanie Caruana.
ⓦ **reptile.users2.50megs.com/research/ r102799d.html** "The Skeleton Key to the Gemstone File" in full. One of many Web-published versions.
ⓦ **www.sumeria.net/politics/opal.html** The text of the "Opal File". Non-Kiwis may find the New Zealand material oddly parochial for a universal conspiracy theory. But then, so is the Gemstone File, from a non-American perspective.

The EU

This book's most surprising agent of conspiracy has to be the European Union. Al Qaeda – fine; the CIA – naturally; the Knights Templar – frankly, no, but we take your point. But the giant bureaucracy that is the European Union? Really? From one viewpoint, of course, the EU is a kind of conspiracy, inasmuch as it's an agreement between powerful nations to order affairs to their own advantage. As a legal entity ratified by parliaments, however, it's not exactly secretive or malevolent – the usual conditions for a "conspiracy" to be labelled as such. Eurosceptics – particularly of the "Little Englander" variety – might disagree, claiming that the EU, like a kind of political vampire, feeds on national sovereignty in order to grow. Unlike European national parliaments, such Eurosceptics say, the EU is neither properly democratic nor practicably accountable. Hence it may behave like a power-hungry, conspiratorial cabal.

But all this is politics, not conspiracy theorizing. Maybe the EU is democratic, maybe it isn't. Maybe its advocates do want to create a European superstate, maybe they don't. True conspiracists see more esoteric dangers. In Northern Ireland, for example, Ian Paisley's pro-British, ultra-Protestant Democratic Unionist Party likes to put about the idea that the EU is ... a Catholic plot. Professor Arthur Noble, a DUP-backed speaker, is quoted on Paisley's website as saying: "The European Union was intended from the outset as a gigantic confidence-trick which would eventually hurtle the nations of Europe into economic, social, political and religious union." Thus far, most British Conservatives might agree. But Noble goes on to state that the "prime mover

behind the EU conspiracy" is none other than "the Vatican". Surely not even the most Europhobic Tory could get behind that argument. In August 2003, however, Adrian Hilton – later the Conservative candidate for the Slough constituency – wrote in the *Spectator* magazine that "a Catholic EU will inevitably result in the subjugation of Britain's Protestant ethos to Roman Catholic social, political and religious teaching". (And this in the EU that so vehemently opposed inscribing any mention of religion into its new constitution.) Hilton was quickly deselected.

But neo-Paisleyan anti-Catholicism is nothing compared to some of the rhetoric coming out of evangelo-hysterical America. One conspiracy blog site recalls Revelation: "Then I saw another beast, coming out of the earth. He had two horns like a lamb, but he spoke like a dragon." The beast, it seems, has been "pretty well pegged as the second-coming of the Holy Roman Empire based out of Europe". Someone, the writer suggests, "has to run this new Holy Roman Empire from the political side" (apparently not realising that, as Voltaire put it, the Early Modern political conglomeration that was the Holy Roman Empire was "neither holy, nor Roman, nor an empire"). The beast's master, of course, is "aspiring Marxist dictator" – to quote another US-based website – Javier Solana, the EU's High Representative for foreign and security policy. Elsewhere, Solana's "meteoric rise to power" is compared to that of the Antichrist, and his office is blamed for a massive hacking attack on a good, Christian (and anti-EU) blogger. Luckily "her firewalls held", and Solana was thwarted.

Behind this kind of frothy-mouthed rhetoric seems to lie a recognition that the EU is becoming a serious challenge to US unilateralism and power. EU support for absurd, unscientific notions like climate change or international law is interpreted as a cynical move to limit the US's freedom of action. And not just by the wacko fringe. An adviser to George W. Bush, Myron Ebell of the Competitive Enterprise Institute (funded by Esso to the tune of $1.5 million a year), claimed on BBC Radio 4's flagship *Today* programme that the concept of global warming was EU propaganda aimed at disrupting the US economy.

Confusingly, left-wing Eurosceptics, especially in France, protest that the EU is behind a *right*-wing conspiracy to impose free-market neo-liberalism on Europe. Meanwhile, former British Secretary of State for International Development, Clare Short, has accused the EU of being behind a massive conspiracy that keeps Africa impoverished, thanks to the generous agricultural subsidies that effectively close European markets to African farmers. Which seems pretty much spot on – though the Common Agricultural Policy isn't exactly a secret.

The European Parliament at Strasbourg

SOURCES

Books

T.R.Reid The United States Of Europe: The New Superpower And The End Of American Supremacy (2004). The former *Washington Post* Europe chief calls the EU a "waking giant" with more people, wealth, trade, leverage in international organizations and better-loved than the US. As the Euro

may yet undermine all America's military supremacy and end America's global dominance, Reid rings the warning bell of the threat the EU poses to the US, that Americans have been oblivious to for too long.

Websites

The official website for the European Union is ®**http://europa.eu.int/** and news of its development is followed at ®**www. euobserver.com**. But an unofficial, unsanitised investigation of the more sinister workings of the EU is at ®www. freemasonrywatch.org/eu.html

The Council on Foreign Relations

The Council on Foreign Relations describes itself on its website www.cfr.org as "an independent, national membership organization", where policy makers, government figures, leading thinkers, journalists and others can "better understand the world and the foreign policy choices facing the United States". From its offices in New York and Washington DC, the CFR disseminates books, articles and its journal, *Foreign Affairs*, and also runs programs to develop "the next generation of foreign policy leaders".

While the calibre and breadth of the CFR's 3605-strong membership is comparable with the World Economic Forum (see p.237) or the Bilderberg Group (see p.235) – and there's considerable crossover between the three – the CFR is exclusively American. The *Washington Post* has called it "the

nearest thing we have to a ruling establishment in the United States", which has "for fifty years managed our international affairs and our military-industrial complex". Around five hundred of the members are current or former US government officials, including all CIA directors, former Secretary of State Colin Powell, his successor Condoleezza Rice, Vice President Dick Cheney, former Secretary of Defense Richard Perle, former Assistant Secretary of Defense and new World Bank president Paul Wolfowitz, and Bill Clinton and practically everyone in his administration. Indeed, all US presidential candidates of the two main parties between 1948 and 1972 (with the exception of Barry Goldwater) were members, while all US members of the Bilderberg Group steering committee from 1955 to 1971 were CFR members as well.

The rest of the CFR membership is composed of bank chiefs, university deans, diplomats, newspaper and news network executives and operatives, captains and executives of civilian and military industries, and the like. Professor Carroll Quigley of Georgetown University, who Bill Clinton praised as his mentor in 1992, called the CFR a bastion of policy continuums in US government, irrespective of which party was in office. Its purpose, he wrote in 1966 in *Tragedy And Hope*, was that "the two parties should be almost identical, so that the American people can 'throw the rascals out' at any election without leading to any profound or extensive shifts in policy".

Officially, the CFR was founded in 1921 in Paris by several Americans who had taken part in the negotiations that produced the post-World War I Treaty of Versailles. However, the CFR was not a completely spontaneous concoction. Quigley called it an "international Anglophile network" set up as the US counterpart to the Royal Institute of International Affairs (the RIIA, with around 1,800 members and reporting in *The World Today* and *International Affairs*), a.k.a. Chatham House, the source of the "Chatham House Rule", whereby participants can freely use the information received but not reveal the identity nor affiliation of who said it or who was there.

Indeed, the RIIA says on its website www.riia.org that it was at Versailles that "the idea of an Anglo-American Institute of foreign affairs to study international problems with a view to preventing future wars" was conceived, with the RIIA set up in 1920 prior to its "sister institute". One theory is that some English Round Tablers, who were mostly of aristocratic stock, formed the Cliveden Set, who, led by Edward VIII, disgraced themselves by consorting with Hitler and advocating appeasement in the 1930s. Likewise, the CFR is said to have had senior government figures working with Nazis not only pre-1941 (as Ambassador Joe Kennedy and Prescot Bush advocated), but also immediately after the war, against the Communists (except, of course, for those members of the US government suspected of being Communist agents – see below). After a while it seems the CFR is guilty of something simply because it exists.

According to Robert Gaylon Ross's conspiracy manual *The Who's Who Of The Elite*, however – which identifies the Bilderberg Group, the Trilateral Commission and the CFR as the "three major secret organizations" in the global Elite, which he contends has David Rockefeller as first lord of the CFR and Czar of the Elite – the RIIA and the CFR weren't spontaneous set-ups so much as modernised versions of the nineteenth-century Round Table groups. These were under the umbrella of the International Secret Society, and all established by Imperial Britain's most successful venturer and diamond magnate, Cecil Rhodes. There were Round Tables in India, Canada, Australia and elsewhere in the English-speaking Empire to keep the gaggles of the imperially minded up to speed on how England sought to run the world, and their role in it. The Round Tables then morphed into those countries' Councils on Foreign Relations or Institutes of International Affairs.

Former US Navy admiral and former CFR member Chester Ward has lambasted the CFR as a gang of bankers in the pocket of those other bankers at the Bilderberg Group, all bent on global domination. Ignoring both the banking and the Anglophile angles, the right-wing US magazine *New American* (www.newamerican.com) has by contrast called it "a coterie of internationalists" – read Communists – and the "architects of the New World Order", who have been "working furtively for decades to undermine America's nationhood and constitutional order" under an endless procession of UN treaties and laws. *New American* also charges that every successive "loss" to Communism, from China, Korea, Cuba, and Vietnam to the failure of the 1956 uprising in Hungary and the sending of aid to Communist Poland and Romania, was engineered by CFR members in the US government. The list of alleged conspirators includes the Dulles brothers, John J. McCloy, Dean Rusk, Robert McNamara, Richard Nixon, Henry Kissinger, Zbigniew Brzezinski, Cyrus Vance, Warren Christopher, George Shultz and William J. Casey. By this reckoning, the CFR is the US sector of the "Internationalist Power Elite" responsible for tens of millions of deaths in World War II, Korea, Vietnam, the Gulf War, the War in Iraq and others, and also for the "Global Order" of the League of Nations, the Atlantic Charter, NATO, the UN, the IMF and the World Bank.

SOURCES

Books

Carroll Quigly Tragedy And Hope (1996). This is positively the Bible of proof for conspiracists of the thinking and plotting behind everything from the New World Order and the International Banking Conspiracy. Quite simply, Quigley's thesis is that the planet is governed by international laws and financial flows which are governed by a select, unelected, unaccountable few, but whether he is advocating this system or merely reflecting it is a matter of debate among theorists and detactors.

Robert Gaylon Ross, SR. Who's Who Of The Elite? (2002). Ross bookends a massive list of Bilderberg, Trilateral Commission and Council on Foreign Relations members (the "three major secret organizations") with discourses on their origins, ulterior purposes and position in the global Elite, which he contends has David Rockefeller as its Czar.

Websites

⊛**www.newamerican.com** An oasis of conspiracy theories about the CFR. The magazine evidently has little time or respect for the institution, but some interesting kernels of information float up in its foaming copy.

⊛**www.cfr.org** The council's own website, which has a list of sources on its views on the globe's hot spots and issues.

The Trilateral Commission

Another major cabal of colluding conspirators, according to conspiracy theorists, is the Trilateral Commission. The Commission was established in 1973, when international economic pressures such as the oil crisis were piling pressures on the US as the world's major capitalist superpower. As the Commission itself puts it on its website www.trilateral.org: "There was a sense that the United States was no longer in such a singular leadership position as it had been in earlier post-WWII years, and that a more shared form of leadership – including Europe, and Japan in particular – would be needed for the international system to navigate successfully the major challenges of the coming years."

Thus the Commission consists of the EU, North America and Japan (originally alone but now head of the Asian sector, which currently includes China, New Zealand, Indonesia and Malaysia) – the three main centres of industrialized, democratic power – and meets annually in the capital of a member nation. The European sector has expanded to include

Eastern European states such as Estonia, Poland and Slovenia.

The Trilateral Commission was conceived by David Rockefeller, the former chairman of the Council on Foreign Relations (CFR), who funded Polish geopolitical analyst Zbigniew Brzezinksi to establish and direct it from 1973 until 1976. The then-governor of Georgia, Jimmy Carter, was also in on the group's foundation: when he became president in 1976, he appointed Brzezinski as his national security affairs adviser, defence adviser and National Security Council chief. These events are repeatedly cited in such conspiracy books as Pat Robertson's *The New World Order* and James Perloff's *The Shadows Of Power* as proof of the power of the Trilateral Commission, as well as that of the "Elite" in building a New World Order – not that the Elite was able to stop Carter losing office in 1980 to non-Trilateralist and non-CFR member Ronald Reagan. It's also suggested that the Trilateral Commission is involved in some rivalry with the Council for Foreign Relations, so there can be dissenting, competing views in the quest for world dominance.

Senator Barry Goldwater, the defeated Republican presidential candidate in 1964, later dismissed the Trilateral Commission as "Rockefeller's newest international cabal". He charged that it helped Carter to win both the presidential nomination and the presidency by mobilizing "the money power of the Wall Street bankers, the intellectual influence of the academic community – which is subservient to the wealth of the great tax-free foundations – and the media controllers represented in the membership of the CFR and the Trilateral". The Commission has been further attacked by right-wingers as a coterie of bankers, stemming from the loans totalling $52 billion that were made to the developing world at the time of the oil crisis, which were allegedly spearheaded by David Rockefeller's Chase Manhattan Bank.

The Trilateral Commission certainly has a very strong economic orientation, and while its actual policy direction or constituted powers (if any) are not known, it does serve as an extraordinary networking institute. Its European chairman is Peter Sutherland, the chairman of BP plc and Goldman Sachs International, a director of the WEF and a former Director General of GATT/WTO. His impressive portfolio is paralleled by many other TC members, who include the great and the good (or not-so-good) from past and present US governments – George H. W. Bush, Dick Cheney, Bill Clinton, Paul Wolfowitz, Henry Kissinger, Alan Greenspan – plus (at some time) Ken Lay of Enron, and to maintain the presence of the original founder's family, Senator John D. Rockefeller IV.

Other members of the Commission include directors, CEOs and presidents past and present of US, European and East Asian companies such as Mobil Corp, Exxon, CNN, Time Warner, Chase Manhattan Bank, Citibank, Citigroup, Citicorp, N. M. Rothschild & Sons, J. P. Morgan Chase, the Carlyle Group, RAND Corp, Bechtel, Halliburton Co, Banca Sella, First National Bank of Chicago, German Council on Foreign Relations, Carnegie Endowment for International Peace, French Institute for International Relations, World Trade Organization, New York Times, Fuji Xerox, and Banco Itau SA of Brazil. The list grows longer all the time, and with it, inevitably, suspicions about its intentions, influence and power.

SOURCES

Books

Pat Robertson The New World Order (1991) and **James Perloff The Shadows of Power** (1988). Both tomes are of a similar ilk, lambasting the secret world of decisions taken behind closed doors in smoke-filled rooms.

Websites

ⓦ **www.trilateral.org** The commission's official (and not particularly detailed or revealing) homepage, that has publications, purpose and up-coming meeting fixtures, plus membership details if you're interested

Organized crime

The very notion of organized crime implies conspiracy and corruption. Drug trafficking, gambling, loan sharking, protection rackets, prostitution... These unsavoury practices feature in countless conspiracy theories, in large part due to the shadowy profiles of the men behind them (understandable as most of the activities they're engaged in are illegal).

The Mafia

"Mafia" – "hostility to the law" or "boldness" in Sicilian dialect, while "Mafioso" means "man of honour" – is now used as a general term for secret criminal organisations, but the word originally referred to the Italian and especially Sicilian family gangs that formed both there and in the US. (The term Cosa Nostra, or "this thing of ours", is also used.) It's been claimed that the first Mafia families came to prominence in medieval times as part of the resistance to Turkish, French and later Spanish rule, but by the late 19th century there were powerful Mafia groups across Italy, which developed organically in the US through Italian emigration, principally to New York and Chicago.

The Mafia became made men in the land of opportunity during Prohibition, profiting enormously from the illicit production, smuggling and distribution of booze, while having not a few shootouts with each other and the civic authorities (which ultimately led to the formation of the FBI). Post-Prohibition, this enabled many families to move into new ventures like gambling, loan sharking and eventually drug dealing and extended their purchasing power from bent policemen to politicians.

In World War II, the Allied invasion of Sicily and Italy in 1943 supposedly depended on the US Army working with big US-based Mafia groups still tied to their homeland. This was a good quid pro quo, as Fascist dictator Benito Mussolini had caused many Mafia men to flee to the US in the first place, so they returned backed by US Army firepower on the ultimate vendetta. Gangsters like Joseph "Joe Bananas" Bonanno and "Lucky" Luciano profited handsomely from the new power and honour this gave them, which carried over into the postwar battle against Communism.

The Mafia is also widely believed to have muscled in on American labour unions, particularly the Teamsters, led by Jimmy Hoffa, who mysteriously disappeared without trace in 1975. (He was officially declared dead in 1983, one theory being that his body was run through a Mob-controlled fat-rendering plant.) Postwar, the FBI and CIA may have fought the Mafia, but also employed a few of them as heavies in the war against Cuba (see p.20 and Northwoods p.329), and they've been linked to the deaths of Marilyn Monroe, Martin Luther King and both John F. and Robert Kennedy. In Italy, the Mafia has been blamed for the murders of many Italian judges and politicians, and investigations have reached into the upper echelons of Italy's government.

The Triads

With a similar worldwide reach are the Chinese Triads, secret criminal groups that have dominated the Chinese underworld for centuries. Based on sworn brotherhood and built on kinship, the Triads derive their name from the triangular shape – symbolising man, heaven and earth – of the Chinese character for "secret society" that they use as an emblem, although the name was first applied to them by the British colonial government in the Triad stronghold of Hong Kong.

Triads first emerged in the seventeenth century as underground political organizations fighting the Qing dynasty to restore their Ming predecessors. After the Qing fell, the Triads lost public support and financing along with their original reason for existing, but being men of violent means, they turned to earning their daily rice through extortion and other rackets.

The Communist victory in China's Civil War in 1949 made the Triads head for Hong Kong and to Macau and Chinatowns beyond. These days it's reckoned that there are up to 60 triad groups and 100,000 members, with major groups like the 14K Triad or Sun Yee On having several tens of thousands of members globally. Initiation ceremonies can involve drinking the blood of a beheaded cockerel before an incense-burning altar, and numbers are used to denote role and rank. Smaller groups use tricks like wearing right-handed white gloves for recognition (the imaginatively titled White-glove Gang).

Triads are now moving back into the Chinese mainland and profiting (in various legal and not-so-legal ways) from China's rapid economic growth, with key figures in place in financial institutions and government. As a result, sources of Triad income are changing from smuggling to legitimate business investments in southern China (although tactics like leaking key information are causing consternation for foreign multinationals based there). Indeed, the Communists seem to tolerate this, as in 1997, one Chinese official law officer acknowledged the Triads as true patriots.

One big issue is China's unwillingness to address issues of intellectual property, and much Triad income derives from trading fake CDs and DVDs. However, they also make money from drug smuggling, racketeering bus and taxi companies, and karaoke bars. They are also involved in the traffic of illegal immigrants to North American and Europe, through affiliated gangs referred to as "snakeheads".

Gangsters they may be, but Triads have a strict code of conduct, worshipping the Confucian qualities of humanity, wisdom, loyalty, righteousness and obedience embodied in the ancient Chinese hero Lord Guan (also a deity to the Hong Kong police). Apparently it's this code and the fact that disorderly society makes for bad business that has made the streets of Vladivostock so much safer in the twenty-first century, as Triads have moved in to take over the city's illicit businesses from the brashly violent Russian Mafia.

Indeed, it's reported that hundred of millions of dollars are passing through underground banks into the Russian Far East, not just into casinos, hotels and hostess bars, but also into logging and fishing enterprises. However, neither the Chinese nor the Russians stray much into drugs, dominated as it is by Tajiks, Kazakhs, Chechens smuggling heroin from Afghanistan and some North Korean government officials.

The Russian Mafia

The ethnic mix of groups operating across Russia belies the generalisation "Russian Mafia", which covers all the gangs and groups that sprang up in the vacuum after the USSR's collapse. With many ex-Soviet officers, soldiers and KGB officials finding themselves unemployed in the early 1990s, crime was the surest route to riches for some and a matter of basic survival for others, such as the sportsmen and martial arts experts who became their henchmen.

Across Russia and its ex-Soviet satellites in Central Asia and Eastern Europe, numerous networks of trafficking in drugs, prostitution and illegal workers have sprung up, reaching into the EU and North America.

Even the ethnic identity of many Russian Mafiosi has been obscured by numerous bogus (but successful) applications for Israeli passports, and billions of dollars have gone to Israel by that route. Arms also sell well, with stockpiles and ex-Soviet factories still producing dirt-cheap but efficient weaponry. It's been feared that the profusion of Soviet missile and nuclear warheads could end up being pawned off by dodgy Army units and their Mafia friends.

In Moscow at least, you can tell a Mafioso by the fact they tend to dress darkly and wear black flat caps, with minders in bomber jackets and "officers" in long, plush coats. Some seek to show off their status by, for example, having car horns that play the theme-tune to *The Godfather*. For ordinary Russians, though, it's no joke.

The Yakuza

A similar level of power infiltration was once enjoyed by Japan's Mafia, the Yakuza, the backbone of a weird nexus of ultra-right-wing military officers, gangsters and government officials that used espionage, terrorism and assassination to control Japan's colonial dominions in East Asia, while profiting from the opium trade, gambling and prostitution. Post World War II, the Yakuza moved into the black market to such an extent that they came to control major seaports and beat off efforts by the occupying Americans to close them down.

It was all a far cry from the loose community of pedlars and gamblers from whom the term Yakuza originated (Ya-Ku-Sa, or eight-nine-three, the value of the worst hand in a Japanese card game called Oicho-Kabu that's similar to Blackjack, suggesting the value of Yakuza to society and the seediness of their past). Roaming Samurai and Ronin warriors, employed as vigilante groups to protect villages, sometimes ganged up, but most were drifters who were pushed into cities by Japan's industrialisation, where they engaged in commercial ventures and moved in to red-light districts – if not directly investing, then "protecting" them.

These days the larger Yakuza groups also dabble in property speculation, banking and extorting stock from shareholders, and such is their quasi-legitimate presence that their offices have signs outside denoting their purpose. (The major Yakuza chapter in Kobe was instrumental – and far more effective than the civic authorities – in providing relief after the earthquake there.) In person, however, the easiest way to identifying Yakuza is through their lack of fingers, as it's a Yakuza penance to cut off your digits. Ironically, this has led to problems with imported cartoons such as *Postman Pat* and *The Simpsons*, whose three-fingered characters apparently convey gangster connotations to their infant audiences.

SOURCES

Books

John Dickie Cosa Nostra: A History Of The Sicilian Mafia (2004). Dickie maps the rise of the Sicilian Mafia from gangs on Palermo's streets to "tolerated" status under Italy's post-war governments and an unnerving role in the US as an economic and political enemy-ally to the government.

Websites

The likelihood of the major Mafia groups having their own official websites promoting their activities isn't great, as is borne out by a dearth of them online, so much of the information about them comes from the law enforcement agencies that (supposedly) are battling these various mobs. The FBI and Interpol websites are ® www.fbi.gov and ® www.interpol.int respectively.

A general interest website concerning all matters mob and mafia, historical and updated with news stories both big and small-fry, is at ® www.mobmagazine. com. The stories carried don't display their source (as in the original publicaion, not the name of the snitch).

Secret services

It's almost a surprise to read a conspiracy theory that doesn't involve the CIA somewhere, such is the tentacular reach on the imagination of that secretive organisation. But it's not the only agency to register on the conspiracy theorists' radar; when theorists twitch the curtains, they're also often looking for the agents of Russia, Britain and Israel.

The KGB

The KGB, or *Komitet Gosudarstvennoy Bezopasnosti* (Committee for State Security) was the USSR's secret service agency. The agency had been around since 1917 (when known as the Cheka), a secret police to liquidate so much as a dissenting thought against the Communist rulers, and carry out missions against enemies abroad. The KGB, based in the imposing Lubyanka office-cum-prison and torture chamber in Moscow, was divided into various directorates (foreign operations, internal political control, military counter-intelligence and so on) also provided bodyguards and patrolled the USSR's borders.

The KGB successfully bloodied its American and British counterparts' noses many times. Two apparent KGB spies were Americans Ethel and Julius Rosenberg, executed for giving the Soviets atom bomb secrets enabling the Soviets to build their own nukes. Then there was the 1960s "Cambridge spy ring" in the British Secret Intelligence Service, which included the head of MI6's Counter-Espionage unit, Kim Philby. He saved more than a few Soviet agents while allowing scores of British to be caught and killed. Another was George Blake, captured by the Chinese during the Korean War to become a

"Manchurian Candidate" on his return to the UK, informing the KGB of tunnel operations for defectors in Vienna and Berlin. Caught, the British hadn't the chance to try him – Blake was busted from jail and escaped to Moscow.

In the end, however, the KGB got too big for its boots. In August 1991, KGB chief Colonel Vladimir Kryuchkov helped orchestrate the hardline Communist coup attempt against Mikhail Gorbachev. The coup failed, Kryuchkov was arrested and the KGB shortly disbanded and replaced by the *Federalnaya Sluzhba Bezopasnosti* (FSB), though there is precious little difference in practice between the two organizations, and the ignominy of the betrayal didn't stop former KGB chief Vladimir Putin from becoming president of Russia later on. Only in Belorussia under the Stalinist dictator Lukashenko is the secret service still called the KGB, but to the locals it's the "association of crude bandits".

The idea that AIDS was a US military concoction was in part put about by the KGB, and the man who shot Pope John Paul II in 1981 was supposedly on the KGB payroll. It's also been suspected, but officially discounted, that Lee Harvey Oswald was a KGB agent. But the *Komitet* was capable of its own conspiracy theories, however. *The Sword And The Shield: The Secret History Of The KGB,* by Christopher Andrew and Vasili Mitrokhin, describes how Soviet leaders and KGB chiefs, having never lived in the West, could never really understand it, or how America's levels of economic production and innovation were achieved with so little apparent regulation. Defector Arkadi Shevchenko noted: "Many are inclined to the fantastic notion that there must be a secret control center somewhere in the United States. They themselves, after all, are used to a system ruled by a small group working in secrecy in one place."

SIS-MI6

The Secret Intelligence Service (SIS), *aka* MI6 or Military Intelligence [section] 6 since WWII, or Her Majesty's Secret Service, is the UK's external secret service agency, founded in 1909. The SIS coat of arms, with the motto *semper occultus* ("always secret"), shows a grey brain contained within a green "C", a letter that stands for the SIS's founder Sir Mansfield Cumming. Every SIS director since has been referred to by the first letter of their surname (like "M" in the Bond books – Bond himself is an MI6 man). Indeed, the SIS's real-life HQ in Vauxhall, London, a yellow and green pile of blocks known as "Legoland" to those who work there, featured in the Bond film *The World Is Not Enough*.

In the 1920s SIS agents were billeted to embassies as "Passport Control Officers" – not the most convincing of covers, and it wasn't too long before they were rumbled. A notable early SIS venture was backing the Russian-born "ace of spies" Sidney Reilly and ex-terrorist Boris Savinkov in their bid to bring down the Soviet government, but both Reilly and Savinkov were caught and executed in 1925. Later "successes" attributed to covert SIS action include the overthrow of the elected Iranian leader Mohammed Mossadeq in 1953 (in a joint venture with the CIA) and Patrice Lumumba in the Congo in 1961; triggering paramilitary conflict in the Lebanon in the 1980s and providing duff intelligence to justify the Iraq War in 2002. But the SIS doesn't figure much in conspiracy theories, bar an attributed role in a plot to kill Princess Di.

Mossad

Maybe it's because the SIS doesn't have the fearsome reputation of Israel's spy unit, "The Institute for Intelligence and Special Operations" (its English title), or Mossad (Hebrew for "institute") to most people. "Where no counsel is, the people fall, but in the multitude of counsellors there is safety" (Proverbs XI/14) is the organization's motto, and Mossad's "counsellors" engage in everything from diplomacy and intelligence analysis to covert action and counter-terrorism. It also works to bring Jews to Israel from countries where official agencies to facilitate Jewish migration aren't allowed, notably Syria, Iran and Ethiopia.

The institute was created amid the chaos of the Palestine Mandate as the *Shai* or information service, and given official sanction in 1949 by Prime Minister Ben Gurion. With its base in Tel Aviv and some 2000 staff, Mossad is part of the Prime Minister's office and reports directly to him.

Mossad successfully located and kidnapped top Nazi Adolf Eichmann from South America, bringing him back for trial. Mossad also found and killed all those responsible for the Munich massacre of Israeli athletes at the 1972 Olympic Games. Mossad kidnapped the Israeli nuclear scientist Mordechai Vanunu from Italy (Vanunu had let on that Israel had nuclear bombs) and set up Iraq's Osiraq nuclear reactor for air strikes in 1981. Mossad agents with fake Canadian passports were caught in Jordan in 1997 trying to poison a Hamas leader, and a number of assassinations of Palestinian nationalists can no doubt be laid at their door.

Conspiracy theorists have also put Mossad behind the assassination of John F. Kennedy, apparently over his opposition to Israel developing nuclear weapons. Mossad has even been blamed for the 9/11 attacks by anti-Semitic conspiracy theorists, who claim that many thousands of Jewish workers at the World Trade Center were absent on the fateful day. Czech-born British newspaper tycoon Robert Maxwell was supposed to be a KGB agent, rescued by Communists from the Nazis, but also a Mossad agent, and when Mossad found out about his KGB connection, Israeli frogmen are said to have assassinated Maxwell on his yacht. Apparently, it was also Mossad that did it for British Cabinet minister David Mellor after he made a pro-Palestinian statement in

1988. Mossad tapped Mellor's phone and rumbled his extra-marital affair; when the press learnt of Mellor's philandering antics, he resigned.

SOURCES

Books

Christopher Andrew, Oleg Gordievsky KGB: The Inside Story of Its Foreign Operations from Lenin to Gorbachev (1992). Coming out just as the Cold War ended, this tome, co-written by an ex-KGB colonel, uncovers quite how successful – or not – the Soviet's shadowy spies were at recruiting foreign traitors, setting up coups and "liquidating" opponents. Somewhat academic in tone, it's worth a read.

Christopher Andrew, Vasill Mitrokhin, Vasili Mitrokhin The Sword and the Shield: The Mitrokhin Archive (2000). Andrew returns to his subject with KGB defector Mitrokhin and unveils more covert ops from those pesky Russkies to discredit every American in the public eye, from Martin Luther King to Ronald Reagan, while leaving deepcover sleeper agents strewn across the West, along with boobytrapped caches of arms and little side-shows such as trying to link Lee Harvey Oswald to the CIA.

Stephen Dorril MI6: Inside the World of Her Majesty's Secret Intelligence Service (2002). A book the UK government apparently sought to suppress, Dorril portraits a blundering British spy organisation that can't quite put together plots to kill or bring down Libya's Colonel Qaddafi, Albania's Enver Hoxha or Serbia's Slobodan Milosevic, but can employ Nelson Mandela to tell all on Libya's funding for the IRA.

Websites

The KGB expired before the Internet got to Russia, but by then the KGB had become the FSB, so Cyrillic-script readers can find it at ⊛**www.fsb.ru.**

⊛**www.bbc.co.uk/crime/fighters/mi6.shtml** has a good brief on the service, from the UK's state broadcaster.

Mossad's homepage is at ⊛**www.mossad. gov.il/**

MI6 lacks a homepage although ⊛**www.five. org.uk/security/mi6org/** also has some interesting – but not entirely reverent detail. All have interesting write-ups on their past and present espionage capers at the Federation of American Scientists' Intelligence Resource Program, ⊛**www.fas.org**

Miracles, secrets and lies: conspiracies of religion

The great conspiracy: patriarchy and the Great Goddess
Jesus the myth
The suppressed Apostle: Mary Magdalene as feminine divine

Miracles, secrets and lies: conspiracies of religion

Easily the oldest conspiracy in this book, pre-dating the assassination of Tutankhamun (see p.4) by thousands of years, is the suppression of *matriarchal religion*. Not until the last fifty years have women, in the shape of female archeologists, finally started to fight back, but things still haven't changed much. Men – or at least male academics – appear to have closed ranks to deny that the so-called *Great Goddess* ever existed. Archeological infighting was also a key feature of the *Dead Sea Scrolls* controversy. Some claimed that these ancient Jewish texts, discovered near Jerusalem in the 1940s, could seriously undermine Christianity. Unfortunately, the Vatican was busy burying the evidence as fast as it could be dug up.

And that wouldn't be the first time: the early church supposedly conspired to suppress the alternative, "gnostic" accounts of Jesus's crucifixion, some of which maintained that Jesus had never died at all, or that he was only a man, and not a god. Gnostic theories were revived by the medieval Cathars – who were exterminated by the established church. Modern theologians, meanwhile, attempted to prove that "Jesus" was nothing more than a water-walking collection of myths.

Parallel to the Jesus story is the conspiracy theory that early Christians covered up the truth about Mary Magdalene, who's said to have been Jesus's true apostle, or his wife, or even his divine consort in a male–female holy union. That at least was the tale *trumpeted* by Dan Brown's super-selling thriller *The Da Vinci Code*, which resurrected some ancient conspiracy theories, while finding time to publicize some new ones too. The book did little for the repu-

tation of Opus Dei, a severe and some would say secretive Catholic group, but at least it took the heat off the Jesuits, the long-term historical also-rans to the Masons in the conspiracy stakes.

The medieval Cathars are also a long term favourite of the conspiracist's imagination deemed to have been the guardians of an unmentionable secret, whilst Pope Benedict XVI is the focus of a lot of current highly questionable speculation.

The great conspiracy: patriarchy and the Great Goddess

The idea that patriarchy has suppressed the fact that women once ruled the world while goddesses ruled the roost in the heavens is the original mega-conspiracy. The main argument, put forward by some controversial archeologists, is that European Paleolithic and Neolithic culture, dating from around 25,000 BC until 2500 BC, was at root matriarchal, and the chief objects of worship were fertility goddesses, or even some original Great Goddess. This theory, of course, runs directly counter to Judaeo-Christian mythology, and the debate is hot: the "Goddess" thesis encompasses not just a millennia-long conspiracy to oppress

women and suppress the worship of the feminine, but a live, ongoing academic conspiracy to conceal the alleged discovery of that original, patriarchal conspiracy.

Early Amazons

From around the seventeenth century, evidence began to filter back from travellers that the patriarchal social structure of Europe might not be the only possible form human society can take. The first to put forward a theory of an early, female-dominated culture was a Swiss philologist, Johann Jakob

Bachofen, who in 1861 published the catchily titled *Mutterrecht*, or *Mother Right: An Investigation Of The Religious And Juridical Character Of Matriarchy In The Ancient World*. Bachofen speculated that at some point in the distant past, women revolted against an earlier epoch of sexual subjugation and established matriarchy through the institution of marriage, and that in turn, this "Amazonian" world had evolved into the patriarchal society of his day.

The earliest apparent evidence of matriarchal societies emerged during the first half of the twentieth century, when archeologists dug up endless apparently ritual figurines of women at megalithic sites across Europe, and indeed all over the world. Paleolithic and Neolithic statuettes were found with emphasized feminine characteristics such as breasts, buttocks and vulvas, or pregnant bellies. Some were apparently sitting on what may be altars or thrones, or with animal heads – often seen as indicating the portrayal of a deity. Others were surrounded by eggs and animals, which are fertility symbols, or depicted actually giving birth.

Gods and goddesses

From the 1950s onwards, religious historians and anthropologists began to provide corroboration in the form of myths of men overthrowing female power, which are particularly common among so-called "primitive" peoples in Australia, Melanesia, Africa and the Amazon basin. And there are parallels within Indo-European culture: the Minoans, Etruscans and early Greeks, for example, all seem to have had elements of goddess or nature worship in their ideology, while legends of male priests taking control of the female Oracle were attached to the great shrine of Apollo. Some have tried to demonstrate through the analysis of parallel symbolism that the powerful goddess figures worshipped across the Mediterranean region – Isis, Artemis, Astarte – all refer back to one Great Goddess or god-mother.

Similarly, in Hinduism, the many goddesses are supposed to refer back to one original Devi, sometimes called "Ekakini, the Only. And the cultures of many "tribal" peoples of India contain elements of matriarchal society and goddess worship, albeit variously intermixed and overlaid with patriarchal beliefs, allegedly of later, "Aryan" origin. Some historians of Judaism claim that in the distant past, the early Israelites worshipped a goddess called Asherah. The Jewish scholar Raphael Patai even maintained that her statue stood in the Temple for hundreds of years, before being driven out by the god who was once her consort, and later became the monotheistic, jealous god of the Hebrews. In Arabia, the triumph of Islam is sometimes described as a victory over a triad of goddesses: as Mohammed said in one of the *hadith* sayings, before the revelation of the Qu'ran the Arabs worshipped only women. And Christianity may have its own alternative tradition (see p.164).

Even more controversial is "evidence" drawn from modern anthropology. Many contemporary hunter-gatherer societies, it has been found, have relatively emancipated gender relations – a fact which runs counter to the popular intuition of man the hunter as man the master. Perhaps, then, it was when people settled down into an agrarian society that men started lording it over women. Unfortunately, this notion is bound up with a suspect, maybe racist assumption that modern hunter-gatherer societies are somehow more "primitive" and closer in culture to earlier humans.

Pornographic statuettes

Opponents of the Goddess theory have come up with endless alternative explanations for all those Neolithic and Paleolithic statuettes. They could be pornography, toys, sex-education aids, dolls or even, as art historian LeRoy McDermott maintains (claiming the anatomical distortions aren't so much

Mother-godess figurine, Venus of Willendorf, c.28,000–25,000 BC

Some archeologists think that there are just as many male, gender-neutral or animal figures anyway. Why postulate a Great Goddess, they ask, when there could be any number of other kinds of deities? Others point out that even if the figurines are overwhelmingly, buxomly female, this could point to the existence of a widespread fertility ritual, and that the leap to Europe-wide goddess-worship is a leap of faith not of reason. A kind of reverse sexism, perhaps. As for drawing on later Indo-European myths to find out the myths that went before, they say, that's just sloppy methodology – pursuing a feminist agenda by comparing like with unlike.

Feminists and archeologists

The eminent archeologist Jacquetta Hawkes described how, before World War II, she was advised to keep quiet about her discoveries of material that seemed to suggest female-led societies. No one, she was told, would take her seriously. Eventually, in 1945, she published *Early Britain*, which speculated about generalized worship of a European "Great Goddess" in the megalithic era.

But the totemic figure who really developed the Goddess theory was Marija Gimbutas, Professor of Archeology at UCLA for a quarter of a century. She developed the leading hypothesis about the origins of Indo-European people and practically invented a new discipline (never a good idea in academic circles), which she called archeomythology. In 1974, her book *Goddesses And Gods Of Old Europe* – her publisher changed the title of the first edition to *Gods And Goddesses Of Old Europe* – set out her stall for a wider public. According to Gimbutas, peaceful, "matristic" Paleolithic and Neolithic Europe was suddenly invaded by the warlike, patriarchal Indo-Europeans. Europe inherited most of its religious ideas from the invaders, but key elements of Goddess worship survived underground and in folk tales, leaving only hundreds of thousands of femi-

about ritual fertility as familiar female fears about fat bums and heavy thighs), self-portraits. And the more theories emerge, the more confident mainstream archeologists become that it's all just speculative interpretation and that no one can actually *know* what these figurines were used for.

nine figurines as evidence of Old Europe's once-dominant belief-system.

Curiously, Gimbutas's theories only became truly controversial *after* the feminist movement got going. "Some people", she claimed, "are automatically not accepting" her ideas now. In fact, the debate over her work is so politicized and heated that some archeologists claim they can't even discuss it without being sidelined, as if there were a conspiracy to undermine her work. But while it is true that some male archeologists advancing similarly bold, speculative theories have been treated rather differently – with admiration or at least indulgence – many archeologists frown on *all* interpretations or speculations about religious and social beliefs, whether they concern goddesses or not.

And feminists, too, have been known to gang up on the Goddess theory. Religious scholar Cynthia Eller thinks it is an "ennobling lie" that ultimately shoots feminism in the foot because it buys into the oppressive idea of societies naturally evolving towards an "advanced" patriarchal society. Or as feminist historian Gerda Lerner put it: "The creation of compensatory myths of the distant past of women will not emancipate women in the present and the future."

SOURCES

Books

Cynthia Eller The Myth Of Matriarchal Prehistory: Why An Invented Past Won't Give Women A Future (2000). A feminist attempts to demolish the Goddess theory, with some success, and a lot of publicity.

Marija Gimbutas The Goddesses And Gods Of Old Europe, 6500–3500 BC (1974). The original and classic – overreaching but fascinating nevertheless. The Language Of The Goddess (1989) focuses on the actual figurines, with beautiful photographs.

Merlin Stone When God Was A Woman (1976). The improbably named Stone argues that a patriarchal conspiracy has perverted Goddess worship from its real origins in the devotion to wisdom and fertility.

Websitses

ⓦ www.belili.org/index.html Another good site dedicated to Gimbutas, set up by Starhawk, the eco-activist and reviver of Wicca, or Goddess worship.

ⓦ www.levity.com/mavericks/gim-int.htm Site devoted to Marija Gimbutas, with a fascinating interview.

ⓦ www.suppressedhistories.net/articles/eller.html Sustained and well-argued defence of the Goddess theory against Cynthia Eller's published attack.

Dead Sea cover-up

The story of the discovery of the Dead Sea Scrolls reads like a Hollywood yarn, featuring an elusive Jewish sect, lost treasure and the Arab-Israeli war. A vicious academic spat, complete with accusations of texts going missing and evidence being suppressed, ensured that the affair was widely publicized, but what really seized the public imagination was the idea that locked away in the scrolls was a lost truth about Jesus.

Bedouins, Dominicans and lost scrolls

In early 1947 – or possibly late 1946, no one is quite sure – a Bedouin shepherd of the Tacâmireh tribe, Mohammed "the Wolf", was searching for a lost goat in crags near the shore of the Dead Sea, in what is now the occupied West Bank. Throwing a stone into one of the many small caves in the area, he was surprised to hear the sound of breaking pottery. By chance, he'd hit a jar containing an ancient scroll. It was the first of many. Through various intermediaries in nearby Jerusalem – including the antiquities dealer known only as Kando, and the more extravagantly named Mar Athanasius Yeshua Samuel, the Archimandrite of the Syrian Orthodox monastery of St Mark – Mohammed and his friends managed to sell a handful of scrolls and fragments.

News of the discoveries in the desert slowly leaked out over the next year, and by the spring of 1948 academics had seen enough scroll fragments to date them tentatively to around the first century BCE. Unfortunately, the eruption of the Arab-Israeli war in May of that year ruled out the possibility of a proper archeological survey of the Qumran cave site. Meanwhile the Bedouin kept searching. By the early 1950s, the situation was calmer, and a series of expeditions and digs led by Roland de Vaux, a Dominican Biblical scholar based in Jerusalem, uncovered a total of eleven caves containing every known book of the Hebrew Bible, as well as the related works sometimes called the Apocrypha and Pseudepigrapha. At last, scholars had a chance to compare the text of the Bible as it has survived today with early – and perhaps less corrupt – versions.

There were also a number of hitherto unknown texts, which suggested that the Qumran site belonged to a sect with ideas and scriptures of its own. A document containing laws regulating the life of the Qumran community was named the "Community Rule". An apocalyptic text was dubbed the "War Scroll", while a text describing an ideal temple city became known as the "Temple Scroll". Most famous of all was the "Copper Scroll", whose metal construction long resisted attempts to open

MISCELLANEOUS FOR SALE

By 1954, the Archimandrite Mar Athanasius Yeshua Samuel clearly hadn't managed to shift all the scrolls he'd bought from his Bedouin contacts, because on June 1 he placed an advertisement in the *Wall Street Journal*, under the category Miscellaneous For Sale. "THE FOUR DEAD SEA SCROLLS", it read. "Biblical Manuscripts dating back to at least 200 BC are for sale. This would be an ideal gift to an educational or religious institution by an individual or group. Box F206."

Fragment from a Dead Sea scroll

and read it. (It turned out to be a treasure map – though no one has yet successfully deciphered it, and many think it describes a fictional treasure.)

Academic rivalry or Vatican censorship?

While all the finds from Mohammed the Wolf's "Cave 1" had been released by 1956, material found in other caves took a surprisingly long time to see the light of day. Roland de Vaux had set up a team of eight scholars to study, edit and publish the forty thousand scroll fragments from the richest trove, Cave 4. Outsiders were jealously kept in the dark under a so-called "secrecy rule". Some claimed this

was for political reasons – de Vaux and some others on the team had refused to co-operate with Israeli scholars in the highly charged atmosphere of the time. Others argued that it was all about academic rivalry, with every team member anxious to announce their own career-gilding discovery.

Others smelled a more troubling conspiracy. The French academic André Dupont-Sommer had pointed out a number of parallels between Jesus and a figure called the Teacher of Righteousness in the texts, and in a BBC broadcast of 1956 maverick team-member John Allegro went further still, claiming that the Qumran sect worshipped a crucified Messiah. He went on to accuse de Vaux, among others, of suppressing texts that contained evidence of similarities between the Qumran sect and Christianity. (In later life, Allegro really went for the jugular, claiming that Christianity had originated as a hallucinogenic mushroom cult.)

Pauline propaganda?

For Professor Robert Eisenman – one of the key figures in freeing the Scrolls from the clutches of the original team and releasing them into the public sphere – the community that produced the Scrolls didn't just pre-echo Christianity, it *was* a Christian group. Eisenman identified the "Teacher of Righteousness" as James the Just, the brother of Jesus and the original founder of the Christian tradition. He saw the "Man of the Lie" described in the Scrolls as Paul, who in the eyes of the Qumran community, was a Roman agent conspiring to obscure and discredit the claims of James and his co-religionists. Given Paul's crucial role in disseminating the Word, this opened up the possibility that Jesus's "original message" had been lost, concealed – or even perverted.

In a grand-scale conspiracy finale, the hokey religion journalists Michael Baigent and Richard Leigh worked up Allegro's complaints and Eisenman's theories into their best-selling *The Dead Sea Scrolls Deception: Why A Handful Of Religious Scholars Conspired To Suppress The Revolutionary Contents Of The Dead Sea Scrolls*. According to them, de Vaux was a tool of the Vatican, bent on destroying texts that revealed the truth about Paul, and therefore the truth about Jesus.

Anti-Semitism at work?

While the presence of Protestants among the scholars originally chosen by de Vaux makes the Baigent and Leigh theory of a Vatican conspiracy look more than a little shaky, it is odd that the team chosen to analyze the most important collection of Hebrew Biblical texts ever discovered did not contain a single Jewish member. It's hard to imagine the outcry that would have ensued if the Gnostic gospels discovered in Egypt in 1945 (see p.164) had been examined only by Muslim scholars. Let alone if one of such a team had described Christianity as a "horrible religion", which is what Dead Sea Scroll scholar John Strugnell called Judaism in a 1990 interview for the Israeli newspaper *HaAretz*...

Digging – and covering up

The furore wasn't limited to the scrolls alone. Archeologists debated the nature of the "monastic" ruins adjacent to the cave sites with equal fervour, with a few mavericks challenging the majority view that it was the home of the Qumran community

that had written the Scrolls. Some Israeli scholars accused de Vaux of suppressing finds such as jewels and cosmetics, which if they existed would have undermined the consensus theory that Qumran was the home of the Essenes. It seems that this strict and ascetic Jewish group, which may have been related to the followers of John the Baptist, wouldn't have had much truck with self-beautification.

In 1995, Professor Norman Golb of the University of Chicago even alleged that de Vaux and other scholars had "buried" archeological evidence confirming Golb's own theory that the Dead Sea Scrolls were *not* a treasured collection of coherent sacred texts but instead a miscellaneous collection drawn from the library of the Jerusalem Temple. If Golb was right, the dramatic conclusions some scholars and commentators had drawn about the "nature of Judaism/early Christianity" wouldn't amount to a hill of beans.

Publish and be damned

The Dead Sea Scrolls were finally published in 1991. Admittedly, when the Huntington Library in California released a complete set of photographs, this was against the wishes of the official team, but nevertheless, an official microfiche edition soon followed, in 1993. Unless you believe the unsubstantiated – and unverifiable – theories that key scrolls have been destroyed or buried in the Vatican library or, like a very few bloody-minded scholars, you can conjure entire gospel texts out of a few fragmentary Greek letters on scraps of untested scroll, the fact of official publication pretty much lays the old conspiracy theories to rest.

But the most tenacious of anti-Vatican theorists like to try one last argument in favour of the suppression theory. Even if the Scrolls predate Christ, they say, they still reveal some worryingly familiar facts about the Qumran community. They believed that the end of the world was approaching, that private property was iniquitous, that ritual meals should involve the blessing of food and wine, and that enemies should be loved. This, the theorists claim, was the uncomfortable truth that de Vaux and his Vatican backers wanted to suppress: Christianity wasn't all that original. Except that Christian scholars knew that already. And, for Christians, similarities with earlier Jewish practices are positive *proof* of Christianity's fulfilment of history in the New Covenant. Divine history, they say, works that way.

Carbon-14 controversy

As for those who believe that the Qumranites were actually Christians, Carbon-14 dating on the linen coverings of fourteen scrolls has now shown that they were all made in the last two centuries BCE, a dating that agrees with the earlier paleographic and archeological evidence. Of course, some people maintain that the tests were faked, or that the scrolls must have been supernaturally buried at Qumran outside normal timeframes – presumably by the same whimsical power that hid fossils in rocks at the Creation.

Media attention built on conspiracy theories has all but died away, allowing the real importance of the scrolls to be publicized. They are still, by about a thousand years, the oldest Hebrew writings to have been discovered. They reveal the diversity of Jewish thought around the time of Jesus. They prove that many Biblical texts originally came in different versions, and that variations in the earliest Bible translations may reflect differing originals rather than mistranslations. They show that Greek thought had influenced Jewish religion long before anyone realized. And they demonstrate that texts are wide open to interpretation, and that it's almost impossible to impose an official view.

SOURCES

Books

John Marco Allegro **The Dead Sea Scrolls And The Christian Myth** (1979). Allegro plays up the Essenes and pagan myth, and plays down the originality of the Jesus story and the historicity of Jesus' life. And he includes the chapter title "Will the real Jesus Christ please stand up?"

Michael Baigent and Richard Leigh **The Dead Sea Scrolls Deception** (1991). The original conspiracist version of the history of the Scrolls.

Robert Eisenman **James The Brother Of Jesus: The Key To Unlocking The Secrets Of Early Christianity And The Dead Sea Scrolls** (1992). Almost a thousand pages of serious early Christian history, but essential conspiracist reading. Up James; down Paul.

Robert Eisenman and Michael Wise **The Dead Sea Scrolls Uncovered: The First Complete Translation And Interpretation Of 50 Key Documents Withheld For Over 35 Years** (1992). The best-selling translation, plus controversial editorial commentary.

Barbara Thiering, **Jesus & the Riddle Of The Dead Sea Scrolls: Unlocking The Secrets Of His Life Story** (1992). A contentious version of the events, which makes the Qumranites Christians, dates the Scrolls in New Testament times, and employs an esoteric "*pesher*" method of reading to uncover a radically different version of Christianity.

Geza Vermes **The Dead Sea Scrolls In English** (1987). Exactly what it says it is.

Websites

ⓦ **www.ibiblio.org/expo/deadsea.scrolls. exhibit/intro.html** The website of the Library of Congress exhibition, showing photographs of a few key scrolls along with accompanying translations.

ⓦ **www.historian.net/4Q285.html** Photograph of the controversial "Slain Messiah" fragment, with a suggested translation.

THE JESUITS

The Jesuits were not originally supposed to be "the shock troops of the Counter-Reformation". When St Ignatius Loyola began to gather followers in Paris in the 1530s, it was with the idea of imitating the life of Jesus. Then came Pope Paul III, who helped transform Loyola's idealists into the missionary, militant "Societas Jesu", or Society of Jesus. At first, the Jesuits were sent to win converts across the world, but they were soon operating secretly in Protestant countries.

The earliest conspiracy theories about Jesuits stem from their zealous efforts at conversion and the fact that, uniquely, they came under the direct control of the Pope. They were accused of hair-splitting, morally evasive logic, and Machiavellian plotting. It was said that they followed the motto "the end justifies the means", and they were thought to have a finger in every political pie – they even acquired the role of private confessors to Europe's kings. It quickly became as common to "blame the Jesuits" as the Jews. (In England, of course, the Jesuits really were conspiring against the Protestant monarchy.) The Society's reputation in France was damaged by the vicious, early seventeenth-century theo-logical spat between Jesuits and Jansenists, which was fuelled by wild allegations – at one point, the Jesuits accused the Jansenists of meeting secretly in a monastery at Bourg-Fontaine to discuss a conspiracy to overthrow nothing less than Christianity itself, and to establish Deism in its place.

Over in the New World, the Jesuits were more the victims of a conspiracy than the instigators. They had set up missions among native Americans in the colonial possessions of Spain, Portugal, France and England, and for 150 years, from 1609, administered the huge Republic of Paraguay, where Guarani Indians lived free of slavery. Their work threatened Spanish and Portuguese commercial interests, and from the mid-eighteenth century they were gradually expelled from countries across the New and Old Worlds – thrown out of Portugal in 1759, Louisiana in 1763, France in 1766 and Spain in 1767. In 1773 the order was officially suppressed by Pope Clement XIV, under heavy pressure from half the monarchs of Europe. As the French Revolution ignited, the Jesuits were suspected of fanning the flames in revenge – and they remain prime candidates for conspiracy theorists' accusations.

Either them or the Jews. Or the Masons.

When the Society was finally restored in 1814, under Pope Pius V, the European nations hadn't lost any of their suspicions. French novelist Eugène Sue's *The Wandering Jew*, published in 1844, recycled old anti-Masonic and anti-Semitic myths, but substituted a mysterious, conspiratorial Jesuit under the command of a "Black Pope" as the villain. In the US, the anti-Masonic hysteria of the 1820s and 1830s swept up the Jesuits along with it, with Protestant preachers seemingly convinced that American doors were big enough for Jesuit as well as Masonic bogeymen to hide behind. Later in the century, Jesuit machinations were once again seen everywhere in France, and the order was variously accused of being behind the Franco-Prussian war of 1870–71, the Dreyfus affair and a number of assassinations.

The most famous element of anti-Jesuit conspiracy theories is alive and well in the twenty-first century: the so-called "Jesuit Oath" or "Oath of the Knights of Columbus" can be found reprinted all over the Internet, often with portentous references to its appearance in the Congressional Record. It's red-hot stuff: "I do … promise and declare that I will, when opportunity presents, make and wage relentless war, secretly and openly, against all heretics, Protestants and Masons … that I will spare neither age, sex nor condition, and that I will hang, burn, waste, boil, flay, strangle, and bury alive these infamous heretics; rip up the stomachs and wombs of their women, and crush their infants' heads against the walls in order to annihilate their execrable race. That when the same cannot be done openly I will secretly use the poisonous cup, the strangulation cord, the steel of the poniard, or the leaden bullet."

Like any good regional news item, the website of the gravel-voiced, ultra-Protestant Northern Irish politician, Ian Paisley (www.ianpaisley.org), adds some locally specific information at the end: "That if two Catholics are on the ticket I will satisfy myself which is the better supporter of Mother Church and vote accordingly. That I will not deal with or employ a Protestant if in my power to deal with or employ a Catholic … That I will provide myself with arms and ammunition that I may be in readiness when the word is passed." Luckily for Paisley – and all the other Protestants (and Masons) at risk of being hanged, burned, wasted and boiled – the Jesuit Oath was in fact a seventeenth-century forgery aimed at thwarting the accession of the Catholic monarch James II. The author was one Robert Ware, a "literary skunk", as the nineteenth-century writer and Catholic convert Father Thomas Edward Bridgett dubbed him in *Blunders And Forgeries*.

As for the Oath's appearance in the Congressional Record, it turns out to be a document submitted as evidence for a quarrel between two Congressional candidates in Pennsylvania in 1912, Democrat Eugene C. Bonniwell and Republican Thomas S. Butler. Bonniwell lost the election, then protested that Butler should be disqualified as he'd (illegally) campaigned against Bonniwell's Catholicism, using the Oath as a supporting document. Both men accepted that the Oath wasn't authentic, but there it remains, forever in the Congressional Record. These days, allegations that politicians belong to conspiratorial Catholic organizations seem to have shifted their focus away from the Jesuits towards a relative newcomer, Opus Dei (see p.171).

Pope Paul III accepting the Jesuit Order into the church

Jesus the myth

At the core of Christianity lies belief in a miracle: Jesus was crucified and, three days later, rose from the dead. Christians see this miracle as proof that Jesus was the Son of God. Sceptics, of course, think it proves the opposite – people just don't come back to life, and thus there was no resurrection. If, then, they can undermine the bedrock of the resurrection, they should be on their way towards bringing the whole church crashing down. As a result, the story of the Passion has attracted as many conspiracy theories as any event – or non-event – in history. It's the original JFK, the dark wood where anyone with an axe to grind soon finds themselves thrashing about wildly among the trees.

The hero of a thousand faces

The simplest theory states that Jesus never existed – or at least existed only as a man, and not as the Son of God – and that the early church concocted the whole story out of earlier myths. Variations hold that, divine or not, Jesus was never actually crucified, or never came back from the dead. Most shocking of all is the theory that the resurrection was an elaborate fake by a group of cunning conspirators.

Many scholars and researchers have pointed out that much of Jesus's story is surprisingly reminiscent of earlier "pagan" myths. (For Christian apologists, of course, this just shows how Christ fulfils the divine plan and, not incidentally, supersedes all other wisdom figures.) In his quixotic search for what he called the "Monomyth", mythologist Joseph Campbell came up with the idea that behind the major myth systems of the wider Mediterranean

region was a figure he dubbed "The Hero of a Thousand Faces". Ever since, sceptical researchers have trawled through what we know of early, non-Christian religions, cults and myth groups in search of material that might undermine Christianity's claims to uniqueness. Prime candidates for proto-Jesus status are Mithras, the hero-god of Roman soldiery; the Egyptian gods Osiris and Horus; the Greeks' Dionysus and Adonis; the Babylonian Tammuz; and even Hinduism's Krishna.

Crucifixion of Jesus c.1480

Dionysus

Bearing in mind that if you pick and choose your versions of a story from a wide enough area, you can pretty much come up with anything, it nevertheless looks pretty striking that, for example, Dionysus was allegedly born to a virgin in a cave in mid-winter; he miraculously turned water into wine; he rode an ass through a crowd waving branches; and died as a sacrificial victim at around the spring solstice, before descending to hell and rising to heaven after three days.

On closer examination, however, the parallels aren't as straightforward as claimed. The December 25 or January 6 datings of Christmas are well known to be later pagan borrowings anyway. Dionysus, according to most versions, wasn't exactly born to a virgin but from his father Zeus's thigh – more like Buddha than Jesus. He is the wine god, so many of his miracles obviously involve making wine magically appear, and in any case the earliest known story of the Dionysus wedding miracle dates from well after Jesus, so the argument could just as well be reversed. As for the entry to Jerusalem on a donkey, Jesus could be making a deliberate symbolic statement about his kingship, relying on his audience's knowledge of older myth patterns. The Dionysian "Easter" is based only on a loose link with spring in a few reported early festivals, and Dionysus is hardly a redeeming figure, even if he does personally rise up to heaven thanks to his father, Zeus. And again, the Jesus of the gospels *deliberately* chooses the Jewish (spring) Passover festival to enact his Passion – he wasn't the first to note that it seems the most spiritually appropriate time.

Throw enough copycat incidents together from obscure references in Frazer's myth-soup book, *The Golden Bough*, however, and you get what Timothy Freke and Peter Gandy, the authors of *The Jesus Mysteries*, call "nothing less than the greatest cover-up of all time. Christianity's original Gnostic doctrines and its true origins in the Pagan Mysteries had been ruthlessly suppressed by the mass destruction of the evidence and the creation of a false history to suit the political purposes of the Roman Church." Their argument is oddly reminiscent of the second-century writer Tertullian's view that "the devil, whose business is to pervert the truth, mimics the exact circumstances of the Divine Sacraments ... Let us therefore acknowledge the craftiness of the devil, who copies certain things of those that be Divine."

Jesus the man

Throughout the two-thousand-year life of Christianity, more than a few radicals and sects have argued that Jesus was no Son of God, but simply a revered prophet – much as Muslims view Mohammed. Today, some scholars even argue that this was actually the original "Christian" message and that all of the "redeeming Saviour" stuff came later. In the earliest gospel version of all, it seems, there may have been no talk of virgin mothers, angels, mangers and wise men, and no mention of Last Suppers, trials, crucifixions and empty tombs. History, they theorize, was literally rewritten, and compelling new material presenting Jesus as the Son of God was woven into the gospels. Paul, it's pointed out, says surprisingly little about crucifixions.

The alternative version of Jesus' story seems to have survived at least until the third or fourth century, when the church successfully drove it into the darkest corners of human memory. However, it came to light once again in 1945 when a dozen ancient codices were found by chance near Nag Hammadi in Egypt (see p.164). One of the texts discovered, the *Gospel Of Thomas*, seemed much simpler and more basic than the gospels of the New Testament. In *Thomas*, Jesus is no Messiah, no Son of God, just a prophet announcing the arrival of God's kingdom. Was this a version of the lost "Q", a text scholars think may have been used as a source by the gospellers? Or was it a later, boiled-down version of the gospels?

Crucifixion cover-up

One of the Gnostic texts even makes the astounding claim that the man on the cross between the two thieves was not in fact Jesus, but Simon of Cyrene, acting as a remarkably generous stand-in. So instead of there being a conspiracy between Pharisees and Romans to get rid of Jesus, the conspirators were in fact Jesus and his own followers, staging a dramatic endgame scene to fool the onlookers. The *Second Treatise Of The Great Seth* has Jesus saying: "It was another, Simon, who bore the cross on his shoulder. It was another upon whom they placed the crown of thorns. But I was rejoicing in the height over ... their error ... And I was laughing at their ignorance."

The Gnostic *Apocalypse Of Peter* takes a slightly different line, claiming that while the crucifixion took place, it was only of a "Living Jesus", a kind of physical projection of the real, divine Jesus projected onto earth for the benefit of humanity, thus keeping the wicked flesh and pure spirit nicely separate, in the Docetic tradition. "He whom you see above the tree, glad and laughing, is the living Jesus", the *Apocalypse of Peter* adds. "But he into whose hands and feet they are driving the nails is his fleshly part, which is the substitute." This story seems to be the origin of a theory common in Muslim countries, and found in the tenth-century Quran commentary of Tabari, that a switch was made, and someone else was crucified in Jesus's place. According to some Muslim traditions, the substitute was a disciple-volunteer; according to another it was a divine punishment for a would-be assassin; elsewhere it's said that God made all the disciples look the same as Jesus and the Romans crucified only one of them – which wasn't altogether cunning.

The *Acts Of John* – a Gnostic text which the fifth-century Pope, Leo the Great, wanted "not only forbidden, but entirely destroyed and burned with fire" – finds the bodily crucifixion and resurrection similarly distasteful. It argues that Jesus was a purely spiritual rather than a physical figure, whose appearance changed depending on who was looking at him. He was a man who left no footprints and who never blinked.

Passover plots and shrouds of conspiracy

Maybe, then Jesus only *seemed* to be crucified. Maybe it only *appeared* as if he came back to life. Hugh Schonfield's *Passover Plot* imagines Jesus at the centre of his own conspiracy. Knowing the Messianic prophecies backwards, as a good rabbi would, he apparently deliberately shapes his own life in order to fulfil the scriptural predictions. Unfortunately, the grand finale of crucifixion and resurrection goes wrong, as he doesn't expect to be speared in the side. The disciples are then forced to cover up the debacle by staging the resurrection themselves.

Even further out on the left field – she creatively uses an archaic Jewish method of interpretation known as *pesher* – is Barbara Thiering. Not only does she believe that Jesus was in fact crucified, but at Qumran, the home of the Dead Sea Scrolls (see p.154–157), rather than in Jerusalem, but she says he didn't die but went on to have children with Mary Magdalene (see p.167).

Jesus having an extended post-crucifixion afterlife is a common theme, with many writers weaving theories about the Turin Shroud and the legends that Jesus went to southern India or Kashmir into a lurid tapestry. Best of the lot is Kersten and Gruber's *The Jesus Conspiracy*, which uses "scientific" analysis of the Turin Shroud to reveal a shocking truth: Jesus was still bleeding when he was stitched up in it, and therefore *still alive*. Of course, according to the authors, the shroud isn't a medieval fake (as the official carbon-dating tests showed) but the real thing – thus bringing the Vatican into an apparently perverse conspiracy to prove that its own relic is a fake. Kersten and Gruber point the finger at gravemen Joseph and Nicodemus as the prime conspirators, while the centurion of the gospels was apparently in on the fraud, too, giving Jesus an unusually quick three-hour crucifixion and helping him to stage his "death" with a heavy dose of opium, delivered in the famous vinegar-soaked sponge. Upon burial in the tomb – or rather upon being evacuated to the hospital cunningly disguised as a tomb – Jesus, still bleeding, was wrapped in a cloth soaked in healing myrrh and aloe according to a secret Essene recipe. (How do the authors know this? Because they've recreated the shroud's image using a similar concoction.) For the grand finale, there's Jesus's reappearance three days later – a case of recuperation rather than resurrection.

Did he or didn't he?

However indigestible sceptics have found the idea of a crucifixion and resurrection, they've had a surprisingly hard time arguing against it. The most detailed, apparently authentic evidence there is comes from the gospel writers, who of course believed it. Even the non-Christian Roman writers Tacitus and Josephus mention the crucifixion of Christianity's founder as fact. The controversial Gnostic texts (see p.164) have been brandished high as crucial counter-evidence, but it's hard to get round the fact that they postdate Matthew, Mark et al.

The upshot, then, is pretty much the same as it has been for two thousand years: if, like the earliest Christians of all, you believe that Peter and the other apostles saw the bodily resurrected Jesus, you'd better get yourself to a church. If you believe they didn't see what they said they saw, or what they saw wasn't what they believed it to be, you don't need to bother. Incidentally, it wasn't in fact Peter who saw the raised Jesus first, it was Mary Magdalene (see p.164). But according to the early church only certain sightings – all by male apostles – count. Which is another conspiracy theory in itself.

SOURCES

Books

Acharya S. The Christ Conspiracy: The Greatest Story Ever Sold (1999). Fanciful and poorly written book, by, as her website (www.truthbeknown.com) puts it, "scholar, visionary" Acharya S. Jesus was apparently the product of a conspiracy of secret societies and mystery schools to create a single Roman state religion. The heavy reliance on astrology will hardly convince sceptics.

Earl Doherty The Jesus Puzzle (1999). Doherty pushes the view that Western society has been "the victim of the greatest misconception in history". Namely, that Jesus was conjured into existence by Paul and his co-conspirators as proof for their Christ myth.

Timothy Freke and Peter Gandy The Jesus Mysteries: Was The "Original Jesus" A Pagan God? (1999). It's difficult to think about the New Testament in the same way after reading this, though many of the "facts" about pagan religions have been used creatively.

Holger Kersten and Elmar R. Gruber The Jesus Conspiracy: The Turin Shroud And The Truth About The Resurrection (1992). See p.174.

Hugh Schonfield The Passover Plot (1963). This conspiracy theory was turned into a film (see opposite), with Zalman King as Jesus and Donald Pleasence as Pontius Pilate, washing sticky dates off his hands.

A.N. Wilson Jesus (1993). Sober but superbly readable biography, which covers speculation that Jesus may have been married.

Films

The Last Temptation of Christ (Martin Scorsese, 1998).

The Passion of the Christ (Mel Gibson, 2004). Gibson's pet project focuses – relentlessly – on the physical suffering of Jesus (Jim Caviezel). Nothing particularly conspiratorial about the film itself, though Gibson's private beliefs as a Sedevacantist and conspiracy theorist shade off into some murky areas.

Websites

ⓦ www.bede.org.uk/jesusindex.htm Run by a "Christian intellectual", this website boils down lots of arguments for the authenticity of mainstream Christianity based on "faith and reason".

ⓦ www.tektonics.org Another Christian apologetics site, managed with a high regard for accuracy and rigour by the burgeoning Internet celebrity, J.P. Holding. Lots on the Jesus myth.

The suppressed Apostle: Mary Magdalene as feminine divine

In Dan Brown's multi-million-selling novel *The Da Vinci Code*, historian Leigh Teabing reveals to the book's hero, "symbologist" Robert Langdon, the existence of a set of ancient, leather-bound manuscripts found in Egypt in 1945 that reveal the truth about Mary Magdalene. She was, he explains, the bride of Christ, and the manuscripts are the sole remnant of "thousands of pages of unaltered, pre-Constantine documents" which perished in a presumed firestorm unleashed by the early church.

Teabing seems to have got his plot largely from a dubious book by Lincoln, Baigent and Leigh (notice anything about those last two names?) called *Holy Blood, Holy Grail*, whose high-octane ingredients include Mary Magdalene, Leonardo da Vinci, the Holy Grail and a mysterious/spurious quasi-Templar society called the Priory of Sion. But how much of this mega-theory is true? Was Mary Magdalene married to Jesus? Was she ever revered as the feminine divine? And did the church really conspire to suppress knowledge of her true status – whatever that was?

The finds at Nag Hammadi

In December 1945, an Egyptian peasant called Muhammad 'Ali al-Samman was out in the Jabal al-Tarif, a rugged upland near the town of Nag Hammadi, digging for a special kind of soft soil for fertilizer. He hit upon a three-foot earthenware jar buried in the earth, inside which were more than a dozen leather-bound papyrus books. The story is strangely parallel to that of the Dead Sea Scrolls (see p.154). He took the codices home, where his mother used some as kindling for the fire (holy smoke indeed). What was left found its way to the antiques dealers of Cairo, and thence to the Coptic Museum, where they were discovered to be fourth-century copies of the long-lost gospels from the second-century Gnostic tradition of early Christianity.

Just as the Dead Sea Scrolls were to present a new picture of Judaism, the Gnostic texts of Nag Hammadi showed that early Christianity was far more heterodox than previously believed. They were a collection of theological tracts and alternative "gospels", probably dating from around 150 to 250 years after Jesus' death, which shared an influence from Greek philosophy and an emphasis on personal spiritual insight or understanding – in Greek, *gnosis* means "knowing". They contain some provocative ideas. At times, god is described as Father *and* Mother; elsewhere Jesus's crucifixion is interpreted as symbolism rather than literal fact (see p.160).

Most controversial of all, in the cultural context of the postwar West, is the emphasis some of the Nag Hammadi gospels place on the role of Mary Magdalene. In the *Gospel Of Philip*, a theological-spiritual tract probably dating from around the middle of the third century (though some say it's a hundred years older), Mary appears as a deeply spiritually significant figure. Symbolically, she represents the psyche, the wisdom goddess Sophia, the spiritual consort of Jesus and the unique recipient of a tradition of alternative wisdom.

The most controversial passage of *Philip* goes further still, declaring that Jesus, as "the partner of Mary Magdalene, loved her more than all the disciples and often kissed her on the mouth" (63.34–35). This, her supporters say, is proof that Mary Magdalene was not just spiritually but literally the bride of Christ.

Looked at more closely, however, there are problems with this interpretation. In the New Testament, the same Greek word for "partner" refers to a companion rather than a sexual partner, and in Gnostic terms it means something more like "spiritual consort". Kissing on the mouth was probably more like giving a kiss of peace or of spiritual initiation rather than a sexual kiss. And in fact the damaged papyrus actually reads as follows: "the companion of the ... Mary Magdalene ... her more than ... the disciples ... kiss her on her m...".

And yet ... The same text goes on to describe the disciples asking Jesus why he loves Mary more than them. His answer, while extremely cryptic in typical Gnostic style, segues into a discussion of marriage. There's even a *Gospel Of Mary*, which may date from the early second century. According to this text, Mary Magdalene tells how she had a private vision of Jesus who passed on hidden knowledge to her (frustratingly, four pages are missing at this point, so we never found out what it was). An angry Peter questions why Jesus would have given secrets to a woman, but Levi defends Mary, saying: "Surely the Savior knows her very well. That is why he loved her more than us."

Patriarchs, heretics and conspirators

Peter's jealousy, conspiracists allege, was just the start of two thousand years of suppression of the alternative, Mary Magdalene-focused version of Christianity. In the *Pistis Sophia*, one of the few Gnostic texts still in circulation before the finds at Nag Hammadi, Mary Magdalene tells Jesus that she is afraid of Peter "because he is wont to threaten me and hateth our sex". Elaine Pagels, scholar and author of the best-selling *Gnostic Gospels*, sees this rivalry as a metaphor for the power struggle being fought out between the authoritarian church hierarchy, headed by Peter, and the Greek-influenced, spiritual tradition represented by Mary Magdalene, Jesus's mystical consort. Peter "the Rock" in the red corner; Mary "the spirit" in the blue. Karen King, of the feminist Harvard Divinity School, claims that it's no coincidence that the *Gospel Of Mary* and Paul's woman-subjugating *Letter To Timothy* were (possibly) written at the same time.

Things only got worse for the Gnostics. Powerful figures in the early church declared their ideas to be heretical and their "gospels" to be invalid. As the *Second Treatise Of The Great Seth*, a Gnostic text found at Nag Hammadi, puts it: "We were hated and persecuted, not only by those who are ignorant, but also by those who think they are advancing the name of Christ." In his *Against Heresies* of 187, Irenaeus raged against Gnostic beliefs in such fuming detail that, ironically, his writings were the chief source of modern knowledge about Gnosticism – until the Nag Hammadi codices came to light. Tertullian's *Prescription Against Heretics*, from around 200AD, takes up the cudgel with enthusiasm, taking some hefty sideswipes at women for good measure, protesting that heretical women are "wanton ... bold enough to teach, dispute, exorcize, heal, even baptize". Perhaps even bold enough to tell a different story about Mary Magdalene.

In 325, bishop Eusebius furthered the cause of orthodoxy by promoting the idea of a single church doctrine at the Council of Nicea. He also drew up a list of which gospels were divine and which, he thought, would be better on a bonfire. Following his lead, in 367 the bishop Athanasius of Alexandria commanded the monks of his diocese to destroy all the unorthodox writings found in their libraries. It's

THE CATHARS

Whether or not you believe the church conspired to stamp out Gnostic heresies in the early years of Christianity (see p.164), there's no doubt that it brutally suppressed a medieval outbreak of Gnosticism, the Albigensian heresy of the early thirteenth century. Like their Gnostic fore-bears, the Albigensians lauded the feminine principle in religion, condemned luxury and plea-sure, held that Jesus was only a kind of Holy Ghost unsullied by human flesh and, most danger-ously of all, rejected the need for priests to intercede between man and God. Though known to contemporaries as Albigensians, on account of their stronghold town of Albi, in southern France, they called themselves Cathars, from the Greek *katharos*, or "pure ones".

If the Cathars stood for "purity", Pope Innocent III was firmly on the side of the impure. The Cathars were decried in much the same terms as the Templars would be in the following cen-tury – accused of heresy (true enough), devil worship (well, they did hold that the creator of the world, the God of the New Testament, was the Demiurge or devil) and buggery (perhaps be-cause of their alternative name of Bougres, or Bulgarians, a name acquired through the theology they shared with the Bogomils of Thrace). These attacks quickly developed into a kind of civil war between those northern French nobles aligned with the Papal cause and the local opposition, and culminated in entire Cathar towns being sacked and burned. The most infamous massacre was at Béziers, where the Papal legate instructed Simon de Montfort's besieging forces to spare none of the townspeople, neither Cathar nor Catholic. "Kill them all", he said; "God will know His own."

Modern Cathar conspiracy theo-ries have less to do with the con-spiracy to wipe out the Cathars and more to do with the belief that they were guardians of a secret that gave them great power. In 1885, Berenger Saunière, the vil-lage priest at Rennes-le-Château, deep in Cathar country, claimed to have discovered a group of parchments in a hollow column underneath the altar. Saunière took his find to Paris, where he moved in wealthy circles – oc-cult mysteries have always been fashionable in Paris – before returning to Rennes-le-Château. He had somehow become an occult expert – and a wealthy man. Local legend, bolstered by pseudo-historical books like *Holy Blood, Holy Grail* (see p.169), has it that Saunière discovered the legendary Cathar treasure hoard.

Was this the very same treasure that the Templars had discovered in Jerusalem (see p.73)? Was it the Holy Grail itself – whatever that was (see opposite)? Or was it, as the author of *The Jesus Conspiracy* believes (see p.162), evidence that the Cathars had been the guardians of the Turin Shroud and its mysteries?

In extreme conspiracy circles, the Cathars are spoken about in much the same way as the Templars, the Masons or the Bavarian Illuminati. All survived faked or unsuccessful con-spiracies to exterminate them. All possessed powerful secrets. All are now players in the battle for world domination. Ironically, if the Cathars hadn't been such implacable opponents of worldly power, the idea of playing a part in a grand battle between good and evil would have fitted right in with their world view…

---

presumed that similar orders went out all over the Christian world. Was this a conspiracy to suppress the truth? Or the cleaning up of a later, decadent tra-dition that risked perverting the truth about Jesus as reported by those who knew him best? Were the Gnostic gospels a hidden, elite tradition? Or, as Catholic historian Raymond Brown put it, "the rubbish of the second century"? (He added, sniff-ily, that they were "still rubbish".) Whatever their reasons, somebody disobeyed Athanasius and bur-ied the forbidden texts in a cave at Nag Hammadi, where they remained hidden for almost sixteen hundred years.

Pope Gregory "the conspirator"?

Even if the Gnostic gospels aren't saying that Mary Magdalene was Jesus's consort – or even if they are and they were wrong – she is still a crucial figure in the story of Jesus. In the four orthodox gospels, it is the women in Jesus' group – unlike the male disciples – who do not flee the Roman soldiers at Jesus' arrest, who witness the crucifixion and buri-al, who discover the tomb, and who are first with the news of the resurrection. And yet by the sixth century, women in general were shunned by the church, and Pope Gregory "the Great" had declared that Mary Magdalene was in fact an ex-prostitute. Which, for anyone trying to discern an undercurrent of Magdalene-hating in the confused waters of early church history, is the equivalent of coming across some serious rapids.

Gregory announced that three women in the Bible – Mary Magdalene, Mary of Bethany and an unnamed "sinner" forgiven by Jesus immediately before the Bible's first mention of Mary Magdalene – were in fact one woman. The Magdalene was the sinner and the sinner was a whore. For Mary – once herald of the resurrection and guardian of Jesus's secret tradition, but now, as author Susan Haskins put it, "an effective weapon and instrument of propaganda against her own sex" – this was some fall from grace.

But was Gregory really conspiring to bury the feminist, Gnostic truths believed by early Christians? Religious historian Jane Schaberg sees the sexual denigration of powerful women as such a common historical pattern that she has created a word specially for it – harlotization. Or was Gregory just trying to simplify the Bible? Was his conspiracy nothing more than an attempt to paper over confusing cracks in its narrative? One problem with the patriarchal conspiracy theory is that Mary continued to be a significant and hugely popular devotional figure even after Gregory's declaration, albeit as a penitent sinner.

Holy smoke, holy fire

According to Michael Baigent, Richard Leigh and Henry Lincoln, the authors of *Holy Blood, Holy Grail*, after pulling off the mock crucifixion stunt (see p.160), Jesus and his family fled from Palestine and the clutches of the quasi-fascist St Peter. Jesus' wife, Mary Magdalene, apparently washed up in France, where she founded the Merovingian dynasty, a family line that still preserves the *Sang Réal*, aka Holy Blood, aka the Holy Grail. This is the alternative version of history long hidden (but recently revealed) by a secret (yet self-publicizing) society called the Priory of Sion. The entire existence of this society is predicated on some 1950s typescripts allegedly deposited in Paris's Bibliothèque Nationale and dubbed the *Dossiers Secrets* (though they can't be all that secret if they've been submitted to a public library) by an odd crypto-fascist and hoaxer called Pierre Plantard.

The admirably erudite historian Marina Warner famously called *Holy Blood, Holy Grail* "a heap of hooey". Whatever the truth of its claims, its tactics are certainly dubious, and the authors have a peculiar logical tic. When they can find no substantiating evidence for their claims, they say this only shows how powerful the conspirators were, and how successful in covering their traces. Genealogical links become evidence of a conspiracy; people who "must have met" other people are transformed into co-conspirators; anagrams are wielded as coherent proofs; and no smoke is left to drift away without throwing its imagined fuel onto the conspiratorial bonfire.

The Holy Grail

The idea of a Holy Grail was dreamt up by the twelfth-century French poet Chrétien de Troyes, in his *Conte du Graal*. As Umberto Eco snorted in a television interview: "The historical reality of the Holy Grail is the same as the reality of Pinocchio and Little Red Riding Hood." Some of Chrétien's themes and symbols may be drawn from earlier traditions – the setting in the kingdom of the Britons is taken from Geoffrey of Monmouth's reinvention of stories about a legendary King Arthur, written some fifty years previously – but otherwise there's no evidence anywhere that the idea of a Holy Grail existed before Chrétien wrote about it. Unless you're willing to believe that the poet was the inheritor and maverick first publicist of a secret tradition, that is, or that some medieval entity with a secret agenda managed to systematically destroy all earlier texts that mentioned the Grail.

As for the idea that the Holy Grail was not, as all medieval authors stated, the chalice used by Jesus at the Last Supper and later reused to catch his blood at the Crucifixion, but in fact a code word referring to the bloodline of Mary Magdalene, this seems to have been concocted by the authors of *Holy Blood, Holy Grail* in the 1980s. The main ingredient of their story seems to be an ancient, nationalistic French legend that a pregnant Mary Magdalene had fled from Palestine to France (a legend paralleled by many other countries' "founding myths" which, when put together, would have half the figures in the gospels magically transported all over the Mediterranean in boats in various states of ruin and decay – rudderless, sail-less, leaky, made of stone and so on). Add a whimsical bit of false etymology by translating Chrétien's *saint Graal* not as "Holy Grail", but as "holy blood" (*sang royal*), via a corruption of the Old French *sang réal*, and you've got a marketable tale.

Picknett, Prince and the Da Vinci connection

The notion of Leonardo da Vinci as the guardian of the secret Magdalene tradition was another idea concocted by Baigent, Leigh and Lincoln in *Holy Blood, Holy Grail*, on the basis of the dodgy *dossiers* of the "Priory of Sion", which list the artist as one of the Nautonniers, or Grand Masters. The theory was further investigated by Lynn Picknett and Clive Prince's *The Templar Revelation*, which also draws on the Gnostic gospels to promote Mary as the object of quasi-goddess worship. Ignorant, perhaps of the artistic tradition that John the Evangelist is typically portrayed as a youthful, beautiful, beardless figure, Picknett and Prince seize on John's feminine features as painted in Leonardo's *Last Supper* as proof that "he" is in fact "she", and she is actually … Mary Magdalene.

Skirting gingerly round the whole Priory of Sion

chimera, it's not hard to lance this rather swollen theory. Even on a casual visual impression, John/Mary could just as easily be a young man as a woman. And the extremely fragile Last Supper fresco has been restored so many times – eight, to be exact – that it's pretty doubtful whether anything much of Leonardo's original paintwork actually survives. And if the contentious figure *isn't* John, where is he? And even if Leonardo did paint a figure of a woman beside Jesus in his *Last Supper*, it doesn't mean she was actually there at *the* Last Supper. As for all the pseudo-art theory that bolsters the idea, such as the "V" composition between Jesus and John/Mary (recalling the vagina), and the red and blue colours of their robes (supposedly suggesting royal blood), it's an enticing taste of flamboyantly ingenious art criticism, but nothing more.

Admissions and restorations

Whatever its past misdemeanours, the Catholic Church now recognizes that Mary Magdalene and the "unnamed sinner" are two different women. Of course, it hasn't gone as far as accepting the authenticity of the Gnostic gospels, and continues to stick with Eusebius's notion that only the gospels actually written by apostles count. That said, the Vatican also admits that the four principal gospels weren't actually written by Matthew, Mark, Luke and John, only written "according to" their version of events. Even supporters of the authenticity and importance of the Gnostic Gospels don't buy the *Holy Blood* idea that Jesus was married. As Elaine Pagels, of Princeton University, stated in a television interview on ABC News: "If I were guessing, and we are guessing, I would guess that there was a special relationship between Mary Magdalene and Jesus. I would also guess that it did not take a sexual form."

The various theories haven't done Leonardo's reputation much harm, mostly just reinforcing his celebrity status as the artist-genius *par excellence*, according to the familiar romantic myth. Unfortunately for Leonardo conspiracists, the Last Supper fresco was revealed after a twenty-year restoration in 1999 with many of the previously usefully murky details clarified. The old smudges on John/Mary that could have been said to look like the swelling of a breast were gone. End of story? No; Lynn Picknett apparently believes that someone took advantage of the restoration to literally clean away the evidence...

As for the Priory of Sion, in the hands of conspiracy theorists it has mushroomed into a vast secret society accused of being on the verge of establishing a United Theocratic States of Europe. Pierre Plantard would have been delighted.

SOURCES

Books

Michael Baigent, Richard Leigh and Henry Lincoln Holy Blood, Holy Grail (1982). The fertile source behind Dan Brown's *The Da Vinci Code*.

Richard Barber The Holy Grail: Imagination And Belief (2004). The true biography of a medieval myth. Serious and reliable.

Dan Brown The Da Vinci Code (2003). See p.164 & 391.

Bart D. Ehrman Lost Christianities: The Battles For Scripture And The Faiths We Never Knew (2003). Reliable, earnest and fascinating account of the withering of early Christian beliefs in the face of orthodoxy and the authorized New Testament.

Timothy Freke and Peter Gandy Jesus And The Lost Goddess: The Secret Teachings Of The Original Christians (1999). Freke and Gandy analyze the Gnostic gospels as the springboard for their own theories about the "original" Christianity as another manifestation of the god-man/god-woman dualism inherent in all religion.

Michael Haag and Veronica Haag The Rough Guide to The Da Vinci Code (2004). This pocket-sized guide to the not-so-wonderful world of Dan Brown has a wide brief, encompassing everything from the truth about heresies to the real locations in Paris, London and elsewhere.

Susan Haskins Mary Magdalene: Myth And Metaphor (1993). Scholarly, readable history of Mary and her place in art, history and literature.

Elaine Pagels The Gnostic Gospels (1980). Original and best. Pagels is the leading authority on the Nag Hammadi texts, and remains open to their potential significance while resisting the lure of sensationalizing them.

Lynn Picknett and Clive Prince The Templar Revelation: Secret Guardians Of The True Identity Of Christ (1997). Key source for Dan Brown – the book even appears on Teabing's bookshelves – and rather less wildly credulous than Baigent et al. Lynn Picknett went on to write *Mary Magdalene: Christianity's Hidden Goddess*, which uses fascinating facts to reach far-out conclusions, for instance that Mary Magdalene "was probably a black woman from Ethiopia, who bore Jesus' mixed race child".

Margaret Starbird The Woman With The Alabaster Jar: Mary Magdalene And The Holy Grail (1993). Starbird sees beyond the squabbles about Mary's role and into a sacred world where the feminine divine is celebrated and worshipped. The Grail becomes the idea of the vagina.

Barbara Thiering Jesus The Man (1992). Based on an idiosyncratic reading of the Dead Sea Scrolls, Thiering has Jesus married to Mary Magdalene with two sons and a daughter – before she leaves him and he remarries. Some ambitious leaps of argument, such as claiming that "the Word of God increased", from Acts 6:7, refers to Jesus having more children.

Films

The Last Temptation of Christ (Martin Scorsese, 1988) Based on Nikos Kazantzakis's novel of the same name, this finely crafted biopic caused huge waves of controversy for its dream-sequence on the cross, in which Jesus (Willem Dafoe) imagines how his life would have been as an ordinary man – including the love affair he could have had with Mary Magdalene.

Websites

ⓦ www.beliefnet.com This US-based open religious discussion site has lots of Magdalene-related chatter, including articles by Sandra Miesel and Margaret Starbird.

ⓦ www.milano.arounder.com See for yourself: Milan's official tourist site contains a link to a high-resolution image of the Last Supper.

ⓦ www.gnosis.org Website of the LA-based Gnostic Society, with endless information on Gnosticism including translations and photographs of the Nag Hammadi codices.

ⓦ www.newadvent.org/cathen/09761a.htm Mary Magdalene, the authorized version, according to the authoritative Catholic Encyclopedia.

ⓦ www.ordotempli.org/priory_of_sion.htm Reams of unfiltered pseudo-fact on the Priory of Sion from one of the many groups that like to make out they are the modern-day Knights Templar.

ⓦ www.religioustolerance.org/cfe_bibl. htm Handy overview of Jesus' teachings regarding women, from a liberal website aiming to break down fundamentalism based on the lack of information.

BENEDICT XVI : THE PANZER POPE

In the aftermath of Cardinal Joseph Ratzinger's election as Pope Benedict XVI, the *Times* collected some choice quotations. At various points in his long career, the new Pope has called homosexuality an "intrinsic moral evil", declared rock music to be a "vehicle of anti-religion" and announced that Anglicanism and Protestantism are "not proper churches". Oh, and he thinks that Turkey joining the EU is "an enormous mistake". But liberal sneers at conservative Catholic views don't amount to conspiracy theories.

What *is* unashamedly conspiracist is the "Panzer Pope" theory, which imagines Ratzinger as having a Nazi agenda on the basis that the Bavarian-born Cardinal was a "former Nazi". He was, in fact, a member of the Hitler Youth. At age 14. At a time when it was illegal for young Germans not to join. In reality, his father was an active opponent of Nazism. Similarly, Ratzinger's service in the German flak (anti-aircraft) corps was more a matter of conscription than conviction, and he deserted shortly before the German surrender.

Some conspiracists also like to make out that Ratzinger was complicit in the "murder" of Pope John Paul I (see p.48) – not that there's any evidence. At best, the man they call the "Killer Cardinal" was one of the conservatives who weren't supposed to be too pleased about having a liberal pope poking his nose around the Vatican Bank's accounts, or its lists of Masonic members.

There's rather better evidence for Ratzinger's involvement in a cover-up of the Catholic Church's sex-abusing priests scandal. As Prefect of the Congregation for the Doctrine of the Faith (CDF) – or Chief Inquisitor, to give the job its old-fashioned name – it was Ratzinger's job to handle all sex abuse cases. On May 18, 2001, the Cardinal sent a letter – written in Latin – to all the church's bishops pointing out that sex abuse investigations were a matter for the CDF alone, and that all details were to remain strictly confidential. On April 23, 2005, the *Independent* reported that nine separate sex abuse allegations made against Marcial Maciel, the founder of the Legion of Christ, had been ignored by Ratzinger on the grounds that "One can't put on trial such a close friend of the Pope's as Marcial Maciel". The cases were eventually reopened in December 2004.

As Prefect of the CDF, Ratzinger was also instrumental in promulgating the Vatican's policy on birth control and condom-use. Following the publication of "The Many Faces Of AIDS" by the National Conference of Catholic Bishops' Administrative Board, Ratzinger wrote a widely publicized explanatory letter to Archbishop Pio Laghi on May 29, 1988. Discussing the church's position on educational programs about condoms in government schools, he wrote: "one would not be dealing simply with a form of passive toleration"; this was "a kind of behaviour which would result in at least the facilitation of evil". (Whereas telling a woman whose philandering husband is HIV-positive that if they use a condom she will go to hell is pure goodness.)

It must also have been Ratzinger's conservatism that made him write to US bishops in June 2004, declaring that priests must refuse the sacrament to "pro-choice" politicians. Supporting abortion laws was "a grave sin". Ratzinger specifically mentioned "a Catholic politician consistently campaigning and voting for permissive abortion and euthanasia laws". No names, of course – that might unfairly influence Catholic voters in the upcoming presidential election. An American who voted for a pro-choice candidate would be "guilty of formal cooperation in evil and so unworthy to present himself for Holy Communion." (Himself? Presumably the Cardinal temporarily forgot that women also vote.)

Chris Floyd of the *Moscow Times*, writing at conspiracyplanet.com, thought Ratzinger had other reasons to support Bush. He seized on a newsday.com article of April 21, 2005, which revealed that the Cardinal sat on the board of the Swiss Foundation for Interreligious and Intercultural Research. Also on the board was none other than Neil Bush, the President's younger brother, a man best known not for his contributions to religious debate, but rather for his business failures, notably as a director of the failed Silverado Savings and Loan bank, whose collapse cost the federal government $1 billion.

Floyd thought it fishy that the foundation was registered as a "management trust" rather than as a religious foundation. "A cynic", he wrote, "i.e. anyone with the slightest acquaintance of Bush business practices – might think that a 'management trust' masquerading as a religious charity would be an excellent place to launder money or park assets away from the taxman's prying eyes." Was Ratzinger paying a debt to the US when, in May 2005, he appointed the conservative Archbishop of San Francisco, William Levada, to the recently vacated post of Prefect of the Congregation for the Doctrine?

At the crazier end of the conspiracy scale was the story, reported in the obscure *Hertfordshire Mercury* on April 29, 2005, that a "German former cardinal" had called a historian at Hertfordshire's County Hall for details of the "Hertfordshire branch" of the Knights Templar. A certain Tim Acheson, one of the Hertfordshire Knights, commmented that "perhaps it is the revenge of the Templars that the Church fears, since the origin of Freemasonry is rooted in the persecution of the Templars by the Church." Or perhaps Ratzinger was recruiting? Acheson also pointed out that the Pope's birthplace, Bavaria, was also the home of the mysterious Illuminati (see p.85)…

OPUS DEI: THE HOLY MAFIA

Latin countries have been hearing dark whisperings about *Opus Dei*, "the work of God", for decades. In Spain, where the Catholic group was founded in 1928, it was dubbed the "Holy Mafia". Members virtually controlled the economic policies of Franco's fascist government during the 1960s, and resurfaced under the recent conservative leadership of José María Aznar, whose wife was close to the organization. In Italy, Opus Dei was rumoured to have had connections with the P2 Masonic conspiracy and with the rescue of the Vatican bank (see p.124).

In Peru, the group was a motivating force in a coalition that bankrolled (corrupt) President Alberto Fujimori, while the hard-line conservative Peruvian archbishop, Juan Luis Cipriani, became Opus Dei's first cardinal in 2001. Peruvian conspiracy theorists have attempted to link Cipriani with the murder of his predecessor, liberal Jesuit Augusto Vargas Zamora – a "killing" allegedly orchestrated by Fujimori's jailed spy chief, Vladimiro Montesinos. In the Vatican, the speedy canonization of the organization's founder, Josemaría Escrivá de Balaguer y Albás, in 2002 – just 27 years after his death – was seen as evidence of the extent of Opus Dei's power, as was the fact that in 1994 John Paul II kneeled in front of the coffin of Escrivá's successor, Alvaro del Portillo, who is now in the process of being canonized.

In the Anglophone world, by contrast, the group only made headlines after it was caricatured in Dan Brown's conspiracy thriller, *The Da Vinci Code*. Seemingly, no one had noticed the seventeen-storey US headquarters Opus Dei had built on New York's Lexington Avenue, at a cost of an estimated $42–54 million (viewable at http://maypinska.com/pages/projects/buildbodylex.htm). But suddenly, the group was everywhere. In the UK, New Labour education secretary Ruth Kelly was forced to admit that she was a "Supernumerary" (see below), while rumours circulated that Cherie Blair, the wife of the Prime Minister, was involved at some level, along with her husband, Tony, on the grounds that he was alleged to be on the point of conversion to Catholicism. In the US, a number of conservative politicians have close links with Father C. John McCloskey III, an Opus Dei priest with a big media presence, while Supreme Court justice Antonin Scalia is widely rumoured to be a member (which he denies), as is former FBI director Louis Freeh – though largely on the grounds that Freeh's son went to an Opus Dei school, and that his career was paralleled by FBI agent, Opus Dei member and Russian spy, Robert Hanssen.

Just what is so sinister about Opus Dei? Is it the cult-like techniques – semi-secrecy, peer pressure, cutting of family ties, staged "crises", threats of damnation, censored exposure to media – that surround membership and recruitment? Is it Opus Dei's advocacy of corporal mortification using the cilice (a spiked belt worn around the thigh) and the discipline (literally, a whip for your own back)? However repellent, these aspects don't amount to a conspiracy theory.

The problem, as always, is power. Opus Dei's stated aim is to "sanctify work", creating a new model for an active religious life in the professional community. Opus Dei's critics, however, claim its *real* project is to recruit high-flyers – government ministers and congressmen, for instance. The resulting mixture of religion, tightly controlled organization and political influence would be potent – like the Masons, only with the fires of hell added for encouragement. On its website, www.opusdei.org, the group declares that members separate their professional decisions from their private religious life anyway. Websites such as the Opus Dei Awareness Network (www.odan.org), however, counter with a quotation from the Spanish founder of Opus Dei, St Josemaría: "Have you ever bothered to think how absurd it is to leave one's Catholicism aside on entering a university or a professional association or a scholarly meeting or Congress, as if you were checking your hat at the door?".

Politically, Opus Dei has been linked with Fascism. Its emphasis on work is certainly reminiscent of Fascist ideology, as is the commitment to a charismatic leadership, the emphasis on purity, and the deeply hierarchical internal structure. Escrivá's own writings make clear he is no friend of socialism or modernism, and he is alleged to have said "Hitler against the Jews, Hitler against the Slavs – this means Hitler against Communism". As the Spanish theologian Juan Martin Velasco commented bitterly: "We cannot portray as a model of Christian living someone who has served the power of the state and who used that power to launch his Opus, which he ran with obscure criteria, like a Mafia shrouded in white."

Opus Dei is certainly building a powerful network of conservative Catholics. It has some 83,000 lay members, three thousand of them in the US. These include celibate "Numeraries", who have ordinary jobs but live in single-sex, monastic-style houses and give over all their income to Opus Dei, and "Supernumeraries", who can be married and merely hand over large portions of their salaries. That's quite an army. It remains to be seen whether *The Da Vinci Code* will dent or swell the ranks.

The
land of
the free

Watergate: a third-rate burglary
Ronald Reagan and the October Surprise
Clintongates: ruining people is
considered a sport
OKC: the Oklahoma City bombing

The Land of the Free

For sheer presence, the United States is by far and away the leader in conspiracism. American domestic politics, the focus of this chapter, is rife with conspiracy theories. They have even been blamed for a generalized breakdown in trust in the political system. Conspiracists counter that it's not the *theorists* that are to blame so much as the actual conspirators...

The US even gave the world a word for a conspiracy theory whose proof leads to a politician's downfall: a Watergate. Nixon's original Watergate affair didn't just create a new word; it also set the pattern for three decades of American presidential conspiracy theories based on dirt-digging and the obvious corollary, mud-slinging. Most damaging perhaps were the various "gates" that dogged Bill Clinton's presidency. The heat that emanated from Republican-funded researchers was intense enough for Hillary Clinton to declare that there was a "vast right-wing conspiracy" to bring her husband's administration down. Politicized conspiracy theorists were no less hard at work during George W. Bush's presidency. In 2000, his very election was enmired in conspiracy

theories about the electoral and legal processes that had brought him to power, not to mention the secret societies such as the Skull and Bones that supposedly backed – or controlled – him.

It wasn't the first time that conspiracy theories had swarmed around a presidential election. Ronald Reagan's inauguration speech in 1980 was magically blessed by the simultaneous release of American hostages in Iran, but in future years this October Surprise became more of a curse on Reagan's reputation, as theories about the timing of the incident refused to die down. The rumours were underpinned by the very real conspiracy behind the Iran–Contra affair, which in turn buttressed the long-running theory that the CIA were behind an elaborate scam to bring crack cocaine into the US and support the Contras at the same time.

The most radical right-wing American conspiracy theorists dismiss talk of Bush, or Reagan, or Clinton, as the mere rumblings of partisan politics' grubby underbelly. Left-wing theorists may concoct conspiracies with Reagan or Bush at their centre, they say, and right-wingers can do the same for Clinton, but their targets are no more than front men for the sinister federal machine.

In the eyes of ultra-right "Patriot" or "Christian Identity" groups, the machine's workings have been exposed by manifestations of federal evil such as the Jonestown massacre of 1978, or the Waco killings of 1993. Conspiracy theories about the latter actually inspired Timothy McVeigh to carry out the Oklahoma City bombing of 1995 – about which the ultra-right have plenty more conspiracy theories.

Note that America's role in foreign conflicts – from Pearl Harbor to the second Gulf War – is covered separately in the "Warplay" chapter (see p.325),

while American weapons technology is discussed under "Real Weapons of Mass Destruction" (see p.265). For conspiracy theories centred on alleged assassinations, including those of Robert Kennedy, Malcolm X and of course John F. Kennedy, see the dedicated chapter (see p.3). Alleged CIA plots to kill Allende, Castro and Romero are also covered under "Assassinations", while the CIA gets a whole well-deserved section to itself under "Mega-conspiracies" (see p.109).

Watergate: a third-rate burglary

These days, a botched break-in at a fancy Washington hotel doesn't sound like a big deal. But we're not talking about just any burglary. This was a genuine conspiracy whose uncovering brought down a president, the *original* "-gate" scandal, the one that lent its name to every sleazy *affaire* in American politics that followed and inspired a generation of investigative journalists – as well as conspiracy theorists who like to imagine they're investigative journalists. Remember Travelgate, Filegate, Contragate, Zippergate and Fajitagate? Or Britain's Squidgygate and Camillagate? Not forgetting the Clintons' Whitewatergate, of course, and San Francisco's less well-known Watermelongate.

It all began in the early hours of June 17, 1972, when a security guard spotted a piece of tape holding a door unlocked in the basement stairwell of the Watergate complex, a Washington DC hotel and apartment building heavily patronized by the political establishment. Suspicious, he called the police, who in short order discovered five burglars in the offices of the Democratic National Committee. Two were CIA-trained Cuban exiles; another, James McCord, claimed to be an ex-CIA agent (as if they're ever "ex"...). The "black bag" team were apparently adjusting or replacing bugging equipment. The story made headlines in *The Washington Post*, but President Nixon's press secretary dismissed the story as a "third-rate burglary", and it probably wouldn't have run much further had two staff writers not done a bit of checking.

Bob Woodward and Carl Bernstein at *The Washington Post*

All The Washington Post's Men

On June 19, Bob Woodward and Carl Bernstein of *The Post* published an article pointing out that McCord was not just a former spook, but the actual, current, right-now security chief for Nixon's re-election campaign, the Committee to Re-Elect the President, aka CRP – or CREEP, as the press put it.

The dynamic duo kept on digging, helped by an anonymous inside source who was dubbed "Deep Throat" by *Washington Post* insiders, after a porn film making headlines at the time. He advised them to follow the money trail, and repeatedly confirmed what other, single sources were saying – which, as sceptics point out, was all rather convenient for the two

journalists. Woodward and Bernstein linked a White House consultant, E. Howard Hunt, to at least two of the burglars, and discovered that a CRP consultant and former FBI agent, G. Gordon Liddy, had been fired shortly after the incident. On August 1, they reported another puzzling fact. A $25,000 check earmarked for the Nixon campaign had somehow found its way into the account of one of the Watergate burglars, through funds managed by former Attorney General John Mitchell. Bernstein called Mitchell for comment, only to have his ear blistered with the response: "Katie Graham's gonna get her tit caught in a big fat wringer if that's ever published."

Katie Graham was the *Post*'s publisher, but she put her tits on the line. On October 10, her rising-star reporters' article opened with a thunderous (if awkwardly phrased) salvo: "The Watergate bugging incident stemmed from a massive campaign of political spying and sabotage conducted on behalf of President Nixon's re-election and directed by officials of the White House and the Committee for the Re-election of the President." But outside Washington, the American people didn't seem to have noticed. On November 7, 1972, "Tricky Dicky" was re-elected in a landslide.

Lies and audiotape

The Watergate burglars, along with Hunt and Liddy, went on trial in January 1973, and were duly convicted of conspiracy, burglary and wiretapping. Facing thirty years, McCord confessed that CREEP had conspired not only to plan the burglary, but to pay off the burglars to plead guilty and keep shtoom in court. McCord started to finger more and more of the "President's Men" for involvement. The fire was spreading upwards, fast. On April 30, desperate to clear a firebreak beneath him, Nixon fired several senior White House and campaign staff.

But White House Counsel John Dean turned on his former boss, testifying to Nixon's involvement before a televised Senate committee of inquiry. Then, on July 13, a presidential aide casually mentioned that the White House had made tape recordings of every single presidential conversation. The Senate and newly appointed Special Prosecutor Archibald Cox pounced, subpoenaing Nixon for the tapes. Nixon refused, ordering Cox to drop the subpoena. On October 20, 1973, after Cox refused to back down, Nixon went on the rampage, sacking first Cox and then official after official in an attempt to find someone who'd do what he was told. The president declared: "I am not a crook."

In March 1974, a grand jury named Nixon – off the record – as a "co-conspirator", and in April Nixon was forced to give up 1200 (expurgated) pages of transcripts of the White House tapes. A wide-eyed public could now hear its president plotting how to pay off blackmailers and get conspirators off the hook, swearing profusely (or at least apparently saying "expletive deleted") and fulminating against blacks and Jews.

And what on earth was missing from one particularly glaring eighteen-and-a-half minute gap? The White House claimed that Nixon's secretary, Rose Mary Woods, had accidentally erased the tape by pushing a foot pedal while answering the phone. Photo reconstructions in the newspapers, however, showed this to have been ergonomically impossible, while scientific analysis of the original tape revealed that the "gap" had been erased not once, but over and over again.

Finally, the famous "smoking gun" tape was released, showing Nixon had known about the cover-up within one week of the original break-in. The House Judiciary Committee voted 27–11 to impeach the president on three articles: obstruction of justice, abuse of power, and contempt of Congress. Before the Senate could try him, however, the famously grudge-bearing, paranoid president resigned on August 8, 1974, saying: "I have never been a quitter. To leave office before my term is completed is abhorrent to every instinct in my body. But as President, I must put the interest of America first ... let me say I leave with no bitterness toward those who have opposed me."

Entrapment Theory

As a conspiracy unmasked, Watergate has plenty of sleazy allure, but one fact has struck generations of commentators: the game wasn't worth the candle. Why would the president risk everything just to find out a few details of his rival's campaign? Or was there more to it? For a start, Liddy claims they were bugging Larry O'Brien, the chairman of the Democratic campaign. Hunt and the Cubans, however, say that another area of the office was being targeted. Nixon summed up the most common conspiracy theory himself. "The whole thing was so senseless and bungled", he wrote in his memoirs, "that it almost looked like some kind of a set-up." He guessed that the Dems had *known* about the break-in, and had set up Nixon for a fall. The Senate investigation, he pointed out, had found some evidence that Larry O'Brien's deputy had been tipped off about a spying job.

The focus of the "Democratic Entrapment" theory, though, is Carl Shoffler, the policeman who answered the Watergate security guard's call. It was Shoffler's birthday – and yet he'd signed up for an eight-hour night shift. Who would do such a thing unless they'd been paid off? Shoffler himself had a simpler explanation: "I just felt like it", he said. More murkily, a friend of Shoffler's called Edmund Chung claimed that Shoffler had suggested to him over dinner that he'd known about the burglary in advance. Shoffler counter-claimed that Chung had offered him $50,000 if he'd confess to foreknowledge. But where did that kind of money come from? Perhaps Nelson Rockefeller, soon to rise to new heights of wealth and influence as Gerald Ford's (unelected) vice president. Or perhaps – as Nixon himself suspected – Howard Hughes. Others turn the last theory on its head, claiming that the real aim of the break-in was for Nixon to find evidence of Hughes' undoubted financial connections to the Democrats...

Secret agenda, silent coup

Jim Hougan, author of *Secret Agenda*, thinks that the visible evidence we've seen is just the tip of a murky iceberg. McCord, he believes, was trying to sabotage the original break-in, possibly to cover up a separate CIA bugging operation aimed at collecting details of Democratic sexual indiscretions. Hougan's line was spun into a giant web by Len Colodny and Robert Gettlin, whose book *Silent Coup* was the last, Nixon-defending word in Watergate conspiracy theory literature – a theory so far out that the *Washington Post* didn't even see fit to report

it. A White House insider the book alleged, had arranged the Watergate break-in to find and presumably destroy evidence of a prostitution ring which compromised a close acquaintance. Only afterwards did Nixon jump in to protect his aides.

The *Silent Coup* theory led to a welter of lawsuits Most have been settled out of court, with the result that *Silent Coup* has been withdrawn from publication . It's hard to avoid one major problem with Colodny and Gettlin's theory. Integral to their allegations was the notion that Nixon's chief of staff, Alexander Haig, was the legendary "Deep Throat", and that Watergate was the conclusion of a campaign led by Haig and his CIA/Pentagon backers to bring down a president who wanted out of the Vietnam War. Oops. In May 2005, Deep Throat revealed himself to be not Haig but FBI number two, Mark Felt.

From Watergate to Dealey Plaza, via the Bay of Pigs

Much has been made of the backgrounds of the Watergate burglars. Three of them, Frank Sturgis and two Cuban exiles, had been heavily involved in anti-Castro plots – as had their handler, ex-CIA asset E. Howard Hunt. Sturgis had surfaced in the conspiracy world once before, when he ran a media campaign to blame JFK's assassination on Cuban Communists. And there were other, more puzzling links with Cuba. The White House tapes revealed that Nixon had sent his Chief of Staff, H.R. Haldeman, to persuade Richard Helms at the CIA to pressure the FBI into dropping the Watergate investigation. Nixon threatened, mysteriously, that if the FBI proceeded, it would "open up the whole Bay of Pigs thing again". What about the Bay of Pigs? Were the Watergate gang connected to the CIA plots to kill Castro (see p.20)? Or were they connected to an even more sinister assassination plot? H.R. Haldeman claimed in *The Ends Of Power* that "the whole Bay of Pigs thing" was actually coded talk for "the whole JFK thing". Howard Hunt and Frank Sturgis, it's pointed out, look rather like two of the famously over-dressed three hoboes (see p.28) arrested in Dealey Plaza and promptly released. And strangely, Nixon himself was in Dallas that day, working as a lawyer for the Pepsi Corporation...

The system prevails

On September 8, 1974, Nixon's successor Gerald Ford granted him an official pardon, thus making him the only major player in the Watergate affair to avoid prosecution. That forty government officials involved in the scandal were indicted or jailed is evidence, according to the establishment, that integrity prevailed in the system. The press and the law courts did their jobs. Sceptics wondered about the handy timing: Nixon's fall provided symbolic closure for the Vietnam war, sparing America any real soul-searching about what had gone wrong. It has also been suggested that Nixon's pardon had been a pre-condition of his offer to make Ford his vice president in December 1973, fol-lowing the resignation of the disgraced Spiro Agnew.

After Watergate, major changes were made in campaign finance law, and in rules relating to the disclosure of private financial information by government figures. Government, as a result, is supposed to be cleaner. Certainly, bugging is no longer routine (or if it is, it's well hidden) and no one tapes the White House. Which is lucky for Bill Clinton and Monica Lewinsky. It's fascinating to compare Clinton and Nixon. Both have been called the greatest – and most flawed – presidents of their generations. Both tried to bury a relatively minor incident, only for the cover-up itself to become the issue. There was one key difference: Tricky Dicky fell on his sword, while Slick Willy lived out his full term.

Today, the original White House tapes are still being released and new conspiracy theories are sure to follow. Sadly, one mini-conspiracy theory industry has now shut up shop. On 31 May 2005, former FBI deputy director Mark Felt outed himself as Bob Woodward's famous source, "Deep Throat." Many conspiracy theorists felt oddly disappointed; others refused to believe it.

SOURCES

Books

Carl Bernstein and Bob Woodward All the President's Men (1974). A gripping, novella-like exposition of Woodward and Bernstein's investigation.

Fred Emery Watergate (1994). Uses memoirs and newly released White House tapes to tell the whole story afresh. Pulls no punches when it comes to describing the details of Nixon's fall, but is equally focused on the political context of the scandal.

H.R. Haldeman and Joseph Dimona The Ends Of Power (1978). Since disavowed by former White House Chief of Staff "Bob" Haldeman as ghost-written and sensationalizing, it has also been called a rare moment of clarity from an insider who defends Nixon without whitewashing him. "Most of us would have been willing to sacrifice ourselves", says Haldeman, "to save the Presidency that we believed in."

Stanley I. Kutler Abuse Of Power (1998). In 1996, Kutler and the advocacy group Public Citizen won a landmark decision to release the tapes. Using this new source, Kutler shines a new light into the dark workings of Nixon's White House.

Websites

ⓦ **www.archives.gov/nixon/tapes/ transcripts.html** The original transcripts, courtesy of the US government.

ⓦ **www.asianweek.com/2002_08_30/ opinion_emil.html** Watermelongate. You read it here first. (You won't find it anywhere else.)

ⓦ **www.washingtonpost.com/wp-srv/** national/longterm/watergate/chronology. htm Handy timeline containing links to the original *Washington Post* stories. All the mucky details, straight from the horse's mouth.

ⓦ **www.whitehousetapes.org/**... or the real thing – downloadable audio versions.

Films

All the President's Men (Alan J. Pakula, 1976). All the gritty glamour of Bernstein (Dustin Hoffman) and Woodward's (Robert Redford) relentless investigation. A hugely watchable advert for journalism, though it doesn't much clear up what actually went on at Watergate.

Watergate: The Secret Story (1992). CBS News with *The Washington Post*, naming FBI director L. Patrick Gray as Deep Throat.

Jonestown

At the end of the 1960s, California was the epicentre of the worldwide "hippy scene". Many adherents had gathered together to live in large communes, run according to belief systems far removed from the accepted norms of Main Street America. Prominent among those infused by strong religious or mystical elements was the People's Temple, a utopian, agrarian community in Ukiah, near San Francisco. Its founder, lay preacher Jim Jones, was originally from Indiana, where his father had been a Klansman. A flourishing, well-funded development, the Temple propounded a peaceful, multiracial mission of harmonious, godly existence, and became a haven for the poor. Hundreds lived and worked on the camp, while thousands more followers spread the Temple's message throughout California.

However, lurid tales in the press spoke of beatings at the camp, and alleged that followers were subjected to brainwashing and ritual abuse. There were even rumours that escapees were being murdered. Jones had already used the Temple's not inconsiderable funds to buy a large plot of land in Guyana, and when the state began to investigate his tax affairs in 1977, he decided to take his whole flock. The heart of the Guyanese jungle was just the place for the spiritual fiefdom of Jonestown to prosper.

Horror stories continued to filter back from Guyana, via the press and the concerned relatives of followers, telling of abuse, torture and murder. A worried California congressman, Leo Ryan, decided to investigate, and arrived in Guyana with a group of journalists on November 14, 1978. Together with the deputy from the local US embassy, Richard Dwyer, they toured Jonestown without incident. As the party returned to the airport the next day, however, all except Dwyer were shot dead in an ambush by Temple followers.

Then the massacre began. At the camp, Jones reportedly told his followers to drink cups of Kool-Aid laced with cyanide, or face execution from his armed guard. Jones shot himself in the head. Photos depict hundreds of dead bodies, dressed in apparently clean, casual clothes, laying in an eerie orderly array, as though sleeping among the huts and trees. Most were women. Most were black. There were 913 victims in all, including 276 children.

The official verdict

In 1979, back in the US, the House Foreign Affairs Committee concluded that the massacre was the result of Jones's "extreme paranoia". Its 782-page report detailed what it called a mass suicide at Jonestown, a verdict already reached by two books written with astonishing speed in 1978, *The Suicide Cult* and *Guyana Massacre*, and by similarly themed 1979 articles in *Time*, *Newsweek* and *Rolling Stone* that described a crazy cult of death.

Too many dead people

But not everyone agreed. The *New York Times* and *Baltimore Sun* originally reported that four hundred bodies had been found at Jonestown, while around seven hundred people had fled into the jungle. Yet a week later, the dead numbered over nine hundred. Local papers like the *Guyanese Daily Mirror* reported that over a hundred Guyanese troops, as well as several score US Green Berets and members of the UK's

Black Watch, were on exercise in the jungles around Jonestown at the time. Doing what, exactly? What happened, the *Mirror* asked, to the followers who ran into the jungle but came out dead?.

The gun that killed Jones was found 200ft from his body, while the rest of the bodies, laying face down in neat rows, showed no signs of the contorted rigidity induced by cyanide. As reported in The *New York Times* and the *Miami Herald*, Guyanese pathologist Dr Leslie Mootoo told the coroner's court that he found gunshot wounds on some victims, but strange, needle-like puncture wounds on many, many more. Nonetheless, the US Army said that as the cause of death was not in dispute – suicide by drinking cyanide – no autopsies were required. The bodies rotted in the sun, were stripped of identification, and then flown to a remote US base with sev-

eral corpses lumped into each casket. Many were embalmed or cremated post-haste. According to the National Association of Medical Examiners, the military "badly botched" procedures.

The CIA

Several theories about Jonestown involve the CIA, with the most prevalent seeing it as a CIA-backed exercise in mind control and brainwashing. According to John Judge in his article *The Black Hole Of Guyana*, Guyana was also a CIA hotbed: its government was installed by a CIA-backed coup, the US embassy was a CIA HQ, and Dwyer, who escaped the killing at the airport, was a CIA agent. Judge relates that Jonestown survivor Teresa Buford,

The dead at Jonestown

who was Jones's mistress and financial manager of the Temple in California, as well as being the daughter of a former naval commander and spy, described brainwashing and mind-control methods in the Temple. Another senior Jonestown member was Larry Layton, whose father ran the US Army's Chemical-Biological Weapons Research unit. The stashes of drugs found at Jonestown included many used in the CIA's MK-ULTRA programme, which involved experimenting with the use of drugs for brainwashing and mind-control, and which the agency *claimed* to have stopped in 1973.

The story runs that Jones was employed by the CIA in Brazil, under the auspices of the CIA-linked charity World Vision. He then moved to California, where he founded a children's home before establishing the Temple at the behest of the CIA. After being forced to re-locate to South America when the Temple's activities attracted too much public opprobrium, Jones developed acute megalomania. The leader's loss of control meant that the CIA risked having its programme exposed, so the agency terminated the Temple in the most effective way imaginable: everyone was killed. Former Jonestown director Joyce Shaw called it a mass experiment in brainwashing and exterminating blacks.

A variation supported by Robert Sterling in *The Jonestown Genocide* and Michael Meiers in *Was Jonestown A CIA Medical Experiment?* argues that Jonestown was not only instigated by the CIA, but was still under CIA control at the time of the massacre, when it was about to be exposed by Ryan – who was therefore killed at the airstrip. It is a fact that Ryan had been behind the Hughes-Ryan amendment bill, which would have forced the CIA to disclose covert operations before carrying them out, and the link between this bill, his apparent antipathy to the CIA, and his death has also been made in the Church of Scientology magazine *Freedom*. Despite the self-evident dangers of Jonestown, Ryan wasn't provided with a US military escort; and when he died, so did the bill.

The threat that Ryan would expose Jonestown has been given another twist on the Internet: it's alleged that fugitive Nazis Dr Josef Mengele and Martin Bormann were overseeing experiments at Jonestown, which would obviously have embarrassed the CIA if anyone had found out. Some say, on the other hand, that the CIA destroyed Jonestown as a threat to the US when it cottoned on to the Nazi connection.

If Larry Layton was a CIA operative, his high connections didn't save him from receiving a life sentence in 1986. After two trials, in which he pleaded not guilty, Layton was jailed for his part in the killings at the airstrip – having got to the airport by pretending to Ryan that he wanted to defect, he produced a gun and shot and injured two people. Larry's sister Deborah, the Temple's financial director, had indeed defected in May 1978, and told the US government and the CIA in a 37-page affidavit that Jones was drilling for a mass suicide. However, the House Select Committee on Intelligence concluded in 1980 that Jones had never had anything to do with the CIA, and that the agency had no prior knowledge of the impending massacre.

The Soviets

There are also reputed links to the Soviets. Around $500,000 was allegedly taken from Temple funds and given to the Soviet embassy in Guyana shortly before the massacre, while Jones met frequently with officials from the Soviet and Cuban embassies. Was that what spurred so much interest from the CIA, or was the colony just a front to lure in Communist interests?

Conspiracist Dr Peter Beter told his listeners just weeks after Jonestown that the mass deaths were a cover for a large military operation against a Soviet missile base in Guyana. Jones was actually a Jew, who had organized Jonestown like a kibbutz, and had been spirited back to Israel by Israeli troops working with US in the strike.

The Californian conspiracy

Jones also had strange links in Californian politics. A week after the massacre, *The Washington Post* described Jones as a "West Coast power", referring to the presence and utilization of Temple followers in Californian politics. *The Washington Times* reported that President Jimmy Carter's wife Rosalynn had invited Jones to dinner. Jones's twenty thousand followers in California were pivotal political foot-soldiers, albeit crooked. The *New York Times* and *San Francisco Examiner* detailed how multiple ballots were cast to rig the 1975 San Franciscan mayoral election for Jones's ally, Democrat George Moscone.

Further rigged votes, threats and blackmail got more Temple men into public office in San Francisco, enabling the funnelling of $26 million from welfare and housing into offshore bank accounts. Just days after Jonestown, Moscone and prominent gay activist Harvey Milk (who at one time was a Temple follower) were shot dead by disaffected civic councillor Dan White, who later "killed himself". *USA Today* economics editor Jeff Schnepper has said that White was not the kind to commit suicide, and his death was "never investigated fully". The *New York Times* carried a charge from then-Governor Ronald Reagan that Jones "was close to Democrats". Was Jones so close that his Californian corruption ultimately got him killed?

John Judge makes another odd connection, arguing that Jones became Temple leader around the time Richard Nixon moved into the White House and set in place a massive increase in covert FBI surveillance and infiltration of political groups. Jones installed uniformed, armed guards in the Temple and used various techniques of coercion and blackmail against followers – sinister methods which Judge insinuates may have had Federal origins. One theory on the Web suggests that Jones fell between the stools of a Republican sting and Democrat politicking. Although if Jones, Moscone and Milk were all murdered for their supposed corruption, surely Jones could have been silenced without having to kill a thousand innocents as well?

Today

Little new evidence concerning Jonestown has emerged in recent years, though theorists are tantalized by the fact that five thousand documents from the HFAC hearings in 1979 have remained classified ever since. The committee's chief consultant, George Berdes, told CNN in 1998 that the documents would be declassified soon, but there's still no sign. At that time, CNN described the relatives of the dead as still asking questions and demanding answers, despite the prevailing media consensus of mass suicide. In 2004, the BBC reported the poignant fact that 412 bodies of the dead have never been claimed. They remain buried in a mass grave in Oakland, California.

SOURCES

Books

Jim Keith (ed) Secret And Suppressed (1993). Worth seeking out for John Judge's long, very detailed article, "The Black Hole Of Guyana", cited by virtually all subsequent works on Jonestown.

Michael Meiers Was Jonestown A CIA Medical Experiment?: A Review Of The Evidence (1989). Although Meiers' claim that Jonestown was a CIA medical experiment remains unsubstantiated, he shows that there was much more to Jones, the Temple and Jonestown than is usually covered.

Websites

Ⓦ www.deborahlayton.com Deborah Layton's own account of life in the People's Temple, also published in 1999 as **Seductive Poison: A Survivor Of Jonestown Shares Her Story**.

Ⓦ jonestown.sdsu.edu/AboutJonestown/Articles/conspiracy.htm This site by Rebecca Moore covers many of the major conspiracies about Jonestown.

Ⓦ www.parascope.com/articles/0997/jonestown.htm Robert Sterling's *The Jonestown Genocide* is now on the Net.

Ronald Reagan and the October Surprise

On January 16, 1979, following mass street protests, Shah Reza Pahlavi fled Iran. Islamic opposition leader Ayatollah Khomeini returned from exile to fill the power vacuum, imperilling the country's long-cosy relations with the US. In November, pro-Khomeini student revolutionaries seized the US embassy in the capital, Tehran, denouncing US support for counter-revolutionaries. They took more than sixty hostages and promised not to release them until the Shah was returned to Iran for trial and President Carter's administration unfroze $12 billion in Iranian assets held in US banks. The plight of the hostages – 52 of them, once a number of women were released – consumed the attention of the American public.

A year later, with the November 1980 presidential election approaching, the hostage crisis was the key issue of the campaign. Seeking a second term, Jimmy Carter was facing strong opposition from the Republican ticket of Ronald Reagan and his prospective Vice President, CIA chief George H.W. Bush. Polls showed the two parties racing neck and neck. Bush commented that he feared an "October Surprise" by the Democrats, whereby they would somehow pull off the hostages' release by the end of the month. (So the "October Surprise" label actually refers to a conspiracy theory that didn't happen, rather than one that allegedly did.) Meanwhile, Carter had declared an oil and weapons embargo and was negotiating hard with Khomeini's government. Iran was just as eager as the US to find a solution – it urgently needed weapons to resist an invasion by Iraq in September.

However, Carter's negotiations somehow broke down in October, and on November 4, 1980, Reagan won the election. The Republicans entered new talks with Iran through Algerian intermediaries. Reagan's inauguration speech of January 20, 1981,

trumpeted new beginnings: "Let us begin an era of national renewal", he said. "Can we solve the problems confronting us? Well, the answer is an unequivocal and emphatic 'yes'." Within minutes, it was announced that the hostages had been freed. That day, the Republicans had unfrozen $8 billion of Iranian assets. In the weeks that followed, the US government secretly began selling billions of dollars worth of weapons to Iran, mostly through the good offices of Israel.

The theory

So had regime change in the US simply resolved the impasse? Or, as conspiracy theorists charged, was there more to it than that? Was the 1980 election, as one commentator alleged, a "covert political coup"?

The theory runs that Reagan's team secretly negotiated with the Iranian revolutionary government behind Carter's back – aiming not only to release the hostages but also deliberately to undermine Carter's own efforts. The Republicans supposedly made a deal: if the Iranians would delay the good news until inauguration day, the new Reagan administration would make sure they were handsomely rewarded. At the heart of the story are the Hashemi brothers, Jamshid and Cyrus, Iranian arms dealers and businessmen who claim they brokered secret meetings between Khomeini's representatives and Reagan's campaign director, William Casey. (An American spy chief during World War II, Bill Casey went on to become Reagan's CIA chief.) Contact was made first in July and August 1980, in Madrid, and the deal firmed up at a Paris hotel (which one depends on whose version of events you believe) on either October 18, 19 or 20 (again, depending on whose account you follow). Which was exactly when Carter's

IRAN–CONTRA: NO THEORY

In 1979, the *Frente Sandinista de Liberación Nacional*, aka the Sandinistas, concluded their war against Nicaragua's brutal and corrupt Somoza government by taking power. They established a paternalistic, left-wing regime and, in 1985, held and won internationally recognized democratic elections. Against them, right-wing loyalists branded "Contras" (from "contra-revolutionary") were fighting a brutal campaign – in 1982 a Congressional intelligence committee reported that they "raped, tortured and killed unarmed civilians, including children". They had been trained and funded by the CIA. Under the 1983 Boland Amendment, however, Congress banned the spending of federal money on the Contras.

Faced with the ongoing hostage-taking of Americans in Beirut, the Reagan administration stepped up its programme of arms sales to Iran in return for Iranian help in freeing American hostages held by pro-Iranian militias. By November 1985, General Colin Powell was attempting to sell Iran five hundred HAWK anti-aircraft missiles through the Israeli government. As the value of the deal topped $14 million, however, Powell realized it would have to be declared to Congress. Spotting a way to kill two birds with one stone, Reagan's campaign chief, Bill Casey, devised the so-called Iran–Contra scheme, originally known only to a few top officials under the code name "the Enterprise". The

money from the missile sales would be diverted directly to the Contras to avoid awkward questions, troublesome domestic laws and UN agreements. The hostages would be freed and Nicaragua liberated from left-wing oppression. Everyone's a winner.

On November 3, 1986, the Beirut weekly *Ash-Shiraa* scooped the world with news of the scheme. On November 21, Oliver North, the National Security Council member responsible, began to shred documentary evidence. Four days later, US Attorney General Edwin Meese confessed to the Contra side of the scheme, and on November 26 Reagan announced the opening of the Tower Commission to examine the affair. As with the Watergate controversy, the key issue was how much Reagan knew, and how early. Handsome Colonel Oliver North, aide to National Security Advisor John Poindexter, became the public whipping boy – and media darling – of the affair, but Congress's final report, released on November 18, 1987, failed to clarify the extent of Reagan's knowledge. This was despite Reagan's diary entry of January 1986, which clearly stated "I agreed to sell TOWs to Iran", and North's testimony that he'd written five memos for the president describing the Contra angle. Reagan even delivered a bizarre apology to the American people on March 4, 1987: "A few months ago I told the American people I did not trade arms for

hostages. My heart and my best intentions still tell me that's true, but the facts and the evidence tell me it is not."

North and Poindexter were convicted on numerous counts of lying, conspiracy and obstruction of justice, but their convictions were overturned on appeal on the grounds that their testimony to Congress had been used against them despite a grant of immunity. The CIA emerged without a stain on its reputation, though it's widely assumed that it played a key role, possibly to the extent of providing extra

covert funds for the Contras by assisting their drug-trafficking business (see p.196). A 1988 Senate inquiry found that at the very least US officials had turned a blind eye to Contra involvement in the drug trade.

Much about the Iran–Contra scandal makes the October Surprise theory look worryingly plausible: Casey's involvement, the use of CIA contacts, the conduct of secret negotiations with Iran, and the evident willingness of the Reagan administration to work secretly and in contravention of both US and international law.

Oliver North testifies

negotiations stalled. It's claimed that George H.W. Bush was present at one or all of the meetings, possibly along with CIA agents Donald Gregg and/or Robert Gates – who went on to become Bush's director of the CIA.

A conspiracy of journalists: the prosecution on trial

From its inception, the October Surprise conspiracy theory was pieced together – or, if you prefer, concocted – by journalists. By now, everyone wanted to be a Woodward or a Bernstein. *Executive Intelligence Review*, the mouthpiece of Lyndon LaRouche's leftist/crypto-fascist/conspiracy theorist political group, was the first to publish, as early as December 1980. However in these pre-Internet years the rumours remained largely as word-of-mouth whisperings until an article by Gary Sick, former navy captain and Carter's White House aide for Iran during the hostage crisis, appeared in the *New York Times*, on April 15, 1991.

Sick attracted support from former President Carter himself, but how reliable is he? A leading sceptic of the October Surprise theory, the *Village Voice*'s Frank Snepp, pointed out that much of his information seems to have come from correspondence with another journalist, Martin Kilian, the Washington correspondent for Germany's leading political review, *Der Spiegel*. For his own book, Sick apparently interviewed only half the sources he quotes. As Snepp put it in 1991, he "built them into the scaffolding of his conspiracy theory, thus erecting an edifice of compounded error".

Snepp has come up with a sophisticated counter-theory that penetrates right to the heart of the problem with conspiracy theories in general. He claims that researchers and journalists cross-fed each other information and, worse still, allowed their sources in turn to cross-reference between each other. "The truth", Snepp writes, "may be lost to the confusion they generated." It was an unwitting conspiracy of journalists and sources. Sick responded that "there was no conspiracy ... this was a voluntary group of people working on the story which I regard as almost the best of investigative journalism."

The evidence: American alibis

The revelation of the Iran–Contra scandal (see opposite) made the October Surprise theory "feel" very substantial. But it wouldn't be enough in court – it's all circumstantial. Investigative journalists have spent thousands of person-hours trying to place Bush, Gregg, Casey and Gates in the right place at the right time. Bush's alibi seems fairly sound: he is known to have campaigned in Pennsylvania and New Jersey on October 17, and to have visited his Washington country club, Chevy Chase, on October 19 – between 10.29am and 11.56am, according to Secret Service logs. But, it's alleged, he *could* have made it to Paris and back between times, if he'd had use of a military jet. Donald Gregg's alibi seems even more solid. He was on vacation in Delaware, spending most of his time down on the beach. But as German journalist Martin Kilian pointed out, weather reports for the days in question describe overcast, cool conditions – as low as 55 degrees.

None of this would stand up in court, but some find it curious that no one has yet produced an alibi for Casey. And there is some troubling circumstantial evidence. In 1983, a Congressional subcommittee headed by Democrat Don Albosta was set up to examine "Briefing-gate", a scandal that centred on the theft of President Carter's briefing book during the 1980 campaign. It uncovered a network of Reaganite "foreign policy consultants" who appeared to have deliberately leaked disinformation about the progress of negotiations in an attempt to unnerve the Iranians and perhaps prevent an October Surprise. The campaign was headed by William Casey.

The evidence: witnesses

On the one hand, the alleged conspirators are CIA-linked Republicans who all vociferously deny involvement. On the other is a bizarre line-up of businessmen, arms dealers and self-described ex-intelligence operatives who all claim – just as loudly – to have been key players. The arms dealers Jamshid Hashemi and his brother Cyrus are often cited as key witnesses. Cyrus, unfortunately can't talk – he was murdered in London in July 1986. That hasn't stopped Jamshid, however, who confirmed details of the October Surprise meetings to journalist Craig Unger. Nor another arms-dealer and witness, Hushang Lavi, who was reported as having helped to open negotiations with the Iranian government.

Meanwhile, voluble Oregonian businessman Richard Brenneke places himself in Paris and Madrid as a kind of fixer. Brenneke's story is backed up by one Heinrich Rupp, who said (while under trial for bank fraud) that he was a CIA pilot and had flown Casey to Paris on October 18, where he'd caught sight of George Bush waiting at the airport. Brenneke cross-confirms his story. Bush himself, along with Donald Gregg, is supposed to have been flown home by one Gunther Russbacher, also said to be a former CIA flier, who says Bush attended one meeting at the Hôtel Crillon and another at the George V, negotiating with Hashemi Rafsanjani (Khomeini's number two) and Saudi Arabian businessman Adnan Khashoggi. Russbacher named $40 million as the price for the delayed release of the hostages.

The US arms sales to Iran were to be channelled through the Israeli government, an angle of the deal covered by the self-confessed presence in Paris of Ari Ben-Menashe – by his own account a former Mossad agent working as a fixer for the Israelis. He claims to have met Casey, Bush, Robert Gates *and* Donald Gregg at the Paris Hilton on 19 or 20 October. Supposed Mossad man Ahran Moshell makes similar claims.

An authoritative-sounding source for the October Surprise theory was Abol-Hassan Bani-Sadr, the first president of Iran under Khomeini. (So, no axe to grind there.) Speaking to researcher Barbara Honegger in 1988, he said that his knowledge of the affair came from a message he'd been sent by the Iranian foreign minister in September 1980. Bani-Sadr also believes that Carter's National Security Advisor, Zbigniew Brzezinski, helped Saddam Hussein plan the invasion of Iran. (Which isn't all that unlikely – in 1998, after all, Brzezinski publicly admitted that the CIA started arming the Afghanistani Mujahadeen in July 1979, six months *before* the Soviet invasion.)

In the witness box: the sources on trial

Self-described intelligence freelancer, Oswald "Razine" LeWinter, is central to the theory's claims. He originally told researchers Martin Kilian and Barbara Honegger that he'd read a secret memo about the affair in a CIA report. Later, he said that he'd been employed to get rid of evidence that the Paris meeting(s) had ever taken place. Later still, he placed himself in Paris at the time. Why did his story keep changing? Perhaps it was because he was a chronic myth-spreader – he once claimed he'd been paid $40,000 in 1988 to propagate the October Surprise theory. Later in his career, he materialized as a witness to the PanAm Flight 103 conspiracy theory (see p.301), and was jailed for trying to con $10m out of Mohamed al-Fayed for "proof" that Dodi al-Fayed and his girlfriend, Princess Diana, were assassinated by MI6 (see p.59).

LeWinter is not the only witness whose role seems to have grown over the years. Talking to a researcher in 1980, Jamshid Hashemi discussed the October Surprise theory without mentioning his own presence at Paris, and later changed his story regarding the presence of Bill Casey at negotiations. It's also strange that in 1984 he was indicted by a grand jury for smuggling small quantities of petty arms to Iran in 1980. Would he have been involved in such a job, it's asked, if he was simultaneously at work on the multi-million arms-to-Iran deal? As for Ari Ben-Menashe, he has never been able to prove his presence at the Paris hotel, and his credibility may be somewhat undermined by his boast of having planted a homing device at Iraq's Osirak reactor to enable Israeli planes to locate and destroy it – an unsubstantiated story that's too James Bond for some stomachs.

The other pilot regularly named as a witness, Gunther Russbacher, turns out to have been found guilty of misuse and misappropriation of government properties and misuse of government jets. Is his claim of involvement in the October Surprise the desperate squirming of a guilty man trying to get out of trouble? Or is he the victim of trumped-up charges designed to discredit him?

Conspiracy to create a conspiracy theory?

Quite apart from their individual credibility gaps, some detect a problem in that many of the main sources for the October Surprise theory knew each other and had dealt together in the past. A US Customs sting operation in April 1986, for instance, nabbed Brenneke and LeWinter, among others as illegally exporting arms to Iran. The insider informant was one Cyrus Hashemi... Did Lewinter and Brenneke want to pay the Americans back? Or clean up their reputations by association with something bigger than minor fraud and petty arms dealing? Or did Brenneke just want to make some money from the book he was planning?

Or were there other more pressing reasons for inventing such a scam? In 1988 Brenneke had to testify at a case where two Customs informants had supposedly claimed fraudulent expenses for a separate sting that had gone wrong. Brenneke supported his friend Heinrich Rupp's claim that he thought he had been acting under CIA instructions, citing his own involvement as a CIA agent flying arms into Iran in 1980–82. Both men testified to each other's involvement in the October Surprise negotiations. Unimpressed, the government charged Brenneke with perjury – only for Brenneke to repeat his claims, bringing George H.W. Bush into the picture too. Brenneke was cleared on five counts of lying – though journalists later showed that the prosecution could have proved from Brenneke's credit-card receipts that he was nowhere near Paris in mid-October 1980. As Steve Emerson and Jesse Furman put it in a *New Republic* article of November 18, 1991, "The Conspiracy That Wasn't", these super-sources had "discovered that it was possible to get away with any allegation in the national security area ... if an intelligence agency, already suspect in the public's mind, denied something, that merely reinforced the authenticity of the charges." The observation has since become an axiom of conspiracy theorizing.

Counter-theories: Carter's surprise

One Iranian theory brilliantly turns the tables on Carter. Far from being the victim of an evil electoral fraud, it's claimed that he was partly responsible for the hostage crisis in the first place – not to mention the Iranian revolution itself. The evidence? The quick-slow, stop-start speed of the Iranian students marching on the US embassy. It seems their procession was being controlled by a mullah – who was receiving commands by radio from the Iranian government. These delays were aimed at giving the Americans time to destroy crucial documents, and for senior diplomats to take refuge in the Iranian foreign ministry. But why would the revolutionary government have done this favour for the Americans? Because, it seems, they owed Carter one after he had secretly withdrawn support for the Shah, who had refused the Americans' demands for oil kickbacks.

This may be an outlandish theory, but there's some evidence that Carter's team may have undermined their own negotiation efforts by simultaneously pursuing arms deals – perhaps through none other than Cyrus Hashemi.

Lingering suspicions

In 1992, after pressure from former hostages and President Carter himself, the House of Representatives investigated the "October Surprise" charges, concluding that "there was no October Surprise agreement ever reached." The ensuing Senate Foreign Relations Committee inquiry, published as *The "October Surprise" Allegations And The Circumstances Surrounding The Release Of The American Hostages Held In Iran*, agreed that "the credible evidence now known falls far short of supporting the allegation of an agreement between the Reagan campaign and Iran to delay the release of the hostages". And yet, as journalist Robert Parry has pointed out, Congress received one crucial report too late for inclusion. It came from the Russian government, who disclosed that their own intelligence files confirmed the tale of an October Surprise deal.

Also "too late" to be included was material from journalist David Andelman's biography of Alexandre de Marenches, the legendary director of France's intelligence agency SDEC (now renamed the DGSE). According to Andelman, De Marenches acknowledged helping Casey to set up hostage talks with Iranian officials – in Paris, in October 1980. Similarly, Palestinian leader Yasser Arafat told President Carter that the PLO was also approached by Republican emissaries for a brokerage role. Of course Arafat and De Marenches may have had their own reasons for spreading the rumours. Or perhaps, as a US government spokesman said of the Russian report, their ideas were "based largely on material that has previously appeared in the Western media".

A matter of faith

John Barry's *Newsweek* cover story on November 11, 1991, "Making Of A Myth" commented that the October Surprise theory "reflects back at your own political biases. If you revile the Reagan-Bush epoch, you'll find an administration founded on ultimate treachery. If you admire Reagan's reign, these tales come across as the hallucinations of crazed publicity hounds." Such partisan interpretations of news events were to become the hallmark of the Clinton presidency. The truth, Barry said, had "become so complicated and so hideously detailed that no reasonable person can say with absolute certainty that there was no conspiracy and no deal." A feeling that anyone trying to pin down the truth about conspiracy theories will find horribly familiar...

The evidence for the October Surprise doesn't stand up to close scrutiny – the witnesses, especially, could hardly be a less reliable bunch. On the other hand, the timing and the coincidence of the Iran–Contra scandal absolutely stink. As journalist Craig Unger, in an October 1991 *Esquire* article, reported a congressional staffer as saying: "You'd have to be the village idiot to believe Iran released them at that time without talking to the Republicans." Another Unger source, Scott Thompson – a Tufts University professor who worked with Bill Casey in the 1980 Reagan-Bush campaign – puts it even more forcefully: "So people finally figured it out. What the fuck did they think was going on?"

OCTOBER SURPRISES

The phrase "October Surprise" has lent itself to a number of post-1980 US elections. George H.W. Bush's 1992 campaign was supposedly hijacked by the Democrats' timing of the indictment of Defense Secretary Caspar Weinberger on Iran–Contra conspiracy charges – four days before the election. In 2000, it was George W. Bush's turn, with the "discovery" of his old arrest for drink-driving. In 2004 accusations were hurled by both sides. There was the well-timed release of the story that US troops had allowed huge quantities of explosives to disappear from an Iraqi warehouse, and the equally well-timed delay in the release of the results of the Iraq Survey Group, which failed to find any WMD. Widespread suspicions also held that Bush would suddenly announce the capture of Osama bin Laden. In fact, only a video appeared, in which bin Laden directly addressed the American people – "I tell you in truth, that your security is not in the hands of Kerry, nor Bush, nor Al Qaeda. No. Your security is in your own hands." It wasn't much of an October Surprise, however, as commentators failed to agree which side bin Laden's intervention had favoured.

SOURCES

Books

Barbara Honegger October Surprise (1989). The first October Surprise book. A former researcher for the Reagan–Bush campaign team, Honegger claims to have heard a senior figure on Reagan's team boasting that the Republicans had "cut a deal" to prevent Carter's October Surprise. Her principled resignation from the Reagan administration and her detailed investigations followed.

Robert Parry Trick Or Treason (1993). Gutsy, persuasive book written by a campaigning journalist and true believer in the October Surprise conspiracy theory. Lots of material on the gaps in the schedules of the prime suspects.

Gary Sick October Surprise: America's Hostages In Iran And The Election Of Ronald Reagan (1992). The best-researched and most convincing version of the October Surprise conspiracy, from an expert on US policy in the region. Lots of fascinating context on the background to the Iranian situation.

Websites

⊛ archives.cjr.org/year/92/2/october.asp Fascinating analysis of the sourcing of a trio of pieces of investigative journalism into the October Surprise affair. Reveals how conspiracy theories can be created and sustained by journalists.

⊛ www.consortiumnews.com/archive/xfile.html Links to a series of pro-October Surprise articles by journalist Robert Parry, plus one or two others.

MK-ULTRA

The notion of a programmable agent who robotically carries out assassinations for the CIA, and then has no memory of who told him to do so, has cropped up in speculative theories about the killings of many prominent people. However, it has its roots in a real-life program, MK-ULTRA, which was worked on by the CIA and US Army Chemical and Biological Weapons division for two decades.

Origins

Congressional investigations and the declassification of archives have revealed that US military and intelligence agencies have been dabbling in mind control ever since the end of World War II. Project Chatter was instigated by the US Navy in 1947, following news of successful Soviet experiments with truth drugs. The CIA's mind-control experiments began with Project BLUEBIRD, which evolved into Project ARTICHOKE. This involved the use of hypnosis to induce amnesia in subjects, with the aid of magician John Mulholland. MK-ULTRA, the largest and most infamous such programme, was created when CIA director Allen Dulles amalgamated the various projects in April 1953, and set aside six percent of CIA funds to pay for it.

MK-ULTRA was given added impetus by reports of the Chinese and Koreans "brainwashing" US prisoners during the Korean War. It was feared that such brainwashing might have re-programmed certain POWs to defect or come back as Communists, or as "sleeper" spies who could be activated by trigger words or signals to carry out some heinous task

– hence the 1959 novel and subsequent film *The Manchurian Candidate*.

It's been suggested that the term "brainwashing" was actually invented by a magazine writer-cum-CIA-agent who was aiming to introduce the concept to Americans, but make it appear to be a cruel Commie invention. Be this as it may, the fear of what the enemy might do was enough to spur the CIA to try to do it too. As well as seeking the ultimate interrogation techniques and truth serums to use on enemy spies, the CIA wanted to be able to programme its own agents under altered states of consciousness. Not only could they then be activated by a click of the fingers, but their knowledge couldn't be tortured out of them, and ultimately their memories could be wiped clean.

Experiments

Many of the experiments carried out under MK-ULTRA were performed without the knowledge or consent of their subjects, who ranged from CIA employees to prostitutes and ordinary citizens. Some were supposedly coerced into "volunteering" by being entrapped in brothels set up by the CIA. Dr Sidney Gottlieb, a Bronx biochemist who was supposedly the inspiration for the mad scientist in Stanley Kubrick's film *Dr Strangelove*, was at the helm of MK-ULTRA during its first eleven years.

Gottlieb oversaw some truly bizarre experiments. Subjects were hypnotized and given drugs such as LSD, ketamine, psilocybine, heroin, marijuana, scopolamine, mescaline and alcohol, as well as electro-convulsive shocks, implanted electrodes, lobotomies, and radiation. Volunteers were locked in

Manchurian candidate? A US POW is released in Korea

sensory deprivation chambers, or had their "therapy" sessions recorded and played on a loop through headphones, all while doped on LSD. One volunteer was given LSD for 77 days straight. Another technique was to pump someone first with barbiturates and then with amphetamines, yanking the subject from near-sleep to consciousness.

Sometimes the human guinea pigs "talked" and revealed everything they knew; sometimes they just died. Experiments with heat, cold, and atmospheric pressure – uncannily reminiscent of similar experiments by the Nazis – were also conducted, on around 150 subjects in total. Programme officers "tested" LSD on each other, spiking drinks at parties – one such incident is said to have resulted in the suicide of Dr Frank Olson, as described on p.15 – and Gottlieb "experimented" with LSD by taking copious amounts himself, when working at Fort Detrick and Edgewood Arsenal (see Secret Bases, p. 283).

Applications

Even as the recreational use of LSD flourished during the 1960s, Major General William Creasy, the chief of the Army Chemical Corps, was advocating its use to poison the water supplies of enemy cities, as a kinder alternative to nuclear weapons. MK-ULTRA drugs, administered via poisoned cigars or handkerchiefs, were considered as weapons for assassinating Cuba's Fidel Castro, Patrice Lumumba in the Congo, and Iraq's Abd al-Karim Qasim (a.k.a. Abdul Kassem – see p.22); the latter two were ultimately dispatched by other means. Although there's no published evidence that any MK-ULTRA programmed agent had any success, the project has also been linked to the killings of Robert Kennedy (see p.37) and John Lennon (see p.55), the shooting of Ronald Reagan in 1981 and the Jonestown Massacre (see p.181).

Most of Gottlieb's records were destroyed, possibly on his orders, after the programme finished in 1972, a well-timed pre-emption of the Congressional Church Committee and the Rockefeller Commission, which investigated the CIA's domestic activities and uncovered MK-ULTRA not long after. President Gerald Ford formally prohibited further such activities in 1976.

Mengele and Montauk

So far, so factual. However, some conspiracy theorists of a more luridly imaginative bent have inevitably thickened the plot, speculating that the evil genius behind MK-ULTRA was none other than Nazi doctor Dr Josef Mengele (supposedly brought to the US under the legendary Operation Paperclip. The story goes that Mengele perfected his mind-control techniques by working on tens of thousands of kidnapped children, who were kept in iron cages stacked floor to ceiling in his secret underground base. Many, it's claimed, were enslaved for tasks from sex to assassinations, but just as many were slaughtered in front of the other children for Mengele's pleasure.

The largest of perhaps as many as 25 MK-ULTRA underground bases is said to have been at Montauk, on Montauk Island (see p.284), where around 250,000 teenage boys were allegedly brainwashed under the so-called "Montauk Project" from 1976 onwards (although some believe that the project also involved setting up a time-portal to receive the sailors teleported aboard the USS *Eldridge* – see Philadelphia Experiment p.268). Many of these "Montauk Boys" supposedly went on to lead normal and indeed successful lives as journalists, radio and TV personalities, businessmen, lawyers and judges, unaware that they were just agents of a higher power.

In fact, there have been and still are children's summer camps around Montauk on Long Island. Unsurprisingly, though, it's not been reported in the mainstream press that any of these camps are part of some crypto-fascist plot to create a race of brainwashed Americans.

MK-ULTRA victims

Candy Jones, who was a well-known model during the late 1940s and 1950s, claimed in her book *The Control Of Candy Jones* to have been one of the first to be programmed under MK-ULTRA. Her claims, however, pale in comparison with those of Brice Taylor, the pseudonym of Susan Ford, who purports to be an MK-ULTRA subject who recovered her senses in 1985, after an "accidental" car crash failed to kill her and reawakened dormant memories instead.

In *Thanks For The Memories*, Taylor states that she is the survivor of a NASA-CIA program of "ritual abuse and government mind control", instigated for both business and pleasure by shadowy governmental figures who were involved in bringing about the New World Order. Her handler, golfing comedian Bob Hope, supposedly loaned her out to every president from Kennedy to Clinton, and others besides, sometimes as a favour and sometimes to ensnare them in the bigger Illuminati trap. She also says that she was a drugs courier and part-time human computer for Henry Kissinger, no less, and that her children were "taken to parties where the elite or anybody who wanted to have sex with them was able to".

Another mind-control slave who claims to have known Taylor was Cathy O'Brien, who was supposedly "rescued" in 1988 by Mark Phillips, a self-styled intelligence insider. Together, O'Brien and Phillips have released a shelf-load of books, videos and CD-ROMs about the programme of brainwashing slaves for courier work, pornography and prostitution. By their account, Ronald Reagan's trigger-word for O'Brien to perform sex acts was "kitten", while deviant sexual practices are also attributed to George H.W. Bush, Dick Cheney and Hillary Clinton (presumably not together). According to her posts on Amazon.com, Ms Kathleen A. Sullivan knew O'Brien "as a fellow government mind-control victim", and worked with Phillips to deprogramme her. As she puts it: "I am reasonably certain Cathy's recollections ... are probably valid."

Messing with the mind

It has also been alleged that many prominent advocates of LSD, including Ken Kesey (author of *One Flew Over The Cuckoo's Nest*), Timothy Leary, Allen Ginsberg and Baba Ram Dass (Richard Alpert), not to mention future Unabomber Theodore Kaczynski, were introduced to the drug under the MK-ULTRA programme. The book *Acid Dreams* suggests that LSD was deliberately allowed to spread among the rebellious youth of the 1960s, in order to space them out and melt their minds into submission. When the programme backfired, and turned out to encourage critical thinking and the questioning of authority, "bad trips" and bad tabs were used to scare users away again. The full truth of MK-Ultra is unlikely to be revealed any time soon. In the meantime conspiracy theorists, many of who claim to have been under its influence, will no doubt continue to provide their own accounts – or hallucinations, as the case may be.

SOURCES

Books

Richard Condon The Manchurian Candidate The Cold War paranoia novel that penetrated – or perhaps inspired – the dark heart of MK-ULTRA.

Bruce Shalin and Martin A. Lee Acid Dreams The history of LSD in America, from the social effects on the hippy scene, the literary genius unleashed and the whole sinister CIA plot behind it all.

Websites

ⓦ http://mdma.net/mk-ultra/sidney-gottlieb.html Gottlieb's obituary from the *LA Times*. RIP, Dr LSD.

ⓦ ww.mindcontrolforums.com/radio/ckln23.htm An interview with the aforementioned Brice Taylor. Either incredibly imaginative fantasy or even more incredible fact.

ⓦ www.trance-formation.com/ The website of Cathy O'Brien and Mark Phillips not only gives you a glimpse of their stories but many opportunities to buy materials on MK-ULTRA in book, audio and CD.

The White Alliance: the CIA, the Contras and cocaine

Rumours that the CIA keeps a hand in the international drugs trade have circulated for decades, ever since the Agency's alleged co-operation in Southeast Asia's opium "Golden Triangle" during the Vietnam War, and its backing for Afghani drug-warlords who fought for the Mujahadeen against the Russians. But the rumour vultures are thickest in the air closer to home, over Central America, where a trail of corpses and cocaine-stained banknotes leads back to shady narco-regimes and coca-guerillas who were the recipients of generous US government support in the 1980s. Scratch a freedom fighter and you'll find a drug baron; scratch the drug baron, it seems, and you'll see the CIA disappearing out of his back pocket.

The Contras and the CIA

On the face of it, allegations that the CIA was in cahoots with cocaine traders are absurd. The US government spends billions every year on drug suppression, with the Drug Enforcement Agency heavily involved in million-dollar programmes of coca-crop eradication and the pursuit of traffickers across South and Central America. Why would one hand of the government palm off what the other was trying to smash with an iron fist? The answer, say critics, goes back to 1983 and the Boland Amendment, which banned federal funding of the

Contras, the Nicaraguan militias dedicated to the overthrow of the left-wing Sandinista government. The CIA responded by devising the so-called Iran–Contra scheme (see p.186), swapping weapons for Iranian cash and backhanding the proceeds to their Nicaraguan terrorist friends. But this wasn't enough, so the Contras had to rely on drug money for their funding as well. According to which conspiracist or journalist or politician you ask, the CIA helped the Contras maintain their coke-fuelled campaigns by not worrying unduly about their allies' finances, failing to pass on evidence of trafficking to the DEA, or even facilitating cocaine shipments itself. And knowledge of the programme supposedly went right to the top, reaching George H.W. Bush and Ronald Reagan. Seems it's not called the White House for nothing...

Mercurial news

According to the most extreme theorists, the CIA made use of so-called "rogue agents" to actually import cocaine into the US. The agency, they charge, had a taste for two-birds-one-stone schemes like Iran–Contra. Just for the sake of a little powder on its hands, it could fund the Contras and simultaneously guarantee a cheap supply of a debilitating drug that would keep the downtrodden masses – inner-city black communities in particular – nicely in their place.

If this kind of outright evil plotting seems unbelievable now, it might have felt more credible in South Central LA in the early 1980s. Communities literally came under attack as lethal addiction and violent crime took over the streets, under the influence of crack cocaine. It seemed implausible that a drug with such destructive effects had just rolled in out of the blue, impossible that users were bringing all this misery on themselves unaided. Conspiracy theories that crack cocaine was a new kind of weapon of mass destruction joined the conspiracy theories about KFC and Snapple, or the AIDS virus. None was given mainstream credibility by reporters until August 1996, when investigative journalist Gary Webb published a three-day series of articles under the headline "Dark Alliance" in the *San Jose Mercury News* – a respected paper with Pulitzer prizes under its belt.

Webb didn't claim the CIA was actually flying crack into LA, but he did trace a process of policy decisions and dubious activities that, he believed, had allowed the cocaine explosion to occur. LA's drug supplies, he said, could be traced back to Nicaraguan drug producers with close links to the Contras. And those Contras were being protected by their CIA handlers. The article caused a blizzard of protest and vehement denial. By May 1997, *Mercury News* executive editor Jerry Ceppos was calling the story "oversimplified" – while claiming he'd never read it – and protesting that the newspaper had always been worried by a lack of corroborating sources. But the genie was out of the bottle. Inevitably, a bunch of government committees began trying to force it back in. And, just as inevitably, a crowd of "witnesses" and "ex-CIA assets" began coming forward, laying claim to key roles in the affair.

The heroin angle: Bo Gritz and Prof McCoy

Surely the most glamorous and controversial figure to take the stand against the US government was Bo Gritz. A highly decorated Vietnam vet, he became the inspiration for "Rambo" as the hero of (failed) missions to find fellow veterans missing in action, whom he suspected were being held in Laos as unacknowledged prisoners of war. He later became a fierce anti-government campaigner and Christian Identity fundamentalist. While Gritz's "evidence" didn't exactly relate to Central America, it did suggest that federal agencies were not averse to a bit of drug trafficking. According to his sensational account, as part of a secret mission to northern Burma he held talks with the warlord Khun Sa, who controlled the Golden Triangle opium trade, and hence most of the heroin flowing towards the Americas. Khun Sa told Gritz that his main client was … the US government, working through regular conspiracy suspects such as Santos Traficante, boss of the Florida Mob, and Richard Armitage, the bodybuilding veteran of Vietnam, Iran and the State Department.

Flanking Bo Gritz is the incongruously academic figure of Alfred McCoy, professor of Southeast Asian History at the University of Wisconsin-Madison, and author of *The Politics Of Heroin* (see p.201). He too had made an investigative trip deep into the heroin jungle. As a graduate student, he had discovered that French intelligence had funded itself by selling opium during the colonial wars in Indochina. After that, in his own words, "It was basically pulling a thread and keep tugging at it and a veil masking the reality began to unravel." The reality he uncovered was that the CIA routinely recruited upland warlords as allies in the war against Communism, from northeastern Burma in 1950, through Laos during the Vietnam war, to the Afghan resistance to the Soviet invasion. Coming under the wing of the CIA allowed these allies to operate without fear of investigation, and their role in the heroin trade followed the same pattern each time, mushrooming from smaller-scale local production to massive international trading.

Nothing could be allowed to come between the CIA and its fight against the red menace. The DEA would always concede priority to the bigger campaign. In Honduras, for example, a DEA agent called Tomas Zepeda gathered evidence that the military were corruptly allowing drug barons to fly shipments to the US. His reports threatened a Contra supply line and he was withdrawn. "Faced with the choice", McCoy says, "the United States government chose the cold war over the drug war." It wasn't difficult to arrange: as McCoy points out, the DEA and CIA had their origins with the same personnel and their "institutional relationship" remains close.

Whistleblowers: Castillo, Palacio

The most ubiquitous witness – his testimony is pinned up all over the Internet – is Celerino "Cele" Castillo, who claims that he personally caught CIA agents red- (or rather white-) handed while working as a field agent for the DEA in the late 1980s. Castillo has impressive credentials, including stints in Central America working alongside Hector Antonio Regalado – aka "Dr Death", the death-squad specialist and supposed trigger-man for Roberto D'Aubuisson, the alleged murderer of Archbishop Romero (see p.52) – and the infamous Felix Rodriguez, the self-confessed murderer of Che Guevara, who carried the revolutionary's Rolex as

a souvenir. While stationed in El Salvador, Castillo recorded a number of suspicious flights taking off from Ilopango airfield on which known drug traffickers appeared to enter and return from the US on CIA-provided visas. The operation came under the command of Lt Col Oliver North, of Iran–Contra fame. Castillo claims that he tried to file reports but was repeatedly warned off investigating further on the grounds that drug running was necessary for Contra funding.

One such warning came from the DEA's Latin America chief, just a month before the Iran–Contra hearings. Castillo says that he was even told the operation was protected by the White House, and was ordered not to close his files on the Contras so that they could continue to be active, and thus protected from Senator John Kerry's Subcommittee on Terrorism, Narcotics and International Operations. Castillo was never called to testify. Instead, he was arrested on drug charges. As an October 1986 cable to Langley from the narcotics coordinator at the US Embassy in Tegucigalpa stated: "The DEA believes ... he will attempt to use publicity of his alleged [US Government] ties to defeat any prosecution." But Castillo *was* a former DEA agent!

Another "eyewitness" was FBI informant Wanda Palacio, previously with Colombia's notorious Medellin cartel. In 1983 she claims she was stand-

DID NOT SNORT: COCA-CLINTON AND THE "MENA" AFFAIR

With Iran–Contra and the CIA–cocaine allegations, the liberal left has pretty much had a monopoly on political mud to chuck around. On the drugs turf, the best right-wing theorists have been able to come up with is the Mena scandal. It blatantly piggybacks on CIA drug-flight theories, claiming that drug-smuggling Contra pilots regularly used the Intermountain Regional

Airport at Mena, Arkansas. Based on the dubious statements of characters such as the notorious drug smuggler and DEA informant, Barry Seal, and Richard Brenneke, of October Surprise fame, Mena emerges as the centre of a multi-million-dollar drug smuggling network.

The twist in this tale is the location: Arkansas. "Patriotic"

conspiracy theorists would have it that the whole operation must have been overseen, protected and covered up by the then-Governor of Arkansas, Bill Clinton, in league with various state banks. The left came right back with a counter-conspiracy: the whole Mena conspiracy theory, it's said, is the result of an *actual* conspiracy by Richard Mellon Scaife and other

right-wing figures to smear Clinton, and a very well-funded conspiracy at that. At this point, the arguments go round in circles. The least that can be said is that next to known conspiracies such as Oliver North's Enterprise (see p.199–200) and the downfall of BCCI (see p.230), "Mena" simply doesn't cut the mustard.

ing beside Colombia's drug supremo, Jorge Ochoa, as cocaine was loaded onto a Southern Air Transport plane. The company had previously been owned by the CIA, and Palacio says she was told that it was still being used by the CIA to exchange Contra drugs for guns. Senator Kerry passed Palacio's statement on to William Weld, the Assistant Attorney General for Criminal Affairs, who reportedly laughed and passed the story off as a rumour, or the work of "bum agents", later comparing Palacio's credibility to "a wagonload of diseased blankets". When, in October 1986, the famous plane was shot down by the Sandinistas over Nicaragua – the so-called Hasenfus incident, named after the pilot that died – Palacio claimed she recognized the co-pilot that survived, Wallace "Buzz" Sawyer, as one of the men she'd seen loading cocaine three years before. President Reagan denied any connection between the government and the Hasenfus plane, but within a month the Iran–Contra scandal had broken. Was there a drugs angle to Iran–Contra? Or was Palacio an opportunist taking a chance to give her story a little credence?

Public investigations

Witnesses could be ignored, but the revelation that Iran–Contra was a real, CIA-backed scheme galvanized a few politicians into action. In 1987, Vietnam veteran turned Democratic Senator John Kerry headed a subcommittee of the Senate Foreign Relations Committee under the brief of "Narcotics, Terrorism and International Operations". The "Kerry Committee" reported in December 1988. While it didn't state that US officials ran drugs, it did conclude that Oliver North had set up a privatized network to supply the Contras, and that this had been used by drug barons as a cover for smuggling. North's network turned a blind eye to such an extent that it had blithely worked with known drug traffickers. But as with Iran–Contra, the buck

stopped with Ollie North. It was left to conspiracy theorists to trace the white lines upwards, towards Donald Gregg and George H.W. Bush.

Kerry's report was deeply critical of the CIA, but many smelled whitewash anyway. The *San Jose Mercury News* furore sparked a new wave of investigations, including three inquiries by the Office of the Inspector General – one at the Department of Justice and two at the CIA. In October 1998, the CIA's report on itself again denied the allegation that it had been involved in drug smuggling, or that its employees had "conspired with or assisted Contra-related organizations or individuals in drug trafficking to raise funds for the Contras or for any other purpose". At least, that's what the summary said. As journalist Robert Parry has pointed out, the detail of the report painted a subtly different picture – more murky grey than whitewashed. Frederick Hitz, the CIA's Inspector General, made it clearer than ever that the Contras were deeply involved in drug trafficking, and that the CIA had frequently failed to pass on their knowledge of this to the Justice Department or Congress. It had even blocked drugs investigations that threatened intelligence work.

But the CIA argued that this was quite proper. CIA Director Bill Casey had actually negotiated an exemption from the legal requirement to report drug smuggling by Agency assets to the Justice Department – "in view of the fine cooperation the Drug Enforcement Administration has received from CIA", as the Memorandum of Understanding puts it. Casey's request was granted in February 1982, two months before Reagan authorized CIA support for the Contras. It's not just that the War on Drugs ceded place to the War on Communism, it seems, but that the War on Communism allowed drug barons to operate without having to worry about squads of Special Forces helicopters suddenly descending on their ranches, or their freight planes being shot down.

In the second year of his investigation, Kerry turned to the BCCI – the utterly discredited Bank of Credit and Commerce International. By the time he reported, in 1992, he had exposed an utterly corrupt institution that the CIA had routinely used for secret payments. The bank's web of complicated connections – extending from the bin Ladens to the Bushes, and from Saddam Hussein and Manuel Noriega to Richard Helms and William Casey – is disentangled on p.230.

White lines and Shining Paths: the case of Vladimiro Montesinos

The coke trail doesn't stop on the north side of the Panama canal. On September 14, 2000, Peruvian TV viewers were amazed to see a leaked video of their intelligence chief bribing an opposition politician to join President Alberto Fujimori's ruling coalition. The resulting mega-scandal saw Fujimori sacked by a Congress that declared him "morally unfit" to govern, and intelligence chief Vladimiro Montesinos going on an eight-month fugitive-run across Central America. It also saw yet more evidence emerge that the CIA tolerated the drug trade. Montesinos, it transpired, had been paid $1m a year as a CIA asset to fight narco-trafficking. Did the CIA not know that he had profited to the tune of hundreds of millions from deals with Colombian drug barons?

It seems someone did. A DEA document written in August 1996 has recently emerged showing that the agency was aware that Montesinos was taking bribes from drug barons to go after their competitors – these were the anti-drug campaigns that were being funded by the CIA. Montesinos had been cultivated by the CIA since 1974, and rose steadily to become head of the SIN, the Peruvian intelligence service, in the early 1990s. International criticism of his methods – including sponsorship of death-squad killings – was always tempered by CIA and DEA support. Critics of US policy have long suspected that the real reason for this backing was Montesinos's bloody, ruthless campaign against Peru's Maoist guerilla movement – the *Sendero Luminoso* or "Shining Path" – a twenty-year war that, the Peruvian Truth and Reconciliation Commission concluded in August 2003, had killed an estimated 69,280 people.

US policy-makers also favoured Montesinos's support for the right-wing counter-insurgency in Colombia. Some commentators believe that it was only after the CIA discovered in August 2000 that Montesinos had double-crossed them (by smuggling ten thousand AK-47 rifles from Jordan to the Colombian rebel group FARC – the very rebels that Washington was funding him to suppress) that they pulled the plug on his operation. Peruvians certainly haven't failed to notice that the leaked video came at a suspiciously useful time for the CIA, which suddenly wanted to get rid of a liability. Other critics, including the Jordanians, claim that the shipment couldn't have happened without CIA support. An anonymous Peruvian judicial source was widely quoted as saying: "How can people doubt that the CIA is capable of something like this. Did the Iran-Contra scandal teach you nothing?"

At the time of writing, Montesinos was languishing in a naval base near Lima, slowly accumulating

GANGLAND PENINSULA

Central America has a burgeoning problem with street gangs. Two of the biggest, Mara 18 and Salvatrucha, may have as many as 100,000 members across Honduras, El Salvador and Guatemala. Modelled on US gangs like LA's famous Bloods and Crips, they're deeply involved in the drug trade – though gang members are forbidden to become users themselves on pain of vicious punishment beatings. The gang culture is partly homegrown, born of rural families who fled the US-backed civil wars of the 1980s and whose children grew up on city streets. But it's also an imported phenomenon.

more and more years to his sentence. Convicted of conspiracy, embezzlement and corruption, he has yet to answer the drugs charges. More shocking revelations seem likely to emerge, though his defence team's appeal for George Tenet, ex-CIA Director, to testify fell on deaf ears.

In the early 1990s, Bill Clinton encouraged US immigration officials to deport gang members back to their home countries – at the height of the programme, hundreds of young El Salvadoreans were arriving in San Salvador alone, every month. Some Central American conspiracists have called it a deliberate campaign by the US to destabilize the region. Others believe that the gangs are funded and supported by Columbian cartels, keen to flex their muscle in the US's backyard. The end of the era of CIA-protected narco-regimes certainly created a gap in the market for an alternative network of distributors...

The upshot

In 2000, a House Intelligence Committee investigation set up to report on the truth of the *San Jose Mercury News* articles declared that "the CIA as an institution did not approve of connections between Contras and drug traffickers, and, indeed, Contras were discouraged from involvement with traffickers". (One wonders what this discouragement involved.) But then the Committee was headed by Porter Goss, a CIA employee whom George W. Bush rewarded with the post of Director of the CIA in September 2004... The report said that "CIA offi-cers on occasion notified law enforcement entities when they became aware of allegations concerning the identities or activities of drug traffickers", but admitted that in some cases "CIA employees did nothing to verify or disprove drug trafficking information, even when they had the opportunity to do so. In some of these, receipt of a drug allegation appeared to provoke no specific response, and business went on as usual."

As for allegations that the CIA was responsible for the crack explosion in LA, the House report concluded that the traffickers and dealers named by reporter Gary Webb were not CIA agents or assets. The two most significant, Norwin Meneses and Danilo Blandon, were sympathetic to the Contras, it said, and had made donations of thousands of dollars, but their role was not significant. To sum up, there was "no evidence that any other US intelligence agency or agency employee was involved in the illegal supply or sale of drugs in the Los Angeles area".

Perhaps the theory of a CIA-inspired eugenic campaign to force-feed drugs down the necks (or up the noses) of US citizens is a little paranoid. The social and economic costs of drug use are so appalling that it seems preposterous that any government agency would knowingly promote the drug trade. Encourage a criminal, violent, volatile and, worst of all, untaxable, underclass? Talk about shooting yourself in the foot. But then if the whole Contra debacle showed one thing, it's that during the Reagan era the CIA would have sold its soul if it would have helped it fight the Reds. Assuming it had a soul in the first place, of course.

SOURCES

Books

Celerino Castillo and Dave Harmon **Powderburns: Cocaine, Contras And The Drug War** (1994). "Cele" Castillo's ghostwritten testimony. A drug dealer's fantasy? Or the most serious indictment of the CIA–cocaine affair?

Michael Levine **The Big White Lie: The CIA And The Cocaine/Crack Epidemic – An Undercover Odyssey** (1993). Former DEA agent Levine acts as both witness and prosecutor in this fictionalized, highly personal story detailing CIA complicity in the drug trade.

Alfred McCoy **The Politics Of Heroin: CIA Complicity In The Global Drugs Trade** (2003). A serious history of CIA involvement in the heroin trade in Southeast Asia. Some of the material is twenty years old, but new chapters cover Afghanistan and Central America. A virtual conspiracy Bible.

Robert Parry Lost History: Contras, Cocaine, The Press & "Project Truth" (1999).

One of the foremost journalists writing on the Iran–Contras–CIA–cocaine connection, Parry has also been accused of being a leading conspiracy theorist. Well-written and researched.

Peter Dale Scott and Jonathan Marshall Cocaine Politics: Drugs, Armies And The CIA In Central America (1998). At the political and serious end of the scale – co-written by a UC-Berkeley professor and an economics journalist. Updated with a preface covering the *Mercury News* story.

Gary Webb Dark Alliance: The CIA, The Contras, And The Crack Cocaine Explosion (1999). The exposé that launched a thousand others – but it's six hundred pages long, and now a little out of date.

Websites

ⓦ www.consortiumnews.com/archive/crack.html Robert Parry was one of the journalists who broke the original Iran–Contra story for Associated Press. This is the online archive of his articles on the crack cocaine angle.

ⓦ www.csun.edu/CommunicationStudies/ben/news/cia/main.html Huge database of CIA/cocaine-related news articles. Comes under the banner "Cocaine Import Agency" – in case you were wondering which side of the fence this site's author was on.

ⓦ www.fas.org/irp/cia/product/cocaine/ The official answer to Gary Webb's news articles: aka the Office of the Inspector General of Investigations Staff's report on "Allegations of Connections Between CIA and The Contras in Cocaine Trafficking to the United States" (January 29, 1998). For Volume II "The Contra Story" (October 8, 1998), see www.cia.gov/cia/reports/cocaine/

ⓦ www.odci.gov/cia/reports/cocaine/pilots.html. The CIA's response to claims by Castillo and others. On the main CIA site, www.cia.gov, searching under "Contra" brings up a number of detailed reports.

ⓦ www.usdoj.gov/oig/special/9712/ "The CIA–Contra–Crack Cocaine Controversy: A Review Of The Justice Department's Investigations And Prosecutions" (December, 1997).

Clintongates: ruining people is considered a sport

"I do believe that this is a battle." So said First Lady Hillary Clinton, on NBC's *Today* show, on January 27, 1998. Instead of covering her husband's peccadilloes and misdemeanours, she said, journalists should be writing about "this vast right-wing conspiracy that has been conspiring against my husband since the day he announced for president", a conspiracy designed "to undo the results of two elections." Those two elections, in 1992 and 1996, had really hurt the Right. Bill Clinton was not just a Democrat, he was a liberal-leaning, saxophone-playing, glad-handing scumbag. His wife was worse. Practically a *feminist*. They had to be stopped.

Fostergate

The first attack came right at the start of President Clinton's first administration. In the "Travelgate" scandal, seven White House travel office workers were fired on the pretext of minor corruption – allegedly so that they could be replaced with travel agents from Little Rock, Arkansas. As deputy White House legal counsel, Arkansas lawyer Vincent Foster investigated the issue. After a hostile *Wall Street Journal* editorial attacked him for alleged complicity in a cover-up, Foster apparently became depressed. On July 20, 1993 – six months after Clinton's inauguration and a day after he had contacted his doctor for treatment – he was found dead with a gunshot wound to the head. A week later, a resignation letter was discovered in his briefcase. "Ruining people", it said, "is considered a sport."

Conspiracy theorists pounced. Some said the letter was a forgery. It was widely claimed that Foster had shot himself with the wrong hand, that his body had been moved, that he'd been drugged, that there wasn't enough blood on the scene – the usual allegations that circle round every celebrity corpse. But the most baroque theory behind Foster's death does in fact hold that he killed himself.

This is the so-called "Norman-Grabbe" or "Fostergate" theory, from the pens of journalists James R. Norman and J. Orlin Grabbe. A former editor at *Forbes* magazine – which rejected his story – Norman claims that Vince Foster killed himself because he was about to be unmasked as an Israeli spy. By this account, Foster had been working for the National Security Agency on behalf of Systematics Inc, the company behind the infamous PROMIS software, which supposedly allows the NSA to hack into the world's banking transactions. Norman contends that Systematics was really a global money-laundering operation, and that Foster was working for Israel, possibly on its acquisition of US nuclear codes. Using a Cray supercomputer, CIA hackers had broken into a Mossad database, found Foster's name, and traced it to a Swiss bank account that they covertly emptied and repaid to the US Treasury. Apart from the obvious plot holes – hackers use Crays? Mossad keep their NOC-lists online? Swiss bank accounts can be accessed with a password and a double click? – Norman and Grabbe have a problem with their sources, all of whom are prolific conspiracy theorists themselves.

Whitewater-gate

Some theorists allege the Norman-Grabbe theory is itself a conspiracy, a deliberate disinformation leak to hide the fact that Foster was murdered by his former friend, Bill Clinton. With the President under increasing pressure to come clean about the so-called Whitewater affair, they say, Foster knew too much. Following every rapid of the Whitewater-gate story is a painfully dull paperchase. It's a tawdry tale of Arkansas land deals, bank loans and transactions between the Clintons and their business partners, the McDougals, in which the basic charge is that Clinton abused his position as Arkansas governor to advance his own business interests. By January 1994, the affair had become a right-wing *cause célèbre*, and Clinton was forced to request that a special prosecutor investigate. Attorney General Janet Reno appointed one Robert B. Fiske, who concluded in June that Foster's death was suicide, and that the White House had not broken any laws. But that wasn't enough. By July, Whitewater was the subject of both House and Senate Banking Committee hearings, and in August Kenneth Starr was appointed as a new special prosecutor. The big dog was off the leash.

The Senate Whitewater probe drew to a close in June 1996. Republicans alleged suspicious obstruction by the Clintons, but could find no smoking gun; Democrat Senators separately concluded that the Clintons' water was whiter-than-white, and that they were victims of a Republican smear campaign.

Pick a side. Either way, Whitewater was a damp squib – but Kenneth Starr kept going. On October 10, 1997, he released a new report on Foster's death. He found the death to be suicide, and declared the reports of funny business with the corpse – wrong hand, no blood, faked note, you name it – to be untrue. And if Kenneth Starr thinks Foster killed himself, surely the rampant right can be satisfied.

Monica Lewinsky and the path to impeachment

Despite everything, the Starr juggernaut kept rolling on. On January 12, 1998, government worker Linda Tripp contacted the special prosecutor directly to let him know that she had tape-recorded conversations with White House intern Monica Lewinsky. (Tripp, it transpired, had been prompted to make the tapes by her literary agent friend, Lucianne Goldberg – a name familiar to Watergate buffs, as Goldberg had worked as a writer for Democrat George McGovern during his presidential campaign against Richard Nixon, while secretly reporting to Nixon aide Murray Chotiner.) Tripp said that the tapes proved that Lewinsky and Clinton had had an affair, and that a Clinton aide had told Lewinsky to lie about it in Paula Jones's (unsuccessful) sexual harassment lawsuit against Clinton. By January 16, Kenneth Starr had obtained permission from Janet Reno to expand his enquiry into examining whether Clinton had lied under oath. That news emerged just a day later on the Drudge Report, a contentious Internet news-sheet. Had Starr's office deliberately leaked the story? Was Starr a tireless campaigner for standards in public life? Or was he simply out to hang Clinton for whatever could be pinned on him?

In August, after earlier denials, Clinton admitted that he'd misled the American people, perjured himself, and had indeed had an "inappropriate" relationship with Lewinsky. Finally, after more than four years and at a cost of almost $40m, the *Starr Report* was released on September 9, 1998. On December 11, Starr's recommendation that Clinton be impeached was approved by a House Judiciary Committee vote that split straight down party lines. Congress duly sent the case to the Senate. In February 1999, ten Republican Senators joined the solid mass of Democrats in voting that Clinton had not committed

THE CLINTON BODY COUNT

During the summer of 1998, an email and Web-based list of some fifty suspicious deaths of people said to have been associated with Bill Clinton appeared as if from nowhere. It seems to be an expanded version of a list compiled by an Indianapolis lawyer, pro-gun activist and conspiracist called Linda Thompson, which was circulated to Congressmen by former California representative William Dannemeyer in 1994. Thompson admitted to having "no direct evidence" that Clinton had anyone killed – but that scarcely mattered. *The Clinton Chronicles*, a video version of the list compiled by arch Clinton-hater and religious conservative Jerry Falwell, is no more rigorous in its sourcing. The anonymous, silhouetted journalist giving "evidence" on the tape was later revealed to be the video's producer.

Clinton was not the first US president to be attributed such a Machiavellian record – which either shows that politicians are a bunch of murdering maniacs, or that you can make up a list of this kind for anyone with enough high-profile connections, if you trawl widely enough. Take name no. 30: Dr. Stanley Heard, a high-flying chiropractor who treated Clinton's mother, stepfather and brother. His private plane caught fire and crashed, killing him outright. Maybe Clinton's stepdad let something slip while his back was being manipulated…

But however dubious individually, after you've waded through fifty suicides, plane crashes and "mysterious" accidents, you'll be tempted to lean towards the latter part of the list's usual subheading: "Coincidence or the Kiss of Death?". Two questions, however, spring to mind: if Clinton's allies are such psychos, how come they never took out Gennifer Flowers, or Paula Jones, or Monica Lewinsky? And if Clinton could be impeached for getting a blowjob in the Oval Office, why did no one ever think of trying him for multiple murder?

perjury, while five Republicans stood behind Clinton in rejecting the charge that he had obstructed justice in the Paula Jones case. In both instances, that was a long way from the two-thirds majority required to remove Clinton from office.

A vast right-wing conspiracy?

Hillary Clinton's allegation of a "vast right-wing conspiracy" sounds like the words of someone who is under siege and feeling the pressure. It could equally be a political smokescreen, an attempt to turn media attention around. She could also have been entirely serious. Even Attorney General Janet Reno apparently considered investigating the Whitewater affair as a campaign to smear the Clintons. Was Kenneth Starr a pawn of the right? A Texan minister's son, Starr had worked under Ronald Reagan's first attorney general, and had gone on to become solicitor general in the first Bush administration.

Although friends called Starr dogged and honest, perhaps his thoroughness was manipulated by a well-funded campaign to bring down Clinton. Multi-millionaire and deep conservative Richard Mellon Scaife has been fingered as a force behind the anti-Clinton campaigns. As the owner of the *Pittsburgh Tribune-Review*, he was able to push the Fostergate story. According to investigative reporters Jonathan Broder and Murray Waas of *Salon* magazine, Scaife was also paying off David Hale, the key Whitewater witness, and publicizing the Mena scandal, in which Clinton was supposed to have profited from a CIA-Contra cocaine-for-arms deal operating out of Mena airfield in Arkansas. The conservative Rutherford Institute funded Paula Jones's case against Clinton, while the right-wing Citizens for Honest Government paid for the video version of the "Clinton body count" list (see opposite) – and supposedly paid off Arkansas state employees on the side.

Hillary and Bill Clinton: who wears the trousers?

More troubling (and more demonstrable) is the idea that Clinton's enemies didn't even need to pay for their campaign. Ever since Watergate (see p.176), a part of every American political journalist has wanted to be a Woodward or a Bernstein. In June 1997, the Clintons' Whitewater lawyer, David Kendall, accused the Starr office of an outright "leak-and-smear" campaign to damage his clients, a campaign that he alleged even broke grand jury secrecy rules. But leaks can't survive on their own, and papers like *The Washington Post* and *New York Times* played their part in propagating stories that once would have barely made it on to scandal sheets or scurrilous websites.

Some commentators tried to turn Hillary Clinton's words right back on her, claiming that the whole Foster-Whitewater-Lewinsky affair was in fact a left-wing conspiracy to obscure a secret agenda. Bill Clinton was a Communist! Didn't he make a trip to Moscow as a student? Bill Clinton was a would-be Hitler! He planned to bring the country's political system to its knees and then proclaim martial law – just as the Y2K bug struck. Or perhaps Hillary Clinton is the real prime mover, bringing down her own husband to set herself up for the presidency. According to the Conspiracy Nation Newsletter, Hillary was – still is, perhaps – a member of a powerful but shadowy Feminist Intelligence Network, a movement that counts Linda Tripp, Monica Lewinsky, Madeleine Albright and Maya Angelou among its members.

The dust settles

There's no question that a lot of powerful people believed that Clinton had to be unmasked. The question is, when does a negative political campaign become outright skulduggery? When the facts are blatantly cooked? When the campaign can't wait to have its chance at the next election? Many liberals have an enduring sense of outrage. After miles of newsprint, millions of dollars and endless lawsuits and hearings, all that was officially found wrong with Clinton's presidency was a few blowjobs and a misplaced cigar. Even though Clinton survived impeachment, however, the Republican campaign in 2000 successfully leveraged conservative, "moral" issues to the forefront. George W. Bush was in the White House, and Hillary Clinton was out of the picture.

Mud had stuck, maybe, but it was also left all over the hands of its slingers. An ABC News poll found that 56 percent of Americans thought Kenneth Starr had been more interested in damaging the president than discovering the truth, and that half the population believed a right-wing conspiracy had tried to discredit Clinton. Some of the leading Republican lights behind the impeachment campaign lost their seats at the next election. There may have been no stains on their interns' dresses, but manhandling Lewinsky's hadn't looked good.

SOURCES

Books

Sidney Blumenthal The Clinton Wars (2004). This memoir from the Assistant to the President from 1997 to 2001 puts you right inside the White House at the time of the impeachment. Sympathetic but not entirely uncritical.

Bill Clinton My Life (2004). You'd think even 1000 pages wouldn't be enough to cover Clinton's life, but you'll want to skip some of those pages – too many deadweight reminiscences – for those on Starr and the "vast right-wing operation" to spoil the Clinton presidency.

Hillary Clinton Living History (2003). A thousand pager, but it's only a couple of pages that anyone wants to read. Except extreme conservatives, of course, who have taken to this book like historians to *Mein Kampf*.

Joe Conason and Gene Lyons The Hunting Of The President: The Ten-Year Campaign To Destroy Bill And Hillary Clinton (2000). Two veteran hacks from the *New York Observer* and *Arkansas Democrat-Gazette* breathlessly tell the story of the characters (and dollars) behind the campaign to discredit Clinton. It wasn't a conspiracy as such, they say, more a "loose cabal".

Ann Coulter High Crimes And Misdemeanors: The Case Against Bill Clinton (1998). Arch-conservative lawyer and liberal love-to-hate-figure Ann Coulter mounts a rampantly aggressive and highly partisan attack on Clinton, hoovering up the same old controversy canards and a bunch of new ones – Wampumgate, anyone?

Carl Limbacher Hillary's Scheme: Inside The Next Clinton's Ruthless Agenda To Take The White House (2003). Investigative journo claims Hillary has

plotted for decades for the top job. So what's new? Ah, her underhand methods.

Richard Poe Hillary's Secret War (2004). Noble, courageous, public-spirited Internet journalists expose the truth about Hillary "Blofeld" Clinton's Stasi-style infiltration and intimidation of the courts and media. Somehow her reach didn't extend as far as stopping this book.

Kenneth Starr The Starr Report (1998). Also published as *Clinton: The Starr Report*, this is the definitive article, comprehensive and scrupulously footnoted. With a few years' hindsight, however, it seems oddly over-

comprehensive and perhaps a little too full of scruples.

Websites

ⓦ **archive.salon.com/news/1998/03/cov_ 17news.html** The *Salon* article fingering Richard Mellon Scaife.

ⓦ **thomas.loc.gov/cgi-bin/query/z?c105: h.res.611.rh:** Congress's original articles of impeachment.

ⓦ **www.snopes.com/inboxer/outrage/ clinton.htm** Utterly sceptical investigation of the body-count list.

Waco

April 19, 1993: a huge and spellbound TV audience watched as the 51-day siege of the rural compound of Mount Carmel, near Waco, Texas, ended in a hellish inferno. At least 85 people perished in the blaze, including 21 children. Such an horrific end to a siege that had received massive daily media coverage left many unanswered questions, ultimately leading to allegations of conspiracy and cover-up.

The standoff was between Mount Carmel's occupants – men, women and children of the Branch Davidians, a Christian group formed by Seventh Day Adventists in the 1930s – and agents from the FBI and the Bureau of Alcohol, Tobacco and Firearms (ATF). It had begun on February 28, when ATF agents attempted to raid Carmel in search of

illegal stashes of firearms and other weapons. But the Davidians, led by the charismatic preacher David Koresh, fought back. Four ATF agents were killed and sixteen wounded, while a half a dozen Davidians were left dead.

The FBI took over and began prolonged negotiations with Koresh. At first, everything seemed to be going well and a few Davidians were let out, but the negotiations soon turned sour. Mount Carmel's power, water and food supplies were cut; bright lights and deafening noise tapes were beamed at the buildings at night; no more Davidians were released, and as the days turned into weeks, it seemed the Federal side at least was pushing harder and harder for resolution. On April 19, FBI tanks rolled into the compound and started knocking holes in the main building, firing CS or tear gas inside. Then around midday the deadly fire broke out, rapidly engulfing the compound's buildings.

Investigations

The US government and its agencies contended that Koresh had ordered the fire to be started as an act of mass suicide – or mass murder, seeing as many who died in the fire had no choice in the matter. In October 1993, the Justice Department's investigation into the FBI and its own role in the affair concluded that Koresh wanted his flock to die on a martyrs' pyre. Koresh was portrayed as a fraud, a failed rock star and predatory sex fiend who had brainwashed his followers into believing that he was the "Lamb of God", sexually exploiting their daughters as he preached apocalypse.

It was reported that FBI bugs picked up conversations of Branch Davidians in the compound discussing plans to set it on fire for hours before the blaze. Arson investigators found traces of gasoline, lighter fluid and stove fuel around the compound. Davidians were said to have shot at agents and firefighters trying to approach the blaze, and prevented anyone inside the compound from getting out alive. Investigator Edward Dennis concluded that FBI agents had exhibited "extraordinary restraint" and acted with "great professionalism" throughout the siege. An investigation into the BATF demonized the Branch Davidians as "cold-blooded killers" who "knew ATF agents were coming" and "prepared a deadly ambush".

Attorney General Janet Reno told Congressional hearings that she took responsibility for ordering the CS gas to be fired, but admitted no mistakes and

The Branch Davidian complex at Waco burns

stayed in her job. Two federal agents were suspended as a result of the investigations. They were later reinstated.

Things don't add up

In September 1995 top FBI investigator Robert Matthews called the Waco investigations a "whitewash." Davidians testified that Mount Carmel was a peaceful Bible study centre, while according to one survivor, Koresh was a "serious religious scholar", who only prolonged the siege in order to finish a tract on the Book of Revelations.

The first assault on Mount Carmel certainly seemed ill conceived. The ATF stressed that the mission needed to be a "surprise" to work. Yet not only did the Davidians know that ATF agents were coming, but the ATF knew that they knew – because they had an agent, Robert Rodriguez, inside Mount Carmel. As a weeping Rodriguez later admitted in a Congressional hearing, he had told his ATF superiors that the Davidians knew about the impending raid after his cover had been blown and Koresh had asked him to leave. Any remaining element of "surprise" had been destroyed by helicopters flying over the compound hours beforehand and by the numerous local TV camera crews outside Mount Carmel.

There was also doubt as to who shot at who. Former US Attorney General Ramsey Clark told a Waco memorial gathering in April 1996 that infrared video from the FBI helicopters showed agents firing heavily into the compound as the blaze started – exactly when anyone inside might have been trying to escape. Despite media reports to the contrary, Clark said, the Davidians did not shoot at the FBI tanks: it was the FBI, not the Davidians, who had prevented the fire department from approaching the compound to put out the blaze. The FBI said later that they had been forced to keep everyone back because of the "million rounds of ammo" waiting to go off in the compound. This did not, however, prevent the still smouldering remains of the compound from being bulldozed within a matter of days, with the result that – as at Oklahoma City – any remaining evidence was destroyed.

It was widely reported that many of the children died of "blunt force trauma", having been beaten to death by their parents. But pathologist Dr. Rodney Crowe told the *Maury Povich Show* in late 1993 that the children and their mothers were either crushed to death or suffocated by falling concrete after a tank rammed the room they were hiding in. Medical examiner Nizaam Peerwani concurred with Crowe's reports, and the charge was repeated in the documentary *Waco: The Rules Of Engagement*.

As the London *Times* reported, the FBI had bugged the entire compound, so it would have known where the women and children were, as an FBI agent later confirmed. The 1995 Congressional hearings showed a tank repeatedly ramming the compound wall where the bunker was – the purpose of which, the Justice Department claimed, was to inject CS gas inside and create exits for Davidians to escape. That the dead women and children were found in that concrete-enforced room isn't disputed. That Koresh would have the most vulnerable herded into the toughest, most flame-resistant room doesn't fit with a man apparently bent on mass murder.

The media

A local man, Ken Fawcett, has claimed that TV stations mis-stated the time of the raid on February 28 by two hours, so that the ATF could edit the tapes. As agents climbed into the building that day, some of their weapons misfired. Other agents thought they were under attack and let rip, while a helicopter bombed the room. The agents essentially killed themselves and a few Davidians by using "spray and pray" tactics – firing blindly through walls – the last resort if one man is being pursued, but if dozens of children's lives are at stake?

Many of the charges and other powerful questions over the siege were put in William Gazecki's film, *Waco: The Rules Of Engagement*, which every Waco site refers to, but Gazecki was incensed by the total indifference he received in Hollywood in trying to get backing and distribution for the film. Dr Alan A. Stone wrote in the *Boston Review* that Gazecki "seemed not to realize that in the jungle of Waco the liberal [*sic*] establishment was his natural enemy". Stone, a Harvard professor of psychiatry who sat on the government's investigative panels on Waco, added that he himself was assured that his services "[would] never again be needed in Washington". The reason being that he thought that the investigations didn't add up either.

Stone rounded on the psycho-war tactics used at Waco, mainly sleep deprivation with bright spotlights beamed onto the compound and all-night broadcasts through loudspeakers of rabbits being slaughtered, teeth being drilled and Tibetan prayer chants. That these methods may have only reinforced the Davidians' solidarity and unwillingness to come out, and could also produce nerve deafness in children, wasn't something the Justice Department or FBI was aware of, Stone reported. (One conspiracy rumour is that microwave antennas were deployed around the compound, subjecting the Davidians to mind control that bade them to react violently and ensure their own destruction, to all appearances by their own hand.) It was the cutting off of electricity, on the other hand, that forced them to use stoves and lanterns, hence the presence of liquid fuel drips around the compound .

CS gas cover-up

Stone also objected to CS gas being fired into buildings with unprotected children in them. CS gas can kill in confined areas, which is why it's used outside to disperse rioting adults. Toxicologist Dr William Marcus told the Congressional Hearings that CS converts to hydrogen cyanide when burned. CS particles are often dispersed with kerosene or methyl chloride, both highly flammable. Yet CS gas was fired into the confined, wooden interiors of Carmel over a period of six hours, with only a muzzle flash needed to ignite the lot.

The government, however, blamed Koresh for the fires. Attorney General Janet Reno, FBI Director Louis Freeh and their subordinates repeatedly told congressional committees, federal courts and the public that the federal government used nothing capable of starting a fire on April 19, something Reno was saying up to July 1999. Then the following month, former FBI official Danny Coulson told *The Dallas Morning News* that pyrotechnic grenades had been used. The Texas Rangers also had evidence of M-651 CS tear gas grenades, set off by a burning explosive capable of sparking fires, being fired at the compound on April 19. Coulson and the FBI insisted that the grenades were fired at dawn "in a direction far away from the compound", while the fire started around noon, as arson experts verified – although their conclusion was in part based on FBI assurances that no pyrotechnic devices were used.

Reno ordered a new investigation, headed by Missouri Republican Senator John Danforth. In his 2000 report, Danforth criticized the FBI's false statements about the grenades, saying that "the result ... is that people who want to believe the worst about government say, 'Aha! This is something that's really bad'" – hence a 1999 poll showing that 61 percent of Americans blamed the government for the fire. He concluded, however, that there had been "no massive conspiracy or cover-up" and that "the government did nothing evil".

The bigger picture

For many conspiracy theorists, Waco is part of a wider plot. One anti-Koresh theory is that he was a neo-Nazi aiming to resurrect the Third Reich and deserved to die in the defence of liberty. Members of the National Rifle Association, on the other hand, have suggested that Waco was deliberately pushed into a calamitous bloodbath to swing the public behind the tightening of gun laws. Many right-wing fringe groups take this argument a stage further, seeing Waco as the first phase in a conspiracy to impose the New World Order (see p.234), which seeks to destroy US sovereignty and bring the world under the control of the UN. The Federal government, they believe, provoked Waco to justify a strong clampdown on arms ownership and civil liberties, leaving Americans defenceless in the face of this assault.

Rumblings

Murmurs about misdeeds at Waco also rumbled behind General Wesley Clark's nomination as a Democratic presidential candidate in 2004. Clark commanded the III Corps Cavalry Division at Fort Hood when the Fort supplied tanks to the FBI, and officers advised both Texas governor Ann Richards

and Reno on raiding Waco before April 19. What substance, if any, there was to these later dark mutterings about Clark at Waco never materialized; Clark was out of the 2004 race early on.

In the same month as the conclusion of the Danforth investigation, Ramsey Clark led about a hundred Davidian survivors and relatives in a $675m suit against the US government over charges that Federal agents used excessive force to end the siege. A Texas jury cleared the government of blame. The BBC's Washington correspondent reported that the finding probably wouldn't silence America's "many conspiracy theorists and anti-government activists". These include Clinton-haters, the National Rifle Association and religious and political right-wingers who in print and on air stir up fears of Federal war on US citizens.

BBC Online, however, omitted to mention that the second anniversary of Waco was marked by the blasting to smithereens of the Alfred P. Murrah federal agency office building in Oklahoma City. The man convicted and executed for the bombing, Timothy McVeigh, cited Waco as one of the reasons for his rage against the State.

SOURCES

Films

Waco, The Rules Of Engagement (William Gazecki, 1997). This has footage of David Koresh not as a wild-eyed hellfire and brimstone preacher, but as a mild-mannered man explaining the Book Of Revelation to his followers.

Websites

ⓦ **www.salon.com/news/ feature/1999/09/09/waco/print.html** A Davidian talks about life in Waco.

ⓦ **www.serendipity.li/waco.html** The editorial content sometimes alarms (George W. Bush is described as a "psychopath" and

the "insane" John Ashcroft as "Bush's Himmler", with no reference to Waco), but this website is continually updated and has copious links to mainstream news websites reporting criticism of Waco and unfolding investigations.

OKC: the Oklahoma City bombing

On the morning of April 19, 1995, two years to the day after the deaths at Waco, a Ryder hire-truck pulled up outside the Murrah Federal Building, in Oklahoma City, home among others to offices of the FBI, Drug Enforcement Agency, and the Bureau of Alcohol, Tobacco and Firearms (ATF). Inside the truck, thousands of pounds of fertilizer were mixed with motor-racing fuel, to make a crude but very lethal bomb. When it exploded at 9.02am it destroyed a third of the building, including the federal employees' creche on the second floor. A total of 168 people were killed, victims of what was then the most serious terrorist act ever committed on US soil.

Two hours later, former soldier and alleged paramilitary Timothy McVeigh was pulled over seventy miles from OK City for driving without number plates. At gunpoint, he calmly handed over a hidden Glock pistol. Traces of explosive were later found on his clothing, and his prints discovered on a receipt for two thousand pounds of fertilizer. Not a shining example of covering one's tracks. Two days later, an accomplice and militia-member called Terry Nichols gave himself up. At his farm were found detonators, fertilizer, and a number of guns later revealed to have been stolen from a man named Roger Moore. Strangely, Nichols also stole Moore's quilt. On May 23, 34 days after the bombing, the remains of the Murrah Building were bulldozed.

McVeigh was tried by a federal court in the spring of 1997. His sister, Jennifer, testified that he had boasted shortly before the bombing that "something big is going to happen". At first, McVeigh publicly pleaded his innocence, telling Time magazine in 1996: "I enjoy guns as a hobby, I do gun shows and I follow the beliefs of the Founding Fathers. If that means I was involved in the bombing, then ... about a billion other Americans were involved in the bombing as well." After he had been found guilty of eight counts of murder in June 1997, however, he confessed in letters sent from prison that "the bombing was a retaliatory strike: a counter-attack, for the cumulative raids (and subsequent violence and damage) that federal agents had participated in over the preceding years (including, but not limited to, Waco)".

McVeigh was killed by lethal injection in 2001 – the first time that the federal government had (officially) executed one of its citizens since 1963. Terry Nichols escaped the death sentence, but Judge Richard P. Matsch sentenced him to life in prison in January 1998, calling him "an enemy of the constitution". At a subsequent state trial in 2004, Nichols reportedly confessed during plea bargaining that "McVeigh told me what to do", which didn't go down any better in court than it does in most infant schools. He also denied that there were any co-conspirators. The jury found him guilty of 161 counts of murder, but could not agree to impose the death penalty.

Doubts: John Doe 2

Following the federal trial, Judge Matsch stated that "there are many unanswered questions. It would be very disappointing to me if the law enforcement agencies of the United States government have quit looking for answers in this Oklahoma bombing tragedy." There seemed to be too many loose ends. The FBI's case was built largely on McVeigh and Nichols' phone records. But were there accomplices? A number of witnesses claimed to have seen another man with McVeigh on the morning of the crime. The FBI spent millions of man-hours chasing the suspect, dubbed John Doe 2, before finally concluding that he probably didn't exist. Former Grand Juror Hoppy Heidelberg, thrown off the case for talking to the media, claims some witnesses were never called at the trial in order to conceal the identity of John Doe 2 – as a government agent or informant.

Could there have been John Does 3, 4 and 5, as well? Charles Farley, testifying for the defence, claimed to have seen a second truck and a brown car parked with the Ryder truck at an outdoor recreation centre a day or two before the bombing. Five men, he claimed, were handling bags of fertilizer. A Kansas deputy sheriff called Jake Mauck claims he firmly identified the John Doe 2 sketch as of a local "patriot" whom some have linked to previous FBI sting operations against paramilitaries.

Explosive evidence

Suspicions about federal involvement in the bombing focused on the bomb itself. Various explosives experts, would-be experts and supposed experts expressed their doubts that the fertilizer bomb described by the authorities could have been put together by McVeigh and Nichols, or whether it would have worked if they had managed to. The conspiracists' star witness is Brigadier-General Benton Partin (USAF-retired), expert witness on munitions to the Oklahoma City Bombing Investigation Committee, a pressure group run by an Oklahoma State Representative. His report claims that the damage caused to the building had to have been caused by demolition charges placed on the internal structural columns. But as one conspiracy website ponders, if it's demonstrably true that the truck bomb couldn't have done the damage, why didn't McVeigh's lawyers make this the cornerstone of the defence?

The two-bomb theory

Early media reports that other bombs were found inside the ruins of the building were later withdrawn. If you don't believe that those reports were simply checked and rejected, you can see that as evidence of government coercion. David Hall, part-owner of KPOC-TV in Oklahoma and a campaigner against the government conspiracy at Waco, believes that firefighters found a second, unexploded bomb in the rubble. But then he also reckons that he heard the original arrest call for a "1978 Mercury, no license plate, involved in OK bombing" while he happened to be listening to a local police scanner.

A more authoritative source of what has become known as the two-bomb theory was the University of Oklahoma's Geological Survey, which was initially puzzled as to why seismographic records seemed to show a second explosion following roughly eight seconds after the first. But as the Survey's Director, Dr Charles Mankin, later reported, "the second shock was from the same occurrence that caused the first, which had travelled through a different and more dense layer of the earth".

More evidence of a conspiracy supposedly comes from the Ryder truck. CCTV footage showed a UPS truck parked where the Ryder truck should have been – though it turned out that the camera's clock was wrong. A photograph by a sergeant from the County Sheriff's office was hailed as an incriminating "before and after" shot – though in fact they're just two similar pictures from very different dates stuck together. An aerial photo supposedly shows the Ryder truck parked in a military facility, but looks suspiciously fake. The truck axle found at the site is alleged to have been moved or planted, or to have had its vehicle identification number doctored to implicate McVeigh.

Federal Bureau of Misinvestigation

Rumours circulated in Oklahoma that the FBI had warned the fire department, or ATF employees, or local judge Wayne Alley, who was originally assigned to the trial before it was moved out to Denver, to take "special precautions" shortly before the bombing. The Feds' alleged sluggishness in hunting down John Doe 2 is seen as proof that they were hiding one of their own men. By that account, this supposed agent was the prime mover behind an elaborate sting operation that went tragically wrong when McVeigh et al actually succeeded in setting off their bomb. Others – still angry, like McVeigh, about the Waco killings – blame the Bureau of Alcohol, Tobacco and Firearms. Was the bomb designed to destroy records of the ATF's role in the Waco affair? Supposedly, no ATF staff were in the building at the time – though in fact five ATF staff were killed.

Some have turned the spotlight on Oklahoma governor Frank Keating. As a former FBI man and Bush loyalist he couldn't fail to have had a finger in the pie, surely. And the fact that his brother Martin Keating wrote a thriller called *Final Jihad* about terrorist attacks on the US homeland just proves it. Supposedly written before the Oklahoma bombing, it was in fact published a year after the event, while the claim that its hero is called "Tom McVey" is simply false.

More genuinely disturbing documents emerged just days before McVeigh's scheduled execution in May 2001, when the FBI let slip that it had "accidentally" withheld some three thousand pages from the defence team, blaming both staff who thought them "irrelevant", and a "computer glitch". Attorney General John Ashcroft immediately postponed McVeigh's execution and ordered an inquiry. In September, Gore Vidal wrote a J'Accuse-style article in *Vanity Fair* criticising right, left and sundry, and the FBI in particular. However, the inquiry concluded that while there were "serious deficiencies" in the FBI's handling of the case, the missing paperwork could not have affected McVeigh's conviction.

Hardline anti-government activists believe the government deliberately destroyed the Murrah Federal building as the perfect smokescreen for the introduction of laws cracking down on "patriot" militias. Comparisons were made with the Nazi's Reichstag fire of 1933, which allowed the Nazis to assume control of Germany. McVeigh, they claim, was nothing more than a patsy. Or possibly a CIA agent. Or even a Manchurian candidate, controlled by a microchip implant implanted during his time in the army. The clincher? That he was strangely cold and subject to mood-swings.

After the bomb, Oklahoma City

9/11 rehearsal?

Perhaps the most disturbing theory stems from Jayna Davis, a reporter for KFOR-TV in Oklahoma City at the time of the bombing. Citing witness statements and intelligence reports, she claims that "olive-skinned" John Doe 2 was a former Iraqi Republican Guard. KFOR-TV showed a digitally blurred photo of the man during a news broadcast, whereupon he stepped forward and sued for defamation of character. The court ruled for KFOR-TV, and the plaintiff supposedly upped sticks and went off to work at Boston's Logan International Airport – from where Mohammed Atta took off on 9/11. Whether or not, as Davis goes on to allege, a Middle Eastern terrorist cell operated in Oklahoma City, and whether or not Terry Nichols had made contact with Islamic Filipino terrorists linked to Osama bin Laden, no court has yet tried to determine. Was this just an angry city turning on the foreigners in its midst?

The sword of justice

On April 24, 1996, almost a year to the day after the Oklahoma bombing, President Clinton signed the Anti-Terrorism and Effective Death Penalty Act. It allowed the State Department to label organizations as "terrorist", and the FBI to launch criminal investigations of people who gave them financial support.

Immigrants could be deported without the need for public hearing of evidence, and federal review of state death penalty cases was eliminated.

Web-based rumours that liberal Congressman (now Senator) Charles Schumer's 1995 bill HR 2580 would have imposed a prison sentence for "publishing or transmitting by wire or electronic means baseless conspiracy theories regarding the Federal government of the United States" turn out to be exaggerated. The bill did indeed blame paramilitary violence on "baseless conspiracy theories regarding the government", but it didn't actually suggest sending people to jail for speculating.

The final word has to be that of the Oklahoma County grand jury investigation, which concluded in December 1998. "We have observed a tremendous amount of journalistic overlap in a number of magazines, books, talk radio shows and Internet websites", it observed. "The same misprinted information is repeated over and over again without anyone validating its veracity. Sadly, these organizations and individuals have glorified those convicted in federal court by vilifying the federal government and increasing the public's distrust of its government by providing half-truths, uncorroborated, and oftentimes outright false information ... As Americans we do not want to believe that fellow Americans could plot, scheme and carry out such a cowardly act in the name of protest. Tragically this is the current reality of the world in which we live."

SOURCES

Books

Jayna Davis The Third Terrorist: The Middle Eastern Connection To The Oklahoma City Bombing (2004). Davis pushes the Islamic terrorist thesis, suggests that McVeigh and Nichols had shadowy backers, and asks why the FBI shut down the investigation.

David Hoffman The Oklahoma City Bombing And The Politics Of Terror (1998). Five hundred pages of hearsay evidence leads Hoffman to conclude that it can't have been a fertilizer bomb, and that neo-Nazis, and possibly Middle Eastern terrorists, were behind McVeigh and Nichols.

Stephen Jones and Peter Israel Others

Unknown: Timothy McVeigh And The Oklahoma Bombing Conspiracy (1998). The title says it all. Jones was chief defence counsel for McVeigh, and holds the torch for those still looking for John Doe 2 – possibly an Islamic extremist.

Kenneth S. Stern A Force Upon The Plain: The American Militia Movement And The Politics Of Hate (1996). From one of the influences behind Charles Schumer's anti-militia law. Written as a wake-up call not just to the threat of the militias to the United States, but to right-wing conspiracizing itself. Currently out-of-print, which says a lot about the agenda shift towards international terrorism.

Gore Vidal Perpetual War For Perpetual Peace (2002). Collection of virtuoso essays attacking the US government from a liberal but original perspective. Two fascinating

pieces on McVeigh suggest that he cannot have worked alone. Interesting to see the possible links between liberal and right-wing libertarian thinking.

Websites

ⓦ**www.mcveightragedy.com** Pushes McVeigh as the victim of a stitch-up. Technically high-end: you can browse photos of smiling Tim from the gallery while a midi version of "Bohemian Rhapsody" plays.

ⓦ**www.okcbombing.org** The sceptical, conspiracy-minded Oklahoma Bombing Investigation Committee

ⓦ**www.oklahomacounty.org/treasurer/ GrandJuryBombingReport.htm** Scotches almost all the theories, but leaves open the door leading to John Doe 2. If you don't believe Oklahomans, who do you believe?

The elections of George W. Bush

On the night of the US presidential election, November 7, 2000, exit polls showed that with three states too close to call – Florida, New Mexico, and Oregon – George W. Bush could count on 246 electoral votes to Al Gore's 255. In total, Gore had received almost half a million more individual votes across America than Bush, but the presidency is determined not by the popular vote, but by votes received in the electoral college, delivered as a block from each state. To win in 2000, either candidate needed 270 electoral votes; and thus whoever won Florida's 25 votes would also win the overall race. On the basis of exit polls that predicted a Gore victory in Florida, several TV networks that night "called" the presidency for Gore.

As ultimately counted, the vote in Florida was close enough to force a machine recount – which, on November 10, put Bush ahead by just 327 votes. Gore called for a manual recount in four largely Democrat counties, and the process immediately started in hotly disputed Volusia and Palm Beach. Bush's team countered by applying to a federal court to block the recount. At this point, Florida's Secretary of State, Katherine Harris – a Republican – stepped in, declaring that she would set a deadline of November 14 for any hand recounts. She also applied to Florida's Supreme Court to block manual recounts entirely.

By November 16, almost thirty separate court cases were underway. It was legalized chaos: some courts ordered recounts, others ruled that for selective recounts to be held in a few largely Democratic counties would be unfair. Eventually, the most significant cases were combined at the

US Supreme Court, which decided on December 12, by seven votes to two, to stop recounts on the grounds that different counties shouldn't have different voting standards. On the issue of whether or not new recounts should be ordered, however, the court split 5:4 – right down party lines. The five conservative judges decided that to impose a standard on Florida would be to change rather than interpret Florida law – a constitutional no-no for the Supreme Court. They were sorry, but their hands were tied. Katherine Harris therefore gave Florida's 25 electoral college votes to George W. Bush, who thus became America's first Republican president for eight years.

The super-bright spotlight of media and legal attention in November and December 2000 ensured that the slightest molehill in the road to the presidency threw a mountain-sized shadow back onto TV screens and newspapers. And there were plenty of molehills. Some dug up by pretty scary moles.

Butterflies, chads and spoiled votes

The voting systems in a few Florida counties in 2000 were seriously flawed. The infamous "butterfly ballot" in Palm Beach County was designed so badly – albeit by a Democrat – that over 5000 votes were cast for the surprising cross-party duo of Al Gore and Reform Party candidate Pat Buchanan. It was also Florida that gave us the word "chad", as courts weighed whether punch-card votes still counted if those itsy bits of paper were left hanging from the card, rather than being punched right through.

Gadsden County, where the population has a particularly high proportion of African Americans, suffered from a strange excess of spoiled ballots. Papers there were machine-read by an optical "Accuvote" system which rejected any that were wrongly completed – such as having any extra marks on them. Unfortunately for Gadsden voters, the machines recording the vote had a tendency to leave just such marks. Worse still, the "reject" mechanism telling a voter that they'd accidentally spoiled their own ballot was switched off. As a result, one in eight ballot papers in Gadsden County failed to pass muster. In Tallahassee County, by contrast, the (largely white) voters were warned to try again if they accidentally spoiled their ballot. One in a hundred was spoiled in Tallahassee. According to the US Commission on Civil Rights, over half of the spoiled ballots in Florida 2000 belonged to African-Americans, who make up just eleven percent of the population. Most media commentators blamed that statistic on "lack of education"...

Scrub lists: the crime of being a black voter

During the run up to November 2000, the politicos knew that the results were going to be close, and that any advantage could be crucial. Luckily for George W. Bush, his brother Jeb was Florida's Governor, while two successive Secretaries of State, Sandra Mortham and Katherine Harris, were political associates. They commissioned a company called DBT (whose parent company ChoicePoint specialized in conducting manhunts for the FBI) to prepare a "scrub list" of criminals who, under Florida law, would not be eligible to vote. Florida paid DBT $2.3m – just $2,294,300 more than the last company that did the same job. Statistics show that roughly nine out of ten felons prefer Democrat – and quite legitimately, the Republicans didn't want to lose the state thanks to the illegal votes of a bunch of criminals.

What looks a whole lot less legitimate is how the list was drawn up. Florida voters' names were matched with known felons by comparing names, birthdays and genders. Crucially, near-matches were included, and never crosschecked – Florida officials told DBT it wasn't necessary. Campaigning journalist Greg Palast claims to have found a handwritten note in Katherine Harris's files saying "DON'T NEED", right next to DBT's proposals for checking.

It didn't help that middle initials were excluded from the computer matching process. A felon called George V. Bush, for example, could be matched with a Florida voter called George Bush, whatever his middle name actually was. And, because racial ID is included on voter rolls in Florida, if George V. Bush was African-American he could knock off African-American George Bushes from the rolls – but not white George Bushes. Palast even found 325 names with conviction dates in the future. In all, 57,746 people were listed as felons and therefore denied the vote, and a disproportionate number of them were African-American or Hispanic. At least fifteen percent of the list, it seems, was incorrect – enough to have swung the election. The one county that independently cross-checked its felons list found that it could only confirm 34 out of 694 names as those of people genuinely ineligible to vote. That's an error rate of 95 percent.

For the 2004 presidential election, the state of Florida once again commissioned a "potential felon" list, or as it was popularly known the "black purge" list. The second time around, media pressure forced officials to abandon the plan.

The early call

Some of the stories circulating about the 2000 election are more "theory" than "conspiracy". On election night, the big news channels relied on the Voter News Service to report early results and exit polls. At the conservative-minded channel Fox News, an analyst called John Prescott Ellis was working on the VNS's results. He owed the "Prescott" part of his name to his grandfather, Prescott Bush – another of whose grandsons was up for president that night... Conspiracists allege that it was Ellis's sole responsibility to call the Florida result for Fox. Apparently – or not – he spoke repeatedly with both George and Jeb Bush on election night.

Fox News was the first network to call it for George Dubya, at 2.16am, and the other networks soon followed. Did Ellis single-handedly swing the election analysis in favour of Bush, thus leaving the future president in a strong position in the legal fight for the White House that followed? Republicans point out that Ellis worked on just one team on one news channel; that Fox had also been the first to call it for Gore, before retracting the announcement; and that in any case the decision was based on real figures from the VNS. No one, they say, "made the call" for Bush.

Towards 2004: the age of the machine

In 2000, electronic voting machines were relatively new-fangled and uncommon. One of the few counties using them was Volusia, Florida. According to campaigning author Bev Harris, of *Black Box Voting*, it was the announcement by the computers there, during the early hours of November 8, of a huge Bush lead of 51,000 that prompted the networks' early call of a Bush victory in the state. That figure was later corrected, giving Bush some 16,022 fewer votes. The manufacturers blame a faulty memory card for the inaccurate early result. But how often does bad memory selectively alter a few numbers on the data it stores? Harris claims to have found official voting records in the trash at Volusia County's offices, as well as official voting tapes designated for shredding, and memory cards just lying about. Confusion? Or collusion?

Volusia County's machines were manufactured by Diebold Inc. On November 9, 2003, the *New York Times* quoted one Walden W. O'Dell as saying in a letter to fellow Republican loyalists, each of whom had raised over $100,000 for the Bush campaign, that "I am committed to helping Ohio deliver its electoral votes to the president next year". Mr O'Dell's talents were not restricted to fund-raising; he was also chief executive of Diebold, the second largest company providing voting machines in America.

The *largest* voting-machine company, responsible for roughly half of US polling stations, was ES&S, which grew out of American Information Systems. One of AIS's first financial backers, Howard Ahmanson, also helped to finance the Chalcedon Institute, dedicated to "restoring the Christian Faith and Biblical law as the standard of all of life", and guiding Christians "in the task of governing their own spheres of life in terms of the entire Bible: in family, church, school, vocation, arts, economics, business, media, the state..." Another controversial ES&S figure is Chuck Hagel, a former chairman who subsequently ran for the Senate as a Republican candidate in Nebraska in 2002. After 24 years of Democratic senators, Hagel won his seat in a landslide. ES&S had supplied vote-counting machines for around eighty percent of those Nebraskan votes.

Maybe Hagel just ran a great campaign. So perhaps did the Republican candidate for the Governorship of Georgia, in 2002. After 130 years of Democratic Governors, and months of opinion polls in favour of the Democratic candidate, Republican Sonny Perdue marched into office with the help of a sixteen percent swing in the four days leading up to the election. Georgia's touch-screen voting systems, in use for the first time, were made by Diebold. Mysterious software patches were reportedly downloaded onto the systems shortly before the election; afterwards, conspiracists protested that the computers' memory cards had been formatted. And of course there could be no recount. Unlike their ATMs and other electronic data systems, Diebold's DRE (Direct Record Electronic) voting machines leave behind no messy paperwork, no "paper trail".

Suppress the vote 2004

Although the election of George W. Bush in 2004 was not as controversial as that of 2000, allegations of a conspiracy to suppress the Democratic vote weren't lacking. Most notoriously, Michigan Republican state representative John Pappageorge was quoted in the *Detroit Free Press* as saying, "If we do not suppress the Detroit vote, we're going to have a tough time in this election." Detroit is almost 85 percent African-American. Pappageorge later clarified that all he'd meant was that the Republicans needed a good campaign in order to win Democrat votes.

In Ohio, the key swing state for 2004, some voters reported receiving phone calls or letters telling them to vote on a different day or at a different location; others were told that they could register their vote there and then on the phone. When it came to election day, Democratic areas were alleged to have been poorly supplied with voting booths or voting machines, causing long queues to form. In the pouring rain of a wet November day in Ohio, this was a major disincentive to vote. Republicans were filmed waiting by the booths to challenge voters' legitimacy. Republicans pointed out that they were simply stopping non-registered or fraudulent voters; Democrats complained that they were only doing so in black or Democratic areas, and that amounted to intimidation. As Jesse Jackson put it, "suppose five hundred black folks came into a white neighborhood to challenge votes. It would be totally unacceptable."

In the final result, the Democratic turnout in Ohio was well below the Republican figure. In Franklin County, precincts won by Kerry had an average turnout of fifty percent, whereas those won by Bush registered sixty percent. Was this ten percent gap due to the famous Republican-red surge? Or was it, as some claimed, a statistical impossibility? Or just the predictable consequence of the illegal assignation of more voting machines per head to Republican-leaning areas than Democratic ones?

Some turnout figures seemed even more surprising. Ohio's Secretary of State, J. Kenneth Blackwell – who combined his electoral role with a position as co-chair of the Bush-Cheney campaign in the state – certified turnouts of 124 percent in two precincts of Republican-leaning Perry County. The figures were explained as statistical anomalies caused by the difference between electoral districts and county boundaries. Blackwell had been busy before the election too, challenging 35,000 new voter registrations – before the move was blocked by a federal judge – and attempting to ban registrations made on the wrong weight of paper. He also allegedly targeted presumed-liberal universities and colleges for provisional ballot voting, setting rules so that the slightest error on these ballots would result in their being automatically rejected.

Some say that Blackwell is a tough politician; others, that he was behind outright vote-rigging. Conspiracists say that he only got away with it thanks to the new paperless DRE voting machines, whose software was full of security loopholes, and whose manufacturers' neutrality was questionable. Without a paper-trail, it was hard to find firm evidence of fraud. Avid number-crunchers turned instead to discrepancies between exit polls and final results. Thus Ohio's exit polls had predicted a Kerry victory, by a figure that exceeded their margin of error. But when the final results came in, Bush had won. What had changed?

Politics as usual?

In 2001, news organizations including CNN, The *New York Times* and *The Washington Post* commissioned the University of Chicago's National Opinion Research Center to examine what would have happened had the Supreme Court allowed various recount scenarios. The NORC concluded that Bush would actually have won if the partial recounts wanted by Al Gore had gone ahead. A full statewide recount, however, would have given Florida to Gore. But as liberal film- and trouble-maker Michael Moore put it in *Fahrenheit 9/11*, it doesn't really matter "just as long as all your daddy's friends on the Supreme Court vote the right way". In 2003, Moore refreshed his reputation for infamy by calling Bush a "fictitious president" while picking up an Oscar.

One result of the 2000 controversy was the Help America Vote Act of 2002, which caused billions of tax dollars to be spent on voting machines. Was this a decent, fair-minded attempt to consign chads permanently to the trashcan? Or did a few Republican legislators expect a payback from the companies who made the machines?

SOURCES

Books

Vincent Bugliosi The Betrayal Of America (2001). Trial lawyer Bugliosi argues that the Supreme Court's 5:4 decision to stop the Florida recount was "treasonous" and a "judicial coup d'état".

Ann Coulter Slander: Liberal Lies About The American Right (2003). For Coulter, the conspiracy is that the liberal media stifles real debate by screening out radical, conservative voices like hers. Unfortunately, the fact that Coulter's face is all over the news channels undermines her own argument.

Bev Harris Black Box Voting: Ballot Tampering In The 21st Century (2004). This clarion-call alert to the problems of electronic voting systems, not to mention the vested interests behind them, was published just too late for the 2004 election,

but in time to get a lot of people talking about the next one.

Greg Palast The Best Democracy Money Can Buy (2002). Subtitled "An Investigative Reporter Exposes the Truth About Globalization, Corporate Cons, And High Finance Fraudsters", Palast's all-encompassing attack covers Bush scandals such as Enron and the revelation of the Bush family's Saudi Arabian connections, as well as the 2000 election.

Websites

ⓦ **www.blackboxvoting.org** The leading campaigning website, run by the profoundly energetic Bev Harris, including a well-trafficked chat forum.

ⓦ **www.countthevote.org** Website campaigning against paperless voting machines, gunning for Diebold in particular.

ⓦ **www.gregpalast.com** "George Bush's nightmare" and "New Labour's Public Enemy Number One", Palast has acquired plenty of epithets in the course of his combative, anti-establishment reporting career. His coverage of the Bush election itself achieved news-item status.

ⓦ **www.naacp.org** Click on "The Long Shadow Of Jim Crow" for the National Association for the Advancement of Colored People's analysis of attempts to suppress the black vote.

ⓦ **www.norc.uchicago.edu/fl/** The official site of NORC's Florida Ballot project – with enough "what if" stats to boggle a Supreme Court judge.

ⓦ **www.verifiedvoting.org** Mainstream campaign for a papertrail – look under "2004 Theories And Counter-theories".

Skull, Bones and Bush

When lantern-jawed Senator John Kerry won the Democratic nomination for the 2004 presidential election, conspiracy theories could hardly believe the evidence of their on-line news reports. The contest would pit one "Bonesman" – or member of Yale's Skull and Bones fraternity – against another, George W. Bush. To most observers, the society's ex-

istence is powerful evidence of a disturbing truth: that expensively educated, emotionally immature private schoolboys are liable to grow up to be expensively educated, emotionally immature college frat-boys. These kind of clubs – and there are scores of them at campuses all over America – exist to provide a reassuring sense of elite-ness for rich kids struggling to come to terms with the levelling, meritocratic atmosphere of higher education – and an excuse to drink a lot. Period.

Others see the Skull and Bones as visible proof of a sinister, conspiratorial network of the rich and powerful. Even though it has been around since 1832, the society, aka "Chapter 322", aka the "Brotherhood of Death", only achieved its current high profile after the elections of George H.W. Bush (he of the "New World Order", see p.234) and, later, his son George W. Bush. The Internet is now crawling with conspiratorial lists of Bonesmen. Early twentieth-century president William Howard Taft is a prominent name, but otherwise most lists simply feature a smattering of banking-dynasty scions and high-fliers in US intelligence – pretty much what you'd expect of Yale – as well as scores of wealthy lawyers and accountants of whom you've never heard.

Reports of ghoulishly absurd initiation rituals are just as ubiquitous. Ceremonies are held in the campus building of Jonathan Edwards College, nicknamed "The Tomb" – for once the media has a theory it can back up with real pictures. These reportedly centre on heavy doses of quasi-Masonic flimflammery involving a skull, supposedly looted from the grave of Apache warrior Geronimo by Prescott Bush (George H.W.'s father) in 1918. Following Native American demands for its return, however, tests revealed that it was no such thing.

Other rituals are, predictably, heavily sexualized, involving an acted-out murder, the nude confession of previous sexual misdemeanours, and masturbation while lying in a coffin.

The more profoundly stupid their actions, the less likely initiates will be to confess them, it seems. Or is there a darker edge? Is the adoption of cod Masonic or Satanic symbolism proof of real links to Masonic or Satanic societies? In *America's Secret Establishment*, author Anthony Sutton traces the society's links back to the mythical Bavarian Illuminati (see p.85), through the popularity of German-style secret societies in 1830s America. But then Sutton also claims he started his researches after he was mysteriously sent bound volumes of the membership list, which – sadly for anyone wanting to check his evidence – he had to give back within 24 hours. And those Masonic lending libraries are so strict about returns...

Some point out, quite reasonably, that the connotations of the Skull and Bones motif are more than a little sinister. Is it linked to the "death's head" *Totenkopf* sported by the Waffen-SS? Is it a sign that Skull-and-Bones members will "take no prisoners" in their future careers – careers helped along by an alleged "donation" to graduating members? Are members ideologically committed to militaristic notions of death before dishonour? Or is it all just boyish posturing?

SOURCES

Books

Alexandra Robbins Secrets Of The Tomb: Skull And Bones, The Ivy League, And The Hidden Paths Of Power (2003). The supposed inside story, from a photogenic Yale graduate.

Antony Sutton America's Secret Establishment (1986, updated 2002). Before you buy, check out the interview with Sutton at www.freedomdomain.com/ secretsocieties/suttoninterview.html.

Websites

ⓦ **politicalgraveyard.com/group/skull-bones.html** Purported "very incomplete" list of Skull and Bones members.

ⓦ **www.bilderberg.org/skulbone.htm** Giant scrapbook of news articles and opinion pieces, with lots of Web links too.

ⓦ **www.freemasonrywatch.org/bones. html** Full text of a 2001 **New York Observer** piece by Ron Rosenbaum – chief investigator, and the man behind CBS's **60 Minutes** exposé of the Skull and Bones.

Films

The Skulls (Rob Cohen, 2000) Frat-boy movie relying heavily on conspiracist thinking.

Corporate clampdown

COMMITTED TO IMPROVING THE STATE OF THE WORLD

The international banking conspiracy
Perpetual war on perpetual energy
Microsoft
A cure for cancer

Corporate clampdown

One of the most basic and widely held conspiracy theories – it's almost an urban myth – is that of the eternal light bulb. Somewhere in the world exists the design for the bulb that'll never pop, only the greedy light-bulb manufacturers have bought the patent and sat on it, forcing everyone to continue to buy their duff, continually blowing bulbs for perpetuity and keep them in business. (There's always low-energy light bulbs, of course, but naturally they cost proportionately more and never seem as bright.) A similar charge is made at the oil industry, seen as keeping the lid on clean, efficient technologies like the direct injection Elsbett engine – which can run on vegetable oil as well as diesel – so that drivers keep on using the dirtier, duffer petrol-powered variety. In the same vein, computer software manu-

facturers (mainly Microsoft) have been repeatedly accused of all sorts of cunning ploys to do down their rivals and keep their customers buying expensive upgrades. Computer geeks have also been blamed for the Millennium Bug, with Y2K suspected of having been a big moneymaking hoax on a global scale.

A conspiracy theory about something so big and co-ordinated (all the world's computers were supposed to melt down simultaneously) might suggest someone was a little paranoid or that the Y2K initiative was simply a triumph of clear-sighted commercial pre-emption.

Preventitive policy, however, doesn't alsways seem to have been applied in the case of cancer. More generally it's suspected that the pharmaceutical companies make such a mint out of treating sick people that the last thing they want is for them to get better – or even worse, for them not to get ill in the first place. That drug companies actively seek to make people ill is a heady charge, but as part of the toxic chemical industry, it's certainly worrying that the process of making medicine may also be creating the need for it.

This is also a charge levied at those seeking to fluoridate the planet, a decades-old row that's seen many a good, rational argument buried under rants about Communist plots and right-wing nuts. The fluoride debate, like the cancer controversy, is sustained by the fact that there is little *definitive* proof that factor X causes disease Y.

Such conspiracies can't, of course, be hatched in isolation: there have to be opportunities for all the interested parties to get together to decide how to cover up their dirty deeds and what new ones they're going to commit in the future. This is where groups like the World Economic Forum come into the picture: annual meetings of the world's big bankers, industrialists and politicians.

Where some point the finger at the WEF, others suspect the existence of a centuries-old conspiracy of international bankers, a notion that epitomizes the best and the worst of conspiracy theories, from detailed, complex discussions of hidden history to foaming racist diatribes. But when you learn about the real-life case of the BCCI bank and the fate of Nazi gold, you might be tempted to conclude that some seemingly paranoid conspiracy theories appear positively plausible in comparison. At that point, it might be best to turn out the light and hope no one sees you're in.

The international banking conspiracy

Reginald McKenna, one time British Chancellor of the Exchequer and chairman of the Midland Bank, once said: "They who control the credit of the nation direct the policy of governments and hold in the hollow of their hands the destiny of the people." That alone is enough for Web writer Christopher Mark to fulminate that the Bank of England, the Bank of France, the World Bank and the International Monetary Fund are all "bastard siblings" of that "hideous constitutional monster" the Federal Reserve. With the UN as "the ultimate front for international banking interests", the international bankers' mission is "to enslave the entire population of the planet". And all through loans, too. This is the world of the international bankers' conspiracies.

The central banks

According to Gerry Rough, a prolific debunker of banking conspiracies: "The Bank of England holds a special place in the hearts of New World Order conspiracy theorists." He goes on to discuss the "idea that the conspirators had enormous power even as far back as three hundred years ago, and have been gaining power and global influence ever since".

Charging interest on money loans has offended people since long before Christ (when it was simply deemed usury). For some, however, the more recent phenomenon of privately owned banks charging governments interest on loans is even more insidious. According to R. Robertson's *The New World Order*, the bankers struck their first decisive blow in 1694, when Scotsman William Paterson set up a joint stock company to loan £1.2 million at eight percent interest to King William III, so that he could wage war against Louis XIV. When Paterson then won the charter for the Bank of England, he effectively won power over England's monetary systems, with the result that the country's tools of monetary policy were now in private hands. The English government, having been suckered into debt by "international bankers", was then obliged to establish income tax to pay it off. The rot had begun.

Revolution

But England's bankers let greed cloud their judgment, says Mark. He writes that Britain's American colonies didn't use Sterling but their own paper money known as "colonial Scrip", printed locally as required to keep the economy in tick. It wasn't a currency issued with interest charged on it, and more to the point, England's bankers weren't profiting from it. So the Bank of England pressurized Parliament to outlaw it and make the Bank's interest-bearing monies the currency of the day – reverting monetary control back to England while causing a sharp downturn in colonial economic fortunes, thus precipitating the American Revolution. According to Alexander Hamilton, one of the founding fathers of the US: "The Colonies would gladly have borne the little tax on tea and other matters had it not been for the poverty created by the bad influence of the English Bankers on the Parliament, which has caused in the Colonies hatred of England and the Revolutionary War." For Mark, the reason why this isn't the version of history taught in American schools is the bankers' continuing control of the media.

Assassinations

President Andrew Jackson later called bankers "vipers and thieves!" and sought to undermine the single national, privately owned bank. It's said that it was these anti-bank moves that led to an assassination attempt on Jackson, and that the bankers then did their best to denigrate his character. "Wildcat banks" joined in by creating bad debts, hyperinflation and high interest rates that would tip Jackson's presidency into an economic depression. As Abraham Lincoln was to comment, banking "denounces as public enemies all who question its methods or throw light upon its crimes".

President Lincoln himself sought to pay for the Civil War by issuing "greenbacks" on the same basis as scrip. As Christopher Mark tells it, the issuance of "greenbacks" was so incendiary to Europe's banks, who would otherwise have happily funded the Civil War, that it provoked France and Britain to mass their troops in Mexico and Canada. Their intervention was only averted, the story goes, by Lincoln's appeals to the Russians: "I have two great enemies, the Southern Army in front of me and the bankers in the rear", Lincoln complained. He of course was subsequently assassinated, as was President Garfield, who also opposed the international moneychangers and noted: "Whoever controls the volume of money in any country is absolute master of all industry and commerce." A century later, a plan by John F. Kennedy to pay off the Federal debt using "U.S. Notes", a US government-printed currency that the Federal Reserve (se p.230) must supposedly accept, also apparently led to his assassination.

Wars and debts

In his 1971 rant *None Dare Call It Conspiracy*, Gary Allen argues that the bankers' battle in the US is just part of a bigger plot. He quotes Carroll Quigley's *Tragedy And Hope* – cited by many as "proof" of conspiracies to take over the world – as saying that "the heads of the world's chief central banks were ... the technicians and agents of the dominant investment bankers of their own countries, who had raised them up, and who were perfectly capable of throwing them down", by means of coup d'état or war.

This theme has been developed by Professor Stuart Crane, who argues that the biggest profits are derived from making interest-bearing loans to governments – and that the largest loans of all tend to be for arms and wars. But how can a bank ensure that it collects on a loan, when it's dealing with a well-armed, sovereign government? Its most obvious recourse if a government defaults is to lend more money to another foreign power, again of course at a profitable rate of interest, to finance a war against the defaulter.

Crane says that the architect of this system was Frankfurt banker Meyer Rothschild, who dispersed his sons to Paris, London, Vienna and Naples to finance wars between the governments of Europe during the eighteenth and nineteenth centuries. The House of Rothschild was the first and most prominent of several European banking families who were granted state monopolies over their respective nations' central banks. The Rothschilds went to finance the North during the US Civil War, while their relatives the Erlangers financed the South (which flies in the face of Christopher Mark's contention that European banks weren't able to fund the North because of Lincoln's "greenbacks").

With what could appear to be overtones of anti-Semitism, Minister Muhammed of the UK-based Islamic group Final Call To Prayer alleged to his followers in 2004 that the Rothschilds and Warburgs financed England and Germany in World War I, whereas historian Antony C. Sutton claimed that Winston Churchill colluded with banker J.P. Morgan to embroil America in the war by arranging for the liner *Lusitania* to be sunk. Sutton argues that the Korean and Vietnam Wars were not about fighting Communism, but about generating multi-billion-dollar arms contracts, and that Wall Street bankrolled both the US and the USSR.

Sutton charges that "the financial elite knowingly and with premeditation assisted the Bolshevik Revolution of 1917 in concert with German bankers", who financed Lenin in order to end Russian involvement in World War I. The subsequent default of Russian debts led all of Wall Street to back the Allied war against the Bolsheviks in 1919 and 1920; similarly, some allege that the hottest spells during the Cold War came when the USSR defaulted on later loans, causing banks to double their lending for US armaments.

Sutton further alleges that Wall Street engineered and profited from Germany's 1923 hyperinflation and the 1929 Wall Street Crash, while the Depression of the 1930s was a bankers' plot that put tens of millions of people into poverty and bankrupted nations, but pushed land and assets into the possession of the banks. Wall Street supposedly backed Franklin D. Roosevelt in the US *and* Adolf Hitler in Germany; according to Muhammed and Allen, the Warburgs and the Rothschilds financed Hitler, a charge spun by one Internet writer to suggest that Hitler was simply their agent. By that account, both Roosevelt's New Deal and Hitler's Four-Year Plan were near-identical "plans for fascist takeovers of their respective countries". Accordingly,

Wall Street also wanted war between France and Germany, which Hitler delivered, and war between the US and Germany, which Roosevelt and Hitler also provided.

Harvard Professor Richard Pipes has called Sutton's research too "uncomfortable", and it's regularly either ignored or dismissed as "extreme". That said, although Sutton is written off by many as the arch-conspiracy theorist, he's not alone in depicting Wall Street as a cabal of banking families. In 1899, M.W. Walbert's *The Coming Battle – The International Monetary Conspiracy Against The United States* described how European banking families were attempting to siphon away America's riches, by controlling the Treasury via the banks. Allen outlines a detailed, nearly incestuous series of marriages around 1900 between the Warburgs, the Loebs (of Khun, Loeb & Company), the Schiffs (who'd shared digs with the Rothschilds), and their US agent, J. Pierpont Morgan. There was also John D. Rockefeller, who married the daughter of Senator Nelson Aldridge, and whose grandson, also named Nelson, was to become both vice president and governor of New York. Warburg backed Aldridge to set up the Federal Reserve in 1913, and writer Michael Edwards claims that eight banking families own about eighty percent of the Fed to this day (the Rockefellers being the biggest holders). The top seven families at the Fed are European in origin, says Mark.

The Jews

Of course, where some write "European", others write "Jewish", and pick out the Rothschilds, Warburgs, Schiffs and Loebs over the Rockefellers and Morgans. The association of Jews with banks and insidious activities has been one of the most enduring, pernicious conspiracy theories, called by the Anti-Defamation League a "timeworn, classic" anti-Semitic myth, which nonetheless still reappears across a swathe of sources.

Jewish bankers figured very high on Hitler's hate propaganda. He also hated the Bolsheviks of course, who Sutton claims were lent $20 million in 1917 by Jacob Schiff. This in part has given rise to theories that the Bolshevik Revolution was in fact a Jewish plot, and hence that the international bankers were Jewish Communists engaging in a "bigger conspiracy to control the world". In a somewhat analogous situation, it's been said that recently stirred-up fears about the threat of Islamism are just a cover for the core potential economic threat of an Islamic finance bloc stretching from the Middle East to Malaysia, as pioneered by Malaysia's ex-premier Mahathir Mohammed. Yet, in another scarcely ironic twist, the Simon Wiesenthal Center says that Mahathir's diatribes about Jewish finance "would have made Hitler and Goebbels proud".

A pervasive anti-Semitic conspiracy theory in the US alleges that Jews control the Federal Reserve (see p. 230). In his 1931 book, *The Truth About The Slump*, A.N. Field claimed that "the Money Power that rules the world" is a "German-Jew engine of control", which enslaved the US by controlling the Federal Reserve. In *Called To Serve*, James Gritz, who was the Populist Party's presidential candidate in 1992, charged that "eight Jewish families control the Fed". Three years later, the Nation of Islam's Louis Farrakhan concurred, adding that the Rothschilds "financed both sides of all the European wars".

Eustace Mullins in 1983 and Gary Kah in 1991 both claimed that the Federal Reserve is controlled by those who own and control its largest regional branch, the New York Federal Reserve Bank. Kah's "Swiss and Saudi Arabian contacts" told him that the NY Fed is owned by the banks of Rothschild, Lazard, Israel Moses Seif, Warburg, Goldman Sachs, Lehman Brothers and Kuhn-Loeb – it's easy to see where this is going – while Mullins cites a cabal called the "London Connection", which controls the NY Fed by owning its eight biggest shareholders, and thus makes "the most powerful men in the US answerable to ... the House of Rothschild."

Nazi gold

Both writers, however, ignored the fact that the NY Fed has only one vote of the twelve on the board of the Federal Reserve, and that the Federal Open Market Committee must also approve any changes to interest rates. Kah lists mostly foreign or investment banks, which cannot own Fed stock by law. The Anti-Defamation League has called Mullins an "anti-Semitic propagandist" (www.adl.org/special_reports/control_of_fed/print.asp).

The Federal Reserve

The Federal Reserve is the regulatory agency that governs the US banking industry, setting monetary policy and influencing the business cycle through changing interest rates, issuing currency or purchasing government bonds. However, it's alleged that the Fed too was created in conspiracy. Gary Allen alleges that J.P. Morgan created a series of banking panics such as the "Panic Circular" of 1893,

which read "You will at once retire one-third of your circulation and call in one half of your loans...", as well as rumours of insolvency at the Knickerbocker Bank and the Trust Company of America in 1907.

Paul Warburg and Senator Nelson Aldridge used such "panics" to lobby for a single national bank, which was set up in the 1913 Federal Reserve Act under President Woodrow Wilson. An attempt to pass a similar act had been made under the previous administration of President Taft, but Taft had it defeated. So, the theory goes, international "banksters" backed Woodrow Wilson for office and split the Taft vote by backing ex-President Teddy Roosevelt to run. With the Wilson administration successfully installed, the Act was passed, albeit with most of the opposition on Christmas vacation. Congressman Charles A. Lindbergh, Sr called it an act that legalized "the invisible government by the money power". New York mayor John Hylan echoed that claim in 1922, when he decried the Federal Reserve as an "octopus" headed by Rockefeller-Standard Oil and powerful banking houses.

BCCI

The Bank of Commerce and Credit International SA saga is one case where reality outdoes the most paranoid of conspiracy theorists' imaginings. The short career of this infamous bank began in 1972, when it was founded in Pakistan by Agha Hasan Abedi with backing from sheikhs in Abu Dhabi. Presenting itself as a "Third World Bank" with the remit to invest and foster prosperity in corners of the globe usually beneath the interest of Western capitalism, BCCI would end up with over a million depositors, using four hundred branches worldwide, on every continent except Antarctica, and at one point claimed assets of $25 billion. Such was the claim, but the gargantuan scale of its criminal operations and the bank's tentacular reach were real, and really quite awesome.

Throughout the 1970s, the bank grew speedily,

NAZI GOLD

Since 1945, legions of treasure hunters have plumbed the depths of Lake Toplitz in Austria, hoping to find the truckloads of Nazi gold supposedly dumped there during the closing days of World War II. Many have died in the process, and the lake has had to be sealed off with only occasional, officially sanctioned dives permitted.

However, the Nazis hid away a lot more gold than that, and some of it is much easier to find. Vast sums were deposited in the banks of those countries that remained neutral during the war, countries which by accepting bullion from the Third Reich helped the Nazis to fund their war effort. In 1997, the World Jewish Congress and the US Senate Banking Committee uncovered a sordid saga of wartime transactions. Gold from all kinds of sources – looted from invaded countries, or taken from the bank deposits, jewellery, spectacle frames or dental fillings of the millions of people who were exterminated in Nazi concentration camps – was melted down into bullion, and stamped with false pre-war dates to make it appear legitimate.

About $400 million dollars' worth of gold, in 1945 terms, went into Switzerland's Swiss National Bank, and more into the Basel-based Bank for International Settlements. Both served as conduits through which $500 million dollars in assets and $300 million dollars in gold were channelled into central banks in Portugal, Spain, Argentina, Turkey and Sweden, as payment for trade. As William Clarke tells it on www. bigeye.com, while the Allies monitored these triangular deals, they either did not, or could not, do anything to close them down.

Although the Swiss National Bank denied taking any "tainted gold" in 1945, the directors of the Reichsbank and the US Military Government in Germany disagreed. The latter concluded that "the Bank for International Settlements accepted looted gold ... [and] was dominated by Axis interests". In 1998, a Swiss government report confirmed that the country's central bank made no effort until late in the war to ensure that gold paid in had not been taken from Holocaust victims. Swiss bankers also initially denied, then severely understated "heirless

deposits", which is to say accounts held by those who fell victim to the Holocaust, which should by rights have passed to their families after the war. According to one estimate, made in 1997, the Swiss held between $6 and $20 billion dollars' worth of Nazi gold. Faced by class action suits launched from the US against Swiss banks, and the threat that Swiss assets would be frozen and Swiss banking licences in the US revoked, the Swiss government set up a $5 billion-dollar fund to pay annual compensation to the victims of *all* human catastrophes, including the Holocaust.

Not that the Swiss had all the Nazis' gold. The governments of the US, Britain and France set up the Tripartite Gold Commission after the war to reimburse captured gold. However, only around two thirds of it was claimed. That leaves some three and a half tons of gold in the Bank of England, and two tons in the Federal Reserve Bank of New York.

In 1999, the US undertook its own efforts to restore assets stolen during the Holocaust to

their rightful owners or heirs. Clinton's Presidential Advisory Commission on Holocaust Assets (www.pcha.gov) listed property worth hundreds of millions of dollars, including looted books that had found their way into the Library of Congress, a painting in the National Gallery of Art, and several thousand dormant bank accounts. Much of that may have been acquired and/or neglected in all innocence.

But there was one spectacular exception. In 1945, the US Army in Austria appropriated twenty-four boxcars of paintings, sculptures, gold and possessions that had been stolen by the Nazis, and were then valued at up to $200 million dollars. In 2001, tens of thousands of Hungarian Holocaust survivors formed a class action suit against the US government, charging that the goods had been falsely classified as unidentifiable or enemy property. Survivors were told lies about the fate of their possessions, which in many instances had ended up in officers' homes. The US government settled in 2004.

---

pursuing asset growth over profits – seeking high net-worth individuals and regular large deposits, splitting holdings between Luxembourg and the Grand Cayman, and acquiring other banks in Switzerland. (This, according to conspiracy theorist Lyndon LaRouche's magazine *Executive Intelligence Review*, brought BCCI into the orbit of Rothschild

Bank AG; see International Banking Conspiracy p. 226.) By then, it's thought, BCCI was already teetering on the edge of bankruptcy, and using deposit cash to fund operations instead of investing, but that didn't stop its expansion into Africa and Asia, and in 1977 it arrived on the shores of the US (although, as the *Review* tells it, BCCI was originally conceived with the connivance of the CIA and the Bank of America). There, BCCI swiftly, secretly and illegally used nominees and friends in high places to buy four banks, which operated in seven states and the District of Columbia, and included the First American Bank. BCCI largely restricted its US operations to laundering drug-money.

By early 1985, the US Drug Enforcement Administration, IRS and CIA were all separately pointing to BCCI involvement in laundering heroin money from BCCI branches in Colombia, Central America and Southeast Asia. Even so, the CIA used both BCCI and First American for its own operations. The 1992 report *The BCCI Affair* (fas.org/irp/congress/1992_rpt/bcci), from a Senate Subcommittee investigation led by Senator John Kerry, stated that former CIA directors Richard Helms and William Casey, together with other CIA luminaries, "float in and out of BCCI at critical times in its history", as Helms and Casey were involved in equally critical episodes such as the Camp David peace talks and the Iran-Contra affair (see p.186). Saudi-CIA intelligence agents, meanwhile, worked in BCCI's commodities affiliate, Capcom, which laundered billions of dollars from the Middle East to the US.

Kerry's investigation, however, didn't begin until the late 1980s. Although the CIA told the State, Treasury, Commerce and Justice departments about the drug-money laundering in 1985 and 1986, no investigations were launched at that time, and *The BCCI Affair* later slated belated intra-departmental investigations as being confounded by incompetence, inter-agency turf wars, and obstruction by members of various government departments with something to hide. Federal prosecutors in Florida, the US Customs Service, the Federal Reserve, the State Department, the Treasury Department and the Justice Department all contrived or conspired to obstruct outside investigations.

All the while, BCCI remained reputable enough for Harken Energy, of whom George W. Bush was then a director, to borrow $25 million from its joint ventures in 1987. Around this time, however, the fact that Manuel Noriega, the disgraced president of Panama, used the bank to launder drug money was uncovered, and it was then that the Senate Subcommittee on Terrorism, Narcotics, and International Operations instigated Kerry's investigation. With assistance from New York District Attorney Robert Morgenthau, the subcommittee uncovered a criminal enterprise of a breathtaking scale and reach.

BCCI, the report stated, boasted an impressive roster of allies who had a "material impact" on its ability to operate, including lawyers and government officials who lobbied to keep the bank afloat, diverted investigations and impugned the motives and integrity of investigators. Among those on the list were former Secretary of Defense Clark Clifford, former senators and congressmen Stuart Symington, John Culver, Mike Barnes, federal prosecutors, and State Department, White House and Federal Reserve officials, and even Jimmy Carter and the Rev. Jesse Jackson. One former BCCI director, James Reynolds Bath, was part-owner of Arbusto Energy, which was co-founded by his National Guard friend, George W. Bush. Bath also purchased Houston Gulf Airport on behalf of one Salem bin Laden, one of Osama bin Laden's cousins. Kerry was repeatedly pressured to close the investigation, not just by the Foreign Relations Committee but even – according to "Follow the Money", a *Washington Monthly* piece by David Sirota and Jonathan Baskin – Jacqueline Kennedy Onassis, who was inspired to phone Kerry up in person.

In 1990, the Bush administration admonished, but didn't close down, BCCI over its involvement in money laundering (the net was closing in on BCCI as its covert CIA purpose to fund the Mujahadeen against the Soviets had been completed, according to LaRouche). That same year, a deal between a concerned Bank of England and major BCCI shareholder Abu Dhabi to prevent the collapse of BCCI withheld information from Federal Reserve investigators as well as BCCI's million depositors, most of whom were entirely innocent and ignorant of the bank's extraordinarily broad criminal activities. The deal, which *The BCCI Affair* said exhibited "extremely poor judgement" by the Bank of England, also allowed records and witnesses to escape from British government control to Abu Dhabi.

Only in July 1991 were Kerry's committee, US and UK regulators and the Federal Reserve finally able to close BCCI down, and indict the group for grand larceny, bribery, and money laundering. By then, the bank had laundered money in most of the 73 countries in which it operated, using shell companies, banking secrecy laws and bribes to facilitate its operations; worked with Iraqi arms dealer Sarkis Sarkenalian, and arms traffickers and terrorists in Syria and Palestine; worked with drug traffickers in Syria, Afghanistan, Pakistan, Burma and Panama, and was involved (with the connivance of the CIA) in funnelling heroin trafficking proceeds to fund the Mujahadeen's fight against the Soviet Union in Afghanistan; and had financed and trafficked technology for Pakistan's nuclear programme. It had also been implicated in the 1980 "October Surprise", when the release from Iran of 52 American hostages just so happened to coincide with the inauguration of Ronald Reagan as US president – Reagan having defeated President Jimmy Carter largely over his failure to get the hostages released (see p.185).

According to the Senate report, BCCI had also had its fingers in "prostitution, income tax evasion, smuggling, and illegal immigration", while the CIA later discovered that its customers included Osama bin Laden, members of his extended family, dozens of his comrades and companies thought to have funded Al Qaeda. The great irony, of course, was the extent to which the bank, for all its American friends in high places and collaboration with the CIA, was actively funding anti-Western groups. Indeed, its only limits, said the report, were in the "imagination of its officers and customers" – or at least a few of them. Shutting down BCCI closed off an extraordinary international conduit for dirty money to fund equally dirty deeds, but hundreds of thousands of innocent customers and employees suffered as a result.

The IMF and the World Bank

Michael Edwards charges that the "big money" that finances both the Republicans and the Democrats is controlled by "a collection of mostly banking family reps known as the Bilderberg Group" (see p.235), who all belong to what's effectively an exclusive club that also dominates the Council on Foreign Relations and the Trilateral Commission (see p.137 and p.139 respectively). Rear Admiral Chester Ward complained that the Council on Foreign Relations is dominated by "Wall Street international bankers" who "want the world banking monopoly from whatever power ends up in the control of global government". That government is the infamous "New World Order" (see p.234), and among the large, venerable institutions often accused of being mere instruments of this global conspiracy are the World Bank and the International Monetary Fund (IMF).

Both the World Bank and the IMF were set up in the aftermath of World War II, with headquarters in Washington DC. Their aim was to oversee the reconstruction and development of the worldwide economy, the IMF by steering monetary policy and setting the conditions for loans, and the World Bank by alleviating poverty. However, by 2004, some 85 countries owed $97 billion to the IMF, despite the fact that since 1996 the IMF and World Bank have been working, via the Heavily Indebted Poor Countries (HIPC) Initiative, to ensure that "no poor country faces a debt burden it cannot manage".

Which poses the question: what were the lending policies during the preceding fifty years, which have led to so many countries staggering under debt, instead of being happy capitalist countries kick-started into prosperity by judicious lending?

THE NEW WORLD ORDER

The New World Order (NWO) crops up in countless conspiracy theories. While the detail varies as to which institutions or individuals are involved, and to what ends, the basic premise seems to be that a group or groups are seeking to establish a single, all-powerful global government (hence the theory's other moniker, the One World Government). According to Dr John Coleman in his 1992 book *Conspirators' Hierarchy: The Story Of The Committee Of 300*, the NWO is a group of "permanent non-elected hereditary oligarchists", elected by some "feudal system" to enforce globally uniform laws, through courts and a military force.

As such, the United Nations is in the frame for many US conspiracy theorists as the ultimate expression of the New World Order, being an unelected institute of global governance, pushing its economic diktats through the IMF, the World Bank (see p.233) and the World Economic Forum (see p.237), its laws through the World Court and International Criminal Court, and enforcing its rule through NATO bombers and UN peacekeepers. Other institutions supposedly in on the plot are the Bilderberg Group (see opposite), the Trilateral Commission (see p.139), the Council on Foreign Relations (see p.137) and related bodies.

The NWO's agents are said to be responsible for nearly all of the major wars, economic successes and maelstroms of the last century, and to have profited greatly from each. The Great Depression of the early 1930s, both World Wars, the Bolshevik Revolution, the Cold War, the Soviet Union's collapse – all, apparently, were NWO projects, with Communists and far-right US Republicans as part and parcel of the same conspiracy. Famine and disease, like AIDS (see p.277), are also supposedly NWO weapons to control and cull the world's population and reduce pressures on finite resources.

In the US, other calamities – like the chaos the Y2K Millennium Bug was supposed to bring (but didn't, see p.248), or supposedly government-manufactured terrorist events like the Oklahoma City bombing (see p.212) and 9/11 (see p.360) – have been engineered to justify the imposition of martial law under the Federal Emergency Management Agency (FEMA, see Secret Bases p.283). This would quell the few who can't be brainwashed through mind-control methods such as MK ULTRA (see p.192).

The idea of a One World Government is often associated with Professor Carroll Quigley, a specialist in twentieth-century US history cited approvingly by President Bill Clinton in one of his speeches. Part exposé of, part apologia for rule by the elite, Quigley's 1300-page tome *Tragedy And Hope* – which ironically favours the cock-up rather than the conspiracy theory of history – advocates a single body of global governance.

The current manifestation of such a body, of course, is the UN, but for other conspiracists the NWO's origins reach back to mystical groups like the Illuminati (see p.85) and the Freemasons (see p.76), both of which are now said to control the NWO. One Christian conspiracy theorist, Pat Robertson, traces its origins back to before the Tower of Babel, when one government and one language unified the world (or so the Old Testament has it). A single global government is also apparently foretold in the Bible's Book of Revelations, so Robertson argues that today's NWO is the work of Satan, an interpretation supported by the prevalence of war, famine, pestilence and death, the Four Horsemen of the Apocalypse.

Other conspiracy theorists claim that the expression "New World Order" is part of the currency – literally so, being inscribed in Latin on the US dollar bill amid all the supposedly Masonic imagery (see p.119) as *Novus Ordo Seculorum* (although the expression actually means "New Order of the Ages"). It also became a catchphrase of President George H.W. Bush, who told Congress in January 1991 that what was at stake in the impending Gulf War (see p.372) was "a big idea – a new world order, where diverse nations are drawn together in common cause to achieve the universal aspirations of mankind: peace and security, freedom and the rule of law".

The Gulf War, authorized by the UN Security Council and waged by its main members, is thus seen by some as the first *overt* NWO war, with the White House – and the Bush family – at its helm. From this perspective, the New World Order is less about the UN subverting the power and sovereignty of the US, than the US exploiting the UN to enforce the Order of the New World – a conspiracy theory that, for political realists, might seem to come uncomfortably close to the truth.

According to John Perkins, in *Confessions Of An Economic Hit Man*, the World Bank and IMF served as channels through which huge loans were directed to poor countries by the CIA and the National Security Agency, to fund grand but utterly useless infrastructural projects. The loans were made conditional on the relevant contracts being awarded to US corporations, which ensured that the loan capital was returned straight to the US, while the debtors were never expected to repay the loans. The point was that when, inevitably, they defaulted, the World Bank or IMF could step in, and dictate that country's spending on everything from social to military security, and even how it voted in the UN. Resistance will get the country's leadership "removed". Failing that, a war would be engineered so that US forces could go in as bailiffs and reclaim control of the capital.

Perkins claims that this strategy, in which "economic hit men" such as himself worked through civilian consultancies like the Boston-based Chas T. Main, enabled the creation of a new US empire. Thus because half of Ecuador's GDP is owed in debt, the US can say, as Perkins put it to *Democracy Now* in 2002: "Look, you're not able to repay your debts, therefore give our oil companies your Amazon rain forests, which are filled with oil." He added: "We literally have them over a barrel." He alleges that Ecuador's president Jaime Roldes was assassinated over non-payments of debt, while President Omar Torrijos of Panama was killed for awarding a canal contract to a Japanese company rather than a US corporation.

Perkins concedes that he may be derided as a conspiracy theorist. Even so, it does seem strange that so many developing countries have somehow contrived to be so consistently inept for so long under the aegis of capitalism that "austerity measures" have to be imposed by the World Bank and IMF. Over 140 countries, including Brazil, Mexico and Argentina, can only receive continued credit if they lower their subsidies to producers of domestic staples and export commodities, devalue their currencies, and demolish their social welfare programmes, utterly irrespective of what their governments were voted in for.

More than fifteen years after the Cold War ended, a billion people remain undernourished, and a bil-

lion live in slums. The main beneficiaries of stable economic prosperity from this system seem to have been the US, Europe and Japan, which all have permanent directors at the World Bank – and by a long-standing informal agreement, the president of the World Bank is always an American (currently former Under-Secretary of Defense and notorious neocon Paul Wolfowitz, who succeeded James Wolfensohn), while the IMF chief is European.

The Bilderberg Group

During the early 1950s, with postwar Europe divided and the Cold War turning violent in Korea, prominent Americans such as John J. McCloy – the head of the Office of Strategic Services, the predecessor of the CIA – and C.D. Jackson, the chief of President Eisenhower's unit on psychological warfare, felt that economic and security issues of joint concern to western Europe and America were not getting enough attention. Backed by the CIA, and the Rockefeller and Ford foundations, they decided to instigate informal, unofficial top-level meetings that might foster prosperity and help to avert wars.

Prince Bernhard of Holland hosted the first meetings at the Hotel de Bilderberg in The Hague in 1954, and the Bilderberg Group was born (although subsequent meetings have varied in location, Bilderberg's headquarters are still in The Hague). As the BBC described it in 2004, Bilderberg is an "elite coterie of Western thinkers and power-brokers": the cream of North Atlantic statesmen, royals, bankers, industrialists, pressmen and generals, continue to meet annually to discuss world issues, and select and invite favoured individuals for membership.

According to Reuters, both Tony Blair and Bill Clinton came to international attention as speakers at Bilderberg meetings before they achieved power, as did former World Bank president James

Wolfensohn. The list of American big-hitters is impressive. Of George W. Bush's neo-conservative clique, Richard Pearle, Richard Armitage, Paul Wolfowitz and Colin Powell are all Bilderbergers.

One prevalent theory, originating in the early 1960s from books like right-wing American Phyllis Schlafly's diatribe *A Choice Not An Echo: The Inside Story Of How American Presidents Are Chosen*, is that membership of the Bilderberg Group is key to getting the White House. By extension, it's said that George W. Bush's Bilderberg backers secured him the presidency in 2000 over non-Bilderberger Al Gore. George H.W. Bush lost in 1992 to Bilderberger Bill Clinton, while another member, Gerald Ford, managed to become vice-president and president without being elected for either job.

But the theory of omnipotent Bilderberger power doesn't always hold up. Ford lost the presidency in 1976 to non-Bilderberger Jimmy Carter, who was a member of the Trilateral Commission, which is the target of its own secret clique conspiracy theories (see p.139). Although not a Bilderberg member, George H.W. Bush won in 1988, while Bilderberg members John Kerry, John Edwards, John McCain and Gary Hart have all been stymied. In any case, many Bilderbergers are also Trilateralists, as well as members of the Council of Foreign Relations and the World Economic Forum, so which group has more power and how that ultimately matters is a blurry subject with different spins coming depending on who's having a go at which group (if not all of them) on the day. The catch-all theory is that they're just different names for the same old gangs colluding behind closed doors, funded by conspiracy theorists' favourite David Rockefeller, Exxon, IBM and the Carnegie Endowment fund.

While the real significance of Bilderberg membership is debated, however, the theories about its power can have an impact. Schlafly's book surfaced during the presidential campaign of fellow-Republican Barry Goldwater in 1964. Schlafly ranted that many *Republicans* were part of the northeastern establish-

ment and were just puppets of Bilderberg's godless Communists. That dissent in the party's ranks may have contributed to Goldwater's defeat. Over thirty years later, William Rees-Mogg wrote in *The Times* of American evangelist Pat Buchanan's belief that his presidential bid was finished when he snubbed Bilderberg membership.

But that may all be another conspiracy again. Right-wing writer Chip Berlet has argued that to devise conspiracy theories about the Bilderberg Group merely distracts from a systematic analysis of how wealthy elites control the world's economy and politics. Economist and Bilderberger Will Hutton says that the Group does exactly that, likening the group to the World Economic Forum (indeed, Goldman Sachs chairman and WEF board member Peter Sutherland presided over the 1999 Bilderberg meeting), where "the consensus established is the

The WEF at Davos

THE WORLD ECONOMIC FORUM

Although likened to the Bilderberg Group, the World Economic Forum is in fact a Swiss-based non-governmental organization (NGO) that describes itself as the "foremost global community of business, political, intellectual and other leaders of society committed to improving the state of the world". Representatives from the world's top thousand companies make up half of the two thousand participants at the WEF's annual meeting in Davos, Switzerland, along with heads of state, NGO chiefs, academics and journalists, working in the "collaborative spirit of Davos" to "improve the world" through business.

There are few specific theories about the WEF, but it certainly attracts the world's top guns. Davos 2005 was attended by 2500 guests, includ-

ing ex-president Bill Clinton, UK Prime Minister Tony Blair (as president of the G8) and European Commission president Jose Barroso. Issues such as Equitable Globalization, Global Governance and Islam, and United States Leadership and Weapons of Mass Destruction were discussed, with the likes of Bill Gates and the CEOs of Citigroup and the New York Stock Exchange in the chair.

Bono of U2, Angelina Jolie, Sharon Stone and Lionel Richie also pitched in their views, raised some money and added glamour to the meetings. Executives from ChevronTexaco, Coca-Cola, Dell, Nestlé, Nike, PricewaterhouseCoopers, Saudi Aramco and Sony rubbed shoulders with directors from Amnesty International, Human Rights Watch and World Vision

International, while presidents and deans from Harvard University, the London School of Economics, Peking University and Yale University's Center for the Study of Globalization mixed with chairs and editors-in-chief from – amongst others – Agence France Presse, Al Jazeera, BBC News, *China Daily*, the *India Today* group, Novosti, Reuters and *Time*. The WEF board arranges it all, staffed by luminaries ranging from Peter Sutherland, the chairman of Goldman Sachs International, and Henry McKinnell, chair and CEO of the world's largest pharmaceutical research company, Pfizer, to Queen Rania of Jordan and George Carey, the former Archbishop of Canterbury.

The WEF is also organising a forum of Young Global Leaders, a group of 1,111 – a number of

unknown significance – people aged under 40, "who share a commitment to shaping the global future ... [and are] destined for future greatness". As well one might be if deemed so by the WEF and asked to engage in the "2020 Initiative" to formulate the "roadmap" to "spearhead change" (see www.weforum. org or www.younggloballeaders. org to find out who these youthful movers and shakers are). Although there isn't necessarily anything sinister in this, there's nothing remotely democratic about it either: the WEF's projection of the balance of power in the world of 2020 is suggested by the fact that it has identified more Young Global Leaders in Europe and North America than in Africa, Asia, Latin America and the Middle East put together. No change there then.

backdrop against which policy is made worldwide". According to Lord Denis Healey, former Labour chancellor in the UK and founding member of the group, however, Hutton's idea is "crap".

Others hold the Bilderberg Group responsible for creating the 1957 Treaty of Rome, which formed the first building block of the European Union and the euro-zone. Serbian news agencies reported in May 1999 that the war in Kosovo, which ultimately brought down Serbian president Slobodan Milosevic, was plotted as a "Balkan Vietnam" at Bilderberg's 1996 meeting in Scotland by a "supra government" including Margaret Thatcher, Helmut Kohl, Valery Giscard D'Estaing, Henry Kissinger, David Rockefeller and Baron Rothschild. They wanted Serbs to be tried for war crimes at The Hague, and

also, said the Serb press, war with Russia (although the benefits of such a war weren't fully explained).

It's easy to find a more positive spin on Bilderberg's work. Senior editors and correspondents from CBS, ABC, the *Financial Times*, *The Wall Street Journal*, the *LA Times*, *The New York Times* and *Time* all attend meetings, though they're not permitted to report on them, and the minutes of the meetings do not state who said what (not that they're publicly available). The venues are kept secret, there is no website – which explains how the conspiracy website www. bilderberg.org came to have that auspicious address – and the telephone line is a terse answerphone. The meetings are serviced by the group's own barracks of cooks, bodyguards and police.

All of this adds to a mysterious aura that helps

to fuel the myth of its omnipotence. This in turn, according to the BBC, has proved potent enough for the likes of Timothy McVeigh and Osama bin Laden to point at Bilderberg in their violent rages. Bilderberg has also been called the ultimate club for the architects of the New World Order (see p.234), and a talking shop for liberal Zionists plotting world domination, although for some theorists the two ideas are interchangeable.

You can find out more about the group (and how to join it) by writing either to Bilderberg Secretariat, 1 Smidswater, The Hague, or to Bilderberg Meetings, Amstel 216, 1017 AJ Amsterdam. By a curious coincidence – or perhaps not – its US base was once next door to two other institutes of ill-boding for conspiracy theorists, the Trilateral Commission and the Carnegie Endowment, but it's now at 477 Madison Ave, 6th floor, New York 10022.

Don't bank on any of it

The phrases "invisible government" and "money power" recur throughout anti-banking literature, as do explicit references to Jews. Anti-Semitism is often so clearly bubbling beneath the surface that you have to wonder whether bigots use the label "European" as a code word to make their views seem more acceptable in public. Are some writers reproducing ancient slurs in new disguises, perhaps unwittingly, or are extremists hijacking ideas that do not deserve to be dismissed on those grounds

Men in ties: G7 finance ministers gather for a summit meeting, Washington, 2004

alone? Allen argues that the "anti-Semites have played into the hands of the conspiracy", in that by portraying the banking conspiracy as being the work of Jews they've made it an unacceptable topic for historians to tackle, and that the backlash from the Anti-Defamation League has served to distract attention from the fact that J.P. Morgan and the Rockefellers, for example, were white Christians. At this level of logic, snakes eat their own tails, and as Gerry Rough repeatedly points out, conspiracy literature about banking can be a hideous web of misinformation and politically malign scholarship.

And yet in monetarized economies, the moneymen do have great power, as US founding fathers Madison, Jefferson and Hamilton were all too aware. No one can do much without financial backing of some kind, but banks are rarely accountable to anybody. Within a week of taking office following the 1997 UK election, New Labour handed monetary policy back to the Bank of England (a decision taken by chancellor Gordon Brown, a Scotsman, in a coincidental sop to the Paterson conspiracy), to keep it "free of politically motivated decisions" – effectively removing whatever UK government control it had in the first place.

To believe, however, that banks deliberately conspire to manipulate national economies to their own ends, by allowing or even forcing them to go broke, requires you also to believe that they're omniscient or omnipotent enough to do so. What's indisputable is that they're in the business (and usually it's a very successful business) of profiting hugely from the time-honoured practice of lending money and charging for it – and that they continue to profit while their decisions power economies from boom and bust to boom and bust, over and over again. Busts that remove families from their homes, and governments from power.

SOURCES

Books

Gary Allen None Dare Call It Conspiracy (1995). As the title suggests, this is an excitable tome, packed with fascinating detail (especially if it's true), and liberally sprinkled with block capitals and exclamation marks.

Websites

ⓦ**iresist.com/cbg/battle.html** The webpage for Michael Edwards "The Battle America Lost In 1913", an interesting if rather sprawling piece on the rise of the banks.

ⓦ**www.antonysutton.com** Links to many of the works of Antony C. Sutton, a prolific writer on banking conspiracy theories.

ⓦ**www.floodlight.org** A site dedicated to debunking conspiracy theories of a far-right bent, with writer Gerry Rough clinically demolishing banking theories.

ⓦ**www.prisonplanet.com/analysis_mark_022803_deception.html** Check out Christopher Mark's passionately expressed views on international banking and "The Grand Deception and the Theft of America".

Perpetual war on perpetual energy

The industrialized world needs energy, energy for which many people expect to be paid a lot of money. But what if energy suddenly became free, or available in quantities boundless enough to threaten one of the big suppliers? Perhaps conspiracies really are afoot, to ensure that the world remains dependent upon the filthiest, most expensive, and most violently sought-after fuels.

Tesla

The Croatian electrical genius Nikolas Tesla (see also p.291) registered numerous patents for free energy devices, power sources, propulsion systems and weapons. Most of them, and the "free energy" sources in particular, failed to attract investors; it's said that J.P. Morgan and John D. Rockefeller sought to suppress any such threats to their own industries. According to conspiracy lore – and lore it is – Tesla invented an on-board electro-propulsion system, using the globally present force of "ether", which was powerful enough to propel machines such as flying saucers with incredible speeds and manoeuvrability.

By this account, the Nazis developed practical applications of Tesla's system during the 1930s. The US managed to keep abreast of these developments through scientist Werner von Braun, who supposedly secretly visited the US in the late 1930s (he certainly came to the US at the end of WWII). The thousands of flying saucer sightings since then, it's claimed, are real enough, but UFOs are built and flown, not by aliens, but by earthlings.

American physicist and author William Lyne, who has written extensively on the alleged suppression of Tesla's work, describes in baffling scientific detail a power source that's small and cheap enough for everyone to have one, but a world of individuals zipping around in personal flying saucers would be a world without roads or borders. (It would also be a world with a lot of flying saucer crashes, but hey...) This would destroy the oil and automobile industries – among others – at a swoop, and also fatally damage the ability of governments to control their own people. The CIA and NASA have therefore quashed any dissemination of the technology, using tactics developed by the Gestapo's *Reichssich erheithauptamt*.

Wind farms, an alternative energy source: not as glamorous as "ether" power

To Lyne, the scale of the conspiracy is immense. Academics and universities suppress Tesla's ideas, and instead propagate conventional theories in physics and engineering that sustain the industrial status quo, with the media in on this "misinformational conspiracy" to keep Tesla's plans quiet. Most of the talk of aliens and extraterrestrials is just a ploy to distract the public, while UFO-logists and paranormalists are government agents, coming up with ludicrous ideas for other government agents posing as sceptics to shoot down. Anyone who really does have an interest or belief in UFOs, let alone actual proof, can thus then be written off as a crank.

Lyne claims that another power source developed by American physicist Thomas Townsend Brown in 1921 has also been suppressed. Brown discovered what was later called the Biefeld-Brown effect, in which a vacuum tube with two asymmetrical electrodes produces an X-ray-based force when powered with high voltage. During his career in the military, Brown made flying discs up to 70cm wide, powered by this strange force. He believed that this power source could be what was propelling UFOs, and Lyne and others say he was right.

However, if – as Lyne argues – the information is out there, and certain people not only know about it, but have the know-how to build such a machine, then why haven't they? Such super-fast craft couldn't be intercepted as they flew over the world's cities, and showed everyone on the planet what they'd been missing.

Garabed's hoax

In contrast to the alleged conspiracies to keep Tesla and Brown down, Armenian-born Garabed T.K. Giragossia's "free energy generator" was a conspiracy to wind the US government up. Garabed claimed in 1917 that his generator was a machine that would "perform the miracles of the Arabian Nights" and "revolutionize the world's affairs and lift civilization to a higher plane".

A machine born of twenty years of toil and no engineering knowledge whatsoever, it was "intuition" alone that inspired Garabed to create in his little Massachussetts shop an engine that was run by a "mysterious and hitherto unknown force ... waiting to be utilized". He declared that a 48-acre field could provide enough free power "to drive all the industrial machinery in the world", as well as locomotives, ships, and even ungainly aircraft. Without any proof of this whatsoever, Garabed somehow persuaded the US government of the feasibility of his project.

In 1918, President Woodrow Wilson signed a bill from the House and Senate which offered Garabed protection from conspiracy, on condition that he "[could] demonstrate the practicability of his discovery" to a panel of scientists. And what was this incredible energy source revealed to be? A giant flywheel, which charged up over several minutes and then spat back out its kinetic energy in a second. The project was swiftly killed off.

Unseen powers

The Japanese Mafia, or Yakuza, is said to have kept at least three Japanese-developed "overunity systems" off the market. An overunity magnetic motor not only powers itself but also produces excess energy to power other loads, achieving the Holy Grail of perpetual energy and more. Japanese engineer Tuero Kawai reportedly invented one that was confirmed to be workable by Hitachi engineers, and in 1996 a US company in Huntsville agreed to develop and market his engine globally. Within a day of the agreement, however, Yakuza gangsters arrived and scared Kawai's men into scrapping the deal.

In 1972, Texan bulldozer-operator Richard Clem unveiled a vegetable-oil turbine capable of driving a car 115,000 miles on eight gallons of chip fat. As a local newspaper reported, "that might come as a shock to Detroit and the petroleum industry". Ford Motors objected when Clem installed his prototype engine in his Ford Falcon, which should have tipped him off to the possibility that some people wouldn't take kindly to his invention. Soon enough, big men came and told Clem that his next drive would be in the back of a hearse if he didn't ditch his fat-fuelled engine. He died shortly afterwards of a heart attack, and only the efforts of his daughter have kept the story alive.

Elsbett

The fate of Clem's engine bears an uncanny resemblance to the rumours that surround the Elsbett diesel engine. This was patented in 1977 by German engineering company Elsbett AG, to run on either fossil diesel fuel or bio-diesel – vegetable oil. (For that matter, the first diesel engine of all, patented by Rudolf Diesel in 1893, ran on peanut oil). Most diesel engines run exclusively on one or the other, and can be converted from one to the other, but the Elsbett can run on both. Bio-diesel is carbon neutral and a fraction of the price of fossil diesel, so why isn't the world powered by Elsbetts? Because, the theory goes, oil companies who don't want their fossil-fuel monopoly upset by bio-fuel vehicles have run the Elsbett into the ground with unfair practices.

Elsbett's website charts the glittering career of engineer Ludwig Elsbett and his company, including over four hundred patents filed, countless corporate and government awards, and engineering partnerships with Volkswagen and Scania, design licences from Malaysia to Russia, and a six-million-dollar Citibank-backed conversion project in Brazil. Not bad for a firm with six employees, and no mention of any conspiracy. Admittedly, few companies would promote themselves with stories some might consider to be paranoid fantasy. But amid all the self-promotion and success, Elsbett AG's site cryptically mentions one fact that the site says pertains to the date Herr Elsbett was born: "On September 29th, 1913, Rudolf Diesel disappears overboard from a ferry between Antwerp and Harwich" – a startlingly incongruous mention.

Elsewhere, *Forbes* magazine speculated that Diesel was "probably bumped off by the German secret service", as he was heading for talks with the British Admiralty, even though his engine was "key to the new German weapon, the U-boat". Pondering alternatives to petrol, *Forbes* asked: "Is there a message here for us today? ... Just remember what happened to Rudolph when he tried to share his knowledge." So what might Elsbett be referring to?

Powering on

As the main US automobile manufactures don't make diesel cars, the "conspiracy" against Elsbett may amount to no more than the fact that there's no market for diesel cars in the US, and no one's going out of their way to create one. On the other hand, bio-diesel is in fact taking off in the sector that actually makes the stuff, and stands to make a fortune from it – farming.

Bio-diesel is commercially available in most oilseed-producing American states – farm states, the "red" states that always vote Republican – and is making dramatic gains as a farm fuel. Between 1997 and 2002, output increased 35-fold to 3.5 million gallons, while tax credits and the drive to reduce pollution could push that up to one billion gallons by 2010. Meanwhile, *Forbes* points out, forty percent of Western European cars run on diesel, which suggests a huge potential in Europe for carbon-neutral conversion. In the UK, a growing number of owners of diesel cars are already said to be filling up at chip shops. It may not be quite as glamorous or thrilling as "ether" power, X-ray propulsion or a perpetual motor, but bio-diesel could have a major impact on energy use and emissions – if it's allowed to.

Books
William Lyne Occult Ether Physics (1998).
An outline in sometimes mind-numbing detail of the theories and mathematical problems that lie behind perpetual energy, together with some interesting pages of conspiracy insight.

Websites
www.hsv.com "The Master Principle Of

Overunity And The Japanese Overunity Engines: A New Pearl Harbor?" – an article by Tom Bearden, who specializes in micro-energy sources, from the *Virtual Times*, January 1996.

The eternal light bulb and the Phoebus Cartel

The suppression of an "eternal" light bulb that never burns out is one of the most widely held conspiracy theories. The fact is that light bulbs are pretty low-tech devices, involving a strip of metal (the filament), sitting in an airtight glass bulb filled with an inert gas, being heated to glowing point by electric current. But while millions are made every day, your average household 100-watt bulb shines its light for only 1000 hours. Surely something so simple could be made in such a way that it lasted forever? The problem is, of course, that such an "eternal bulb" would mean that people would only need to buy light bulbs once, putting light-bulb manufacturers out of business. So, the theory runs, the manufacturers have bought up and sat on all the world's patents for eternal bulbs to protect their profits.

The Phoebus Cartel

Unless someone ever delves into the vaults of the world's light-bulb makers and finds eternal bulb designs in a file marked "suppressed", the theory will remain just that – a theory. There is, however, a kernel of truth to the thinking behind it. In fact, the US had a light-bulb price-fixing cartel from the late nineteenth century, when six light-bulb makers formed Incandescent Electric Lamp Manufacturers, whose purpose, according to social scientist Patrick

Gaughen, was to "fix prices, set output, and divide markets".

The biggest manufacturer, General Electric Co, shared the Edison patent for light-bulbs with its main competitor, Westinghouse Electric Company, and agreed with light manufacturing equipment makers to buy their goods and charge GE's competitors inflated prices. GE soon bought out the other association members and eighteen rivals, and controlled eighty percent of US light-bulb output before moving on to Europe.

There, the short-lived Internationale Glühlampen Preisvereinigung price-fixing cartel collapsed in 1924, but some chicanery from International GE led to its resurrection as the Swiss-based Phoebus SA Compagnie Industrielle cartel, with leading bulb-makers such as Osram, Philips, Tungsram and Associated Electrical Industries. Phoebus divided the world into three markets, and companies dominating particular regions colluded to fix prices locally. Members also had sales quotas depending on their usual market share, and profits were redistributed to companies that hadn't met their quotas, skewing production to quotas instead of demand. As Westinghouse observed in 1937: "The goal ... is to make as much money as possible out of those units we are permitted to sell. It is much more advantageous for us to make a profit of 5 cents per unit on 4,000,000 units than 2.5 cents on 8,000,000 units."

Although the eternal light bulb had yet to be invented, Phoebus also had industry-wide "quality control standards". One GE engineer cast light on what this meant in 1932: "The battery manufacturers went part way with us and accepted lamps of two battery lives instead of three [lives] ... We have been continuing our studies and efforts to bring about the use of one battery life lamps ... [which] would result in increasing our flashlight business approximately sixty percent." So the industry conspired to make shoddier bulbs with shorter lives, increasing sales and turnover. GE's participation in Phoebus ended in 1939, when the Justice Department broke GE's domestic US monopoly in the US vs General Electric case. The Phoebus cartel subsequently played a significant role in the plot of Thomas Pynchon's novel *Gravity's Rainbow* (1973).

The upshot

Could an eternal bulb be built? Subjected to continual, random cycles of being heated to several hundred degrees centigrade in a split second, the simple structure of blown glass and metal would most probably always break in the end. What's not clear is how much of an improvement would be needed to the current design and materials that would make bulbs last significantly longer without being substantially more expensive. (Energy-efficient bulbs are a bright idea in theory, but dim in practice, and of course the long-term savings are reflected in higher prices.)

But there are ways the life of a conventional light bulb can be lengthened. A five percent cut in operating voltage, reducing wattage by a fifth, can double the bulb's life. So, a 100-watt, 1000-hour bulb lit at half voltage could glow on for nearly 7000 years – albeit with a dingy 15-watt glow. Light bulbs may be made to blow rather than glow to the end of time, but a little TLC can help them shine long and fine. Otherwise, every time a bulb goes, declare in the darkness "it's a conspiracy!"

SOURCES

Patrick Gaughen Structural Inefficiency In The Early Twentieth Century: Studies In The Aluminium And Incandescent Lamp Markets (1998). Despite its dreary academic title, this sheds some interesting light on a murky episode from Europe and America's industrial past.

Microsoft

How many times have you opened a program on your PC, only to be told that your "version" of the program needs upgrading, because it's no longer compatible with a newer and fractionally more innovative version that can now be purchased for a modest sum? Or found that a new program requires an upgrade of your operating system for it to run at all (like users of Windows 98 being unable to use Google's desktop search function)?

A widely held conspiracy theory among computer users – more of an entrenched belief, really – is that software companies deliberately build in obsolescence. New versions of software may be genuine improvements, but each new version or update that adds bits here and there also incrementally detaches users from their old software. Bit by bit, little things like fonts, formats, symbols, all change and morph until the day comes when nothing works, and an entire new software program is required. Trusting souls argue that updating fiascos just happen to happen, perhaps because "patches" are churned out in haste for what were already dodgy products.

A more sinister interpretation of what's going on first arose in the 1970s, following the introduction of AT&T's UNIX operating system. Many companies bought the new system because it was inexpensive and portable, but UNIX also turned to be unreliable and far from secure, which meant that companies which had already become dependent on UNIX had to keep buying upgrades from AT&T. Some have likened UNIX to a computer virus that's spread by market forces rather than disks and networks.

The Microsoft conspiracy

Microsoft is by far and away the biggest, most successful, and most dominant computer software company in the world. According to the *Financial Times*, it's the second largest company in the US in terms of global brand value, at $61.3 billion. IBM (before it was bought by the Chinese) and Intel followed it in the top five, at $53.8 billion and $33.5 billion respectively. Microsoft is ranked fifteenth in the world's top five hundred companies, while since 1991 its operating software is reputedly now installed in over ninety percent of the world's desktop computers.

Set up by Harvard dropout Bill Gates and his friend Paul Allen in 1977, Microsoft made its first million dollars in sales within a year. In its rise to the number one spot, the company has often been accused at times of underhand dealings. During the early 1980s, for example, Microsoft's Multiplan spreadsheet program lost market share to its rival Lotus 1-2-3. In James Wallace and Jim Erikson's 1993 book *Hard Drive: Bill Gates And The Making Of The Microsoft Empire*, it is alleged that Microsoft programmers deployed various underhand tactics to stay ahead of competitors.

While this may have been mere corporate backbiting, the following decade saw Microsoft pitched against no less than the US government, the Justice Department, nearly half the states of the US, and nearly all of its IT competitors. The Federal Trade Commission began to probe suspected collusion between Microsoft and IBM in the PC software market in 1992. The Department of Justice (DoJ) took up the suit in 1993, and a series of suits, counter-suits and appeals involving Microsoft and anti-trust and anti-competition charges lasted for the rest of the decade. Anti-competition suits mounted up over a proposed merger between Microsoft and Intuit, which was later abandoned; over a $200m dollar investment by Microsoft in Apple Computers and Internet firms; and over Microsoft's sale of versions of JAVA software that would not work with any other competitor's software, stymying the business of Microsoft competitor Sun Microsystems.

The longest battle of all raged over charges that Microsoft had used the near-monopoly held by its Windows platform to destroy its competitors. Microsoft was repeatedly hauled up for threatening PC makers that if they didn't carry the Web browser Internet Explorer, they would lose their Windows distribution licences. The DoJ fined Microsoft at the rate of a $1 million per day. Microsoft was sued for bundling Explorer "free" with Windows, wrecking the market for other browsers such as Netscape Navigator. They had to be downloaded or bought, whereas Explorer was subsidized by raising the prices of Windows or other Microsoft products.

Although Explorer and Windows were initially sold separately, Microsoft tearfully proclaimed in court that the one couldn't operate without the other, and showed videos of Explorer-less Windows computers breaking down. When the court ordered the Windows 95 platform be sold to PC manufacturers without Explorer, Microsoft appealed to get the injunction lifted on the "improved" Windows 98 platform, which was coincidentally launched for sale that year. When the court made the same order once again, Microsoft offered old, busted, unusable versions of Windows. Twenty US states then joined the DoJ in pursuing Microsoft.

In 1999, Judge Thomas Penfield Jackson ruled that Microsoft had harmed the market, its competitors and consumers, and should be split in two. That ruling was overturned in 2001, on condition that Microsoft shared its software codes with rivals. Nine states, plus Washington DC, dissented, because Microsoft was not banned from tying new software to Windows in future.

A conspiracy against Microsoft?

The Clinton years were long, hard and litigious for Microsoft. There lies the rub. Microsoft argued both in court and in advertisements in the *New York Times* and *Washington Post* that the suits were not backed by consumers, but by industry competitors. In *Pride Before The Fall*, John Heilemann argued that the actions of the Clinton DoJ formed part of a "corrupt, underhanded trick perpetrated by Microsoft's sour-grapes competitors" to bring Microsoft down. Behind the ballyhoo of the PC market being ruthlessly dominated by the Microsoft empire, everyone in software was making a killing. The problem for Microsoft's green-eyed competitors was that Gates's company was making the biggest killing of all.

Heilemann claimed that in 1997, Netscape, Sun Microsystems and Novell met and enlisted US senators, members of the US Senate Judiciary Committee, and top Clinton administration figures and allies, including the White House chief of staff, and formed a joint project to sue Microsoft into oblivion. According to Heilemann, a mock case drawn up against Microsoft by Sun Microsystems at a cost of $3m, named "Project Sherman" after the Sherman Antitrust Act, was adopted "almost verbatim" as the DoJ's case. Project Sherman advocated the break-up of Microsoft, just as Judge Jackson eventually ruled.

Yesterday, the West; today, the rest

The DoJ's charges were strangely paralleled some years later by the competition authorities of the European Commission. They levied anti-trust suits against Microsoft that cost the company $600m, and ordered it to share software codes with its rivals and strip Windows of its "free" audio and video-playing capabilities.

Undeterred, Microsoft is expanding out of the litigious industrialized world into the more grateful developing world. Under its Unlimited Potential scheme, it has agreed with dozens of NGOs, such as UNESCO and UNDP, to plug the developing world into the digital economy by supporting computing and Internet centres and instilling new skills. Gates has spoken passionately at the World Economic Forum about how business can alleviate poverty, so Unlimited Potential is pure altruism, surely?

Gates vs God

There are opponents of Microsoft who believe that Bill Gates is so evil, he must be Satan. If you write "Bill Gates" using the ASCII computer code (www.asciitable.com), you get: 66 + 73 + 76 + 76 + 71 + 65 + 84 + 69 + 83. Add 3, as in the 3 from William Gates III, and you get a total of 666, the number of the Antichrist in the Book of Revelations! The same

Bill Gates: antichrist?

also goes for "Windows 95" (rather inconveniently, it doesn't seem to work with later versions). Other omens include the fact that one of the characters in the occultist Aleister Crowley's novel, *Moonchild*, is called Bill Gates, and that Bill is an abbreviation of Bavarian *Ill*uminati...

Gates vs death

Alex Hidell hated Gates so much that he shot him dead on December 2, 1999, in Los Angeles. Hidell fired from a hotel window as Gates was crossing a plaza, and then shot dead a police officer before being fatally cut down himself. However, the report of the subsequent inquiry by Los Angeles County District Attorney Gil Garcetti was strewn with inconsistencies and fuelled numerous conspiracy theories. Filmmaker Brian Flemming documented them in his movie *MacArthur Park*, and public action group "Citizens For Truth" was set up (see www.billgatesisdead.com and www.garcettireport.org).

The whole thing, of course, was a hoax, a parody of the JFK assassination, but it was convincing enough for the newspaper China Daily and three South Korean TV channels to be fooled when they picked up the story from a spoof CNN site in April 2003. When they ran with it, the Seoul stock market fell by US $3 billion in a single day – which makes you wonder what would have happened if the story had been true.

Linux

The supposed machinations of Microsoft against the rival operating system Linux have inspired the "comic" website Humorix, home of the Humorix Vast Conspiracy Theory Research Division, to create scores of theories. One of its more hilarious "discoveries" is that Microsoft has pressured Internet providers to give terrible broadband service, forcing consumers to stick with their slower dial-up services and thus making them less likely to download Linux. Using

dial-up exposes up fewer holes in Windows, whereas broadband can unleash a plague of worms on PCs.

SOURCES

Books

James Wallace and Jim Erikson Hard Drive: Bill Gates And The Making Of The Microsoft Empire (1993). A surprisingly riveting account of the rise of the world's most powerful geek. Originally published in 1993, it misses out on the main legal battles of the 1990s, but shows how the seeds of the unrest and revolt against Microsoft were sown.

John Heilemann Pride Before The Fall (2003). Deals with the other side of what fired the legal war on Microsoft.

Websites

humorix.org/articles/2004/08/conspiracy/ link The home of the Humorix Vast Conspiracy Theory Research Division.

Cyberdisease and Y2K

As described earlier, many conspiracy theorists accuse computer companies of inventing problems simply in order to make a profit out of "solving" them. Thus while computer viruses and worms may wipe billions of dollars from the global economy, they also generate huge revenues for PC fixers and virus-killer programs. Is the computer industry simply a large-scale version of the old scam in which glaziers smashed windows by night and fixed them by day? Major software firms make a big show of employing former hackers – even Bill Gates started out as a hacker – to test out their products, so why don't these poachers-turned-gamekeepers do it better, and actually make software bugproof before it's sold worldwide?

The prime example of the artificial creation of a digital disease – or at the very least, of an overhyped panic – has to be Y2K. Remember the so-called "Millennium Bug", which threatened to take down every computer on the planet on the stroke of midnight, December 31, 1999?

Where Y2K came from

The first computers were simple things with limited memories. As a shortcut to maximize the space available for data, many used only the last two digits of a year to store the date: thus the year 1999 was stored as "99". As 2000 AD approached, the fear began to grow that computers with this system would not be able distinguish between 2000 and 1900, and that the world would be swept away by a tsunami of digital nervous breakdowns.

The havoc that this "Y2K" bug might wreak was thought to be stupendous. It might cause the international banking system to crash; airplanes to fall out of the sky; power stations to blow up; and thousands of nuclear missiles to launch themselves spontaneously.

An International Y2K Co-operation Centre (IY2KCC) was set up, supported by the UN and 190 countries. The estimated cost of preparing for Y2K, including spending on new software, hardware and debugging facilities, came to $250–600 billion. As the great day grew nearer, governments around the world announced that they had cleansed their networks of Y2K, and were ready for the new millennium.

An impending apocalypse

In October 1998, the BBC reported that thousands of Americans were stockpiling food, weapons and ammunition to resist the coming of the New World Order, which they believed would be ushered in by the anarchy caused by the collapse of the global computer system. UN troops were said to be planning to move in to disarm the American population and restore order. Various state militias were up for the fight.

Meanwhile, talk in Internet chatrooms described Y2K as an Illuminati plot to create mass chaos and make people beg for a police state. Joseph Farah,

the editor of *WorldNetDaily*, detected the hand of the White House at work. In the John Birch Society magazine, *New American*, he asked: "Much like the Reichstag fire, could the Millennium Bug provide an ambitious President with an opportunity to seize dictatorial powers?"

Bible literalists and Christian fundamentalists had a field day with Y2K. In 1993, twenty percent of Americans are said to have believed that the Second Coming would occur around 2000. Y2K was written up in lurid apocalyptic terms in books such as Gary North's *Y2K And Millennial Pinball* and Michael Hyatt's *The Millennium Bug: How To Survive The Coming Chaos*.

According to website Y2K Storm Watch, set up to monitor the storm of activity to deal with Y2K as much as any actual damage wrought by the glitch, 11.59pm on December 31, 1999 marked a unique moment in world history. For once, the mysterious step into the unknown was enough to cause " ... New Age Prophets, Fundamentalist Christians and Agnostic Computer Geeks to actually agree on something!"

WorldWideWindup

The trouble is, nothing happened. In the US, the world's most computer-dependent nation, a handful of power stations had to reset their clocks, a few hundred slot machines seized up, and a customer in a New York video store was billed $91,000 because the store computer thought his video had been loaned out since 1900. Hardly Armageddon.

If the problem of omitting "00" had been known about since the dawn of computing, why, conspiracy theorists wonder, was nothing done about it before? And why had the bug continued to be left in millions upon millions of new machines? Perhaps it was because that's the way the computer industry wanted it: designers and manufacturers knew that the bug would generate an avalanche of profits at the turn of the century.

BAR CODES

Bar codes – those odd little grilles of bars and numbers on the sides of shop goods – were, the masses are led to believe, invented for the purposes of scanning prices and stock control. When a product is passed over the trapezium of red laser lights at the checkout, the price is registered and a computer takes note that another one needs to be ordered. But for the conspiracy theorist, such an explanation is far too simple. According to the website www.davidicke.com, bar codes are but one major step to the mass monitoring of everyone on the planet. Post offices also use bar codes to track mail, and can do so, it's said, from satellites in space. Similarly, it's argued, bar-coded goods can be tracked from purchase to consumption, or from the store to your home, meaning that someone somewhere may well know exactly what's in your cupboard.

Already, credit cards can log what you bought, where and when, and on the day that cash is finally dropped in favour of smart cards the government will know the very contents of your shopping bag. Bar codes also supposedly have a Satanic significance, with the lines of varying thickness somehow being computed to give the number 666, the mark of the Antichrist, and the trademark of the backers of a cashless economy: "He also forced everyone, small and great, rich and poor, free and slave, to receive a mark in his right hand or in his forehead, so that no one could buy or sell unless he had the mark, which is the name of the beast or the number of his name ... His number is 666" (Revelation 13:16). Of course, the next stage from being cashless is smart chips implanted under the skin, and hell on earth will be established.

Hysteria or just hysterical?

John Koskinen, who was in charge of the Y2K debugging effort in the US, claimed that the campaign was a victim of its own success. The US government spent $8 billion on the problem, including a $50m command centre for Koskinen's team. But was the problem overstated? Koskinen dismissed such speculation: "Corporations don't naively spend hundreds of millions of dollars."

According to top conspiracist Jim Marrs, Y2K did have one notable effect. As Marrs reported, "congressional testimony [in 1999] revealed that none of our oil refineries would be ready for the Y2K rollover", and indeed a worldwide series of refinery fires, explosions and broken pipelines brought production down and forced prices up. The subsequent and predictable rise in oil prices boosted the oilmen's profits several times over (most OPEC countries had ordered US-made computer chips en masse).

WorldWideWaste of money

In the event, and notwithstanding a few billion hangovers, the world of January 1, 2000, was much the same as that of December 31, 1999. Had Y2K been cooked up by spotty, bespectacled computer geeks as a desperate ploy to make themselves appear heroic?

By some accounts, the global campaign on Y2K was a success story on the scale of the eradication of smallpox. By others, the world fell victim to its own propensity for hysteria, or rather, its propensity to believe hysteria whipped up by the very industry that stood to profit the most. Possibly over half a trillion dollars was spent on Y2K that could have gone on Millennium celebrations – just ask the Y2K de-programmers how much champagne that can buy.

SOURCES

Books

Sherman S. Smith Lie-2K: Why The Alleged End-of-the-World Year-2000 Computer Crisis Is Really Just A Hoax. (1999). And doesn't it all seem so obvious now?

ECHELON and the World Wide Web

The World Wide Web is a wonderful tool, linking tens of millions of computers and enabling the citizens of the world to communicate – for commercial, academic, scientific, political, military, criminal reasons or just plain fun. However, it was developed by the US military, who (together with all governments) remain very much "online" and interested in what we do on the Web and say in our emails.

Dark origins

The phenomenal growth of the Web during the 1990s served to obscure its murky origins. The Web was created on the back of the pre-existing Internet – the name is short for "interconnected network" – developed from the 1960s onwards by the US Department of Defense, which wanted a communications network impervious to nuclear attack. The DoD's Advanced Research Projects Agency Net (ARPANet) connected university and military computers and sites, before being divided in 1981 into ARPANet and a purely military network.

Alarmed especially by the involvement of every conspiracy theorist's favourite multinational, the RAND Corporation, more than one writer has put forward – on the Web, naturally – the view that the World Wide Web is a prime component of the Technopoly Conspiracy. That, according to writer Neil Postman, is a society in which "culture seeks its authorization in technology, finds its satisfactions in technology, and takes its orders from technology". Those who thrive in a technopoly exalt technological achievement above all else, while society itself becomes technology's slave.

Lies about Google – and the truth about ECHELON

The military roots of the Web have prompted some to allege that the Google and Yahoo! search engines are both spin-offs of a National Security Agency plan, Operation Prometheus. Supposedly, this monitors online activity to detect any user or data that could harm the US, and tracks the details of users who enter particular "keywords" in their searches. The theory continues that search engines deliberately ignore certain sites so that users will never see them, perhaps firewalling or deleting them, or even attacking their hosts with viruses. This makes the search engines surveillance, censorship and propaganda machines rolled into one.

In fact, the story is a hoax. But even so, the Internet *IS* monitored, on a global scale. Every email, as well as, for that matter, every fax and phone call, whether via landline, cell, microwave, fibre-optic cable or satellite, is monitored by a vast global system known as ECHELON. While there are monitoring bases in Canada, the UK, New Zealand, Australia, Germany, and Japan, the hub is the US, where ECHELON is maintained and overseen by the National Security Agency. Originally established to monitor Soviet communications traffic, and supported when militarily necessary by countless submarines and satellites, the program's remit has been extended and revitalized to monitor rogue states and anything or anyone deemed of interest – be they civilians, senators, Amnesty International, Greenpeace or Christian Aid. Massive computers using voice-recognition and optical character dictionaries filter for keywords, and messages are flagged up, recorded and transcribed for analysis.

In 1998 the European Union released a report that gave details of ECHELON; in response to the extensive monitoring of its citizens and corporations, it invested millions of euros on encryption software.

The military-industrial complex

ECHELON couldn't pay for its upkeep simply by pursuing terrorists. Instead, it's said, many of the same corporations that helped to build it have benefited from intelligence that it has picked up, forwarded via a liaison office in the Department of Commerce. Thus journalist Patrick S. Poole has alleged that in 1990, AT&T received a cut of a $200m deal between Indonesia and Japanese satellite-maker NEC Corp, thanks to ECHELON-derived intelligence and the help of President George H.W. Bush. Similarly, the giant Raytheon corporation got a slice of a $1.3-billion radar deal between Brazil and a French radar company, courtesy of the CIA and NSA intercepts, while US carmakers benefited from CIA information on Japanese makers of zero-emission vehicles. The NSA and FBI are said to have bugged the entire Asian-Pacific Economic Conference in Seattle in 1997, to learn more about hydroelectric dam deals in Vietnam.

As the *Economist* reported in 2000, ECHELON is indeed a favourite of "conspiracy theorists". The magazine claimed that "concrete examples of companies that have gained – or lost – because of this surveillance system are rarely offered", but one German MEP has charged that European businesses have so far lost over twenty billion dollars. The French press has accused ECHELON of involvement in Boeing winning contracts over Airbus, while Tom King, former UK defence secretary and chair of the Commons intelligence committee, has blamed ECHELON for "bad blood" between the Americans and the French over industrial espionage. According to the UK Foreign Office, the interception of the kind of data on which ECHELON snoops is permitted for "economic well-being".

As for its anti-terrorism brief, ECHELON is said to have "played a key role" in the arrest of the alleged September 11 mastermind Khalid Sheikh Mohammed in Pakistan in March 2003 (together, according to the *Guardian*, with an $18m bribe to an "Al Qaida foot soldier"). ECHELON monitored Mohammed's dozen-odd mobile phones; just the sort of tracking which the 9/11 hijackers hoped to evade by using pre-paid Swiss cellular phones not registered in any name.

PROMIS and the future

It's not known whether ECHELON's capacities extend to the ability to predict individuals' thoughts and actions. That facility has however been ascribed to the "brainstorm" version of the software program PROMIS, developed by Inslaw for the Department of Justice to co-ordinate and track disparate data on separate systems. Rumour has it that PROMIS can also track submarines, and even predict the movements of global stock markets.

The Web is the ultimate purveyor of paranoia – one website even contains instructions on how to "build your own conspiracy theory". The great irony is that in being a global source of paranoid information, it worries governments so much that they've created a worldwide system to monitor it. For once, it seems the paranoid foot soldiers of the conspiracy theory world might have a point.

SOURCES

Websites

ⓦ http://fly.hiwaay.net/~pspoole/echelon.
html Patrick Poole sums up the powers and the perils of ECHELON.

Fluoride

Since the mid-twentieth century, putting fluoride into city water supplies, the process of fluoridation, has been a policy proposed by countless municipal governments and national health authorities across the US and in other countries. It's said to be good for teeth, the reason being that it helps to prevent decay. But others aren't convinced, claiming that fluoride is bad for bones, human reproduction and overall health. Fair enough, but others have claimed that fluoridation is a Nazi-Communist-CIA – malevolent government – industry conspiracy, leading to counter-claims that the anti-fluoridation lobby is a bunch of crackpots and right-wing loonies. Yet, in the US at least, in the six decades that fluoridation has been going on, sixty percent of voters have been against fluoridation, and less than two thirds of America's cities have fluoridated water – which suggests either a frightening number of crackpots, or that the story is more complicated than commonly presented.

The obstructers of progress

"Fluoridation is the most monstrously conceived and dangerous Communist plot we have ever had to face! ... A foreign substance is introduced into our precious bodily fluids without the knowledge of the individual – certainly without any choice. That's the way your hard-core commie works!" So said foaming nut General Jack D. Ripper from Stanley Kubrick's 1964 satire, *Dr Strangelove*.

Forty years later, San Diego's civic authorities could fluoridate the city's water only after California governor Arnold Schwarzenegger indemnified them from prosecution for it. San Diego's inhabitants previously voted against fluoridation "amid conspiracy theories about plots to poison the water", said the *San Diego Union Tribune* paper, which also reported without concern that fluoridation was backed by a "local fluoridation coalition and the California Dental Association offering a large grant to San Diego". When fluoridation cropped up in local elections in Connersville, Indiana in November 1999, CNN chortled: "It's a fluoride conspiracy ... Conspiracy theories are flying [while] teeth are decaying."

The American Dental Association claims to have "continuously endorsed the fluoridation of community water supplies". US public health agencies including the Environment Protection Agency, the American Medical Association and the National Academy of Sciences all endorse the National Research Council fluoride review *Health Effects Of Ingested Fluoride,* which is cited by doctors, dentists, researchers and public health officials, and which underlies the safety of fluoride and the benefits of fluoridation.

For Phoebe Courtney, author of the 1971 pamphlet *How Dangerous Is Fluoridation?*, fluoridation was a ploy by the confectionery industry to allow children to "eat all the candy and sweets they want". This was despite, Courtney said, fluoride's ability to kill rats and cockroaches and eat through car engine pipes. As such, fluoridation was also a Communist plot, Courtney said: "Anyone who promotes and supports fluoridation can be considered a 'radical'". When fluoridation came to Wichita, Kansas in the mid-1970s, leaflets went out about "Fluoridation: A Tool Of The Communists", asking "Shall we give the communists the machinery and the materials to destroy us by simply opening a valve in our water supply?"

Communists like fluoridation, suggests Ian Stephen in *Nexus* magazine, because "repeated doses of infinitesimal amounts of fluoride will in time reduce an individual's power to resist domination by slowly poisoning and narcotising a certain area of the brain, making him submissive to the will of those who wish to govern him." This effect, he claims, also attracted the Nazis, who used fluoridation to subdue the populations of the countries they occupied in WWII; it also had the bonus of sterilising them, preventing inferiors and undesirables from reproducing. According to some theorists on the Internet, the American Aluminium Company (Alcoa), which produced sodium fluoride by the kiloton as a by-product of aluminium, transferred technology to Germany's IG Farben chemical company, whose Frankfurt HQ miraculously escaped damage from Allied bombing in WWII. After the war, the US Army and CIA's MK-ULTRA programme showed much interest in behaviour-controlling drugs, and brought over pro-fluoridation Nazi scientists to pick their brains.

Would the CIA's interest in population control (both mind and reproduction) extend to fluoridating the country's water supplies? Why would the lawmakers on Capitol Hill drink only unfluoridated, bottled water? The person who should be asked is Dr George Estabrooks, apparently a one-time adviser to the US government on hypnotism, who later chaired the Department of Psychology at Colgate University (yes, Colgate, the world's biggest producer and advocate of fluoridated toothpaste). Furbies, electronic bear-like toys that mutter to their child owners, have also been linked to the mind-control plot, standing accused of being tools for indoctrination by the State. One theory has it that the kids of US government employees have been banned from owning Furbies (as well as drinking unfluoridated water) to prevent them from succumbing to their subliminal messages.

Nuclear teeth

Some allege there may have been an even more poisonous plot afoot. In a 1998 *Nexus* magazine article, medical journalist Joel Griffiths and BBC and ABC reporter Chris Bryson told the history of how fluoride had been promoted as a "safe" by-product that was of great benefit to the nation's dental health. The allegation is that the evidence for fluoride's dental benefits came from that unlikely source of good health, the atom bomb programme and a certain "Program F".

The story goes that in 1944, industrial company E.I. DuPont de Nemours in New Jersey was producing bomb-grade uranium for the Manhattan Project. A major by-product of the process was the pollutant fluoride, which was producing death and disease on nearby farms. The farmers set out to sue DuPont, but this could have closed the company and meddled with America's destiny of A-bombing its way to global power. No way, said DuPont, the Food and Drug Administration, Agriculture and Justice departments, the Manhattan Project, the US Army and the War Department. While the US Army's Chemical Warfare Service undertook fluoride testing round New Jersey, Manhattan Project directors convinced the farmers, including those suffering from fluoride poisoning, of the government's good faith, before the government spiked their lawsuit by concealing how much fluoride DuPont had let fly: "Disclosure would be injurious to the military security of the United States."

Meanwhile "Program F", set up under Dr Harold Hodge, was spreading the word that fluoride was great, benefiting children's bones and teeth. The information was sourced from the Manhattan Project's fluoride toxicology studies and a Rochester University study of the toxicity of uranium, plutonium and fluoride – both of which Hodge chaired. "Program F" was further supported by evidence from a ten-year study (cut short halfway) into fluoridated water around Newburgh. This was used by the Manhattan Project to fight litigation, and was chaired by none other than ... Harold Hodge. Documents pertaining to "Program F", the DuPont trial and others have since "left" national archives.

From industrial pollutant to a world of healthy teeth

Or maybe it wasn't uranium after all, but aluminium. In 1992 *Covert Action Quarterly* asked "Fluoride: Commie Plot Or Capitalist Ploy?" and claimed that fluoridation was simply the aluminium industry dumping toxic fluoride waste at a profit (a view also supported by the UK's National Pure Water Association). Who, in 1939, had reported an "amazing sodium fluoride/dental caries prevention discovery" (in rats, at least)? The Mellon Institute. What was the Mellon Institute? Like the Rockefeller, Carnegie and Ford Foundations, which all allegedly investigated population control methods, it was a "philanthropic" research body. Who had founded the Mellon Institute? The Mellon family, who happened to have made their millions as founders of... Alcoa, the American Aluminium Company.

And that's not all. In 1941 the United States Public Health Service licensed fluoride dumping in rivers. Who headed the Service at the time? One-time Treasury Secretary Andrew Mellon (yes, from the same family). Who, when he succeeded Mellon, had the water of 87 cities fluoridated? Oscar Ewing, who also happened to be a lawyer for... Alcoa. The Water Works Association, meanwhile, likened fluoride's toxicity to that of lead and arsenic. In 1951 the American Dental Association reported that dental fluorosis, an unsightly mottling and cracking of teeth enamel caused by excessive fluoride intake, required extensive and expensive correction work. (This was while Procter & Gamble were comparing Crest toothpaste with the discovery of penicillin.)

A setback was hydrogen fluoride gas being linked to the 1947 Donora Death Fog in Pennsylvania, which killed seventeen people and left 6000 ill, and to London's Great Smog in 1952, which killed thousands. So, in US cities where industrial fluoride pollution was found (including, Pittsburgh, Chicago, Philadelphia, San Francisco and Oklahoma City), the US Public Health Service backed water fluoridation, spinning "pollution" into "health benefit" – with the aluminium industry supplying the medicine. After the abandonment of a social medicine programme, Oscar Ewing got Congress and the American Medical Association to support nationwide fluoridation, which became a global issue in 1953 when it was pushed for by the World Health Organization committee. Who was the US representative on the committee? Blow me if it wasn't our old friend, Dr Harold Hodge.

Fluoride isn't that safe

Both accounts of the hidden history of the push for fluoridation are pretty dark tales of industrial companies seeking to spin their toxic dumping into a profitable health benefit. Yet the National Pure Water Association, like the New Zealand Pure Water Association and Fluoride Action Network, has multitudes of links to esteemed publications casting doubts on the veracity of fluoridation's healthiness, while these organisations' websites and lists of well-qualified supporters don't shout "wild-eyed paranoiacs".

In the UK, water companies have been allowed to fluoridate only since 1985, but, ten years later, Yorkshire Water refused to fluoridate, not because they thought anti-fluoridators were a bunch of cranks but rather because, they said, "we know which way public opinion rides". Welsh Water has also refrained, calling fluoride a "toxic and potent chemical", as has UK Water. In 2002, the Medical Research Council reported to the Department of

Health that while fluoridation benefited teeth, "much of the current evidence on the benefits of fluoride comes from research conducted several decades ago … Little high quality research had been carried out on the broader question of fluoride and health." By 2003, only five million Brits had fluoridated water.

The war continues

In 1971, the year of Phoebe Courtney's diatribe, US Green Party spokesman Ralph Nader said: "There are better ways to cut down the dental caries in the subject population [namely, children] without exposing eighty or so percent of the population to it." Any new elements should be introduced into the ecology only with "awfully good reason", a position he still supported in 2000. The environmental group the Sierra Club is also concerned by fluoridation. The US National Research Council has said that up to eighty percent of children may have dental fluorosis. Some doctors have paralleled the symptoms of "chronic fatigue syndrome" – fatigue, memory loss, mental dullness and apathy – with those of fluoride poisoning. A 1989 National Toxicology Program study for the Environmental Protection Agency (EPA) linked fluoride with bone and liver cancer, but when senior advisor William L. Marcus exposed this, he was fired. A court ruled that he had "publicly questioned and opposed EPA's fluoride policy".

The John Birch Society (JBS), deemed by some to be a hot-bed of foaming anti-Red sentiment and which has been placed by others as behind the paranoid Wichita campaign, has complained that mass fluoridation is simply an involuntary mass medical treatment that violates individual rights. In 1992, the JBS-affiliated magazine *The New American* railed against fluoride as a "highly toxic and probably carcinogenic substance". And while the report *Health Effects Of Ingested Fluoride* found that overall, *current* concentrations of fluoride do not have clear effects on cancer rates or birth rates, it also noted that fluoride accumulates in bones and that more research is needed. As for the effect on teeth, the report states that there has been an increase in the prevalence of dental fluorosis. So, in the US at least, the process of fluoridation inexorably grinds on, but on a case-by-case basis, because – cranky and mad though the detractors of fluoridation may be portrayed to be – a lot of people believe them.

SOURCES

Articles

Ian E. Stephen "Fluoridation: Mind Control Of The Masses?" *NEXUS* magazine, August-September 1995. Why would there suddenly be such global concern about having bright and shiny teeth? This article suggests the more sinister reasons for mass fluoridation.

Organizations

UK National Pure Water Association Rose Court, 180 Milton Road, Hoyland, Barnsley, S. Yorkshire, S74 9BW; email: info@npwa.freeserve.co.uk

Websites

ⓦ fluoride.oralhealth.org/papers/1999/cnncom110199.html *San Diego Union Tribune* article that sums up the view that opposition to fluoride is a concern of the paranoid, even today.

ⓦ www.aislingmagazine.com/aislingmagazine/articles/TAM26/Fluoridation.html A view from Down Under, from *Australian Fluoridation News*.

ⓦ www.fluoridealert.org Website of the Fluoride Action Network, a sober, well-sourced site about what the problem with fluoride is.

A cure for cancer

In the West at least, cancer is the biggest natural killer. "A cure for cancer" is the Holy Grail of medical research – assuming that a catch-all cure existed, whoever found it would save millions of lives and make tens of billions of dollars in the process. Some suspect, however, that numerous cancer cures have already been found, but are being suppressed by drug companies and other bodies who have a vested interest in continuing to provide their own particular (and expensive) treatments. There are claims that some of these companies and bodies prefer palliative treatments to curing or preventing it in the first place, because their profits would suffer as a result.

Every year six million people die from cancer. One in three Westerners will contract some form of the disease in their lives, and one in four will die from it. Of the several score of known cancers, breast and cervical cancer are the biggest killers of women, while stomach, lung and prostate cancer figure highly in male cancer rates. It's certainly not down to lack of research. Since President Nixon launched his "War Against Cancer" in 1971, US government funding on cancer research has increased more than tenfold from $223m to over $3bn in 1998, a fraction of what medical companies themselves spend. Meanwhile, in the US at least, incidence rates for cancers like stomach and cervix cancer have declined by almost eighty percent. Lung and breast cancer rates have also fallen, seeming to suggest that on some fronts at least, the war against cancer is gradually being won.

In the case of lung and breast cancer rates, however, the decline is from all-time peaks. In 1940 the death rate from breast cancer was 1 in 20 women. Now it's 1 in 8. From 1973 to 1990, overall cancer death rates in the West rose by 7.5 percent. Worldwide, over 10 million people are diagnosed with cancer annually, but the World Health Organization estimates this will rise to 15 million new cases by 2020. With all this money, research and awareness of health risks, how can cancer incidence be *rising*? Some theorists have said that it's no coincidence that Nixon's War Against Cancer was launched at Fort Detrick, a place usually associated not with benign public health programmes but bio-warfare developments (see Secret Bases p.283), leading to the idea that some cancers have been developed and are being used as weapons on the unsuspecting citizens of the US and the world (AIDS has been seen as a similar, though more targeted weapon – see p.277). In most cancer conspiracy theories, however, it's financial and professional – rather than political – interests that are said to be behind it all.

The heretics of cancer will burn

One big theory is that new treatments are held back because of the threat they pose to the medical establishment. For Dr Alan Cantwell, an American doctor who is best known for suggesting the existence of an AIDS conspiracy (see AIDS p.277), the massive investment – both financial and psychological – in conventional treatments has led to a "cancer conspiracy" to discourage research into possible bacterial causes of the disease. In *The Cancer Microbe* (1990), Cantwell claims: "The recognition of microscopic cancer bacteria at this late date would be an embarrassment to the medical profession", leading to "expensive and questionable radiation and chemotherapy" being dumped.

Cantwell cites two earlier researchers into cancer-causing bacteria as victims of this "cancer conspiracy": Dr Virginia Livingston-Wheeler, whose 1984 book *The Conquest Of Cancer* led to her being labelled a quack, and the Freudian-trained psychoanalyst Dr Wilhelm Reich. Both claimed to have found bacterial microbes in cancers, though Livingston-Wheeler's professed ignorance of Reich's earlier work in the field has been questioned. Having outlined his theory that cancerous cells had lower levels of "orgone energy" than healthy cells in his 1948 book *The Cancer Biopathy*, Reich was successfully prosecuted in the 1950s for manufacturing and selling "orgone accumulators". His books and papers were burnt by the Food and Drug Administration (FDA), and he died in prison.

According to "alternative newspaper" publisher Barry Lynes, an even worse fate befell Dr Raymond Rife and his followers, who posed a similar threat to "organized medicine". In the 1930s, Rife not only claimed to have discovered cancer-causing viruses with his self-made microscope, but also invented an electromagnetic energy device, the Rife Ray Tube, to kill them. As Lynes tells it, the University of Southern California proved the worth of Rife's Ray Tube by curing sixteen terminally ill patients, but the adulation of the medical profession was short-lived. Pro-Rife doctors were murdered and their laboratories burnt, as drug and insurance companies, hospitals and doctors, facing ruin, colluded in "deep, criminal activities". (Rife, it's alleged, was murdered by an "accidental" overdose of Valium and alcohol.) Lynes unearthed the story in 1985, but found that no one in Congress wanted to know. Still, Lynes claims that his own books have successfully brought Rife's treatments – whose significance he compares to that of "Galileo and Martin Luther King" – to thousands of cancer sufferers, despite a "virulent" counter-offensive from science, government and "mysterious private interests".

One problem with Cantwell's conspiracy theory is that finding a bacterial cause for cancer would ac-tually open up a whole new area of research funding and profitable treatments. Nor can Cantwell speculate that any breakthrough in this area would render chemotherapy redundant, because different cancers need different treatments. Lynes's view that Rife's treatments are so cheap that they would threaten industry is also a bit odd. If Rife's devices cost so little to manufacture, surely this would only help to increase profit margins: the $64,000 question is whether Rife's treatments really work. Lynes says they do, and that the problem was Rife's refusal to sell the designs to a certain Morris Fishbein, who then, he claims, went on to destroy Rife's instruments, his career and life.

Harry Hoxsey and the Fishbein connection

Fishbein's name crops up regularly in the conspiracy literature of the medical establishment versus alternative medicine. Perhaps that's because Fishbein – who, apparently, originally studied to be a clown – ended up as the head and sole stockholder of the powerful American Medical Association (AMA), despite never having treated a patient in his life. Drug advertisements helped make the AMA's journal one of the most profitable publications in the world, but another leading advertiser was tobacco giant Philip Morris, whose ads boasted that "More doctors smoke Camels than any other cigarette". As AMA chief and editor of the journal, Fishbein became the "voice of American medicine" for four decades.

"Of all the ghouls who feed on the bodies of the dead and the dying," declared Fishbein in a 1947 editorial, repeating a phrase he had already used in a *March of Time* newsreel, "the cancer quacks are the most vicious and most heartless." Fishbein's principal target was "cancer charlatan" Harry Hoxsey, an American alternative healer who became rich and famous in the 1920s for his various tonics and poultices for cancer, but was hounded by Fishbein, AMA journalists and the Food and Drug Administration for years. In 1950, the FDA got the courts to stop Hoxsey's interstate shipments and in 1956 put up 46,000 "Public Warning Against Hoxsey Cancer Treatment" posters in post offices across the US. "Organized medicine" forced the Hoxsey clinic to relocate to Mexico, and in 1964 the FDA spent millions having Hoxsey's treatments banned nationwide.

What caused officialdom to pursue Hoxsey so vigorously was the dark brown liquid "Hoxsey's Tonic", used to treat internal cancers. For decades Hoxsey – a former coal miner with no medical training – wouldn't reveal what was in the tonic, before finally divulging that his great-grandfather had developed the formula after one of his horses had apparently cured itself of cancer by eating a particular combination of plants. For bodies like the AMA and FDA, naturally enough, this proved their case.

The real question, however, is whether "Hoxsey's Tonic" actually worked. Even if it wasn't the product of conventional scientific research, this needn't have stopped the AMA and FDA from carrying out their own. In fact, the tonic contained many traditional herbal ingredients, such as pokeweed, barberry, buckthorn and Stillingia root. As *The Lancet*, *Pediatrics* and *Nature*, and researchers in Japan, the US and Germany have since reported, all of these ingredients have effective anti-tumour properties. Was Hoxsey, then, a case of the medical establishment getting the government to gun down alternative treatments?

If Hoxsey's defenders – including Kenny Ausubel, who has written a book and made a film on the subject – are to be believed, it would certainly seem so. According to Hoxsey, a "senior member of the AMA" tried to muscle in on his business, in a deal that would have given Fishbein and his cronies all of the profits for the first ten years, and Hoxsey a small percentage thereafter – but only if they were satisfied that it worked. This implied either that Fishbein was sufficiently vicious and heartless himself to exploit what might turn out to be another quack remedy for all it was worth – or that he knew all along that Hoxsey's concoction wasn't just snake-oil.

When Hoxsey (unsurprisingly) refused the deal, Fishbein had him arrested over a hundred times in a period of sixteen months for practising without a licence. Not only were the charges consistently thrown out of court, however, but also Fishbein himself was finally forced to admit that Hoxsey's herbal cancer remedy worked, on skin cancer at least (because there have never been proper tests, the jury is still out on its effectiveness in treating internal cancers). Eventually, multiple scandals forced Fishbein to resign, but not before his campaign against an unlikely but potentially effective alternative treatment had succeeded.

"I know these guys, they wouldn't do something like that"

According to cancer sufferer Michael Higgins, any "workable alternative cures would be adopted without cover-up". Higgins writes that he *knows* "there isn't any cancer conspiracy" at www.MyCancerFacts.org ("set up by people living with cancer for people living with cancer"), because it would require hundreds of thousands of compassionate medics to systematically lie about possible cures.

That pharmaceutical companies control medical knowledge and their employees is "ridiculous", states Higgins – governments would welcome cheap cancer treatments and fewer people to treat. The money that governments and tobacco companies make from cigarettes is countered by the money spent on public education about smoking hazards. Tobacco companies were wrong to suppress research linking smoking and cancer, but despite the fortunes at stake, he says, "the truth was not suppressed for long".

With no disrespect to Higgins, however, the millions spent by governments on persuading people not to smoke is a drop in the ocean compared with the billions earned in revenue from tobacco. And when he says that "the truth was not suppressed for long", he's talking about a period of over thirty years.

A rather different view is given by Dr Jeffrey Wigand, research director at US tobacco giant Brown & Williamson, who earned $300,000 for the privilege of researching "safer" cigarettes. In 1994, he went public, telling CBS's *60 Minutes* that B&W and their partner British American Tobacco had known since the mid-1960s that smoking could cause disease (emphysema, heart disease, lung cancer…) and that nicotine was addictive. But references in B&W research to making "safer" cigarettes were removed by company lawyers, as it implied that the company *knew* its products were unsafe – a fatal admission in any future product liability suits. B&W's CEO Thomas Sandefur told a US Senate sub-committee in 1994: "I believe that nicotine is not addictive."

The *60 Minutes* episode, however, was almost never aired because CBS's parent company Westinghouse objected. Meanwhile Wigand was subjected to a horrendous smear campaign led by B&W and picked up by much of the US media, down to the last parking ticket. The story was grittily depicted in Michael Mann's 1999 film *The Insider*, which gave many Americans their first opportunity to hear Wigand's explanation of why millions had died. Thanks to the mainstream media's obsession with the O.J. Simpson trial, that bit of the story had been largely – and for the tobacco industry, conveniently – overlooked.

"Don't ask why they're ill, just make them better"

The best way to reduce the incidence of the various cancers associated with smoking – lung, mouth, throat – is, of course, to dissuade people from smoking in the first place. Indeed, no less an authority than the former US National Cancer Institute director Samuel Broder has declared that prevention is "the most cost-effective way to deal with any disease[s]".

It might be thought, then, that every effort would be concentrated on prevention rather than cure. As far back as the 1950s the WHO estimated that eighty to ninety percent of cancers could be environmentally caused, and today states that enough is known "to prevent at least one-third of all cancers". Yet the WHO also estimates that cancer rates will increase by fifty percent by 2020, mostly in industrializing countries.

So where is the prevention? In a special 1998 issue of *The Ecologist* magazine, Ross Hume Hall and Dr Samuel Epstein argued that a "medical-industrial" complex – including the "cancer establishment" of the American Cancer Society and (despite the views of its ex-director Samuel Broder) the National Cancer Institute (NCI) – are set on discouraging research into how industrial pollutants cause cancer by contaminating food, water and air.

In 1999, Hall and Epstein pointed out, 99 percent of the NCI's $3.2 billion budget went on diagnosis and treatment. Although industrial chemical output increased five-hundred-fold by the 1980s from the half-million tons produced in 1940, less than ten percent of new industrial chemicals have been tested for their carcinogenic properties and only five percent of five hundred carcinogens found in animals have been studied by the NCI. The same chemical industries supplying pharmaceutical companies also benefit from zero-cost chemical waste dumping, and the scientific research justifying the "safety" of dumping pollutants is skewed by the chemical industry paying for the research.

The same issue of *The Ecologist* cited the work of doctors and missionaries over centuries in noting the absence of cancer among the locals in Gabon, Senegal, Portugal, northern Canada and Alaska. As

Zac Goldsmith asked, "how can it be, by anyone's logic, that while breast cancer today afflicts one in eight women in the US, there has been virtually no sign of it among traditional people living traditional lives?" There again, who knows for certain what factors are involved?

No single problem, no single answer

That is the problem with cancer. There is no single form of cancer, and no single cause for the West's biggest "natural" killer – be it dietary, environmental, genetic, viral or (as some claim) bacterial. It follows that there is no single cure. The complexity of the diseases collectively known as "cancer" is reflected in the range of different approaches to finding their causes, then treating – or preventing – them.

If there is a "cancer establishment" crushing numerous avenues of research and treatment, it has failed to stop, for example, the research that the WHO's estimates about preventable cancers are based on, or the research at Columbia University that in 2000 linked Polycyclic Aromatic Hydrocarbons (PAHs, or compounds found in soot and fossil fuel fumes) to genetic damage leading to breast cancer, as the Breast Cancer Fund reported.

There seems little doubt, however, that the treatment industry gets better funding than prevention. This may partly be because treatment is, for want of a better term, sexier (compare your grey-suited fire safety officer with your muscled, smoky, sweat-beaded, hose-wielding fireman). As with measures to protect the environment, cancer prevention also means radically changing the behaviour of individuals and industries – perhaps the whole Western lifestyle – and as with restrictions on smoking, it could take a long time to achieve the critical mass of opinion in favour of making the necessary changes. In the meantime, prevention may be better than cure, but treatment remains the more popular and profitable option.

SOURCES

Books and journals

Dr Alan C. Cantwell The Cancer Microbe (1990). A friend and admirer of Dr Virginia Livingstone-Wheeler defends her controversial and unorthodox theories on cancer (and those of the wacky Wilhelm Reich). Worth reading to get a measure of the opposition faced by doctors who take on the medical establishment.

The Ecologist Vol. 28, No. 2, March/April 1998: "Cancer: Are the experts lying?" A disturbing special issue with well-documented arguments, suggesting that there is a conspiracy by the "cancer establishment" – largely funded by the chemical, nuclear and pharmaceutical industries – to direct research away from environmental pollution as the main cause of cancer and towards areas of financially profitable treatment. (See also edwardgoldsmith.com/page23.html)

Robert Lynes The Cancer Cure That Worked: 50 Years Of Suppression and **The Cancer Conspiracy: Betrayal, Collusion And The Suppression Of Alternative Cancer Treatments** (1987). Lynes sets out to save the world by championing the cause of the Rife Ray Tube.

Films

The Insider (Michael Mann, 1999). An excellent film noir-ish treatment of research scientist and whistleblower Dr Jeffery Wigand's decision to spill the beans on his employer, tobacco giant Brown & Williamson. With Russell Crowe as Wigand and Al Pacino as the TV producer responsible for getting the story aired on CBS's *60 Minutes*.

Websites

- curezone.com/art/read.asp?ID=91&db=5&C0=779 "When Healing Becomes A Crime", a 2001 article by Kenny Ausubel on the Hoxsey case, which he turned into a book and a film of the same name.
- www.jeffreywigand.com/insider/60minutes.html Videoclip and transcript of Wigand's extraordinary TV revelations.
- www.rense.com/general19/enemy.htm "Morris Fishbein – AMA: Enemy Of American Health." Bob Wallace's comprehensive attack on Fishbein discusses the Rife case in some detail and also brings in the Hoxsey affair.

The "official" viewpoint on cancer, its causes and treatment is given by the US government and the World Health Organisation at www.cancer.gov and www.who.org respectively.

Real weapons of mass destruction

The Black Death
The Philadelphia Experiment
Secret Bases
HAARP

Real weapons of mass destruction

With all the talk of the threat of "weapons of mass destruction" – whether biological, chemical or nuclear – falling into the hands of terrorists or rogue states, it's easy to forget just how long such weapons have at least been believed to exist. It was a familiar tactic in medieval sieges, for example, for attacking armies to hurl anything and everything, including disease-ridden beasts, into the besieged camp. When the plague or Black Death hit Europe in the mid-14th century, the belief – sometimes stirred up by cynical governments – that some malign "foreign" influence was responsible led to even more deaths than might otherwise have occurred.

Imperial Japan's Unit 731 really did inflict plague, as well as anthrax, botulin and typhoid, on Chinese and Korean villages and US prisoners-of-war in World War II. If this has received less publicity in the West than contemporaneous Nazi medical experiments, this may be because many of the Japanese involved ended up being employed in the US's own bio-warfare programs, co-ordinated by the Pentagon and carried out in secret bases such as Fort Detrick or Edgewood Arsenal.

The fruit of these dastardly projects, some believe, was what they suspect to be the most cunningly designed biological weapon yet – AIDS. While conspiracy theories about the origin of AIDS extend from Moscow to the US Army to Big Pharma, belief in some theories is having a palpable effect on the battle against the disease, with AIDS drugs being blocked because recipients are seen as just "guinea pigs" in a big race-based conspiracy. The explosion at Port Chicago in 1944 is suspected of being not only the world's first atomic bomb blast, but also a case of the military carrying out hideous experiments on its own personnel, though ironically the more fantastical Philadelphia Experiment – to make ships invisible – was stopped because of the horrible effects it had on servicemen.

There are also questions over the real purpose of HAARP, a massive Alaskan-based field of antennae supposedly built to monitor the upper atmosphere and make phone calls less crackly, but which has been blamed for everything from power-cuts across the US to the Asian tsunami of 2004. False threats being used to justify real weapons; false threats leading to self-destructive violence; real stories of genocide being covered up; friends becoming foes overnight (and vice versa); the enemy abroad and the enemy within – all are part of the rhetoric of WMD.

The Black Death

Although bubonic plague has swept through Europe many times, the most devastating outbreak, in terms both of the total number of deaths and the proportion of the population who died, was in the mid-fourteenth century. The "Black Death" is estimated to have killed some 25 million people. As a contemporary German historian wrote: "In some lands everyone died, with the result that no one was left. " Ships were found adrift at sea, still laden with cargo but with the crew all dead – and it was ships such as these, coming from the East, that are thought to have found their way into Mediterranean ports, carrying the plague with them. The disease spread into France, Spain and Britain by mid-1348, then into northern Europe and Russia in 1351. Curiously, Poland and Flanders were largely spared.

In a continent that was – not surprisingly – gripped by panic, stories spread that the Black Death was the deliberate work of some enemy, in what would now be called biological warfare. From a modern perspective, such an interpretation seems like paranoia, but it provides an object lesson in how irrational fears can be whipped up into hatred and used to justify genocide.

An act of war over trade?

According to contemporary speculation, the various princedoms of India, which had recently been expanding their trade with numerous European states, had become disgruntled at the terms on which they were obliged to operate. They therefore placed plague-laden rats on Europe-bound ships, hoping to inflict massive depopulation, especially near the major Mediterranean ports. Meanwhile, an Indian army would be heading that way, to take over if not the whole continent, then at least large swathes of it.

It's certainly true that areas of northern India were succumbing to plague at the time, and it may have spread to Europe from India aboard European ships. The biowarfare theory doesn't bear much scrutiny, however: there's a world of difference between seeking to redress trade grievances and attempting to wipe out most of your export market. And the Indians were as prone to the disease as anyone else, so for them to infect the land their army was supposedly seeking to take over might well have proved counter-productive. In any case, the Indian invasion never materialized.

Black Death bubos

Enemies without and within

One invading force that actually turned up on Europe's borders around the time did come from the East. In the aftermath of the Black Death, some accounts blamed the Mongols for carrying the disease west from an outbreak in the central Asian steppes, while others write that the Mongols then catapulted plague-ridden corpses into the besieged Crimean city of Kaffa, which was under Genoese control. From there, the plague was inadvertently shipped to Genoa itself in 1347, whence it spread across Europe.

By the autumn of 1348, however, the rumour spread through Europe – much like the disease itself – that the plague was the work of the Jews. They were said to be deliberately infecting wells, springs and other water sources used by Christians. The Count of Savoy took it upon himself to inves-

tigate, and ordered the arrest of Jews living around Lake Geneva. One such, Agimet of Geneva, "confessed" under torture to having poisoned wells in Venice, Calabria, Toulouse and elsewhere around the Mediterranean. He said that he had been bidden to do so by Rabbi Peyret of Chambéry, in the Savoy, who had sent other well-poisoners to France, Switzerland and Italy, as part of a bigger plot hatched by Jewish elders in the enclave of Toledo.

The story is steeped in anti-Semitic superstition: the Jew as scapegoat. In Strasbourg, which had yet to be afflicted, two thousand Jews of all ages were murdered to pre-empt the threat they allegedly posed to the city's wells. All debts owed to them were cancelled, and their possessions and wealth seized and redistributed among the peasants and city traders, who passed their profits on to the Church. A contemporary account – thought to be by Strasbourg historian Frederick Closener – was quite blunt about the real motive for the slaughter: "The money was indeed the thing that killed the Jews. If they had been poor and if the feudal lords had not been in debt to them, they would not have been burnt." If you have a creditor and a debtor, who gains from the death of the other? And it makes no sense for city-dwellers to poison their local well: it's simply suicidal. In any case, Strasbourg's pre-emptive strike failed: the plague came and wiped out sixteen thousand inhabitants.

As news of the supposed confessions spread, tens of thousands of Jews, young and old, were tortured, stabbed, drowned or burned in hundreds of towns and hamlets around the Mediterranean, and in France, Germany and Switzerland. Sometimes there was a "trial", sometimes not.

The message was clear. It was the enemies of white Christian Europe who were responsible for the plague, it was "them", whether Indians, Mongols, or Jews. The disease itself, of course, made no distinction as to whom it killed, or where, wiping out millions across Asia and Africa.

SOURCES

Books

John Kelly The Great Mortality: An Intimate History of the Black Death, The Most Devastating Plague of All Time (2005). Kelly richly details the squalor of life in Europe's Medieval cities and shows what prime venues they were for disease to spread and prosper. No conspirators, you just had to be there to get the sniffles and watch your skin fall off. Grim reading about Europe's greatest visit from the Grim Reaper.

Websites

ⓦ www.fordham.edu/halsall/jewish/1348-jewsblackdeath.html Paul Halsall's comprehensive account of how the Jews came to be blamed for the plague.

The Philadelphia Experiment

Many believe that the US military has led from the front in pushing the frontiers of science. If it's to be believed, however, the Philadelphia Experiment is one case in which even the US military went too far, meddling with forces it couldn't control.

The story of the experiment – for there are few facts as such – runs something like this. During World War II, the US Navy sought to discover the ultimate camouflage for its warships: invisibility to radar, achieved by generating an intense magnetic field around a ship. The operation, known as "Project

Rainbow", aimed to utilize new theories of physics that involved "magnetic resonance". Experiments were conducted at the Philadelphia Naval Yard, where the destroyer USS *Eldridge* was equipped with an array of electronic gadgetry that, according to the outlines of Albert Einstein's "Unified Field Theory" – which neither Einstein nor anyone else has ever proved – would make it invisible. The switch was flicked in June 1943. Engulfed by a mysterious green mist, the *Eldridge* remained invisible to both radar and the naked eye for a good fifteen minutes. However, the crew of the *Eldridge* fell sick, and some of those aboard reported seeing some other port during the experiment. Evidently some unknown frontier had been crossed; the Navy resolved to ensure that it obtained radar invisibility and nothing more.

When the rejigged *Eldridge* was tested again in October, it once more disappeared from radar and normal vision in a green fog (though a green fog is not exactly invisible), with its hull imprinting the water. Then, with a blinding blue flash, the ship completely disappeared, and teleported from Philadelphia to Norfolk, Virginia, over two hundred miles away. There it sat for some minutes, in view of men aboard the ship SS *Furuseth*, before returning to Philadelphia in another flash. This time, crew members were not just ill but crazed into the bargain, while a handful were fused to the ship's metal and some were even missing altogether. Surviving sailors suffered bouts of invisibility, "freeze-framing" into positions for days on end, and spontaneous combustion. Suitably frightened, the project scientists and its military backers concluded they were meddling with forces they didn't understand, and abandoned all hope of finding a crock of gold at the end of "Project Rainbow".

The Navy denies everything

The US Navy has always rebuffed questioning about the Philadelphia Experiment. The Office of Naval Research (ONR) stated in September 1996 that "ONR has never conducted investigations on invisibility, either in 1943 or at any other time". Pointing out that the ONR was not established until 1946, it denounced the story as "science fiction". The master of the *Furuseth*, Lieutenant Junior Grade William S. Dodge, has written that neither he nor his crew saw anything strange going on in Norfolk. The Navy's Naval Historical Center has added that the *Eldridge* wasn't launched until late July, so it couldn't have been experimented on in June (though conspiracy theorists respond that its paperwork could have been faked so that it could be used for experiments). And neither was it ever in Philadelphia during the alleged times, being on convoy duty in the Atlantic. It was in Norfolk on November 2 and 3, but the *Furuseth* wasn't.

Moore to the story

The best-known source for the story, *The Philadelphia Experiment, The True Story Behind Project Invisibility*, was published in 1978 by Charles Berlitz and William Moore. (Moore, a "relentless researcher", subsequently had to "retreat to a remote area of the United States to live quietly".) They in turn drew heavily on the work of UFO investigator Morris K. Jessup. His 1955 book *The Case For The UFO* attracted reams of fan mail, including a series of letters from Carl M. Allende, who said he'd seen the *Eldridge* from on board the *Furuseth*.

Although Allende's letters claimed to come from Texas, they were addressed from Pennsylvania and elsewhere. He stressed his points by liberal use of multi-coloured pens, writing whole texts in upper case, with much underlining and total disregard for grammar and punctuation. He had also changed his name from Carlos Allende to Carl Allen. After the Office of Naval Research received a copy of Jessup's book in early 1957, replete with scribbled ideas about teleportation and Philadelphia, they invited him to Washington. The scribbles proved to match the handwriting on Allende's letters to Jessup, and a couple of dozen copies were circulated around the ONR. At that point, however, the openness and interest of the ONR abruptly stopped, and Jessup's subsequent investigations were stonewalled. Puzzled into a mental breakdown, Jessup committed suicide in 1959. Others involved are said to have died in "freak" accidents, disappeared, or told their stories only on pain of total anonymity.

Sailors' stories

According to Berlitz and Moore, there's one slither of fact in Allende's account, in that he cites a story from a Philadelphia newspaper about a brawl that involved *Eldridge* sailors in the "Seamen's Lounge" bar. Berlitz and Moore say that "presumably still exhibiting the effects of the field", the sailors vanished mid-fight into thin air! They supposedly found the relevant clipping after a long and tortured search, though they fail to include a photo of it in their book, and its date and source remain unknown.

A source not cited by Berlitz is an unnamed sailor who offers a different explanation. He claimed he was at that bar fight, but being a minor, was pushed out the back by staff fearing a bust for under-age drinkers – hence the "disappearing" sailors. He adds that the *Eldridge* did indeed disappear that night, but only to Newport, not Norfolk, along the Chesapeake-Delaware channel, and that it returned the next day.

Neither the colourful presentation of the multi-monickered Allende's theories, nor Jessup's subsequent mental collapse, adds much to the credibility of Berlitz and Moore's case. The Berlitz-Moore book is not exactly convincing either, concluding after 192 pages that "perhaps, as the Navy has so insistently contended, the entire incident is a legend and never took place". Finally, some people have drawn connections between Berlitz and Moore's work and the novel *Thin Air*, by George Simpson and Neil Burger, which came out the year before.

Montauk

One theory that's been put about is that the *Eldridge* teleported not just in space but also in time. After disappearing through a "time-hole", it's claimed, the ship re-appeared in 1983 off Montauk, Long Island (see p.284). Sailors who swam ashore were greeted by Dr von Neumann, the original director of "Project Rainbow", who had waited forty years just to say "I've been expecting you". After a few tests, he sent them and their ship back to 1943. However, he hadn't used the intervening decades to address the problems of men being killed, driven mad, or welded to the ship.

A story shrouded in fantasy

The whole saga appears to be a bizarre case of fact and fiction becoming confused and conflated. Berlitz and Moore's book remains widely known and still in print, and the story has been expanded upon in numerous Discovery Channel documentaries; a 1984 feature film, *The Philadelphia Experiment*; and an episode of *The X Files*, *Dod Kalm*. The 1980 movie *The Final Countdown* gave it another spin, with Kirk Douglas commanding an aircraft carrier that teleports back to Pearl Harbor, 1941, where a couple of the carrier's F-14 jet fighters shoot down the Japanese air force.

SOURCES

Books
Charles Berlitz and William Moore

The Philadelphia Experiment (1998). A vaguely entertaining exercise in imaginative rhetoric, inevitably short on substantive evidence.

Port Chicago

The propensity for the military in various countries to test out new weapons on human guinea pigs is well established. In the UK, Porton Down tested nerve gas on conscripts; the Japanese tested bio-weapons on hundreds of thousands of Chinese; and the US got GIs to stand and watch atomic explosions. However, the story of Port Chicago hints at an even greater zeal for such tests, suggesting that the US may even have nuked one of its own towns.

An explosion of unprecedented power

The port of Port Chicago was constructed in haste after 1941 near the town of the same name, 35 miles north of San Francisco. It served as a major ammunition transit point for US forces fighting in the Pacific. Every day, thousands of tons of bombs, bullets, mines and lethal explosives were transferred from trains to ships. Just before 10.20pm on the evening of July 17, 1944, as two merchant ships, the SS

The Port Chicago disaster

EA Bryan and the SS *Quinault Victory*, were being loaded, a cataclysmic blast wiped the whole place out. The *Bryan* and a train on the pier were vaporized, while pieces of the *Victory* were blown 500m away. A 20m deep, 200m long crater was blasted out of the river bottom. A total of 320 people were killed instantly, and 400 more injured. Body parts were found a mile away. Buildings in Port Chicago town, two miles distant, and across fourteen counties were damaged. Locals thought the blast was an earthquake; indeed, tremors measuring 3.5 on the Richter scale were recorded in Nevada.

Newspapers reported a "dazzling", "sun-like flash" and a "mushroom-like cloud". A few days later, an Army pilot told a Navy Court of Inquiry of having seen a white flash, a smoke ring and a "ball of fire" that reached 12,000ft, with white-hot pieces of metal as large as houses flying past. It appeared that there were two explosions. The first was on the pier next to the *Bryan* – loaded with 4600 tons of munitions, half being high explosives – which held several thousand tons of diesel and 429 tons of munitions, in sixteen box cars. A distinct sound and brilliant flash suggested that a cluster or depth bomb detonated the explosives on the pier, which in turned caused everything aboard the *Bryan* to explode.

After 39 days, the Court of Inquiry said that the explosion probably happened because "a supersensitive element [ie some explosive] was detonated in the course of rough handling by an individual or individuals". Other possible causes mentioned included bad loading procedures, defective munitions, and the neglect of safety procedures to speed things up. With all the evidence blown to smithereens, it was easier to blame the workers, predominantly black enlisted men who were dismissed as "poor quality ... poor material". Their white officers, by contrast, were praised for making the port work. The Inquiry's conclusion remains the only official verdict on the event.

No ordinary blast, and maybe no accident?

The Army pilot who saw chunks of town fly past two miles up, however, had been ordered aloft "to observe Port Chicago". What exactly was there to observe, as the port went about its business in the darkness of the evening? Later A-bomb explosions in water produced a condensation cloud, or "smoke ring", much like that at Port Chicago. Then there was the sun-like flash, the tremor, the scale of the devastation... Did Port Chicago fall victim to the world's first A-bomb blast?

That theory derives from the diggings of Peter Vogel, who in 1980 made a Hollywood-esque find at a jumble sale in New Mexico. He came across a box from Los Alamos Laboratories, where the atomic bomb was created, which contained photographs and a paper labelled "History of 10,000-ton Gadget". Dated September 1944, drawings on the paper resembled workings for an A-bomb, with the note: "ball of fire mushroomed out at 18,000 feet in typical Port of Chicago fashion."

Port Chicago? Embarking on a twenty-year quest, Vogel reported his findings in the online book *The Last Wave From Port Chicago*, which unearths a lot of curious pointers. Vogel himself had studied physics under Dr Edward Teller, the so-called "Father of the Atomic Bomb". When he interviewed Teller, and asked him to explain the markings on the paper, Teller replied that the interview was over, and that he would forever deny seeing it.

On visiting Concord Naval Weapons Station, as Port Chicago was renamed, Vogel was informed that there was a film of the blast, but that it was a recreation made by Hollywood filmmakers in the 1960s for the benefit of the military. Unfortunately, he was told, the footage was on fragile nitrate-based film, and therefore could not be viewed. Which is strange, because nitrate film hasn't been used since 1950. Vogel did eventually get to see the film, which he was convinced showed a real atomic blast, but the Navy subsequently destroyed it.

Los Alamos scientists did indeed take a great deal of interest in Port Chicago. Thus Captain William Parsons – who later became bombing officer on the *Enola Gay*, and as a rear admiral, oversaw the Bikini nuclear bomb tests – submitted a report on the Port Chicago disaster within a week. His main concern in September 1944 was that the war would finish before the A-bomb could be tested in anger. Desert demonstrations would be an expensive "political and military fizzle", he wrote: "Such a demonstration ... would not be held one thousand feet over Times Square, where the human and material destruction would be obvious". Anything other than the kind of carnage seen at Port Chicago would be an "intense disappointment".

However, while Parsons may have been gung ho, perhaps almost psychotically so, he didn't say, "let's test another bomb, this time on New York". And perhaps his enthusiastic interest in the Port Chicago blast is only to be expected from someone working on the ultimate bomb a couple of states away.

Just a few kilos of uranium

The earliest A-bomb prototypes were small affairs known as "gun bombs". The director of the Manhattan Project, James Conant, suggested shelving the Mark II gun-bomb to concentrate on the next model, following an unidentified test in July 1944. The damage reported for this test parallels the damage assessment at Port Chicago. But there are no records of any such test, so what was Conant talking about?

Although the US government claimed, referring to Port Chicago, that it didn't have enough bomb-grade uranium in 1944 to test A-bombs, a gun-bomb only needs fifteen kilos of uranium. Department of Energy records show that 93 kilos of uranium were available in 1944. Los Alamos destroyed the consignment records for two of the boxcars at Port Chicago. Did they contain a gun-bomb? What's more, the *Bryan* was bound for Tinian, in the Mariana Islands, which is where the *Enola Gay* B-29 bomber that dropped the A-bomb on Hiroshima was to take off in 1945.

The Concord Naval Weapons Station – Port Chicago, as was – lies in a county that, even today, has one of the highest cancer rates in the US. Given that the base cleaned and decommissioned ships that were exposed to other Pacific test blasts, a high level of radioactive contamination might be expected. As Vogel contends, however, it might also mask its earlier contamination by an A-bomb.

An A-bomb or just any bomb?

Was it a deliberate A-bomb test? The first official atomic test took place in July 1945 in the heart of the New Mexico desert – a remote location, difficult to spy on, with nothing valuable to be damaged; in short, ideal test conditions. A port on an ocean brimming with enemy spotter craft, on the other hand, would make a very public testing ground for such a major new weapon, while vaporizing a major munitions hub makes little strategic sense, to say nothing of the mass of other explosives around distorting the results of any "test".

So was an A-bomb accidentally discharged in transit? That seems unlikely too. Shipping a workable yet untested bomb towards an enemy who could capture it intact, if they didn't sink the little merchant ship carrying it – which was also carrying a load of volatile explosives – seems unnecessarily rash. When the Hiroshima bomb "Little Boy" was carried across the Pacific, it was entrusted to the towering battleship USS *Indianapolis*. Even that was sunk as it returned home, when the war was basically over.

Vogel believes that the damage inflicted on Port Chicago could only have been done by a nuclear blast, saying that the cited quantity of conventional explosives just wasn't sufficient. In November 1944, however, four thousand tons of explosives accidentally detonated in an underground bunker at RAF Fauld in the UK. That explosion left a 12-acre crater, while the ground shock was recorded by seismographs as far away as Casablanca.

A blast in the past

The reason why neither the Navy nor the US government has bothered with any further investigations or denials is largely because there's been little public clamour for them to do so. Port Chicago has not seized the public imagination, and it's not even big in conspiracy circles.

However, the theory has been cast in a new light by Vogel's work with Robert L. Allen in *The Black Scholar* (www.theblackscholar.org), a journal of black studies and research. They have reminded the world that the worst wartime blast in the US was swiftly followed by the largest mutiny. By September 1944, many survivors from Port Chicago were re-billeted to Mare Island to load ammunition, but 258 men refused to carry out what they regarded as lethal work. Two hundred and eight of them were summarily court-martialled, and the rest tried for mutiny.

SOURCES

Websites

Ⓦ www.portchicago.org Peter Vogel's

handsomely presented, exhaustive site benefits from a wealth of behind-the-scenes

documents from the Manhattan Project.

Chemical cover-ups

Gas, of course, was used as a weapon in the trench warfare of World War I, but one of the Nazis' most hideous innovations in World War II was to use it to exterminate millions of innocent civilians in the death camps of occupied Europe. Nazi doctors also conducted vile medical experiments on human guinea pigs, a practice that still solicits worldwide opprobrium. Outside China and Korea, however, the comparable activities of the Nazis' counterparts in Imperial Japan have been barely remarked upon – indeed, for many years, these crimes have been actively hushed up. History may be written by the victors, but the victorious Americans seem to have agreed with the vanquished Japanese not to mention what the latter did both before and during the war.

Unit 731

The Japanese Imperial Army first revealed its enthusiasm for biological warfare in the experiments conducted by Unit 731 between 1932 and 1945 in Japanese-occupied Manchuria and beyond. Much of the testing was carried out in a prisoner camp at Ping Fang, near Harbin in northeast China, where Unit 731 operated under the name of the Water Purification Bureau. Up to three thousand Chinese and Korean nationals are thought to have died here, infected with diseases ranging from anthrax, cholera, typhoid and tuberculosis to bubonic plague. Human vivisections were performed along with such psychopathic experiments as freezing prisoners' limbs to observe the progress of frostbite. Unit 731's commanding officer, Lieutenant-General Ishii Shiro, also experimented on US POWs at a camp at Mukden. In addition, Japanese planes dropped plague-infected fleas onto several Chinese cities in 1940, and attacked hundreds of hamlets with germ bombs. Japanese troops also dropped cholera and typhoid cultures in wells and ponds, killing an estimated two hundred thousand Chinese and Korean civilians. Unit 731 was stockpiling botulism and anthrax when the war ended, and has fittingly been described as the Asian Auschwitz.

Postwar whitewash

The work of Unit 731 was raised only once at the Tokyo war crimes tribunal in 1946-48, and that was by surprise, when the treatment of US prisoners was raised. When the presiding judge asked "How about letting this item go?", the US lawyer replied 'Well, then, I'll leave it'. The Soviets carried out their own war crime trials in Khabarovsk, but neither Ishii nor his co-officers were ever tried. That was because the US military found their research just too fascinating to give up, describing their data on humans as "invaluable".

Dr Norbert Fell and Lieutenant Colonel Arvo Thompson, both of General Douglas MacArthur's intelligence team at Fort Detrick, offered Ishii and his men immunity from prosecution if they assisted the US's own bio-weapons program. That immunity saw certain doctors from Unit 731 return to handsome positions in postwar Japan's medical community. Ishii's successor as commander, for example, Dr Masaji Kitano, became head of Japan's largest pharmaceutical company, the Green Cross.

Masking the trail

During the Korean War, the Chinese and Korean governments accused the US of using chemical and biological weapons on North Korea in 1951, charges which the International Scientific Commission said had a strong basis. B-29 pilots are said to have launched from Okinawa, while Ishii was allegedly in South Korea orchestrating bio-weapons for the US Army.

Ishii's men went on to lecture for the US Army and form the basis of President Kennedy's Project 112, which evaluated chemical and biological weapons for "limited war applications". However, Ishii's own involvement has always been denied. In his 1981 book *Japan's Biological Weapons 1930-1945: A Hidden Chapter In History*, American journalist John W. Powell alleged a US government cover-up, only for the relevant chapter to be cut from the US edition. Sheldon Harris made similar charges in *Factories Of Death*. It seems that only Japan's right-wingers dare mention Unit 731, and even then only in the context of complete denial. Unlike Germany's children, who learn the horrors of their country's past, Japan's bio-warfare program is not taught in schools or mentioned in history books. A 2002 trial in a Tokyo court acknowledged for the first time that Unit 731 and other units had engaged in "cruel and inhumane" biological warfare in China, but the judges said that the 180 plaintiffs' claims for compensation were without legal foundation. Meanwhile, Ishii's legacy continues: in late 2003, 29 Chinese were hospitalized after buried chemical shells were uncovered in Heilongjiang.

Porton Down

Such conspiracies were by no means confined to the US or Japan. One of the longest-running Cold War cover-ups in the UK centred on the testing of chemical weapons on unwitting Britons at Porton Down in Wiltshire (where Dr David Kelly once worked; see p.64). The base had been testing poison gas since 1916, but thousands of military personnel, or "live guinea pigs", were exposed during the 1950s and 1960s to nerve gas, mustard gas and other chemicals. One soldier, twenty-year-old Ronald Maddison, died in May 1953, after Sarin nerve gas was dripped onto his arm in an experiment presented to volunteers as seeking a cure for the common cold. A secret inquest held weeks later ruled that his death was an "accident". Only in December 2004, when the inquest was re-opened, did a jury unanimously rule that Maddison was unlawfully killed. The UK government still insisted that Porton scientists had done no wrong. Proving that old habits die hard, the Ministry of Defence is seeking to overturn the new verdict, without stating its reason. Further charges that soldiers were duped into these lethal experiments are under investigation.

SOURCES

Books

Sheldon H. Harris Factories Of Death: Japanese Biological Warfare 1932–1945 And The American Cover-up (2002). The best-known (and best-received) book on Japan's bio-warfare experiments.

Robert Gomer, John W. Powell and Bert V.A. Roling Japan's Biological Weapons 1930–1945: A Hidden Chapter In History.

Bulletin of the Atomic Scientists (Oct 1981). This survey of the complicity between the US Army and Japanese war criminals is a faster read than Harris's book.

Websites

ⓦ www.fas.org/nuke/guide/japan/bw/ This is an easy-to-read summary of Japan's bio-weapon crimes and the US's postwar complicity in cover-up and development.

ⓦ www.theage.com.au/articles/2002/08/28/1030508070534.html Shane Green's article from the Australian newspaper *The Age* outlines how the Japanese authorities continue to deny and dismiss the charges of bio-warfare crimes laid against their empire.

AIDS

AIDS, or Acquired Immuno-Deficiency Syndrome, is the final, fatal, though not inevitable stage of infection for people with Human Immunodeficiency Virus (HIV). Sufferers die as a result of having their immune systems wiped out, which makes them susceptible to conditions that are normally either extremely rare or not serious. Pneumonia, tuberculosis and Kaposi's sarcoma, a form of skin cancer, are common in the end stages.

AIDS was first identified by doctors in the US in 1982, when previously healthy, young homosexual men began dying of obscure cancers and pneumonia. Shortly afterwards, two distinct HIV viruses were discovered – HIV-1 and HIV-2 – and it was established that HIV could be contracted by sexual intercourse, direct contact with infected blood, or perinatal transmission. The first drug to treat AIDS to be approved by the Food and Drug Administration (FDA) was AZT in 1987, but although various treatments can slow the growth of HIV and thus stave off AIDS, no cure has yet been found.

UNICEF has called AIDS "the worst catastrophe ever to hit the world". According to the World Health Organization, just under forty million people were living with HIV/AIDS in 2004; at least two million of them were aged fifteen and under. That year, up to 6.4 million people became infected, and over three million people died, bringing the total deaths since 1981 to 24 million. Sixty percent of all cases –

25 million – are in sub-Saharan Africa, which holds just ten percent of the world's population.

Where did it come from?

The precise origin of HIV remains unknown. According to one broadly accepted scientific theory, the disease originated among green monkeys in Africa, and somehow became transmitted to people, possibly because they hunted and ate the monkeys as "bush meat". However, not everyone goes along with this explanation. Many link the higher prevalence of HIV/AIDS in Africa and among homosexuals to something more sinister.

AIDS in Africa: love with care

In conspiracist circles, two documents are often cited as proof that darker forces were at work. The first is a July 1969 Department of Defense appropriation request for funding from the US Senate for $10 million to develop synthetic biological agents, or bio-warfare weapons. US Army bio-warfare expert Dr Donald MacArthur told the Senate: "Within the next five to ten years, it would probably be possible to make a new infective micro-organism [that] ... might be refractory to the immunological and therapeutic processes [depended upon] to maintain our relative freedom from infectious diseases" – in other words, a virus that would kill the immune system. The second document is National Security Memorandum 200, "Implications of Worldwide Population Growth for US Security & Overseas Interests", dated December 10, 1974 and declassified in 1989. In it, National Security Adviser Henry Kissinger is reported as arguing that "Depopulation should be the highest priority of US foreign policy towards the Third World", to secure mineral supplies for the US. How this depopulation was to be achieved was not specified.

The WHO: vaccinations that spread disease

In 1986, Dr Robert Strecker alleged that the US military distributed its HIV bio-weapon by means of the World Health Organization's smallpox vaccination program, under which tens of millions of Africans were vaccinated by injection during the late 1970s. HIV was then introduced into the US population via United States Public Health Service Hepatitis B vaccinations on gay and bisexual men, carried out between 1978 and 1981 in New York, Los Angeles, San Francisco, St. Louis, Denver and Chicago. Those cities subsequently developed the US's highest AIDS rates.

Time magazine denounced Strecker's theory, but it has since been supported by various doctors, including author Dr Alan Cantwell, and Dr Robert Gallo, who is credited with having been the first to isolate HIV, at Fort Detrick in 1984. Gallo commented in 1987 that the smallpox-HIV link was "interesting and important", adding that "live vaccines such as that used for smallpox can activate a dormant infection such as HIV". Dr Johnathan Mann of the WHO's AIDS program responded that the smallpox vaccine-HIV link just doesn't fit, while the *British Medical Journal* sardonically commented that the theory came from the same source as the Hitler Diaries, ie it was bogus.

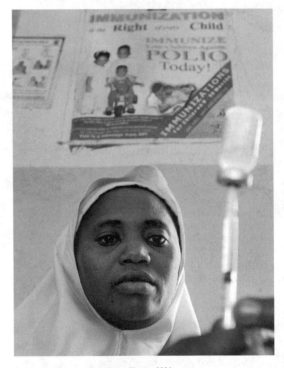

A nurse prepares a needle in Kano, Nigeria, 2004

Charges that the disease may inadvertently have been spread by vaccinations surfaced in February 2003. A team of US doctors led by Dr David Gisselquist wrote in the *International Journal Of STD And AIDs* that only around thirty percent of pre-1988 AIDS cases in Africa resulted from sexual transmission, not the ninety percent usually claimed, while over half the cases were spread by unsterilized needles. The team says that the evidence was discounted because of "preconceptions about African sexuality and a desire to maintain public trust in healthcare". The London *Times*, however, quoted Professor Michael Adler of University College London Medical School as being "extremely doubtful" that needles could have caused so much damage. The WHO estimates that unsafe injections are responsible for five percent of HIV infections. Experts point out that if dirty needles were responsible, then hepatitis B would be growing faster than AIDS in Africa and Asia, and that dirty needles would affect all age groups, whereas AIDS overwhelmingly affects sexually active age-groups.

Cold War or big business?

According to Dr Boyd Graves (www.boydgraves. com), AIDS is a joint US-USSR plot to obliterate blacks and homosexuals. The plot, known as the Special Virus Program, was apparently first hatched in 1960, though a joint agreement to implement it was only made in 1972. He links the Gulf War Syndrome to AIDS, saying that both were spread by giving contaminated vaccines to soldiers. Graves also claims that he himself contracted AIDS and cured it with "colloidal silver", but that this and other known cures are being suppressed (significantly, he singles out an Israeli medical institute and an Israeli pharmaceutical company, hinting at a Zionist conspiracy).

Similarly, the unfortunately named Dr Gary Glum writes in *Full Disclosure* that liquorice extract, essiac tea and an olive-leaf extract are viable treatments, but are being suppressed by pharmaceutical companies. He argues that AIDS was concocted at Cold Spring Harbor, New York, around 1978, as part of a plot by the Olympians, a pro-eugenics sect of the Illuminati, to wipe out non-whites. For that matter, he also says that AIDS can be transmitted through kissing, mosquito bites and "casual contact", in which case nearly all of us should be dead by now. Such nonsense doesn't disprove his other theories, but hardly makes them more plausible. Neither is it clear why a company would suppress a highly lucrative AIDS cure, unless there's more money in continuous, long-term care than there is in a cure.

Kissinger, Rockefeller, Mengele and Malta

In *Emerging Viruses: AIDS & Ebola: Nature, Accident Or Intentional?*, Dr Leonard Horowitz alleges that the twin co-funders and inventors of AIDS were Fort Detrick, home to the National Cancer Institute, and the Rockefeller Institute for Medical Research. Aided by defence companies such as Litton Bionetics, they set out to target Jews, blacks, Hispanics and gays. Horowitz suggests that Kissinger's 1974 memo arguing that the US should actively seek to depopulate the Third World was based on the plans of various prominent individuals at the Council on Foreign Relations. He argues that various parties had already carried out their own cancer tests on Puerto Rican patients, so such eugenics-based work would be nothing new. As Nazi scientists had been brought to the US under Operations Paperclip and Sunshine, US taxpayers were thus funding Dr Mengele's protégés to concoct genocidal diseases. The flesh-eating disease Ebola was another example.

Horowitz rather loses his thread when he traces the US eugenics program back to the quasi-Masonic Sovereign Military Order of Malta. However, his contention that Gallo may have actually discovered HIV back in the early 1970s, but that his work was suppressed, is echoed by Richie and Rosalind Chirimuuta in *AIDS, Africa And Racism*. They argue that much of the literature about AIDS in Africa is racially biased, and wonder why the possibility that AIDS was a lab construct has not been more fully investigated. They also note the similarity between HIV and the sheep virus, Visna, hinting at some lab-induced mutation.

Soviet disinformation

In his 1986 pamphlet *AIDS: USA Home-Made Evil*, Jacabo Segal, biology professor at Humboldt University in East Berlin, suggested that HIV was created at Fort Detrick in 1977, when the sheep virus Visna (see above) was spliced together with HIV-1. The resulting concoction was then tested on "volunteer" prisoners, in exchange for early release. HIV then spread to the population through gays. Fort Detrick promptly denied Segal's theory, while KGB defector Vasili Mitrokhin subsequently denounced it as a KGB disinformation program. According to Norman Covert's *Cutting Edge*, Mikhail Gorbachev himself apologized to Ronald Reagan for the rumours.

Jews against Blacks

Both Louis Farrakhan of the Nation of Islam and the New Black Panther Party have charged that AIDS is a Jewish plot to wipe out blacks. The Anti-Defamation League's director Abraham Foxman replied that Farrakhan was "a relentless racist and anti-Semite" who has accused Jewish bankers of financing the Holocaust, Jewish doctors of infecting Black babies with the AIDS virus, and has claimed that the Jewish community controlled the African slave trade. According to Nation of Islam lore, whites are 'blue-eyed devils' created in a failed laboratory experiment.

The Vatican fails to help

In late 2003, the Catholic Church instructed people in AIDS-stricken countries not to use condoms, because they're not impermeable to HIV. The head of the Vatican's Pontifical Council for the Family, Cardinal Alfonso Trujillo, told the BBC that HIV was small enough to pass through the "net" formed by condoms. The WHO countered by stating that correct condom use reduces HIV infection by ninety percent, and that while condoms can break or slip, they're impermeable to the virus.

Bush and Big Pharma

In January 2003, President George W. Bush announced a five-year, $15 billion aid package to fight AIDS in Africa and the Caribbean. However, Oxfam has criticized the Bush administration's refusal to allow poor countries to import low-cost generic drugs to treat HIV/AIDS, and some say that the program is a massive bung to major US pharmaceutical companies, intended to squash attempts elsewhere to produce cheaper, generic versions of the drugs. It's also been alleged that the money would be made provisional on acceptance of Christian-sourced education and agreement to pro-US trade rules.

Further connections

South Africa's president Thabo Mbeki and the ruling African National Congress party have claimed that white-owned drug companies deliberately infected people with AIDS during drug experimentation. The South African government has interfered with AIDS drug distribution programmes, and the

ANC has accused the country's HIV/AIDS treatment advocacy group, Treatment Action Campaign, of plotting "to market unsafe drugs". After massive protest, in 2003 the ANC allowed the distribution of AIDS drugs, but it has still accused the US of treating Africans like "guinea pigs", and "entering into a conspiracy" with drugs makers over AIDS treatments that may have caused deaths but have been covered up.

In 2004, reports appeared that there was a resurgence of polio in numerous African states, despite the sixteen-year-old, $3 billion WHO campaign to eradicate it. As the *Baltimore Sun* reported, Muslims in northern Nigeria were refusing polio vaccines, considering them to be contaminated with either an anti-fertility agent or with AIDS, in "an American plot to depopulate the developing world". One WHO doctor explained that the war in the Middle East had aggravated the situation. "If America is fighting people in the Middle East, the conclusion is that they are fighting Muslims." Polio cases in Nigeria rose during and after the wars in Afghanistan and Iraq: three in 2001, 54 in 2002, and 74 in the first eleven months of 2003. Three predominantly Muslim Nigerian states banned the vaccines for periods in 2004, prompted, said the *Baltimore Sun*, by "doctors, imams, political leaders and professors who endorse the conspiracy theory". New polio outbreaks in countries like Ivory Coast, Benin, Cameroon, Togo and Chad, all once Africa's leading polio-free countries, were traced back to Nigeria, the *New York Times* said. Nigerian polio cases quintupled to 259 new cases in 2004, while global cases reached 339, double that of 2003.

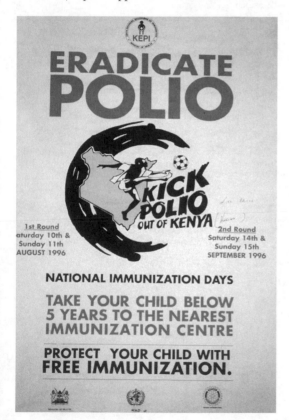

Kick polio out of Kenya

No end in sight

While the origins of HIV may never be discovered, it seems all too conceivable to many people that it could have been made in a laboratory and then released, deliberately or not. There's more to the destructive power of AIDS than its effect on individuals. Whether or not the disease is a bio-weapon being used for eugenic purposes, it's certainly being used as a rhetorical weapon, to stir up hate between people of different races, religion or sexuality, or to promote moral agendas.

In early 2005, the *Washington Post* published the results of a survey of five hundred African Americans that had been carried out by Oregon University and the RAND Corporation. Over half of those ques-

SARS

AIDS and Ebola are not the only contagious diseases suspected of being man-made. The precise cause of Severe Acute Respiratory Syndrome, or SARS, which caused death, panic and mayhem across East Asia and beyond in 2003, hasn't been discovered, but the line supported by the Chinese government for one is that it may be a variation on a virus carried by those cat-like creatures, civets.

One local theory, however, is that SARS was deliberately manufactured to slow the region's prodigious economic growth and power. The death toll from SARS in 2003 was in the few hundreds, most of whom were in China, where the health system is relatively basic. The real impact of the disease was economic, in that the attendant fear and disruption caused financiers and businessmen to steer clear of the region. According to the financial services company J.P. Morgan, SARS caused greater damage to Asia's economy than the 2004 tsunami. Some Chinese find it suspicious that SARS did not appear to return during the warmer months of 2004. One rumour has it that this is because anyone suspected of having SARS is simply whisked away by the Chinese police and shot.

tioned believed that HIV was man-made; over a quarter said they believed that AIDS had been produced in a government laboratory; and more than a tenth believed that it had been created and spread by the CIA. The survey also reported that many believed that cures for AIDS were being withheld from the poor, and that those who took new HIV medicines were government guinea pigs, while some said that AIDS was genocide against blacks.

SOURCES

Books

Dr Alan Cantwell AIDS And the Doctors Of Death: An Inquiry Into The Origin Of The AIDS Epidemic (1992) and Queer Blood: The Secret AIDS Genocide Plot (1993). In much the same vein as Horowitz (see below), Cantwell makes some interesting if excitably written arguments.

Richard & Rosalind Chirimuuta AIDS, Africa And Racism (1997). The authors blame a pernicious combination of imperial ambition and racist attitudes for the notion that AIDS originated in Africa and that the continent is ravaged by the disease (although parts of it undeniably are).

Leonard G. Horowitz Emerging Viruses AIDS & Ebola: Nature, Accident Or Intentional? (1996). Horowitz seemingly manages to interview every expert and cite nearly every theory on AIDS in this grittily detailed (if at times flailing and over-personalized) polemic, which insists that AIDS was manufactured.

Websites

⊕ www.boydgraves.com. Dr Boyd E. Graves expounds his views on the genocidal function of AIDS as a weapon, with a fascinating chart of the origins of AIDS, which he claims can be traced back to the nineteenth century.

Secret bases

Conspiracy literature is permeated with references to scores if not hundreds of "secret bases" scattered around the world. These include government bunkers, command centres, test sites and depots for spectacular and awful weapons, hideouts and bases for desperadoes from this world ... and others. The same names keep recurring, showing the powerful grip these places have on the imagination of conspiracy theorists. And every now and then, as in the case of Fort Detrick for example, there really is a lot of dark history for the imagination to feed on. What follows is a handy primer to the most (in)famous secret bases.

Heart of darkness: The Pentagon

The iconic Pentagon, located just outside Washington DC in the state of Virginia, was constructed during World War II to house the War Department, the Office of Strategic Services (the predecessor of the CIA), and other ministries previously dotted around the US capital. Its main proponent, John McCloy, who was also at times chairman of the Council on Foreign Relations and Chase Manhattan Bank, ensured that it was built despite opposition from President Roosevelt. These days, 29,000 employees of the CIA and Department of Defense work in the Pentagon. It's an ugly but tough building, strong enough on September 11, 2001, to absorb the Boeing 757 that crashed directly into it.

Officially, the Pentagon is pentagonally shaped due to the constricting layout of surrounding roads on the original design site. However, the Pentagon can be seen as being shaped around a five-pointed star – the symbol of Freemasonry (and of the fifty states on the US flag). Most of the Founding fathers were Freemasons, and the entire city of Washington is said to have been laid out along Masonic symmetries by Masonic architect Pierre Charles L'Enfante. The five-pointed star is also Satanist, and the Pentagon is built on a marsh called Hell's Bottom. To some conspiracists, that suggests that it's actually a huge ringpiece or anus, which in turn alludes to sodomy, the favourite sexual practice of Satanists.

It's a certainly evil enough place for some to require an exorcism, as some hippies attempted in 1967 as part of a 70,000-strong peace demonstration. The hippies sought to rid the building of the evil spirits within by singing and chanting until it levitated and turned orange (because it's a nice colour?). It didn't work.

The building is allegedly full of symbolism reflecting numbers that have a Masonic meaning, such as 5 (for the star), 7 (it doesn't take longer than seven minutes to get from any point in the building to another) and 11. According to www.freemasonrywatch.org, 11 puts the Pentagon in the frame for 9/11, as construction of the Pentagon began on September 11, 1941 – exactly 60 years before 9/11. (Also, 9/11 is $9 + 1 + 1 = 11$, and the 254th day of the year, $2 + 5 + 4 = 11$, leaving 111 days. Flight 11 was the first plane to hit the towers. The words The Pentagon, New York City and Afghanistan all have 11 letters, and the World Trade Center resembled an 11.)

The Pentagon is also apparently mathematically appealing to Pythagoreans and MJ12 (see p.314), which some also suspect to operate from there. Others claim that it played a role in Operation Paperclip, under which former Nazi scientists were brought to the US during the Cold War, continuing their experiments to develop weapons at their

Edgewood Arsenal base. It's even been claimed that the Pentagon was built at the request of several Nazis who came to Washington in the 1930s, and wanted a base for their eventual return after the war – a request said to have been backed by rocket scientist Jack Parsons and his spiritual mentor, Aleister Crowley.

Crowley and Montauk

Crowley is also said to have worked (in an undisclosed capacity) with Nazis who are ended up at the mysterious mega-lab of Montauk Point, Long Island. This takes its name from its original inhabitants, the Montauk Indians, who according to the courts no longer exist as a tribe, though they themselves continue to insist that they do. Supposedly a defunct Air Force base, Montauk was at one point supposed to be reopening as a New York state park, but that didn't happen. Instead, high power and high-capacity phone lines have apparently been seen being taken into the sealed-off underground complex – which suggests to some theorists that electromagnetic experimentation is continuing. Montauk is allegedly where the time-travelling USS *Eldridge* reappeared (see p.268), and it's indubitably near where TWA 800, SwissAir 111 and EgyptAir 990 crashed into the ocean (see p.306). Those incidents are said to be the joint work of a Masonic sect from the National Security Council and Nazis who were left there after U-boat operations during World War II.

Give the Nazis a home

Nazis are also believed by some to be still living in parts of Antarctica. Two German expeditions to the continent were made in 1938 and 1939, allegedly in the hope of finding Aryans – who had supposedly kicked out the previous inhabitants, the Knights Templar – living under the ice. A U-boat base was built there, and U-boats were supposedly spotted heading in that direction after the war. The US is said to have sent a task force of 1400 men in pursuit, entitled Operation High Jump and ostensibly searching for coal deposits. The leader of the mission, Admiral Byrd, apparently succeeded in meeting with Aryan representatives, and agreed to keep their secret safe. The man behind the plan, Navy Secretary James Forrestal, was outraged, but he was "retired" to a psychiatric isolation ward, where he killed himself. This, it's said, explains why drilling on the continent is banned – it's so that the civilization beneath it won't be discovered. Some say that Nazis shot down Kiwi airliner TE 109 in 1979 for spying. Although Antarctica is not usually prone to the vagaries of tectonic shifts, an earthquake was detected there in 1998 that measured 8.1 on the Richter scale. This has been attributed to massive nuclear blasts as part of Aryan subterranean construction work.

The Underground Government of America

The Nazis aren't the only ones who are big on big bunkers. As part of America's "Continuity of Government" programme, which was set up during the 1980s to prepare for the possibility of nuclear war or some other calamity, the US government has built a network of deep underground nuclear-proof bases. The program falls under the aegis of the Federal Emergency Management Agency (FEMA), which certainly exists, and apparently had the tunnels built in cooperation with the RAND Corporation and the Mining Bureau.

The "Continuity of Government" plan calls for the president, cabinet and the entire executive branch to relocate to a self-sustaining underground base beneath Mount Weather, Virginia, sixty miles from Washington DC. Under the Joint Emergency Evacuation Plan, special teams equipped with war plans and military codes would accompany several dozen designated constitutional successors to the president and disperse to a hundred secret command posts countrywide, including Pennsylvania, West Virginia, Maryland, North Carolina and another being built in Napa County, California. All are linked via satellite, ground-wave and microwave relay systems.

That much is known. What some conspiracy theorists speculate, however, is that FEMA also has over six hundred prison camps across the US, all ready to receive prisoners under the imposition of martial law. The camps are all said to be connected by road and rail, and some have mini-airstrips. Most, apparently, can house twenty thousand prisoners, but one in Fairbanks, Alaska, can take two million. These camps were built under the Rex 84 Program, designed to deal with a mass exodus of illegal aliens (from Mexico, rather than outer space). However, they're now claimed to be part of two conspiracies run by FEMA, Operation Cable Splicer and Garden Plot, which will enable the government to control the population when the New World Order begins, abetted by fleets of hidden United Nations tanks.

Forts and weapons centres

A military base that undeniably exists and has attracted the attention of a lot of conspiracy theorists over the years is Fort Detrick, located in Frederick County, Maryland, only an hour's drive from Washington DC. Fort Detrick is now home to the United States Army Medical Research and Materiel Command, the National Cancer Institute (NCI-Frederick), and other biomedical organizations. It has also worked on population control, and was where Dr Frank W. Olson fell victim to the Special Operations Division's experiments with LSD and other incapacitating drugs (see p.15). Until 1969,

Fort Detrick was the US Army's main base for research into chemical and biological weapons, a programme that was then, officially, destroyed. It was reopened by President Nixon in 1971 as the Frederick Cancer Research Facility.

Detrick's dirty past was revealed by the 1977 Congressional report, *US Army Activities In The U.S. Biological Warfare Program*. The fort's website openly describes the Army's experiments with dispersing bacterial spores into the Pentagon, San Francisco and in the subways of New York. Detrick's work has been associated with Dugway Proving Ground, Utah; Edgewood Arsenal, Maryland; Pine Bluff Arsenal, Arkansas; Rocky Mountain Arsenal, Colorado, and others. It has also been suggested that Detrick is where HIV/AIDS and the strains of anthrax that hit the US in the wake of 9/11 were developed. In addition, Detrick has been linked to Porton Down laboratories in the UK, where nerve gas was tested on "volunteer" soldiers during the 1950s (see p.276) and where the military use of gas had been investigated since World War I. The various projects undertaken at Detrick may just have been too evil – or idiotic – to have ever received publicly supported funding, but then that's what the infamous "black budgets" are all about – secret flows of money with no public trail.

It's these "black budgets", according to conspiracists, that fund astounding new weapons in the outback of the US. It is reported that electronic weapons systems are developed at places such as Nellis, Las Vegas, an airbase and munitions facility where two hundred nuclear warheads are stored, and where nuclear devices used to be kept for testing in Nevada. The Nellis complex also incorporates the Tolicha Peak Electronic Combat Range and the Tonopah Test Range, where the Department of Energy tests artillery shells, bombs, cruise missiles and rockets, and was home to the first squadron of F117 Stealth fighters. These were developed around Antelope Valley, southern California, home to research facilities for aircraft industry giants

Lockheed, McDonnell Douglas and Northrop, and these companies have, so the conspiracy theorists say, all dabbled in testing anti-gravity propulsion systems and other exotic engine designs.

It's said that Lockheed has its own hothouse in "Plant 42" at Groom Lake, Nevada, where exotic new breeds of stealth and hypersonic aircraft use two two-mile runways. Big airforce transporters fly in and out with cargoes during the night, while base workers – supposedly told to deny that they work at Groom Lake – are flown in from Las Vegas by day. Northrop Corporation's equivalent is the Tejon Ranch below the Tehachapi Mountains, in Lancaster, California. No livestock is visible on this supposed "cattle ranch", which Northrop admits is an "electromagnetic research facility" – as shown by the large radar and microwave dishes on its surface – and which has 42 levels underground. There are also said to be tunnels to other nearby installations, including Edwards Air Force Base, a hundred miles northeast of Los Angeles.

Aliens among us

You might think that with Russia out of the arms race and other contenders left trailing behind, there would be little need for the US to keep on developing ever more sophisticated and high-tech weaponry. As UFO-inclined theorists see it, however, the US military is preparing to repel space invaders – with friendly aliens helping to upgrade weaponry they regard as primitive.

Although the command centre for the US Space Command is at the Peterson base in Colorado, the space weapons being built for the SDI program, supposedly designed to defend Earth from alien attack, are apparently being developed at the Kirtland base in Albuquerque. The Wright Patterson base, near Dayton, Ohio, is where the US Air Force allegedly investigated UFOs under Project Blue Book, logging up over seven hundred yet "unidentified" sightings. But sightings aren't the only activity going on there. Wright is also said to be an aviation research centre that holds UFO wreckage from the Roswell incident (see Roswell p.311), and is linked (in the conspiracist's mind) to the most famous "secret" military base of all, Area 51 in Nevada. Supposedly, aircraft that incorporate designs pilfered from crashed UFOs are built and flown here using the world's longest runway – the base itself is as big as Switzerland – while signs outside say "trespassers will be executed".

Alien spacecraft are also said to be housed ten miles from Area 51 at Site S4, hidden under mountains near an alien base of Lemurians under Mount Shasta in California. (The Lemurians are not to be confused with another group of underground-dwelling interstellar migrants, the Terras, who, it's said, prefer to live a thousand miles beneath the Earth's crust.) More UFOs are thought to be garaged two miles beneath the Jicarilla Apache Indian Reservation near Dulce, New Mexico, which some believe is the world's first joint Earth-Alien biogenetics laboratory. A similar co-stellar project is said to be based on a French Polynesian island, where since the 1950s the Bilderberg Group and the Council for Foreign Relations have apparently allowed the aliens to maintain a base to observe earthlings, and vice versa. Finally, it's been claimed that aliens also marked out and built their own Middle Eastern kingdom, Kuwait, the borders of which were drawn to ensure that, from space, the country bears the profile of the Lord of the Sith, Darth Vader. Which explains, of course, why the Pentagon stepped in so valiantly to rescue Kuwait in 1991.

Websites

ⓦ **www.AboveTopSecret.com** This site charts allegations of what FEMA's true purpose may be; compare it with the US government's official site, www.fema.gov.

ⓦ **www.boblazar.com** One man's own collection of places you couldn't visit even if you knew they existed.

ⓦ **www.detrick.army.mil** Fort Detrick's website is adamant that the fort has a benign influence on its neighbourhood, being Frederick County's largest employer and helping it be "the third fastest growing county in Virginia".

ⓦ **www.mod.uk/issues/ portondownvolunteers/history.html** The official, Ministry of Defence version of what happened with the volunteers at Porton Down.

ⓦ **www.mutanex.com/reconalpha.html**

Six State Tour Of Secret Bases & Secret Technologies Bases. This fascinating reportage of one man's odyssey around America's alternative arsenals steps into the unknowns of UFOlogy.

ⓦ **www.secret-bases.co.uk** Alan Turnbull's absorbing tour of secret bases in the UK, written with a tinge of wide-eyed wonder.

HAARP

On its projected completion in 2007, HAARP, or the High Frequency Active Auroral Research Program, will consist of an orderly array of 180 antennae, spread across 33 acres. Officially this massive transmitter is designed to watch and observe happenings in the ionosphere, the great layer of sky that starts thirty miles above the earth's surface and stretches for six hundred miles into space. That needs a lot of power, and HAARP needs ten megawatts to deliver its 3.6 million watts of radio frequency power and one gigawatt of electro-radioactive pulse power.

As well as being the largest such transmitter in the world, HAARP is one of the most remote, being located eight miles north of Gakona, Alaska. Managed by the Air Force Research Laboratory and the Office of Naval Research, it also enjoys scientific and research input from the University of Alaska, UCLA, Cornell, Stanford and the universities of Maryland, Massachusetts, MIT and Tulsa, among others. According to Alaska University, HAARP exists "to further advance our knowledge of the physical and electrical properties of the Earth's ionosphere which affects our military and civilian communication and navigation systems". The ionosphere interests scientists, business and the military because it disrupts ground-to-satellite signals, mangles radio and radar signals, and can induce power surges and outages. HAARP's work could lead to improvements in communications, for example with submerged submarines, says Alaska University. There's a broad range of ionospheric conditions over Alaska, while HAARP's transmitting and observing gadgetry needs a quiet electromagnetic location away from cities.

That HAARP is being backed by the US Department of Defense, the Air Force and the Navy doesn't lend much conviction to the idea that it's solely a "civilian" project. Why are quite so many academic bodies involved? What is such a device doing in the middle of nowhere? Is HAARP something more than just a big experiment involving the upper atmosphere? Are the Alaskan-based antennae in fact a weapon of mass destruction, able to manipulate the planet's meteorology to the malign ends of its masters? Whatever it is, it's got a lot of conspiracy theorists very excited indeed.

A mega-weapon of the modern age?

According to theorists like Jerry E. Smith (author of *HAARP: The Ultimate Weapons Of The Conspiracy*), HAARP is anything but a grand exploration of the atmosphere for the sake of science and better phone calls. An offshoot of the Strategic Defense Initiative, it's uncannily similar to a weapon designed by Texan physicist Bernard Eastland – US Patent 4,686,605 – which could "alter" the upper atmosphere by "transmitting electromagnetic radiation" and enable eavesdropping on, interfering with and destroying enemy communications without interfering with one's own. What's more, Eastlland claims, the device can be used in "missile or aircraft destruction", and its long-range Electro Magnetic Pulses (EMP) can knock down power grids.

That patent is owned by ARCO Power Technologies Inc., a subsidiary of major defence contractor ARCO-Atlantic Richfield – which is the company contracted by the Pentagon to build HAARP. Eastland's patent claims that "weather modification is possible". Alaska University, however, insists that "HAARP will not affect the weather", possibly in response to rumours that it could fundamentally affect agriculture by doing just that, fostering crop growth on previously barren land but also inflicting drought and famine elsewhere. The university states that HAARP's transmitted energy has practically no effect on the weather-producing troposphere or the stratosphere. Electromagnetic interactions only occur in the ionosphere, the size and capricious magnetic stability of which reduce the effect of HAARP to the level of an "immersion heater in the Yukon River". HAARP's operations are not meddlesome but "strictly passive".

However, in 1998 Congress increased funding for HAARP to examine "the utility of the ionospheric modification", to be used in "military, intelligence, counterproliferation, counterterrorism and counternarcotics missions ... [supporting] military and intelligence requirements identified in the Joint Vision 2010 Defense Science and Technology Strategy", involving "Full Spectrum Dominance and the Joint Warfighting Capability", to "assess initial capabilities of Stochastic Resonance for Defense and intelligence applications." Whatever all that means in practice, it hardly sounds passive. And as for the weather, a paper given at the 1997 Intersociety Energy Conversion Engineering Conference declared that "the effects of HAARP on the weather are completely unknown", adding that "heating the jet stream over Alaska could have profound results on the weather in Denver or Miami".

Earthquakes and tsunamis

And then there's the whole business of "stochastic resonance". Eastland's patent has its roots in the work of Nikolas Tesla, whose experiments with

MICROWAVES

Conspiracy theorists claim mini-tech mind control now lies well within the capacity of earthling inventors. Fillings, spectacle frames, pencils, earrings – all have been cited as the carriers of tiny "silent radio" transmitters. Just like dog whistles, these transmitters are said to work on high frequencies that lie beyond normal human audibility but can still vibrate into the subconscious, and make victims act according to their instructions. Ultra-paranoid conspiracists warn that street and traffic lights are really disguised cameras spying on you, while the worst offender of all is your TV. You think you are watching them on it, but in fact they are using it to watch you. Never mind, have some cereal – just not Kellogg's Lucky Charms or Count Chocula, because the CIA uses them to conceal millions of sub-molecular nanite chips in the marshmallows in order to implant children.

A more convenient system of control, and a major tenet of conspiracy theories, is that human behaviour is affected from a distance by using pulse-modulated electromagnetic radiation, or microwaves. By this reckoning, microwaves mimic the extremely low frequency electrical waves that occur as part of the brain's natural function. Thus by duplicating the waves you can alter the state of mind of targeted people. It's claimed that Wilhelm Reich – who also reported discovering cancer bacteria (see p.258) – stumbled across the controlling powers of microwaves during the late 1940s. When he learned that the CIA was using his work to control Americans, the story goes, he rebelled, only to die mysteriously in Federal prison in 1957.

Radiation as a form of mind-control device was indeed experimented with as part of the MK-ULTRA program (see p.192), which it's said identified the 450 MHz microwave range as the optimum control frequency. Thus some theorists view mobile phone networks as strategic mind-control devices, for use against the population as necessary. Certainly, mobile phones do seem to force people to talk loudly about incredibly dull or personal things, causing mass irritation and embarrassment, though it's hard to be sure whether that's a conspiracy.

MI5, the UK's counterintelligence agency, supposedly possesses mobile microwave units, which it can beam at homes or offices to induce cancer, strokes, heart attacks or nerve damage, as well as mental breakdowns and suicide. That makes microwaves the ultimate traceless murder weapon, cited for example in the deaths of 25 Marconi scientists who worked on the Strategic Defense Initiative. Other victims who proved bothersome to the British establishment, such as David Icke, Princess Diana and Bill Clinton, were simply induced into humiliating public behaviour. Conspiracy theorists also point to the use of microwaves in MI5's war on Harold Wilson's Labour government in the 1970s (see p.41); in manipulating voters to support John Major in the tight 1992 election; and in killing Labour leader John Smith in 1994. By that reckoning, Tony Blair must have somehow won MI5 over since 1997.

In the US, the Ground Wave Emergency Network (GWEN) was constructed in the 1980s, ostensibly to maintain communications in the event of a nuclear Armageddon. However, its eighty sites across the continent are said to emit high levels of dangerous electromagnetic radiation, and their locations are well known, so they'd presumably be targeted in any nuclear attack. That leads conspiracist Jerry Smith to suspect that GWEN's real purpose is "producing behavioural alterations in the civilian population". Smith is an expert on HAARP, the Alaskan observer of the ionosphere, which theorists also believe is a mega mind-control machine. Both GWEN and HAARP are said to have their roots in the designs of Nikolas Tesla, from whose notebooks the Soviets plundered their own microwave beam, which they fired at the US embassy in Moscow and thereby induced an inordinately high cancer rate among its workers. By the 1970s the Russians were reportedly using a short-wave beam nicknamed the "Russian Woodpecker" to interfere with global radio signals. Somehow that long-range mind-disruption, mind-control device was not effective enough to stop the citizens of the USSR abandoning the whole Communist enterprise in 1991.

It's been claimed that chips were inserted into Gulf War soldiers to monitor their brain waves; some remote controller could then change frequencies to affect their nervous systems and fighting ability. During the Vietnam War, soldiers were supposedly implanted with a "Rambo chip" that increased adrenaline flow into the bloodstream, while Timothy McVeigh is said to have claimed that a chip inside him commanded him to bomb Oklahoma City. Prisoners in Sweden were supposedly implanted with mind-control brain chips during the early 1970s, and it's certainly true that many convicts on remand or probation are "tagged" to keep their whereabouts known.

stochastic resonance in New York around 1900 are said to have nearly destroyed several buildings. Is HAARP an attempt to harness the same technology on a global scale?

Some conspiracy theorists suspect that HAARP may be able to peer deep into the earth and spy on the underground secrets of enemies. And if earthquakes can disrupt the ionosphere and magnetosphere, could radio waves blasted through the Earth have the same effect? It has even been suggested that HAARP was behind the massive earthquake in the Indian Ocean in December 2004, which caused a devastating tsunami. This not only struck the major east Asian economies – burgeoning competitors to the US – but gave the Bush administration the chance to ride to the rescue in a region that's simmering with anti-American sentiment. Rohan Gunaratna of the Institute of Defense and Strategic Studies in Singapore has pointed out that in both the worst-hit areas, Aceh and southern Thailand, Islamic separatist groups are fighting their respective governments. He told CNN that with terrorist groups literally washed away, the tsunami afforded "a golden opportunity" for the US to step in and win the war of ideas. Then-designate Secretary of State Condoleezza Rice concurred, telling the US Senate in January 2005: "I do agree that the tsunami was a wonderful opportunity to show not just the US government, but the heart of the American people, and I think it has paid great dividends for us." Democrat Senator Barbara Boxer reminded her that the tsunami "was one of the worst tragedies of our lifetime".

Professor Ali Hassan of the University of Malaysia suggested that earthquakes could be provoked by submarine nuclear tests conducted by the superpowers. Britain's *Big Issue* magazine reported in February 2005 that oil corporations in Southeast Asia in the days preceding the quake had been continually firing huge "air shots" into the ground to chart the underlying geology. Whether the air shots had caused the quake, no oil company or geological surveyors would say, the magazine added.

Power cuts, mind control and the New World Order

On August 11, 2003, power cuts blacked out eastern Canada and the northeastern United States, bringing chaos and darkness to New York, Detroit, Toronto and Ottawa, and a total of fifty million people. The Canadians blamed a fire at a power plant near Niagara, the US blamed a power transmission problem from Canada. The University of Tokyo, however, recorded a testing of HAARP that began at 4pm, just eleven minutes before the blackout began. Was HAARP flexing its muscles? Concerned citizen Michael Kane wrote to the Department of Energy, but received no reply, and then put his fears on the Web.

While HAARP is officially a high-frequency research device, theorists like Smith say that HAARP can use the same electromagnetic low-frequency (ELF) radiation and radio waves that both Western and Soviet researchers have reportedly shown to be the frequencies at which the human brain operates – thus enabling it to be tapped into from a distance. Carrying no ionizing radiation and low heat, and having no visibly grotesque manifestations in terms of physical deformities or vicious diseases developing (at least not in any immediate sense), ELF signals cannot be detected.

As Smith argues in his book on HAARP, this makes them "ideal for covert use". He claims that the US government is researching their use "as a handle on mind control". He isn't alone in claiming that many former Soviet scientists were involved in setting up HAARP and are engaged in its research, which taps into the "one world" theory of the New World Order (see p.234). According to Smith, HAARP is the ultimate, largely untraceable, weapon of mass destruction, able to smite troublesome countries with floods and droughts (as seen in China and North Korea) or earthquakes (Japan, Iran and Southeast Asia). HAARP thus forms the biggest part of the

THE ORIGINS OF HAARP

HAARP is said by some theorists to be an updated version of the inventions of Croat-born engineer Nikolas Tesla, who features in a number of conspiracy theories (see p.240). An electrical genius, Tesla moved to the US in 1884, where he worked for Thomas Edison and Westinghouse Power. By the time he died in 1943, he had amassed over seven hundred inventions, ranging from fluorescent lights and alternating current generators to power systems and flying machines.

In 1900, with private backing,

Tesla set about building the hideous 187-ft Wardenclyffe Tower on Long Island. An octagonal pyramid, spearing up into something that resembled a huge, sagging fly's eye, it was designed to broadcast electricity worldwide from surrounding power stations. Financier J. P. Morgan, one of its principal backers, withdrew when it occurred to him that Wardenclyffe might damage his own electricity monopoly. Even so, the structure was finished by 1904.

What Tesla was up to at Wardenclyffe over the next few

years isn't clear, but, in April 1908, something vast exploded in Tunguska, Siberia, wiping out half a million acres of forest. The official theory – and it's still no more than that – is that a piece of Encke's Comet rammed into the Earth. However, some say the blast was a misfiring from Wardenclyffe, beaming trillions of watts of power into the wrong area. The tower was demolished in 1917, as German U-boats were reportedly using it to navigate by.

Tesla returned in 1934 with what the *New York Times* called a "death beam", which could melt

enemy bomber engines 250 miles away and cause armies of millions to "drop dead in their tracks", while powering flying machines to defend the homeland and bomb the enemy. However, the paltry $2 million needed to build the beam didn't materialize. Indeed, many of Tesla's designs were never constructed and he died in poverty in 1943. Fifty years later, however, Tesla's "death beam" concept resurfaced in the weapon patent taken out by Dr Bernard Eastland, which referenced Tesla's earlier works on wireless energy transmission.

Strategic Defense Initiative, which might appear to be a feeble missile defence system, but which, some conspiracy theorists claim, is actually a raft of weaponry to control people on every front.

The End of Days

Sadly, we won't really know what HAARP is truly capable of until it's completed and operational – and by then, presumably, it will be too late. We can only hope that when we've eaten the last of our crops by candlelight, our minds are melted before the floods wash our cities and corpses away. On the other hand, the HAARP program is unclassified, its Environmental Impact Process documents are public, and indeed, the facility is open for tours for two days at the end of each summer. And if your communications are interfered with by HAARP, you can always report it to the Federal Communications Commission, on 001 907 822-5497.

SOURCES

Books

Jerry E. Smith **HAARP: The Ultimate Weapon Of The Conspiracy** (1998). An entertaining, "fact"-packed account of HAARP's allegedly dubious history and sinister purpose.

Websites

ⓦ www.bariumblues.com/haarp_patent.

htm Eastland's original patent.

ⓦ www.haarp.alaska.edu Alaska University's summary of HAARP's official, civilian work.

Sea, air and space: calamities and cover-ups

The Titanic
Lockerbie
Roswell and Majestic-12
The Apollo moon landing

Sea, air and space: calamities and cover-ups

Introduction

Sea, sky, space: the big blue bits that surround the continents and the world, and on and through which people and goods are propelled in carriers both large and small. But their routes from A to B aren't all that's plotted – if some theorists are to be believed, there's also many a mean conspiracy that has been carried out in these vast, cold arenas.

It's said, for example, that the *Titanic*'s fatal collision with an iceberg was actually an insurance fraud that went horribly wrong, when more than 1500 people lost their lives instead of being rescued as planned. Just three years later, in 1915, the *Lusitania* was sunk by a German torpedo. But again, some suspect that this was what the perfidious Brits wanted, because the loss of the ship and its American passengers might have sparked sufficient anti-German resentment to bring the US into World War I. If that was the plot, however, it didn't work – not immediately, anyway.

Before the end of the century, ocean liners had been supplanted by airliners and torpedoes would evolve into missiles. In 1996 passenger flight TWA 800 took off from New York, heading east over the Atlantic, only to suddenly explode and crash into the dark ocean. It was an accident, said the US government; no, said others, it was "friendly fire" – the US military had accidentally shot the plane down during a training exercise.

After 9/11 and in the build-up to the war in Iraq, theorists and high-ranking politicians tried to link terrorists to the TWA 800 disaster, though the US government had spent years and millions of dollars before concluding that the plane, had, in effect, fallen apart.

One air disaster that certainly wasn't an accident happened over the previously obscure Scottish town of Lockerbie, when Pan Am flight 103 was blown up by a bomb in a suitcase in December 1988. Lockerbie became the centre of a web connecting Frankfurt, London, Beirut, Washington, Tehran and Tripoli via the CIA, MI6, Mossad and other organizations. The Libyans were the ones who were ultimately blamed, punished and fined for the bombing, but despite paying up, they *still* deny their involvement. Syrians, Palestinians, Iranians and Americans have all been suspected of being in on the plot.

Like the Cold War, the space race also had its fair share of conspiracies and cover-ups. It's thought, for instance, that Yuri Gagarin *wasn't* the first man into space, but rather the first man to come back alive... As for the first moon landing itself, in 1969, there are plenty of people who believe that it was a massive hoax. It's alleged that the US astronauts apparently walking on the moon were really filmed out in the American desert – a case of one small step for man, but one giant step for special effects. If the allegation is true, it must be the biggest con trick ever.

A different sort of obsession is displayed by the UFOlogists who believe that aliens crashed a spaceship at Roswell, New mexico, in 1947, an incident they claim has been covered up by the US government ever since. Officials have always claimed that the "flying saucer" was just a weather balloon – but then they would say that, wouldn't they?

The Titanic

For sheer symbolism as well as scale, the tragedy of the Titanic can hardly be surpassed. A massive luxury ship embarks on its maiden voyage, carrying thousands of passengers, ranging from the obscenely rich to the abjectly poor, from the Old World to the New, only for most of them to die in the freezing waters of the black Atlantic night. The incident has inspired countless novels and many films including James Cameron's (1997) box-office titan starring Kate Winslet and Leonardo DiCaprio. The film's tagline was "Collide with destiny". But was fate really the culprit or was the Titanic disaster the result of epic hubris, utter folly or a conspiracy to commit an almost unimaginable fraud?

When the RMS *Titanic* was launched in early 1912 from Belfast shipbuilders Harland & Wolff, it was, at 852 ft long and 46,329 tons, the largest ship in the world. It had been commissioned for the White Star Line, to ply the highly competitive Atlantic route between Europe and America, and for first-class passengers at least it was said to offer the last word in luxury. Because its hull had a series of virtually watertight bulkheads, four of which could be filled without sinking the ship, it was said to be "practically unsinkable" (rather than simply "unsinkable", as later accounts suggested).

On April 10, 1912, the *Titanic* left Southampton

The *Titanic*'s suspicious sister, the *Olympic*

for New York, under the command of Captain Edward J. Smith and with 2224 passengers and crew on board. Four days later, just before midnight on the night of April 14, the ship struck an iceberg around four hundred miles south of Newfoundland, which tore through the *Titanic*'s starboard side and ruptured five bulkheads. By 2.20am, the ship had sunk with the loss of 1503 lives.

Incompetence and ill fortune

The Cunard liner *Carpathia* arrived on the scene eighty minutes after the *Titanic* sank, a fatally long time in near-freezing waters. Inquiries in both the US and UK revealed that another ship, the *Californian*, was sitting less than twenty miles away from the *Titanic* the whole time. However, its radio operator was not on duty to hear the *Titanic*'s SOS, which was not in any case sent out until 35 minutes after the collision.

Because it was categorized with ships weighing only ten thousand tons, the *Titanic* was equipped with a mere sixteen lifeboats, only enough to carry 962 people – even though it was built for 3511 passengers and crew. It also had a further four collapsible boats, increasing capacity to 1178. And the first boat was only launched ninety minutes after the collision, a fatal delay.

Why did the first SOS and the first lifeboat launch take so long? And what was the *Californian* doing there? It later transpired that the *Californian* was owned by the financier J.P. Morgan, who in part owned White Star, and was carrying some three thousand thick woollen jumpers and blankets, and had been dispatched to that spot. A curious mission, especially during a coal strike that curtailed all but the most essential or most profitable shipping. It was widely reported that Morgan himself had been due to travel on the *Titanic*, but had cried off the trip on the grounds of being "ill" (although this excuse was later revealed to have been just

that: an excuse). Also, why did five hundred crewmen from Belfast refuse to rejoin the *Titanic* from Southampton, despite the coal strike that had put thousands of crewmen out of work?

A Titanic insurance fraud...

Something was up. If a shipyard worker nicknamed "Paddy the Pig" was to be believed, the *Titanic* never sank at all – instead, its slightly older sister ship, the *Olympic*, was sunk as part of a huge insurance scam. The design differences between the *Olympic* and the *Titanic* were absolutely minuscule, and the *Olympic* was disguised as the *Titanic* then deliberately sunk. Where the plan went awry was that so many died.

The main proponent of this theory is Robin Gardiner, who has written three books on the subject, including *The Titanic Conspiracy*. He argues that the problem with the *Olympic* was that it had collided with a Royal Navy cruiser, *HMS Hawke*, in Southampton a few months earlier, damaging the *Olympic*'s starboard hull enough for the liner to be written off. However, the Navy's inquiry, not surprisingly, absolved the Navy of any blame. The *Olympic* was therefore unusable and uninsurable, and White Star would remain uncompensated. That would ruin the company, already struggling in its battle with the leaner, faster Cunard liners.

So, shortly before the *Titanic* was launched, the *Olympic* was taken to the same Belfast shipbuilders for a week in dry dock, ostensibly for repairs to its propeller (which should only have taken two days). That's when, the theory goes, the switch was supposedly made, involving a few minor cosmetic changes, changing the name and some paperwork – even the linen and plates aboard weren't ship-specific, all being labelled "White Star". The two ships were so alike that to this day many of the images which purport to show the *Titanic* are actually re-labelled footage of the *Olympic*. And no one

THE LUSITANIA

The British passenger ship SS *Lusitania* was sunk off Ireland by the German submarine U-20 on May 7, 1915, with the loss of 1198 lives. Although Britain and Germany had been at war for some months, transatlantic passenger services like the New York-London route being plied by Cunard's liner continued. This was despite warnings from Germany, published in American newspapers (and on May 1, when the *Lusitania* sailed), that England-bound ships were fair game for their submarines. So the US public couldn't say they weren't told, and the sinking of the *Lusitania* bloodily underscored the danger. There was righteous outrage in the US, not only that the filthy Huns would sink a civilian ship, but that they would dare to kill 128 Americans aboard

too. But the *Lusitania*, hit by one torpedo, sank in just eighteen minutes. (By contrast, the *Titanic*, holed by an iceberg, had taken two hours to sink.) What kind of damage had the torpedo done to make the ship sink so quickly? Suspicion turned on the idea that the *Lusitania* had been carrying a huge consignment of contraband munitions that neutral America shouldn't have been supplying to Britain. But then another suspicion arose: did the Brits conspire to have the ship sunk and sting the US into entering the war on Germany?

The key event cited by conspiracist historians is an Admiralty conference on May 5, attended by then First Lord of the Admiralty Winston Churchill, at which the destroyer meant

to escort *Lusitania* into harbour was ordered to be withdrawn. While the Admiralty War Diary doesn't record who ordered the destroyer's withdrawal, it notes that four other destroyers in the Bristol Channel were assigned to escort duties instead. But that never happened, and the *Lusitania* sailed unprotected into U-boat infested waters to meet its fate. Was Churchill hoping for the ship to be sunk and the US to be spurred into war? The problem with this theory is that it rests on some big assumptions. First, that Churchill could be pretty sure that the *Lusitania*, going full speed and zigzagging to avoid subs, would indeed be sunk by one of a handful of U-boats in the broad, rough seas of the Atlantic. Second, that he could also be sure that the US would be provoked into war as a

result – a provocation that, in the event, President Woodrow Wilson resisted. As for the possible presence of contraband munitions, US Secretary of State William Bryan had made it clear that Germany was entitled to stop contraband reaching the Allies, writing that a "ship carrying contraband should not rely upon passengers to protect her from attack". And surely, if the *Lusitania* had been carrying munitions, the British would not have wanted it to be sunk en route. In any case, Wilson went on to win re-election in 1916 on a neutrality platform, and kept the US out of the war as long as Germany kept its U-boats well away from America's coast and ships. When the Germans started sinking American ships again in early 1917, however, the US entered the war on the Allies' side.

was paying much attention. The *Titanic* received its seaworthiness certificates after half a day of tests, instead of the usual mandatory two full days. And it passed those tests despite smoke pouring from every porthole, due to a fire in one of its coalbunkers!

The plan was to dispatch the *Olympic* disguised as the *Titanic*, sail it close to an iceberg, then explode a hole in its hull. The hole would be blamed on colliding with the berg, and the ship would slowly sink, allowing the nearby *Californian* to rescue everyone on board. However, on the night, the *Titanic* did in fact hit an iceberg, causing the ship to sink far faster than planned. Smith and his crew then panicked for a fatal half hour, and finally launched a real SOS.

... or Titanic blarney?

The insurance story only surfaced in 1995, ten years after the wreck of the *Titanic* (or *Olympic*) was found two and a half miles down on the ocean floor, in two huge pieces. But then maritime researchers Steve Hall and Bruce Beveridge set out to debunk Gardiner's theory in *The Olympic & The Titanic: The Truth Behind The Conspiracy*. The *Olympic*'s ship number was 400 and the *Titanic*'s was 401, and it was the latter number that was found on one of the propellers on the Atlantic floor. The number and location of portholes on the ships differed, and those on the wreck conform to the arrangement on the *Titanic*. The front of the wheelhouse on the *Olympic* was bowed, but the *Titanic*'s was straight – and the wheelhouse on the wreck is straight, too. And if it was known that the *Titanic* would be sending out an SOS, why didn't the *Californian* have anyone on duty to pick it up? Finally, the theory requires fifteen thousand people who worked on the ships to have kept quiet about the switch, with the single exception of "Paddy the Pig", whose real name was nowhere to be found on the workmen's records for either vessel.

However, the evidence that Hall and Beveridge say proves that the ship on the ocean floor is the *Titanic* – like the portholes, propeller and bridge – are all essentially cosmetic details, just the kind of minor alterations that Gardiner contends were "fixed" when the ship was in dry dock. And neither would fifteen thousand shipbuilders need to have been involved. Only a few would be employed to make the cosmetic alterations, and unless they were au fait with the *Olympic*'s insurance problems, which is highly unlikely, the sinister significance of filling in a porthole here or there, wouldn't necessarily have occurred to them. That's not to say Gardiner's theory is true, but neither does *The Truth Behind The Conspiracy* completely sink it.

The reckless racing myth

A longer-standing theory holds that the *Titanic* was racing to reach New York in record time, and that it sank because caution was sacrificed for speed. J. Bruce Ismay, chairman and managing director of the White Star Line, is said to have ordered Captain Smith to "make a record crossing". Ismay, who was aboard the ship, was also singled out for cowardly behaviour, it being claimed that he pulled rank to get himself into one of the first lifeboats.

However, Smith, who was the highest paid commander in the mercantile marine and was on the final voyage of his career, would have been unlikely to defer to Ismay on navigation. And it was Smith who failed to heed the warnings of ice, and allowed partly filled lifeboats to leave the sinking ship. In fact, Ismay helped to fill the boats, and was among the last to leave the *Titanic*.

In any case, White Star competed on bulk, not speed: the top speed of the *Titanic* was still five knots slower than that of the Cunard liners, and not all its boilers were lit. Ironically enough, it was taking the longer southern route precisely to avoid icebergs. The charges of reckless racing stemmed from the newspapers of William Randolph Hearst, who is said to have had a personal antipathy for Ismay, and prosecuted a "vicious" campaign against him. According to BBC Online in 2002, "stories were invented and witnesses, wishing to strengthen exorbitant insurance claims for lost baggage against the company, declared that Ismay ordered Smith to make a record crossing".

Horrible Huns and creepy clairvoyance

In the light of the fact that the First World War broke out a mere two years after the sinking, some have charged that the Germans wanted to test out their U-boat submarine designs, and expose the myth that the *Titanic* was unsinkable. Thus a U-boat torpedoed the *Titanic* as it passed the iceberg – the iceberg took the blame, while the U-boat slipped away.

In 1898, meanwhile, clairvoyant and novelist Morgan Robertson had written a disaster novel about a luxurious British liner, "the largest craft afloat", plying the Atlantic route. Kitted with "water-tight compartments", the three-propeller, multiple-bulkhead 800-ft ship was "unsinkable", and embarked in April with its full complement of three thousand passengers. But days into the maiden voyage, near midnight, it hit an iceberg that cut through its starboard side like a tin-opener. Thousands died as a result of its inadequate provision of lifeboats. The ship's name? The SS *Titan*.

A century later

As things stand, the insurance-scam theory has received little coverage beyond the small community of *Titanic* enthusiasts. To most of them, it's an amusing oddity of a story, not something to be seriously entertained. However, serious changes did result from the *Titanic* tragedy. Maritime laws were changed in 1913, requiring ships to have lifeboat space for everyone on board, to hold lifeboat drills every voyage, and to maintain a 24-hour radio watch. A warning system about icebergs in North Atlantic shipping lanes was also set up. But it's the fate of the *Titanic* itself that continues to grip the imagination.

SOURCES

Books

Robin Gardiner **The Titanic Conspiracy** (1998). This builds on two earlier books by Gardiner, *The Ship That Never Sank* and *The Riddle Of The Titanic*.

Steve Hall and Bruce Beveridge **The Olympic & The Titanic: The Truth Behind The Conspiracy** (2004). An efficient but not entirely conclusive debunking of Gardiner's claims.

Website

ⓦ www.encyclopedia-titanica.org This aptly named website is full of all things *Titanic*.

Lockerbie

Officers from the RAF, CID, Scottish police and CIA spent the Christmas of 1988 combing the bleak lowlands around Lockerbie, Scotland. They were looking, over 850 square miles, for remnants of Pan Am flight 103, which had left London's Heathrow airport on the early evening of December 21. The Boeing 747, the Maid of the Seas, had 259 passengers and crew aboard, 189 of whom were Americans, and was on the Atlantic leg of a Frankfurt-London-New York-Detroit flight.

Just after 7pm, the *Maid* entered Scottish airspace at around 30,000 feet, out of sight and sound as it approached the small town of Lockerbie. Then, at 19.03pm, 38 minutes into the flight, a bomb in the forward luggage hold exploded. The disintegrating plane hurtled earthward, with the fuel-laden wings exploding onto Lockerbie's homes and killing eleven townsfolk. Although it's thought that some 150 passengers survived the initial explosion, everyone on board was killed on impact.

Police and intelligence services from the US, UK, Germany and the Middle East joined in the search for the killers, focusing on Syria, Libya, Germany, Scotland, London, Beirut and Washington. But not until November 14, 1991 were two Libyan intelligence officers, Abdelbaset Ali Mohmed Al Megrahi and Al Amin Khalifa Fhimahmen, indicted for blowing up PA 103 by the Scottish Crown Office and the State Department. Then it was another ten years before a Scottish court, which Libya insisted should be set up in neutral Holland, could try the two men for murder and conspiracy to destroy an aircraft.

In January 2001, after an eight-month trial with three judges but no jury, Al Megrahi was found guilty and Khalifa Fhimahmen was cleared. The case took so long to come to court because the Libyan government persistently denied the charges, and for seven years, refused to hand over the pair, despite the imposition of punitive UN economic sanctions in 1992. These sanctions were finally lifted in August 2002, after the Libyan government offered to pay $2.7 billion in compensation for PA 103.

As Libyan Prime Minister Shokri Ghanem told BBC radio in February 2004, however, the reason why Libya paid up was to get the sanctions lifted, not because it accepted guilt. Evidently, those who thought Libya's official statement accepting responsibility "lacked remorse" were right. But the Libyan government isn't alone in protesting its innocence, and many believe that the country was victim to far bigger conspiracies.

The case against the Libyans

The prosecution had charged that Al Megrahi and Fhimahmen had placed a Samsonite suitcase with a Toshiba radio filled with plastic explosive onto an Air Malta flight to Frankfurt. There, it was alleged, the case had been transferred onto PA 103. The bombing was said to be in revenge for the April 1986 US air attack on Tripoli, itself revenge for Libya's supposed involvement in the bombing of a Berlin nightclub frequented by US marines.

Under the mercurial Colonel Qaddafi, Libya was considered perfectly capable of such outrages. By the mid-1980s he was seen in the West as a madman who had turned his oil-rich country into the world's number one terrorist state (an image sufficiently

familiar for Libyan terrorists to feature in the 1985 comedy film, *Back To The Future*). Qaddafi's delusions of Pan Arabian grandeur and of breaking the West's hold on the Middle East marked him out as an international troublemaker.

Libya wasn't the first, or biggest suspect

During the trial, Al Jazeera reported that former Iranian intelligence official Ahmad Behbahani claimed responsibility for international attacks carried out by the Iranian Government, including Lockerbie. The news agency's notion that this might "have an impact on the current trial in the Netherlands" wasn't borne out, and anyway, Al Jazeera suggested that Behbahani might have some desire for revenge against the Iranian government. Both the Organisation of African Unity and Nelson Mandela, however, have questioned the validity of the conviction, with the latter visiting Megrahi in his Glaswegian prison in 2002. In the trial, the pair pleaded they were innocent and blamed Syrian-backed Palestinians.

Most tellingly, the German government refused to back the US and UK indictment of the Libyans. Investigations by the then West German police into the Frankfurt link had pointed to an offshoot of the Palestinian Liberation Organisation, the Syrian-backed Popular Front for the Liberation of Palestine–General Command (PFLP-GC). Police raids on PFLP-GC cells in West Germany prior to the bombing had uncovered radio bombs and barometric (altitude-triggered) fuses. Indeed, by late 1989, there was "virtually no disagreement" among investigators and intelligence agents that the PFLP-GC was responsible, as David Johnston reported that year in his book *Lockerbie: The Tragedy Of Flight 103* – a claim repeated in Steven Emerson and Brian Duffy's *The Fall Of Pan Am 103* the following year.

The supporting theory was that the PFLP-GC had

been co-sponsored by the Iranians, in revenge for the erroneous shooting down in July 1988 of an Iranian airbus by the US Navy ship USS *Vincennes*, killing 290 people aboard. Iran's Ayatollah Khomeini had vowed that the skies would "rain blood" in revenge.

An unlikely coincidence over the Gulf war and Western hostages

In early 1991, US President George H.W. Bush asked British Prime Minister Margaret Thatcher for this PFLP-GC-Syria-Iran investigation to be "toned down". Days after the Libyans were indicted that year, Bush said that Syria – which had backed the US's first Gulf War in 1991 – had taken a "bum rap" over PA 103; meanwhile, the State Department said that Libya – which condemned the Gulf War – had tried to frame Syria and the PFLP-GC by planting false leads. The UK Foreign Office chimed in by stating that Libya was the sole and prime suspect for the bombing. In the following days, as this shift in blame was being digested, the last Western hostages in Beirut were released.

This pretty neat coincidence was picked up on by the BBC's 1993 documentary, *Silence Over Lockerbie*, which debunked the case against Libya and blamed Syria and Iran. Libya, it concluded, had been framed in favour of the US's Gulf War "allies". The film *The Maltese Double Cross,* withdrawn from the 1994 London Film Festival and investigated by the FBI, was based on the same theory. *The Maltese Double Cross* was later aired on Channel 4 in 1995, with the support of Dr Jim Swire of PA 103 victim support group UK Families Flight 103, Labour MP Tam Dalyell and Tory MP Sir Teddy Taylor. It was quite something, one journalist wrote, when "a right-wing Tory MP openly accuses his own government and the USA of conspiring to cover up the truth".

The FBI, meanwhile, attacked the film's objectivity, saying that it was part-financed with Libyan money and that key witnesses were "known fabricators", some being criminals indicted by the US government for fraud and drug-dealing. This, however, touched on an interesting point.

Syria, the CIA and a case of drugs

Among the debris scattered across the moors, searchers found $500,000 in cash and a case of cannabis and heroin. These were taken away by an American helicopter-borne troupe of CIA agents, who also removed an unidentified body. One tagged body was moved from one site to another; another body disappeared altogether.

The CIA had arrived at Lockerbie within just two hours of the crash, looking for the members of a CIA team who had been on the flight after working in Beirut to secure the release of US hostages held in that war-torn city. British soldiers had found a map locating two such hostages, and the map, together with other papers, was being carried by US Army Special Forces Major Charles McKee. CIA officers took the papers, along with McKee's suitcase, but their "disregard for the rules" of investigation meant that the case had to be returned.

Aviv's investigation

The possible significance of this was brought out by an investigation that Pan Am commissioned from Juval Aviv, a former agent of the Israeli secret service organization Mossad (see p.145). This suggested that "rogue" CIA agents had allowed a Syrian arms dealer to smuggle heroin into the US on PA 103, in exchange for the release of US hostages in Beirut. McKee's team were couriering the drugs, but the drugs were switched for a bomb during a stopover in Frankfurt – not Malta – a bomb meant specifically to take out McKee's team. As Al Jazeera reported years later, Aviv was able to find this out because Mossad had helped to set up the Syria-drugs-CIA triangle.

The Syrian drugs link in Aviv's report was leaked to the press via an Ohio congressman, and was given a further twist in a *Time* magazine piece in April 1992, "The Untold Story Of Pan Am 103", published after the indictment of the Libyans. *Time* had McKee's team coming off not as dirty-dealing spooks but as good guys, going to expose the Syrian drug trafficker-rogue CIA unit link and being killed by the PFLP-GC for their pains. The magazine suggested that McKee's team weren't from the CIA but the DIA (Defense Intelligence Agency), and that the CIA blew up the DIA before the DIA could blow the CIA's operation.

An alternative (and unsourced) Internet theory explaining the presence of drugs on PA 103 is that the Pan Am Frankfurt-US flights were a regular drug trafficking route for a London-based criminal gang enjoying high-level protection from US and UK intelligence. The Samsonite suitcases were said to be marked with symbols to assist their identification and passage by baggage handlers at airports. An investigation into this link to PA 103 by British authorities was then, supposedly, covered up.

Was it ... President Bush?

In *Cover-up Of Convenience – The Hidden Scandal Of Lockerbie*, published in 2002, journalists John Ashton and Ian Ferguson also back the theory of an Iranian revenge attack, suggesting that the Syria-backed, Germany-based PFLP-GC group was brought in to carry out the bombing because of its experience in this area. The Libyans were blamed later out of geopolitical expediency. They imply, however, that it wasn't just the CIA who would have been embarrassed by the exposure of the Syria-drugs-CIA ring.

In 1986, the Iran-Contra arms-drugs-hostages scandal had nearly sunk President Reagan and his vice president, ex-CIA director George H.W. Bush.

Bush survived Iran-Contra to be elected president in 1988, just weeks before Lockerbie. How desperate would he and his old agency have been to avoid another humiliating exposure? Enough to blow up an airliner? Predictably, the CIA denounced the Syria-drugs-CIA explanation as "rubbish", and have dismissed subsequent variations on it as "conspiracy theories". As far as is known, there has been no State Department or Senate investigation into the allegations.

Some warnings were heeded, others not

In 1989, a US State Department ambassador told a Senate subcommittee that if there had been any foreknowledge of an attack, the Beirut team would not have taken the flight. Yet despite the fact that many Americans were going home for Christmas at the time, the ill-fated PA 103 flight was only two-thirds full. This was because, victims' relatives alleged, many State Department employees had cancelled their reservations and flown on other airlines.

An anonymous call had been made to Helsinki's US embassy on December 5, 1988, warning that within two weeks an American airliner from Frankfurt to New York would be bombed. The State Department and the UK government said that at the time, the warning had been considered to be a hoax. A researcher for a House Transportation subcommittee, however, found that the State Department hadn't considered the warning to be a "hoax" until *after* Lockerbie, and that it had been circulated to numerous US agencies and embassies, suggesting a retrospective cover-up.

The researcher, Sheila Hershow, and her boss were later fired, but her investigation also unearthed a 1986 report by security consultants KPI Inc, stating that Pan Am's luggage and passenger security were "vulnerable to most forms of terrorist attack".

This vulnerability had not been addressed, despite a battery of Federal Aviation Administration bulletins from November and December 1988, which relayed vague concerns about hijackings and possible terrorism after the West German police raids on PFLP-GC cells. As one State Department official said: "What sort of security officer is not going to phone his wife and say 'take the kids off the flight' or phone his buddies and pass on the warning to them?"

Somehow, the warnings that so many US government employees seemed to act upon didn't translate into saving PA 103 from being bombed. The presence of the McKee team on the plane may have been an uncanny coincidence that then exposed other nefarious CIA dealings, or the plane may have been deliberately targeted by the CIA, which would mean that CIA agents had the reach and the PFLP-GC contacts to get that exact flight bombed. As for blaming Libya, it's said that the policy of pre-arranging groups to blame for heinous deeds was developed in the early 1980s by the CIA's Vince Cannistraro, working in tandem with Iran-Contra architect Oliver North. Hatching such a conspiracy is one thing, however: actively pursuing it over more than a decade is another matter.

A P2 connection?

Some parts of the Italian press linked the bombing to the quasi-Masonic group P2 (see p.125), claiming that it had teamed up with the CIA in an extended effort to frame Libya and make Qaddafi pay compensation for seized Italian assets in the country (Qaddafi had thrown the Italians out of Libya – once an Italian colony – in the 1970s).

Another Internet rumour is that the oil-rich Libyans were blamed and had sanctions imposed on them to force them to pay compensation far in excess of the paltry $75,000 per person Pan Am would otherwise have paid (had the airline not gone bust). The only people to benefit from such a scheme, however, would have been the victims' relatives – hardly the most likely candidates for a conspiracy.

The aftermath

It's odd that the Libyans would endure ten years of economically painful sanctions, then give up the suspects and pay a $2.7 billion fine, yet *still* protest their innocence. Obviously, they were acting out of self-interest in taking the "reward" of economic and diplomatic rehabilitation in return for accepting responsibility for Lockerbie, but having done so, you might think that they would prefer not to risk rocking the diplomatic boat by reviving the controversy.

But what a difference an hour makes. Had Pan Am flight 103 taken off on time, the bomb aboard would have detonated over the Atlantic, sending the plane and all its evidence irretrievably to the bottom of the sea. Instead, it blew up over land, and so began a terrible, twisted tale involving Washington, Tripoli, Frankfurt, Beirut, Damascus and the hitherto obscure Scottish town of Lockerbie.

From another viewpoint, the passing of over a decade since the bombing has seen some remarkable changes, and yet also a sense of things staying the same. At the time, the bombing of PA 103 sealed the notoriety of Colonel Qaddafi's Libya as the world's worst terrorist state, and President George H.W. Bush stood allied with President Hafez al-Assad of Syria. In the new millennium, Qaddafi is still in charge of Libya, but now the country is treated like an international paragon, enjoying close diplomatic ties and an influx of Western investment, led by the US, the UK and Italy. Now it's Syria, under Hafez's son Bashar al-Assad, and Iran that are regarded by the US (under George W. Bush) as the world's top terrorist states.

Books

David Johnston Lockerbie: The Tragedy Of Flight 103. An early, slightly salacious account of the then ongoing investigation and its controversies, with suspicion pointing nowhere near Libya. For a denser read, see Stephen Amerson and Brian Duffy's *The Fall Of Pan Am 103*. Then move on a decade with John Ashton and Ian Ferguson's *Cover-up Of Convenience: The Hidden Scandal Of Lockerbie*, to see how the story has changed.

TWA 800

On the evening of July 17, 1996, TWA Flight 800 left New York's JFK airport for Paris, carrying 212 passengers and 18 crew. About twelve minutes after take-off, at around 13,000 feet, a catastrophic event caused the Boeing 747 to disintegrate and explode over the northern Atlantic. The blazing bulk smashed into the ocean twenty miles southeast of Long Island, at about 8.30pm. Debris and bodies showered the dark, cold water over three miles. There were no survivors.

Three agencies and four years

In the course of several months, over ninety percent of the shattered aircraft's remains were recovered and reconstructed in a hangar at Calverton, Virginia. Separate investigations by the FBI, Federal Aviation Authority (FAA) and the National Transportation Safety Board (NTSB), led to several pronouncements that some kind of electrical short circuit caused a fire and explosion in the aircraft's central fuel tank, holing the 25-year-old 747 beneath seat rows 17 to 28. Half a minute later, the tank blew up and destroyed the plane. In August 2000, the NTSB's open hearing delivered what it considered the most likely, but still unconfirmed, conclusion: "The 230 men, women and children on board TWA 800 lost their lives not as a result of a bomb or a missile or some other nefarious act but as a result of a tragic accident."

Or was it was a missile?

That same month, however, the two hundred-strong TWA 800 Eyewitness Alliance group ran a full-page ad in the *Washington Times*: "We the eye-witnesses, know that missiles were involved ... for some reason our government has lied and tried to discredit all of us to keep that question from being addressed", it declared, adding that the FBI, CIA and NTSB were involved in a cover-up. According to the FBI, these were mostly "credible" witnesses, who had seen a "missile" or "streak of light" heading towards TWA 800. Evidence in favour of the theory included a photo from the night, which showed something bright heading skyward, and the fact that luggage from the plane was strewn across the ocean earlier on its flight path than the main explosion could have thrown it – so something must have made a hole big enough for suitcases to be sucked through. What's more, the very first reports of the crash, from the Pentagon no less, suggested a missile. And only four days later, the *Jerusalem Post* reported speculation from French military defence experts that if a mis-

sile was responsible for TWA 800's doom, it could only have been a US military missile, adding "it is unlikely that the US army will admit it".

The NTSB explicitly attempted to rebut the notion that TWA 800 was shot down by a US Navy missile. Theorists charge that neither the Navy nor the government could admit that a missile was behind the crash without risking massive public wrath. Likely consequences would include curbs on the military's right to carry out exercises wherever they wanted, the cancellation of an expensive new missile system and a mountain of lawsuits.

In August 1996, retired United Airlines pilot and former crash investigator Richard Russell wrote a memo in which he suggested, apparently on the basis of information from a friend who had attended a high-level briefing on the crash, that "friendly fire" had downed the 747. As he later told the *New York Times*, he emailed the memo to some friends, most-

TWA 800: reconstruction of the fuselage

ly air accident investigators like himself The problem was that Russell's memo subsequently found its way on to the Internet, gaining international attention in November 1996, when it was cited as a crucial piece of evidence for the Navy missile theory by former White House press secretary and ABC News correspondent Pierre Salinger.

Salinger claimed that a French intelligence source with good US official contacts had told him that TWA 800 *had* been accidentally shot down by a US Navy missile, and had given him a document describing what had happened. Unbeknown to Salinger, however, this turned out to be Russell's memo, rather than an official report, and when both men refused to reveal their sources, Salinger's allegations lost credibility. The fact that Russell's memo had previously been posted on the Internet (which, it was widely believed, was where Salinger had found it) even led to the christening of the "Pierre Salinger syndrome", defined as the tendency to believe that everything published on the Internet is true.

Salinger, however, returned in March 1997 with radar images and hearsay reports of Navy personnel lamenting their roles in the shoot-down. Claiming that Russian satellites had filmed the incident, he cited a secret 1996 Presidential commission as reporting that missiles had destroyed 26 planes since 1978, killing six hundred people (a vital report even without the context of TWA 800's destruction, but no other news channel has reported on it and its existence hasn't been corroborated). The NTSB responded that claims of "some massive government cover-up" were "irresponsible"; the FBI said that no radar images showed any missiles; the Pentagon called Salinger's work "bunkum". CNN took it upon itself to say that Salinger's report was "littered with errors and misinformation ... and lacked legitimate attributions". Nonetheless, both Salinger *and* Russell stand by their charges.

What wasn't denied was that huge chunks of the Atlantic Ocean were zoned off for US military exercises, and that the multi-billion dollar AEGIS missile system was being tested in zone W-105, perilously close to TWA 800's flight-path. Salinger argued that an unarmed Stinger missile had been launched to hit a target drone, but instead locked on to a far bigger target – TWA 800. The Stinger lanced through the 747, clipping the central fuel tank and starting the fire that led to the fatal explosion.

That same story appeared weeks later in journalist James Sanders' *The Downing Of Flight TWA 800*. The book contained photos showing a reddish-brown crust, the colour and chemical composition of missile fuel, on seat-foam from rows 17, 18 and 19, where a missile had supposedly impacted. According to Sanders, that earned his publishers a subpoena from the FBI. He claimed that the FBI had scoured Calverton and the ocean floor during the winter of 1996 for all missile parts, and impounded FAA radar tapes showing what the FAA called an "unexplained blip" around TWA 800; one FAA source said that there was a "remote possibility" that the blip was a missile. The NTSB, having been initially prevented from seeing the radar tapes, later rejected this possibility – but didn't say what the blip was either.

Different investigations drew different conclusions. Although a January 1997 report by the BATF supported the idea that a short-circuit was responsible, the FBI said in June that a missile, bomb or mechanical problem were still possible causes, while the NTSB couldn't rule out that a "projectile" had struck TWA 800, without elaborating on what kind of projectile knocks down jumbo jets at ten thousand feet. CBS News speculated that the "streak of light" was flaming jet fuel, while the FBI and CIA said that it was probably the 747 breaking up. When the FBI finally closed its sixteen-month probe, it found "no evidence" of any criminal act and endorsed the short-circuit theory. But FBI agents told a 1999 Senate subcommittee that the investigation was "sloppy" and "inept".

Outside experts also got involved. Ex-US Navy commander and crash investigator William

Donaldson scorned the NTSB's findings and presented the House Aviation subcommittee in 1998–99 with evidence supporting the Stinger-missile theory. The subcommittee, however, agreed with the NTSB. The conclusions drawn by the NTSB and FAA led them to recommend design changes to fuel tanks, wiring and associated hardware, inspection and maintenance. Donaldson's group and the eyewitnesses continue to press their case from the sidelines.

Iraq

During the build-up to the 2003 Iraq war, the destruction of TWA 800 was reinterpreted to make a link between Iraq and 9/11. In *Study of Revenge: Saddam Hussein's Unfinished War Against America*, Laurie Mylroie wrote that on July 16, 1996, Iraq's terrorist front group the Islamic Change Movement (ICM) said that it would "deliver the ultimate response" to US threats. The next day, the anniversary of Saddam Hussein's 1969 Ba'athist party coup, Saddam railed against the US and sanctions, while on July 18, the ICM claimed responsibility for "the plane attack of yesterday".

Also on July 17, alleged Iraqi agent Ramzi Yousef was tried in New York for plotting to blow up US airliners over the Pacific in "Operation Bojinka", which involved using airplanes filled with TNT as flying bombs. Colonel Robert Patterson wrote in *Dereliction Of Duty* that the Navy accidentally shot down TWA 800 when trying to hit such a flying bomb flying ahead of it. Author Jack Cashill also put Baghdad behind TWA 800 in *First Strike: TWA Flight 800 And The Attack On America*, co-authored by James Sanders, which gave Sanders' pet subject an updated, newly profitable spin while somewhat undermining his earlier work. Despite all the White House's dubious claims to justify the invasion of Iraq, however, it never suggested that Saddam had been involved in the downing of TWA 800.

Kerry vs Gore

Jack Cashill also contrived another theory in the aftermath of 9/11. After the September attacks, some politicians speculated that terrorists had also destroyed TWA 800. Senator John Kerry did so on *Larry King Live* and MSNBC's *Hardball*, without identifying who the "terrorists" might have been or how they might have brought the plane down. Meanwhile, certain newspapers were alleging that Vice President Al Gore had failed to implement the recommendations of his 1996 commission on airline and airport safety, because the costs to the aviation industry's big players would have "forced" them to curb donations to the Democratic party. The basic charge was that Gore's corruption and/or negligence had left the airports unguarded, and thus made 9/11 possible.

Gore was Kerry's only serious opponent for the 2004 Democratic presidential nomination. Kerry's public speculation about possible terrorist involvement in the downing of TWA 800, claimed Cashill, was an oblique way of pointing the finger at Gore for his alleged failure to implement the airline safety commission's recommendations – an allegation that, given sufficient coverage, could scupper Gore's nomination bid. "Just by hinting that he knows the story," Cashill suggested, "Kerry may be able to put Gore out of the race even before he gets in." Gore, who had won more votes in 2000 than any previous Democrat, dropped out of the race before the primaries even began. By August 2004, the Democrats had chosen John Kerry.

Montauk? Who said anything about Montauk?

In 2000, *The New York Review of Books* reported speculation that TWA 800 was brought down by an electromagnetic radiation beam, possibly fired from the top-secret experimental base at Montauk, Long Island (see p.284). In itself, there was no compelling reason to take the theory seriously, but the same article made connections that appeared to link TWA 800 with two later plane disasters, SwissAir 111 and EgyptAir 990.

A costly cover-up?

Whatever the truth, the NTSB, FAA and Senate all publicly concluded that the TWA 800 disaster was an accident. If they did indeed conspire to cover up the accidental shooting-down of TWA 800, it was an extraordinarily elaborate deception, which led to reams of detailed and costly recommendations to change aircraft design and maintenance procedures

– a hell of a lot of work to make the official explanation seem more plausible. That said, the FAA and NTSB did in fact drop their recommendations in 2001, saying that they were "too expensive" for dealing with "too remote" risks...

While victims' families and independent investigators continue their quest for information, no further government inquiry is underway and no one has sought to curb the military's rights to exercise as it sees fit. It's ironic that, according to the missile theory, a significant part of the danger that threatens civilian aircraft in US skies derives from the activities of the massive forces charged with their protection. Changing an aircraft's design, or tripling the guard at airports, does nothing to stop a missile accidentally fired by your own side.

SOURCES

Books

Laurie Mylroie Study of Revenge: Saddam Hussein's Unfinished War Against America (2001). An interesting work, if only for how much emphasis it places on Saddam Hussein as the architect of most (if not all) terrorist attacks on the US. Mylroie, whose book was published in 2000, chastises the Clinton administration for focussing too much on the likes of Osama bin Laden and other Muslim extremists, and ignoring an over-arching terrorist network called Al Qaeda.

James Sanders The Downing Of Flight 800 (1997).A rapid account of the unfolding controversy over TWA 800

and the conflicting stories, by a journalist whose significant scoops outweigh the somewhat personalized tone. In the later *Altered Evidence*, Sanders charged that his investigations led to him and his wife being framed by the US government. Sanders also contributed to Jack Cashill's *First Strike: TWA Flight 800* and *The Attack On America*.

Websites

ⓦaviation-safety.net/specials/twa800 A collation of various official reports.

ⓦhttp://users.erols.com/igoddard/TWA800/ Although he was later misleadingly reported as having retracted his "friendly fire" theory, seasoned conspiracy theorist Ian

Goddard marshalled an impressive array of eyewitness, circumstantial and physical evidence to support his case, scrupulously documented here.

ⓦwww.twa800.com The website of the late William Donaldson, whose colleagues and supporters are continuing to investigate and press their case that TWA 800 was shot down.

ⓦwww.worldnetdaily.com/news/article. asp?ARTICLE_ID=24734 Jack Cashill's interpretation of why Kerry was beating the terrorist drum, significant in so far as it suggests that Kerry's aim was to obtain political benefit from a totally unsubstantiated theory.

Roswell and Majestic-12

On June 24, 1947, a pilot called Kenneth Arnold was flying over Washington State's Cascade Mountains when he saw what he later described as bat-winged craft, looking like "saucers skipping over water". Unfazed by the odd choice of image (since when did saucers skip about on water?), the news media all over the US seized on Arnold's report. The ground had been well prepared by similar stories in science fiction of the 1930s and early 1940s. By the first week of July 1947, "flying saucers" were on everyone's minds.

The Roswell incident

On July 8 that year, Lieutenant Walter G. Haut, the Public Information Officer at Roswell air base, in Chaves County, New Mexico, told local press that the actual remains of just such a flying saucer, or "disc" as he described it, had been found by local rancher Mack Brazel the previous week. The press release may have been intended as a joke, or, as some claim, as a crude cover story for some military research or nuclear accident. Many UFOlogists believe, however, that the report was genuine. Whichever, it was quickly retracted in a second press release issued the following day, and the debris was dismissed as the remnants of a weather balloon.

Although that explanation satisfied most people, from September 1947 onwards the Air Force began to secretly collate data regarding UFO reports as part of what later became known as "Project Blue Book". Roswell itself was largely remembered only by UFO folklorists. In 1978, how-

ever, UFO researchers Stanton T. Friedman and William L. Moore announced that a certain Major Jesse A. Marcel, an intelligence officer who had been based at Roswell in 1947, maintained that some materials he had discovered at Roswell were very strange, like indestructible aluminium foil. "I still don't know what it was", Marcel recalled. "It could not have been part of an aircraft, [or] any kind of weather balloon or experimental balloon". Marcel added that he'd seen rockets before, and "it definitely was not part of an aircraft or missile or rocket".

Marcel also claimed that he had been sent to show samples of debris to General Ramey, the commanding officer of the Eighth Air Force. He spread out the material on Ramey's desk, then went with him to the map room to talk the general through the site location. When they returned, the debris was gone, and pieces of a weather balloon had mysteriously taken its place. At this point, press officers took the famous photo of Marcel with his supposed findings.

As discussion of the "Roswell Incident" gathered pace once more during the 1970s and 1980s, other witnesses came forward. Most notably, a mortician who had worked at a funeral home near Roswell, Glenn Dennis, claimed that he had been called up by airfield technicians who wanted child-sized coffins and advice on how to stop bodies putrefying. On visiting the base, he'd seen strange engravings on some bits of wreckage before being threatened by military police and escorted off the base. A nurse he met – who has never been traced – described an autopsy she had witnessed being performed on horrific-smelling alien corpses that looked distressingly like "100-year-old Chinese".

Area 51 and alien technology

Major Marcel's story, more or less backed up by various "eyewitness" memories like those of Glenn Dennis, established the basic Roswell story – that an alien craft had crash-landed and that there had been a military cover-up. Speculations as to exactly what the military knew remained just that until 1989, when a certain Bob Lazar revealed on Las Vegas local television that he had worked at the notorious Lake Groom military installation in Nevada, better known to conspiracists as "Area 51". As a physicist from the elite Massachusetts Institute of Technology (MIT), Lazar said he had been employed to "reverse engineer" extraterrestrial spacecraft, ie to work out the principles of alien science by examining their technology. One of the spacecraft he studied – and, yes, there were many – was the "disc" found at Roswell.

There are many, many holes in Lazar's story. For a start, only a fairly naïve non-physicist would take him on his own account. Scientifically speaking, tales of his discovery of "Gravity B" – a force created by manipulation of the nuclear force-field of a new element called "ununpentium" – ring very hollow. And there is no record of Lazar studying physics at MIT (or anywhere else, for that matter). Lazar had the answer to that, of course: his name was scrubbed from the university rolls as part of a government conspiracy to discredit him. The fact that the base at Groom Lake wasn't used between World War II and 1955 (when it was seemingly brought back into service for the testing of prototypes of Lockheed's U2 spy plane), was another problem – and in any case, Lazar himself was only born in... 1959. (Of course, the Roswell disc *could* have been stored elsewhere until Lazar was summoned to examine it.)

Despite Lazar's feeble credibility, the concept of a government with access to alien technology was suddenly fully "out there" in both mainstream and UFOlogist media. So too was the idea that "Area 51" was the ultimate secret base, an all-American version of a master criminal's lair. Ultra-right-wing "patriot" organizations were delighted to acquire yet more evidence that the federal government was malignant and manipulative. According to conspiracy lore, "Area 51" rapidly acquired a massive underground facility and elaborate protection systems, ranging from motion sensors that could also "smell" intruders to black "stealth helicopters" – supposedly developed right on site at the base, with the help of reverse-engineered technology. The existence of armed (and private) security guards, at least, was real, as was the new name for the nearby

The boundary of Area 51, Rachel, Nevada (2000)

ALIEN ABDUCTIONS

Do you suffer from dreams about being beamed aboard UFOs? Are you harassed by aliens at night and men in helicopters by day? Do you act impulsively against your will, while suffering memory lapses and horrific flashbacks of alien or Army interrogation? Do you have muscle pains, panic attacks and nosebleeds, or find that streetlights turn off when you walk past them? Have you ever found weird bits of metal in your teeth, nose, ears or deep within your rectal chamber? Do your children look suspiciously non-terrestrial? Then you may be in the same boat (or ship) as up to two million others – nearly all American, if only because the relevant poll was carried out by the US-based Alien Abduction Research Center (AARC) – who claim to have been abducted by aliens.

Alien abduction has formed the theme of many an X Files episode, as well as the hit series Taken and The 4400. In the real world, abductees can get help and support via endless conventions, Internet chatrooms, and even the cable TV show UFO-AZ. The AARC publishes its own handbook – Alien Abduction: Can It Happen To You? – to help those keen to avoid unpleasant extraterrestrial kidnappings. Dr

David M. Jacobs has made alien abductions his life work for more than forty years, writing books such as The UFO Controversy In America, Secret Life: Firsthand Accounts Of UFO Abductions, and conducting almost nine hundred hypnotic regressions with abductees since 1986. He is not, he earnestly assures us on his website, a crazy.

Gail Seymour, a pioneer of interstellar medicine on the UFOlogy and holistic healing circuits, advertises that she can remove and de-activate alien implants, be they of Grey, Zeta or Reptilian origin. (Greys, we're told, are into abduction and observation, whereas Reptilians like rape and torture. Both engage in vivisecting animals and humans and use earth women to breed their offspring.)

So what kind of implant does Seymour mean? According to the UFO Folklore Center, one model of alien implant, first identified in the late 1950s, is a "stimoceiver," which receives and transmits electronic signals via FM radio. UFO Magazine investigated one such device in 1997, found by a British man, James Basil. After a series of problems including encountering weird humanoids in his neighbourhood, being

bothered aboard spaceships, and seeing "strange lights" outside his home, Basil claimed that aliens had "implanted a small object in his mouth". The problem, as the author pointed out, is that such implants often disappear, perhaps getting lost in the carpet, while nasal "implants" often turn out to be "of earthly biological origin" – bogies, to you or me. So it was with some excitement that Basil's dullish grey implant, suspected of being "miniaturized alien technology", was taken to the author's university colleagues for analysis. Scanned by a stereo light microscope, then an electron microscope, then an Energy Dispersive X-ray Microanalysis, the implant proved to be a mysterious mix of calcium, silicon, mercury, tin and silver – a tooth filling.

It remains unclear who exactly is behind the alleged abduction plots. Abductees' piecemeal recollections of being aboard spaceships are often interspersed with interrogations by earthlings in Army uniforms or black suits (the so-called "Men in Black" – see p.114). But are these earthling interrogators trying to find out what the abductees saw? Or are they trying to delete their memories, to cover up the awful truth of their collusion with aliens, but using meth-

ods that don't quite work? Worse still, are abductees' memories of aliens in fact fake memories, implanted to cover up whatever super-secret project the abductee may have stumbled across, and made deliberately so ridiculous that the abductees will seem crazy to the world at large?

In fact, of course, delusions of alien abduction, and suspicions that anything and everything may be an instrument of mind-control sound like classic symptoms of paranoia. Many victims find their hallucinations are actively entertained and supported, and provide an entrée into a world of like-minded people. Their extremes of loneliness and misery may only seem explicable in terms of a great terrestrial or extra-terrestrial conspiracy to oversee their lives, and imagined attention from aliens seems preferable to the pain of remaining anonymous even to their closest neighbours. In that sense, tales of implants and microwaves are a way to avoid responsibility on a chronic scale. Thus one of Seymour's patients told her of a "long string of motorcycle and automobile accidents" over twenty years that he put down to an alien implant – and not due to his lack of earthly driving skills.

State Highway 375 – it was grandly entitled "The Extraterrestrial Highway" by a Nevada state government eager to cash in on the burgeoning UFO-tourist market.

The Roswell autopsy film

Possibly even less credible than Bob Lazar's "Area 51" story was the infamous film that surfaced in early 1995, purporting to be original grainy footage from an autopsy conducted on the bodies of the Roswell aliens. Even before the film was aired (on the Fox network), things didn't look good. No "witness" had ever mentioned a film of the autopsy before, and the British company promoting it had previously handled Disney movies. When Ray Santilli's film was aired in August 1995, the quality was found to be atrocious – both cinematically and surgically. Film experts thought it strange that the close-ups of the aliens' organs were uniformly out of focus, while medical specialists found the techniques of the "doctors" amusingly amateurish. It was clearly a hoax.

Official conclusions

Such was the public pressure for information that in September 1994 the US Air Force finally published an official report into the Roswell incident. It concluded that the famous debris had indeed come from a balloon, part of a research project codenamed MOGUL, which had used high-altitude balloons to monitor atomic tests in the desert.

Following widespread complaints that witness statements had been swept under the carpet, a second report was issued in 1997. It concluded that "these witnesses are mistaken about when the events they saw occurred, and they are also seriously mistaken about details of the events". Reports of alien bodies were blamed on crash-test dummies recovered from the balloon, and Glenn Dennis's tale

explained away as a confusion of two separate and later events: a burning Air Force tanker incident from 1956, and an accident involving a manned balloon from 1959.

The US government had always denied the very existence of "Area 51", but after satellite pictures were published on the Internet in 2003, Assistant Secretary of Defense Kenneth H. Baconfelt was forced to respond. Asked what he could say about what went on at the facility, he replied "Darn little", adding: "We have a right, as a sovereign nation – in fact, a responsibility to the citizens of the United States – to develop various weapons from time to time. Sometimes these weapons are developed in classified locations." Probed further, he clarified: "I think I can say beyond a shadow of a doubt that we have no classified program that relies on aliens from outer space."

Majestic-12 and the Aviary

In 1984, photographs of a supposed "briefing paper" prepared for President Eisenhower on November 18, 1952 were mailed to a producer of television documentaries called Jaime Shandera. The paper discussed the Roswell incident, letting slip that "news reporters were given the effective cover story that the object had been a misguided weather research balloon." The paper also confirmed that alien bodies had been found, calling them "Extraterrestrial Biological Entities" or EBEs for short, and noting that "although these creatures are human-like in appearance, the biological and evolutionary processes responsible for their development has apparently been quite different from those observed or postulated in Homo sapiens." Without going into any detail, it speculated that Mars was a possible origin for the Roswell spacecraft, "although some scientists, most notably Dr Menzel, consider it more likely that we are dealing with beings from another solar system entirely".

An attached memo from Harry S. Truman agreed that the "Majestic-12" group would be established to preside over the whole affair, and a higher-than-top-secret security classification "MAJIC EYES ONLY" would apply to all relevant documents. Meanwhile, Shandera and his research partner, UFO writer Bill Moore, were apparently receiving communications from disgruntled sources in the military and CIA who wanted to expose the "shadow government" of "Majestic-12" and publicize the truth about alien encounters such as Roswell. To protect their sources' identities, Moore and Shandera gave them bird names such as "Falcon" and "Condor", slowly building up an entire aviary of contacts. They dubbed their network "the Aviary".

The "MJ-12" documents were finally published by UFO writer Stanton Friedman in 1986. For credulous conspiracists, this was the perfect proof of the theory that many had long cherished: that the government knew much more than it was letting on. Unfortunately, the "briefing paper" was an obvious fraud. Aside from its simplistic content, it was riddled with anachronisms, notably the words "media" and "impacted", which only came into use in the 1950s. It also failed to follow the standard formulas for editorial style – the format for giving dates and so on – and was even stamped with the "Top Secret Restricted Information" security classification, which was only introduced under President Nixon. Sceptics also alleged that Bill Moore had suggested to colleagues right back in 1982 that fake UFO documents might be published to help flush out military sources who hadn't yet revealed their secrets; in the same year, Moore had even worked on a novel he called *MAJIK-12*.

Aliens, abductions and arms

The Air Force's officially debunking report(s) and the exposure of both "Majestic-12" and the "Roswell" film only served to fuel further speculation. The presupposition is that these are all part of a massive cover-up, a conspiracy to dupe the world into believing that there has been no alien contact. Meanwhile, the government – in hock to the military-industrial complex (see p.112), obviously – reverse-engineers its way to superior military technology, while failing to make known the more peaceful technological benefits of alien science.

Some suggest that since Roswell the government has actually made contact with live aliens. The spate of abduction claims is seen as further evidence of government-alien collusion, trading American citizens for ever more futuristic weapons. Which is all a long way from the bits of tinfoil and rubber found by Mack Brazel. As he told the Roswell *Daily Record* in the immediate aftermath of the incident, "I am sure what I found was not any weather observation balloon. But if I find anything else besides a bomb they are going to have a hard time getting me to say anything about it."

SOURCES

Books

Charles Berlitz and William L. Moore The Roswell Incident (1991). The original book that set the whole Roswell research circus in motion; these are true believers, in full rumour-chasing cry.

Philip J. Corso with William J. Birnes The Day After Roswell (1997). Corso retired from the US Army as a Lieutenant Colonel in 1963, after working in the "Foreign Technology Division" of the Pentagon's R&D wing. His analysis of the alien debris from the Roswell crash apparently allowed the army to develop everything from Kevlar and Stealth technology to SDI, and to win not just the Cold War but the war against invading aliens too. Full of holes but a bestseller nonetheless.

Stanton T. Friedman Top Secret / Majic: The Story of Operation Majestic-12 And The United States Government's UFO Cover-up (1997). Long-term UFOlogist "exposes" half a century of government cover-ups, and the appalling "truth" behind Majestic-12.

Kal K. Korff The Roswell UFO Crash: What They Don't Want You To Know

(2000). "They", for once, refers not to conspirators, but to the Roswell conspiracy theorists – this is a detailed, well-researched debunking. Lots on the background of high-altitude balloon research. Widely decried as government disinformation, of course – and what about the author's initials?

James McAndrew The Roswell Report: Case Closed (1998). The more detailed "second report", as published by the United States Air Force. Includes lots of stories of heroic experimentation in the early days of USAF research.

Charles B. Moore, Benson Saler and Charles A. Ziegler UFO Crash At Roswell: The Genesis Of A Modern Myth (1997). The main authors are cultural anthropologists, and as such they treat the Roswell Incident as folklore, examining its relation to mythology and religion – and observing how the narrative only becomes clearer and more detailed as time passes. Moore, a physics professor who actually worked on Project Mogul, adds a chapter on the scientific research of the period.

Karl T. Pflock Roswell: Inconvenient Facts And The Will To Believe (2001). A UFO researcher finds his own "will to believe" collapsing in the face of the evidence.

Kevin D. Randle The Roswell Encyclopedia (2000). Four hundred pages of everything you could ever want to know about Roswell. And more.

Websites

ⓦ **www.abduct.com/news/n46.htm** The photo of Jesse Marcel with the debris.

ⓦ **www.bluebookarchive.org/** Over ten thousand pages online so far, and counting…

ⓦ **www.gl.iit.edu/wadc/history/Roswell/ Report/index.html** Links to downloadable pdf version of the USAF's Roswell reports.

ⓦ **ww.majesticdocuments.com** Hundreds of pdf files of "Majestic" documents, "evidence that we are not alone". Includes assessments of the documents' authenticity – usually positive.

ⓦ **www.mufor.org/majestic.html** Facimiles of the "original" Majestic briefing for Eisenhower.

ⓦ **www.truthseekeratroswell.com** Includes lots of archive photos of key players etc.

ⓦ **www.ufoevidence.org /topics/Roswell. htm** "In-depth, quality and scientific research on the UFO phenomenon", ie lots of pro-UFO evidence, including links to scores of Roswell articles and "Majestic" documents.

The Apollo moon landing

On July 20, 1969, astronaut Neil Armstrong stepped onto the moon and proclaimed: "That's one small step for man, one giant leap for mankind." Minutes later, Edwin "Buzz" Aldrin joined him on the surface, while Michael Collins orbited overhead in the Apollo 11 command module.

The Apollo landing was the culmination of President Kennedy's vow to "have men on the moon by the end of this decade", and had required a work force of over 400,000 people and a budget of $30 billion. Kennedy made his pledge at a time when the US was being thrashed in the so-called "space race" by the USSR. The Soviets had been the first to get satellites into space; live animals into space;

live animals back from space; a man into space; a woman into space; and finally complete a multi-crew mission. However, the Americans came back with Apollo, launching seven manned flights to the moon by 1972 – although Apollo 13 failed to land, due to equipment malfunction. As Armstrong unfurled a billowing Stars and Stripes flag, the watching world was agog.

But to some observers, the notion that three men could fly a quarter of a million miles to the moon and back without a hitch seemed to be inconceivable. Armstrong himself only believed that there was only a fifty percent chance that the moon landing would go as planned. And so the doubts crept in: none of the surface photos from the moon shows any stars in the sky, when there should have been a dazzling sea of them over the atmosphere-less planet. How come the lander module's thrusters didn't blast out a large crater on landing? And how come that Stars and Stripes flag was waving, when surely there's no wind on the moon?

A hoax of astronomical proportions

Precisely where the idea that the moon landings had been faked came from, is unclear. However, it was clearly circulating around Hollywood at the time of Apollo; thus James Bond stumbles across a fake moon-landing set in *Diamonds Are Forever*, released in 1971.

As rumours circulated, former aerospace writer Bill Kaysing, who worked for an Apollo engine manufacturer, was asked to write a satire on the

Lights, camera, Apollo II

moon-hoax theories. His 1976 book, presented as a work of non-fiction, *We Never Went To The Moon: America's Thirty Billion Dollar Swindle!* described how NASA had defrauded the world with its Apollo Simulation Project.

In collaboration with the Defense Intelligence Agency, the landings were supposedly filmed in a vast mock-up of the lunar surface in the empty Nevada desert, in the region where the Atomic Energy Commission carried out atomic tests. On launch day, an empty Saturn V rocket took off from Florida, and then fell back into the sea. Meanwhile, the Apollo crew interspersed lunar filming with parties in Mob casinos in Las Vegas, where they gorged on showgirls, booze and roulette. They also attended "guilt therapy" sessions to cope with lying to everyone on the planet. As the Apollo craft supposedly returned to Earth, the astronauts were put in a space pod, pushed out of a cargo plane into the ocean, and hailed as heroes.

By Kaysing's account, astronaut Gus Grissom had been about to expose the whole Apollo programme as a charade in 1967 when he was killed with two others in a mysterious launch pad fire aboard Apollo 1. Grissom is known to have been aggrieved with NASA because it held him responsible for "sinking" his Mercury spacecraft on splashdown, and he therefore received little of the acclaim he felt was his due. Kaysing later contended that the Challenger space shuttle was blown up in 1986 to silence the squealers aboard. The reason why Apollo 13 "failed" – after all, why have a hoax fail? – was to revive public interest, and with it future funding.

It's debatable whether or not Kaysing lost the plot in writing his "satire". As proof that his own publishers were in cahoots with NASA to suppress the book, he submitted a letter from his editor saying that the manuscript wasn't written well enough for publication – but both book and letter were published. "Evidence" for the astronauts being in girlie bars included a full-page spread of an exotic dancer. In 1997 he also tried to sue astronaut Jim Lovell for

calling him "wacky", but the case was thrown out. However, his book may in part have inspired the 1978 film *Capricorn One*, which recasts the theory to apply it to a doomed Mars mission, which leads to a costly and murderous hoax lasting several months.

Fox versus Plait

Bill Kaysing resurfaced in 2001 on Fox TV's *Conspiracy Theory: Did We Land On The Moon?*, hosted by *X Files* actor Mitch Pileggi. Kaysing asserted that NASA was technically incapable of reaching the moon, but the race with the USSR forced them to fake the whole thing at "Area 51" in Nevada. The programme certainly scored an own goal by alleging that the moon-landing filmmakers borrowed film special-effects technology from the film *Capricorn One*, which was made much later. But this was offset by an interview with Grissom's son Scott and his widow Betty, both of whom concurred with Kaysing's suspicions that the Apollo 1 fire was no accident. They had no proof, but that's what they believed.

NASA responded to the programme with an article by Dr Tony Philips that used "rocks and common sense" to prove that Apollo had reached the moon. The rocks – all 841 pounds of them – were peppered with tiny meteoroid hits and cosmic ray isotopes, which Philips said could neither be found nor simulated on Earth (to which Kaysing replied that they could have been made by anyone with a special kiln). As the subject for a future conspiracy theory, Philips jokily suggested: "Did NASA go to the moon to collect props for a staged moon landing?"

The article also pointed readers towards www.BadAstronomy.com, a NASA-approved website run by Phil Plait, an astronomer for Sonoma State University. Plait rejects the Fox programme's contention that a breeze on set caused the flag to wave. The flag may look as though it's waving, but it's just being jiggled as it's twirled into the ground. Any breeze to make the flag wave would also have blown dust around, of which there's no sign.

Plait goes on to discuss a number of other objections. Why don't the photos show the stars that should be dazzling everyone? And if the sun is the only source of light, and there is no air to scatter that light, then the shadows on the moon should be black, but they're not. In addition, photos show objects on the surface with long shadows that aren't parallel, which they should be if the sun is the only light source. Also, the lunar photos are suspiciously well taken and composed, although the cameras were mounted on the front of the astronauts' spacesuits, with no viewfinder. What's more, in some photos, the black crosshairs on the camera's lens appear to be behind the objects being photographed – an impossible feat, unless the photographs have been faked in some way.

Predictably, Plait can offer an explanation for each of these points. The stars are competing with the brightly-lit grey-white lunar landscape and the visitors dressed in white next to a shiny spacecraft. The rapid exposure time needed for decent photos would not take in the brightest starlight. Equally, the lunar surface and objects are bright enough to reflect light all over the place – you don't need an atmosphere to do that. Perspective and wide-angle lenses make parallel objects appear not to be so. And if there are multiple light sources, where are the multiple shadows? Everything, including taking photos, was rehearsed endlessly, and the photos we're familiar with are the best of thousands taken. And any subject that is bright enough overwhelms the film and the imprint of black crosshairs on it.

So what about the lack of a blast crater under the lander's rocket? There is a crater, it's just very small. On earth, any gas discharge displaces surrounding air, which displaces more air and so on; on the moon, where there's no air, only the dust directly touched by the exhaust gas gets displaced. Another charge the programme made was that the astronauts would only have needed to shift in the cabin to alter the lander's centre of balance and cause it to crash, and that the top half of the lander produced no visible flame from its rocket when it took off from the lunar surface. Plait retorts that the lander's exhaust and booster rockets could move to counter shifting weights, while its fuels, hydrazine and dinitrogen tetroxide, burn with a transparent flame.

When viewed at double speed, according to the Fox programme, film of the astronauts walking and driving looks like earth movements at normal speed. So they would, says Plait, but the film also shows dust thrown up by the lunar rover's wheels travelling in a perfect parabolic arc rather than billowing about, as you'd expect in a vacuum. Surely, the Fox programme said, radiation in the van Allen Belts and in deep space would have killed the astronauts, while the searing sunlight on the moon would have baked them. Yes, Plait agreed, if unprotected men had gone up for long enough, they would have died, but the spaceship's metal hull blocked most of the radiation. These scientists have an explanation for everything.

Tricky Dicky and the Vietnam War

In his 2001 movie *A Funny Thing Happened On The Way To The Moon*, Nashville filmmaker Bart Sibrel argued that the Apollo 1 fire demonstrated that the programme was in such a shambolic state that it couldn't possibly have reached the moon two years later. The faked landings were just a distraction from the Vietnam War, he says, pointing out that the man in the White House at the time of Apollo 11 was cover-up king Richard Nixon – even if he had only been in office for six months.

Sibrel's own profile was raised in September 2002, when he buttonholed Buzz Aldrin outside a Beverley Hills hotel and demanded that he "swear on the Bible" that he'd gone to the Moon. Aldrin smashed Sibrel in the face, saying later that Sibrel had similarly harassed other Apollo astronauts. "He has a good punch", Sibrel told Reuters.

Masonic lunacy

Whether or not the moon landings actually happened, some suggest that the whole Apollo programme was the ultimate expression of Masonic power. All the astronauts were Freemasons, and the head of NASA during Apollo, Fred Kleinknect, is now the Sovereign Grand Commander of the 33rd Degree of Scottish Freemasons. A photograph in the House of the Temple in Washington DC is said by one website to show Neil Armstrong on the moon holding his Masonic apron. By this reckoning, Apollo is also "Lucifer", while the Scottish Rite of Freemasonry flag is the United Nations Flag with the nations of the world encircled by the laurel of Apollo.

Meanwhile website www.theforbiddenknowledge.com links the names given to the space shuttles to the Illuminati: "A Colombian Enterprise to Endeavor for the Discovery of Atlantis ... and all Challengers shall be destroyed" – a phrase whose source isn't made clear. What this Illuminati plot is really about, it's claimed, isn't the exploration of space, but conveying to the general public that space travel is possible. Once people believe that, they can more easily believe that aliens are capable of reaching Earth, and because that prospect is both terrifying and unprovable, people can be scared into submissive order, leaving the Illuminati's reign unchallenged. The only people, however, who claim that aliens could come, or indeed have already arrived, aren't the government but true believers like David Icke.

China heads for the moon

Somewhere between six percent (according to Gallup) and twenty percent (according to Fox) of Americans believe that the moon landings were faked. Even so, President George W. Bush has directed NASA's sights towards a manned mission to Mars. Meanwhile, the Chinese, as part of their move towards global superpower status, are pursuing their own manned moon mission. Thus NASA could silence its detractors by asking the "taikonauts", as they're called in Chinese, to bring back pieces of the Apollo vehicles left on the lunar surface. On the other hand, the Chinese could claim that they'd found no evidence that the US had ever been there. But then how long would it be before the world started to doubt whether the Chinese had been there either?

SOURCES

Books

Bill Kaysing and Randy Reid We Never Went To The Moon: America's Thirty Billion Dollar Swindle (1999). The satire that backfired, this is the first and (intentionally?) the funniest exposé of the greatest "hoax" ever.

TV

Conspiracy Theory: Did We Land On The Moon? (Fox TV, 2001). A televised run-through of Kaysing's theories; easier to assimilate, but with less humour.

Film

A Funny Thing Happened On The Way To The Moon (Bart Sibrel, 2001). Sibrel's amusing, irreverent take raises some not completely invalid questions over the landings (see also www.moonmovie.com).

Websites

 science.nasa.gov/headlines/y2001/ast23feb_2.htm This is NASA's "rocks and common sense" piece, somewhat undermined by Dr Tony Philips harping on about what a terrible impact the Fox TV programme had on his mother.

 www.BadAstronomy.com Astronomer Phil Plait's retort to the Fox programme. *Bad Astronomy* is also the title of a book Plait wrote on the subject.

 www.redzero.demon.co.uk/moonhoax/ A useful site with links to the more obscure details supposedly proving or disproving the moon landings.

COMMIE COSMONAUTS

While the Russians offered public congratulations to the US on the moon landings, the Soviet press ran a grumbling campaign claiming that the landings were faked, with many in high places confirming that view; cosmonaut Boris Volynov was still saying so in 2000. But they may just have been jealous. Their own remarkable lead in the space race had included sending the first man into orbit – Yuri Gagarin, who went up in a tiny Vostok spacecraft on April 12, 1961.

However, Gagarin's true feat may have been that he was the first man to return from space alive, and to the right country. According to a *Pravda* article in 2001, cosmonauts Alexis Ledovsky, Serentyi Shiborin, and Andrei Mitkov, flew into space in 1957, 1958 and 1959 respectively, but all three died in the process. A Horizon Channel documentary, *Cosmonaut Cover-up,* further claimed that cosmonaut Vladimir Ilyushin made three orbits five days before Gagarin's

flight, only to crash-land in China, where he was held for a year. Gagarin, crucially, landed back in the USSR.

Gagarin was killed in 1968 when his aircraft spun into the ground. The official story runs that he could have ejected, but he stayed aboard so that he could steer the plane away from a school. However, some say that the Communist Party bumped him off, over a public slanging match he had had with General

Secretary Nikita Khrushchev. Supposedly, despite Gagarin's uncomradely womanizing and drinking, his huge popularity was putting the party's own bigwigs into the shadows. On the other hand, if Gagarin was really killed for arguing with Khrushchev, the confrontation must presumably have taken place when Khrushchev was still president, prior to 1964; for him to have had Gagarin bumped off four years later would seem like a long time to hold a grudge.

War

play

Pearl Harbor
The Kremlin and the Chechen rebels
9/11
Iraq: the real reaons for war?

Warplay

Introduction

The term "gunboat diplomacy" refers to the practice of dispatching a warship to some far-flung outpost of empire when it looks as though simmering problems might be about to boil over. An intimidating piece of weaponry can do wonders to remind the locals just who's the boss. Diplomacy is however a multi-faceted art, and sometimes you can't help suspecting that gunboats have been sent in not so much to keep the peace as to provoke an attack that might justify a war.

Such instances form part of the long-established tradition that no one likes to be seen as actually wanting a war. Even blatant aggressors cast themselves as victims, prompted to fight only in "self-defence". Thus Hitler, for example, found it nec-

essary to stage fake attacks from Poland in order to justify his "counter-invasion" of the country in 1939.

It's also much easier for a democratically elected leader to win popular support for taking his country into war if he can persuade the citizens that they have fallen victim to an unprovoked attack. In two classic examples – the sinking of the USS *Maine* in Cuba in 1898, and the Gulf of Tonkin incident in 1964 – it's unlikely that American vessels were even attacked at all, but both led the US into full-scale war, against the Spanish and the North Vietnamese respectively. Some conspiracy theorists have even charged President Franklin Roosevelt with having deliberately failed to defend Pearl Harbor against an anticipated Japanese attack in 1941, in order to embroil the US in World War II.

More recently, others have suggested that the bomb blasts in Moscow that provoked Russia to invade Chechnya in 1999 were in fact the work of the Russian secret services. In the latest subtle variation, even a fictitious attack is no longer required; it's enough simply to persuade the populace that your "enemy" is so capable of perpetrating some dastardly onslaught that it would be suicidal not to attack them first. As George W. Bush put it on June 1, 2002, preparing the way for the 2003 invasion of Iraq: "If we wait for threats to fully materialize, we will have waited too long."

Granted that war is an expensive business, why would anyone be so keen to get involved? Conspiracy theorists love to cite the profits to be derived from oil as the principal reason for such conflicts as the Gulf War, the Iraq War, Chechnya and even the Vietnam War. Iraq, Iran and North Korea were allegedly demonized as the "Axis of Evil" not because of their WMD programs or unpleasant regimes, but because they switched from dollars to euros.

Theorists go on to argue that when not fought for profit, wars tend to be fought for stark, Machiavellian reasons of power politics, perhaps to knock out an irritating opponent or an imperial competitor. That kind of project appeals to big-money interests far more than to ordinary voters, which makes it necessary to concoct some other excuse – even when such ends as the destruction of Imperial Japan or the toppling of Saddam Hussein also happen to be morally desirable.

Particularly paranoid theorists see the state as benefiting from fear itself. Every conflict is dependent on munitions and financing, so arms manufacturers and banks love war. Appearing to be forever on the brink of conflict with the Soviets, or the North Koreans, or whoever, is part of a huge money cycle; ruling parties spend generously on equipping national armies, while the industries that benefit from their largesse support them in turn, for as long as the money keeps rolling in. What's more, fear not only deters foreign aggressors, but keeps your own people in line and prepared to pay the necessary price, not only in terms of taxes and votes, but in serving as cannon fodder.

The USS Maine and the Spanish-American War

Almost fifty years have now passed since Fidel Castro came to power, sparking the latest round of tensions between the US and Cuba. But it's easy to forget that the first major intervention by the US into the island's affairs was triggered by the destruction of the American warship USS *Maine* a good half-century before that. There's no question that the ship sank, but the issue still remains, who or what was responsible: the Spanish? The Cubans? The Americans? Or simply fate?

As the end of the nineteenth century approached, Cuba still formed part of Spain's overseas empire, but the Spanish grip on the island was loosening, as more and more Cubans took up arms to fight for independence. The guerrilla war in Cuba alarmed not only Spain but the US, which had considerable investment there. An American warship, the USS *Maine*, was dispatched to Cuba in January 1898, to keep an eye on events and evacuate US citizens should the situation deteriorate.

The *Maine* anchored in Havana harbour, in Spanish waters, on January 25. Three weeks later, at 9.40pm on February 15, 1898, a massive explosion blasted the 6680-ton *Maine* out of the water. Of 354 sailors and officers aboard, 262 were killed.

A US Navy court of inquiry was set up by President McKinley the next day, and concluded on March 15 that the *Maine* had suffered an external explosion on the port side bow, which set off a larger internal explosion in the magazine. Whether the external explosion was a floating mine or a torpedo, the inquiry did not determine, and although it cleared the Navy of any "fault or negligence", neither did it explicitly blame the Spanish or the Cubans.

Among certain members of McKinley's administration, however, there was no doubt as to Spanish guilt. Assistant Secretary of the Navy Theodore Roosevelt, who had declared the day after the sinking that "the *Maine* was sunk by an act of dirty treachery on the part of the Spaniards", pressurized the wavering McKinley into asking Congress to sup-

The USS *Maine* goes down in Havana

port a declaration of war. It duly did so on April 25.

The US did very well indeed out of war with Spain, taking control of Cuba, Puerto Rico, the Philippines, and Guam, and supplanting Spain's position and power not only in the Caribbean but also over much of Latin America and the western Pacific. Roosevelt himself did even better: he resigned his political post to serve as lieutenant colonel of the so-called "Rough Riders", the First US Volunteer Cavalry, in Cuba, and parlayed his resultant fame into becoming first McKinley's vice president in 1900, and then America's youngest-ever president when McKinley was assassinated in 1901.

Picking a fight

According to conspiracy-minded historians, the US was already determined to fight Spain, and the sinking of the *Maine* simply provided the pretext for which it had been searching. While it's easy to trace the bellicose spirit in America, there are fewer signs of any Spanish desire for war. The Spanish empire was in terminal decline, and in no position to provoke conflict with the youthfully muscular United States. The Spaniards had agreed to the *Maine*'s visit to Cuba, greeting it with diplomatic niceties and friendliness, and Spanish officers had dined aboard the ship. After the explosion, the Americans were suspiciously quick to point the finger of blame; William Randolph Hearst's newspapers had already been stirring up anti-Spanish sentiments, and well before the inquiry reported one echoed Roosevelt's charge of Spanish treachery by roaring: "The Warship *Maine* Was Split In Two By An Enemy's Secret Infernal Machine!"

A Spanish investigation, which was denied access to the wreck of the *Maine*, attributed the internal explosion to mechanical failure, but was discounted in the US as a whitewash concocted by the guilty party. Admiral Hyman Rickover, who carried out another investigation for the US Navy in the 1970s, concluded that the explosion was probably caused by the spontaneous combustion of coal dust in a storage bunker, which then ignited the ammunition magazine. Some historians dispute whether such spontaneous combustion is possible, or that it could go undetected.

There's obviously a big difference between saying that the US capitalized on the explosion and alleging that it actually blew up its own ship. Irrespective of what destroyed the *Maine*, however, it's clear that the US raced to blame Spain and declare war. Thus the real conspiracy might centre on deliberate attempts to keep the truth behind the sinking from ever reaching the public. In 1912, with the war over some years, the *Maine*'s damaged bow was cut off and replaced with a wooden one, so the ship could be floated out to sea and re-sunk amid great ceremony. The removal of its damaged exterior destroyed any hope that the true cause might be found.

Was it the Cubans?

Some American historians have asserted that Cuban insurgents were responsible for blowing up the *Maine*, in the hope of forcing an American intervention from which they might benefit. It's certainly true that Cuban rebels repeatedly burned American-owned property and sugar plantations, which might have served to provoke US action to protect its own interests, and perhaps depose the inept Spaniards in the process. However, no evidence of Cuban involvement has been unearthed, and to ascribe any such motives to the rebels is purely speculative. They were fighting for independence, not to provoke heavy-handed intervention by another regional power, and the rationale behind attacks on US assets in Cuba need have been no more sophisticated than to weaken the resources available to the colonial occupier.

OPERATION NORTHWOODS

Six decades after the USS *Maine* exploded in Havana harbour, the memory of how its sinking sparked the Spanish-American War remained vivid in the minds of a new generation of American politicians. According to former deputy CIA director Robert Cline, at the start of the 1960s the CIA, the out-going Eisenhower administration and the fledgling Kennedy administration were "obsessing" over removing Communist Fidel Castro from Cuba.

After the failure of the Bay of Pigs invasion in 1961 – planned under Eisenhower but instigated under JFK – the Kennedys set up Operation Mongoose (see p.20), to "stir things up" in Cuba via espionage, sabotage and general disorder. However, such far-fetched CIA schemes as using flaming cats to burn down sugar fields, or sending Castro an exploding cigar, achieved little beyond outraging Robert Kennedy, who dumped the plan in February 1962.

By then, Joint Chief of Staff chairman General Lyman Lemnitzer was drawing up Operation Northwoods, a plot that – but for the fact that it was really hatched – might sound like the paranoid ramblings of a conspiracy theorist. Its aim was to trick public opinion in the US and around the world into supporting a full-scale invasion of Cuba. "We could blow up a US ship in Guantanamo Bay [yes, *that* Guantanamo Bay] and blame Cuba", Lemnitzer proposed: "casualty lists in US newspapers would cause a helpful wave of national indignation".

Further suggestions included creating public ill-feeling towards Cuba by having US armed forces disguised as the Cuban military hijack and harass civilian aircraft and boats around the Gulf of Mexico, and flying a pilotless drone passenger plane over the island, transmitting Mayday recordings as if under attack by Cuban jets, and then blowing it up by remote control, blaming Castro. If war could be provoked between Cuba and its neighbours, a US invasion could be justified as deposing the alleged aggressors. Perhaps something involving the Commonwealth states of Jamaica or Trinidad and Tobago could persuade the UK to attack, or US planes disguised as Cuban bombers could raid Dominican Republic sugar fields, and then "Cuban" messages and arms to the Dominican Communist underground could be "uncovered".

As well as considering blowing up one of their own ships, Lemnitzer's team suggested that Cuban stooges in Cuban army fatigues could attack the US naval base in Guantanamo Bay, and faux "saboteurs" inside the base could blow things up, probably killing some hapless US servicemen in the process. Reconnaissance planes could be sent over for the Cubans to shoot down. It was even suggested that astronaut John Glenn's rocket could be blown up as he prepared to become the first American to orbit the Earth, and Cuba blamed. Worst of all were schemes to set off bombs in Miami and Washington and arrest Cuban patsies, planting documents that proved Castro's support.

Fortunately, Operation Northwoods was never activated, being comprehensively rejected by Secretary of Defense Robert McNamara and President Kennedy in March 1962. Lemnitzer, however, continued to stoke up rage among his generals, for which he was transferred to Europe to head NATO. He later made it back onto President Ford's Foreign Intelligence Advisory Board. After he lied to a Senate committee about Operation Northwoods, Senator Al Gore called successfully for him to be sacked.

The existence of the operation was finally confirmed after author James Bamford sued the National Security Agency for documents on the Cuban missile crisis and wrote up his findings in a book, *Body Of Secrets*. Published in early 2001, the revelation that the US military had considered unleashing terror attacks on the American people came just six months before 9/11.

The press on the warpath

It was the US press that was responsible for arousing sufficient public anger to demand war from Congress. The *Maine* incident, and virulent anti-Spanish coverage, precipitated massive increases in newspaper sales. The "yellower", more jingoistic and more bellicose the journalism, the greater the profits. Was the prospect of war so profitable to press barons such as William Randolph Hearst that they engineered their coverage to that end?

The power of public rage is mentioned at Arlington Cemetery, where the mast of the *Maine* is interred. The memorial there describes the sinking as the "seminal event" leading to the Spanish-American war, acknowledging that: "Although the cause of the explosion (whether a Spanish torpedo or an internal mechanical malfunction) has never been definitively determined, the event enraged American public opinion."

SOURCES

Books

Louis A Perez Jnr. **The War Of 1898, The United States And Cuba In History And Historiography** (1998). A quick history of the conflict, which also covers a couple of conspiracy theories.

Websites

ⓦ www.history.navy.mil/faqs/faq71-1.htm One official account of the *Maine*'s destruction and the mayhem that ensued can be found in the US Navy's online history file.

Pearl Harbor

The US Defense Department calls the 1941 Japanese attack on Pearl Harbor "one of the greatest military surprises in the history of warfare". In 2002, President George W. Bush, in his presidential proclamation on National Pearl Harbor Remembrance Day, said that the attack had come "without provocation or warning". There are those, however, who believe that not only did then President F.D. Roosevelt have forewarning of Pearl Harbor, but also that he deliberately provoked the attack.

Sunday morning, December 7, 1941, Hawaii. The island of Oahu was home to five airfields and the port of Pearl Harbor, the largest US naval base in the Pacific. That day, most of the Pacific fleet, including eight battleships, nine cruisers and 31 destroyers, were in dock. The ships were aligned in positions highly vulnerable to attack, but then the port, like the US, was at peace. However, as dawn broke, just two hundred miles northwest, wave after wave of Japanese bomber and fighter aircraft swooped off the aircraft carriers of Japan's First Fleet.

At 7.55am, the first of over 350 planes hit Pearl Harbor, strafing, bombing and torpedoing the American fleet. It was carnage. Twenty-one ships, including all eight battleships, were sunk or damaged, some three hundred aircraft destroyed, over 2400 people killed, and nearly two thousand wounded. All for a total Japanese loss of 29 aircraft, six submarines and a hundred men. December 7, President Franklin Roosevelt told the nation, was "a date which will live in infamy", and on December 8 Congress declared war on Japan.

One Japanese flight leader was Commander Fuchida, who yelled "Tora, Tora, Tora!" – code for the US being caught by surprise. It would seem, however, that a total surprise it was not.

Warnings

There *were* warnings of an attack. Japan's diplomatic correspondence was encrypted under a code the US military called "Purple". Since the summer of 1940, every Japanese dispatch had been read by the US through its decryption system "Magic". Thousands of intercepts that revealed Japanese preparations for some big hit, somewhere, flowed in during the months preceding Pearl Harbor, in-

cluding many from US, Dutch and French outposts in the Asia-Pacific region. The War and Navy departments in Washington sent out war warnings on October 16 and November 24, while the Secretary of State told the military chiefs on November 27 that negotiations with Japan had failed and that further action would be the responsibility of the military.

On November 27, the Navy and War Departments dispatched a warning that war was imminent: "Negotiations with Japan looking toward stabilization of conditions in the Pacific have ceased ... an aggressive move by Japan is expected within the next few days." On December 6, 1941, a Japanese communiqué stated that the US and UK were "obviously hostile" and that "the American government ... may be said to be scheming for the extension of the war". The military build-up was "perfecting an encirclement of Japan ... which endangers the very existence of the Empire". East Asia had endured Anglo-American imperial dominance for a century, something that "the Japanese government cannot tolerate the perpetuation of". Further negotiations were unacceptable. As FDR put it, "this means war."

Pearl Harbor, December 1941

The intelligence was there, it just wasn't disseminated

But somehow no one told Hawaii. The November 27 and December 6 messages became the twin focuses of eight successive, high-level wartime investigations into the Pearl

Harbor attack, which fingered one top official after another, up the chain of command to the White House.

The Roberts Commission, set up eleven days after the attack at the behest of FDR, was a stitch-up. Commission member Admiral Standley deemed it "crooked", in that it served only to keep the prestige of the Roosevelt administration "fully preserved in the public mind", and Admiral Robert A. Theobald agreed in his 1954 book *The Final Secret Of Pearl Harbor* (Theobald was Commander of Destroyers at Pearl Harbor in 1941 and also attended the commission). In January 1942, Justice Owen Roberts cleared everyone in Washington and blamed the Hawaiian commanders, Admiral Husband E. Kimmel and General Walter C. Short, for dereliction of duty. They'd failed to confer over warnings and failed to implement war plans preparing for outside attack.

However, those plans were the responsibility of the Washington-based War and Navy departments, overseen by General George C. Marshall and Admiral Harold R. Stark. In 1944, the Army Pearl Harbor Board slammed Marshall and the War Department for not keeping Short "fully advised" of rising tensions with Japan, not forwarding intelligence to Hawaii, and particularly for not sending the December 6 communiqué until *after* the attack.

The concurrent Naval Court of Inquiry rebuked Stark in similar terms. Stark coolly observed in 1945 that everything he did before Pearl Harbor, including refusing to forward key Japanese intercepts to Hawaii, he did on "higher orders" – which could only have come from FDR. The president did receive censure, but only after the war was over and he was dead. In May 1946, the Joint Congressional Committee castigated FDR, Stark, Marshall, Secretary of the Navy Frank Knox, Kimmel and Short, while also lamenting that the information it had was glaringly incomplete.

Itching for a fight

Each investigation centred on the fact that intelligence pointing to an imminent attack existed, but that thanks either to incompetence or conspiracy, it was rendered redundant by inaction. With the steady deterioration of US-Japanese relations, some kind of military showdown had been brewing for a long time. Japan's Asian empire was by then threatening the Dutch East Indies, the Philippines, Burma, Singapore and Australia. The US restricted shipments of airplane fuel, scrap metal, machinery and wheat to Japan throughout 1940, and Anglo-American support prevented the Dutch East Indies falling into Japan's economic clutches. Filipino exports of raw material to Japan were halted, and the US, British and Dutch stopped trade and froze Japanese assets following the Japanese seizure of French Indochina. The US oil embargo was enlarged in mid-1941 to become a petrol embargo.

Some of the US moves were justifiable responses to Japanese actions. But some also tally with an "eight-point plan" drawn up for FDR by Lieutenant Commander Arthur McCollum on October 7, 1940. (The plan was later found in Navy archives by former Navy officer Robert B. Stinnet, who cites it in his book *Day Of Deceit*.) Beginning with the words "The United States desires that Japan commit the first overt act", McCollum set out a series of deliberately provocative steps including using and aiding British military bases and forces; deploying US ships in Japan's Asia-Pacific sphere; and financial and militarily supporting China to fight the Japanese, while recalling British, US and Dutch citizens from the region. The trade embargoes and freezing of assets were also McCollum proposals.

During late 1941, the US and Japan were engaged in protracted diplomatic negotiations, but on November 25, Secretary of War Stimson met with FDR to predict war by December 1. On November 26, the US proposed that peace could be sustained if the Japanese withdrew from China and Indochina, guaranteed not to threaten other Western interests, accepted the economic encirclement, and gave up its tripartite alliance with Germany and Italy. It was this proposal that was cited in Japan's December 6 communiqué as the cause of the breakdown in negotiations – negotiations that the US Navy and War departments said had "ceased" on November 27.

Even the press knew

Another shocking revelation made by Stinnet concerns a secret press conference on November 15, 1941, at which Marshall told correspondents from the *New York Times*, *Newsweek*, *Time* and AP that the US had broken Japanese codes – "We know what they know and they don't know we know it" – and that an attack was expected in the first ten days of December. The press, presumably, was required to say nothing at the time. If, however, reporters knew that Pearl Harbor wasn't the surprise that it was said to be, how come they didn't spill the beans later? Perhaps they kept quiet out of a sense of patriotic duty – or perhaps they were muzzled after the event as well.

A Red in the White House

Another theory is that Pearl Harbor was precipitated by Communist agents working for the USSR, who wanted the US in the war not so much to fight Japan as to fight Nazi Germany, which by late 1941 was invading Russia with terrifying speed. The ultimate extension of this theory, as advocated by Mark Emerson Willey in *Pearl Harbor: Mother Of All Conspiracies*, is that FDR himself was a Communist. Playwright George Bernard Shaw once said that "Roosevelt is a Communist but does not know it", which Willey translates into "Franklin Roosevelt was a hard-core Marxist".

Willey argues that Roosevelt's Marxist beliefs were revealed when his administration re-estab-lished trade and diplomatic ties with the USSR in 1933, which had been severed since the 1917 Russian Revolution. FDR called himself an "internationalist", and set up Lend-Lease to allow arms, minerals and credits for the Soviets to fight the Nazis. He overruled Churchill's request to invade Europe through the Balkans to stop Stalin taking Eastern Europe. And at Yalta in 1944, says Willey, FDR "gave over to Communist enslavement 725 million people", from Germany to Korea.

For Willey, all this "treason" proves that FDR "always worked for Stalin's interests". What Willey overlooks, however, is the fact that, whatever else he may have done, FDR did a superb job in serving the interests of the US, taking it from an economic depression to the status of global superpower (and Russia's only rival) in little over a decade, and winning four consecutive elections while defeating two major fascist powers.

Some historians who have always backed the sneak attack story at least agree with Willey and Stinnet's suggestion that war with Japan made it possible for the US to deal with the real threat: the Nazis. As Gordon Prange argues in *At Dawn We Slept*, the US military and state department saw the possibility of a German victory over Britain as a danger to US security. Britain's industries, bases and navy would fall to Germany, and the Nazis would further cement their Atlantic power through economic and political links with Latin America. The problem was that US polls showed ninety percent of Americans wanting nothing to do with "Europe's war" – a view publicly supported by the likes of Charles Lindbergh, Henry Ford and Joe Kennedy (JFK's father). In 1940 FDR himself had been re-elected on an isolationist ticket.

When the time came, however, the tripartite agreement that Hitler had signed with Japan and Italy came into effect. Four days after Pearl Harbor, Hitler declared war on the US, and within a week, America was facing war on two fronts. Not that it was so unprepared. In January 1941, FDR submitted the huge peacetime military budget of $10 billion, to expand the Army to one million men with fifty thousand planes and the Navy to two hundred thousand men, fifteen thousand planes and a fleet fit for two oceans. If not for war, then for what?

Mother of all myths

If a war with Japan was sought, if only as a means to war with Germany, it seems an odd way to start out by knowingly letting your major naval forces be hammered on day one. Warning Pearl Harbor of the attack wouldn't have stopped the attack itself nor removed the justification for war – it would only have limited the damage, so the surprise may have been one of location.

But only of location. It was no surprise when an attack came, and war was arguably something that both sides wanted. The need for the US government to still downplay its active will to war before Pearl Harbor may be part of sustaining the myth that the US is never the aggressor (even in pre-emptive wars), even when – in the case of Hitler and Hirohito, at least – there might be strong grounds for doing so.

And then there is the myth of Roosevelt himself. Even Stinnet says that his own revelations "do not diminish FDR's magnificent contributions to the American people. His legacy should not be tarnished by the truth." The US entry into a global war saw it emerge by 1945 as a true global superpower. If Stinnet's reaction to what he himself calls FDR's awesome duplicity is any indication, then it doesn't matter that a few Americans question the perception held by the overwhelming majority of their fellow countrymen – that Pearl Harbor was a sneaky surprise, not one predicted and possibly provoked by their own president.

Hollywood is certainly keen to perpetuate the myth of a "surprise" attack, as seen in the 2001 blockbuster *Pearl Harbor*. Although the film portrays FDR as so incandescent over Japan's betrayal that he hoists himself out of his wheelchair in rage, this was not among the many historical inaccuracies for which historians lambasted it. Ironically, the flag-waving story of how Americans responded with unquenchable resolve against aggressors was a hit with cinema-goers if not with critics, and with near-perfect timing, it was released only weeks before foreigners launched another sneak air attack on the US seaboard: 9/11.

SOURCES

Books

Robert Stinnett Day Of Deceit: The Truth About FDR And Pearl Harbor (2001). With new access to archives through the US Freedom of Information Act, ex-US Navy officer Stinnett argues that FDR knew Pearl Harbor was coming, because it was what he had wanted all along. A soberly written book, and all the better for it.

Robert A. Theobald The Final Secret Of Pearl Harbor (1988). Theobald's book was first published in 1954, when the war was very fresh in people's minds. His case – that Pearl Harbor was something FDR actively sought – is all the more surprising, considering the seniority of his naval command in 1941 and attendance at subsequent government inquiries/cover-ups.

Mark Emerson Willey Pearl Harbor: Mother Of All Conspiracies (2001). Willey's argument that Pearl Harbor was a set-up becomes almost incidental to his frenetic attempt to prove that FDR was the architect of a global Communist plot. A good read, if only to see the tortuous, twisted arguments that support conclusions that people like Willey espouse.

Website

⊕ www.apfn.org/apfn/pearl_harbor.htm The American Patriotic Friends Network has its own stab at denouncing FDR for his murderous duplicity. A concise online summary of the case against the US government.

THE INVASION OF POLAND

It's well known that World War II broke out in Europe as a consequence of the Nazi invasion of Poland on September 1, 1939 – the UK and France declared war on Germany two days later. However, it's often overlooked that Adolf Hitler was not prepared for his own people to see him as the aggressor. Thus he told a shocked Reichstag on September 1 that Polish forces had invaded Germany, and that the Wehrmacht had been returning fire since 5.45am. Indeed, it was claimed that the bodies of a dozen slain Polish soldiers had been found, which proved the reality of the invasion, and that radio commands in which Polish forces revealed their intent had been intercepted. Germany's armed forces were counter-attacking with great success.

It was all a lie. The SS had taken twelve prisoners out of Buchenwald concentration camp and ordered them to don Polish army uniforms, whereupon they were shot dead. An SS officer announced in Polish over the radio that the Poles were here, invading, then the SS left the bodies as "evidence". The ensuing invasion of Poland followed the plan known as *Fall Weiss*, or Case White, which had been devised earlier in 1939 after the Nazis took Czechoslovakia. The antiquated, outnumbered Polish armed forces were routed, although Warsaw endured eleven days of shelling before falling; the end came with another surprise on September 17 when the Soviets invaded from the east. Polish resistance ended two weeks later. An improbable non-aggression pact between Germany and the USSR had been unexpectedly announced in late August, but the part about dividing Poland wasn't revealed.

Germany's problem with Poland was that the Poles had been given a corridor to the sea after World War I, which incorporated the German city of Danzig and divided Prussia from the rump of Germany. Also, Hitler sought a face-to-face border with the USSR, ready for Germany's invasion in 1941. He had written in *Mein Kampf* that Poles were "inferior", only good as slaves or dead, and six million Poles, including three million Jews, were to die under the Nazi occupation. But the shock for Hitler was that the UK and France finally put their foot down. Having let the Führer spend the latter part of the 1930s retaking the Rhineland, annexing Austria, stealing the Sudetenland and invading Czechoslovakia without a shot being fired, they gave him a final surprise by declaring war.

ODESSA and the Org

In September 2000, the CIA admitted something that scores of journalists, authors, human rights groups and politicians worldwide had been claiming almost since 1945: that after the German defeat in World War II, the CIA and British intelligence had hidden, funded, and rehabilitated thousands of Nazis in a huge counter-intelligence operation against Communism. The idea that a vast, secret network of Nazis were not only at large but working with the CIA, MI6 and even the Vatican had been given scope in numerous conspiracist accusations, novels and films – but, as is surprisingly often the case, it had a basis in fact.

In May 1945, SS General Reinhard Gehlen, Adolf Hitler's chief of Eastern Intelligence, surrendered to American forces advancing into Germany. With some insouciance, he insisted on speaking only with American Counter-Intelligence Corps (CIC). Considering that Gehlen was wanted by the USSR for war crimes, he risked nothing but the harshest treatment before being thrown to the Russians. However, he had something to offer CIC – all his organization's intelligence about the Soviets (safely stashed in the Alps), and the agents and spy networks in now Soviet-dominated areas.

Gehlen offered it all to the US in return for immunity from prosecution, the recruitment of some of his persecuted colleagues, and the right to continue running his networks. With a massive fight against Communism in the offing, the CIC agreed. Dressed as a US army officer, Gehlen was flown to the US, and at Fort Hunt, Maryland, he dined with officers and directors of the OSS, the forerunner of the CIA. Future CIA director Allen Dulles was particularly taken with Gehlen, and the CIA would eventually channel over $200 million into Gehlen's Bavaria-based organization, aka the Org. (According to conspiracy theorist Mae Brussell – see p.132 – Dulles had been running his own Org-esque programme, Operation Sunrise, since 1942.)

In return for fighting Communism, thousands of Gestapo, Wehrmacht and SS veterans, many indicted for war crimes, had their pasts whitewashed and were given their freedom. Big names on the CIA payroll included SS Commander Karl Wolff, who dispatched three hundred thousand Jews to Treblinka, and the notorious SS officer Klaus Barbie, the "Butcher of Lyon", who was wanted by the French for sending Jewish children to Auschwitz. Barbie ultimately "escaped" to South America, but was handed back to the French courts by Bolivia in 1983. Dulles justified the programme with the words: "[They're] on our side, and that's all that matters." So respectable did the Org become that it was openly incorporated into the West German government's intelligence organization, the *Bundesnachrichtendienst*, in 1955.

The Org tapped into underground fascist networks to become NATO's main intelligence source within the Warsaw Pact. After all, countries like Hungary, Bulgaria and Romania had had fascist governments dependent on Nazi Germany, and had contributed militarily to the 1941 invasion of the USSR. Early Org successes included information about Soviet jet fighter development and tip-offs about the remilitarization of East Germany. The Org also apparently helped the CIA to bring about the 1953 coup in Iran, deposing the democratically elected premier Mossadegh (who had unwisely nationalized Iran's oil industry) and reinstalling the pro-Nazi Pahlevi family. As the Shah of Iran, Mohammed Reza Pahlevi remained a major US ally for almost three decades.

The programme also brought technological benefits for the US. Under Operation Outcast (later Operation Paperclip), the Army's Field Intelligence Agency Technical unit sought out the Nazis' finest scientists to boost American economic development – in effect, a form of war reparations. The most famous of the Nazi boffins to have their wartime CVs rewritten by the Pentagon, and to be given employment in the US, was Werner von Braun. Having led the development of the V2 missile that bombed London and Antwerp, von Braun was rewarded by the US to lead America's rocket programs at NASA. Other Nazi scientific research that continued in one form or another in the US included work salvaged from Germany's atomic bomb programme, and experiments on humans involving gas, varying atmospheric pressures, sterilization and mind-control. These became the basis of research at Edgewood Arsenal (see p.284) and MK-ULTRA (see p.192).

It's not clear whether the notorious shadowy counterpart to the Org known as ODESSA – the *Organisation der Ehemaligen SS-Angehörigen*, or the Organization of former SS officers – ever actually existed. According to rumour, ODESSA was an escape-route set up by the Nazis during the final days of World War II and run by Hitler's top SS commando, Otto Skorzeny from Lisbon or Buenos Aires. It supposedly helped notorious Nazis such as Adolf Eichmann, Martin Bormann and Dr Josef Mengele to flee to Latin America. Dedicated Nazi-hunter Simon Wiesenthal certainly believed in ODESSA, and acted as a consultant to Frederick Forsyth on his novel *The Odessa File*, in which ex-Nazis help Egypt to develop plague-laden missiles to fire at Israel. In *Blowback: The First Full Account of America's Recruitment Of Nazis*, however, Christopher Simpson says that ODESSA was not so much an organization in its own right as a gaggle of extra-Org networks, which functioned to obtain ex-Nazis gainful employment as "security advisers" in the Middle East or in various Latin American death squads.

According to Mark Aarons and John Loftus's book *Unholy Trinity*, in the first years after WWII the Vatican was so afraid of Communist clampdowns on Catholicism in Eastern Europe and Latin America that it used churches and monasteries to funnel fascist war criminals to places where they could serve as "freedom fighters" against Communism. These included Treblinka commandant Franz Stangl, "mobile gas chamber" inventor Walter Rauff, and Croat dictator Ante Pavelic. The scheme was overseen by Pope Pius XII, directed by Giovanni Montini (later Pope Paul VI) and aided by British and US intelligence under the codename Operation Ratlines. The Vatican also channelled Nazi gold and looted treasures into Swiss banks (see p.231), in the full awareness of the Bern-based Allen Dulles, while the "ratlines" served as the working template for the Iran-Contra system.

The journals *Covert Action Information Bulletin* and *The Rebel* describe an even murkier version of the story, in which the Vatican used its *Pro Deo* intelligence network in Portugal and OSS-funded branches in New York and Rome to assist ODESSA. By this account, Gehlen, OSS director Bill Donovan and the improbably named future CIA director James Jesus Angleton were all linked through a quasi-Masonic sub-sect, the Sovereign Military Order of Malta; its chief, Pope Pius XII, awarded the trio the order's highest honour.

Employing ex-Nazis was never exactly a risk-free business. To what extent Gehlen deliberately fuelled Western fears of Communist domination to justify the existence of the Org, and how much the Org simply passed on Soviet disinformation, may never be known. According to Simpson, Org-supplied intelligence that Soviet forces were massing to attack in 1948 nearly started a calamitous war, and it's also claimed that the Org was the source of the Soviet disinformation that led to the "missile gap" scare of the 1950s and 1960s (see p. 340). Some Org agents were simply Soviet double agents who hated democracy more than Communism, and used the Vatican's ratlines to penetrate Western intelligence. Gehlen's ultimate game may simply have been to save his Nazi comrades, employing some and distracting the CIA from finding the rest. Mae Brussell, on the other hand, attributed the shooting of John F. Kennedy to a powerful Nazi cabal.

The sheer horror of not only enabling former Nazis to evade justice, but actually re-employing them in jobs that in some cases were no less evil than their war careers, was justified as being necessary in the cause of fighting what was seen as the greater global threat of Communism. It was all in the name of freedom, even if the fight paradoxically involved the creation and sustenance of fascist networks. By a bitter irony, it may have been these fascist war criminals that exaggerated the threat of Communism in the first place.

SOURCES

Books

Mark Aarons and John Loftus **Unholy Trinity: The Vatican, The Nazis, & Soviet Intelligence** (1998). A depressing but fascinating exposé of the depths the Cold War could descend to.

Christopher Simpson **Blowback: The First Full Account Of America's Recruitment Of Nazis And Its Disastrous Effect On Our Domestic And Foreign Policy** (1988). The title says it all: a seminal work, charting the birth of the Org and its often malign impact on its US sponsors.

Websites

⊛ http://dir.salon.com/news/ feature/2000/05/03/nazi/index.html "Our Nazi Allies", by Ken Silverstein. A fascinating article that details Silverstein's efforts to trace Nazis in the US, and the years of indifference he encountered from the CIA and FBI.

The Cold War conspiracy

For nearly fifty years, the US and its allies waged the Cold War against what President Reagan called the "Evil Empire". That war extended from the polar icecaps to the equatorial jungles of Southeast Asia, from submarines at the bottom of the ocean to satellites in space, from the bleak expanse of Greenham Common to the urban monstrosity of the Berlin Wall, and even to the cosy surroundings of America's libraries and film studios. It was a colossal scrap. But was it a real one?

Reds under the bed

On February 9, 1950, Wisconsin Senator Joseph R. McCarthy unveiled what he claimed to be a massive Communist conspiracy. He triumphantly revealed to the Republican Women's Club in Wheeling, West Virginia, that he had a "list" of 205 individuals who were "either card-carrying members or certainly loyal to the Communist Party", mostly in the State Department. Over the following fortnight, as McCarthy's numbers plummeted to 57 then nudged back up to 81, he hammered on, insisting that the Truman administration was rife with Communists.

McCarthy didn't mention that the "list" was drawn from "loyalty boards" set up by Truman to screen Communists from federal employment, and neither did he heed a Senate investigation that found no Communists in the State Department. Indeed, on June 14, 1951, he railed to the Senate that chief of staff General George C. Marshall and Secretary of State Dean Acheson were "marching side-by-side with Stalin", helping the Communists take over the world as part of "a great conspiracy", one immense enough to "dwarf any previous such venture in the history of man", a "world-wide web ... spun from Moscow", with Truman "their captive". The allegations were truly outrageous and unfounded, but at first they were hardly questioned. People believed them.

Stalin had tried to blockade West Berlin; Eastern Europe and China had gone Communist; and Chinese and Soviet-backed North Koreans were slugging it out against the US-led UN forces in Korea. What was worse, the USSR had the atom bomb, thanks to secrets supplied by Americans Julius and Ethel Rosenberg (who were later executed as spies, although debate continues as to their guilt). The House of Representatives' Un-American Activities Committee (HUAC) set out to find so-called "Reds" in libraries, schools, colleges, the church and Hollywood, and thousands of professionals, some well-known, were sacked, blacklisted, or pushed either abroad or to the point of suicide. Senior State Department official Alger Hiss was tried by HUAC for spying for Russia, and was ultimately convicted of perjury.

McCarthy's Government Operations Committee, supplied with information by Red-hating J. Edgar Hoover's FBI, effectively gave the government employees it interrogated the choice between naming "Communists" or losing their jobs. Any senators, usually Democrats, who denounced the charges as smears were simply smeared themselves as Communists, which cost a few their re-election and scared others into silence. As historian Elmo

Richardson later put it, "Americans believed charges that the Democrats had allowed Communists to gain high government posts".

Dwight Eisenhower, the Republican presidential candidate in the 1952 election, campaigned on the theme "Korea, Communism and corruption", and handsomely defeated Democrat Adlai Stevenson. And while President Eisenhower lamented McCarthy's desire to burn "Communist" books, he didn't publicly criticize the senator. This bitter era of paranoia and distrust in government, based on cavalier accusations of treasonable crimes, came to be termed "McCarthyism". McCarthy, however, never made his list public, and of the thousands of federal employees he accused, not one was identified as a Communist.

The real conspiracy was McCarthy's. Before the 1950 elections, the senator, worried on account of his lacklustre Senate career, flimsy war record and bribery charges, held a dinner with allies.

Senator Joseph McCarthy, witchfinder general

According to his biographer, "McCarthy talked with his guests for a while before bringing up the subject of the need for an issue. The group discarded quite a few before choosing Communism, suggested by [Father Edmund] Walsh, an ardent anti-Red. 'That's it,' McCarthy said. 'The government is full of Communists. We can hammer away at them.'" Only when McCarthy accused the Army in 1954 of "coddling Communists" did his public support evaporate, and the Senate took the chance to vote him down for "conduct unbecoming a senator". When he died three years later, one young senator from his Government Operations' Committee admitted that he would have voted down McCarthy, if he hadn't happened to be "ill" that day. His name was John F. Kennedy.

The "missile gap"

During the late 1950s, there were widespread fears that a so-called "bomber gap" had left the Soviets with more long-range nuclear bombers than the US. After this was disproved by U-2 reconnaissance flights over the USSR, the notion arose instead that there was a "missile gap". Furthered by USAF reports and the Congressional Gaither Committee in 1957, it became a hot potato in the 1960 election.

By now, Senator Kennedy was campaigning as the voice of vigorous youth to replace the avuncular but ineffective President Eisenhower. During televised debates with vice president Richard Nixon, Kennedy blamed Eisenhower for the supposed disparity between US and Soviet weapon stockpiles. "I believe there is a missile gap between the United States and the Soviet Union", he declared. He believed it, the voters believed him, and he became president.

There were indeed missile and bomber gaps – but in fact they were in favour of the US, several times over. As Kennedy oversaw the greatest expansion of US military might since 1945, reaching the level of 220 inter-continental ballistic missiles (ICBMs) and three thousand intercontinental bombers, the disparity with the Soviets' hundred missiles and two hundred bombers increased still further.

Then, however, the new-fangled spy satellites and a National Intelligence Estimate dramatically reduced the accepted counts of Soviet ICBMs. On December 5, 1962, shortly after the Cuban missile crisis, Kennedy and his advisors complained that they had been duped. With both sides possessing enough nuclear warheads to wipe out life on the planet, Kennedy commented: "I don't see quite why we're building as many [ICBMs] as we're building."

When Defense Secretary Robert McNamara presented Kennedy with the 1964 defence budget – set at an unprecedented $54.4 billion, 48 percent of discretionary government expenditure – he expressed concern. He suggested that the Pentagon might, to prevent any slowdown in spending, concoct some harmful story about US military weakness, just as they had over the missile gap: "A myth ... created by, I would say, emotionally guided but nonetheless patriotic individuals in the Pentagon." Laughing, Kennedy replied that he'd been "one of those who put that myth around – a patriotic and misguided man!"

The intelligence that originally supported the "missile gap" had come through agents, possibly in the so-called "Org" of ex-Nazi Reinhard Gehlen (see p.335). According to CIA spy Victor Marchetti, as quoted in Colin Simpson's *Blowback*: "Gehlen provided us [the CIA] with specific reports on the Soviet ICBM program ... He said, 'We have two reliable reports confirming this, and they [the Soviets] have just installed three missiles at that site', et cetera, claiming that they had contacts among the German scientists captured by the Russians at the end of the war."

It was a story the Pentagon and the press were all too ready to believe. The US missile industry, headed by former SS rocket scientist Werner von

Braun, secured further funding in 1955 after another former Nazi, missile-maker Walter Dornberger, published an article about Soviet sea-launched missiles – which wasn't true, but was part of the currency at the Pentagon. Did the Org make up the information to justify its existence, or did it simply pass on Soviet propaganda designed to deter attack? Some say that by late 1963, Kennedy was inclining towards both disarmament and disengagement from Vietnam. After Kennedy's assassination, however, President Johnson rejected both policies, stressing the need for war to counter the "threat" of Vietnamese Communists (see p.343).

A lack of evidence doesn't prove anything

Whatever Kennedy's intent on ICBM production, missile output flourished under his successor, and the Soviet-US nuclear missile race reached fever pitch. By the time that Richard Nixon was elected President, people were getting worried that the expanding stockpile of bigger and bigger weapons was making war by accident all the more likely. Nixon abandoned ideology in favour of détente with the USSR and China, accepting political differences in the interest of achieving a balance of interdependent peace. A brake on missile development was applied in 1972, when Nixon and USSR premier Brezhnev signed the Anti-Ballistic Missile treaty.

However, as Adam Curtis argued in the 2004 BBC TV documentary series, *The Power Of Nightmares*, the neoconservative disciples of the political philosopher Leo Strauss were waiting in the wings. Paradoxically, Strauss – a German-Jewish émigré who lectured at Chicago – had been influenced by the anti-Semitic political philosopher Carl Schmitt, a Nazi as early as 1933, who believed that politics was (and should be) a life-and-death power struggle: political parties and countries became strong by fighting an enemy. Applying this principle to America, Strauss believed that if the US was to avoid descending into liberal decadence, it had to have such an enemy, even if it were a mythical one. That enemy, of course, was the Soviet Union.

As the smoke of trauma from Vietnam and Watergate still swirled across America, President Gerald Ford's neocon Defense Secretary Donald Rumsfeld, his Chief of Staff Dick Cheney, and analyst Paul Wolfowitz began preaching the new gospel – which was, of course, a revival of old American fears of Communist plans for world domination. In 1976, Rumsfeld declared that the Soviet Union had been secretly building newer and better weapons in greater numbers than ever before. A neoconservative group, Team B, was organized to prove this hidden threat to America. Its chairman, Richard Pipes, was convinced that Soviet statements and weapons were meaningless. What mattered was "the Soviet mindset", which was bent on conquering the US.

Just because there was no evidence of illegal, aggressive weapons procurement, that didn't mean they didn't exist; it just meant that the Soviets were hiding them very well. Dr Anne Cahn of the Arms Control and Disarmament Agency summarized Team B's approach like this: "'We can't find evidence that they're doing it the way that everyone thinks they're doing it, so they must be doing it a different way. We don't know what that different way is, but they must be doing it.' No evidence didn't mean it didn't exist, it just hadn't been found." While the CIA insisted that Soviet air defences, like the Soviet economy, were heading for collapse, Team B argued that this was just a ruse, and their air defences worked perfectly – it said so in the Soviet training manual.

The supposed Soviet threat was further extended to terrorist groups such as the PLO, Hezbollah and the IRA, which the neocons said were not fragmented units fighting their own causes, but part of a secret network coordinated from Moscow. Neocons cited Clair Sterling's book *The Terror Network* to convince CIA chief William Casey, even though his CIA subordinates were sure there was no such network. The CIA's former Soviet Affairs chief, Melvin Goodman, said of Sterling's work that "very clear episodes where CIA black propaganda – clandestine information that was designed under a covert action plan to be planted in European newspapers – were picked up and put in this book". In other words, the CIA knew the book was nonsense because they had written the lies themselves.

Casey, however, became a believer. Armed with Pipes's dossier on the hidden terror network, he persuaded President Reagan to implement a new policy of covert wars abroad in 1983. A huge increase in funding and arms for military dictatorships soon followed. "Death squad paramilitaries", trained at the US's School of the Americas, murdered and tortured supposed "left-wing terrorists" in Colombia, Chile, Honduras and El Salvador. Grenada was successfully invaded. The Sandinista government of Nicaragua, which President Carter had supported against the previous Somoza dictatorship, was still fighting Somoza's Contras. But Reagan saw the Sandinistas as Communists, and backed the Contras through such murky means as the Iran-Contra conspiracy (see p.186). Around fifty thousand civilians died in a war the World Court denounced as "unlawful".

Reagan also praised Afghanistan's Mujahadeen guerrillas as "freedom fighters" and gave them billions of dollars in arms and funds to fight the Soviet occupiers. (In fact, as Steve Coll outlines in his 2004 book *Ghost Wars: The Secret History Of The CIA*, President Carter's security advisor Zbiginiew Brzezinski had engineered US aid to the Afghan government to begin in mid-1979, hoping that US aid would provoke a Soviet invasion and get the USSR into an unwinnable war – a war that would eventually cost 1.8 million Afghan lives.) Ironically,

the Soviets' ultimate defeat in the CIA-supported *jihad* in Afghanistan enabled the extremist elements in the Mujahadeen to establish the Taliban regime, and attracted followers to such political mavericks as Osama bin Laden.

After the USSR collapsed in 1991, President George H.W. Bush gloated to the Senate: "We won the Cold War!" Years of warnings from the likes of Mikhail Gorbachev and Melvin Goodman that the USSR was heading for economic implosion were conveniently overlooked, as was the fact that the US was about to tip into a recession that would cost Bush the 1992 election, thanks to the tripling of the national deficit. Instead, the reputations of hawks like Cheney, Wolfowitz and Rumsfeld were assured. After an eight-year interlude of Democrat rule, the neocons returned to power under George W. Bush, just in time to fight the evil terrorist mastermind Osama bin Laden and his worldwide terror network, Al Qaeda. The neocons are now allegedly behind Proactive, Preemptive Operations Group (P2OG), which mounts covert missions to "stimulate reactions" from militant groups – ie incite them to violence in order to justify a US "counterattack".

Conspiracy to exaggerate?

The Cold War was all about mutual paranoia. To suggest that the Communist threat was exaggerated by the US, however, is not to say that it didn't exist. Nor is it to deny the terrible totalitarianism of most Communist regimes (though the right-wing dictatorships of a great many of the US's anti-Communist allies were equally appalling in their own way). But in overestimating the Communist menace, the US expended vast resources and blighted millions of lives by attacking states and people, at home and abroad, who actually posed no threat at all.

SOURCES

Books

Edward S. Herman **The Real Terror Network: Terrorism In Fact And Propaganda** (1982). An eloquent, impassioned rebuttal of Clair Sterling's **The Terror Network** and the role of propaganda in "creating" terrorism (and keeping people terrified)

David M. Oshinsky **A Conspiracy So Immense ... The World Of Joe McCarthy** (1985). A witty attack on the life and lies of Joe McCarthy.

Richard H. Rovere **Senator Joe McCarthy** (1996). A work of its time, written shortly after McCarthy's death, that still divides its critics in its reprinted edition.

Film

The Power Of Nightmares: The Rise Of The Politics Of Fear (Adam Curtis, 2005). An edited version of the award-winning BBC TV documentary series (the original can be downloaded – with Curtis's blessing – from various Internet sites). A brilliantly told and absolutely compelling story of how US (and latterly UK) politicians came to tighten their grip on power, not by selling dreams of a better future but by playing on people's fears – first of Communism, then of an international terror network.

Websites

⊛www.jfklibrary.org The official site of John F. Kennedy's library hosts a growing archive of materials from his presidency.

⊛http://hnn.us/articles/1204.html **When People Fall For Conspiracy Theories: A Rumination**, an interesting piece by Don B. Kates on the power of conspiracy theories.

The Gulf of Tonkin incident and the Vietnam War

A so-called "incident" in the Gulf of Tonkin in August 1964, in which North Vietnamese vessels allegedly fired on US warships, provided the pretext for the US to step up its involvement in Vietnam. Up to that point, US personnel in Vietnam were officially described as "military advisors" to the South Vietnamese government, but from then on, the Americans were engaged in a full-scale conflict – though never, technically speaking, a war. The incident merits close examination, not merely because it was so obviously fabricated, but also because it swiftly became clear to the conspirators that they had bitten off much more than they could chew.

Communism dominoes across Asia

By early 1964, the US government was becoming worried that its ally, South Vietnam, was losing its fight against Communist Vietcong guerrillas, supported by Ho Chi Minh's government in North Vietnam. President Lyndon Johnson and Defense Secretary Robert McNamara were concerned that if South Vietnam fell to the Communists, it would precipitate a "domino effect" under which further regimes across Asia might succumb to the Reds. They therefore provided the South Vietnamese with fast patrol boats and the necessary training. Ostensibly these were for defensive purposes only, but in practice – under Operation 34A, co-ordinated in Washington and Saigon – they were used to attack North Vietnamese radar stations, ships, bridges and other military targets. US ships, tacking along the North Vietnamese coast in international waters, provided the intelligence to direct these attacks.

On August 2, 1964, the USS *Maddox* was carrying out just such operations in the Gulf of Tonkin when it was attacked by three North Vietnamese torpedo boats. The *Maddox* was hit by two machine-gun bullets; in response, the North Vietnamese boats were shelled and strafed by fighter-jets. The destroyer *Turner Joy* was dispatched to support the *Maddox*, and during the night of August 4, the warships reported that several fast craft fired almost a dozen torpedoes at them. The Pentagon declared this to be a second attack by North Vietnamese PT boats; calling the two attacks an "outrage", Johnson went on national TV to denounce North Vietnam's "open aggression on the open seas". Air strikes against North Vietnam were announced, with carrier planes from the Seventh Fleet bombing oil facilities and ships that day.

"They started it!"

According to the *LA Times*, "the Communists, by their attack on American vessels in international waters, have themselves escalated the hostilities", while a *Washington Post* headline described the air strikes as a "Move Taken to Halt New Aggression". With impressive speed, the Gulf of Tonkin Resolution was written and passed by Congress on August 7, opposed by only two senators. It authorized the president "to take all necessary measures to repel any armed attack against the forces of the United States and to prevent further aggression", and "to take all necessary steps, including the use of armed force, to assist any member or protocol state of the Southeast Asia Collective Defense Treaty requesting assistance in defense of its freedom". Although this did not constitute a declaration of war, a sustained campaign of heavy bombing was instigated almost immediately, and by early 1965, the first of hundreds of thousands of US combat troops were arriving in South Vietnam.

The USS *Maddox* attacked by three North Vietnamese torpedo boats

"Shooting at whales"

The North Vietnamese attacks were hardly unprovoked, as Johnson readily acknowledged. He described the coastal raids as something "I imagine [the North Vietnamese] wanted to put a stop to". Yet neither ship sustained any damage or casualties from the August 4 attack. Was there even a "second attack" at all?

The US Navy Historical Center now concedes that "North Vietnamese naval forces did not attack *Maddox* and *Turner Joy* that night". Even at the time, there were doubts. The captain of the *Maddox* spoke of "freak weather conditions" messing with the radar, while before Johnson's TV announcement, Admiral Grant Sharp of the Pacific Fleet sent word back to the White House that "many of the reported contacts and torpedoes fired appear doubtful". Citing the weird weather, and hyped-up personnel aboard the American ships, Sharp said: "A lot of these torpedo attacks were from the sonar operators!"

Squadron commander James Stockdale, a Navy pilot who later became a POW and Ross Perot's 1992 vice-presidential candidate, had "the best seat in the house" that night. In his book *In Love And War*, he wrote that "our destroyers were just shooting at phantom targets – nothing there but black water and American fire power". Lyndon Johnson admitted in 1965 that "for all I know, our Navy was shooting at whales out there", while McNamara went much further in the 2001 documentary *The Fog Of War*. Declaring with surprising contrition that "we initiated the action", he reflected that the geopolitical intentions of the North Vietnamese had been "misjudged", and the dangers to the US "exaggerated". That same film revealed a phone conversation between Johnson and McNamara, some weeks before Tonkin, in which Johnson expressed the desire to manipulate the North Vietnamese government into doing something provocative, declaring "I want to be able to trap these people".

As for Congress's speedy resolution, it clearly had its origins in a resolution drawn up in May 1964 by Undersecretary of State George Ball, who oversaw Operation 34A. His draft endorsed "all measures, including the commitment of force", to defend South Vietnam and Laos, should their governments seek help. The National Security Council responded at the time by suggesting that it would fare best in Congress after the 1964 civil rights bill had gone through in July. According to Daniel Hallin in *The Uncensored War*, the shoddiness of the case for war was clear. Journalists had "a great deal of information" contradicting the official Gulf of Tonkin account, but it simply wasn't used. Hanoi had complained about boat and aircraft attacks on August 1, but was ignored.

Oil, the Kuomintang and Kennedy

McNamara and Johnson's inflated perceptions of the threat of Communism may have meant that, for them, the end of war justified the means. However, in his 1972 book *The War Conspiracy*, Professor Peter Dale Scott argued that a more complex web of arms and oil corporations had pushed the US government into war in Vietnam, seeking control of the "considerable offshore oil deposits in the South China Sea", mainly south of South Vietnam.

Also involved, apparently, were elements of Chiang Kai-shek's Kuomintang (KMT) dictatorship in Taiwan, who were eager to regain the lost Chinese mainland. According to Dale: "The only way the KMT imagined they could get back into China would be if they somehow involved America in a war in that area" – provoking turmoil in Indochina through the diaspora of Chinese exiles, linked and funded by drug trafficking, as well as through Chinese dissidents in the CIA.

Dale highlighted two National Security Action Memorandums: NSAM 263 was signed by President Kennedy in early October 1963, to withdraw sixteen thousand US military personnel from Vietnam by 1965; NSAM 273, signed by Johnson three days after Kennedy's assassination, purported to continue the withdrawal policy by referring to the previous memo, as the *New York Times* and *Washington Post* reported. But it actually referred to a separate, non-binding advisor's report, while escalating US military assistance to South Vietnam. The timing of the NSAMs was alarming: Dale remarked that "the Kennedy assassination was itself an important, perhaps a crucial, event in the history of the Indochina war conspiracy", and claimed that pressure on his publishers from the CIA blocked the distribution of his book for several years.

On the other hand, it seems bizarrely indirect for the Taiwanese to start trouble simply to get the US "into the region". If the hope was to divert mainland China and keep its expansion plans in check, then it has to be said that the US defeat in Vietnam didn't lead to a Chinese invasion of Taiwan.

Dale's speculation as to the profit motive behind the war might seem to be supported by the action of the South Vietnamese government in 1973, just as the US Senate refused to fund further military operations in Indochina, in awarding oil exploration contracts (never fulfilled) to Mobil, Exxon, Shell and others. That's hardly a smoking gun, and seems a bit belated considering the war had already been going for a decade. It is however true that the South China Sea holds enormous oil and gas reserves, estimated at over 210 billion barrels of oil, a third of the size of the Persian Gulf reserves. Since the early 1970s, arguments as to who controls its islands have led to increasingly frequent naval clashes between Vietnam, China and the Philippines. Six countries contest ownership of the Paracel and Spratly Islands, none of whose claims are recognized by the US. American historian Howard Zinn has also pointed to the chain of US bases in the Philippines, Taiwan, Japan and South Korea which have been rendered "precarious" by increasing Communist control, as has the US hold on tin, oil and rubber from Indonesia and Malaysia.

Bankers backing losses and unlikely Communists

Some theories circulating on the Internet are clearly bonkers. These include the notion that the Vietnam and Korean Wars were *deliberately* lost, in order to scare other non-Communist states worldwide into supporting the US and NATO, and rope them into the US dollar economy and the international banking system. Given the uncertainty of the desired outcome on the one hand, and the huge loss of men, money and prestige on the other, this hardly seems cost-effective, to put it mildly.

Another suggestion, put forward by the *New American* magazine, is that the Vietnam War was never intended to be winnable, because McNamara, Henry Kissinger and President Nixon, all members of the Council on Foreign Relations, were Communists who wanted Communist victories in Indochina. In which case you have to wonder why they had a war at all.

An enduring legacy

Around 58,000 US military personnel and 1.25 million Vietnamese soldiers from both sides were killed in the Vietnam War, along with hundreds of thousands of civilians who died as a result of either direct action or the attendant chaos. In addition, 750,000 Cambodians perished following Richard Nixon's illegal bombing of their country. Although the calamitous costs of the war, and the resultant domestic unrest in the US led Lyndon Johnson not to seek re-election in 1968, he was never called to account for the fabricated "incident" that started it all.

Vietnam – a poor, predominantly agricultural

country – had more bombs dropped on it than Nazi Germany, and a massive dose of dioxin-laden defoliants that still cause hideous birth defects today. To rub salt in the wound, the US then subjected it to a further twenty years of economic sanctions. Cambodia, meanwhile, was taken over by the genocidal Khmer Rouge regime, overthrown in 1979 when the Vietnamese invaded after several years of murderous Khmer incursions. This prompted the US and UK governments to send arms and SAS instructors for Pol Pot's forces on the Thai border.

The plight of Cambodia was famously depicted in Roland Joffe's film *The Killing Fields*, based on the experience of journalist Sydney Schanberg and his friend Dith Pran. During the first Gulf War, Schanberg recalled the Gulf of Tonkin fabrications and warned: "We Americans are the ultimate innocents. We are forever desperate to believe that this time the government is telling us the truth."

SOURCES

Books

Peter Dale Scott The War Conspiracy: The Secret Road To The Second IndoChina War (1972). An angry if not always persuasive diatribe against the larger forces that, Dale claims, conspired to make war in Southeast Asia.

Daniel Ellsberg Secrets: A Memoir of Vietnam And The Pentagon Papers (2003). This prizewinning book by an insider who decided to blow the whistle begins with the Gulf of Tonkin incident. Ellsberg worked in the Defense Department and later on the top secret McNamara study of US decision-making in Vietnam, later known as the Pentagon Papers.

Film

The Fog Of War: Eleven Lessons From The Life Of Robert S. McNamara (Errol Morris, 2002) Morris's Oscar-winning documentary is based on extended interviews with McNamara, the charismatic US Defense Secretary from 1961 to 1968, and covers the Cuban Missile crisis as well as Vietnam. Don't hold your breath for a sequel featuring Donald Rumsfeld.

Websites

ⓦ **www.eia.doe.gov/emeu/cabs/schinatab. html** Detailed documentation on energy reserves in the South China Seas.

The Israeli attack on USS Liberty

The gains made by Israel during the June 1967 Six Day War were truly remarkable. Within less than a week, the Israelis attacked and comprehensively defeated the armed forces of Jordan, Syria and Egypt, quintupling its territory by retaking the Golan Heights, the Gaza Strip, the West Bank and the Sinai Peninsula. What's more, those victories were won single-handedly, with no direct military support from the US.

But that's not the whole story. In what's largely a forgotten footnote to the conflict, Israeli military forces actually attacked the US Navy intelligence ship USS *Liberty*, killing 34 servicemen and injuring 174 more. This mysterious incident, which eight successive US presidents, from Lyndon Johnson to George W. Bush, have publicly acknowledged to have been a mistake, is regarded by some as evidence of an intricate conspiracy at the highest levels of the US and Israeli governments.

It was on June 8, three days after the start of the war, that the USS *Liberty* of the Sixth Fleet found itself under attack a dozen or so miles off the Sinai coast. At about 2pm Sinai time, as the *Liberty* was gathering radio intercepts from the chaos ashore, Mirage jet planes appeared, circled it, and then began to bomb and strafe it. They were later joined by Israeli torpedo boats, in a protracted attack that lasted over an hour.

"It was a mistake"

Although both Egypt and the USSR were initially suspected of carrying out the attack, Israel took responsibility within days, claiming that its aircraft and boats had mistaken the *Liberty* for an Egyptian vessel, the *El Quseir* – a civilian cargo ship a quarter the size of the *Liberty*. Among the barrage of reports that backed the story were the Israelis' Ram Ron Commission of Inquiry, which said on June 16 that the attack was "a bona fide mistake", and a US Navy Court of Inquiry, which concluded two days later that it was "mistaken identity". A month later, the Clifford Report for the Foreign Intelligence Advisory Board said that "information thus far available" suggested that the attack was not knowingly carried out against a US vessel.

The USS *Liberty*

The "mistake" version fails to hold water

In his 1976 book, *Assault On The Liberty*, a survivor of the attack, Lieutenant Commander James Ennes, argued that the *Liberty* was obviously American, and located in international waters. He suggested that the Israelis deliberately attacked the US intelligence ship in order to stop the Americans learning about a surprise assault on Syria. The theory was further expanded on Ennes's USS *Liberty* Memorial website (www.ussliberty.org), and by the History Channel's 2001 documentary, *Cover Up: Attack On The USS Liberty*.

The Israelis alleged that the *Liberty* was not flying a flag, and that no markings were discernible to the Israeli pilots and boat crews. However, the Court of Inquiry, the Clifford Report and the Salans Report all agreed that a 5ft by 8ft flag was visible, as were hull markings on the bow and stern. Ennes additionally stated that there was enough wind to blow the flag aloft. Attacking unidentified ships in neutral waters would in any case be a war crime, while it's claimed that one flight recognized the ship as being "possibly American or Soviet", and non-hostile, before the main air attack began. According to Ennes, witnesses aboard the *Liberty* reported that the Israeli planes were so close at times that the pilots could be seen in their cockpits, and that they had waved at the planes. The *Liberty*'s crew were supposedly told to stay quiet or face court martial at the very least.

The CIA replies

In August 1977, accusations that the assault on the *Liberty* was being covered up prompted the CIA to declassify its own conclusion, reached five days after the attack, that the attack had been accidental, and caused by the resemblance between the *Liberty* and the *El Quseir*. That September, CIA director Stanfield Turner appeared on ABC's *Good Morning America* to say the Israeli government had no knowledge of the *Liberty*'s existence prior to the attack, and he further wrote in 1978 that the attack "was not in malice".

Operation Cyanide

The Liberty Veterans Association (LVA), formed in 1982, claimed that the attack was deliberate. Concocted between the US and Israel, it was a ruse designed to blame Egypt and justify a massive, nuclear retaliation by the US on the Arab world, thereby ensuring (eternal) victory for Israel. This was also the case argued by a former *Sunday Times* journalist, Peter Hounam, in *Operation Cyanide: How The Bombing Of The USS Liberty Nearly Caused World War III*, and in the TV documentary *Dead In The Water*. He stated that the *Liberty* was in international waters, flying its flag, when attacked by unmarked planes. Only because it failed to sink, carrying all the evidence and witnesses to the bottom of the sea, was Israel forced to admit to the attack. Supposedly, LBJ knew all about it in advance, while the White House twice recalled rescue planes heading for the *Liberty*, and Secretary of State Dean Rusk said it was no accident.

Judge Cristol defends the "mistake" theory

US civil judge A. Jay Cristol, a former navy pilot and lawyer who wrote *The Liberty Incident: The 1967 Israeli Attack On The US Navy Spy Ship*, has become the most prominent advocate of the "mistake" case. His view, reported at length by both the *Jerusalem Post* and the Anti-Defamation League, is that the *Liberty* was marked on the Naval Intelligence map board at Haifa, only to be removed shortly before the attack. That decision was made at "tactical level", while defence minister General Moshe Dayan was at lunch in the countryside. Israeli torpedo boats were seeking a "grey ship" suspected of shelling Israeli forces, which had been spotted heading for Port Said.

Air strikes began just after 2pm, but after fourteen minutes the flight leader noticed that the ship's hull markings were not in Arabic, and stopped attacking. When Israeli torpedo boats arrived soon afterwards, signals from the *Liberty* were unfortunately obscured by smoke. The order to "hold fire" was interpreted as "open fire", and the boats replied with torpedoes. The *Liberty* was identified first as Egyptian, then Soviet, and then Egyptian again, before an Israeli helicopter pilot finally confirmed it as being American at 3.12pm.

In 2003, Cristol sued the National Security Agency to obtain transcripts of communications between Israeli helicopter pilots, intercepted by an EC-121 aircraft flying nearby between 2.30pm and 3.27pm. These transcripts, drawn from before, during and after the attack, reveal the same confusion he'd previously reported. No tape has been found to confirm the claims of conspiracy theorists that Israeli pilots identified the ship as American before they attacked. Senator John McCain, whose father took part in the Navy Inquiry of June 18, 1967, and Senator Bob Graham of the Senate Select Committee on Intelligence, concurred with Cristol's findings. Cristol states that a total of ten US and three Israeli investigations have now concluded it was a case of mistaken identity.

The battle gets ugly

According to Internet writer William Hughes, the helicopter pilots' views as to mistaken identity are irrelevant, because they arrived after the attack. The NSA intercepts released in 2003 show one he-

licopter hearing at 2.30pm that the ship was "unidentified', and then ground control telling them all at 2.42pm that it was an Egyptian cargo ship, without mentioning the name *El Quseir*.

For the pilots to appear so comfortable attacking the ship despite the doubt as to its identity is frightening. That would be against international law, and surely common sense. And it does seem strange that they could tell that the ship's name, written in two-foot high letters, was not in Arabic, but were unable to discern that the writing was in English, notwithstanding the six-ft high identification numbers on the ship's sides. In addition, the fact that the *Liberty* was removed from the Israelis' war map shows that at some point they knew that the ship existed, which contradicts the version of events given by the CIA in 1977.

Something to hide

In his 2000 book *Body Of Secrets*, former ABC TV *World Tonight* reporter James Bamford wrote that radio intercepts gathered by the EC-121 show that the Israeli pilots saw the American flag. Bamford suggested that US servicemen were not the only ones being murdered, and that the *Liberty* was attacked in order to stop it from learning that Israeli forces on Sinai were massacring Egyptian prisoners. If that's the case, Israel would have had to weigh the possible consequences of attacking a major ally, and perpetrating a war crime, to cover up a war crime that was taking place somewhere else.

Cristol countered in the *Jerusalem Post* that while Bamford quoted linguist Marvin Nowicki, aboard the EC-121, about the intercepts, he failed to quote a letter from Nowicki to Bamford stating that the intercepts proved the accident theory. Arguing that "Mr. Bamford's writings are much closer to fiction than to history", Cristol questioned how any electronic intelligence ship could overhear murders happening miles over the horizon, for which in any case no supporting evidence such as graves, or even allegations from Egypt, has ever appeared. Cristol added that the Liberty Veterans Association was "very active" in supporting conspiracy theories, and was founded by Congressmen Paul Findley of Illinois, a politician sympathetic to the Palestinian cause, and Paul N. McCloskey.

The Moorer inquiry indicts Israel

Despite Cristol's rebuttal, Bamford's interpretation of the radio messages was taken seriously by the Liberty Alliance investigation in October 2003, which was led by former Joint Chief of Staff chairman Admiral Thomas Moorer and backed by Marines General Raymond Davis, Rear Admiral Merlin Staring and ex-ambassador to Saudi Arabia, James Akins.

According to the Moorer inquiry, Israel wanted to blame Egypt for the sinking of the *Liberty*, and thus provoke the US into joining the war. It concluded that the movements of the *Liberty* were watched for eight hours, before it was attacked by a dozen Mirage jets using napalm, 30mm cannon and rockets. As Israeli vessels subsequently unleashed their torpedoes and machine-guns, distress messages were jammed. According to Captain Joe Tully of the carrier USS *Saratoga*, and Rear Admiral Lawrence Geis, the White House withdrew a Sixth Fleet intervention to rescue the *Liberty*.

Captain Ward Boston, counsel to the 1967 Navy Court of Inquiry, added that Secretary of State John McNamara and President Johnson instructed the inquiry to reach the conclusion that it was a case of mistaken identity, and compressed the necessary six months into a mere ten days. Boston also claimed that Admiral Kidd, the chairman of the inquiry, privately admitted that his hand had been forced. Dean Rusk, former CIA director Richard

Helms, and two former NSA directors agreed.

While Moorer arguably prejudiced his own inquiry by stating back in 1993 that "I can never accept the claim that this was a mistaken attack", this does nothing to impugn the testimony of the various senior notables who supported his conclusion.

The Anti-Defamation League responded to Moorer's charge by arguing that Israel didn't need the US to intervene in the war. The Israelis had already destroyed the Egyptian air force, and were racing across the Sinai, with victory just hours away. Neither did Israel conceal its responsibility for attacking the *Liberty*. Both the ADL and Cristol refer to Admiral Kidd's remarks as "alleged", and argue that because he's dead they're not valid testimony. They suggest that the *Liberty*'s radio was not jammed, but tuned to the wrong frequencies, with its cables and antennae damaged by gunfire, and finally, that if the Israelis had really wanted to sink the *Liberty*, they would have succeeded.

Insults and arguments

At a January 2004 State Department hearing, Bamford and Cristol clashed in person, trading arguments and insults. Protestors who shouted "whitewash" and "cover-up" when the hearing once more concluded that the attack was a "mistake" had to be forcibly removed.

In June 2004, the ADL described the *Liberty* issue as "popular among anti-Israel conspiracy theorists" seeking to undermine Israel. That same month, the *Jerusalem Post* published "exclusive transcripts" from the Israeli jet pilots, claiming that they proved that the attack was a "tragic mistake". The highlights of the new transcripts centre on what ground controller Colonel Mushuel Kislev told the jet pilots, with all timings on Sinai time.

At 1.50pm Kislev says: "If it's a warship then screw it." At 1.54pm a weapons officer asks: "What is this? Americans?" – but his guess is dismissed. At

1.56pm a pilot queries: "What is it? What is it? A destroyer? A patrol boat? What is it? ... I can't identify it, but in any case it's a military ship." He then begins strafing with 30mm cannon, before other pilots enter the affray with bombs and napalm.

At 1.58pm Kislev is surprised that the ship isn't returning fire, and at 2:02pm he advises that "if there is a doubt, don't attack". After a colleague gives the go-ahead, he concludes at 2.03pm "you can sink her". Then his colleagues change their minds again, and at 2.04pm the attackers are told to hold back because "[the Navy] want to get close and have a look". Kislev suggests at 2.09pm that they should "look for a flag if they can see one", but the pilots then misread the *Liberty*'s identification letters. Only at 2.14pm, amid serious alarm that the ship may be "apparently American", does Kislev order the air attack to be stopped.

Neither the transcripts nor the *Post* mentioned that the boat attacks continued after Kislev stopped the air attacks, and neither did the *Post* mention the *Liberty*'s exact location. The transcripts don't fully fit the events laid out by either Ennes or Cristol's NSA transcripts, which report doubts on the ship's identification at 2.30pm and then call it "Egyptian" at 2.42pm.

A controversy without end

After four decades and dozens of books, documentaries and inquiries, the bitterness of the arguments over the *Liberty* seems only to have increased. There has still been no Congressional-level investigation, and a lot of very senior US political and military figures believe that a conspiracy of some kind took place. Quite what the purpose of that conspiracy may have been, however, remains unclear – contradictory theories suggest that the aim was either to embroil the US in the war or to keep it out. Some also argue that whether the attack was deliberate or not, Johnson and successive presidents have publicly accepted it as a "mistake" in order not to antagonize the Jewish vote in the US.

Furthermore, debate as to the precise facts has become increasingly incidental to nastier arguments. Cristol is not alone in believing that the incident has been stirred up by enemies of Israel. Michael Oren, author of *Six Days Of War*, argues that conspiracy theories about Israel and the Jews are "immortal" because "they tap into the notion or belief of an international Jewish cabal, the Protocols of the Elders of Zion thing". The Liberty Alliance has accused powerful pro-Israeli interests of thwarting proper Congressional investigation, while the USS *Liberty* Memorial website prints comments from "its critics and certain self-hating Americans".

SOURCES

Books

James Bamford Body Of Secrets (2002). Bamford analyzes radio transcripts in immense detail in a bid to prove Israel's culpability.

A. Jay Cristol The Liberty Incident: The 1967 Israeli Attack On The US Navy Spy Ship (2003). Judge Cristol, a stalwart proponent of the "mistake" theory, reports on his personal fifteen-year investigation.

Peter Hounam Operation Cyanide: How The Bombing Of The USS Liberty Nearly Caused World War III (2005). Perhaps the most paranoid of all *Liberty* literature, seeing the attack as an attempt to bring about nuclear war.

Websites

ⓦ **www.adl.org/Israel/uss.asp** The response of the Anti-Defamation League to the ongoing controversy.

ⓦ **www.ussliberty.org** The definitive "conspiracy" site on the *Liberty*, detailing most of the theories and offering links to yet more.

The Kremlin and the Chechen rebels

"Kremlinology", the old-fashioned art of divining which way the wind was blowing in Russia from almost imperceptible clues, was supposed to have died with the collapse of the USSR. Arguably, however, the philosophy that underpinned Kremlinology long predated the Soviet Union; indeed, it may have shaped the twilight-grey shades of Communist politics, rather than vice versa. The current president of Russia, former spy and KGB chief Vladimir Putin, is the latest *eminence grise* of the Kremlin's black arts. His time as Prime Minister and President has been characterized by a series of bloody disasters and terrorist attacks, not exclusively but not least in and around Chechnya. Some observers, however, claim to discern an appalling conspiracy of terror, and trace the chain of events back to Putin himself.

A Russian conspiracy in the Caucasus?

During the summer of 1999, Vladimir Putin, then Russia's new acting Prime Minister, was confronted by renewed conflict in the unstable mass of mini-republics in the Caucasus, in southern Russia. Militant Muslim forces from Chechnya – the tiny breakaway republic that, during its fight for independence, between 1994 and 1996, had fought the Russian army to a standstill and caused President Yeltsin to hit the vodka bottle even harder – were raiding next-door Dagestan.

That August, BBC Online reported a rumour that the Dagestan incursion was a "well-orchestrated conspiracy involving senior figures associated with the Kremlin". By that reckoning, the leader of the insurgency, Chechen warlord Shamil Basayev, was acting on Kremlin orders to create trouble. The incursion served to justify a state of emergency, and the postponing of Russian parliamentary elections in December, while also providing a chance for Putin to blood himself by driving the insurgents back into Chechnya. The BBC's Dagestan correspondent gave more credence to the notion that militant Islamic forces were broadening their *jihad* against "infidel" Russians, and that the incursion was the first phase in building an Islamic republic of states via which Chechnya would gain access to the Caspian Sea. Three years after fending off the Russians at horrific cost, he suggested, Chechen separatists were harbouring suicidal delusions of grandeur.

Someone's bombing Moscow

Then the bombings began. On September 4, a bomb destroyed a block of flats in the southern Russian city of Buinaksk, killing 62 people. Two apartment blocks in Moscow were blown up on September 9 and 13, killing 222 men, women and children in their beds. Finally, on September 16, a further seventeen people were killed by a blast in the southern city of Volgodonsk. With impressive speed, the Russian secret service, the FSB, posted a computer-generated picture all over the capital of a Chechen man, Achimez Gochiyaev, who had rented ground floor space in the Moscow blocks. According to the FSB, Gochiyaev was working for Chechen warlords Shamil Basayev and Khattab.

On October 1, 1999, Putin ordered a wholesale

"anti-terrorist operation" in Chechnya, and the Russian army moved in en masse. Overnight, Putin's public image changed from being a grey non-entity handpicked by Yeltsin to a powerful macho leader. Promising to restore stability to Chechnya, he won the presidential election in March 2000 with over half the vote. His Communist opponent and runner-up, Gennady Zyuganov, accused the government of falsifying the results.

A fifth bomb is foiled

However, the Russian authorities never produced any significant evidence that Chechen terrorists were behind the Moscow bombings. No terrorist group claimed responsibility, and no one has been brought to trial. Some men have been arrested, but none of the alleged "ring-leaders". Respected British journalist John Sweeney reported that bull-dozers obliterated the second bombsite just three days after the blast, destroying any remaining evidence.

The strangest detail of all was the "thwarting" of a fifth bomb in the southern city of Ryazan. A resident of an apartment block there saw a car with a Moscow licence plate, containing a Russian-looking couple who drove off when approached. The police were called, and discovered three sacks of hexogen powder – the explosive used in the other four bombings – and a timing device in the basement. The building was evacuated. FSB men confiscated the sacks, before announcing the next day, a hundred miles away in Moscow, that the whole thing was an "exercise" and that the sacks contained sugar. Two Russians were arrested and then released.

Considering that real bombs were blowing up real people, that's a hell of an "exercise". The Ryazan police were adamant that the timer and hexogen were real. If it was just a drill, why were the two Russians arrested at all? One resident said that he didn't know who was behind the foiled attack, but pointed out that "the government started bombing Chechnya the next day."

Pointing the finger

The mystery of the "fifth bomb" was reported by John Sweeney, the *LA Times*, and author David Satter, who argued in *Darkness At Dawn* that for Chechens to blow up apartment blocks made absolutely no sense. Boris Berezovsky told the press in London in March 2002 that the FSB had carried out the bombings, with Putin's complicity, in order to justify a second Chechen war and boost Putin's profile. As evidence, he presented documents showing that the Russian Explosives Conversion Centre had in 1999 and 2000 purchased large quantities of hexogen from military units, and shipped it all over Russia.

Businessman Berezovsky repeated his charges in the film *Assassination Of Russia*, while the Russian newspaper *Novaya Gazeta* quoted GRU agent Alexei Galkin as saying that the FSB and GRU (Russia's military intelligence service) were behind all the blasts. According to an Agence France Presse report in July 2002, the chief suspect, Achimez Gochiayev – who came not from Chechnya but Karachayevo-Cherkessia, and remains in hiding – claimed that a school friend thought to be an FSB agent had advised him to rent the premises in the apartment block. Former KGB colonel Konstantin Preobrazhensky commented that "Chechen rebels were incapable of organizing a series of bombings without help from high-ranking Moscow officials".

The FSB however denied all involvement in the bombings. Berezovsky for one had an axe to grind. He had fled Putin's Russia to the UK, finding himself wanted for "economic crimes" despite having used his TV stations to help Putin become president. In September 2004, a *Financial Times* article by Martin Wolf argued that "we make common cause with Putin at our peril", because "the bombings that preceded his first election and then as conveniently ceased gave him the presidency". The British Helsinki Human Rights Group responded that "Boris Berezovsky's well-funded conspiracy theory" overlooked the fact that the Chechen separatists' invasion of Dagestan had already happened.

The Moscow siege

On October 23, 2002, a 41-strong gang of Chechen rebels took over the Moscow's Dubrovka theatre. The hostage-takers, armed and strapped with explosives, were seeking to focus world attention on the plight

War damage in Grozny, Chechnya, April 1995

of Chechnya. The siege ended when Russian security services pumped a mysterious gas into the theatre, knocking out everyone inside, and then stormed the building. They refused to disclose what kind of gas it was even to the hospitals treating the hostages. A total of 129 people died in an incident that the Russians called their own 9/11.

Although all the hostage-takers were among the dead, they were not killed by the gas, which had successfully immobilized them. Instead, according to British Conservative MP Dr Julian Lewis, they were shot in cold blood. As he asked the House of Commons in June 2003: "If those people were so incapacitated ... that they could not explode their devices, why did the Russian authorities not act [to take them alive], if not from any sense of simple humanity, then from the common-sense desire for the intelligence that might be gained from interrogating captives who had mounted such a damaging, dangerous and destructive operation ... Why were those considerations put aside and the people executed on the spot while unconscious?"

That question was prompted by former Soviet dissident Vladimir Bukovsky and allegations reported by Agence France Presse and *Novaya Gazeta* that April. A Chechen rebel leader and former Russian spy claimed that former Chechen journalist Khanpach Terkipayev was among the hostage-takers and had been placed there by Russian security services. Moscow supposedly needed the siege because Western capitals were promoting the idea of negotiating with Chechnya's separatists. Dr Lewis warned dissenters that "all I would say is that that is not just my conspiracy theory", adding that the Moscow apartment bombings "conveniently" provided the perfect *casus belli* for the second Russian invasion of Chechnya.

Murder and mayhem – and the mysterious Basayev

The Caucasus seemed to be calming down, until on August 28, 2004, two Tupolev passenger jets on internal Russian flights crashed within hours of each other, killing ninety people. Two female Chechen suicide bombers, one aboard each plane, were officially blamed, and when a bomb subsequently exploded at a Moscow metro station, Chechens were blamed once again.

Then came the worst atrocity of all. On September 1, 2004, thirty-two men and women, armed with guns and homemade bombs, took over an elementary school in Beslan in the state of North Ossetia, which bordered Chechnya. A thousand hostages, most of them children, were held for three days before the siege ended amid explosions and gunfire. Over half of the 330 who were killed were children.

According to a website that claims to serve as his official mouthpiece, www.Kavkazcenter.com, the Chechen warlord Shamil Basayev has claimed responsibility for the plane crashes and the Beslan school seizure. Holding the Russians accountable because of their war in Chechnya, he promised more to come.

Vilified in the Russian media for his alleged links to Al Qaeda, Basayev has been called "Russia's homegrown version of Osama bin Laden" by CBS News. He first came to prominence when he seized control of a Russian hospital in 1995. Although a hundred hostages died in the ensuing battle with security services, Basayev and his men managed to escape. He is also said to have claimed responsibility for the Moscow theatre siege and for the killing of Kremlin-backed Chechen president Akhmad Kadyrov in 1999, but he blamed Dagestanis for the Moscow bombings.

Although Basayev is thought to have left Chechnya just twice in a decade, the Americans are sufficiently worried about him for Secretary of State Colin Powell to have called him, in August 2003, a "threat to US national security", as well as American people, policy and economic interests. Tall, often depicted with a peaked cap, a hedge of a beard and a massive cigar, Basayev is currently aged around forty and resembles a youthful Fidel Castro. His most distinctive feature is that he only has one leg, having lost the other while escaping Russian forces who chased him through a minefield in 1999. The Russian authorities have repeatedly failed either to catch him or to forestall his attacks, despite offering a $10m reward.

Some liberal Russian political figures allege that the Russian government doesn't really want to capture Basayev, as his presence and antics justify continued fighting in Chechnya. Anatol Lieven of the Carnegie Endowment for International Peace dismissed such rumours as similar to suggestions that President Bush's administration was behind 9/11. As he told the Associated Press news agency: "You can oppose these conflicts without yielding to irrational conspiracy theories."

A third force

Despite Basayev's claim, and despite the widespread assumption that Chechens were responsible, Russia's defence minister Sergei Ivano has admitted that there were no Chechens among the hostage-takers at Beslan. Former Chechen President Aslan Mashkadov's envoy Akhmed Zakayev has denied Chechen responsibility, blaming "a third force that brought Russian President Vladimir Putin to power" for all three incidents. Their motive was supposedly to destabilize the North Caucasus by creating animosity between the Christians of North Ossetia and the Muslims of Chechnya, thereby justifying the continued presence of Russian soldiers.

In Internet chatrooms, a story has circulated that the hostage-takers were not "international terrorists" but local mercenaries, let into the school by local police who knew them. Once inside, they then dug up arms from under the gymnasium floor, where they had been buried by builders months before. By this reckoning, the ensuing massacre was simply a mistake. A bomb detonated by accident, bringing down the roof and panicking parents and police into storming the building.

In late January 2005, the British *Independent* newspaper reported that hundreds of Beslan residents were blocking roads to protest about what they called "official apathy" over the atrocity, and denounce suspected Russian complicity in the attack. On January 28, Interfax News and the BBC reported Aleksandr Torshin, the deputy speaker of the Federation Council (upper house), and the chairman of a Russian parliamentary commission investigating Beslan, as telling journalists that "a terrorist atrocity on a scale such as this could not have been committed without accomplices." He stated that the accomplices must have held ranks higher than major or lieutenant colonel.

According to Vladimir Kulakov, another senator and commission member, the terrorists had accomplices not only in Beslan, but also at federal (ie Russian) level, and that the latter were "still in their posts". Meanwhile, an amateur video was given to CBS TV, apparently showing talks in progress between the Ingush ex-president, Ruslan Aushev and the terrorists. How a US TV channel had come to acquire this video was not made clear. At the time of writing, the official inquiry was continuing its investigations.

Putin blames the US

On September 4, 2004, responding to the Beslan school siege, Putin told Russia that the country's borders were no longer safe "from East or West". He accused the US of supporting terrorists, trying to disarm Russia's nuclear capability, and scheming to diminish its territory. "Some would like to cut a juicy piece of our pie", as he put it; "terrorism is just one instrument they use". The allegation seemed strange in view of the official US stance depicting Basayev as being in cohorts with Osama bin Laden, and the fact that at that same moment, the siege was being cited at the Republican National Convention as the kind of Islamic extremism which justified the global "war on terror".

The conspiracist magazine *The Insider*, on the other hand, depicted Beslan as forming part of the "terror" war that has enabled Putin to become ever more authoritarian, diverting attention from the economic liberalization that has privatized medicine, closed schools, worsened unemployment, and failed to deliver pensions. Putin has also been busy reinforcing the powers of the FSB, creating an anti-terrorism ministry, tightening the grip of the Security Council, and reinstating the "vertical" rule of the Communist era, by appointing regional governors instead of having them elected.

There's oil in them there mountains

So what makes Chechnya and the other tiny fragmented mountain states of the Caucasus – like Ossetia (north and south), Ingushetia, Kabardino-Balkaria and Karachaevo-Cherkessia – so important to the Russians? The Chechens themselves are in no doubt. After Dzhokar Dudayev was elected president of Chechnya in 1991, on a constitution based on "US principles" of government, his government suffered a dozen assassinations and coup attempts, which he claimed were Russian-backed. Then came the first Russian invasion, from 1994 to 1996. Dudayev wrote in the *Washington Post* in 1995 that "the lure and importance of the Chechen oil and pipeline [through the Caucasus states] have prompted Moscow to use brutal force ... to seize control of our capital Grozny".

Putin is clearly alarmed by the increasing US military and economic presence in the independent ex-Soviet states of Azerbaijan and Georgia, just south of the Russian Caucasus – which constitute a critical route for oil and gas pipelines from the Caspian Sea and Iran – and by further NATO encroachment into former Soviet satellites. Both Russia and the US have described Azerbaijan's Pankisi Gorge as a hotbed of Islamic militancy that justifies intervention from both countries.

The poison of power

In retrospect, Putin's complaint that territories were being encouraged to secede from Russian influence were given an eerie resonance by events on September 5, 2004, in the former Soviet state of Ukraine. With Beslan still dominating the headlines, Ukraine's opposition leader Viktor Yushchenko was invited to dine with the chiefs of the country's security service. In a grisly assassination attempt, he was fed soup containing dioxin, which swiftly turned his handsome face into a ghoulish mask. Yushchenko survived, after treatment in Austria, but "lost" Ukraine's presidential election in November.

Worldwide attention then focussed on Kiev, as demonstrators poured into the streets. It was eventually declared that the first ballot had been rigged in favour of the incumbent pro-Putin Prime Minister, Viktor Yanukovich, and Yushchenko won a re-run in January.

Had Yushchenko died as planned, in September, would the wider world have noticed? And who stood to gain the most from a pro-Putin premier in Ukraine? According to the official Russian perspective, the US has been exerting too much untoward influence in the country. Thus, in 2003 and 2004, the Americans spent $65m in Ukraine subsidizing democratic institutes and meddlesome NGOs

– such as the Poland-America-Ukraine Cooperation Initiative – that the Russians see as "blatantly" favouring Yushchenko.

A war without end

Since 1994, around 250,000 Chechen men, women and children have died either directly or indirectly as a result of the war in Chechnya. Dozens of Russian soldiers, mainly conscripts, are killed each week. While questions may have been raised among the international community, however, neither the governments of Yeltsin nor Putin have received any significant censure or opprobrium.

What concerns have been expressed have focused principally on the threats Putin's centralizing reforms pose to Russian democracy. Thus in January 2005, US Secretary of State Condoleezza Rice described "the concentration of power in the Kremlin to the detriment of other institutions in Russia" as "a real problem", saying that "the path to democracy" was uneven and far from assured.

Alarm has also been voiced about diminishing media freedoms, the persecution of Russia's oligarchs, and Russian attempts to influence Ukraine's elections. Russian Foreign Minister Sergei Lavrov has dismissed all such criticisms, arguing that critics merely hated the idea of Russia becoming economically strong and independent, and wanted a new Cold War. Meanwhile, the country's GDP has been rising fast, thanks largely to rising sales of oil and gas.

SOURCES

Books

Anna Politkovskaya Putin's Russia Russian journalist Politkovskaya stands apart, not least for her bravery in exposing the darker side of recent government policy, but also for her ability to be in the right place at the right time. As well as witnessing atrocities in Chechnya, she was a negotiator at the

Moscow siege, and might have made it to Beslan, had she not been nearly fatally poisoned en route.

Websites

ⓦ http://eng.terror99.ru/publications/072. htm The place to look for all the latest theories about the Moscow bombings.

ⓦ www.theinsider.org/mailing/article. asp?id=575 An interesting piece on the political capital Putin gained from the Beslan school siege.

ⓦ www.truth-and-justice.info/theater.html A broad selection of alternative perspectives and links on what really happened in the Moscow theatre siege.

THE GREAT GAME: AFGHANISTAN AND CASPIAN GAS

In October 2001 a US-led military force invaded war-torn Afghanistan in order to overthrow the cruel, oppressive Taliban regime, which had refused to hand over Osama bin Laden, the mastermind of 9/11. By Christmas, the Taliban had been brought down, and a new UN-backed government installed.

Instead of being the first victory in George W. Bush's "war on terror", however, perhaps this was just the latest round in what Rudyard Kipling called the "Great Game" – the secret struggle to dominate Central Asia. Some conspiracy theorists argue that Afghanistan was invaded not so much because it was a haven for terrorists, but because it was an invaluable transit route for oil and gas from the huge reserves in the land-locked Central Asian states of Azerbaijan, Kazakhstan, Turkmenistan, and Uzbekistan.

Rather than pipe their fuel through such highly undependable countries as Iran and Russia, Western oil companies suggested building pipelines to Pakistan, via Afghanistan. For that to be a viable proposition, however, the Taliban would have to be removed. And removed they were, with such alacrity that one has to suspect that the forward planning was in place before 9/11 provided the excuse to move in.

In a BBC report broadcast just before the invasion of Afghanistan, analyst Malcolm Haslett attacked this hypothesis as being "flawed" and favoured by those with "a fondness for conspiracy theories". While "the importance of Central Asian oil and gas has suddenly been noticed", he declared, Afghanistan is not the only potential route out. Thus, a pipeline has been built from the Caspian in Azerbaijan through Georgia to the Mediterranean coast of Turkey. In any case, Afghanistan still isn't stable enough for a pipeline, and Western powers have rendered pipeline deals considerably less likely with their criticisms of "human rights abuses" by Central Asia's authoritarian regimes.

Actually, Central Asian fuel reserves had hardly been "suddenly noticed". In December 1997, for example, Taliban officials met in Texas with oil corporation Unocal to discuss the construction of a gas pipeline from Turkmenistan across Afghanistan to Pakistan. Unocal announced that it had agreed with Turkmenistan to sell its gas and with Pakistan to buy it, and had begun training Afghan staff to build and maintain the line. A BBC correspondent described the deal as part of an "international scramble" to profit from developing the rich Caspian Sea energy resources.

An April 1998 paper from the James A. Baker III Institute for Public Policy of Rice University reported: "Senior Administration officials have delivered well-publicized policy declarations on the importance of Central Asia and the Caucasus to the United States. And a US military exercise in the region, though long-planned and small in scope, has been cited both there and here as a signal of our strategic interest in the region." According to some observers, the paper noted, that interest was seen as compelling enough for the region to require "a new and more assertive US policy towards it ... Why? Oil and gas. The Caspian Basin is rich – perhaps very rich – in both."

As for the need for stability, it was originally felt that if the Taliban regime could deliver it, that would be good enough. Pakistan's Prime Minister Nawaz Sharif argued that if the US recognized the Taliban, and Unocal was permitted to build the pipeline, this would create a virtuous circle of investment and stability. Things began to go wrong when Clinton authorized the bombing of Al Qaeda terrorist camps in Afghanistan in late 1998, in response to the bombing of US embassies in Tanzania and Kenya. World opinion turned decisively against the Taliban when they started blowing up historic Buddhist statues, and 9/11 completed the process.

Post-Taliban, the first US envoy to Afghanistan was former Unocal risk analyst Zalmay Khalilzad. An Afghan émigré, Khalilzad had previously been employed by the Reagan administration and Unocal to work *with* the Taliban in connection with their anti-Soviet activities and the proposed pipeline respectively. (A founding member of the Project for the New American Century – see p.381 – he subsequently served as George W. Bush's special envoy to postwar Iraq and was finally named US ambassador to Afghanistan in September 2003.)

As envoy to Afghanistan, Khalilzad worked hand-in-glove with interim president Hamid Karzai, himself a former oil industry analyst, as feasibility studies for oil and gas pipelines were drawn up. Karzai met with Turkmenistan's President Niyazov and Pakistan's President Musharraf in 2002 to approve a gas pipeline from Turkmenistan's Dauletabad gas field to the Pakistani port of Gwadar.

Present-day Afghanistan remains deeply troubled. Warlords, Al Qaeda and tribal groups are still competing for territory and power, and fighting US and Allied troops. But the $2.2 billion pipeline, worth over ten percent of the country's GDP and surpassing all foreign aid contributions, is going ahead. It would seem that pipelines don't need stability so much after all. The terrible Taliban regime has been overthrown, another reserve of fossil fuel has been opened up to the world, and everyone from Kabul and Islamabad to Houston gets rich. So what's the problem?

9/11

On August 31, 2004, the Reuters news agency's polling company, Zogby International, found that just under half (49.3 percent, to be exact) of New York City residents believed that senior officials in the Bush administration knew about the 9/11 attacks in advance and had "consciously failed" to act. Two thirds (66 percent) wanted investigations reopened, and only just over a third (36 percent) believed that the 9-11 Commission had "answered all the important questions about what actually happened".

Like the assassination of John F. Kennedy, the terrorist attack on New York's "Twin Towers" delivered a massive, epoch-making shock to the US. It wasn't only America's sense of security that had been punctured, but its sense of self. Conspiracy theorists' response to 9/11 was also disturbingly similar to JFK. When a second event of the magnitude of "JFK" came around, theorists just followed forty years of training. They pored over the tiniest minutiae of the attacks, chipping away at the timing, questioning the motives, cross-referencing the words and actions of government officials. Each finding was released back into the churning conspiracy media, now swollen by the Internet and innumerable cable TV channels. Even the government seemed to be obeying the JFK rules, when it set up the 9-11 Commission to answer public doubts. Like the 1963–64 Warren Commission, of course, its report, issued in July 2004, was dismissed as a whitewash. Perhaps its strongest charge was that the Clinton and Bush administrations had "not [been] well served" by the FBI and CIA.

The morning of September 11

At around 8.15am on September 11, 2001, American Airlines Flight 11 went off course shortly after it had taken off from Boston. Within five minutes, the plane's identification transponder beacon was switched off and a flight attendant alerted a colleague on the ground that hijackers had taken control. Almost twenty minutes later, at 8.38am, Boston air traffic controllers alerted North American Aerospace Defense Command (NORAD). At 8.42am, the transponder of United Airlines Flight 175 also blinked off, and at 8.46am, two F-15 fighter jets were scrambled from Otis Air National Guard base near Falmouth, Massachusetts.

At 8.46am, Flight 11's Boeing 767 ploughed into the North Tower of New York's iconic World Trade Center building, striking on the north side, just fourteen stories from the top. Within a minute, Flight 77 had changed its course and started heading back east. Meanwhile, confused and excited reporters were trying to make sense of the image of a burning North Tower on news networks around the world. Evacuations had already begun in the WTC's South Tower when, at 9.02am, it was struck in turn by another Boeing 767, as Flight 175 smashed into the corner of the building at the eightieth floor, causing a massive explosion of fuel and debris. It was watched by an audience of millions. Most were horrified; some cheered at this obviously symbolic blow against US hegemony and world capitalism.

At 9.06am, while President George W. Bush was sitting in on a second-grade class at a school in Florida, his chief of staff went over and whispered in his ear: "A second plane hit the other tower, and America's under attack." Bush continued with the now notorious "pet goat" reading lesson until 9.11am, when the two F-15s arrived over New York. At 9.30am two F-16s were scrambled from Langley, Virginia, and five minutes later a third plane, American Airlines Flight 77, began a spiralling descent before smashing into the side of the Pentagon. At 9.59am, the South Tower of the World Trade Center pancaked down on itself, sending giant clouds of ash and smoke across Manhattan. Three minutes later, a fourth hijacked plane, United Airlines Flight 93, plunged into the ground near Shanksville, Pennsylvania. And at 10.23am, the North Tower of the World Trade Center finally collapsed.

Responsibility

In all, 2749 people were confirmed dead or missing as a result of the four hijackings and the WTC collapse. The Bush administration very quickly blamed the Al Qaeda network of extremist Islamic terrorists, and the charge was soon supported by a video discovered in Afghanistan in November 2001, on which Al Qaeda's chief, Osama bin Laden, admitted full knowledge of the attacks. Final confirmation only came in April 2002, however, when Khalid Sheikh Mohammed told Al Jazeera reporter Yosri Fouda: "I am the head of the Al Qaeda military committee ... and yes, we did it."

Some felt Khalid Sheikh Mohammed missed a trick. If he'd said instead that Al Qaeda had nothing to do with 9/11, conspiracy theorists would have had a field day. Even as early as April 2002, the web was crawling with allegations of sinister conspiracies. Some had even struggled out of the online mire onto the relative dry land of print. At the simplest level, some conspiracy claims seemed to stem from sheer disbelief. As millionaire's son and arch-9/11 conspiracy theorist Jimmy Walter bluntly announced: "It wasn't nineteen screwups from Saudi Arabia who couldn't pass flight school who defeated the United States with a set of

Flight 175 approaches the WTC South Tower

box cutters." Or as Moroccan-born Canadian Adil Charkaoui put it, just after he was released from two years' detention on suspicion of being a terrorist: "I'm not an expert but from what I read some guy living in a cave doesn't have the means to plan an attack against the most powerful nation in the world."

Asked who he thought *was* responsible, Charkaoui told Federal Court Justice Simon Noël: "maybe it was done by ultra-conservatives in the United States for economic gain. It was the world's biggest conspiracy." This was the classic "insider" theory, in which 9/11 is seen as a "false-flag operation" – a covert action carried out in order to be blamed on the enemy. There are plenty of alleged precedents – from the Reichstag fire of 1933 to Pearl Harbor (see p.330), and from Operation Northwoods (see p.329) to the Gulf of Tonkin incident (see p.343) – but relatively few commentators, however cynical, could bring themselves to believe that the Bush administration was warped (or brilliant) enough to actually plot the 9/11 attacks. The more common claim, therefore, was that Bush's team knew about the plan in advance, and for broad strategic reasons allowed it to go ahead.

The hijackers

The weakest link in the official version of events concerned the hijackers themselves. So little was known about them, and so much of what was known was classified. Why had they been allowed into the country, when it was discovered that only four out of nineteen involved had managed to fill in a proper visa application form? Why had they enrolled in flight schools in the US when they could have learned more cheaply and more safely elsewhere? Was it true that this group of "religious extremists" had celebrated on the night of September 10 by calling up prostitutes and drinking in bars? Why had the ringleader, Mohamed Atta, left incriminating documents behind in his car, including a copy of his will and (it was said) flight simulation manuals? How had they managed to board the planes without showing up on CCTV cameras? And if the hijackers had used aliases, how had the FBI managed to track some of them down to their flight schools within a day of the Twin Towers' collapse? Were they already being watched? And *allowed* to proceed?

For conspiracy theorists, the biggest absurdity was a piece of much-touted evidence. The passport of one of the hijackers was conveniently found in the ruins of the World Trade Center. Somehow, a bit of laminated cardboard had survived a fire that was capable of melting solid steel and destroying the plane's indestructible "black boxes".

The World Trade Center

The extent of the fires in the Twin Towers became a very contentious question. Innumerable pundits, few with any expertise, claimed that the burning aviation fuel was not hot enough to melt the WTC's steel support structures. Scientific-minded conspiracists pointed out that the smoke was "sooty" and therefore not the product of a super-hot inferno. Firemen were quoted as saying that they had thought the fires could be controlled, and photos of workers looking out of gaping holes in the tower were used to demonstrate that the temperatures inside must have been tolerable. Better-informed commentators painstakingly demonstrated how the fires caused the angle clips supporting the floors to fail, leading to an unzipping effect that caused one floor to "pancake" down into the next, ultimately bringing down the entire building.

There were even reports of explosions and seismic tests showing that bombs had gone off just before the buildings collapsed, leading some to allege that the collapse was the result of a controlled demolition – either to save the rest of Manhattan, or to bury the evidence of an inside job. Curiously, these bomb reports echo similar allegations made about the Oklahoma City Bombing (see p.212). Another accusation relied on video evidence of Flight 11 crashing into the tower. A white-hot fireball or "mysterious burning object" visibly shoots ahead of the plane, trailing black smoke. Was it debris launched by aviation fuel exploding under pressure? Or evidence of the use of depleted uranium? Or was there a mysterious "pod" visible in one photograph under Flight 175, as conspiracy theorist Dave vonKleist alleges?

The Pentagon under attack

VonKleist's 911inplanesite.com website and associated video/DVD are typical of post-disaster conspiracy theorizing. Photographs and video and audio footage – even seismographic readings – are ripped out of context, given an amateurish forensic examination and the inevitable "anomalies" revealed to an eager public. Few have tried it on with the World Trade Center, given the abundant film footage of a jetliner very visibly slamming into the South Tower. When it comes to Flight 77 and the Pentagon, however, the field is wide open: all the relevant video and CCTV footage was confiscated by the FBI.

The notion that "there was no plane at the Pentagon" was bubbling away on conspiracy newsgroups within weeks of the disaster. The story hit the big time in April 2002, when French writer Thierry Meyssan published L'Effroyable Imposture, or "The Horrifying Deception" (though the English title was The Big Lie). In Paris, the book sold out its initial print run of 20,000 within two hours of going on sale.

Meyssan's theory sprang from photos of the Pentagon taken by a computer worker called Steve Riskus and posted in the immediate aftermath on the (now defunct) criticalthrash.com. The hole made in the outer wall looked bizarrely small for one punctured by a dive-bombing Boeing 757. As one French aviation expert commented: "It's like imagining that a plane of this size could pass through a window and leave the frame still standing." The grass in front of the building looked green and unscorched, and there were no signs of any wreckage. Meyssan's answer? The damage was not caused by Flight 77, but by a missile. Shot by the Pentagon at itself. (The WTC attacks were explained by the use of future-tech remote-control planes – presumably no one could be found for the suicide mission.)

Pentagon theories

Partly in response to public pressure, the Pentagon finally released five frames of the attack. The effect was like pouring aviation fuel on a smouldering fire. Conspiracy theorists asked why only *five* frames. And why, if the Pentagon had lots of good footage, which it surely must, were these five frames so ambiguous, showing first off empty skies and then a blast next to the building, with no clear shot of anything resembling an airliner in shape or size in any frame? Why hadn't the Pentagon's reputed air defences shot down the incoming jetliner? Why were workers at the site shown wearing full body suits? Did they know that there was depleted uranium lying around in the wreckage? Surely the bits of airline debris weren't what the Pentagon said they were? What had happened to the plane's wings? Why was there no footage of the actual crash?

In Brazil, where the "missile" theory was seized on even by official news media, much was made of witnesses who reported that the incoming plane was strangely quiet. Photos of what appeared to be a wrecked jet engine were not, it was claimed, the auxiliary power unit of a 757, but the remains of a Rolls Royce Allison AE3007H jet, which had (about) the same diameter. And this engine was used on the Global Hawk, a futuristic drone or unmanned aerial vehicle. Awkward eyewitness accounts of an American Airlines jetliner were explained by the alleged addition of red and blue stripes.

If it wasn't Flight 77 that had smashed into the Pentagon, sceptics asked, then where had Flight 77 (and all its passengers) gone? Pentagon officials described exactly how the airliner had bounce-crashed into the ground right in front of the building, how the wings had snapped, and either burned up or been driven into the building. The photos were confusing because they were taken with super-long lenses, creating a distorting sense of distance, and they were partly concealed by smoke or the water from fire hoses. Aerial photos showed that the plane before successfully flying the 757 so low over the ground that it decapitated exterior light stands as it approached the Pentagon. Some stunt. And this from a rookie pilot whose skills were so weak that he had been refused permission to rent a small plane a month earlier.

Pennsylvania: Flight 93

Flight 93, which crashed relatively unspectacularly into the ground near Shanksville, Pennsylvania, received relatively little coverage until it was announced that passengers had heard about events in Manhattan on their mobile phones, and had told relatives that they were going to tackle the hijackers. It was widely reported that they had succeeded, and nobly crash-landed the plane in the countryside to prevent any further loss of life. Only later was it officially concluded that the hijackers had destroyed the plane themselves.

Hit by a Boeing 757: the Pentagon, 9/11

had done far more damage than the hole visible in the initial snapshots, slamming its way though the newly reinforced outer wall and on into the first five "rings" of the building.

Undeterred, conspiracy theorists now asked how a mere 757 had done so much damage. They seized on a new picture of the inside wall of the second-to-innermost ring, punched through by an almost perfectly circular, heavily scorched hole. A missile's exit wound? No, Pentagon officials said, it was damage from an aircraft engine that had broken free of its moorings, creating an air hole that sucked the firestorm through it.

A more troubling allegation was based not on "I'm not expert but that's how it looks to me" analysis, but on reports of the extraordinary manoeuvre that brought Flight 77 down from the air and into the Pentagon. The hijacker pilot, Hani Hanjour, had pulled off an amazing descending-spiral turn

Some doubted if this was in fact the case. It was reported that in the aftermath of the attacks, Vice President Dick Cheney finally ordered the military to shoot down any further hijacked planes, and told Defense Secretary Donald Rumsfeld: "It's my understanding they've already taken a couple of aircraft out" – who "they" were, he didn't say. And in 2004, Rumsfeld told US troops in Baghdad during his Christmas Eve address that "the people who attacked the United States in New York shot down the plane over Pennsylvania." If he was stating that Flight 93 was *shot* down, presumably by the US military, didn't this imply that they had carried out the New York attack as well? Pentagon officials claimed that Rumsfeld "misspoke".

Cheney and Rumsfeld: drills and stand-down orders

If Cheney's understanding was correct and Rumsfeld's "slip" in saying that Flight 93 was shot down was true, it would prove that US air defences were not quite as leaden-footed as is often claimed. It would also prove that Rumsfeld and Cheney were not in fact arch-villains who had planned the whole thing. In the absence of clarification on this point, however, the apparent failure of NORAD to scramble fighter jets early enough to shoot down the hijacked airliners is pointed to as evidence of the Bush administration's complicity. According to some theorists, even when the jet fighters were scrambled, they must have flown at a fraction of their top speeds to explain the timescales, despite the evocative (too evocative?) soundbite from one of the pilots, who said they had flown "like scalded apes". Surely the US could not have been so incompetent as to let 9/11 happen. Surely somebody, somewhere, must have issued a "stand-down order".

According to Michael C. Ruppert, author of *Crossing The Rubicon*, that somebody was Dick Cheney, and the somewhere was the White House Situation Room. With a puppet president conveniently trapped at a schoolroom photo opportunity (and later sidelined on an unprotected Air Force 1 chicken flight), Cheney had free rein to run the whole operation. He was a shadow government of one.

These kinds of allegations received some circumstantial support when it was revealed that the National Reconnaissance Office had actually scheduled a war-game-style exercise involving a corporate jet crashing into the NRO's headquarters in Chantilly, Virginia – just a few miles from Washington D.C. In 2004, former National Security Council counter-terrorism chief Richard Clarke revealed in his book that this exercise was only part of a bigger war game called Vigilant Guardian.

Bizarrely, it involved all three 9/11 crash sites, and ensured that Clarke and Cheney were already in the White House Situation Room when the terrorist attacks occurred.

Some, including *October Surprise* conspiracy writer Barbara Honegger, believe that Vigilant Guardian must have included hijack scenarios, because the key decision-makers in the White House were not at first surprised when they heard the news of the 9/11 attacks. It explains Bush's otherwise unconscionable delay in that Florida classroom. Had the hijackers found out about the war-game plans? Had they been tipped off? One final piece of "evidence" was President Bush's bizarre claim at a press conference that he had seen the first plane hit the WTC. Was this confusion, or posturing? Or had he seen simulations beforehand? Was the hijack scenario the US government's own idea?

Rumours

In the wake of 9/11, the world, and New York especially, was swept by rumours. Some were apparently convincing, notably the story that there had been a surge in WTC-related financial transactions just before the attacks – suggesting that somebody knew what was going to happen. "Insiders" were alleged to have made millions of dollars in profit by short-selling stocks in United and American Airlines shortly before the crashes, and similarly by buying "put" options (effectively a bet that a share price will drop) for the airlines' parent companies. The amount of trading was supposedly suspiciously high. Was this the terrorists themselves, cashing in? Or Wall Streeters with inside knowledge? The 9/11 Commission declared that the sales were "innocuous".

Other rumours lacked even basic substantiation. Workers from the Federal Emergency Management Agency (favourite target of the ultra-right) were supposedly sent to New York on September 10. At least, this was what was construed from Dan Rather's *CBS Evening News* interview with Tom Kenney, a FEMA worker from Massachusetts who had been one of the very first teams at the site. Kenney said: "We arrived on late Monday night and went into action on Tuesday morning". It's hardly surprising he got his days muddled: at the time of the interview he had been working in the rubble for two days straight.

One widespread rumour in particular had more to do with racism than fact. New Yorkers heard that there were no cabs (many driven by Muslims) near the WTC on the morning of September 11, or that all the (Arab-run) coffee shops and newsstands nearby were closed. The entire Muslim population of New York, these theories suggested, had stronger allegiances to extremist terrorists than to their own city.

Four thousand Jews

Equally racist was the notorious "4000 Jews" conspiracy-theory rumour that exploded onto the streets of the Middle East, then onto Middle Eastern conspiracy websites before working its way back to the West. It began as a generalized whisper that Israel, or its intelligence agency Mossad (see p.145) was behind the attacks – a conspiracy theory that routinely follows pretty much every disaster or terrorist attack involving Muslims.

On September 14, Major General Hamid Gul, ex-chief of Pakistan's ISI secret intelligence agency was reported in *Newsweek* as declaring that "Mossad and its American associates are the obvious culprits. Who benefits from the crime?" The benefits would be the attacks that the US would feel free to unleash on a "guilty" Muslim population... Confusingly, he also suggested that Israel had masterminded the WTC attacks against its American allies: "the Israelis don't want to see any power in Washington unless it's subservient to their interests", he said, "and President Bush has not been subservient". Other

Middle Eastern theorists saw the hidden hand of the "Elders of Zion" (see p.100) at work. Some alleged that Mossad had known in advance and failed to pass on the information to the US authorities.

The more specific conspiracy theory that Israeli workers were warned to stay away from their offices in the World Trade Center originated in a story in the *Jerusalem Post*'s Internet edition, which said that the Israeli foreign ministry had gathered the names of four thousand Israelis thought to have been in the vicinity of the World Trade Center and the Pentagon on the morning of September 11. Through a system of conspiratorial Chinese whispers, the story morphed into the allegation that four thousand presumably forewarned Israelis had failed to turn up for work that morning, as reported by Hezbollah's Al Manar network on September 17 and by largely (but far from exclusively) Middle Eastern news services in the following weeks. "Israelis" soon became "Jews". In fact, the proportion of Israelis among the victims of the attack was roughly equivalent to the proportion of Israelis in the population of New York. Many more victims were Jewish.

Foreknowledge

The conspiracy theory that the Bush administration had known about the attacks in advance actually gained in currency as press releases and leaks filtered through from the 9-11 Commission, which was set up in November 2002 – despite initial opposition from President Bush, on the grounds that it would cover "sensitive information". Were these reports evidence of massive incompetence on the part of the FBI and CIA, as the 9-11 Commission would later suggest? Or of a more sinister, orchestrated campaign to shut down investigations that could prevent the 9/11 attacks?

Intelligence reports from April and May 2001 had the titles "Bin Laden planning multiple operations", "Bin Laden threats are real", and "Bin Laden network's plans advancing". In August, an intelligence briefing for President Bush warned that bin Laden might hijack commercial airliners. It was entitled "Bin Laden Determined To Strike In US" (though administration officials speaking to the press later somehow left out the word "in"). Also in the summer of 2001, George Bush was personally warned that Islamic terrorists were capable of crashing an airliner into the summit building of the Genoa G8 conference, which he was attending. At around the same time, Russian intelligence warned the CIA that suicide pilots were training for attacks on US targets, while Israel's Mossad actually gave the agency a list of terrorists who had infiltrated the US – and four of the names on the list were of 9/11 hijackers.

Among the most significant dead-end leads was the July 2001 "Phoenix Memo", sent to FBI bosses by Agent Kenneth Williams from Phoenix, Arizona. It warned of the possibility that Osama bin Laden might place agents in US flight schools. At around the same time, later that month, a threat assessment led to Attorney General John Ashcroft refusing to make any flights on commercial airlines. And on September 10, a group of top Pentagon officials suddenly cancelled their travel plans for the following morning. Rumours that this was because of security alerts were denied. It seems that Pentagon officials travel very frequently, and almost as frequently change their plans. That's why they have first-class tickets.

Whistleblowers

The various intelligence reports of the summer of 2001 were explained away as bits of flotsam in a sea of contradictory intelligence. It was patiently explained that there were thousands of similar reports raising the possibility of terrorist attacks that never happened. But at the least, they proved that protests by senior officials that the attacks were a *total* surprise, an event that could not have been foreseen, were disingenuous. Condoleezza Rice, speaking two weeks before she appeared in front of the 9-11 Commission, said: "We had no specific information." Challenged by FBI translator and whistleblower Sibel Edwards, she clarified: "I made a mistake. I should not have said 'we'. I should say that I personally did not have specific information."

Edwards also alleged that in her role as an FBI translator (in Farsi, Turkish, and Azerbaijani) she had seen or heard about evidence that senior US government figures were "directly involved" in the financing of the 9/11 attacks, to the extent that they were financially implicated in drug trafficking and money laundering. Another FBI whistleblower, Coleen Rowley (who later became *Time* Person of the Year – the magazine was evidently congratulating itself for running her story) accused FBI bosses of deliberately blocking her attempts to investigate Zacarias Moussaoui, the so-called "twentieth hijacker". Edwards and Rowley are far from lone voices, but if the US government really did attack itself, it's strange that no whistleblower has come forward with proof of the massive planning that would have been required.

Why?

Thrown together in this way, the flimsy pieces of circumstantial evidence seem for some to form a coherent picture of US government complicity in – or even direct responsibility for – 9/11. What's less clear is why the US government would be involved in such a massive conspiracy. There are, of course, plenty of theories. It is (correctly) pointed out that the WTC attacks swung world opinion behind the neoconservatives' aggressive military agenda, and that they loosened the diplomatic ties that fettered America's hands. The international, loosely left-liberal view holds that the US needed unrestricted supplies of oil, as well as strategic bases in the Middle East, and that 9/11 allowed it to go get what it wanted, first in Afghanistan and then in Iraq. Someone – the Bush administration, Dick Cheney, the CIA, the military-industrial complex (see p.112), the neocons, the PNAC (see p.381) or a combination of these – must therefore have planned it.

From the conspiracist libertarian right comes the alternative theory that the federal government planned 9/11 or allowed it to happen as an excuse for tightening its chilly grip. The same arguments were trotted out in the wake of the Oklahoma City bombing (see p.212). Fears of a declaration of martial law weren't borne out, but the Patriot Act, rushed into law in October 2001, certainly made serious inroads into civil liberties.

In June 2004, right-wing conspiracy websites were awash with reports that a former aide of Republican Senator Bob Dole, the controversial Stanley Hilton, had filed a $7 billion lawsuit on behalf of "hundreds" of victims' families. Hilton was quoted as citing "Bush and his puppets" for being involved "not only in aiding and abetting and allowing 9/11 to happen but in actually ordering it to happen". Hilton supposedly claimed that he'd done his senior thesis on how the US could be turned into a "presidential dictatorship" by a bogus Pearl Harbor. And he had been to college with many senior neocons, including Donald Rumsfeld... Maybe they had peeked at his notes? "The goal", Hilton was quoted as saying, "is to make this a one-party dictatorship in this country, to pursue their dubious ends with their blood brothers like the Saudi royal family. And also, historical blood brothers, such as Nazi Germany and Communist Russia."

Blood brothers? The Saudi connection

The Saudi "blood-brother" claim was not a new one. Anti-Bush activists have attacked the family's oil and business relations with Saudi Arabia for years. In his vastly popular film *Fahrenheit 9/11*, liberal filmmaker Michael Moore claims that "six to seven percent of America is owned by Saudi Arabians", and he traces numerous links between Saudi Arabian companies and Bush family interests. The same links are painstakingly uncovered by Craig Unger's best-selling *House Of Bush, House Of Saud*, which alleges "brilliantly hidden agendas and purposefully murky corporate relationships" between the two families. "With the Bush family", the blurb claims, "the Saudis hit a gusher."

Conspiracy theorists attribute the "success" of the young George W. Bush's oil firm Arbusto to Saudi investment. Most notoriously, they allege that George W. Bush's fellow "draft-dodger" in the Texas Air National Guard, James R. Bath, invested not his own money in Arbusto, but money on behalf of various influential Saudi businessmen. White House officials later seemed to attempt to conceal George W's connections with James R. Bath by blanking out his name when they released Bush's military service records.

Despite Osama bin Laden's well-documented status as the rogue or black sheep of his vastly wealthy family, *House Of Bush, House Of Saud* and *Fahrenheit 9/11* also made a big noise about the movements of the bin Laden family in the wake of 9/11. It was alleged that they had departed the US before national airspace had reopened – and without being interviewed. Who had pulled those strings, if not Bush? The 9-11 Commission countered that while members of the bin Laden family were airlifted to assembly points, they were at least "made available" for interviews with the FBI, and were only actually flown out of the country on September 14, after flights resumed.

It was widely hinted that the claims of FBI whistleblower Sibel Edwards related directly to the involvement of Saudi Arabian government figures in the financing of the 9/11 attacks. Unfortunately, the gag orders imposed on her by Attorney General John Ashcroft – on the basis of "state secret privilege" and "diplomatic relations" – meant that she couldn't name either anyone she claimed was involved or their country of origin. The most she could say was that what she knew was connected to BCCI and international securities fraud.

Mega theories and counter-theories

As for "blood brothers", David Icke and his ultra-conspiracy crowd have a mega-theory that traces a real (and non-human) blood connection between the Houses of Bush and Saud. According to Icke, the attacks were "co-ordinated by forces within U.S. borders. Those responsible are possessed by non-human entities and have no regard for human life any more than most humans have regard for the death and suffering of cattle."

Out there flanking Icke on the loony fringe are the theorists who believe that 9/11 was a conspiracy to "prepare people's minds for the arrival of extraterrestrial visitors", or that it related in some mystical sense to the number eleven – in addition to the date and the flight number of the plane that hit the North Tower, the towers themselves could be said to resemble a giant figure eleven. Another theory claims that there were 911 days separating September 11, 2001 and the Madrid train bombings. (Were there? Does anyone care?)

Most magnificently, one web-based author declared that Al Qaeda had deliberately recreated the "Falling Tower" card from the Tarot deck, and that "maybe" bin Laden was therefore an "evil Masonic sorcerer who just killed the secret spell that has held the US together these many years". Tugging on the same Masonic chain, radical, London-based cleric Abu Hamza al-Masri declared that the "business lobby" wanted a third world war. Plenty of people would agree with him, but perhaps not his conspiratorial belief that "most of them are Freemasons loyal to the Zionists".

A number of campaigning groups have complained that the wilder conspiracy theories muddy the waters. Some suspect they are part of a deliberate propaganda campaign. According to 911review. com, the 9/11 attack was "a complex psychological operation carefully designed to conceal the truth", relying on the dissemination of *memes* – ideas that, like genes (or germs) can be transmitted from person to person. One of the most important memes, the site claims, "is the idea that all people who question the basic tenets of the official story are loony conspiracy theorists, whose ideas are not worthy of consideration".

The biggest problem with all 9/11 conspiracy theories that pin the ultimate blame on the Bush administration rather than Al Qaeda is that they never explain why the World Trade Center needed to be destroyed. Maybe the Bush administration did want to attack Iraq (and Afghanistan). Maybe they did want a Patriot Act. There's little evidence, however, that it wouldn't have been able to achieve both goals without 9/11. And why, if the administration was capable of faking or setting up a massive terrorist attack on New York, couldn't it make a few FBI intelligence reports from the summer of 2001 disappear? (Or were these supposed to have been left lying around on purpose?) Most obviously, if the Bush administration was as duplicitous and cynical as we are asked to believe, why couldn't it simply have planted a few WMD in the Iraqi desert?

SOURCES

Books

Richard Clarke Against All Enemies: Inside America's War On Terror Written by a true Washington insider who served every president from Reagan to George W. Bush, this is a fascinating insight into official anti-terror measures, and a harsh indictment of the Bush administration's failure to take Al Qaeda seriously.

Noam Chomsky 9/11 (2001). Not Chomsky's best – a hundred-odd-page rush job. Despite conservative allegations, Chomsky doesn't say that the 9/11 attacks were justified, but that they can be explained as a reaction to imperialist US foreign policy.

David Icke Alice In Wonderland And The World Trade Center Disaster (2002). David in fairyland, more like. Icke cashes in with more of the same old conspira-lunacy.

Peter Lance Cover Up: What The Government Is Still Hiding About The War On Terror (2005). A serious investigative reporter takes the 9-11 Commission to task, detailing the national security failures in the lead-up to 9/11 and the agendas behind the cover-up of the final report. Asks some trenchant questions.

Jim Marrs Inside Job: Unmasking The Conspiracies Of 9/11 (2005). Amateurish production and rather unbalanced in tone, but a great overview of the details of the main conspiracy theory arguments nonetheless.

Thierry Meyssan 9/11: The Big Lie (2002). Originally published in France as *L'Effroyable Imposture*. Discussed in detail above.

Michael C. Ruppert Crossing The Rubicon: The Decline Of The American Empire At The End Of The Age Of Oil (2004). In preparation for "Peak Oil: an economic crisis like nothing the world has ever seen", insiders in the Bush administration – ie Dick Cheney and his cronies – pulled off an amazing false-flag operation. Six hundred pages long.

Paul Thompson The Terror Timeline: Year By Year, Day By Day, Minute By Minute: A Comprehensive Chronicle Of The Road To 9/11 – And America's Response (2004). The title says it all (it's certainly long enough). Gripping.

Craig Unger House Of Bush, House Of Saud: The Secret Relationship Between The World's Two Most Powerful Dynasties (2004). An experienced investigative journalist exposes the "brilliantly hidden agendas and purposefully murky corporate relationships" between the two vastly wealthy families.

Websites

ⓦ **cooperativeresearch.org** This website is a serious research tool: "the Center for Cooperative Research seeks to encourage grassroots participation and collaboration in the documentation of the public historical record using an open-content model." Features the famous "Complete 9/11 Timeline", plus well-attended discussion "phorums".

ⓦ **911research.wtc7.net** An excellent, extraordinarily detailed analysis of exactly how and why the Twin Towers collapsed, with detailed structural diagrams and photos.

ⓦ **slate.msn.com/?id=116813** Tracks the fascinating spread of the "4000 Israelis" rumour.

ⓦ **www.crisispapers.org/essays/911-testimony.htm** Hilarious fictional transcript of the Bush-Cheney testimony to the 9-11 Commission.

ⓦ **www.defenselink.mil/photos/Sep2001/** Official photos of the Pentagon crash.

ⓦ **www.english.aljazeera.net/NR/exeres/79C6AF22-98FB-4A1C-B21F-2BC36E87F61F.htm** Full transcript of bin Laden's videotaped speech, released on November 1, 2004.

ⓦ **www.globalresearch.ca.myforums.net/** Popular 9/11 conspiracy-theory discussion site.

ⓦ **www.michaelmoore.com** Michael Moore's homepage. Includes links to www.fahrenheit911.com, where you can buy DVDs and even teaching packs.

ⓦ **www.9-11commission.gov/report/911Report.pdf** A downloadable PDF version of the 9-11 Commission report. All 585 pages' worth...

ⓦ **www.911review.com** One of the best "sceptical" websites – and sceptical cuts both ways. Includes detailed evidence that the Pentagon/missile claims are phoney.

ⓦ **www.911truth.org** An excellent place to start further digging. 911Truth.Org campaigns "to educate the public about the Sept. 11th cover-up and inspire popular pressure to ... expose the truth surrounding the events of 9/11; namely, that elements within the US government must have been complicit, or worse". Excellent links in the "Web ring" to campaigning groups and official resources alike.

ⓦ **www.pentagonstrike.co.uk** Smartly put-together flash video presenting the basics of the Pentagon/missile theory.

ⓦ **www.time.com/time/covers/1101020603/memo.html** Coleen Rowley's whistleblowing memo to FBI Director Robert Mueller.

Iraq: the case for war

On March 20, 2003, a US-led coalition of military forces stormed into Iraq in an invasion codenamed "Operation Iraqi Freedom". The war would swiftly bring down the brutal dictatorship of Saddam Hussein and lead to his capture (see p.388) and imprisonment, while a system of multi-party democratic government was eventually established in the country. But although the war officially ended in May 2003, Iraq is, at the time of writing, still occupied, mainly by US forces, and still suffering a brutal, bloody insurrection.

The war has also engendered bitter political opposition across the globe, not because people supported or sympathized with Saddam, but because many believed that the US government in particular had a hidden agenda. What follows, then, is first an examination of the "official" reasons given for going to war, and then a look at the alternative explanations that have been put forward, some of which have been publicly dismissed as "conspiracy theories".

The official version(s)

Although the British Prime Minister Tony Blair has sometimes talked as though he decided to remove Saddam single-handedly, there is no doubt that the initiative came from the Bush administration, and that Blair, for whatever reason(s), decided to stand "shoulder to shoulder" with the Americans. In the December 2004 edition of the British magazine *Prospect*, Paul Wolfowitz, then Deputy Secretary of Defense, and the man widely regarded as the architect of the Iraq war, recalled that when President George W. Bush first went to the UN to seek approval for war, he had made three arguments: "He talked about terrorism, he talked about WMD and he talked about abuse of the Iraqi people."

Wolfowitz had identified the same three "fundamental concerns" in an interview for *Vanity Fair* in 2003, when he said that "for reasons that have a lot to do with the US government bureaucracy we settled on the one issue that everyone could agree on, which was weapons of mass destruction". In his *Prospect* interview, however, Wolfowitz cited the need to try and gain UN backing as the reason for focusing on WMD ("The UN was what forced us down the WMD path"). Whatever the case, there was always more than one official reason for going to war.

Weapons of mass destruction

Let there be no doubt about this: Saddam *had* had WMD, and had been continuing to develop them. On December 9, 2002 the *Guardian* reported that, prior to their departure from Iraq in December 1998, UN weapons inspectors had destroyed or made unusable "48 long-range missiles, 14 conventional missile warheads, 30 chemical warheads, 'supergun' components, close to 40,000 chemical munitions, 690 tonnes of chemical weapons agents and the al-Hakam biological weapons plant". They had also discovered "evidence of a nuclear programme that was more advanced than previously expected".

To get things into perspective, however, it is worth remembering a number of points about the US's own possession and use of WMD. First, the US has by far the world's largest arsenal of nuclear weapons, and is the only country to have used them, at Hiroshima and Nagasaki in 1945. Second, although the US ratified the Geneva Protocol in 1975 and the

THE FIRST GULF WAR

The common perception of the first Gulf War is that in invading Kuwait, Saddam Hussein failed to take account of the likely US (and world) reaction to his unprovoked aggression against Iraq's tiny neighbour. There are those, however, who believe that the US administration of George H.W. Bush deliberately encouraged the invasion.

In August 1990, Saddam Hussein ordered the armies of Iraq to annex Kuwait and its oilfields. He claimed that Kuwait was part of Iraqi territory, and that it had been illegally taking oil from the Iraqi portion of the Rumaila oilfield on the Iraq–Kuwait border. The main reason seems to have been that annexing Kuwait would enable Saddam to use its immense wealth to pay off debts accrued during the Iran–Iraq war (during which, ironically, Kuwait had aided Iraq and had been bombed by Iran as a result). If oil prices rose, so much the better.

While Saddam's annexation of Kuwait attracted nearly universal condemnation – the PLO was a notable exception – the US seemed to have particular reason to feel aggrieved. Throughout the 1980s, the US had supplied Saddam with arms, commodity credits, loans and military intelligence to fight Iran – and this was how he repaid them. In January 1991, a US-led UN coalition of forces from 28 countries, including France, Saudi Arabia, Syria and the UK, bombed Iraq's munitions factories and armed forces into the sand, before sweeping the Iraqis out of Kuwait in February.

It so happened, however, that April Glaspie, the US ambassador to Iraq had met Saddam one week before the invasion, as Iraq's forces were massing on the Kuwaiti border. Excerpts from a document described by Iraqi government officials as a transcript of the meeting were subsequently given to ABC News and published by the *New York Times* (see www.chss.montclair.edu/english/furr/glaspie.html). Translated from the Arabic, Glaspie is reported as telling Saddam that "we have no opinion on the Arab–Arab conflicts, like your border disagreement with Kuwait" – and that this view reflected the instructions of Secretary of State James Baker.

According to the website whatreallyhappened.com, which gives a different version of part of the document, (unidentified) British journalists got hold of the transcript and a tape of the meeting and confronted Glaspie as she left the US embassy in Baghdad. Glaspie is quoted as saying: "Obviously, I didn't think, and nobody else did, that the Iraqis were going to take all of Kuwait." As one journalist is said to have asked, didn't this imply that she thought he was going to take *some* of it?

Glaspie later said that she was the victim of "deliberate deception on a major scale," and denounced the Iraqi transcript as "a fabrication" that distorted her position, though it contained "a great deal" that was accurate. Iraqi deputy prime minister Tariq Aziz said later that Glaspie had not given Iraq a green light for the invasion.

The *Washington Times*, however, reported that the conversation had become a central "article of faith" among Arab conspiracy theorists as indicating American willingness to turn a blind eye to the invasion of Kuwait. Although conceding in an editorial that it was more likely to have been simply "inept diplomacy",

the paper, usually a staunch Republican Party ally, agreed that relations between Iraq and the US had remained friendly right up until August 2, and that no indication had been given that Saddam's invasion would meet with American disapproval.

According to the late Alistair Cooke on his BBC *Letter From America* radio programme, the Americans were initially against taking military action. It was only a meeting with former British prime minister Margaret Thatcher, said Cooke, that persuaded President George H.W. Bush that Saddam had to be dealt with, as he now posed a threat to Saudi Arabia. Middle East expert Hugh Roberts and Crown Prince Hassan of Jordan later concurred, however, that a diplomatic solution remained possible even after the invasion, but that this possibility was deliberately sabotaged by the US.

Perhaps the last word should be left to Lawrence Korb, assistant defence secretary under Reagan, who shortly before the Gulf War started was quoted by the *International Herald Tribune* as saying: "If Kuwait grew carrots, we wouldn't give a damn."

Chemical Weapons Convention in 1997, it still retains large stockpiles of the types of weapons the convention bans: as of May 2004, according to the US Army Chemical Materials Agency, the US had destroyed less than thirty percent of its original declared stockpile of over 30,000 tons of mustard gas and nerve agents, including sarin and VX. During the Vietnam War, of course, the US made extensive use of chemical weapons, most notably defoliants such as Agent Orange.

The position regarding biological weapons is less clear. In 1975 the US ratified the Biological Weapons

Convention, having already ordered the destruction of its own biological weapons by 1973. In 2001, however, longstanding international negotiations for a verification protocol broke down when the US insisted that such a protocol would interfere with legitimate research into defence *against* biological weapons. Meanwhile the US Army Medical Research Institute of Infectious Diseases, located at Fort Detrick (see p.285) continues to produce biological agents for "research" purposes.

Saddam, of course, had used chemical weapons before – not only against the Iranians in the Iran-Iraq war of 1980–88, but also against Kurdish rebels inside Iraq. Indeed, this enabled the George W. Bush administration to link WMD to the humanitarian issue of Saddam's treatment of the Iraqi people. Thus, in his January 2003 State of the Union speech, President Bush declared: "The dictator who is assembling the world's most dangerous weapons has already used them on whole villages – leaving thousands of his own citizens dead, blind, or disfigured."

What Bush didn't mention was that under Ronald Reagan, the US had supported Iraq during the Iran-Iraq war, despite knowing that – as a declassified November 1983 memo to then Secretary of State George Shultz put it – Saddam was using chemical weapons on an "almost daily basis". And that up to 1989, under the Reagan and George H.W. Bush administrations, the US had sent or sold samples of these agents to Iraq. These samples included anthrax, botulism and West Nile virus, some of which were used by Saddam in his biological weapons research programme. The US knew, in other words, that Saddam had (or had had) biological warfare capability because they – along with France, Germany, Japan and the UK – had supplied him with it.

Halabja

When George W. Bush referred in his 2003 State of the Union speech to Saddam using WMD on his own people, he was referring, above all, to the gas attack on the Kurdish village of Halabja in March 1988, which left more than 5000 dead and has often been cited as an example of Saddam's brutality. Commenting on Bush's speech in the *New York Times*, however, Stephen C. Pelletiere, the CIA's political analyst for the Iran-Iraq war, wrote: "We cannot say with any certainty that Iraqi chemical weapons killed the Kurds." As the Defense Intelligence Agency had reported, recalled Pelletiere, both sides in the war used gas, but what killed the Kurds at Halabja was Iranian cyanide gas – Iraq only had mustard gas.

Oh really? The same month of Pelletiere's article, British journalist Robert Fisk reported in the *Independent* that recently declassified State Department documents revealed that "the Pentagon had pushed US diplomats to blame Iran for Halabja – but not to present details, because the story was a lie". Far from punishing Saddam for Halabja, indeed, both the American and British governments gave him more money: the incoming George H.W. Bush administration doubled Iraq's "agricultural credits" – whatever they were – to $1 billion a year, while the UK approved an extra £340m of credit.

And in July 1988 – just two months after Halabja – the giant California-based Bechtel Corporation won a contract to build a petrochemicals plant near Baghdad, which Saddam planned to use for producing fuel-air explosives and mustard gas; construction was only halted after the Iraqi invasion of Kuwait. More recently, Bechtel has been awarded contracts worth over $2.5 billion for reconstruction in Iraq.

Selling to Saddam

Just how far the Reagan administration had been prepared to go in assisting Saddam was underlined by a now declassified US State Department memo of May 9, 1984, which said that the US was reviewing its policy "on the sale of certain dual-use items to Iraq nuclear entities" and that "preliminary results favor expanding such trade to include Iraqi nuclear entities". As regards other WMD, a Senate committee inquiry into US export policy to Iraq prior to the Gulf War concluded in 1994 that "the United States provided the government of Iraq with 'dual use' (ie civilian and military) licensed materials which assisted in the development of Iraqi chemical, biological and missile-system programs".

According to the report, these materials included "chemical warfare-agent precursors; chemical warfare-agent production-facility plans and technical drawings; chemical-warfare filling equipment; biological-warfare-related materials; missile-fabrication equipment and missile-system guidance equipment." Between 1985 and 1990, in fact, the US Department of Commerce approved 771 licences for exporting $1.5 *billion* worth of such dual-use items to Iraq. As a later joke put it, the Americans knew that Saddam had WMD because they still had the receipts.

Humanitarian concern?

After 1990, of course, when Saddam's invasion of Kuwait sparked off the Gulf War (see p.372), everything changed. The UN Security Council imposed a trade embargo on Iraq and passed resolutions for all of Saddam's WMD stocks and facilities to be destroyed. These "sanctions" were turned by the US and UK into a complete economic blockade, including food and medicine, and accompanied by intermittent bombing.

Compounded by the after-effects of the Gulf War, the results were devastating. In May 1996, CBS *Sixty Minutes* reporter Lesley Stahl, referring to reports that half a million Iraqi children had died as a result, asked Madeleine Albright, then US ambassador to the UN, whether the cost was worth it. Albright replied: "I think this is a very hard choice, but ... we think the price is worth it." Although the figure of half a million deaths and the apportionment of blame continue to be disputed (see, for example, www.reason.com/0203/fe.mw.the.shtml), UNICEF reported in 1997 that nearly a million Iraqi children were malnourished, while the fact that the UN introduced an "oil-for-food" programme in December 1996 speaks for itself.

Meanwhile UN inspection teams were sent in to inspect suspected weapons sites and ensure the destruction of any WMD they found. But Saddam frequently refused to cooperate and after the inspectors pulled out in 1998, complaining of obstruction, there was massive retaliatory bombing by the US and UK. Inevitably, despite the much-trumpeted use of "smart" weapons and supposedly precision targeting, there was significant "collateral damage". According to Amnesty International, a confidential UN report found that over a period of five months in 1999, 41 percent of the victims of US and UK air strikes were civilians. Concern for the Iraqi people would later be cited by the US government as a reason for removing Saddam.

"Things related and not"

In December 2000 George W. Bush was finally declared to have won a presidential election that has spawned its own fair share of conspiracy theories. According to the BBC's *Newsnight* and *Harpers'* magazine, secret meetings planning the ousting of Saddam and discussing likely successors were being held in the US and across the Middle East "within weeks" of Bush taking office in 2001. And then came 9/11.

The reaction of one member of the new Bush administration in particular suggests that he saw the terrorist attack on the Twin Towers as an opportunity to put some long-laid plans into operation. "Barely five hours after American Airlines Flight 77 plowed into the Pentagon," CBS News reported in

2002, "Defense Secretary Donald H. Rumsfeld was telling his aides to come up with plans for striking Iraq – even though there was no evidence linking Saddam Hussein to the attacks."

According to notes taken by one of these aides at the time (see www.cbsnews.com/stories/2002/09/04/september11/main520830.shtml), Rumsfeld wanted "best info fast. Judge whether good enough [to] hit S.H. [Saddam Hussein] at the same time. Not only UBL [Usama bin Laden]". He added: "Go massive. Sweep it all up. Things related and not." Iraq, of course, wasn't related: seventeen out of the nineteen hijackers, like Osama bin Laden himself, turned out to have come from Saudi Arabia – a country that, after his invasion of Kuwait in 1990, the US feared Saddam might attack. According to *Time* magazine, however, Rumsfeld was so set on finding a rationale for attacking Saddam that he asked the CIA to find evidence connecting Iraq to 9/11 on ten separate occasions, but to no avail: the evidence simply wasn't there.

An Al Qaeda connection?

This didn't stop the Bush administration from talking up the terrorist threat that Iraq allegedly posed. Before the war, US Vice President Dick Cheney spoke of "overwhelming evidence" connecting Al Qaeda and the Iraqi government. Condoleezza Rice said "there clearly are contacts between Al Qaeda and Saddam Hussein that can be documented" and told CNN that "Saddam Hussein cavorts [*sic*] with terrorists" (the mind boggles). Bush declared: "We know that Iraq and Al Qaeda have had high-level contacts that go back a decade ... Alliance with terrorists could allow the Iraq regime to attack America without leaving any fingerprint" – which, ironically, would make it impossible to prove Iraq's role in such attacks.

In September 2002, Donald Rumsfeld spoke of "bullet-proof" CIA evidence of an Al Qaeda pres-

ence in Iraq. When a journalist pointed out to White House spokesman Ari Fleischer that Al Qaeda operatives were suspected only in Iraq's no-fly Kurdish zone, over which Saddam had no control, Fleischer replied: "Iraq is Iraq". In June 2004, both Bush and Cheney were still insisting there were strong Iraq-Al Qaeda connections.

The US Senate's 9-11 commission, however, concluded that there was "no evidence" of co-operation between Iraq and Al Qaeda, or of Iraq aiding terrorist acts on the US. CIA analyst Melvin Goodman argued that Iraq's regime didn't support terrorism, and that bin Laden considered Saddam – whose Ba'thist regime was secular rather than Islamic – a "socialist infidel". Other US diplomats have said that Saddam giving WMD to terrorists was "inconceivable".

Bush himself later said that there was "no connection" between Saddam and Al Qaeda, and in October 2004 Rumsfeld told the Council on Foreign Relations: "To my knowledge, I have not seen any strong, hard evidence that links the two." Rumsfeld described US intelligence on the subject as having "migrate[d] [*sic*] ... in the most amazing way", a statement he later said had been "misunderstood".

A nuclear threat?

The alleged threat posed by Saddam also included nuclear weapons. Before the war, Bush warned: "The regime is seeking a nuclear bomb and with fissible ... fissile material could build one within a year" – and in January 2003 he told the US Senate: "The British government has learned that Saddam Hussein recently sought significant quantities of uranium from Africa", and had documents showing that uranium oxide, or "yellow cake", had been sold to Iraq by Niger. However, Colin Powell hadn't considered the evidence for this claim "sufficiently strong" to present it to the UN eight days earlier. CIA director George Tenet had also deleted the

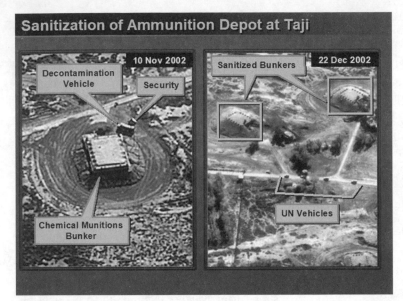

Sanitization of Ammunition Depot at Taji

10 Nov 2002

Decontamination Vehicle

Security

Chemical Munitions Bunker

22 Dec 2002

Sanitized Bunkers

UN Vehicles

Iraq's WMD: the evidence

Niger claim from the draft of a speech Bush had given three months earlier, on the basis that it was unreliable.

UN weapons inspector David Albright said that the photos of Iraq's nuclear sites that Colin Powell presented to the UN as evidence were a decade old; the charges were "complete nonsense". The International Atomic Energy Agency (IAEA) repeatedly asked the US and UK for copies of the allegedly incriminating documents, but were only given them in February. On March 7 – just eleven days before the war began – the IAEA director-general told the UN Security Council that the yellow cake documents were "not authentic", ie they were forged: dates, titles, and the names of government ministers were incorrect and words were misspelled. Condoleezza Rice, meanwhile, told CBS politics show *Meet The Press* that Tenet's deletion

of the Niger claim was something that "people didn't remember ... I didn't remember" when Bush's State of the Union speech was being put together.

Downing Street: behind closed doors

On May 1, 2005 the *Sunday Times* published the top-secret minutes of a meeting held in Downing Street on July 3, 2002, eight months before the invasion of Iraq. It also quoted a briefing paper for the meeting, which proved that Blair had taken the crucial decision to support the US in April 2002. "When the prime minister discussed Iraq with President Bush at Crawford in April," the briefing stated, "he said that the UK would support military action to bring about regime change." As for the Americans, they just wanted to get rid of Saddam, "whether or not he posed an immediate threat", as the *Sunday Times* put it.

This was confirmed at the meeting itself by Sir Richard Dearlove, the chief of the UK intelligence service MI6. Dearlove – identified by his nickname "C" – reported on talks he had had in Washington with the CIA director George Tenet. "There was a perceptible shift in attitude", the minutes record: "Military action was now seen as inevitable. Bush wanted to remove Saddam, through military action, justified by the conjunction of terrorism and WMD. But the intelligence and facts were being fixed around the policy."

For the Foreign Secretary, Jack Straw, this presented a problem: "The case [for war] was thin.

Saddam was not threatening his neighbours, and his WMD capability was less than that of Libya, North Korea or Iran." He then went on to suggest a solution: Saddam should be given an ultimatum to allow the UN weapons inspectors back in, which would also help with the legal justification for the use of force (presumably on the basis that if he refused, it would provide grounds for war).

The attorney general, Lord Goldsmith, however, told the meeting that "the desire for regime change was not a legal base for military action". He explained that there were three legal grounds: "self-defence, intervention to end an humanitarian crisis and a [new] resolution from the UN Security Council". Only the last might apply to Iraq; to rely on an existing UN resolution would be "difficult".

On July 17 Blair told the House of Commons, referring to military action against Iraq: "as I say constantly, no decisions have yet been taken". From one point of view, he was correct: the first conclusion of the meeting was that "we should work on the assumption that the UK would take part in any military action", but that a fuller picture of US plans was needed before any firm decisions could be made. As the briefing for the meeting made clear, however, Blair had already signed up to support US military action: all he was waiting for was the fine print.

Dodgy dossiers: conspiracy and cock-up

The Bush administration wasn't the only one to fit intelligence and facts around the policy of regime change. In September 2002 the British government presented a dossier on Iraq. Among other claims, this stated that Saddam had plans to use biological and chemical weapons and that "some of these weapons [were] deployable within 45 minutes of an order to use them". A second dossier followed in February 2003, entitled "Iraq: its infrastructure of concealment, deception and intimidation", which claimed to be based on numerous sources, including what was described as "intelligence material".

As Cambridge academic Glenn Rangwala discovered, however, the bulk of the February dossier had been directly copied from three previously published articles (not, as widely reported, a PhD thesis). Two of the articles – one dating from 1997 – were from *Jane's Intelligence Review*, an international journal for threat analysis. The biggest debt, however, was to a piece by postgraduate student Ibrahim al-Marashi, based primarily on Iraqi documents captured in the 1991 Gulf War and freely available on the Internet, from where it had been copied complete with grammatical idiosyncrasies and typographical errors. The only substantive changes to the articles were that numbers had been increased or rounded up and particular words replaced to make the claim sound stronger.

The impression, inevitably, was that civil servants – whose identities were revealed in the "properties" section of the computer file – had been given the job of coming up with material to back up a decision that had already been taken. This "dodgy dossier", as it came to be known, was later called "wholly counter-productive" by a House of Commons Foreign Affairs Select Committee. The 45-minute claims of the September dossier were similarly claimed to have been "sexed up" (see Dr David Kelly, p.64) and later found to refer to short-range, battlefield tactical weapons.

The Chalabi connection

Similarly dubious claims about the threat posed by Saddam's WMD were being made on the other side of the Atlantic. In September 2002, Bush told the UN that Saddam had failed to account for over "three tonnes" of material for bio-weapons production, and that Saddam was expanding production facilities for "stockpiles of VX [nerve], mustard and other chemical agents". In his State of the Union address in January 2003, Bush claimed that Saddam hadn't accounted for biological agents that should have been destroyed – enough to make 25,000 litres of anthrax, 38,000 litres of botulin toxin and 500 tons of sarin, mustard and VX nerve agents. Iraq also had mobile biological weapons labs. "We know that", Bush asserted, "from three Iraqi defectors."

Those three defectors, it turned out, had been supplied by the industrious Iraqi exile, Ahmad Chalabi, whom some suspect of having played a colossal confidence trick on the US and UK governments. Chalabi, whose wealthy Iraqi Shiite family had fled Iraq in the 1950s, was educated in the US, where he moved in early neoconservative circles. In 1977 he founded a bank in Jordan, whose collapse in 1989 led to his conviction in absentia for fraud. Fleeing to the West once more, Chalabi founded and became the leader of Saddam-opposition group the Iraqi National Congress (INC).

Chalabi was such a smooth talker that, in 1995, he separately persuaded the CIA and Kurdish groups that he had the support of the other to overthrow Saddam. But this lethal wheeler-dealing came unstuck when he tried to convince the Iranians to join in, showing them the CIA "plans" to depose Saddam. When the CIA found out about this leak, they ditched the plan wholesale, while Saddam killed thousands of Kurds.

Undeterred, Chalabi continued to lobby for the INC, which was the chief beneficiary of nearly $100m of funding given to Iraqi opposition groups under the Iraq Liberation Act in 1998. With the support of influential neocon friends such as Richard Perle and Paul Wolfowitz, Chalabi effectively became the voice of anti-Saddam opposition in Washington. Most importantly, he played a key role in supplying intelligence on WMD – especially from a defector codenamed "Curveball", the brother of one of Chalabi's aides – that was used by the Bush administration to justify the war in Iraq, notably in a presentation given to the UN by then Secretary of State Colin Powell. Chalabi also told the Pentagon that invading US forces would be greeted as "liberators".

"Heroes in error"

When the US-led coalition invaded Iraq, Chalabi was given a position on the country's interim governing council by the Coalition Provisional Authority and even served briefly as its president. It wasn't long, however, before Chalabi's chickens came home to roost. Not only did the occupying forces find themselves facing a bloody insurrection, but also the WMD "intelligence" Chalabi had supplied – and been paid millions of dollars for by the Pentagon and State Department – turned to be bogus. The Robb-Silberman commission into US intelligence failures later said that there was an over-reliance on information from defectors.

Chalabi was unrepentant, telling the British *Daily Telegraph*: "We are heroes in error. As far as we're concerned we've been entirely successful. That tyrant Saddam is gone and the Americans are in Baghdad. What was said before is not important." After CIA chief George Tenet resigned following a number of high-profile intelligence failures, Chalabi was quick to shift the blame: "[Tenet provided] erroneous information about weapons of mass destruction to President Bush."

In 2004 Chalabi was investigated for currency fraud, grand theft and other criminal charges; he has also been accused of passing US state secrets to Iran (with whom he had been in "continuous dialogue"), and even of being an Iranian double agent. Despite polls that once showed him to be by far the least popular member of Iraq's interim governing council, however, he has somehow contrived to become the country's acting oil minister and one of its four deputy prime ministers. Clearly a man to watch.

A last-minute change of advice

By the end of 2002, Saddam decided to allow UN weapons inspectors back into Iraq, following threats from Bush that the US would take military action if he failed to disarm. The ensuing reports from UN weapons inspection chief Hans Blix led to bitter debate as to whether Iraq was in "material breach" of its disarmament obligations. The UN Security Council divided, with China, France, Germany and Russia wanting a diplomatic solution and more inspections. The US and UK governments, however, insisted that Saddam had had enough time, and would only carry on playing games like he had for twelve years.

On the British side, there was one further obstacle. The attorney general Lord Goldsmith continued to argue that regime change could not legally be the aim of war, and on March 7, 2003, he delivered a thirteen-page opinion to that effect. Along with a number of other caveats, this stated that a legal war would probably need a second UN Security Council resolution backing the use of force. But then Goldsmith made a trip to Washington, and on his return to the UK, his advice – now whittled down to one side of A4 – was "unequivocal" in arguing that war was legal, which is what the UK Cabinet were told on March 17, 2003. War began next day.

The Bush blitzkrieg

If Saddam did have any WMD left at the time of the invasion, he didn't use them. US vice president Dick Cheney described the advance of coalition forces as being "dazzling" and "unprecedented" in speed and lightness of casualties (he also drew a favourable – if rather unfortunate – comparison with the 1940 German offensive in the Ardennes).

The corresponding speed of Iraq's collapse, however, prompted rumours in the Arab media of a secret arrangement, or *safqa*, between the Iraqi leadership and the US to finish the war quickly and save lives all round. Muslim pressure group Media Review Network reported that this agreement had been cooked up by Saudi monarch Prince Abdullah, the only Arab leader to be invited to Bush's Crawford ranch.

A simpler explanation, however, is that Iraq's military was collapsing anyway. In February 2001 Colin Powell had said that Saddam "is unable to project conventional power against his neighbours". In July Condoleezza Rice claimed "we are able to keep his arms from him" – and that since the first Gulf War, "his military forces have not been rebuilt". These statements, of course, were made before 9/11. But if they were true, where was the threat?

It's official: no WMD

For months after the invasion, the Iraq Survey Group – led by former UN weapons inspector David Kay with 1400 scientists, military and intelligence experts – combed Iraq for WMD. In September 2004 they concluded that there were no weapons of mass destruction left in Iraq at the time of the invasion. All of Saddam's stockpiles had been destroyed in 1991, and his facilities and programmes dismantled by 1996 – which is what UN weapons inspectors could have confirmed if they'd been allowed to carry on doing their job. The trouble was that Bush and Blair didn't let them. The question is why not. (For Sources see p.391.)

Iraq: the real reasons for war?

The neoconservatives' not-so-hidden agenda

One group of neoconservatives had been planning regime change in Iraq well before George W. Bush came to power, let alone 9/11. In January 1998, the neocon think-tank Project for the New American Century (or PNAC – see opposite) wrote a letter to then President Clinton calling for Saddam's removal. "If Saddam does acquire the capability to deliver weapons of mass destruction," the letter argued, "... the safety of American troops in the region, of our friends and allies like Israel and the moderate Arab states, *and a significant portion of the world's supply of oil* will all be put at hazard" [emphasis added].

The first signatory of the letter was Elliott Abrams. Abrams had escaped prison in 1991 by pleading guilty to failing to tell Congress that he had solicited a $10m contribution for the right-wing Nicaraguan Contra rebels (see p.186) from the Sultan of Brunei. He was pardoned by George H.W. Bush in 1992. At the time of the PNAC letter, Abrams was President of the Ethics [sic] and Public Policy Center; in February 2005 George W. Bush made him deputy national security adviser, with special responsibility for his strategy for... democracy.

The letter's other signatories included:

• John Bolton (later George W. Bush's Under Secretary of State for Arms Control [sic], currently US ambassador-designate to the UN);

• Richard Perle (former Assistant Defense Secretary under Reagan, later chairman – until his resignation in 2003 over allegations of conflicts of interest – of the Defense Policy Board, of which he remains a member);

• Donald Rumsfeld (former and current Defense Secretary, who had met Saddam twice as Reagan's special envoy to the Middle East during the Iran–Iraq war);

• Rumsfeld's deputy, Paul Wolfowitz (Under Secretary of Defense to Dick Cheney in the George H.W. Bush administration, now appointed president of the World Bank).

A further PNAC letter – whose signatories again included all of the above – was sent to the Speaker of the US House of Representatives and the majority leader in the Senate in May 1998. The letter stated: "We should establish and maintain a strong US military presence in the region, and be prepared to use that force to protect our vital interests in the Gulf – and, if necessary, to help remove Saddam from power."

This was followed in 2000 by a PNAC report called *Rebuilding America's Defenses* (RAD), which now reads as a blueprint for George W. Bush's foreign policy. Stating that the US had sought to play a more permanent role in Gulf regional security for decades, the report said [emphasis added]: "*While the unresolved conflict with Iraq provides the immediate justification, the need for a substantial American force presence in the Gulf transcends the issue of the regime of Saddam Hussein.*"

The principal author of RAD was Thomas Donnelly, who subsequently became director of strategic communications and initiatives at Lockheed Martin, the world's largest "defence" contractor (see Military Industrial Complex, p.112). Among the contributors listed at the end of the report were I. Lewis "Scooter" Libby (formerly George H.W. Bush's Deputy Defense Under Secretary, now chief of staff to Vice President Dick Cheney) and Paul Wolfowitz, who supervised the writing of the controversial "Defense Policy Guidance" with Libby for then Defense Secretary Cheney in 1992. Among other things, this had

THE PROJECT FOR THE NEW AMERICAN CENTURY

If it weren't for the fact that it makes no secret of its goals, the Project for the New American Century (PNAC) would be the sort of organization that gives conspiracy theories a good name. A Washington-based foreign-policy think tank and pressure group, the PNAC describes itself as "an educational organization supporting American global military, diplomatic, and moral leadership".

For the likes of former British Labour minister Michael Meacher, former Labour MP Tam Dalyell and many more, however, the PNAC is a sinister and dangerous neoconservative cabal that is bent on achieving American world domination, and which has the George W. Bush administration in its thrall. What is undeniable is that its influence goes to the very heart of the US government.

The origins of the PNAC have been traced back to a controversial "Defense Policy Guidance" or defence white paper drafted under the supervision of Paul Wolfowitz for then Defense Secretary Dick Cheney early in 1992, during the George H.W. Bush administration. The central strategy the document proposed was to "establish and protect a new order" and to maintain the mechanisms capable of "deterring potential competitors from even aspiring to a larger regional or global role".

Scenarios in which US interests could be threatened by regional conflict included "access to vital raw materials, primarily Persian Gulf oil [and] proliferation of weapons of mass destruction". (Examples of where such conflict might occur were North Korea and Iraq, recently defeated in the Gulf War, but with Saddam's regime left in place.) If necessary, the US should act both pre-emptively and unilaterally – and yet, in a classic example of doublethink, in such a way as to "promote increasing respect for international law, limit international violence, and encourage the spread of democratic forms of government and open economic systems".

When the Defense Policy Guidance was leaked to the press, it caused a furore both in the US and abroad. Officials, however, claimed that the document – which described itself as "definitive guidance from the Secretary of Defense" – had not been given final approval by Cheney or Wolfowitz, although both acknowledged that they had played a substantial role in its creation and endorsed its principal views. A new, toned-down version was subsequently produced (see www.yale.edu/strattech/92dpg.html).

In 1997, along with Florida governor Jeb Bush (George W's brother), former and future defence secretary Donald Rumsfeld and other prominent neocons, Wolfowitz and Cheney signed the Statement of Principles issued by the newly formed PNAC. Harking back to the Reagan era, the statement talked of the need to "shape a new century favourable to American principles and interests", and drew four consequences from this – significantly increasing defence spending; challenging regimes hostile to US interests and values; promoting the cause of political and economic freedom abroad; and accepting responsibility for America's unique role in "preserving and extending an international order friendly to our security, our prosperity, and our principles".

The key document for understanding the PNAC's worldview, however, came in September 2000, shortly before George W. Bush became President. *Rebuilding America's Defenses* (RAD) was based explicitly on the earlier Defense Policy Guidance (DPG) masterminded by Cheney and Wolfowitz. Describing the DPG as "a blueprint for maintaining US pre-eminence [...] and shaping the international security order in line with American principles and interests", RAD states: "The basic tenets of the DPG, in our judgment, remain sound." Hardly surprising, perhaps, when one of the project participants listed at the end of the report was Paul Wolfowitz.

Among the core missions for the US military the report identifies are to "fight and decisively win multiple, simultaneous major theatre wars", and "to perform the 'constabulary' duties associated with shaping the security environment in critical regions" – the US as global sheriff, in other words. To fulfil these missions, the US must, among other things, develop and deploy global missile defences "to provide a secure basis for US power projection around the world", and control space and cyberspace. The report even hinted that the US should consider developing its own biological weapons, suggesting that technological advances "may transform biological warfare from the realm of terror to a *politically useful tool*" [emphasis added].

As if all this wasn't creepy enough, the report describes the process of technological transformation of US military capabilities as "likely to be a long one, absent some catastrophic and catalyzing event – like a new Pearl Harbor". Given the suspicions that a previous US administration deliberately *allowed* Pearl Harbor to be attacked (see p.330), conspiracy theorists of a paranoid persuasion (and Michael Meacher) see this as evidence that 9/11 – only a year away, remember – was somehow factored into the PNAC's plans.

Be this as it may, there's no denying that Bush's post 9/11 pronouncements on defence policy seem to be drawn straight from RAD – and, in their claims to the right, to take pre-emptive and unilateral action, to the earlier Defense Policy Guidance. The "Axis of Evil" to which Bush referred in his January 2002 State of the Union address, for

[continued overleaf]

instance, corresponded exactly to the threats identified by RAD, which had said: "We cannot allow North Korea, Iran, Iraq or similar states to undermine American leadership, intimidate American allies or threaten the American homeland itself."

Similarly, RAD called for the US to withdraw from the anti-ballistic missile treaty, to commit itself to a global missile defence system and to increase defence spending to as much as 3.8 percent of gross domestic product – which is exactly what Bush did in 2002. What the PNAC proposed has become US policy.

If you want to find out more about the PNAC, the easiest way is to visit their website (www.newamericancentury.org), from where you can download a copy of *Rebuilding America's Defenses*. It may amaze, anger or appal you, but it certainly won't leave you indifferent.

The PNAC isn't the only neocon think tank on the block, mind. Literally so, in the case of the similarly influential American Enterprise Institute (www.aei.org), which rents office space to the PNAC in its own building. In a speech to the AEI made in the run-up to the Iraq war,

George W. Bush said that its members' minds did such good work that his administration had borrowed twenty of them. AEI alumni include Dick Cheney (whose wife Lynne is a senior fellow) and John Bolton, while current fellows include Thomas Donnelly (principal author of the PNAC's *Rebuilding America's Defenses*) and our old friend Richard Perle. Other important outfits of a similar persuasion include the Heritage Foundation (www.heritage.org) and the Centre for Security Policy (www.centerforsecuritypolicy.org), whose mission is "to promote world peace through American

strength".

One policy group that regularly crops up in conspiracy theories is the RAND Corporation (www.rand.org), which has been going since World War II. Renowned for its handle on statistics and probabilities for war scenarios, more than a few big guns in US politics have had some kind of paid stint there. These days, RAND researches everything from obesity to the military aircraft industry and how to avoid becoming a terrorist target. In comparison, however, the PNAC seems less the stuff of conspiracy theory than of realpolitik fact.

stated that the US should use military power to protect "access to vital raw materials, primarily Persian Gulf oil".

Perhaps the last word here should be left to former PNAC co-chairman Donald Kagan, another contributor to RAD. Acknowledging the probable need for a major concentration of forces in the Middle East over a long period of time, Kagan told reporter Jay Bookman in September 2002: "When we have economic problems, it's been caused by disruptions in our oil supply. If we have a force in Iraq, there will be no disruption in oil supplies." For the PNAC, it was as simple as that.

It's the oil, stupid

On January 15, 2003, three days before a coalition of US-led forces invaded Iraq, Labour MP Dennis Skinner put it to UK Prime Minister Tony Blair that the imminent war was all about "America getting their hands on the oil supplies in the Middle East".

Rejecting what he called "the conspiracy theory idea that this is somehow to do with oil", Blair argued that if this were the issue, it would be "infinitely simpler to cut a deal with Saddam, who I'm sure would be delighted to give us access to as much oil as we wanted if he could carry on building weapons of mass destruction". What the war was about, he insisted, was Iraq's growing arsenal of WMD: in the light of 9/11, the madman of Baghdad had to be stopped.

It was the same story on the other side of the Atlantic. Just a month before Blair's rejection of the oil explanation, US Defense Secretary Donald Rumsfeld was asked by CBS's *60 Minutes* if the coming war was about oil. "Nonsense. It just isn't", he snapped, and called the idea a "myth". Asked the same question on the same programme, however, oil and gas expert Phillip Ellis of Boston Consulting replied: "Of course it is".

The players

The oil theory was lent added weight by the close links between the Bush family and administrations and the oil industry. President George H.W. Bush had spent the 1950s climbing the greasy pole in the Texas oil industry, becoming chief of Zapata Petroleum (which, ironically, took its name from a Mexican guerrilla leader). Before beginning his own political career, his son George W. Bush started up the oil company Arbusto (Spanish for "bush"), which was part-financed by Osama bin Laden's brother.

After the largely unsuccessful Arbusto merged with Harken Energy in 1986, Bush's connections paid off, with Harken winning its first overseas oil-drilling contract in Bahrain. (The Bush family also has strong ties with the Saudi royal family – see p.368 and the Carlyle Group.) Bush eventually became governor of the oil state, Texas, and according to the Center for Public Integrity, six of the ten largest contributors to his presidential campaign came from or had connections with the oil business. Secretary of State Condoleezza Rice, meanwhile, who had been a member of George H.W. Bush's National Security Council, went on to become a board member of Chevron in 1991 and even had a 130,000-ton tanker named after her.

The biggest player, however, has to be Vice President Dick Cheney, who between 1995 and 2000 earned $44m as chief executive of Texas-based Halliburton, the world's largest oil and gas services company. (You have to admire Cheney's chutzpah: in his last year at Halliburton, Cheney also served as the head of George W. Bush's vice-presidential search committee, considering various candidates before finally selecting... himself.)

The Cheney/Halliburton connection has been well explored in a 2004 New Yorker article by Jane Mayer. Both in and out of government, says Mayer, Cheney has been a long-time champion of the private sector, arguing that it can supply cheaper and better services than state bureaucracies. As Mayer points out, his arguments seem to have won the day – in 2002, for example, over $150 billion of public money was transferred from the Pentagon to private contractors. These include Cheney's old firm Halliburton, which is now the largest private contractor for American forces in Iraq, having received contracts worth up to $11 billion for its work there.

This, however, marked the culmination of a process began ten years earlier, when Cheney was Defense Secretary under George H.W. Bush. As Peter W. Singer notes in his book *Corporate Warriors*, when the Pentagon decided to contract out its non-military support services for overseas operations to a single contractor, it paid Halliburton $9m to carry out two studies into this. It came as no surprise that when, in August 1992, the US Army awarded a five-year contract for providing all its overseas support services, the contract went to the same firm that had carried out the studies – Halliburton.

Under Cheney's stewardship, Halliburton nearly doubled its government contracts, from $1.2 billion to $2.3 billion And although Cheney claimed in 2000 that he had had a "firm policy" that Halliburton should not do any business with Iraq, two of its subsidiaries signed Iraqi contracts worth more than $73m while he was CEO. The deals helped to reconstruct Iraq's oil-production infrastructure – the very same infrastructure whose destruction Cheney had supervised as Defense Secretary during the Gulf War.

As regards the Iraq war, the closest thing to a "smoking gun" is a top-secret National Security Council document of February 3, 2001. This instructed NSC staff to offer their full cooperation to Cheney's newly formed Energy Task Force during its consideration of what it described the "melding" of two policy areas: "the review of operational policies towards rogue states" – which naturally included Iraq – and "actions regarding the capture [sic] of new and existing oil and gas fields".

The prize

There's a lot of oil in Iraq. It has proven reserves of 112 billion barrels – the world's largest after Saudi Arabia's – and may have up to 220 billion barrels. Global oil reserves, on the other hand, have peaked, while demand (mainly from Asia) is set to soar. By 2025, meantime, the Department of Energy estimates that the US – the world's largest consumer of oil – will be importing up to 70 percent of the oil it needs. In September 2002 the *Washington Post* reported that ousting Saddam would herald a "bonanza" for American oil companies long banished from Iraq, while scuttling oil deals between Baghdad and Russia, France and China. These three countries – all ambivalent or flatly against the Iraq war – had previously agreed oil concessions with Saddam, to be developed once UN sanctions were lifted.

Faisal Qaragholi, London director of the exiled Iraqi National Congress (INC) opposition (and a petroleum engineer), said the INC wasn't bound by these deals. INC leader Ahmed Chalabi (see p.377) added: "American companies will have a big shot at Iraqi oil". An eve-of-war speech by Bush, ironically published on the White House website under a banner bearing the words "Iraq: Denial and Deception", seemed to reflect the order of priorities. First he warned Iraqis not to destroy oil wells, describing them as "a source of wealth that belongs to the Iraqi people". Only then did he tell them "not [to] obey any command to use weapons of mass destruction", adding that war crimes would be prosecuted.

The Axis of Evil and the dollar/ euro switch

There again, it might not be oil as such, but the currency it's sold in. Saddam Hussein switched to selling oil in euros in 2000, which increased Iraqi prof-

its as the euro rose against the US dollar. When the US put Iraqi oil back on the open market in 2003, the *Financial Times* reported, it switched the trading currency back to US dollars. Iran, meantime, has sold its oil in euros since 2003, while North Korea ditched dollars for euros in 2002. As the journalist Robert Fisk speculated in the *Independent*, Bush's so-called "Axis of Evil" might be an "axis of euro", which – in challenging the supremacy of the dollar as the dominant trading currency for oil – poses a threat to the economic well-being of the US itself.

Officially, one of the most important reasons why Iran should be regarded as part of this "Axis of Evil" is its development of enriched uranium, which can be used both in bombs and power stations. Quite why a country rich in oil and gas needs nuclear power stations is not clear, but doubts have been raised about whether Iran has a nuclear *bomb* programme. In November 2004 the *Washington Post* reported that a "single unvetted source" supplied the intelligence for Colin Powell's accusation of Iranian nuclear bomb-building, while UN weapons inspector Mohamed El Baradei said in February 2005 that the IAEA lacked "conclusive evidence" of such a programme.

According to writer William Clark, however, Iran's nuclear ambitions are just a pretext to attack the country – the real problem with Iran is its setting-up, in direct competition with the London-based International Petroleum Exchange and New York's Mercantile Exchange, of a euro-based oil trading exchange in 2005. This, Clark argues, will further increase the desirability and purchasing power of the euro while sending the dollar into a tailspin of devaluation and dumping from capital markets, hammering the US economy accordingly.

A pro-US regime in Iraq, on the other hand, will help to counter the move towards petroeuros. In the short term, the Iraq war may add to massive US deficits and do nothing to halt the dollar's decline. In the long term, however, the cost of this – borne by taxpayers anyway – is outweighed by the benefits of ensuring that the black stuff continues to be sold in the US's own currency.

A further twist to this theory was added by Al Jazeera, which reported that OPEC's drift towards euros was only stymied by the US's ally Saudi Arabia, something "largely suppressed in the US media". The continued hegemony of the dollar, it would seem, relies heavily on Saudi support. As the euro rises in parity and desirability, increasingly becoming the reserve currency for India, China and Russia, this means that the US in turn is becoming increasingly dependent on Saudi goodwill.

An offer Saddam shouldn't have refused

There's another theory that says that the war was really just sour grapes over Saddam's refusal to play ball in what amounted to a political and financial protection racket. According to John Perkins in *Confessions Of An Economic Hit Man*, the US helps to keep the House of Saud in power in return for the House of Saud helping to keep oil prices stable and investing or spending a large part of its petrodollar income in the US, a scheme benefiting both sides handsomely. Thus the Saudis not only invested heavily in US government securities, but also used US firms to build new cities and infrastructure in Saudi Arabia – and then, of course, there are all those juicy defence contracts.

A similar deal, along with some cheap World Bank loans, was apparently proposed to Saddam, only he turned it down, not realizing that it was an offer he couldn't refuse. According to Perkins, refusing such offers leads to CIA-backed "jackals" fomenting a coup d'état or setting up an assassination. Failing this – and before his capture, Saddam proved a notoriously elusive target – the next stage is, and always has been, war.

The Euro Dollar pit at the Chicago Mercantile Exchange

Zionist conspiracy

Given the close relationship between the US and Israel on the one hand, and the fact that Iraq is an Arab country on the other, it's hardly surprising that the war has been seen by some as a Zionist conspiracy. In March 2003 the *New York Times* reported the theory that a cadre of pro-Zionist zealots in the White House and the media seeking to oust Saddam and make the Middle East safe for Israel had finally succeeded. Congressman Jim Moran declared: "If it were not for the strong support of the Jewish community for this war with Iraq, we would not be doing this." Similarly, the late Professor Edward Said of Columbia University pointed to the "Zionist lobby, right-wing Christians or the military-industrial complex" in Congress who hate the Arab world. However, given the fact that Saddam had attacked Israel with Scud missiles during the first Gulf War, Israel's support for his removal is hardly surprising, and in itself, provides no evidence of a Zionist plot.

Ongoing grief

The most important official reason given for the war on Iraq was the threat posed by Saddam's alleged WMD capabilities. With the benefit of hindsight (which is a wonderful thing), it was a threat that was not so much exaggerated as non-existent: as the Iraq Survey Group confirmed, the weapons and facilities in question had been destroyed following UN inspections in the 1990s.

In the end, however, it wasn't Saddam, but Bush and Blair who had stopped the weapons inspectors from carrying on with their job and finding this out. And up to that point, the US and UK governments deliberately exaggerated the scale of the alleged threat. In the UK at least, people weren't fooled: in September 2003, the *Independent* published an opinion poll that suggested that 59 percent of the British public believed that Blair had lied over Iraq.

George W. Bush and Tony Blair went on to be re-elected in 2004 and 2005 respectively. Serious damage, however, has been done to public trust in both "intelligence" and political leaders. This makes the citizens of the US and the UK less likely to believe their governments if and when a genuine threat emerges in future. As the US Robb-Silberman commission put it: "US credibility was put on the line over the existence of an Iraqi WMD programme – and as a result of nothing being found, it has been severely undermined."

International relations have hardly been helped either, not only in the West, but also between the West and the rest of the world, particularly Islamic countries, and the wave of sympathy for the US that

9/11 created (though not everywhere) has, at best, subsided. For some, the US and the UK's willingness to take pre-emptive, bilateral military action – in what they see as blatant disregard of the UN, international law, and the centuries-old principles of a just war – sets a dangerous precedent.

The financial cost of the war has been estimated at $150 billion for US taxpayers alone, and oil prices have soared. While the American Academy of Sciences has estimated that rebuilding Iraq will cost between $30 and $105 billion, some US construction firms and service providers, "defence" contractors and oil companies – often with strong Washington connections – seem to be doing very nicely, thank you. Meanwhile some unemployed Iraqis are so desperate for work that they're prepared to risk being blown up as they queue for equally dangerous jobs in the police force.

The full human cost of the war and ongoing insurrection is impossible to calculate. At the time of writing, 2000 US, 97 UK and 92 coalition soldiers had been killed, along with 238 contractors. Both the US and UK denied it was their responsibility to try and keep track of Iraqi civilian casualties, although the CIA did finally disclose in October 2005 they had recorded 26,000 to date. Meanwhile, as Terry Jones noted in the *Guardian* in April 2005, a report to the UN Human Rights Commission in Geneva showed that, by the end of 2004, the number of Iraqi children under five suffering from malnutrition had doubled, from four percent under Saddam to eight percent under occupation.

Overall, though, surely it can't be denied that Iraq is better off without Saddam Hussein? That's a question for the Iraqi people to answer, and at least now they have the chance to speak for themselves. But to justify the war in terms of regime change is ultimately equivalent to saying that the end justifies the means. The $64 billion dollar question is what end or ends the Bush and Blair administrations were pursuing *through* regime change – and in whose interests. Whether we suspected Saddam and Al Qaeda of plotting to use weapons of mass destruction, or Bush and Blair of using weapons of mass deception, we're all conspiracy theorists now.

SOURCES

Books

Richard Clarke Against All Enemies: Inside America's War On Terror (2004). Clarke advised presidents Reagan, George H.W. Bush, Clinton, and George W. Bush, and castigates the latter for failing to take terrorism seriously, then turning on Iraq immediately after 9/11 as the "Vulcans" (Wolfowitz, Rice, Rumsfeld) had already been planning all along.

Laurie Mylroie Bush Vs The Beltway: The Inside Battle Over War In Iraq (2004). Mylroie, an American Enterprise Institute fellow who advised Bill Clinton on Iraq during his 1992 presidential campaign, argues that the CIA and State Department, among others, conspired to discredit vital intelligence about the threat from Saddam and his links with Al Qaeda. In her earlier **The War Against America** (2001) – praised by Richard Perle – Mylroie claimed that Saddam was involved in the 1993 World Trade Center bombing.

Stephen C. Pelletiere Iraq And The International Oil System: Why America Went To War In The Persian Gulf (2001). A pretty savage indictment of the US government's motives for its continued interference in the Gulf, by the CIA's own analyst for the Iran-Iraq war.

William Rivers Pitt and Scott Ritter War On Iraq: What Team Bush Doesn't Want You to Know (2002). Ritter (a former UN weapons inspector) and Pitt lay into the neo-cons pushing the US into war, shooting down the Bush administration's arguments about Saddam's WMD – known to be already destroyed – and alleged connections with Al Qaeda.

Randeep Ramesh (ed) **The War We Could Not Stop: The Real Story Of The Battle For Iraq** (2004). British, American and Arabic-speaking journalists detail the historical context to the Iraq War, from the rise of a neo-con cabal in Washington to the UN and Tony Blair's efforts to bring the UK onside with fears of Iraq's WMD.

Geoff Simons Iraq: From Sumer To Post-Saddam (2004). This lays out the history of a nation created, exploited and invaded in the cynical pursuit of Western interests.

Gore Vidal Dreaming War: Blood For Oil And The Cheney-Bush Junta (2003). Bush (with his curious family connections to the bin Laden family) and Cheney are "corporate oil gunslingers" and defenders of the super-rich, who were all too well warned that 9/11 was likely but needed an excuse to take on Iraq. A typically pugnacious piece from the vitriolic Vidal.

Bob Woodward Plan of Attack: The Road To War (2004). Woodward, one of the famous Watergate investigation duo of Woodward and Bernstein, reports from within the White House in the run-up to the Iraq War, detailing the split between the gung-ho Cheney and Rumsfeld and the more cautious Colin Powell and General Tommy Franks. The influence of Saudi Ambassador Prince Bandar emerges particularly clearly.

Films

Uncovered: The Whole Truth About The Iraq War (Robert Greenwald, 2003). A score of experts weigh in with sober judgements on the "threat" from Iraq, against the painful paucity of facts coming from the Bush administration's stars and their use of frightening rhetoric.

Websites

ⓦ **globalresearch.ca/articles/CLA410A. html** "The Real Reasons Why Iran Is The Next Target", an article by William Clark that supports the euro vs dollar theory.

ⓦ **www.americaforsale.org** Carrying the banner "This is not a conspiracy theory. This is history in the making", this two-man site uses mainstream media sources to counter the kind of misinformation and misunderstanding that has led seventy percent of Americans, according to a CNN poll, to believe that Iraqis attacked the US on 9/11.

ⓦ **www.casi.org.uk/discuss/2003/ msg00457.html** Cambridge academic Dr Glenn Rangwala's exposure of the UK government's "dodgy dossier", with links to both the original dossier and one of the three articles (not, as commonly thought, a PhD thesis) it plagiarized.

ⓦ **www.gwu.edu/~nsarchiv/special/iraq/** "The Saddam Hussein Sourcebook: Declassified Secrets From The US-Iraq Relationship", another invaluable Web publication from the US National Security Archive. Go to the bottom of the page and click on "Iraq And Weapons Of Mass Destruction".

ⓦ **www.newyorker.com/fact/content/ ?040216fa_fact** "Contract sport: what did the Vice-President do for Halliburton?", by Jane Mayer (February 16 and 23, 2004). The New Yorker, famous for its fact-checking, delves into the murky connections between Vice President Dick Cheney and government contracts awarded to Halliburton, his former employer.

ⓦ **www.timesonline.co.uk/article/0,,2087-1593607,00.html** "The secret Downing Street memo" – ie the minutes of the May Day 2005 meeting. Details of the briefing paper for the meeting can be found at www.timesonline.co.uk/article/0,,2087-1592724,00.html.

The capture of Saddam Hussein

On December 14, 2003, the US administrator in Iraq, Paul Bremer, announced to a press conference: "Ladies and gentlemen ... we got him!" No one needing telling who Bremer was talking about, and the assembled journalists erupted in cheers – although Western news agencies insisted on reporting that it was the Iraqi journalists who showed most emotion.

The deposed Iraqi dictator, Saddam Hussein, had been on the run since Baghdad had fallen to coalition forces in April 2003. The world was shown a video of him looking gaunt and dishevelled, with his hair and beard overgrown and his eyes glazed, being poked and prodded by surgically gloved hands. He seemed a far cry from the smart, stout man so often seen posing on a palace balcony, or at the head of a long table of minions.

No sooner was the capture of Saddam Hussein announced, however, than suspicions, in certain quarters at least, began to set in. In a region where little can be taken at face value, Saddam's detention unleashed a barrage of scepticism about American duplicity, and revealed that many in the Middle East held Saddam's captors in as much contempt as Saddam himself.

Saddam in a spider hole

According to the official story, Saddam was found near the small Iraqi town of al-Dawr, ten miles south of his hometown of Tikrit. Around six hundred US troops were searching the area in darkness, when they spotted a small walled compound that held a mud hut. In that hut, beneath a tatty camouflage of bricks and carpet, was a "spider hole". Just as the troops were about to throw a grenade into the hole, a figure emerged. "My name is Saddam Hussein. I am the president of Iraq and I want to negotiate", he said. "Regards from President Bush," replied the commanding US officer. It was 8.36pm, Saturday, December 13.

The dictator's hideout, located within view of one of his former palaces, was a mere eight feet deep, and equipped with a vent and extractor fan. Saddam had a classic gangster's stash of around $750,000 in cash, two machine guns, two aides, a briefcase of documents and a taxi parked nearby, but there were no mobile phones or communications equipment. Whatever fighting was going on in Iraq, Saddam wasn't conducting it.

US forces had been scouring the area for months, suspecting that Saddam would hide somewhere in his tribal and political homeland. According to the BBC, interrogations, data analysis and searches narrowed the net, until a tip-off from Baghdad finally led to the spider hole itself. Within 24 hours, DNA tests proved the prisoner to be Saddam.

Gossip about gas

However, a great many respected news sources in the Middle East simply didn't buy the story. Saddam's sister, Nawal Ibrahim Al-Hassan, told the London-based Arabic daily *Al-Quds Al-Arabi* that her brother could only have surrendered so disgracefully if "he was subjected to anaesthetization or nerve gas"; otherwise he would have killed himself. Similarly, his eldest daughter Raghad told Al-Arabiyya TV that Saddam most have been drugged. Others referred to rumours that dead birds and animals were found around the spider hole, suggesting that nerve gas of some kind had been used.

The Pentagon responded that the US military hadn't possessed, let alone used, chemical weapons for several decades, while conjecture grew as to whether the Army had genuinely found Saddam or had been tipped off. To that end, the Saudi daily *Okaz* speculated that Saddam had been betrayed by his second wife, Samira Al-Shahbandar, for the promised $25 million reward. Samira told the British newspaper the *Sunday Times* that she spoke to Saddam weekly from her Lebanese home by phone, and that the last conversation was deliberately prolonged so US intelligence could pinpoint his location.

If there was a tip-off, it's never been clear exactly who, if anyone, received the bounty. The Army dismissed Samira's claim as "rumours", and it's certainly undermined by the fact that no phones were found with Saddam.

Was Saddam in the hole at all?

Other rumours centred on whether Saddam really was captured at that specific time and place. On December 17, the Israeli website www.debka. com (which has the full title "DEBKAfile, Political Analysis, Espionage, Terrorism, Security", suggesting some undisclosed but official status) put forward the theory that Saddam Hussein had in fact been captured weeks before by Iraqis, who then held him underground while they negotiated for the reward.

The Saudi daily *Al-Riyadh*, on the other hand, suggested that the US Army had held Saddam for some time, and only told the world they "captured" him when they did to maximize the story's political impact. It wrote that the timing was designed to "ease the emotional and military pressure by the American forces and give new momentum to the American president just when he needs this kind of event". It also questioned the DNA proof of Saddam's identity, arguing that such tests take longer than 24 hours.

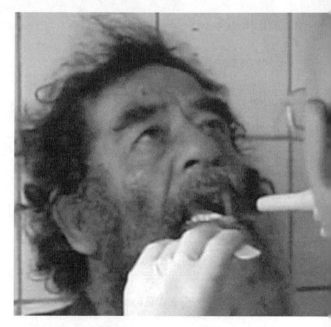

Saddam Hussein, ex-president

Al-Quds Al-Arabi claimed that a photo of GIs around the spider hole showed that Saddam was already in captivity and the "capture" staged. A nearby palm tree held a cluster of yellow dates – the colour they would be in the summer. By December, however, the dates would have long since ripened to dark brown. Saddam's robotic behaviour was also likened to the gas victims who survived the Chechen siege at the Moscow Theatre.

The theory that the US had caught Saddam months before was greeted with derisory laughter by the Republican administration, while the White House responded to the DNA doubts with: "I don't even know if that speculation dignifies [*sic*] comment".

Saddam the super servant

Also on December 17, the Iraqi daily *Al-Shira* opined that Saddam had been a "super servant" of the US since 1963. He had waged war against Iran in 1980 with American backing, while his invasion of Kuwait in 1990 allowed America to reinforce its presence in the Gulf, and ensure US control over Arab oil. Ultimately, the elimination of Iraq would create a regional imbalance of power that would profit the US. Saddam had finally surrendered as a free service for Bush in particular, "in disgraceful pictures that would be used as stickers in the election campaign".

The Washington-based Arabic "media analysts", Middle East Media Research Institute (www.memri.org), described this as an interesting "conspiracy theory". However, but for the fact that after invading Kuwait, Saddam had no longer been an ally but an enemy of the US, the charges are largely true. Why should MEMRI write it off so readily? A senior MEMRI analyst, Dr. Nimrod Raphaeli, argued that "almost every calamity that adversely affects the Arab world prompts conspiracy theories that are quickly woven into intricate shapes and patterns, to demonstrate innocence and blame others for the calamity". The capture of Saddam was indeed a calamity, Raphaeli asserted, as his supporters in Iraq and in the Arab world were "shocked" to see "the knight of knights, courageous and gallant – meek, defeated, and humiliated". Maybe, but then as the Council on American-Islamic Relations told the *Washington Times*: "Memri's intent is to find the worst possible quotes from the Muslim world and disseminate them as widely as possible."

From patsy to poster boy

The idea that Saddam had already been in captivity for some time when he was wheeled out at a moment that would maximize the political benefit for the White House remained in circulation for some time in the West. While the announcement did indeed give George W. Bush a definite bounce in the polls, and boosted support for the war effort, it's hard to see why that precise juncture was better than any other. And was it really worthwhile fabricating a story that, as all stories do, risked being found out?

On the other hand, the well-publicized "rescue" of Private Jessica Lynch from an Iraqi hospital in April 2003 was not all that it seemed. The story dominated TV news headlines in the US, with dramatic footage – shot on a military night-vision camera – of American soldiers heroically storming the hospital to liberate the plucky captive. But then a BBC current affairs programme revealed that the "rescue" was an elaborately staged propaganda exercise: Lynch was a patient rather than a prisoner, and as the Americans had been told the previous day, the Iraqi military had already fled the scene.

"It was like a Hollywood film", said Iraqi doctor Anmar Uday. "They cried, 'Go, go, go', with guns and blanks and the sound of explosions. They made a show – an action movie like Sylvester Stallone or Jackie Chan, with jumping and shouting, breaking down doors." Perhaps Uday himself had seen too many Hollywood films, but that military camera was clearly there for a purpose. The rumbling of this PR stunt, however, did little to dent Bush's popularity, or public faith in the mainstream media.

Global rumour insisted that Osama bin Laden would also suddenly be revealed, encaged, shortly before the US presidential election of 2004, and thus guarantee a landslide win for Bush. Many also believed that another terrorist attack of some kind would hit the US – though no one was sure whether this would strengthen Bush in his War on Terror or make him appear to be losing it.

In the event, bin Laden did make an appearance, just days before the November vote – but in a video he released himself, in which he stood at a podium in a TV studio as though he were a third election

SADDAM AND THE CIA

George W. Bush isn't the first American president to have carried out "regime change" in Iraq. In 1963 the CIA, under President John F. Kennedy, was behind a successful coup in Baghdad, carried out in collaboration with a young Saddam Hussein.

The story was reported by Roger Morris, a former member of the US National Security Council, in the *New York Times* of March 14, 2003. Forty years earlier, according to Morris, the CIA was involved in the overthrow of General Abd al-Karim Qasim (aka Abdul Kassem), who had deposed the pro-Western Iraqi monarchy in 1958. Initially, Qasim's repressive regime was tolerated by the Eisenhower administration because he was opposed to the West's Arab bugbear, Colonel Nasser of Egypt. But in 1959, Qasim suddenly withdrew Iraq from the anti-Soviet Baghdad Pact, began to buy arms from the Russians and gave government posts to Communists.

That same year, Saddam made a botched assassination attempt as part of what the UPI news agency, following an interview with a former State Department Official, called a "US plot" to get rid of Qasim. Ludicrously, the CIA's euphemistically named "Health Alteration Committee" also sent Qasim a poisoned monogrammed handkerchief, though either he never received it or it failed to work.

According to former Ba'thist leader Hani Fkaiki, Saddam was working with the CIA again in 1962 and 1963, when a successful coup was finally staged and Qasim was shot after a hasty trial. On the day the new regime took power, a National Security Council aide wrote to President Kennedy that it was "almost certainly a gain for our side". The Ba'th party then set about systematically arresting and killing large numbers of suspected Communists, using lists supplied by the CIA. Middle East expert Adel Darwish says that the killings were "presided over" by Saddam, who subsequently became head of the Ba'th party's intelligence service.

The new regime was armed by the US, and companies such as Bechtel, and oil companies British Petroleum and Mobil were soon doing business in Iraq. In 1968, however, there was another coup – bloodless this time – which brought the Ba'thist general Ahmed Hassan al-Bakr to power. One of his relatives was Saddam Hussein, who became vice president and then president in 1979 after an ailing al-Bakr stood down – no doubt with more than a little encouragement from Saddam.

---

candidate. He taunted everyone with his "freedom", while denouncing US policies wholesale. Whether this helped to reduce Bush's winning margin to a thin three percent, or gave him victory by inspiring panic and/or patriotism in voters, is hard to say.

SOURCES

Websites

⊚ www.guardian.co.uk/Iraq/
Story/0,2763,956255,00.html An article by
John Kampfner, presenter of "War Spin",
the edition of the BBC Correspondent
programme that exposed the "Saving
Private Lynch" myth. A disturbing insight
into military "news management".

⊚ www.villagevoice.com/news/
0352,mondo5,49601,6.html A *Village Voice*
article by James Ridgway covering many
of the claims and theories about Saddam's
capture. For more, see http://blogcritics.
org/archives/2003/12/22/131524.php

Conspiracy Theory Archive

Material relating to individual conspiracy theories is situated near the individual theories. But of course, there is more to every subject than meets the eye. Here is a selection of the most interesting conspiracy theory books, films and websites to explore and consider.

BOOKS

General reference and theory

David Alexander *Conspiracies And Cover-ups* (2002). A neat collection of essays on the darker histories and stories of the twentieth century, written with a healthy dose of objectivity. Somewhat dry in tone, however, and maybe a little confused about what it's trying to prove.

Michael Barkun *A Culture Of Conspiracy: Apocalyptic Visions In Contemporary America* (2003). A serious but very readable study of the links between mega-conspiracies (Barkun calls them super-conspiracies) and right-wing, neo-fundamentalist beliefs. Thoughtful and alarming in equal measure.

Richard M. Bennett *Conspiracy: Plots, Lies And Cover-Ups* (2003). A compendium of brief historical anecdotes that covers real, acknowledged conspiracies as much as conspiracy theories. There's an excellent spread of subjects, from Nero to 9/11

via Operation Northwoods, but it's not particularly thought-provoking, and the tone is disappointingly bland.

Paul T. Coughlin *Secrets, Plots And Hidden Agendas: What You Don't Know About Conspiracy Theories* (1999). An American Christian attacks right-wing Christian fundamentalist conspiracy theories. Focuses particularly on Waco and Oklahoma, and on the apocalyptic heritage of American fundamentalism.

David Brion Davis (ed) *The Fear Of Conspiracy: Images Of Un-American Subversion From The Revolution To The Present* (1971). Includes brief essays from historians, but this compendium is really an academic sourcebook for classic cries of "conspiracy!" from America's past, from John Robison's anti-Illuminati "Proofs Of A Conspiracy" (1797) and A.J. Warner and H.C. Baldwin's "The British Plot To Enslave The World" (1892) to Senator Joseph McCarthy's astonishing "A Conspiracy Of Blackest

Infamy" (1951) and Robert Welch's John Birch Society tract "The Truth About Vietnam" (1967). Puts the history of conspiracism splendidly in context.

Mark Fenster *Conspiracy Theories: Secrecy And Power In American Culture* (1999). Highbrow literary criticism with conspiracy culture as the text. A handful of essays focus on Bill Clinton, JFK and Christian militias, but Fenster's purpose is to analyse political ideology itself, not its manifestations.

Michael Haag and Veronica Haag *The Rough Guide To The Da Vinci Code* (2005). OK, we're blowing our own trumpet here, but this is the most readable (and most pocketable) of the many "decoding the code"-style books. Includes detailed information on the book's various locations.

Al Hidell and Joan D'Arc *The Conspiracy Reader: From The Deaths Of JFK And John Lennon To Government-sponsored Alien Cover-ups* (1999). These articles from *Paranoia* magazine cover some of the same ground as this book, albeit with a strong emphasis on pop culture. The lack of contextualization, an overview or indeed any concerted effort to distinguish fact from fiction can make this feel like a rather pointless read, however.

Richard Hofstadter *The Paranoid Style In American Politics, And Other Essays* (1952, 1964). Hofstadter is one of the leading historians of postwar American politics. This classic essay on conspiracism on the American Right was the first to use the clinical term "paranoid style" for the conspiracists' view of history, which he compares to clinical paranoia. Brief but fascinating discussions of anti-Illuminati and anti-Masonic panics, and McCarthyism.

Michael Howard *The Occult Conspiracy* (1989). Howard – no relation to the currently outgoing UK Conservative Party leader – takes a well-sourced look at the history, motives and power of secret societies, from Ancient Egypt up to the present day.

Devon Jackson *Conspiranoia! The Mother Of All Conspiracies* (1999). This is a densely written stream-of-consciousness tome, interspersed with near-impenetrable diagrams and symbols and making phenomenal leaps from subject to subject. A good read, nevertheless, offering an insight into how the minds of some conspiracy theorists work.

Jim Keith (ed) *Secret And Suppressed: Banned ideas And Hidden History* (1993). A collection of intensely written, tautly argued pieces on everything from the Jonestown Massacre to sexual symbolism in Masonic worship. It's not always clear whether some of the writers believe the wilder edges of their theories.

Peter Knight *Conspiracy Culture: From The Kennedy Assassination To The X Files* (2000). Not a book of conspiracy theories, but a book of theories about conspiracy theories. Knight's take is thoughtful, and his survey of other academics' thinking on the conspiracy phenomenon is probably the best around. Lots of insightful comments on the rise and development of conspiracy theories in American culture, well illustrated by examples from conspiracy literature on JFK, AIDS, crack cocaine – and even feminism.

Peter Knight *Conspiracy Theories In American History: An Encyclopedia* (2003). This is the last word in conspiracy literature, with 925 pages on over 300 conspiracies. Write-ups come from over 120 mainly academic, specialist contributors; most try to sort the wheat from the chaff. Covers conspiracist culture as much as actual theories, with entries for novelist Thomas Pynchon and "yellow journalism", as well as overview pieces. JFK gets the most detailed coverage, with fifteen pages.

George Monbiot *Captive State: The Corporate Takeover Of Britain* (2000). Britain's leading anti-globalization journalist exposes the pernicious and sometimes malicious influence of corporations on British society, from the imposition of the infamous Skye Bridge and the "economic cleansing" of supermarkets to the role of corporate capital in university research. Angry, but balanced, persuasive and impeccably researched.

Vance Packard *Hidden Persuaders* (1957). Classic exposé of advertising techniques that occasionally slips into conspiracism. Packard protests that they try to invade the privacy of our minds. All the more fascinating for being very dated.

Jane Parish and Martin Parker (eds) *The Age Of Anxiety: Conspiracy Theory And The Human Sciences* (2001). Ten academic sociologists' essays on conspiracy culture. Topics covered include the New World Order, the Patriot movement, viruses and France's Front National, but the book is theoretical for the most part, trying to define conspiracism as a sociological phenomenon.

Daniel Pipes *Conspiracy: How The Paranoid Style Flourishes And Where It Comes From* (1997). The core of the book is a brief but coherent history of anti-Semitic conspiracy theories, but it's surrounded by lots of thoughtful discussion of conspiracism in general. Pipes excoriates the ultra-Right, but doesn't miss the chance to lambast the Left for good measure.

Daniel Pipes *The Hidden Hand: Middle East Fears Of Conspiracy* (1996). Pipes is a controversial figure with a strongly pro-Israeli agenda, but this is one of the best books on Arab conspiracism nonetheless, with lots of examples of conspiracy theories in postwar Middle Eastern history.

Robin Ramsay *Conspiracy Theories* (2000). Ramsay, who is also editor of *Lobster* magazine, looms large in the conspiracy world as an investigative writer with few equals and one with a pretty sane take on theories, their flaws and truths. This is a well-argued super-mini-guide to his preferred conspiracies, with interesting thoughts on what conspiracy theories are, and why they matter.

Jon Ronson *Them: Adventures With Extremists* (2001). In this funny and thoughtful travelogue into the extremes of conspiracy culture, British writer Ronson gets right down into the conspiracy basement with some serious weirdos.

Elaine Showalter *Hystories: Hysterical Epidemics And Modern Culture* (1997). Showalter's fascinating and controversial thesis is that modern epidemics such as chronic fatigue syndrome, Gulf War syndrome, alien abduction and Satanic ritual abuse claims are classic symptoms of hysteria amplified by modern communications and fin de siècle anxiety. Conspiracism, she says, is a psychic problem.

Kenn Thomas (ed) *Cyberculture Counterconspiracy* (1999). These "web readers" are republished articles from the Steamshovel Press conspiracy magazine, and are sometimes authoritative, sometimes wacky, and almost always distinctly conspiracist. Comes in two volumes – take your pick from the contents list.

Jonathan Vankin and John Whalen *The 80 Greatest Conspiracies Of All Time* (2004). As the title suggests, this American-centred tome is written with a keen eye on the popular market. It's actually quite well written, but many of the actual accounts of the theories are very thin – some are little more than brief book reviews.

Francis Wheen *How Mumbo-Jumbo Conquered The World* (2004). Vitriolic, comic but ultimately journalistic rant against UFOs, religion, New Age culture, astrology, self-help ... and conspiracy theories.

Fiction

Dan Brown *The Da Vinci Code* (2003). The book that (re)launched the Christian history conspiracy theories on the world. The writing style isn't for aesthetes, and the plot is clunky, but there's a reason this book sold tens of millions of copies. Covers everything from the bloodline of Jesus and Mary Magdalene to the heritage of the Templars, with lots of what Brown calls "symbology" thrown in. *Angels and Demons* (2000), which imagines a terrorist stand-off between techno-happy Illuminati and the Vatican, may in fact be the better thriller, but the subject-matter feels more hackneyed.

Ian Caldwell and Dustin Thomason *The Rule Of Four* (2004). A kind of middle-brow *Da Vinci Code*, featuring two Princeton students' moderately thrilling quest to trace the secret behind the Renaissance text, the *Hypnerotomachia Poliophili*.

Richard Condon *The Manchurian Candidate* (1959). The satirical political thriller that launched two hit films (see p.395).

Don DeLillo *Libra* (1988). Brilliant and very literary conspiracy novel: two CIA agents plan a false-flag operation to fake an (unsuccessful) assassination of JFK and blame it on the Cubans. Unfortunately, the patsy they choose is called Lee Harvey Oswald. While writing *Libra*, DeLillo has said, "there were times when I felt an eerie excitement, coming across an item that seemed to bear out my own theories. Anyone who enters this maze knows you have to become part scientist, novelist, biographer, historian and existential detective". DeLillo's masterpiece is probably *Underworld* (1997), an 800-page novel that traces – in reverse – five chaotic decades of Cold War culture, using a baseball ball as the lynchpin.

Craig DiLouie *Paranoia* (2001). Zeitgeisty, literary-lite novel charting the descent of an orderly working at a mental health hospital into the world of conspiracy, where paranoia becomes a dangerous addiction and scepticism is no longer an option. Draws chiefly on Illuminati, WMD and presidential assassination conspiracy theories.

Benjamin Disraeli *Lothair* (1870). A glamorous romp through nineteenth-century European high politics, taking in Roman Catholic conspiracies and Italian secret societies. In his alter ego as British Prime Minister, Disraeli frequently warned against conspiracies. You'd have thought he knew a thing or two.

Umberto Eco *Foucault's Pendulum* (1988). The intellectual's *Da Vinci Code*. Eco is the master of the ironic, postmodernist esoteric thriller, and this novel is probably his most challenging and rewarding. It's also drawn straight from conspiracy culture. Three eccentric Italian literary types design their own Templar conspiracy theory and are then horrified to find it appears to be true. Packed with verbal brilliance and abstruse fragments of Renaissance and Jewish occultism.

Giuseppe Genna *In The Name Of Ishmael* (2003). This literary-minded detective thriller tracks two parallel police investigations in Milan, one in 1962, the other in 2001. The researches of the two detectives involved converge ominously on a mysterious and powerful figure called Ishmael, whose murky political and sex crimes seem to be at the centre of decades of conspiracies – both Italian and international.

Robert Harris *Fatherland* (1992). It's 1964 and the Nazis have most of Europe in their grip. Maverick Berlin detective Xavier March starts to uncover clues that lead him to discover the conspiracy buried deep in the Nazi past: the Holocaust. A thrilling, intelligent and fascinating take on alternative history.

Thomas Pynchon *The Crying Of Lot 49* (1965). At just 150-odd pages, this is Pynchon at his most accessible, but it's still pretty meaty stuff – a brilliantly chaotic and often darkly comic maelstrom of pop and conspiracy culture, science and occultism. As the executor of her late boyfriend's estate, Oedipa Maas seems to discover a web of conspiracy focused on a bizarre postal system called Tristero. There's more crazy 1960s Americana in *Vineland* (1990), but for truly serious Pynchon, try the 750-pager *Gravity's Rainbow* (1973), set around a World War II quest for the V2 rocket and with plenty of conspirators on the sidelines.

Robert Shea and Robert Anton Wilson *Illuminatus!* (1975). Inspector Saul Goodman,

Homicide, comes across memos that suggest the Illuminati still exist, and sets out on the trail. Much beloved by computer nerds, this high-camp occultist sci-fi trilogy rolls endless conspiracy theories into its magpie picking at 1960s alternative culture, along with characters such as Padre Pederastia and heavy doses of eschatological humour. The first sentence of Part 1, *The Eye In The Pyramid*, says it all: "It was the year when they finally immanentized the Eschaton."

CONSPIRACY MOVIES

All The President's Men (Alan J. Pakula, 1976). Robert Redford and Dustin Hoffman sweat and snap at each other in this intelligent but wordy depiction of how real-life reporters Bob Woodward and Carl Bernstein battled against newspaper deadlines, editorial jitters and walls of silence to trace the Watergate burglary all the way back to the White House – at considerable personal risk.

The Assassination Of Richard Nixon (Niels Mueller, 2004). As honest salesman Samuel Bicke's life falls apart in the year of 1974, he sees President Richard "Crook" Nixon still occupying the White House. So Bicke (played by Sean Penn) sets out to kill Tricky Dicky in this factually based drama.

Blow Out (Brian de Palma, 1981). In one of his best roles, John Travolta plays a B-movie sound engineer who accidentally records a car-crash that kills a presidential candidate. After rescuing the sole survivor (Nancy Allen), he becomes convinced that the fatal blowout was caused by a bullet, and persuades her to help him unmask the conspiracy. Alludes knowingly both to other films (Antonioni's *Blowup*, Coppola's *The Conversation*) and to theories about JFK's assassination and Teddy Kennedy's "Chappaquiddick incident".

The Bourne Identity (Doug Liman, 2002).

Matt Damon washes up somewhere on the Mediterranean coast with his memory erased, but somehow equipped with incredible skills in evasion and survival. As he tries to piece together how he got there, he is pursued around glamorous European locations (notably Paris and Prague) by dodgy Americans with long coats and a building full of tracking devices. Based on a Robert Ludlum thriller, this film mixes questions about identity with a high-action plot. *The Bourne Supremacy* and *The Bourne Ultimatum* complete the trilogy.

Capricorn One (Peter Hyams, 1977). Elliot Gould plays a reporter who stumbles across the hoax of the century, with NASA faking an entire six-month manned mission to Mars. But when the spacecraft burns up, the astronauts (still on Earth, busy on the film-set) have to be disposed of...

Close Encounters Of The Third Kind (Steven Spielberg, 1977). Suggests not only that friendly aliens have been coming to Earth for years, but that they've been up to all sorts of tricks that the government's been aware of all along. Visually impressive, if a fraction over-long.

Conspiracy Theory (Richard Donner, 1997). Mel Gibson plays nervy, paranoid, rambling New York cab driver Jerry Fletcher, obsessed with both a government mind-control conspiracy and lawyer Alice Sutton (Julia Roberts). Fletcher starts to think he is going mad himself until the government, in the shape of Patrick Stewart, steps in to shut his mouth. Thrilling, and plays provocatively with the idea that a conspiracy theory can have a final validation.

The Conversation (Francis Ford Coppola, 1974). Gene Hackman plays an obsessive covert surveillance expert whose brilliant technical skills help him to piece together a murderous plot involving a mysterious VIP client. Conceived pre-Watergate and made in the wake of *The Godfather*, this is a superb downbeat study in paranoia.

Dr Strangelove (Stanley Kubrick, 1963). This seminal Cold War satire features George C. Scott's lunatic US general taking the world to nuclear war because of his own paranoid fantasies – including a commie plot to fluoridate America's water. Peter Sellers plays nearly everyone else, including a scientist supposedly modelled on Dr Sidney Gottlieb, the LSD-toking chief of the CIA's MK-Ultra project (see p.192).

Executive Action (David Miller, 1973). A cabal of rich old white men plot JFK's assassination in this fictional take on the killing that's colder and far more convincing than Stone's JFK.

Fahrenheit 9/11 (Michael Moore, 2004). This controversial documentary-style one-man political roadshow portrays a pernicious post-9/11 Bush administration cynically spreading a message of fear in order to prepare the electorate for a war on Iraq and blind it to abrogations of civil liberties. Michael Moore spins a suggestive web connecting the Bush family to the House of Saud and Osama bin Laden. The film inspired a right-wing backlash against Moore's "conspiracy theories". Gripping, but you know you're being manipulated by Moore too.

Independence Day (Roland Emmerich, 1996). In this America Saves The World extravaganza, aliens come and zap every capital city on the planet.

Fortunately, the US military has kept all those alien spaceships at the fabled Roswell airbase (see p.311) nicely oiled and tuned-up for just such an occasion.

The Innocent Sleep (Scott Michell, 1996). Based on the Roberto Calvi Italian Mafia / Vatican corruption / P2 affair (see p.50), this thriller centres on down-and-out Alan Terry, who witnesses the murder of a businessman, left hanging from a London bridge. He is drawn into investigating the affair and the corrupt policeman involved. The more he discovers about a major conspiracy, the greater the danger he stumbles into.

The Interpreter (Sydney Pollack, 2005). United Nations interpreter Nicole Kidman overhears a plot to assassinate an African dictator. G-man Sean Penn swallows the urge to say "don't worry, love, happens all the time" and mixes in to stop Kidman and the dictator being killed in a thriller that has more pace than imagination. Added interest comes from being shot almost entirely on location at the UN's HQ in New York.

Invasion Of The Body Snatchers (Don Siegel, 1955; Philip Kaufmann, 1978). People in a small town keep complaining that their spouses aren't their normal selves, the reason being that they've been replaced with alien clones grown from pods. Classic paranoid thriller about the outsiders within, which the remake adds to with icky special effects.

It Came From Outer Space (Jack Arnold, 1953). Easily the most durable of the spate of 1950s sci-fi films about UFOs coming to America. An eccentric amateur astronomer discovers that a meteor crash is in fact a downed spaceship. Nobody believes him, of course, until the local townsfolk start to behave seriously strangely. Heavy anti-Communist undertones, and a good twist in the plot.

JFK (Oliver Stone, 1991). A conspiracy classic, featuring Kevin Costner in one of his best roles, as voice-in-the-wilderness Jim Garrison, a District

Attorney struggling against all the odds to bring a lawsuit against the conspirators behind the JFK assassination. The unashamedly one-sided account is partly explained by the fact that it drew heavily on the conspiracy theories of Garrison himself and Jim Marrs, and partly by Stone's self-proclaimed desire to create not a documentary but a "fable", an emotional counter-punch to the rationalist approach of the Warren Commission. The "magic bullet" courthouse scene is unmissable.

The Manchurian Candidate (John Frankenheimer, 1962; Jonathan Demme, 2004). Korean war veteran and ex-POW Frank Sinatra has nightmares about fellow soldiers carrying out missions for the commies. A cunning plot to use brainwashed POWs as sleeper assassins is uncovered. But is it really the Reds who are behind it? In the 2004 remake, Denzel Washington and Meryl Streep can't quite match the Sinatra/Lansbury team of the original, but the updating of the North Korean setting and Cold War context to Iraq and the military-industrial complex is clever and successful.

Marathon Man (John Schlesinger, 1976). An ex-Nazi in Latin America (played by Laurence Olivier) breaking cover in New York and a secret government agency called the Division conspire to make Dustin Hoffman very confused. A thriller of cross and double-cross that will give you nightmares about your next visit to the dentist – especially if he looks anything like Laurence Olivier's sadistic Szell. Other, lesser films on similar topics include *The Odessa File* (Ronald Neame, 1974) and *The Boys From Brazil* (Franklin Schaffner, 1978), also with Olivier.

The Matrix (Andy and Larry Wachowski, 1999). Keanu Reeves is a slacker computer programmer by day but a whizz hacker by night, until a series of fortuitous discoveries lead him to realize that the human race is living in a virtual-reality dreamworld, unwittingly serving as a giant energy cell to power "the Machines". The sequels add big battle scenes between freed humans and the Machines, but little else to the concept.

Men In Black (Barry Sonnenfeld, 1997). Very silly and sometimes very funny comedy playing up to the mythology of the "Men In Black" alien/FBI conspiracy theory. Will Smith stars as a New York cop recruited to a secretive government agency aimed at suppressing "illegal aliens" – extra-terrestrial-style aliens, that is.

Missing (Costa-Gavras, 1981). Based on the true story of Thomas Hauser, the film follows the search by one American father for his son in the aftermath of General Pinochet's 1973 coup in Chile. In Costa-Gavras's first US production, the audience accompanies Jack Lemmon (excellent) on his journey to the painful realization that his son is as lost as thousands of innocent Chileans in a coup backed by his own government. Condemned by the US State Department, if you need any further recommendation.

Mulholland Drive (David Lynch, 2001). David Lynch's films are famously disorienting and *Mulholland Drive* is the most confusing of them all. As such, it's impossible to summarize, but it's based on the dreams of a suicidal young woman. While this isn't a conspiracy-theory film as such, it's a brilliant riff on how narratives can be twisted by different viewpoints and interpretations, by memories, fantasies and forgetfulness, and it vibrates with a paranoid and deeply conspiratorial style.

National Treasure (Jon Turteltaub, 2004). *Indiana Jones* meets Masonic conspiracy theories. Nicholas Cage stars as a treasure-hunter trying to steal the Declaration of Independence, which conceals a treasure map that will guide him to the Masonic secrets of America's founding fathers. The heavy-footed comedy stops the "action adventure" side of things ever taking off.

The Net (Irwin Winkler, 1995). Hollywood's most successful "cyberthriller". Sandra Bullock plays a somewhat unlikely computer expert whose identity is stolen. As she attempts to get it back, she is dragged out of her safe life into a world of conspiracy. Hackneyed and dated, but satisfyingly tense.

Network (Sidney Lumet, 1976). TV anchorman Peter Finch has a nervous breakdown and suddenly tells his audiences it's all "bullshit". This, of course, only wins viewers and gets Finch his own show, featuring one paranoid man fighting the agenda behind the "real" news. He is unwittingly compromised, however, by a network bent on winning ratings at any cost – including fabricating its own stories. Oscar-winning performance by Finch, backed by Robert Duvall

Nixon (Oliver Stone, 1995). A discomfiting biopic of Richard Nixon – the chronology is jarringly disrupted – sprinkled with Stone's trademark images and fleeting allusions to far bigger, blacker conspiracies. Surprisingly, Nixon (played by Anthony Hopkins) comes across not so much as an arch-villain as an outsider vainly battling to tame the real beasts that run America.

Outbreak (Wolfgang Petersen, 1995). A mutated strain of the Ebola virus is brought to the US by an infected monkey. The truth behind a military WMD experiment and cover-up is revealed. Bog-standard scaremonger thriller just about rescued by good performances from Dustin Hoffman and Rene Russo.

The Parallax View (Alan J. Pakula, 1974). A strange, intensely claustrophobic thriller made around the time of Nixon's resignation, with reporter Warren Beatty delving into a vast, mysterious, extra-governmental conspiracy following the assassination of a Kennedy-style presidential candidate.

The President's Analyst (Theodore J. Flicker, 1967). A zany 1960s spy spoof, with James Coburn as a New York shrink hired to analyse the US president back to sanity, only Coburn nearly goes mad when pursued by the world's finks and spooks seeking to unpick the president's noodle.

Rollover (Alan J. Pakula, 1981). The eerily topical premise here is that the power of the dollar depends on Saudi Arabians selling oil in it and funnelling the profits through the world's banks. But what if they suddenly conspired to withdraw their investments? Murdered banker's widow Jane Fonda and Wall Street troubleshooter Kris Kristofferson join forces to battle the Saudis and the government to avert a global economic depression. Too cerebral for a conventional action thriller, but well worth seeing.

Ruby (John Mackenzie, 1992). Sub-JFK flick focusing on Jack Ruby, Dallas strip-club owner and murderer of Lee Harvey Oswald. Conveys a good flavour of the era's seedy mobster glamour, and includes a great reconstruction of the Dealey Plaza assassination, but unconvincing as a conspiracy theory – Ruby is apparently exposing "the truth" of Mafia-CIA collusion.

Rules Of Engagement (William Friedkin, 2000). Pro-Army propaganda that relocates the mass killings of Somalis by US Marines in Mogadishu in 1993 to Yemen. Commander Samuel L. Jackson is framed by a bent State Department and a long trial ensues. The weird part is the closing credits, which claim that the film is based on fact.

Rush To Judgement (Emile de Antonio, 1967). A documentary from Mark Lane's book of the same name on JFK's assassination, and narrated by Lane as he cuts down the Warren Commission's conclusion. Of interest if only for being one of the earliest conspiracy theories on JFK and to observe what conspiracy documentaries looked like in those days.

Seven Days In May (John Frankenheimer, 1964). The sequel to *The Manchurian Candidate* (see p.395) and every bit its equal. US president "Lyman Jordan" initiates a nuclear disarmament programme alongside the Soviets. Quiet but ruthless General Scott (Burt Lancaster) seems about to launch a military coup to prevent it, but his plans are uncovered by

Jiggs Casey (Kirk Douglas), a Pentagon aide who just happens to be a friend and close associate of Scott's. Tensely plays out ethical dilemmas and conspiracy plots in atmospheric White House/Pentagon settings.

Slacker (Richard Linklater, 1991). A genuinely original independent movie, shot for $23,000 on 16mm film. It's basically a series of semi-comic rants by a long series of quirky counter-culture types, or "slackers", on subjects ranging from UFOs to JFK conspiracy theories and Elvis. What could be incredibly dull is made immediate and absorbing by an improvisational feel and a thoughtful take on conspiracist culture.

Sneakers (Phil Alden Robinson, 1992). Robert Redford's shadowy team of tech-geeks tries to snare evil tycoon Ben Kingsley in his quest to control the world's stock markets with a brilliant gizmo in a box. A pudgy Dan Ackroyd makes a lot of noise as a conspiracy-theory nut in this vaguely amusing caper.

The Stepford Wives (Bryan Forbes, 1975; Frank Oz, 2004). A paranoid feminist's nightmare. All the men in Stepford have conspired to turn their wives into perfectly submissive fantasy women, but Katharine Ross (or Nicole Kidman in the less successful remake) just won't play ball. Funny and disturbing in equal measure.

Thirteen Days (Roger Donaldson, 2000). As the world teeters on the brink of nuclear war during the Cuban Missile Crisis, the Kennedy brothers find that the war-crazies aren't necessarily all confined to Moscow – more than a few work in the Pentagon. A fascinating, taut depiction of real events. For whatever reason, the Pentagon refused to cooperate with filming.

Wag The Dog (Barry Levinson, 1997). Satire on US politics, featuring a spin doctor (Robert De Niro), a Hollywood producer (Dustin Hoffman) and a White House aide (Anne Heche), who join forces to bury the news of the President's molestation of a young girl – a fortnight before the election. Their solution is a nice, distracting – and fake – war in Albania. Predates and anticipates the Clinton-Lewinski saga and the Kosovo War.

Z (Costa-Gavras, 1969). In an unnamed country under right-wing rule – the story is based on real-life events in Costa-Gavras's native Greece – an outspoken opposition leader (Yves Montand) is fatally injured in a traffic accident. Or was he assassinated? Jean-Louis Trintignant is the examining magistrate seeking the truth and uncovering the true mendacity of power. Coming so soon after the killings of the Kennedy brothers and Martin Luther King, this Oscar-winning political thriller resonated with American audiences, becoming one of the highest grossing foreign-language films ever in the US.

WEBSITES

Conspiracy theory sites and magazines

http://rightweb.irc-online.org/index.php
"Exposing the architecture of power that's changing our world." A project of the International Relations Center, this politically oriented US site traces the tangled connections between individual neocons, corporations, government and organizations. Click on "People Web", "Org Web", "Corp Web" and "Gov Web" on the left of the page. You can also sign up for a *Right Web News* e-zine.

http://skepdic.com This "skeptics' dictionary" is an alphabetically arranged list of links for paranormal, mystical and conspiratorial stories.

www.alexconstantine.50megs.comhome.html
Alex Constantine's Political Conspiracy Research Bin is a largely one-man band. Plugs its author's books, but also includes voluminous archives dedicated to unmasking "fascism" in American politics – a term used to mean anything from CIA mind control to the Bush family's big-business connections.

www.bilderberg.org One-man campaign, run from Bristol, UK by a Quaker. Describes itself as a "lobbying organization" against the "power elite". Begins with the Bilderberg group but soon spirals out into attacks on globalization in general and all kinds of conspiracy areas: "It is the facts behind very real groups like the Bilderbergers, the Skull and Bones and the Council on Foreign Relations that must be known before we can best understand how to deal with them on a personal and a global level."

www.conspiracyarchive.com The Illuminati Conspiracy Archive believes in "the occult nature of the ruling elite". Lots of professionally presented articles on Freemasonry, the New World Order and the paranormal. According to the authors, the word "conspiracy, in many cases, should be replaced with policy. Likewise, theory is easily interchanged with documented" – which kind of makes it a "documented policy" site.

www.conspiracyplanet.com The "antidote to Media Cartel Propaganda", this site borrows a lot from other conspiracy websites and mixes intelligent takes on events with the more flagrant fruitcake views.

www.covertactionquarterly.org Formerly the Covert Action Information Bulletin, this is a 70-page mixed bag of broadly lefty, generally well-sourced news pieces and conspiracist articles. Its mission is more to seek out what powers like the CIA or neo-Nazi groups are up to than to indulge in wild-eyed speculation on aliens and Masons. You can subscribe and order back issues online, but most of the recent articles are available for free.

www.davidicke.com Click on the "headlines" link and scroll down past all the book promos to get to the Icke team's wacky take on the news of the day. Lots of good photos and wildly scurrilous allegations. Icke's more seriously conspiratorial work is found in the archive at www.davidicke.net.

www.deepblacklies.co.uk "Bringing in-depth reporting of crime and corruption in high places." The author, David Guyatt, is a former investment banker with a mission to expose the truth about the financing of the international arms trade. From this tight, serious base, the site spirals into discussion of WMD, Nazi gold, Vatican corruption and much more. Lots of World War II conspiracy history.

www.larouchepub.com The official site of Lyndon LaRouche's deeply conspiratorial *Executive*

Intelligence Review. LaRouche is a man on the fringe of the US political scene – his supporters think he's a visionary, but some conspiracists think he's a conspiracy theory in his own right who exists only to spread disinformation and discredit other conspiracy theorists.

www.lobster-magazine.co.uk "The Journal of Parapolitics", "as denounced in the House of Commons". Edited by the tough, sceptical and left-wing Robin Ramsay, who has even less time for bullshit than he has for political chicanery. A proper magazine: you need to subscribe to get access to the articles.

www.maebrussell.com Lots of articles on contemporary conspiracy theories, but the best thing about this site is the downloadable MP3s of Californian conspiracy commentator Mae Brussell's original radio shows. Mesmerizing.

www.namebase.org Amazing searchable index of historical and political books – mostly conspiracy-related – and the people who appear in them. Great tool for researchers – you can even find out which pages of which books your suspect appears on.

www.paranoiamagazine.com *Paranoia Magazine* has been publishing articles on conspiracy theories, the occult and the paranormal since 1992. Leavens the usual fare with pinches of humour and salt. You can browse online, but you'll have to subscribe to receive the full magazine – published three times yearly. Back issues are now published as a book.

www.parascope.com Decent if not exceptional general website featuring lots of articles on conspiracies, aliens and the paranormal. Conspiracy theories you may not have come across before include "Air Force invades NASCAR race", whatever that's about.

www.prisonplanet.com A professionally presented rolling news site with theories and commentaries added. One of many sites linked with the prolific, slick American radio host Alex Jones, a libertarian, anti-New World Order commentator. Jones's official, commercial website is at www.infowars.com.

www.rense.com Radio host Jeff Rense keeps this website continually updated with contentious takes on the news of the day.

www.rotten.com Includes a lot of pretty disturbing images of death and mutilation (as well as lots of hardcore porn), but also includes worryingly fascinating news updates on the most scurrilous events of the day, and the day before. Includes digests of lots of conspiracy theories.

www.rumormillnews.com Alternative news website, with pieces written by "agents", usually with a Christian-conservative, conspiracist leaning. As it notes at the foot of the front page, this site does not contain any classified information – because "Rumor Mill News is a strong supporter of the American Military". There's also a forum area for discussion of news, theories etc.

www.sherryshriner.com Talk show host Sherry Shriner seems to have a thing about aliens and how to make best use of the Bible to smite them. Extends into New World Order, Illuminati, Jews – all evidence of the work of Satan. But fear not: a donation to Sherry – just click – will help her fight the good fight. More of much the same at www.the-watcherfiles.com.

www.steamshovelpress.com A real magazine with its own website (which doesn't present much by way of links or news itself), *Steamshovel Press* mixes full-on conspiracy theories with some fascinating articles into the more plausible – but no less dark – methods of how those in power seek to hold on and profit from it. Attracts some good writers – and a fair few crazies to boot. By subscription.

www.theforbiddenknowledge.com Crammed with intricately detailed pieces articulating anything from the perils of Freemasonry to the computer chips that will take over your life.

www.thisiswhoweare.com A randomly presented but comprehensive selection of links to the classic conspiracy theories.

www.totse.com The bulletin board of the Temple of the Screaming Electron has a distinctly anarchic bent, offering up anti-government theories, hackers' tips and unverifiable information on how to make drugs and things that go bang.

www.weirdload.com The coverage of this one-man site ranges from aliens to the New World Order, with a genuinely offbeat take on the world. The presiding theme is anti-Catholicism; as the author puts it: "I was an 'unlucky' altar boy, having been repeatedly sexually and ritualistically abused by my parish priest. As an adult I long ago fled the Church of Rome and became an ordained priest in the Church of Antioch – Malabar Rite."

Conspiracy forums, blogs and newsgroups

http://groups.msn.com/ConspiracyTheory Hugely popular conspiracy theory newsgroup, with scores of posts every day. If you can't find someone to argue your pet theory with here, you'll just have to talk it through with the voices in your head.

www.abovetopsecret.com A handsomely made website mixing acerbic cut-downs of manipulated news with cover-ups and a few out-and-out fantasies. The site's best aspect, though, is its forum section, including a dedicated conspiracy-related area that attracts lots of relatively informed commentators following the numerous threads.

www.ctrl.org You can sign up to receive the email traffic of the Conspiracy Theory Research List here, but beware – there can be up to around 100 posts a day. The archive section gives you a bit more control, and includes postings of conspiracy-related news items from newspapers, agencies and broad-

casters around the world.

www.dailygrail.com Wide-ranging blog site whose postings range from "astrobiology" and Yonaguni Underwater Monuments through to Votergate, Masonic influences in the US and conspiratorial chat about the day's news.

www.disinfo.com Lots of stories, some very well argued, and lots of links to Disinformation's excellent publications (*Everything You Know is Wrong, The Book Of Lies* etc.), but most interesting as a discussion site for theorists on the dubious side of current affairs.

General resources

www2.gwu.edu/~nsarchiv/index.html Website of the National Security Archive, an NGO and research library based at the George Washington University in Washington, DC Top source for declassified documents acquired through the Freedom of Information Act, and a great resource for conspiracy theorists who want to do their own research.

www.aarclibrary.org The Assassination Archives and Research Center is a privately-run news archive and online library. Thousands of online documents on political assassinations, notably JFK, Bobby Kennedy and Martin Luther King, many released from government records under the Freedom of Information Act. Includes facsimiles of the entire Warren Commission Hearings.

www.adl.org The Anti-Defamation League's homepage has an archive of patiently written rebuttals and shootdowns of the more anti-Semitic theories that continue to make the rounds, as well as taking a few shots at what might be considered fair comment.

www.campus-watch.org Deeply controversial site that "monitors" Middle East-related issues and articles in American universities, and names and shames those it sees as stepping out of line. Opponents would say it conflates anti-Israeli politics with anti-Semitism and attacks free speech. The project itself says it is aimed at "analytical failures, the mixing of politics with scholarship, intolerance of alternative views, apologetics, and the abuse of power over students".

www.fas.org/irp/hotdocs.htm The nonprofit Federation of American Scientists – originally a group of atomic scientists concerned about the accelerating arms race – makes available all the most topical US government documents in the public sphere, from Justice Department memos and press releases to full downloads of the 9/11 Commission and WMD Commission reports. This hotdocs page includes the most requested documents. Hugely popular site.

www.religioustolerance.org As the name suggests, this site is dedicated to giving all religions due respect. Features well-written articles on all things religious, including a number aimed at countering conspiracists' misconceptions about Wicca (a form of neopaganism that rehabilitates witchcraft), Masons, Satanism and so on.

www.snopes.com Witty, accurate and utterly browsable analysis of urban myths, covering anything from "racial rumours" (ie slurs) to "old wives' tales", taking in lots of conspiracy theories on the way. Explodes most myths, but the fun is in seeing exactly how they grew and finding out the real story. Gives ratings for true, false and "undetermined". Fully searchable, but the hierarchical format is well thought out.

General news media

www.aljazeera.com The Arab news network Al Jazeera needs no introduction. This English-language website includes a superb section dedicated to conspiracy theories with a Middle Eastern angle – lots on Iraq and Palestine, of course. Most items are simply speculative or conspiracist-flavoured articles culled daily from the world's news media.

www.commondreams.org Breaking news and views for the "progressive community", this hosts a wealth of taut, leftish essays and alternative (as opposed to flat conspiratorial) takes on political issues worldwide, with some big-name thinkers contributing.

www.consortiumnews.com Serious-minded news/comment website originally set up as "a home for important, well-reported stories that weren't welcome in the O.J. Simpson-obsessed, conventional-wisdom-driven national news media of that time". Run by Robert Parry, an experienced investigative journalist and author with a broadly liberal agenda and a taste for conspiracy.

www.globalismnews.com Journalistic anti-globalization news and comment site. Click on "who dares call it conspiracy" for lots of good links to classic conspiracy theory articles elsewhere on the Web.

www.indymedia.org A site dedicated to real news stories chosen with a more radical, anti-authority perspective.

www.newsmakingnews.com A rolling news service of mainly US and UK media stories with an anti-authoritarian bent, updated daily. The chronological listing gives a somewhat random feel to the site, but it's a good way to gauge which way the wind's blowing.

www.whatreallyhappened.com Less conspiracy, more political controversy. An anti-war site with stacks of links to news sites every day.

Acknowledgements

James and Robin would like to thank Jonathan Buckley, Kris Dent, Mark Ellingham, Kevin Fitzgerald, Donald Kaye, Sally Jones, Terry Jones, Tobias Jones, Angus Kennedy, Charlie Marshall, Kate Rew, Richard Scholar, Iain Stewart, Andrew Vereker and everyone at Milk Studios for support, advice and those crucial tip-offs. Our especial thanks to Andrew Lockett, for indefatigably overseeing the whole project; Neil Foxlee and Greg Ward, our editors; Henry Iles, for his sleek text design; Suzanne Bosman, for finding such great images; Michelle Bhatia and Dan May, for all their typesetting work; and everyone at Rough Guides for giving the project such enthusiastic backing. Finally, a bid personal thank you to Jorinde Chang, Alice Hunt, Rosemary Tudge, Colin Tudge and Ruth West for their encouragement, support, insights – and all those discussions. Any errors are, of course, our own.

Picture credits

AFP/Getty Images 44, 51, 214
Architecture Studio/Vincent Kessler/Reuters/Corbis 136
Archivo Iconografico, S.A./Corbis 159
Bettmann/Corbis 18, 22, 38, 49, 56, 177, 182, 193, 267, 327, 339, 344, 348
Stephen J. Boitano/Reuters/Corbis 238
W. Cody/Corbis 119
Corbis 24, 32, 46, 118, 297, 331
Corbis Sygma 230
Gianni Dagli Orti/Corbis 74
Tony Gentile/Reuters/Corbis 127
Getty Images 57, 101, 278, 312, 376
Tim Graham/Corbis 62, 105
John Gress/Reuters/Corbis 385
Handout/Reuters/Corbis 389
Rob Howard/Corbis 361

Hulton-Deutsch Collection/Corbis 35
Keerle Georges de/Corbis Sygma 355
Pascal Lauener/Reuters/Corbis 236
Wally McNamee/Corbis 186
Maiman Rick/Corbis Sygma 247
Markowitz Jeffrey/Corbis Sygma 155
Matthew Mendelsohn/Corbis 205
Ali Meyer/Corbis 13, 152
Moviestore (Amblin Entertainment/Columbia Pictures Corporation MacDonald/Parkes Productions) 114
NASA/Corbis 317
Reuters/Corbis 65, 113, 208, 307, 364
Patrick Robert/Sygma/Corbis 277
San Diego Museum of Art, USA, Gift of Samuel Henry Kress/Bridgeman Art Library 160
Jon Sparks/Corbis 240
Liba Taylor/Corbis 281
Time Life Pictures/Getty Images 128

Index

10-agora coin 120

9/11 ..... 110, 119, 145, 252, 283, 309, 329, 360–369, 360–370, 374–375

9-11 Commission 366–367

A

Abiff, Hiram 78, 79

A-bomb 271, 272–274

Acquired Immuno-Deficiency Syndrome see AIDS

Afghanistan 342, 359

AIDS (HIV/AIDS) 144, 170, 257, 265, 277–282

Akhenaten 4, 5

Al Qaeda 110, 252, 368, 359, 361, 369, 375

Albigensians 166

Aldrin, Buzz 316, 319

Al-Fayed, Dodi 59, 61

Al-Fayed, Mohamed 60, 61, 188

Allegro, John 155

Allen, Gary 228

Allende, Salvador 43–45

American Medical Association (AMA) 255, 258, 259

anal probe 313

Andanson, James 61

Andreae, Johann Valentin 87

Andreotti, Giulio 124, 125, 126

Angelou, Maya 206

Antarctica 284

Anti-Defamation League (ADL) 91, 351–352

Apollo 11 see Moon landing

Arafat, Yasser 120, 190

Area 51 .... 286, 312

Armenian genocide 98

Ashcroft, John 214

Assassinations Record Review Board 20

ATF (Bureau of Alcohol, Tobacco and Firearms)
.... 207, 212, 214

Aviary, the 314

Aviv, Juval 303–304

B

Banco Ambrosiano 50

Bank of Credit and Commerce International (see BCCI)

Bank of England 226, 227, 232–233, 239

Banking conspiracy, International 226–239, 346

Bar codes 250

Barruel, (Abbé) Augustin de 79, 86

Basayev, Shamil 353, 354, 356

Bay of Pigs 20, 179

BCCI 199, 226, 230–233

Beatles, the 57, 58, 107

Beethoven, Ludwig van 12

Behold A Pale Horse 88

Beirut `eth 220

Blair, Cherie 171

Blair, Tony 59, 67, 235, 371, 377
Blix, Hans 379
Blofeld, Ernst Stavro 131
Blood Libel ....`89–93
Blowback 340
Blue Book, Project 311
body count, the Clinton 204
Boland Amendment 110, 186
Bormann, Martin 29, 183
Brenneke, Richard 188, 189, 198
British Royal Family 105–108
Brown and Williamson 260
Brown, Dan 71, 75, 88, 164, 171
Brown, Gordon 239
Brussell, Mae 29, 55, 57, 131, 132
Brzezinski, Zbigniew 139, 140, 188
Buchanan, Pat 217
Bureau of Alcohol, Tobacco and Firearms (see ATF)
Bush, George H.W. 111, 113, 125, 140, 185, 187, 189,
     191, 195, 196, 222, 234, 236, 252, 303, 304, 372
Bush, George W. ..111, 116, 170, 191, 206, 216–221,
     222, 232, 280, 360, 366–368, 371, 374, 375
Bush, Jeb 217, 218, 381
Bush, Neil 170
Bush, Prescott 218, 222
butterfly ballot 217
Bryan, EA 272–273

C

Cagliostro, Count 86
Calo, Pippo 50
Calvi, Roberto 50, 51, 124
Campbell, Alistair.. 65
cancer 225, 257–261
cannabis 225
Cannon, Martin 134
Cantwell, Dr Alan 257, 258, 278
Carlo, Francesco Di 50

Carlyle Group 113, 140
Carnarvon, Lord 6, 7
Carter, Howard 4, 6, 7
Carter, Jimmy ...46, 53, 140, 185, 187, 189, 190, 232,
     236, 341
Caruana, Stephanie 131
Casey, William J. (Bill) 57, 110, 139, 185–190, 199, 200
Cashill, Jack 309
Casolaro, Danny 128
Caspian gas 359
Castillo, Celerino (Cele) 198
Castro, Fidel 19, 20–23, 25, 27, 179, 194
Cathars 166
Central Intelligence Agency (see CIA)
CFR (see Council on Foreign Relations)
chads, hanging 217
Chalabi, Ahmed 377–378
Chapman, David 55
Charles, Prince 62, 82
Chase Manhattan Bank 140
Chatham House 106, 138
Chechnya 353–358
Cheney, Dick 16, 113, 137, 140, 195, 341, 364,
     381–383
Chip-oil engine 242
Church Committee 21, 27, 57, 109, 194
CIA 3, 15, 18, 20, 25, 26, 28, 33, 36, 39, 43, 44, 50,
     53, 55, 109–111, 114, 123, 176, 182, 183, 186, 188,
     189, 192, 196–202, 203, 214, 232, 233, 235, 240,
     254, 283, 289, 302–305, 307–309, 329, 336–337,
     340, 349, 390
Cigarette industry cover-up 260
Cipriani, Juan Luis 171
Clark, General Wesley 211
Clark, Ramsey 209
Clement V, Pope 73, 75
Clems's engine 241–242
Clinton, Bill ...137, 140, 180, 195, 198, 201, 202–207,
     215, 231, 235, 236, 246, 359
Clinton, Hillary Rodham 195, 202, 205, 206
Club of the Isles, the 106
Colby, William 15

Cold War 235, 338–343
Coleman, John 88
Communists 253, 254, 333
Confessions of an Economic Hitman 234–235
Connally, John 23, 24, 26, 30
Contras 53, 186, 196
Cosmonauts see Vostok
Costello, Frank 19
Council on Foreign Relations .137, 233, 283, 286, 375
Courtney, Phoebe 253–254, 256
crack cocaine 197
Creasy, William 194
Cristol, Judge Jay 349–352
Cuba 327–329
Cubela, Roland 22

Drudge Report 204
Drug Enforcement Agency (DEA) 196–198
Dulles, Allen 25, 27, 30, 192
DuPont 254

D

D'Aubuisson, Roberto 53, 198
Da Vinci Code, The 71, 75, 133, 164, 171
da Vinci, Leonardo 168
Dagestan 353, 355
Davos (see World Economic Forum)
Day of Deceit 332
DEA (see Drug Enforcement Agency)
Dead Sea Scrolls 154–157
Dean, John 178
DeBeers 106
Deep Throat 179, 180
de Gaulle, Charles 29
Department of Defense, US 251, 278, 288
Diamond, Bernard 39, 55
Diana, Princess 59–63, 108, 145
Diebold, Inc 219
Diem, Ngo Dinh 22
DiMaggio, Joe 17, 18, 19
disinformation, Soviet 280
Dodgy Dossier 64
Dr Strangelove 253

E

ebola virus 279–280
ECHELON 251–252
Eco, Umberto 88
E.I. Dupont de Nemours see DuPont
Eisenhower, Dwight D. 112, 329, 391
Eldridge, USS 269–270
Elizabeth I 9
Ellis, John Prescott 218
Elsbett engine 225, 242
Ennes, James 349–352
Environmental Protection Agency (EPA) 256
Escrivá, Josemaría 171
eternal lightbulb 225, 243–244
European Union (EU) 72, 135–136, 237
Evans, Richard 97
Exxon 140

F

FAA see Federal Aviation Authority
Falwell, Jerry 204
Farrakhan, Louis 33, 280
Fauld, RAF 274
Faurisson, Robert 95
FBI 19, 26, 28, 33, 34, 36, 57, 180, 184, 207–210,
 ....212–215, 306–308
FDR see Roosevelt, Franklin Delano
Federal Aviation Authority (FAA) 307–309

Federal Bureau of Investigation (see FBI)
Federal Emergency Management Agency (FEMA)
.... 284–285, 365
Federal Reserve 226, 229, 230
Felt, Mark 180
FEMA, see Federal Emergency Management Agency
Fishbein, Morris 258–259
Flight 175 .... 360, 361, 363
Flight 77 361
Flight 93 364
Fluoride 226, 253–256
flying saucers see UFOs
The Fog of War 345
Ford, Gerald 15, 16, 22, 25, 30, 76, 110, 179, 180, 194
Ford, Henry 102
Fort Detrick 16, 257, 275, 278, 280, 285, 373
Foster, Vincent 203
Fox News 104, 218
Frank, Anne 96
Franklin Bank 50
Franklin, Benjamin 80, 118
Freeh, Louis 171, 210
Freemasonry 13, 14, 30, 50, 51, 52, 76–85, 101, 103,
    117–119, 125, 158, 222, 283, 320, 369
FSB (Federal Security Service of the Russian Federation)
....353–357
Fujimori, Alberto 200

G

Gaitskell, Hugh 42
gangs, Central American 200
Garabed Giragossia 241
Garaudy, Roger 95
Garcetti, investigation 247
Gardiner, Robin 298–300
Garfield, James 227
Garrison, Jim.. 26, 30
Gates, Bill 237, 245–248

Gates, Robert 187
Gehlen, General Reinhard 336–337
Gelli, Licio 124–126
Gemstone File 131
Giancana, Sam 19, 21, 27, 29, 40
Gibson, Mel 52
Gilligan, Andrew 64
Gimbutas, Marija 152
Gnostic gospels 162, 164–168
Godfather, The 21
Golitsin, Anatoli 42
Google 251
Gore, Al 216, 236, 309, 329
Goss, Porter 201
Gottlieb, Sidney 16, 21, 109, 192, 194
Graves, Dr Boyd.. 279
Gravity's Rainbow 244
Great Goddess 150–153
Great Seal 117
Greenson, Ralph 18
Gregg, Donald 187, 188
Gritz, Bo 197
Guantanamo Bay 329
Guevara, Che 33
Gulf of Tonkin Incident 325, 343–347
Gulf War, the First 234, 303, 372

H

HAARP (High Frequency Active Auroral Research
    Program) 266, 287–291
Hagel, Chuck 219
Haig, Alexander 179
Halabja 373
Hamas 103
Harris, Bev 219
Harris, Katherine 216–218
Hashemi brothers.............................. 85, 188
Hawass, Zahi 6

Hayes, Rutherford B. 217
HCSA (see House Select Committee on Assassinations)
Hearst, William Randolph 300, 328–329
Helms, Jesse 92
Helms, Richard 22, 45, 179, 200, 233, 351
heroin 197
Higgins, Michael 259–260
Hitler, Adolf ..94, 96, 97, 102, 228, 229, 325, 333, 334
HIV see AIDS
Hodge, Dr Harold C 254, 255
Hoffa, Jimmy 19, 27, 40, 141
Holocaust denial 94–100
Holy Blood, Holy Grail 164, 166–169
Holy Grail, the 75, 166, 167
Holy Roman Empire 135
Hoover, J. Edgar 19, 28, 29, 36, 40, 56, 133
Horowitz, Dr Leonard 279
House Select Committee on Assassinations 27, 29, 36
Hoxsey, Harry 258–259
Hughes, Howard 131, 133, 179
Humna Immunodeficiency Virus see HIV, AIDS
Hund, Baron von 79, 85
Hunt, E. Howard 28, 177–180
Hussein, Saddam 109, 188, 200, 309, 388–390
Hutton, (Lord) Brian 65, 67
Hutton, Will 236–237

Icke, David 88, 107, 108
Illuminati 77, 85–89, 170, 195, 222, 279
IMF see International Monetary Fund
Imperial Japan 331–334
Indianapolis, USS 273
Inslaw 129
International Monetary Fund (IMF) 233, 234–235
Iran 185, 186, 188, 189, 190
Iran, nuclear threat 382, 384
Iran–Contra 186, 190, 196, 200

Iranian oil 384
Iraq 67, 115, 145, 191, 215, 372, 371–387
Irving, David 97
Israel 348–352
Istituto per le Opere Religiose (see Vatican Bank)

J

Jack the Ripper 82, 105
Jackson, Bruce P. 113
Jackson, Jesse 220
Jackson, Andrew 227
Jacobin Club 80
Japan, 1941 attack on US 330–334
Japanese bio-chemical warfare see Unit 731
Japanese Mafia see Yakuza
Jefferson, Thomas 118
Jessup, Morris K 269–270
Jesuits 53, 85, 158–159
Jesus 7, 160–163, 165
Jews 79, 89–93, 94–100, 100–104, 156, 267
Jews and banks 229–230, 238–239, 366
JFK 30
JFK (see Kennedy, John F.)
John Birch Society 249, 256
John Paul I 48–52
John Paul II 50, 52, 171
Johnson, Lyndon B. ...24, 25, 27, 28, 30, 37, 76, 112,
.... 344–346, 349
Jones, Alex 67
Jones, Jim 181
Jones, Paula 204, 205
Jonestown 181–184
Jowers, Loyd 36
Justice, US Department of 244, 245, 246

K

Kassem, Abdul (see Qasim, Abd al-Karim)
Kaysing, Bill 317–318
Keating, Frank 214
Kelly, David 64–68
Kelly, Ruth 171
Kennedy, Edward (Teddy) 133
Kennedy, Jackie 23, 24, 30
Kennedy, Joe 19
Kennedy, John F. (JFK) . 18, 23–31, 47, 112, 133, 145, 179, 180, 195, 228, 329, 337, 340, 345
Kennedy, John F Jr 31
Kennedy, Robert 18, 19, 21, 29, 37–40, 194
Kerry, John 198, 199, 232–233, 236, 309
KGB 27, 41, 42, 52, 144, 145
Khashoggi, Adnan 188
Khomeini, Ayatollah 185
Khrushchev, Nikita 28
Kim Il-sung 64
Kim Jong-il 64
King Jr., Martin Luther 34–37
Kissinger, Henry 45, 139, 140, 195, 278, 346
Knights Hospitaller 73
Knights Templar 73–76, 77, 78, 166, 170
Kopechne, Mary Jo 133
Korea 16, 192
Korea, North 64, 112, 275, 339
Korean War, ...228, 235, 275, 339
Koresh, David 207–211
Koskinen, John 250
Ku Klux Klan (KKK) 29, 33, 83, 181

L

Lafayette, Marquis de 80
LaRouche, Lyndon 105, 187, 231
Lashbrook, Richard 15
Lawford, Peter 18
Lay, Ken 140
Lazar, Bob 312
Le Pen, Jean-Marie 99
Lefebvre, Marcel 52
Lennon, John 55–58, 194
Leo XIII 81
Lewinsky, Monica 180, 204, 206
LeWinter, Oswald "Razine" 188, 189
Liberty, USS 348–352
Libya 301, 302, 303
Libyan terrorists...................................301–302
Liddy, G. Gordon 177–179
Linares, Oscar Perez 53
Lincoln, Abraham 227
Linux 247–248
Little Hugh of Lincoln 90
Livingstone, Ken 42
Lockerbie 301–306
Lockheed Martin 113, 116
Long, Russell 26
Lowenstein, Allard 39
Loyola, Ignatius (of) 158
LSD 15, 16, 192–195
Luciano, Albino (see John Paul I)
Lumumba, Patrice 22, 109, 145, 194
Lusitania, The 228, 295, 299
Lyne, William 240–241

M

Maddox, USS 344
Mafia, Russian 142
Mafia, the 19, 27, 29, 40, 50, 72, 126, 133, 141
Magdalene, Mary 164–169
Magic Bullet 26, 30
Maheu, Robert 21
Maine, USS 325, 327–330
Majestic 12 311, 314–315

Malcolm X 32–34
The Manchurian Candidate 39, 144, 192, 214
Manhatten Project 254, 255
Manson, Charles 57
Marcello, Carlos 27, 29
Marcinkus, Paul 50, 51
Marenches, Alexandre de 190
Mark, Christopher 226–7
Marlowe, Christopher 8–11
Marrs, Jim 250
Masons (see Freemasonry)
Matriarchy 150
Maxwell, Robert 130, 145
McCarthy, Joe 338–339
McCartney, Paul 58
McCloy, John J. 25
McCord, James 176, 177
McEnroe, John 121
McKee, Charles 303–305
McMartin Pre-School 92
McNamara, Robert 112, 138, 340, 344
McVeigh, Timothy 211, 212–215, 289
Meese, Edwin (Ed) 129, 186
Mellon Institute 255
Mellon, Andrew 255
Men In Black 114
Mena, Arkansas 198, 205
Mengele, Josef 194
Merovingian dynasty 167
MI5 41–43
MI6 .... 42, 145, 188
Microsoft 245–248
microwaves 289
Middle East Research Institute 90, 91
Military-industrial complex 40, 112–116, 252, 341, 345
Millennium Bug (Y2K) 206, 225, 248–250
Miller, Arthur 92
mind control 254, 289
Missile gap 337, 340
MK-ULTRA 16, 21, 39, 55, 183, 192–195, 254, 289
Mohamad, Mahathir 103

Molay, Jacques de 75, 79
Monroe, Marilyn 17–20, 39
Montauk 194, 284, 310
Montesinos, Vladimiro 171, 200
moon landing 316–320
Moore, Michael 113, 220
Morgan, J.P. 229, 230, 240, 282, 291, 298
Morgan, William 81
Mormon Church 82
Moro, Aldo 124
Moscow apartment bombings 353–354
Moscow theatre siege 355
Mossad 15, 130, 145, 188, 203
Mother of All Conspiracies 333
Mothman 114
Mountbatten, Lord 41
Mozart, Wolfgang Amadeus 11–14
Muhammad,Elijah 33

N

Nag Hammadi 161, 164
NASA (National Aeronautics and Space Administration)
.... 240, 318–319
Nation of Islam 33
National Cancer Institute (NCI) 257, 260
National Rifle Association (NRA) 211
National Security Agency (NSA) 251, 350
Nazi Gold 231
Nazis.. 14, 29, 83,
91, 94, 96, 102, 138, 170, 183, 193, 194, 210, 214,
222, 240, 253, 254, 265, 279, 283, 284, 332–335,
335–337
Neoconservatives, neocons 380–382
The New American 249, 256
New World Order ...88, 117, 140, 195, 211, 234, 237,
249, 285
New World Religion 153
Nicaragua 186, 342

Nicea, Council of 165
Nichols, Terry 212
Nixon, Richard ..29, 40, 43, 44, 47, 56, 139, 176–180, 184, 257, 319, 341
Noguchi, Thomas 39
None Dare Call it Conspiracy 228
Noriega, Manuel 200
North, Colonel Oliver (Oli) 186, 198, 305
NSA see National Security Agency
Nuclear weapons 285

O

October Surprise 129, 185–191, 233
Octopus, the 128–130
Odessa 335–337
Office of Naval Research (ONR) 269
oil 28
Oil for food programme 374
Oil in Iraq 382–384
Okhrana 101
Oklahoma bombing 211, 212–216
Oldfield, Maurice 42
Olson, Frank 15–17, 194
Olympic, The 298–300
Onassis, Aristotle 40, 131, 133
Onassis, Jackie – see Kennedy, Jackie
Ono, Yoko 55
ONR see Office of Naval Research
Opal File 133
Operation Gladio 122
Operation Mongoose 20, 329
Operation Northwoods 329
Operation Paperclip 279, 283
Operation Sunshine 279
Opium Wars 107
Opus Dei 50, ... 171
Org, The 29, 335–337, 340
Osiris 7

Oswald, Lee Harvey 23–31

P

P2 ....50, 51, 83, 125, 171, 305
PA103 301–306
Pahlavi, Shah Reza 185, 190
Paisley, Ian 135
Palacio, Wanda 198
Pan Am 103, flight see PA103
Parsons, Captain William 273
Partin, Benton 213
Paterson, William 227
Paul VI 81
Paul, Henri 59, 60
Pearl Harbor 325
Pentagon 283, 286, 362–364
Perkins, John 234–235, 385
Perle, Richard 137
Peru 171, 200
PFLP-GC, see Popular Front for the Liberation of Palestine – General Command
Philadelphia Experiment 194, 268–270
Philby, Kim 42, 144
Philip, Prince 106
Philippe IV 74, 75
Phoebus Cartel 243–244
Piazza Fontana 123
Pike, Albert 82
Pilger, John 115
Pinelli, Pino 123
Pinochet, Augusto 43, 44
Pipes, Daniel 103, 104
Pipes, Richard.. 229, 341
Plantard, Pierre 75, 79
PLO (Palestinian Liberation Organisation) 190
PNAC (see Project for a New American Century)
Poland, 1939 invasion of 335
Polio 281

Popes (see under first name)
Popular Front for the Liberation of Palestine – General
  Command (PFLP-GC) 302–304
Port Chicago 265, 271–274
Port Chicago mutiny... 274
Porton Down 16, 67, 276, 285
Posner, Gerald 61
Powell, Colin 137, 186, 236
The Power of Nightmares 341
Presley, Elvis 46
Princess Diana (see Diana, Princess)
Priory of Sion 75, 164, 168, 169
Program F 254, 255
Project for a New American Century (PNAC) 112,
  119, 380, 381–382
PROMIS (Prosecutor's Management
  Information System) 129, 203
Propaganda Due (see P2)
Protocols of the Elders of Zion79, 83, 92, 100–104, 352
Pushkin, Alexander 13
Putin, Vladimir 143, 353–358

Q

Qaddafi, Colonel 302, 306
Qasim, Abd al-Karim 194
Quigley, Caroll 138, 228, 234
Quinalt, USS, ...272–273
Qumran 154–156, 162

R

Raleigh, Walter 9, 10
Ramsay, Andrew 78
Ramsey, Robin 27, 31, 395

Ratzinger, Cardinal Joseph 170
Rauti, Pino 123
Ray, James Earl 35
Reagan, Ronald.........30, 50, 140, 184, 185, 190, 194,
  195, 196, 199, 232–233, 341, 373
Rees-Jones, Trevor 60, 61
Reich, Dr Wilhelm 258, 289
Reno, Janet 36, 203–205, 208, 210
Reptilians 107
Rhodes, Cecil 107, 138
Rice, Condoleeza 116,137, 290, 376, 379
Riconosciuto, Michael 129
Rife, Dr Raymond Rife 258
Roberts, Bruce 131
Robison, John 81
Rockefeller Commission 15, 27, 194
Rockefeller family 108, 140
Rockefeller Foundation 16, 235
Rockefeller, David 138, 140, 236
Rockefeller, John D 240
Rockefeller, Nelson 179, 279
Rodriguez, Felix 198
Romero, Archbishop Oscar Arnulfo 52–55
Rometsch, Ellen 29
Roosevelt, Franklin D. (FDR) 30, 76, 119, 283, 325,
 330–334
Roselli, Johnny 21, 27
Rosicrucians 77, 87
Rosslyn Chapel 108
Roswell (Incident) 30, 311–315
Rothschild family 108, 228, 229
Round Tables 138
Royal Dutch/Shell Group 140
Royal Institute for International Affairs (see Chatham
  House)
Royal Society 77
Ruby, Jack 24, 25
Rumsfeld, Donald 16, 113, 341, 374–375, 382
Russell, Richard 307–308
Russian Woodpecker 289
Rutherford Institute 205
Rwandan genocide 106

S

Sabra and Shatila 91
Salieri, Antonio 11–13
Salinger, Pierre 308
Sandanistas 186, 199
SARS (Severe Acute Respiratory Syndrome) 282
SAS (Special Air Service Regiment) 60, 106
Satan.. 81, 82, 92
Satanic Ritual Abuse 92
Savings and Loan 170
Scaife, Richard Mellon 198, 205
Scalia, Antonin 171
Schneider, René 22
Scientology 183
scrub lists 217
Secret Bases 283–286
Secret Intelligence Service (see MI6)
Senate, US 232–233, 278
Seventh Day Adventists 207
sexual abuse 92, 170
Shabazz, Betty 32, 34
Shaffer, Peter 13
Shah of Iran (see Pahlavi, Reza)
Shakespeare, William 9
Sharon, Ariel 91
Shaw, Clay 26
Shiro, Ishii 275
Simon of Trent 90
Simpson, Colin 340
Simpsons, The... 84, 143
Sinatra, Frank 18, 19
Sindona, Michele 49, 50, 51, 124
Sirhan, Sirhan 37–39
Six Day War 348–352
Skull and Bones 78, 221
Smith, Jerry 288, 289, 291
Solana, Javier 135
Soviets, the   25, 27, 33, 41, 42, 43, 44, 102, 183, 251
Spain, American war with 327–329
Star Wars 115

Starck, Johann August 79, 86
Starr, Kenneth 203–206
Stasi 29
Stevens, Sir John 61
Stinnet, Robert B 332–333
Stone, Oliver 30
Strauss, Leo 341
Strecker, Dr Robert 278
Sutton, Antony C 228
Swiss banks and BCCI.. 231
Swiss banks and Nazi gold 231

T

Taft, William Howard 222
Taliban 359
Tavistock Institute 88, 107
Teamsters 19
Templars (see Knights Templar)
Tenet, George 110, 200
Tesla, Nikolas 240, 288, 291
Thatcher, Margaret 42
Tilden, Samuel J. 217
Tippit, J. D. 24, 25
Titanic, the 295, 297–301
Tlass, Mustafa 90
Tomlinson, Richard 60
Tonkin, Gulf of 112
Top Gun 115
Traficante, Santos 21, 27, 197
Tragedy And Hope 228
Triads 141
Trilateral Commission 138, 139–140, 233
Tripp, Linda 204, 206
Trujillo, Rafael 22, 109
Truman, Harry 339
Tsunami, Asian 290
Turin Shroud 75, 162
Tutankhamun 4–8

TWA 800 306–310

U

UFOs 114, 240, 241, 311–315
UN Security Council 373–376, 379
Unit 731 265, 274–276
UNIX 245
Unocal 359
US military 251
US Navy missile 307–309
USSR 279, 333, 336–337, 348, 353

V

Vanunu, Mordechai 145
Vatican Bank 49, 50, 124
Vatican 280, 336–337
Vaux, Roland de 154, 155
Vidal, Gore 214
Vietnam 28, 180, 196
Vietnam War 228, 289, 319, 344–347, 372
Villot, Cardinal Jean-Marie 51
Vincennes, USS 303
Vogel, Peter 272–274
Volusia County, Florida 219
Vostok 321

W

Waco 207–211
War on Terror 341, 357

Warburg family 228, 229, 230
Wardenclyffe Tower, the 291
Warren Commission 25, 27, 28, 30
Washington, George... 80, 118
Watergate 133, 176–180
Weapons of Mass Destruction (WMD) 16, 64, 110,
    191, 237, 265, 371–375
Webster, Nesta H. 86
WEF see World Economic Forum
Weishaupt, Adam 85
Whitewater 203
WHO see World Health Organisation
Wigand, Dr Jeffrey 260
Willey, Mark Emerson
Wilson, Harold 41
Wilson, Woodrow 241, 299
Windsors (see British Royal Family)
WMD (see Weapons of Mass Destruction)
Wolfowitz, Paul 137, 140, 235, 236, 341, 371, 380
Woodward, Bob 110, 177
World Bank 233, 234–235
World Economic Forum (WEF) 226, 237
World Health Organisation (WHO) . 255, 257, 278–279
World Trade Center 360–362
World Trade Organization (WTO) 140
World Vision 183
World Wide Web 249, 251
World Wildlife Fund (WWF) 106
Wright, Peter 41
WTO (see World Trade Organization)

X

X, Malcolm (see Malcolm X)
The X-Files 270

Y

Y2K (see Millennium Bug)
Yakuza 143, 241
Yallop, David 48
Yushchenko, Viktor 358

Z

Zamora, Augusto Vargas 171
Zapruder, Abraham 26
ZR/Rifle 21
Zündel, Ernst 98